Other Books and Series by Jeff Bowen

Applications for Enrollment of Choctaw Newborn Act of 1905 Volumes I thru XX

Choctaw By Blood Enrollment Cards 1898-1914 Volumes I thru XIX

Visit our website at **www.nativestudy.com** to learn more about these and other books and series by Jeff Bowen

Other Books and Series by Jeff Bowen

1901-1907 Native American Census Seneca, Eastern Shawnee, Miami, Modoc, Ottawa, Peoria, Quapaw, and Wyandotte Indians (Under Seneca School, Indian Territory)

1932 Census of The Standing Rock Sioux Reservation with Births And Deaths 1924-1932

Census of The Blackfeet, Montana, 1897- 1901 Expanded Edition

Eastern Cherokee by Blood, 1906-1910, Volumes I thru XIII

Choctaw of Mississippi Indian Census 1929-1932 with Births and Deaths 1924-1931 Volume I
Choctaw of Mississippi Indian Census 1933, 1934 & 1937, Supplemental Rolls to 1934 & 1935 with Births and Deaths 1932-1938, and Marriages 1936-1938 Volume II

Eastern Cherokee Census Cherokee, North Carolina 1930-1939 Census 1930-1931 with Births And Deaths 1924-1931 Taken By Agent L. W. Page Volume I
Eastern Cherokee Census Cherokee, North Carolina 1930-1939 Census 1932-1933 with Births And Deaths 1930-1932 Taken By Agent R. L. Spalsbury Volume II
Eastern Cherokee Census Cherokee, North Carolina 1930-1939 Census 1934-1937 with Births and Deaths 1925-1938 and Marriages 1936 & 1938 Taken by Agents R. L. Spalsbury And Harold W. Foght Volume III

Seminole of Florida Indian Census, 1930-1940 with Birth and Death Records, 1930-1938

Texas Cherokees 1820-1839 A Document For Litigation 1921

Starr Roll 1894 (Cherokee Payment Rolls) Districts: Canadian, Cooweescoowee, and Delaware Volume One
Starr Roll 1894 (Cherokee Payment Rolls) Districts: Flint, Going Snake, and Illinois Volume Two
Starr Roll 1894 (Cherokee Payment Rolls) Districts: Saline, Sequoyah, and Tahlequah; Including Orphan Roll Volume Three

Cherokee Intruder Cases Dockets of Hearings 1901-1909 Volumes I & II

Indian Wills, 1911-1921 Records of the Bureau of Indian Affairs Books One thru Seven
Native American Wills & Probate Records 1911-1921

Turtle Mountain Reservation Chippewa Indians 1932 Census with Births & Deaths, 1924-1932

Other Books and Series by Jeff Bowen

Chickasaw By Blood Enrollment Cards 1898-1914 Volume I thru V

Cherokee Descendants East An Index to the Guion Miller Applications Volume I
Cherokee Descendants West An Index to the Guion Miller Applications Volume II (A-M)
Cherokee Descendants West An Index to the Guion Miller Applications Volume III (N-Z)

Applications for Enrollment of Seminole Newborn Freedmen, Act of 1905

Eastern Cherokee Census, Cherokee, North Carolina, 1915-1922, Taken by Agent James E. Henderson   Volume I (1915-1916)
Volume II (1917-1918)
Volume III (1919-1920)
Volume IV (1921-1922)

Complete Delaware Roll of 1898

Eastern Cherokee Census, Cherokee, North Carolina, 1923-1929, Taken by Agent James E. Henderson   Volume I (1923-1924)
Volume II (1925-1926)
Volume III (1927-1929)

Applications for Enrollment of Seminole Newborn Act of 1905 Volumes I & II

North Carolina Eastern Cherokee Indian Census 1898-1899, 1904, 1906, 1909-1912, 1914 Revised and Expanded Edition

1932 Hopi and Navajo Native American Census with Birth & Death Rolls (1925-1931) Volume 1 - Hopi
1932 Hopi and Navajo Native American Census with Birth & Death Rolls (1930-1932) Volume 2 - Navajo

Western Navajo Reservation Navajo, Hopi and Paiute 1933 Census with Birth & Death Rolls 1925-1933

Cherokee Citizenship Commission Dockets 1880-1884 and 1887-1889 Volumes I thru V

Applications for Enrollment of Chickasaw Newborn Act of 1905 Volumes I thru VII

Cherokee Intermarried White 1906 Volume I thru X

Applications for Enrollment of Creek Newborn Act of 1905 Volumes I thru XIV

OGLALA SIOUX INDIANS PINE RIDGE RESERVATION 1932 CENSUS BOOK 1

TRANSCRIBED BY
JEFF BOWEN

NATIVE STUDY
Gallipolis, Ohio
USA

Copyright © 2020
by Jeff Bowen

ALL RIGHTS RESERVED
No part of this publication can be reproduced
in any form or manner whatsoever
without previous written permission from the
Copyright holder or Publisher.

Native Study LLC
Gallipolis, OH
www.nativestudy.com

Library of Congress Control Number: 2020923011

ISBN: 978-1-64968-117-1

Book cover: "The Great Hostile Camp" 1891, Photographer: John C. H. Grabill; Bird's-eye view of a Lakota camp (several tipis and wagons in large field)--probably on or near Pine Ridge Reservation.
All photos including the one for the book cover are complements of the Library of Congress.

Made in the United States of America.

This book is dedicated to
Kent Anderson,
Forever the Faithful Friend
to the Pine Ridge Sioux.

"One does not sell the land people walk on."

Crazy Horse

Photographer: John C. H. Grabill (c. 1891)

Four Lakota women standing, three holding infants in cradleboards, and a Lakota man on horseback, in front of a tipi, probably on or near Pine Ridge Reservation.

Photographer: John C. H. Grabill (c. 1891)

Two Oglala Chiefs, American Horse (wearing western clothing and gun-in-holster) and Red Cloud (wearing headdress), full-length portrait, facing front, shaking hands in front of tipi--probably on or near Pine Ridge Reservation.

Photographer: John C. H. Grabill (c. 1891)

Indian chiefs who counciled[sic] with Gen. Miles and setteled[sic] the Indian War -- 1. Standing Rock Sioux Bull, 2. Bear Who Looks Back Running [Stands and Looks Back], 3. Has the Big White Horse, 4. White Tail, 5. Liver [or Living] Bear, 6. Little Thunder, 7. Bull Dog, 8. High Hawk, 9. Lame, 10. Eagle Pipe. Posed group portrait of Lakota chiefs standing in front of tipi--probably on or near Pine Ridge Indian Reservation.

Photographer: Heyn Photo (c. 1899)
Stella Yellow Shirt and baby.

Photographer: John C. H. Grabill   (c. 1891)

#1 - What's left of Big Foot's band -- Group of twelve Miniconjou (children and adults)--many are looking away from camera--in a tepee camp, probably on or near Pine Ridge Reservation.

Photographer: John C. H. Grabill (c. 1891)

#2 - What's left of Big Foot's band -- Group of eleven Miniconjou (children and adults) in a tipi camp, probably on or near Pine Ridge Reservation.

INTRODUCTION

The best way to start this introduction is to quote author Joe Starita who wrote *The Dull Knifes of Pine Ridge* in 1995. He mentions a gentleman who is on page 106 of this census along with his wife Rosa by the name of Guy Dull Knife, Sr. "'My name is Guy Dull Knife Sr. I am Oglala Sioux.' His people, the Oglala, were once the largest and most powerful of the seven subtribes of Teton Sioux, prairie dwellers who lived farther west than the other tribes of the Great Sioux Nation. In their own language, Teton tribal members traditionally referred to themselves as *Lakota*, 'alliance of friends.'"[1]

"Pushed out by the Ojibwa from their ancestral woodlands home near the headwaters of the Mississippi in northern Minnesota, the displaced Lakota began migrating west and reached the heart of the Great Plains about 1760. By the early years of the nineteenth century, they had become superior horsemen, skilled hunters and fierce warriors, commanding a huge section of the northern plains that at one time stretched from the Missouri River of South Dakota to Montana's Big Horn Mountains."[2]

At one time, the Oglala were the most vast and able-bodied among the seven Teton bands or subtribes, the Brule, Oglala, Sans Arc, Hunkpapa, Miniconjou, Blackfeet or Blackfoot and Two Kettles. For generations they were strongly associated with the Northern Cheyenne through marriage as well as customs, similar dress and rituals. They wintered together within the same mountains and had the same enemies in common. Even with their great numbers and tribal confederations they couldn't hold back the destruction of their mostly peaceful existence. Their life sustaining abundance of food and many uses of the buffalo during the late 1700's to the mid 1800's was about to be destroyed by those coming from the east bringing with them what was thought to be civilization. The buffalo from early times were estimated at 50 million but by the 1870's they were decimated by fur traders and next by hired railroads' private armies of extermination. Then came the government policies of destroying Sioux individualism by finishing off the food supply by having the Army slaughter helpless animals that provided economic stability to the Sioux people. The buffalo wasn't just food for a plains tribe but they provided skins for tipis, clothing, moccasins, bedding, saddle covers, and sinew for bow strings, even a buffalo tongue could be used as a hair brush. The use of the buffalo for the Sioux and other tribes was literally unlimited. The buffalo was a way of life for the people and they watched it disappear before their very eyes just so they could be controlled and have their lands stolen.

---

[1] The Dull Knives of Pine Ridge; Pg. 4 Para. 4-5
[2] The Dull Knives of Pine Ridge; Pg. 4-5 Para. 7

Over the years the Sioux have had to contend with many struggles, one such event was the massacre of Wounded Knee during December of 1890 and, "On the morning of December 29, the U.S. Cavalry troops went into the camp to disarm the Lakota. One version of events claims that during the process of disarming the Lakota, a deaf tribesman named Black Coyote was reluctant to give up his rifle, claiming he had paid a lot for it. Simultaneously, an old man was performing a ritual called the Ghost Dance. Black Coyote's rifle went off at that point, and the U.S. Army began shooting at the Native Americans. The Lakota warriors fought back, but many had already been stripped of their guns and disarmed.

By the time the massacre was over, more than 250 men, women, and children of the Lakota had been killed and 51 were wounded (4 men and 47 women and children, some of whom died later); some estimates placed the number of dead as high as 300."[3]

In bringing up Wounded Knee it's understood that Chief Bigfoot at the time had gotten pneumonia and was extremely ill, therefore not able to keep his promises of turning in the Hunkpapas the next day after he had taken them in when they were in need a Colonel Sumner took it as resistance to follow instructions. But the pressure was great from General Miles who had wired Sumner to gain control of the situation and arrest Bigfoot. Sumner later reported that Bigfoot's people looked so pitiable that he didn't consider them hostile. But he sent a rancher he thought they could depend on to relate to Bigfoot to at least travel to Fort Bennett. This rancher obviously translated the wrong message which seems like it was on purpose and told him to go to the Pine Ridge immediately, 50 miles away, if you want to save your lives. When Sumner had gone to Bigfoot's village looking for him and him not showing up at Bennett, Miles sent a message stating that Bigfoot was clearly being defiant and hostile. Sumner was ordered to arrest and disarm Bigfoot's band immediately. So Miles was in fear that Bigfoot was making for the Stronghold on Pine Ridge and was afraid he would arouse the Ghost Dancer's into a frenzy.

In finishing the story of Wounded Knee and its circumstances it was felt that one last quote from Joe Starita's book was needed to balance out the history of what worth there was to Wounded Knee. "The Reverend Charles Cook hastily removed all the pews and then he covered the floor of the Holy Cross Episcopal Church with a bedding of straw and quilts. The Christmas season was upon Pine Ridge. Garlands and wreaths decked the walls and a homemade sign—Peace On Earth, Goodwill To Men—still hung above the altar of his church. Shortly after 9:30 p.m., the first wagons arrived carrying survivors from the Miniconjou village. When Dr. Charles Eastman, a Santee Sioux in charge of treating the wounded, and the Reverend Cook and his church staff first saw the men, women and children carried in from the wagons, they cried out in anguish. 'All of this,' said Eastman later, 'was a severe

---

[3] Wounded Knee Massacre; Wikipedia

ordeal for one who had so lately put all his faith in the Christian love and lofty ideals of the white man.'

Steals a Running Horse, age five, was among thirty-eight survivors laid out in rows on the church floor that night. Bullets had torn apart the small boy's throat, and when doctors tried to feed him, the food and water came out the side of his neck. Blue Whirlwind had been wounded fourteen times. Her two small sons were shot up, but still alive. Her husband, Spotted Thunder, was dead. Louise Weasel Bear had been one of the first to flee the village for the ravine. 'We tried to run but they shot us like we were a buffalo. I know there are some good white people, but the soldiers must be mean to shoot children and women. Indian soldiers would not do that to white children.' Bertha Kills Close to Lodge, seventeen, ran with her relatives through the ravine, stopping when she heard a burst of gunfire behind her. 'I went over there and it was my sister and her mother was pregnant at that time. I found she was killed. I was wounded but was able to go to where they were. My sister was near death and I stayed with her. When she died I straightened her out, laid her out the best way I could.' Alice Dog Arm saw a soldier on a bay horse riding toward her family. 'I ran and hid in a ditch with my mother and two brothers. My father came and took my older brother to care for him. Soon he came back and said that they had killed my brother. Then my mother cried and as she wanted us all to be together and die together so my father took us to a safer hiding place and then he left us and soon a man named Air Pipe came and told us that my father was killed.' Afraid of Enemy, thirty-six, said she saw an officer on a sorrel horse swing around the left end of the camp. 'I heard him give some command and right after the command it sounded like a lightening crash. That is about all I know. When I became conscious I was lying down. As I rose and started to go I began to get unconscious again. For that reason I do not know a great deal of what took place after this. I have my old cloak and it has nine bullet holes in it.' After the initial cannon salvo, Rough Feather and her family fled toward the ravine under heavy fire. 'My father, my mother, my grandmother, my older brother and my younger brother were all killed. My son who was two years old was shot in the mouth that later caused his death.'

On New Year's Day, 1891, a burial detail rode out of the agency headquarters in Pine Ridge with an army escort. Under contract at two dollars per body, the civilian detail of thirty men spent two days combing the snow-covered battlefield, tossing frozen bodies in the back of wagons drawn by mule teams. They found Chief Bigfoot, wrapped in a thick coat and head scarf, propped up beside the blown-out remains of his army tent, his body frozen in a half-sitting position. Not far away, inside the council circle, was the charred remains of the medicine man, Yellow Bird. Strewn along a trail more than three miles long, they found the remains of three pregnant woman riddled with bullets, another with her abdomen blown away and a young boy whose upper body had been torn apart by a cannon shell.

They also found a baby girl, covered in snow, huddled beside her dead mother. She was wrapped in a shawl, her head, hands and feet severely frostbitten, but still alive. On her head, the eight-month-old infant wore a tiny buckskin cap with a needlepoint design in the shape of an American Flag."[4] In finalizing this study it makes it obvious as to how dark men's souls can be, let alone those in power. As Abraham Lincoln stated, "Nearly all men can stand adversity, but if you want to test a man's character, give him power."[5]

Wounded Knee seems as though it was a precursor to a future of consistent adversities involving a people who just wanted to live on the prairies and be left alone. If it wasn't someone telling them how to live, it was conflict between the American government or tribal government and traditionalism.

But it was always about the land and the resources that were being discovered on that land. To the Government there wasn't a treaty they couldn't break and did. "In 1887, after years of fierce debate, Congress passed the General Allotment Act (the Dawes Act), yet another in the long series of 'reform' laws designed to assist the Indian into the American mainstream by breaking down his traditional means of existence (the act was 'a mighty pulverizing engine to break up the tribal mass,' cheered Teddy Roosevelt, who with the help of his friend J. Pierpont Morgan would later sponsor Edward Curtis's theatrical photographic portraits of "The Vanishing Redman"). Each male Indian in those tribes coerced by the Indian Bureau into accepting allotment would be given 160 acres, with any 'surplus' land to be purchased inexpensively by the government and turned over to white settlers at its own discretion, according to the rules set out by the Homestead Act of 1862. This 'surplus,' as it turned out, comprised most of the remaining Indian land.

By destroying communal guardianship of land, the Dawes Act—first aimed at tribes in Western Indian Territory but eventually affecting more than one hundred Indian groups—destroyed not only the unity of Indian nations but the people's tradition of generosity and total sharing for the common good. Since according to their sacred instructions the Indians could never 'own' a Mother Earth of which they felt themselves to be a part, and since even those willing to go against the Indian life-way—*wouncage*, 'our way of doing,' as the Lakota say—had no experience of the white economy, most of those who tried to adjust to the new system were sooner or later relieved of their land due to innocence, drink, inability to pay off mortgages and taxes, and finally, the hard exigencies of starvation; for by the time the people had been reduced to irregular handouts of flour and lard, the ration of which depended largely on their willingness to cooperate with the agents sent out by the Indian Bureau and their accomplices in the reservation missions. In short the Dawes Act legalized an

---

[4] The Dull Knives of Pine Ridge; Pg. 128-129 Para. 1-5
[5] forbes.com/quotes/76/

arrangement in which, during the next half century, the native people all across the country would lose two thirds of their remaining lands by sale and swindle.

Until World War I, the Lakota managed to resist allotment, but in 1889—the year of the great Oklahoma land rush inspired by the Dawes Act—General Crook was dispatched to his old foes with the proposal that 9 million acres of their remaining land should be turned over to white settlement. The aging Red Cloud refused to sign such an agreement, and so did Sitting Bull, who had returned from political asylum in Canada in 1881 (for a time he appeared in "Wild West" shows with the old railroad hunter Buffalo Bill Cody) and was living at Standing Rock on the Grand River, not far from the place where he was born:

> Friends and Relatives: Our minds are again disturbed by the Great Father's representatives, the Indian Agent, the squaw-men, the mixed-bloods, the interpreters, and the favorite-ration-chiefs. What is it they want of us at this time? They want us to give up another chunk of our tribal land. This is not the first time nor the last time. They will try to gain possession of the last piece of ground we possess. They are again telling us what they intend to do if we agree to their wishes. Have we ever set a price on our land and received such a value? No, we never did. What we got under the former treaties were promises of all sorts. They promised how we are going to live peaceably on the land we still own and how they are going to show us the new ways of living, even told us how we can go to heaven when we die....
>
> When the white people invaded our Black Hills country our treaty agreements were still in force but the Great Father ignored it.... Therefore I do not wish to consider any proposition to cede any portion of our tribal holdings to the Great Father.... My friends and relatives, let us stand as one family as we did before the white people led us astray.

Due mostly to the stubborn resistance of Sitting Bull and Red Cloud, the signatures required for the cession of Indian land were not obtained, and as in the seizure of the Black Hills, it was recommended to the government that it simply ignore the 1868 Treaty, which it did. A few months later President Benjamin Harrison proclaimed an act that dismantled the Great Sioux Reservation, established at Fort Laramie and created the seven reservations that exist today; the Oglala band, which had been the most hostile, was given the dry rolling hill country between the Dakota Badlands and the Sand Hills of Nebraska, now known as the Pine Ridge Reservation."[6]

But in modern times on a positive note, "In 1971 the tribe founded the Oglala Lakota College, one of the earliest tribal colleges in the nation, and part of Native American institution building of the last 40 years. First started as a two-year community college, it has expanded to offer four-year baccalaureate degrees, as well as a master's in Lakota leadership. It is operated by tribal people, with a tribal board. In 2011, it had an enrollment of 1,400."[7]

---

[6] In The Spirit of Crazy Horse; Pg. 18-19 Para. 1-6
[7] Pine Ridge Indian Reservation; Wikipedia

This new 1932 Pine Ridge Oglala Sioux Census contains over 8000 names listing sex, date of birth and age at last birthday, degree of blood, marital status (in most cases giving the wife's maiden name) and relationship to head of family along with the jurisdiction where they were enrolled and if they were a ward to the head of household. Also included is the allotment and annuity numbers.

In 1996, the 1924 to 1932 Oglala Sioux Pine Ridge Birth and Death rolls were published by this author which has long been out of print. This new 1932 Census has been transcribed as *Book I* that will go along with the original Birth and Death Records covering over 4500 names to be re-published as *Book II*. In addition to this census and the forthcoming Birth and Death Rolls you will find a few early pre-1932 photographs from the Pine Ridge Reservation included in both books. You can actually find a few of the names mentioned either in the introduction or on a picture within this 1932 census and possibly the births and deaths.

Also I wanted to thank the authors who worked so long and hard to give me the ability to dig out the facts and circumstances mentioned in this introduction. Without them searching out these materials before us we would have nothing. They give me inspiration to continue while sometimes feeling the tears of so many that didn't want and never asked for such anguish.

The 1932 Census for *Book I* has been transcribed from National Archives film NATIVE AMERICAN CENSUS ROLLS 1885-1940; Pine Ridge (Oglala Sioux Indians): M-595 roll number 378. For *Book II*, the (Oglala Sioux Indians) 1924-1932 with Birth and Death rolls was also transcribed from Indian Census Rolls 1885-1940; M-595 roll number 379.

It is the hope that this work helps many find their ancestors and that it will honor those both past and present.

Jeff Bowen
Gallipolis, Ohio
NativeStudy.com

Census Instructions

INSTRUCTIONS

(*A*) A separate roll is to be made of each reservation; also, of each *rancheria* or reserve, and a separate roll of Indians allotted on the public domain or homesteading. The roll is to be based on enrollment and not on residence.

(*B*) Persons are to be listed by families alphabetically; that is, not only by the first letter of the surname, but also by the second and subsequent letters, when the first letter or letters are the same. For example: Abalon, Abbott, Abcou, Abend, Abict; Ball, Bell, Bill, Boll, Bull; Carfey, Carmen, Carfon, etc. Families having the same surname are also to be listed in this way, e. g.: Brown, Anson; Brown, Bill; Brown, Charles; Brown, David. In the case of English translations of Indian names, such as John *Flying-Elk*, Flying-Elk is the surname and is to be listed under F. In such cases the first word of the translated Indian name determines the alphabetical position. The best way to accomplish this will be to write the names of each family group on a separate card; then, arrange the cards alphabetically and type the names therefrom onto the census roll.

Members of a family are to be listed in the following order: Head, first; wife second; then children, whether sons or daughters, *in the order of their ages;* and lastly, all other relatives and persons living with the family who do not constitute another family group.

Annuity and per capita payment rolls are also to be prepared in the same manner.

(*C*) A family is composed of the following members:
1. Both parents and their unmarried children, if any, living with them; all other relatives and persons living with the family who do not constitute another family group.
2. Either parent and the unmarried children, if the other parent is dead; all other relatives and persons living with the family who do not constitute another family group.
3. A single person over 21 years of age, not living with a relative.

(*D*) For each person the following information is to be furnished:
1. NUMBER.—A number is to be assigned in serial order. Thus, the first person listed is to be numbered as "1," the second, as "2," and so on until the census is completed.
2. NAME.—If there are both an Indian and an English name, the allotment or annuity roll name is to be given. First, the last or surname; then, the given name in full. Ditto marks are to be used under the surname of the head for the surnames of the other members of one family.
3. SEX.—"M," for male; "F," for female.
4. AGE AT LAST BIRTHDAY.—Age in completed years at last birthday is to be shown. For infants under 1 year, age in completed months, expressed as twelfths of a year. Thus, 3 months as $\tfrac{3}{12}$ yr.
5. TRIBE.—Care is to be taken that tribe, not band or local name, is given. Thus, Ute tribe, not Pahvant, which is a band of Ute. Likewise, Hupa tribe, not Bear River, which is a local name for the members of the Hupa tribe living near Bear River.
6. DEGREE OF BLOOD.—"1," for full blood; "$\tfrac{1}{4}+$," for one-fourth or more Indian blood; "$-\tfrac{1}{4}$," for less than one-fourth Indian blood.
7. MARITAL STATUS.—"S," for a single or unmarried person; "M," for a married person; and "Wd," for widowed of either sex.
8. RELATIONSHIP TO HEAD OF FAMILY.—The head, whether husband or father, widow or unmarried person of either sex, is to be designated as such. For the other members, the appropriate term which designates the particular relationship the person bears to the head is to be used.
9. RESIDENCE.—
    (*a*) At *jurisdiction* where enrolled: Yes or no. The term jurisdiction includes all reservations and public domain allotments under the agency.
    (*b*) Or at another jurisdiction. The name of the jurisdiction is to be given.
    (*c*) Or elsewhere:
    1. Post office: Both the proper name of the post office and the class by which it is known (city, town, village, etc.) are to be given. Thus, Lewiston, city.
    2. County.
    3. State.
10. WARD.—Yes or no. Wardship depends primarily upon the ownership of individual property held in trust or upon membership in a tribe living on a Federal reservation. See Circular 2145.
11. ALLOTMENT, ANNUITY, AND IDENTIFICATION NUMBERS.—"Al," for allotment; "An," for annuity; and "Id," for identification, before the appropriate number or numbers. All numbers are to be shown.

(*E*) Rolls not prepared in strict conformity with the above instructions will be returned for correction.

Census of the **Pine Ridge** reservation of the **Pine Ridge, South Dakota** jurisdiction, as of **April 1**, 1932, taken by **James H. McGregor**, Superintendent.

Key: Number; Surname, Given; Sex; Date of Birth-Age at Last Birthday; Tribe (Oglala Sioux, unless stated otherwise); Degree of Blood; Marital Status; Relationship to Head of Family [Last Census Roll Number]; At Jurisdiction Where Enrolled (Yes/No); (If no – Where); Ward (Yes/No, if given); Allotment, Annuity and Identification Numbers (if given).

1; Adams, Alex; M; 1846-86; plus 1/4; Wd; Head 1; Yes; Yes; Al. 345 An. 1

2; Adams, Aloysius Mousseau; M; 1906-27; 1/4; M; Head 2; No; Rosebud Agency, S.D; Yes; Al. 2348 An. 2

N.E. Adams (Neiss, Bernice) Bernice; F; ?; Rosebud Sioux; 1/4; M; Wife; No; Rosebud Agency

3; Adams, Bennie Pete; M; 1894-38; 1/4; S; Head 3; No; No permanent home; travels constantly Elsewhere; No; Al. 460 An. 3

4; Adams, John; M; 1878-38; 1/4; Wd; Head 4; Yes; Al. 459 An. 4

N.E. Adams, Bryan P; M; ?; Hopi; F; Wd; Head; No; Polacca, Navajo Co, Ariz.

5; Adams, Sarah G; F; 12/12/10-22; Sioux & Hopi; plus 1/4; S; Daughter 5; No; Polacca, Navajo Co, Ariz; Al. 6943 An. 8

6; Adams, Byron A; M; 4/26/13-19; Sioux & Hopi; 1/4; S; Son 6; No; Polacca, Navajo Co, Ariz; Id. U-9000 An. 9

7; Adams, Hazel Bernice; F; 5/28/17-15; Sioux & Hopi; 1/4; S; Daughter 7; No; Polacca, Navajo Co, Ariz; Id. U-9001 An. 10

8; Adams, Joseph; M; 1883-49; plus 1/4; M; Head 8; Yes; Al. 338 An. 12
9; Adams (Charging, Laura) Laura; F; 1882-50; 1/4; M; Wife 9; Yes; Al. 5110 An. 13
10; Adams, Noah; M; 10-1911-21; plus 1/4; S; Son 10; Yes; Al. 7184 An. 15
11; Adams, Acron; M; 11/12/12-19; 1/4; S; Son 11; Yes; Id. U-9002 An. 16
12; Adams, Viola; F; 1-1915-17; 1/4; S; Daughter 12; Yes; Id. U-9004 An. 17
13; Adams, Roy Landman; M; 4/25/17-15; 1/4; S; Son 13; Yes; Id. U-9003 An. 18
14; Adams, Maurice; M; 11/9/22-10; 1/4; S; Son 14; Yes; Id. U-12037 An. 19
15; Adams, Virginia; F; 6/3/27-4; 1/4; S; Daughter 15; Yes; Id. U-12541 An. none

16; Adams, Clement; M; 10/7/09-22; plus 1/4; S; Head 16; Yes; Al. 7185 An. 14

17; Adams, Ruddie; M; 1903-29; plus 1/4; Wd; Head 17; Yes; Al. 339 An. 20
18; Adams, Gerry Patrick; M; 1/3/31-1; 1/4; S; Son 18; Yes; Id. U-13679 An. none

N.E. Addison, Burt; M; ?; Arapaho; F; M; Head 0; Yes; [blank]
19; Addison (Clincher, Mary) Mary; F; 1903-29; F; M; Wife 19; Yes; Al. 5318 An. 21
20; Addison, Raymond; M; 1/10/25-7; Sioux & Arap; F; S; Son 20; Yes; Id. U-11453 An. 22
21; Addison, Susanna; F; 10/8/27-4; Sioux & Arap; F; S; Daughter 21; Yes; Id. U-12397 An. none

Census of the   **Pine Ridge**   reservation of the **Pine Ridge, South Dakota** jurisdiction, as of   **April 1**   , 19**32**, taken by   **James H. McGregor**   , Superintendent.

Key: Number; Surname, Given; Sex; Date of Birth-Age at Last Birthday; Tribe (Oglala Sioux, unless stated otherwise); Degree of Blood; Marital Status; Relationship to Head of Family [Last Census Roll Number]; At Jurisdiction Where Enrolled (Yes/No); (If no – Where); Ward (Yes/No, if given); Allotment, Annuity and Identification Numbers (if given).

22; Addison, Esther Veronica; F; 6/13/31-10/12; F; S; Daughter 0; Yes; Id. U-13956 An. none

~~N.E. Adlar, Eugene H; M; ?; White; M; Dead; No; Oakland, Alameda Co, Cal.~~
23; Adlar (Livermont, Florence) Florence; F; 1898-34; -1/4; M; Wife 22; No; Oakland, Alameda Co, Cal; Al. 2543 An. 4069

24; Afraid Of Bear, George; M; 1902-30; F; M; Head 23; Yes; Al. 6110 An. 23
~~N.E. Afraid Of Bear (Kills Crow, Annie) Annie; F; ?; Standing Rock Sioux; F; M; Wife~~
25; Afraid Of Bear, Ernest; M; 3/5/25-7; Sioux; F; S; Son 24; Yes; Id. U-13203 An. none
26; Afraid Of Bear, Joseph L; M; 7/2/26-5; Sioux; F; S; Son 24; Yes; Id. U-11987 An. none
27; Afraid Of Bear, Francis; M; 6/15/28-3; Sioux; F; S; Son 26; Yes; Id. U-10245 An. none
28; Afraid Of Bear, Isaac; M; 1/23/32-2/12; Sioux; F; S; Son --; Yes; Id; U-14078 An. none

29; Afraid Of Bear, Robert; M; 1877-55; F; M; Head 28; Yes; Al. 5098 An. 25
30; Afraid Of Bear (White Wolf, Frances) Frances; F; 1882-50; F; M; Wife 29; Yes; Al. 5099. An. 26
31; Afraid Of Bear, Samuel; M; 1/31/13-19; F; S; Son 30; Yes; Al. 7600 An. 27
32; Afraid Of Bear, Patrick; M; 12/13/17-14; F; S; Son 31; Yes; Al. 5146 An. 28
33; Afraid Of Bear, Chester; M; 8/21/24-7; F; S; Son 32; Yes; Id-U-11325 An. 30

~~N.E. Afraid Of Enemy, Silas; M; ?; Cheyenne River Sioux; F; M; Head; No; Pine Ridge~~
34; Afraid Of Enemy (Wounded Horse, Mabel) Mabel; F; 1897-35; F; M; Wife 33; Yes; Yes; Al. 3528 An. 31

35; Afraid Of Hawk, Cain; M; 1904-28; F; S; Head 34; Yes; Yes; Al. 3005 An. 32

36; Afraid Of Hawk, Emil; M; 1886-46; F; M; Head 35; Yes; Yes; Al. 3036 An. 33
37; Afraid Of Hawk (Hollow Horn, Agie) Agie; F; 1907-25; Yes; Yes; Al. 4752 An. 2958
38; Afraid Of Hawk, Martha; F; 4/20/26-5; F; S; Daughter 37; Yes; Yes; Id. U-11872 An. none
39; Afraid Of Hawk, Eldred; M; 5/2/31-11/12; F; S; Son --; Yes; Yes; Id. U-13826 An. none

Census of the **Pine Ridge** reservation of the **Pine Ridge, South Dakota** jurisdiction, as of **April 1**, 1932, taken by **James H. McGregor**, Superintendent.

Key: Number; Surname, Given; Sex; Date of Birth-Age at Last Birthday; Tribe (Oglala Sioux, unless stated otherwise); Degree of Blood; Marital Status; Relationship to Head of Family [Last Census Roll Number]; At Jurisdiction Where Enrolled (Yes/No); (If no – Where); Ward (Yes/No, if given); Allotment, Annuity and Identification Numbers (if given).

40; Afraid Of Hawk, Richard; M; 1872-57; F; M; Head 38; Yes; No; Al. 3004 An. 35
41; Afraid Of Hawk, (No data), Mabel; F; 1881-51; F; M; Wife 39; Yes; Yes; Al. 2781 An. 36
42; Afraid Of Hawk, Grant; M; 4/14/12-20; F; S; Son 40; Yes; Yes; Al. 6308 An. 40
43; Afraid Of Hawk, Maurice; M; 3/19/14-18; F; S; Son 41; Yes; Yes; An. 7748 An. 41
44; Afraid Of Hawk, Preston; M; 3/19/14-18; F; S; Son 41; Yes; Yes; Id. U-9007 An. 42
45; Afraid Of Hawk, Dorothy; F; 7/15/20-11; F; S; Daughter 43; Yes; Yes; Id. U-9010 An. 45
46; Afraid Of Hawk, Adile Jane; F; 3/3/26-6; F; S; Daughter 44; Yes; Yes; Id. U-11857 An. none
47; Afraid Of Hawk, Daniel; M; 10/15/30-1; F; S; Son 45; Yes; Yes; Id. U-1362 An. none

48; Afraid Of Hawk, Bertie; M; 1908-25; F; S; Head 46; Yes; Yes; Al. 3006 An. 37

49; Afraid Of His Horses, Amos; M; 1877-55; F; M: Head 47; Yes; Yes; Al. 3144 An. 46
50; Afraid Of His Horses (Poor Elk, Elizabeth) Elizabeth; F; 1872-60; F; M; Wife 48; Yes; Yes; Al. 3273 An. 47
51; Afraid Of His Horses, Pugh; M; 3/15/15-17; plus 1/4; S; Son 49; Yes; Yes; Id-U-9011 An. 49

52; Afraid Of His Horses, Frank; M; 1882-50; plus 1/4; M; Head 50; Yes; No; Al. 1264 An. 53
53; Afraid Of His Horses (Red Cloud, Lucy) Lucy; F; 1881-51; F; M; Wife; 51; Yes; Yes; Al. 1265 An. 54
54; Afraid Of His Horses, Zona; F; 1028/08-23; plus 1/4; S; Daughter 52; Yes; Yes; Id. U-9013 An. 55
55; Afraid Of His Horses, Sadie; F; 12/22/10-21; plus 1/4; S; Daughter 53; Yes; Yes; Id. U-9014 An. 56

56; Afraid Of His Horses, Paul; M; 11/11/04-27; plus 1/4; M; Head 54; Yes; Yes; Al. 7798 An. 57
57; Afraid Of His Horses (Fool Head, Lucelia) Lucelia; F; 11/9/13-18; F; M; Wife 55; Yes; Yes; Al. 7802 An. 2314

58; Afraid Of Left Hand; M; 1847-85; F; M; Head 56; Yes; Yes; Al. 1763 An. 58
59; Pretty Woman; F; 1843-89; F; M; Wife 57; Yes; Yes; Al. 5864 An. 59

Census of the **Pine Ridge** reservation of the **Pine Ridge, South Dakota** jurisdiction, as of **April 1**, 1932, taken by **James H. McGregor**, Superintendent.

Key: Number; Surname, Given; Sex; Date of Birth-Age at Last Birthday; Tribe (Oglala Sioux, unless stated otherwise); Degree of Blood; Marital Status; Relationship to Head of Family [Last Census Roll Number]; At Jurisdiction Where Enrolled (Yes/No); (If no – Where); Ward (Yes/No, if given); Allotment, Annuity and Identification Numbers (if given).

~~N.E. Afraid Of Lightning; M; ?; Cheyenne River Sioux; F; [blank]; Head~~
60; Afraid Of Lightning (Bissonette, Amelia) Amelia; F; 1906-26; plus 1/4; M; Wife 58; No; Bridger, Haakon Co, SD; Yes; Al. 7922 An. 60

61; Allen, Arthur O; M; 1906-26; -1/4; M; Head 59; No; Washington, D.C; Al. 4596 An. 61

~~N.E. Allen (Waller, Cricket Ruby) Cricket Ruby; F; ?; Cherokee; 1/4; M; Wife; No; Washington, D.C.~~
62; Allen, William Arthur; M; 9/16/30-1; Sioux & Chero; -1/4; S; Son 60; No; Washington, D.C; Id. U-1363[?] An. none

63; Allen, Charles; M; 1881-51; -1/4; Wd; Head 61; No; Cody, Cherry Co, Neb; Yes; Al. 1103 An. 62
64; Allen, Theodore; M; 1/30/16-16; -1/4; S; Son 62; No; Cody, Cherry Co, Neb; Yes; Id. U-9015 An. 63

65; Allen, Edgar; M; 2904-28; -1/4; M; Head 63; Yes; Yes; Al. 1120 An. 62
~~N.E. Allen (LaFurge, Iris) Iris; F; ?; White; M; Wife~~
66; Allen, Norman E; M; 12/7/24-7; -1/4; S; Son 64; Yes; Yes; Id. U-11567 An. 65
67; Allen, Maxwell; M; 2/10/26-6; -1/4; S; Son 65; Yes; Yes; Id. U-12341 An. none
68; Allen, Wendell Verne; M; 7/31/27-4; -1/4; S; Son 66; Yes; Yes; Id. U-11423 An. none

69; Allen, Joseph; M; 1876-56; -1/4; M; Head 67; Yes; No; Al. 1121 An. 67
70; Allen (Rooks, Rosanna) Rosanna; F; 1880-52; plus 1/4; M; Wife 68; Yes; No; Al. 4653 An. 68
71; Allen, Martin Brace; M; 4/8/12-19; -1/4; S; Son 69; Yes; Yes; Al. 7176 An. 70

72; Allen, Joseph F; M; 1905-28; -1/4; M; Head 70; Yes; Yes; Al. 4643 An. 71

73; Allen, Robert; M; 1888-44; -1/4; M; Head 71; Yes; No; Al. 1106 An. 72
74; Allen (Salvis, Lillie) Lillie; F; 1890-46; plus 1/4; M; Wife 72; Yes; Yes; Al. 2369 An. 73
75; Allen, Cleveland; M; 7/26/13-18; 1/4; S; Son 73; Yes; Yes; Id. U-9016 An. 74
76; Allen, Emma Irene; F; 7/17/15-16; plus 1/4; S; Daughter 74; Yes; Yes; Id. U-9017 An. 75
77; Allen, Clayton V; M; 8/1/17-14; 1/4; S; Son 75; Yes; Yes; Id. U-9018 An. 76

78; Allen, Samuel; M; 1882-50; -1/4; M; Head 76; Yes; No; Al. 1119 An. 77
79; Allen (Carlow, Nellie C); F; 1882-50; plus 1/4; M; Wife 77; No; Bremerton, Kitsap Co, Wash; No; Al. 4623 An. 78

Census of the __Pine Ridge__ reservation of the __Pine Ridge, South Dakota__ jurisdiction, as of __April 1__, 1932, taken by __James H. McGregor__, Superintendent.

Key: Number; Surname, Given; Sex; Date of Birth-Age at Last Birthday; Tribe (Oglala Sioux, unless stated otherwise); Degree of Blood; Marital Status; Relationship to Head of Family [Last Census Roll Number]; At Jurisdiction Where Enrolled (Yes/No); (If no – Where); Ward (Yes/No, if given); Allotment, Annuity and Identification Numbers (if given).

80; Allen, Helen D; F; 7/6/12-19; -1/4; S; Daughter 78; No; Bremerton, Kitsap Co, Wash; Yes; Al. 6987 An. 80

81; Allen, Alma Marian; F; 4/27/15-17; -1/4; S; Daughter 79; No; Bremerton, Kitsap Co, Wash; Yes; Id. U-9019 An. 81

82; Allen, Hilda E. F; 7/28/24-7; -1/4; S; Daughter 80; No; Bremerton, Kitsap Co, Wash; Yes; Id. U-11362 An. 82

83; Allman, Alonzo; M; 9-1897-34; plus 1/4; M; Head 81; Yes; Yes; Al. 212 An. 84

84; Allman (Two Two, Amelia) Amelia; F; 1897-34; 1/4; M; Wife 82; Yes; Yes; Al. 158 An. 85

85; Allman, Janet Eliza; F; 4/18/20-11; 1/4; S; Daughter 83; Yes; Yes; Id. U-9020 An. 86

86; Allman, Margaret T; F; 3/29/22-10; 1/4; S; Daughter 84; Yes; Yes; Id. U-10991 An. 87

87; Allman, Archie Leroy; M; 10/19/24-7; 1/4; S; Son 85; Yes; Yes; Id. U-10800 An. 88

88; Allman, Robert Charles; M; 11/13/27-4; 1/4; S; Son; 86; Yes; Yes; Id. U-12436 An. none

89; Allman, Verna May; F; 1/6/31-1; 1/4; S; Daughter 87; Yes; Yes; Id. U-13663 An. none

90; Allman, Charles; M; 1883-49; plus 1/4; M; Head 88; Yes; No; Al. 216 An. 89

91; Allman, Cornelia; F; 1880-51; plus 1/4; M; Wife 89; Yes; No; Al. 5710 An. 90

92; Allman, Melvina Florence; F; 8-3-13; 1/4; S; Daughter 90; Yes; Yes; Al. 8005 An. 94

93; Allman, George; M; 4/14/20-11; 1/4; S; Son 91; Yes; Yes; Id. U-9021 An. 95

94; Allman, Mabel; F; 7/23/26-5; 1/4; S; Gr. daughter 94; Yes; Yes; Id. U-121562 An. none

95; Allman, Leroy; M; 1906-27; plus 1/4; S; Head 92; Yes; Yes; Al. 5712 An. 96

96; Allman, Louisa; F; 1855-77; plus 1/4; Wd; Head 95; Yes; Yes; Al. 207 An. 98

97; Allman, William A; M; 1904-29; plus 1/4; S; Head 96; Yes; Yes; Al. 6118 An. 111

98; Allman, Samuel; M; 1885-47; plus 1/4; M; Head 97; Yes; Yes; Al. 213 An. 100

99; Allman (Shangreau, Rosa) Rosa; F; 1887-49; plus 1/4; M; Wife 98; Yes; Yes; Al. 214 An. 101

100; Allman, Antoine T; M; 1/1/08-24; 1/4; S; Son 99; Yes; Yes; Al. 6120 An. 102

Census of the **Pine Ridge** reservation of the **Pine Ridge, South Dakota** jurisdiction, as of **April 1**, 19**32**, taken by **James H. McGregor**, Superintendent.

Key: Number; Surname, Given; Sex; Date of Birth-Age at Last Birthday; Tribe (Oglala Sioux, unless stated otherwise); Degree of Blood; Marital Status; Relationship to Head of Family [Last Census Roll Number]; At Jurisdiction Where Enrolled (Yes/No); (If no – Where); Ward (Yes/No, if given); Allotment, Annuity and Identification Numbers (if given).

101; Allman, Corbett Ben;; M; 10/6/09-22; 1/4; W; Son 100; Yes; Yes; Al. 6121 An. 103

102; Allman, Louisa M; F; 7/6/11-20; 1/4; S; Daughter 101; Yes; Yes; Al. 6122 An. 104

103; Allman, Sylvanus C; M; 3/31/12-19; 1/4; S; Son 102; Yes; Yes; Al. 6894 An. 105

104; Allman, Elisnohr; F; 12/13/14-17; 1/4; S; Daughter 103; Yes; Yes; Id. U-9024 An. 106

105; Allman, Francis D; M; 8/13/18-13; 1/4; S; Son 104; Yes; Yes; Id. U-9026 An. 108

106; Allman, Lorenia I; F; 6/25/20-11; 1/4; S; Daughter 105; Yes; Yes; Id. SU-9027 An. 109

107; Allman, Millie M; F; 4/6/23-8; 1/4; S; Daughter 106; Yes; Yes; Id. U-9637 An. 110

108; Allman, Cornelia; F; 4/1/25-7; 1/4; S; Daughter 107; Yes; Yes; Id. U-11554 An. none

109; American Bear, George; M; 10/1/09-22; F M; Head 109; Yes; Yes; Al. 6509 An. 114

N.E. American Bear (Blacksmith, Rosa); F; ?; Cheyenne River Sioux; F; M; Wife

110; American Horse, Alfred; M; 1881-51; F; Wd; Head 110; Yes; Yes; Al. 2297 An. 115

111; American Horse, Benjamin; M; 1876-56; F; M; Head 111; Yes; Yes; Al. 1692 An. 121

112; American Horse, Jessie; F; 1879-53; plus 1/4; M; Wife 112; Yes; Yes; Al. 3717 An. 122

113; American Horse, Charles; 1882-50; F; M; Head 114; Yes; Yes; Al. 619 An. 123

N.E. American Horse (Kills Crow, Louisa) Louisa; F; ?; Standing Rock Sioux; F; M; Wife

114; American Horse, Martha; F; 8/9/24-7; F; S; Daughter 115; Yes; Yes; Id. U-11380 An. 124

115; American Horse, Vernie; M; 11/17/26-5; F; S; Son 116; Yes; Yes; Id. U-12131 An. none

116; American Horse, William; M; 7/18/28-3; F; S; Son 117; Yes; Yes; Id. U-12754 An. none

Census of the __Pine Ridge__ reservation of the __Pine Ridge, South Dakota__ jurisdiction, as of __April 1__, 1932, taken by __James H. McGregor__, Superintendent.

Key: Number; Surname, Given; Sex; Date of Birth-Age at Last Birthday; Tribe (Oglala Sioux, unless stated otherwise); Degree of Blood; Marital Status; Relationship to Head of Family [Last Census Roll Number]; At Jurisdiction Where Enrolled (Yes/No); (If no – Where); Ward (Yes/No, if given); Allotment, Annuity and Identification Numbers (if given).

117; American Horse, David; M; 7/3/31-9/12; F; S; Son ---; Yes; Yes; Id. U-13915 An. none

118; American Horse, Dawson; M; 1880-52; F; M; Head 118; Yes; Yes; Al. 42 An. 125

119; American Horse (no data) Lucy; F; 1880-52; F; M; Wife 119; Yes; Yes; Al. 2273 An. 126

120; American Horse, Stanley; M; 2/14/13-19; F; S; Son 120; Yes; Yes; Al. 6712 An. 129

121; American Horse, Eugene; M; 3/16/15-17; F; S; Son 121; Yes; Yes; Al. 8037 An. 130

122; American Horse, Mary; F; 11/2/17-14; F; S; Daughter 122; Yes; Yes; Id-U-9031 An. 131

123; American Horse, Alice; F; 7/13/20-11; F; S; Daughter 123; Yes; Yes; Id. U-9032 An. 132

124; American Horse, Grace; F; 10/2/10-21; F; S; Head 124; Yes; Yes; Al. 5483 An. 128

125; American Horse, Nancy; F; 1869-63; F; Wd; Head 126; Yes; Yes; Al. 6774 An. 133

126; American Horse, Thomas; M; 1869-63; F; M; Head 127; Yes; Yes; Al. 621 An. 135

127; American Horse (Shot To Pieces, Annie) Annie; F; 1880-52; F; M; Wife 128; Yes; Yes; Al. 5586 An. 136

128; American Horse, Casey; M; 12/8/16-15; F; S Son 129; Yes; Yes; Al. 8268 An. 137

129; American Horse, Wilson; M; 1907-25; F; S; Head 125; Yes; Yes; Al. 2275 An. 127

130; Amiotte, Albert; M; 1892-40; plus 1/4; S; Head 130; Yes; Yes; Al. 5485 An. 138

131; Amiotte, Edward; M; 1878-53; plus; M; Head 131; Yes; Yes; Al. 2271 An. 139

132; Amiotte (Rocks, Delia) Delia; F; 1890-42; 1/4; M; Wife 132; Yes; Yes; Al. 2272 An. 140

133; Amiotte, Alex W; M; 1907-25; 1/4; S; Son 136; Yes; Yes; Al. 2537 An. 141

134; Amiotte, Albert; M; 1/2/18-14; 1/4; S; Son 133; Yes; Yes; Id-U-9033 An. 144

135; Amiotte, Catherine; F; 12/18/19-12; 1/4; S; Daughter 134; Yes; Yes; Id. U-9034 An. 145

Census of the __Pine Ridge__ reservation of the __Pine Ridge, South Dakota__ jurisdiction, as of __April 1__, 19**32,** taken by __James H. McGregor__, Superintendent.

Key: Number; Surname, Given; Sex; Date of Birth-Age at Last Birthday; Tribe (Oglala Sioux, unless stated otherwise); Degree of Blood; Marital Status; Relationship to Head of Family [Last Census Roll Number]; At Jurisdiction Where Enrolled (Yes/No); (If no – Where); Ward (Yes/No, if given); Allotment, Annuity and Identification Numbers (if given).

136; Amiotte, Agnes; F; 6/3/09-22; plus 1/4; S; Head 137; Yes; Yes; Al. 4076 An. 142

137; Amiotte, Zohy E; F; 6/1/11-20; plus 1/4; S; Head 135; Yes; Yes; Ak[sic]. 5475 An. 143

138; Amiotte, Ellen; F; 1886-46; plus 1/4; Wd; Head 138; Yes; Yes; Al. 2331 An. 146
139; Amiotte, Harlan H; M; 3/29/14-18; 1/4; S; Son 139; Yes; Yes; Id. U-9039 An. 151
140; Amiotte, Leo E; M; 12/25/15-16; 1/4; S; Son 140; Yes; Yes; Id. U-9040 An. 152
141; Amiotte, Violet; F; 9/26/18-13; 1/4; S; Daughter 141; Yes; Yes; Id. U-9041 An. 153

142; Amiotte, Philip; M; 1/26/09-23; plus 1/4; S; Head 142; Yes; Yes; Al. 4939 An. 1088

143; Amiotte, Lawrence; M; 4/20/10-21; plus 1/4; S; Head 143; Yes; Yes; Al. 4754 An. 149

144; Amiotte, Ella K; F; 4/6/12-19; plus 1/4; S; Head 144; Yes; Yes; Al. 7001 An. 150

145; Amiotte, Doris; F; 1907-25; plus 1/4; S; Head 145; Yes; Yes; Al. 2332 An. 147

146; Amiotte, Henry; M; 5/14/11-20; plus 1/4; S; Head 146; Yes; Yes; Al. 5466 An. 1087

147; Amiotte, Emery; M; 1907-25; plus 1/4 1/4; M; Head 147; No; Rosebud, SD; Yes; Al. 2191 An. 155
N.E. Amiotte (Looking White, Jennie) Jennie; F; [blank]; Rosebud Sioux; F; M; Wife
148; Amiotte, Hazel Roselle; F; 11/26/31-4/12; Sioux; plus 1/4; S; Daughter ---; No; Rosebud, SD; Yes; Id. U-14079 An. none

149; Amiotte, Emery; M; 1897-35; plus 1/3[sic]; M; Head 148; Yes; Yes; Al. 2584 An. 154
N.E. Amiotte (Wilcox, Blanche) Blanche E; [blank]; White; M; Wife
150; Amiotte, Louise; F; 2/10/19-13; plus 1/4; S; Daughter 149; Yes; Yes; Id. U-12984 An. none

Census of the **Pine Ridge** reservation of the **Pine Ridge, South Dakota** jurisdiction, as of **April 1**, 19**32**, taken by **James H. McGregor**, Superintendent.

Key: Number; Surname, Given; Sex; Date of Birth-Age at Last Birthday; Tribe (Oglala Sioux, unless stated otherwise); Degree of Blood; Marital Status; Relationship to Head of Family [Last Census Roll Number]; At Jurisdiction Where Enrolled (Yes/No); (If no – Where); Ward (Yes/No, if given); Allotment, Annuity and Identification Numbers (if given).

151; Amiotte, Gloria J; F; 7/7/27-4; -1/4; S; Daughter 150; Yes; Yes; Id. U-12962 An. none
152; Amiotte, Wallace Emery; M; 4/7/31-11/12; -1/4; S; Son ---; Yes; Yes; Id. U-13795 An. none
153; Amiotte, Lena; F; 1901-31; plus 1/4; S; Head 151; Yes; Yes; Al. 2586 An. 156
154; Amiotte, Levi Bert; M; 1891-41; plus 1/4; M; Head 152; Yes; Yes; Al. 5484 An. 157
155; Amiotte (Janis, Louisa) Louisa; F; 1892-40; 1/4; M; Wife 153; Yes; Yes; Al. 5755 An. 158
156; Amiotte, Olive; F; 4/29/12-19; 1/4; S; Daughter 154; Yes; Yes; Al. 6889 An. 159
157; Amiotte, Esther; F; 2/11/14-18; 1/4; S; Daughter 155; Yes; Yes; Id. U-9035 An. 160
158; Amiotte, Eleanor; F; 7/13/16-15; 1/4; S; Daughter 156; Yes; Yes; Id. U-9036 An. 161
159; Amiotte, Louise; F; 10/7/18-13; 1/4; S; Daughter 157; Yes; Yes; Id. U-9037 An. 162
160; Amiotte, Walter; M; 1/4/21-11; 1/4; S; Son 158; Yes; Yes; Id. U-9038 An. 163
161; Amiotte, Dallas; F; 2/7/23-9; 1/4; S; Daughter 159; Yes; Yes; Id. U-13048 An. 164
162; Amiotte, Delbert L; M; 8/18/23-6; 1/4; S; Son 160; Yes; Yes; Id. U-11930 An. none
163; Amiotte, Donald L; M; 7/7/27-4; 1/4; S; Son 161; Yes; Yes; Id. U-12398 An. none
164; Amiotte, Erna Belle; F; 11/4/30-1; 1/4; S; Daughter 162; Yes; Yes; Id. U-13664 An. none

165; Andrews, Katherine; F; 1871-61; plus 1/4; Wd; Head 163; No; Ft. Collins, Larmier[sic] Co, Colo; No; Al. 3855 An. 165
166; Apple, Charles; M; 1889-43; plus 1/4; M; Head 166; Yes; Yes; Al. 5128\ An. 172
167; Apple (Lamont, Mary) Mary; F; 1882-50; 1/4; M; Wife 167; Yes; Yes; Al. 5157 An. 173

168; Apple, Dora; F; 1906-27; plus 1/4; S; Head 168; Yes; Yes; Al. 3583 An. 174

169; Apple, Frank; M; 1895-37; plus 1/4; M; Head 169; Yes; Yes; Al. 5129 An. 175
170; Apple (No Neck, Grace) Grace; F; 1886-46; plus 1/4; M; Wife 170; Yes; Yes; Al. 2052 An. 176
171; Apple. Stephen; M; 3/28/17-15; plus 1/4; S; Son 173; Yes; Yes; Id. U-9842 An. 181

Census of the **Pine Ridge** reservation of the **Pine Ridge, South Dakota** jurisdiction, as of **April 1**, 1932, taken by **James H. McGregor**, Superintendent.

Key: Number; Surname, Given; Sex; Date of Birth-Age at Last Birthday; Tribe (Oglala Sioux, unless stated otherwise); Degree of Blood; Marital Status; Relationship to Head of Family [Last Census Roll Number]; At Jurisdiction Where Enrolled (Yes/No); (If no – Where); Ward (Yes/No, if given); Allotment, Annuity and Identification Numbers (if given).

172; Apple, Victoria; F; 7/12/21-10; plus 1/4; S; Daughter 174; Yes; Yes; Id. U-9046 An. 182
173; Apple, Leroy; M; 10/3/28-3; plus 1/4; S; Son 175; Yes; Yes; Id. U-12823 An. none
174; No Neck, Daniel; M; 12/27/15-16; plus 1/4; S; Step-son 171; Yes; Yes; Id. U-9044 An. 179
175; No Neck, Dora; F; 10/12/17-14; plus 1/4; S; Stepdaughter 172; Yes; Yes; Id. U-9045 An. 180

176; Apple, George; M; 1880-52; plus; M; Head 176; Yes; Yes; Al. 3577 An. 183
177; Apple (WhiteLance) Susie; F; 1902-30; F; M; Wife 177; Yes; Yes; Al. 1545 An. 184
178; Apple, Fred; M; 4/19/11-21; plus; S; Son 178; Yes; Yes; Al. 7234 An. 185
179; Apple, Edith; F; 4/11/14-18; plus 1/4; S; Daughter 179; Yes; Yes; Al. 7865 An. 186
180; Apple, Woodrow; M; 3/8/17-15; plus 1/4; S; Son 180; Yes; Yes; Id. U-9047 An. 187
181; Apple, Paul; M; 5/13/21-10; plus 1/4; S; Son 181; Yes; Yes; Id. U-9048 An. 188
182; Apple, Anthony G; M; 10/3/25-6; plus 1/4; S; Son 182; Yes; Yes; Id. U-11786 An. none
183; Apple, Kenneth; M; 3/15/28-4; plus 1/4; S; Son 183; Yes; Yes; Id. U-9604 An. none
184; Apple, Francis D/ M; 9/26/31-6/12; plus 1/4; S; Son ---; Yes; Yes; Id. U-13929 An. none

185; Apple, John; M; 1849-63; plus 1/4; M; Head 184; Yes; Yes; Al. 3578 An. 190

186; Apple (Stirk), Rosa; F; 1858-54; plus 1/4; M; Wife 185; Yes; Yes; Al. 3579 An. 191
187; Apple, John, Jr; M; 9/3/10-21; plus 1/4; S; Son 186; Yes; Yes; Al. 7219 An. 193

188; Apple, Hattie; F; 1908-25; plus 1/4; S; Head 187; Yes; Yes; Al. 3584 An. 192

189; Apple, Joseph; M; 1893-39; plus 1/4; M; Head 188; Yes; Yes; Al. 5140 An. 194
190; Apple (Marshall), Lizzie; F; 1896-36; plus 1/4; M; Wife 189; Yes; Yes; Al. 4538 An. 195
191; Apple, Joseph, Jr; M; 12/22/17-14; plus 1/4; S; Son 190; Yes; Yes; Id. U-9050 An. 197
192; Apple, Martin; M; 4- -21[sic]-11; plus 1/4; S; Son 191; Yes; Yes; Id. U-9051 An. 198

Census of the **Pine Ridge** reservation of the **Pine Ridge, South Dakota** jurisdiction, as of **April 1**, 1932, taken by **James H. McGregor**, Superintendent.

Key: Number; Surname, Given; Sex; Date of Birth-Age at Last Birthday; Tribe (Oglala Sioux, unless stated otherwise); Degree of Blood; Marital Status; Relationship to Head of Family [Last Census Roll Number]; At Jurisdiction Where Enrolled (Yes/No); (If no – Where); Ward (Yes/No, if given); Allotment, Annuity and Identification Numbers (if given).

193; Apple, Francis Kermit; M; 9/26/22-9; plus 1/4; S; Son 192; Yes; Yes; Id. U-11121 An. 199
194; Apple, Marie E; F; 11/9/24-7; plus 1/4; S; Daughter 193; Yes; Yes; Id. U-11531 An. 200
195; Apple, Antione J; M; 4/2/28-4; plus 1/4; S; Son 194; Yes; Yes; Id. U-12720 An. none
196; Apple, Clara; F; 6/2/30-1; plus 1/4; S; Daughter 195; Yes; Yes; Id. U-13540 An. none

197; Arapahoe, David, Jr; M; 1908-24; F; M; Head 196; No; Boston, Suffolk Co, Mass; Yes; Al. 5160 An. 3215
198; Arapahoe (Crow), Julia Lizzie; F; 1910-22; F; M; Wife-197; No; Boston, Suffolk Co, Mass; Yes; Al. 6813 An. 683
199; Arapahoe, Coolidge; M; 11/11/27-4; F; S; Son 198; No; Boston, Suffolk Co, Mass; Yes; Id. U-12675 An. none

200; Arapahoe, David, Sr; M; 1875-57; F; Wd; Head 199; No; Boston, Suffolk Co, Mass; No; Al. 1091 An. 202

201; Arapahoe, Herman; M; 1904-28; F; Wd; Head 200; Yes; Yes; Al. 1093 An. 203

202; Arapahoe, William; M; 1882-50; F; Wd; Head 202; Yes; No; Al. 1094 An. 204

203; Around Him, John; M; 1895-37; F; M: Head 203; Yes; Yes; Al. 1968 An. 208
204; Around Him (Prairie Chicken), Zallie; F; 1901-31; F; M; Wife 3031; Yes; Yes; Al. 5265 An. 3021
205; Around Him, Sallie; F; 9/8/15-16; F; S; Daughter 204; Yes; Yes; Id. U-9054 An. 210
206; Around Him, Dora; F; 1/27/18-16; F; S; Daughter 205; Yes; Yes; Id. U-9055 An. 211
207; Around Him, Anna; F; 1/3/21-11; F; S; Daughter 206; Yes; Yes; Id. U-9056 An. 212
208; Around Him, Christina; F; 5/8/23-8; F; S; Daughter 207; Yes; Yes; Id. U-14036 An. 213
209; Hopkins, Stephen; M; 11/22/22-9; F; S; Stepson 3032; Yes; Yes; Id. U-12025 An. 3022
210; Hopkins, Laevinia; F; 1/7/24-8; F; S; Stepdaughter 3033; Yes; Yes; Id. U-11183 An. 3023
211; PrairieChicken, Eva Lillian; F; 2/11/28-4; F; S; Stepdaughter 3034; Yes; Yes; Id. U-12635 An. none

Census of the **Pine Ridge** reservation of the **Pine Ridge, South Dakota** jurisdiction, as of **April 1**, 1932, taken by **James H. McGregor**, Superintendent.

Key: Number; Surname, Given; Sex; Date of Birth-Age at Last Birthday; Tribe (Oglala Sioux, unless stated otherwise); Degree of Blood; Marital Status; Relationship to Head of Family [Last Census Roll Number]; At Jurisdiction Where Enrolled (Yes/No); (If no – Where); Ward (Yes/No, if given); Allotment, Annuity and Identification Numbers (if given).

212; PrairieChicken, Zallie Eliza; F; 10/13/30-1; F; S; Stepdaughter 3035 (probably daughter); Yes; Yes; Id. U-13740 An. none

213; Around Him, Howard; M; 1868-70; F; M; Head 208; Yes; No; Al. 1966 An. 206

214; Around Him, Victoria; F; 19-872-56; F; M; Wife 209; Yes; Yes; Al. 1967 An. 207

215; Arrow Wound; M; 1852-80; F; M; Head 210; Yes; Yes; Al. 3440 An. 214
216; Arrow Wound (ComesWalking), Emma; F; 1866-66; F; M; Wife 211; Yes; Yes; Al. 3441 An. 215

~~N.E. Artichoker, John; M; ?; Winnebago; 7/8; M; Head; No; Chas. H. Burks Sch. Ft. Wingate~~

217; Artichoker (Lessert), Emily; F; 1901-31; plus 1/4; M; Wife 212; No; Chas. H. Burks Sch. Ft. Wingate; Yes; Al. 975 An. 217
218; Artichoker, Lucille S; F; 10/10/20-11; Sioux & Winne; plus 1/4; S; Daughter 213; No; Chas. H. Burks Sch. Ft. Wingate; Yes; Id. U-9057 An. 218
219; Artichoker, Benjamin D; M; 10/12/26-5; Sioux & Winne; plus 1/4; S; Son
214; No; Chas. H. Burks Sch. Ft. Wingate; Yes; Id. U-11994 An. none
220; Artichoker, John Hobart; M; 1/17/30-1; Sioux & Winne; plus 1/4; S; Son 215; Chas. H. Burks Sch. Ft. Wingate; Yes; Id. U-13316 An. none

~~N.E. Ashley, Joseph Everett; M; ?; Rosebud Sioux; ?; M; Head~~
221; Ashley (Little Whiteman), Nellie; F; 7/29/12-19; F; M; Wife 4057; Yes; Yes; Al. 7735 An. 4042

~~N.E. Austin, Seth; M; ?; Sioux (not enr.); 1/4; M; Head~~
222; Austin (Valandry), Hattie; F; 1891-41; plus 1/4; M; Wife 216; Yes; Yes; Al. 1085 An. 219
223; Austin, Kenneth; M; 5/1/15-16; plus 1/4; S; Son 217; Yes; Yes; Id. U-9058 An. 222
224; Austin, William; M; 7/18/19-12; plus 1/4; S; Son 218; Yes; Yes; Id. U-9059 An. 223
225; Austin, Hobert N; M; 2/23/22-10; plus 1/4; S; Son 219; Yes; Yes; Id. U-10978 An. 224
226; Austin, Charles W; M; 6/20/24-7; plus 1/4; S; Son 220; Yes; Yes; Id. U-11304 An. none

227; Babby, Fred; M; 11/10/82-49; -1/4; Wd; Head 221; Yes; No; Al. 3853 An. 225
228; Babby, Dennis I; M; 4/1/12-20; plus 1/4; S; Son 222; Yes; Yes; Al. 6372 An. 228

Census of the __Pine Ridge__ reservation of the __Pine Ridge, South Dakota__ jurisdiction, as of __April 1__, 1932, taken by __James H. McGregor__, Superintendent.

Key: Number; Surname, Given; Sex; Date of Birth-Age at Last Birthday; Tribe (Oglala Sioux, unless stated otherwise); Degree of Blood; Marital Status; Relationship to Head of Family [Last Census Roll Number]; At Jurisdiction Where Enrolled (Yes/No); (If no – Where); Ward (Yes/No, if given); Allotment, Annuity and Identification Numbers (if given).

229; Babby, Gilbert; M; 7/17/21-10; plus 1/4; S; Son 223; Yes; Yes; Id. U-12086 An. 229
230; Babby, Faith Lorraine; F; 9/2/24-7; plus 1/4; S; Daughter 224; Yes; Yes; Id. U-11440 An. 231
231; Babby, Paul Wayne; M; 11/10/22-9; plus 1/4; S; Son 225; Yes; Yes; Id. U-12085 An. 230

232; Babby, Louis; M; 7/10/02-29; -1/4; M; Head 226; Yes; Yes; Al. 4608 An. 233
~~N.E. Babby (Rumsey), Sophia; F; ?; White; M; Wife~~
233; Babby, Louis Jane; F; 11/28/30-1; -1/4; S; Daughter 227; Yes; Yes; Id. U-13727 An. none

234; Babby, Maurice; M; 10/30/10-21; plus 1/4; S; Head 228; Yes; Yes; Al. 6371 An. 227

235; Babby, Wilbur; M; 4/5/81-51; -1/4; Wd; Head 229; Yes; Yes; Al. 4607 An. 234

236; Back, Simon; M; 1878-54; F; Wd; Head 230; Yes; Yes; Al. 6507 An. 237

237; Backward, Austin; M; 1898-34; F; Wd; Head 231; Yes; Yes; Al. 6141 An. 240
238; Backward, Virginia; F; 11/12/22-9; F; S; Daughter 232; Yes; Yes; Id. U-11203 An. 242
239; Backward, Avril; F; 1/17/24-8; F; S; Daughter 233; Yes; Yes; Id. U-11204 An. 243
240; Backward, Jessie; F; 2/25/27-5; F; S; Daughter 234; Yes; Yes;Id. U-12233 An. none

241; Bad Bear, Howard; M; 1877-55; F; M; Head 235; Yes; Yes; Al. 3345 An. 244
242; Bad Bear, Nellie; F; 1878-54; F; M; Wife 236; Yes; Yes; Al. 3346 An. 245
243; Bad Bear, Alexander; M; 8/12/08-23; F; S; Son 237; Yes; Yes; Al. 3561 An. 246
244; Bad Bear, William; M; 7/18/12-19; F; S; Son 238; Yes; Yes; Al. 7411 An. 247
245; Bad Bear, Jennie; F; 9/18/16-15; F; S; Daughter 239; Yes; Yes; Id. U-9063 An. 248
246; Bad Bear, Albert; M; 11/24/18-13; F; S; Son; 240; Yes; Yes; Id. U-9064 An. 249
247; Bad Bear, Grace; F; 4/18/23-8; F; S; Daughter 241; Yes; Yes; Id. U-14033 An. 250

248; Bad Cob, George; M; 1890-42; F; S; Head 242; Yes; Yes; Al. 4240 An. 253

249; Bad Cob, Roy Thomas; M; 1901-31; F; M; Head; Yes; Yes; Al. 4242 An. 254

Census of the ___Pine Ridge___ reservation of the ___Pine Ridge, South Dakota___ jurisdiction, as of ___April 1___, 19**32**, taken by ___James H. McGregor___, Superintendent.

Key: Number; Surname, Given; Sex; Date of Birth-Age at Last Birthday; Tribe (Oglala Sioux, unless stated otherwise); Degree of Blood; Marital Status; Relationship to Head of Family [Last Census Roll Number]; At Jurisdiction Where Enrolled (Yes/No); (If no – Where); Ward (Yes/No, if given); Allotment, Annuity and Identification Numbers (if given).

250; Bad Cob (Red Elk), Victoria; F; 1906-26; F; M; Wife 244; Yes; Yes; Al. 5651 An. 5428
251; Bad Cob, Sylvester; M; 4/19/23-8; F; S; Son; 245; Yes; Yes; Id. U-13071 An. none
252; Bad Cob, Agatha; F; 6/23/29-2; F; S; Daughter 246; Yes; Yes; Id. U-13199 An. none

253; Badger, David; M; 1898-34; plus 1/4; M; Head 247; Yes; Yes; Al. 803 An. 247
254; Badger (Mousseau), Mary; F; 1897-35; plus 1/4; M; Wife 248; Yes; Yes; Al. 702 An. 258
255; Badger, Evelyn; F; 1/8/20-12; plus 1/4; S; Daughter 249; Yes; Yes; Id. U-9065 An. 259
256; Badger, Sophia; F; 3/10/22-10; plus 1/4; S; Daughter 250; Yes; Yes; Id. U-12059 An. 260
257; Badger, Myrtle; F; 12/12/24-7; plus 1/4; S; Daughter 251; Yes; Yes;Id. U-11397 An. 261
258; Badger, Rebecca; F; 4/10/29-2; plus 1/4; S; Daughter 252; Yes; Yes; Id. U-13128 An. none
259; Badger, Vera; F; 6/20/31-9/12; plus 1/4; S; Daughter 00; Yes; Yes; Id. U-13850 An. none

260; Badgett, Elizabeth; F; 1868-64; plus 1/4; ?; Head 253; No; Morecroft[sic], Crook Co, Wyo; No; Al. 5505 An. 262

261; Bad Hair, John; M; 1891-41; F; Wd; Head 254; Yes; Yes; Al. 1341 An. 263

262; Bad Hair, Louis; M; 10/31/10-21; F; S; Head 255; Yes; Yes; Al. 5424 An. 1700

~~N.E. Bad Hand, Hugh; Rosebud Sioux; Head~~
263; Bad Hand (Shaving Bear), Anna; F; 1897-34; F; M; Wife 256; No; Rosebud, S.D; Yes; Al. 2362 An. 6156
264; Shaving Bear, Noah; M; 10/29/13-18; F; S; Son 257; No; Rosebud S.D; Yes; Al. 7632 An. 6158

265; Bad Heart Bull, Eli; M; 1883-49; F; M; Head 258; Yes; Yes; Al. 3233 An. 266
266; Bad Heart Bull (Left Hand Bear), Cecelia; F; 1892-40; F; M; Wife 259; Yes; Yes; Al. 1251 An. 267
267; Bad Heart Bull, John; M; 2/28/12-19; F; S; Son 260; Yes; Yes; Al. 6166 An. 268
268; Bad Heart Bull, Ida Hattie; F; 4/16/14-17; F; S; Daughter 261; Yes; Yes; Id. U-9067 An. 269

Census of the __**Pine Ridge**__ reservation of the __**Pine Ridge, South Dakota**__ jurisdiction, as of __**April 1**__, 19**32**, taken by __**James H. McGregor**__, Superintendent.

Key: Number; Surname, Given; Sex; Date of Birth-Age at Last Birthday; Tribe (Oglala Sioux, unless stated otherwise); Degree of Blood; Marital Status; Relationship to Head of Family [Last Census Roll Number]; At Jurisdiction Where Enrolled (Yes/No); (If no – Where); Ward (Yes/No, if given); Allotment, Annuity and Identification Numbers (if given).

269; Bad Heart Bull, Tina; F; 5/ /16-15; F; S; Daughter 262; Yes; Yes; Id. U-9068 An. 270
270; Bad Heart Bull, Seth; M; 11/7/18-13; F; S; Son 263; Yes; Yes; Id. U-9069 An. 271
271; Bad Heart Bull, Estella; F; 1/12/21-11; F; S; Daughter 264; Yes; Yes; Id. U-9070 An. 272
272; Bad Heart Bull, Vincent; M; 6/4/23-8; F; S; Son 265; Yes; Yes; Id. U-11627 An. 273
273; Bad Heart Bull, Susanna; F; 3/3/26-6; F; S; Daughter 266; Yes; Yes; Id. U-12234 An. none
274; Bad Heart Bull, Lucy; F; 7/14/28-3; F; S; Daughter 267; Yes; Yes; Id. U-12736 An. none
275; Bad Heart Bull, Julius; M; 3/14/30-2; F; S; Son 268; Yes; Yes; Id. U-13406 An. none

276; Bad Wound, Daniel; M; 1862-66; F; M; Head 269; Yes; Yes; Al. 2131 An. 276
277; Bad Wound, Bessie; F; 1862-66; F; M; Wife 270; Yes; Yes; Al. 5298 An. 275
278; Bad Wound, Daniel; M; 1898-34; F; M; Head 272; Yes; Yes; Al. 2069 An. 276
279; Bad Wound (Monroe), Julia Dorothy; F; 1905-27; plus 1/4; M; Wife 273; Yes; Yes; Al. 2325 An. none
280; Bad Wound, Robert E; M; 4/26/26-5; plus 1/4; S; Son 274; Yes; Yes; Id. U-12505 An. none
281; Bad Wound, James; M; 1/27/28-4; plus 1/4; S; Son 275; Yes; Yes; Id. U-12503 An. none
282; Bad Wound, Fannie; F; 3/17/30-2; plus 1/4; S; Daughter 276; Yes; Yes; Id. U-13438 An. none
283; Bad Wound, Wesley; M; 12/11/31-3/12; plus 1/4; S; Son ---; Yes; Yes; Id. U-13981 An. none
284; Bad Wound, Gilbert; M; 1893-39; plus 1/4; M; Head 277; Yes; Yes; Al. 2095 An. 277
285; Bad Wound (Twiss), Naomi; F; 1902-30; plus 1/4; M; Wife 278; Yes; Yes; Al. 822 An. 278
286; Bad Wound, Bernetta M; F; 12/9/23-8; plus 1/4; S; Daughter 279; Yes; Yes; Id. U-11191 An. 279
287; Bad Wound, Lewis; M; 2/23/28-4; plus 1/4; S; Son 280; Yes; Yes; Id. U-12504 An. none

Census of the __Pine Ridge__ reservation of the __Pine Ridge, South Dakota__ jurisdiction, as of __April 1__, 19**32**, taken by __James H. McGregor__, Superintendent.

Key: Number; Surname, Given; Sex; Date of Birth-Age at Last Birthday; Tribe (Oglala Sioux, unless stated otherwise); Degree of Blood; Marital Status; Relationship to Head of Family [Last Census Roll Number]; At Jurisdiction Where Enrolled (Yes/No); (If no – Where); Ward (Yes/No, if given); Allotment, Annuity and Identification Numbers (if given).

288; Bad Wound, Maggie; F; 1861-71; F; Wd; Head 281; Yes; Yes; Al. 2073 An. 280

289; Bad Wound, Noah; M; 1867-65; F; M; Head 282; Yes; No; Al. 2093 An. 282
290; Bad Wound, Mary; F; 1873-59; plus 1/4; M; Wife 283; Yes; No; Al. 2094 An. 283
291; Bad Wound, Joseph; M; 1/4/15-17; plus 1/4; S; Son 284; Yes; Yes; Al. 8119 An. 286

292; Bad Wound, Oliver; M; 1906-26; F; M; Head 287; Yes; Yes; Al. 2071 An. 237
293; Bad Wound (Short Bear), Cecelia; F; 1894-38; F; M; Wife 288; Yes; Yes; Al. 5222 An. 6202
294; Bad Wound, Jennie; F; 12/18/28-3; F; S; Daughter 289; Yes; Yes; Id. U-12998 An. none
295; Bad Wound, Leroyal Ellis; M; 6/21/30-1; F; S; Son 290; Yes; Yes; Id. U-13524 An. none

296; Bad Wound, Robert; M; 1871-61; F; M; Head 291; Yes; Yes; Al. 2066 An. 288
297; Bad Wound, Day; F; 1876-56; F; M; Wife 292; Yes; Yes; Al. 2067 An. 289
298; Bad Wound, Eva; F; 9/28/11-20; F; S; Daughter 293; Yes; Yes; Al. 7034 An. 291
299; Iron Cloud, Seth; M; 12/2/20-11; F; S; Nephew 271; Yes; Yes; Id. U-9732 An. 3156

300; Bad Wound, Vincent; M; 1895-37; plus 1/4; M; Head 294; Yes; Yes; Al. 2097 An. 293
301; Bad Wound (Brown, Rosa), Rosa; F; 1896-36; plus 1/4; M; Wife 295; Yes; Yes; Al. 2295 An. 294
302; Bad Wound, Louisa; F; 3/19/23-9; plus 1/4; S; Daughter 296; Yes; Yes; Id. U-13003 An. 296
303; Bad Wound, Lavina E; F; 2/3/25-7; plus 1/4; S; Daughter 297; Yes; Yes; Id. U-11556 An. 297
304; Bad Wound, Leroy Albert; M; 8/28/27-4; plus 1/4; S; Son 298; Yes; Yes; Id. U-12381 An. none
305; Bad Wound, Evelyn Mae; F; 11/14/30-1; plus 1/4; S; Daughter 299; Yes; Yes; Id. U-13623 An. none

306; Bad Yellow Hair, Asa; M; 1883-49; F; M; Head 300; Yes; Yes; Al. 7245 An. 300
307; Bad Yellow Hair (Brave Eagle), Lizzie; F; 1894-38; plus 1/4; M; Wife 302; Yes; Yes; Al. 4393 An. 945

Census of the __Pine Ridge__ reservation of the __Pine Ridge, South Dakota__ jurisdiction, as of __April 1__, 19**32**, taken by __James H. McGregor__, Superintendent.

Key: Number; Surname, Given; Sex; Date of Birth-Age at Last Birthday; Tribe (Oglala Sioux, unless stated otherwise); Degree of Blood; Marital Status; Relationship to Head of Family [Last Census Roll Number]; At Jurisdiction Where Enrolled (Yes/No); (If no – Where); Ward (Yes/No, if given); Allotment, Annuity and Identification Numbers (if given).

308; Bad Yellow Hair, Roy; M; 4/15/15-16; plus 1/4; S; Son 301; Yes; Yes; Id. U-10851 An. 302

309; Brave Eagle, Ada; F; 9/29/12-18; plus 1/4; S; Stepdaughter 303; Yes; Yes; Al. 7329 An. 946

310; Bad Yellow Hair, Joseph; M; 1871-61; F; Wd; Head 304; Yes; Yes; Al. 8056 An. 303

311; Baggage, Monoka; F; 1884-48; F; Wd; Head 304; No; Chadron, Dawes Co, Nebr; Yes; Al. 6038 An. 305

312; Baggage, Henry; M; 1/21/19-13; plus 1/4; S; Son 307; No; Chadron, Dawes Co, Nebr; Yes; Id. U-9072 An. 306

313; Bald, Minnie; F; 1863-69; plus 1/4; Wd; Head 308; Yes; Yes; Id. U-9073 An. 308

314; Bald Eagle, Max; M; 1877-55; F; M; Head 309; Yes; Yes; Al. 3195 An. 311

315; Bald Eagle (Mousseau, Agnes), Agnes; F; 1892-40; plus 1/4; M; Wife 312; Yes; Yes; Al. 700 An. 6561

316; Bald Eagle, Delphine; F; 8/12/13-19; F; S; Daughter 310; Yes; Yes; Id. U-9074 An. 315

317; Bald Eagle, Max, Jr; M; 10/9/30-1; plus 1/4; S; Son 314; Yes; Yes; Id. U-13587 An. none

318; Blue Horse Owner, Reuben; M; 1/21/12-19; F; S; Ward 311; Yes; [blank]; Id. U-10465 An. 316

319; Kills Small, Cornelius; M; 1/6/28-4; plus 1/4; S; Stepson 313; Yes; Yes; Id. U-12727 An. none

320; Bald Eagle Bear, Paul; M; 1893-39; F; S; Head 315; Yes; Yes; Id. U-12727 An. none

321; Bald Eagle Bear, Peter; M; 1889-43; F; M; Head 316; Yes; Yes; Al. 1764 An. 318

322; Bald Eagle Bear (Crier, Mary), Mary; F; 1898-34; F; M; Wife 317; Yes; Yes; Al. 4213 An. 319

323; Bald Eagle Bear, Lorine R; F; 12/30/24-7; F; S; Daughter 318; Yes; Yes; Id. U-11504 An. 322

324; Bald Eagle Bear, Frederick; M; 6/9/29-2; F; S; Son 319; Yes; Yes; Id. U-13177 An. none

325; Bald Eagle Bear, Evangeline; F; 9/6/31-7/12; F; S; Daughter ---; Yes; Yes; Id. U-13912 An. none

326; Bald Head; M; 1877-55; F; M; Head 320; Yes; Yes; Al. 52 An. 323

Census of the __**Pine Ridge**__ reservation of the __**Pine Ridge, South Dakota**__ jurisdiction, as of __**April 1**__, 1932, taken by __**James H. McGregor**__, Superintendent.

Key: Number; Surname, Given; Sex; Date of Birth-Age at Last Birthday; Tribe (Oglala Sioux, unless stated otherwise); Degree of Blood; Marital Status; Relationship to Head of Family [Last Census Roll Number]; At Jurisdiction Where Enrolled (Yes/No); (If no – Where); Ward (Yes/No, if given); Allotment, Annuity and Identification Numbers (if given).

327; Bald Head (Lee, Susanna), Susanna; F; 1885-47; plus 1/4; M; Wife 324; Yes; Yes; Al. 2267 An. 3779

328; Bald Head, Wallace; M; 10/5/15-16; F; S; Son 321; Yes; Yes; Id. U-9077 An. 325

329; Bald Head, Antoine; M; 9/25/19-12; F; S; Son 322; Yes; Yes; Id. U-9079 An. 327

330; Bald Head, George; M; 10/24/21-10; F; S; Son 323; Yes; Yes; Id. U-10960 An. 328

331; Bank, John; M; 1901-31; F; M; Head 325; Yes; Yes; Al. 6240 An. 329
332; Bank (Bores A Hole, Dora), Dora; F; 1902-30; F; M; Wife 326; Yes; Yes; Al. 3403 An. 330
333; Bank, Thomas; M; 7/27/27-4; S; Son 327; Yes; Yes; Id. U-12379 An. none

~~N.E. Barker, Wallace; M; ?; Santee Sioux; plus 1/4; M; Head~~
334; Barker (LaPoint, Grace), Grace; F; 1903-29; plus 1/4; M; Wife 328; Yes; Yes; Al. 4679 An. 3693

335; Bartlett, George; M; 1888-46; plus 1/4; M; Head 329; Yes; Yes; Al. 5563 An. 331
~~N.E. Bartlett (Barker, Mabel), Mabel; F; ?; Santee Sioux; plus; M; Wife~~
336; Bartlett, Althia; F; 9/1/24-7; Sioux; plus 1/4; S; Daughter 330; Yes; Yes; Id. U-11336 An. 334
337; Bartlett, Delphine; F; 2/22/27-5; Sioux; plus 1/4; S; Daughter 331; Yes; Yes; Id. U-12235 An. none
338; Bartlett, George, Jr; M; 1/27/11-21; Sioux; plus 1/4; M; Head 332; Yes; Yes; Al. 5565 An. 332
~~N.E. Bartlett (Hand Boy, Allen), Allen; F; ?; Ch. R. Sioux; F ; M; Head 332; Yes; Yes; Al. 5565 An. 332~~

339; Bartlett, Susie; F; 1889-43; plus 1/4; Wd; Head 333; No; Winnebago, Nebr; Yes; Al. 5565 An. 335
340; Bartlett, Pansy; F; 3/31/15-17; plus 1/4; S; Daughter 334; No; Winnebago, Nebr; Yes; Al. 7895 An. 336
341; Bartlett, Ramsey; M; 10/21/19-12; plus 1/4; S; Son 335; No; Winnebago, Nebr; Yes; Id. U-9081 An. 337
342; Bartlett, Minnie; F; 12/16/21-10; plus 1/4; S; Daughter 336; No; Winnebago, Nebr; Yes; Id. U-10850 An. 338
343; Tebo, One Leroy; M; 10-26-27-4; Winnebago & Sioux; plus 1/4; S; Son 337; No; Winnebago, Nebr; Yes; Id. U-9081 An. 337

Census of the __Pine Ridge__ reservation of the __Pine Ridge, South Dakota__ jurisdiction, as of __April 1__, 1932, taken by __James H. McGregor__, Superintendent.

Key: Number; Surname, Given; Sex; Date of Birth-Age at Last Birthday; Tribe (Oglala Sioux, unless stated otherwise); Degree of Blood; Marital Status; Relationship to Head of Family [Last Census Roll Number]; At Jurisdiction Where Enrolled (Yes/No); (If no – Where); Ward (Yes/No, if given); Allotment, Annuity and Identification Numbers (if given).

~~N.E. Bates, Thomas W; M; ?; Yankton Sioux; F; M; Head~~
344; Bates (Good Teacher, Ida), Ida; F; 1902-30; plus 1/4; M; Wife 338; No; Yankton, S. Dak; Yes; Al. 1817 An. 339

345; Bates, Maurice; M; 1908-24; -1/4; S; Head 339; Yes; Yes; Al. 5366 An. 341

346; Bauman, Marie; F; 1892-40; -1/4; Wd; Head 340; No; Columbus, Platte Co, Neb; Yes; Al. 4442 An. 342
347; Bauman, Rose Mary; F; 8/25/23-8; -1/4; S; Daughter 341; No; Columbus, Platte Co, Neb; Yes; Id. U-11135 An. 343

~~N.E. Bauman, Frank; M; ?; White; Head~~
348; Bauman (Brown, Susie), Susie; F; 1899-32; plus 1/4; M; Wife 342; Yes; Yes; Al. 4021 An. 344
349; Bauman, Frank G; M; 11/15/25-6; -1/4; S; Son 343; Yes; Yes; Id. U-12299 An. none
350; Bauman, Marie; F; 7/1/27-4; -1/4; S; Dau 344; Yes; Yes; Id. U-12609 An. none

~~N.E. Bayliss, Clifford Arthur; M; White; M; Head~~
351; Bayliss (Allen, Katherine), Katherine; F; 8/3/09-22; -1/4; M; Wife 345; Yes; Yes; Al. 4652 An. 69
352; Bayliss, Frances E; F; 6/7/27-4; -1/4; S; Daughter 346; Yes; Yes; Id. U-12342 An. none
353; Bayliss, William A; M; 10/26/28-3; -1/4; S; Son 347; Yes; Yes; Id. U-13407 An. none
354; Bayliss, Betty Jean; F; 10/3/30-1; -1/4; S; Daughter 348; Yes; Yes; Id. U-13624 An. none

355; Bear Comes Out; M; 1858-74; F; Wd; Head 349; Yes; Yes; Al. 3011 An. 346

356; Beard, Dewey; M; 1862-70; F; M; Head 350; Yes; Yes; Al. 1775 An. 348
357; Beard, Alice; F; 1878-54; F; M; Wife 351; Yes; Yes; Al. 3642 An. 349
358; Beard, Thomas; M; 9/28/16-15; F; S; Son 352; Yes; Yes; Id. U-9083 An. 350
359; Beard, Carrie Ann; F; 12/31/22-9; F; S; Daughter 353; Yes; Yes; Id. U-12069 An. 351

360; Beard, Agnes; F; 1906-26; F; Wd; Head 354; Yes; Yes; Al. 5096 An. 3495
361; Beard, Agnes; F; 12/25/28-3; F; S; Daughter 355; Yes; Yes; Id. U-12999 An. none

362; Bear Eagle, Rosa; F; 1860-72; F; Wd; Head 357; Yes; Yes; Al. 1811 An. 354

Census of the __Pine Ridge__ reservation of the __Pine Ridge, South Dakota__ jurisdiction, as of __April 1__, 19**32**, taken by __James H. McGregor__, Superintendent.

Key: Number; Surname, Given; Sex; Date of Birth-Age at Last Birthday; Tribe (Oglala Sioux, unless stated otherwise); Degree of Blood; Marital Status; Relationship to Head of Family [Last Census Roll Number]; At Jurisdiction Where Enrolled (Yes/No); (If no – Where); Ward (Yes/No, if given); Allotment, Annuity and Identification Numbers (if given).

363; Bear Eagle, James; M; 1895-37; F; M; Head 358; Yes; Yes; Al. 43 An. 356

~~N.E. Bear Eagle (Jandron, Grace), Grace; F; ?; Yankton Sioux; F; M; Wife~~

364; Bear Eagle, Legene; M; 7/2/17-14; Sioux; F; S; Son 359; Yes; Yes; Id. U-0985 An. 359

365; Bear Eagle, Laura; F; 8/4/31-8/12; Sioux; F; S; Daughter ---; Yes; Yes; Id. U-13930 An. none

366; Bear Foot, Mary; F; 1862-70; F; Wd; Head 361; Yes; Yes; Al. 4782 An. 361
367; Sun Bear, Talbert; M; 1/4/16-15; F; S; Grand-son 362; Yes; Yes; Id. U-10513 An. 6696

368; Bear Killer, Frank; M; 1894-38; F; M; Head 363; Yes; Yes; Al. 1065 An. 363
369; Bear Killer (Fast Eagle, Jessie), Jessie; F; 1899-32; F; M; Wife 364; Yes; Yes; Al. 739 An. 564
370; Bear Killer, Sampson; M; 5/19/25-16; F; S; Son 365; Yes; Ues[sic]; Id. U-11726 An. none
371; Bear Killer, Charles; M; 6/9/29-2; F; S; Son 366; Yes; Yes; Id. U-13200 An. none

372; Bear Killer, Hazel; F; 11/17/10-21; F; S; Head 267; Yes; Yes; Id. U-9087 Al. 7644

373; Bear Lays Down, Bennie; M; 1853-79; F; Wd; Head 268; Yes; Yes; Al. 173 An. 365

374; Bear Nose, Frank, Jr; M; 1898-34; F; M; Head 369; Yes; Yes; Id. U-9093 An. 370
375; Bear Nose (White Bear Claws), Julia; F; 1905-27; F; M; Wife 370; Yes; Yes; Al. 6185 An. 371
376; Bear Nose, Floyd; M; 4/13/23-9; F; S; Son 371; Yes; Yes; Id. U-13057 An. 372
377; Bear Nose, Arnold; M; 2/13/25-7; F; S; Son 372; Yes; Yes; Id. U-11539 An. 373
378; Bear Nose, Alvina; F; 7/14/31-9/12; F; S; Daughter ---; Yes; Yes; Id. U-13881 An. none
379; Bear Nose, Joe; M; 1902-29; F; S; Head 373; Yes; Yes; Id. U-9094 An. 374

380; Bear Nose, Louisa; F; 1856-76; F; Wd; Head 374; Yes; Yes; Al. 8232 An. 375

381; Bear Nose, Roy; M; 1899-33; F; M; Head 375; Yes; Yes; Id. U-9095 An. 376

~~N.E. Bear Nose (Burnell, Violet), Violet May; F; Canadian Indian; ?; M; Wife~~

382; Bear Nose, Peter; M; 3/30/20-12; F; S; Son 376; Yes; Yes; Id. U-9096 An. 378

Census of the __Pine Ridge__ reservation of the __Pine Ridge, South Dakota__ jurisdiction, as of __April 1__, 19**32**, taken by __James H. McGregor__, Superintendent.

Key: Number; Surname, Given; Sex; Date of Birth-Age at Last Birthday; Tribe (Oglala Sioux, unless stated otherwise); Degree of Blood; Marital Status; Relationship to Head of Family [Last Census Roll Number]; At Jurisdiction Where Enrolled (Yes/No); (If no – Where); Ward (Yes/No, if given); Allotment, Annuity and Identification Numbers (if given).

383; Bear Nose, John; M; 1/22/22-10; F; S; Son 377; Yes; Yes; Id. U-10844 An. 379

384; Bear Robe, Augustus; M; 1872-60; F; M; Head 378; Yes; Yes; Al. 2433 An. 384

385; Bear Robe, Kate; F; 1871-61; F; M; Wife 379; Yes; Yes; Al. 8229 An. 385

386; Bear Robe, Charles; M; 3/26/12-20; F; M; Head 389; Yes; Yes; Id. U-9098 An. 398

387; Bear Robe (Clincher, Naomi), Naomi; F; 4/10/17-15; F; M; Wife 1454; Yes; Yes; Id. U-9352 An. 1499

388; Bear Robe, Jessie; F; 1875-57; F; Wd; Head 388; Yes; Yes; Al. 6461 An. 396

389; Bear Robe, Lena; F; 9/27/14-17; F; S; Daughter 390; Yes; Yes; Id. U-9099 An. 399

390; Bear Robe, Mary; F; 2/13/20-12; F; S; Daughter 391; Yes; Yes; Id. U-9100 An. 400

391; Good Soldier, Victoria; F; 11/30/26-5; F; S; Granddaughter 392; Yes; Yes; Id. U-12861 An. none

392; Bear Robe, John; M; 1881-51; F; Wd; Head 281; Yes; Yes; Al. 3208 An. 388

393; Bear Robe, Stella; F; 9/8/13-18; F; S; Daughter 382; Yes; Yes; Al. 7654 An. 391

394; Bear Robe, John, Jr; M; 5/13/17-14; F; S; Son 383; Yes; Yes; Id. U-9097 An. 392

395; Bear Robe, Samuel; M; 9/29/21-10; F; S; Son 384; Yes; Yes; Id. U-10874 An. 393

396; Bear Robe, Noah; M; 1907-25; F; M; Head 385; Yes; Yes; Al. 2438 An. 394

397; Bear Robe (Long Soldier), Virginia; F; 3/20/09-23; F; M; Wife 386; Yes; Yes; Al. 5913 An. 4223

398; Bear Robe, Verena; F; 9/18/29-2; F; S; Daughter 387; Yes; Yes; Id. U-13260 An. none

399; Bear Robe, Leo Bernard; M; 5/13/31-11/12; F; S; Son ---; Yes; Yes; Id. U-13851 An. none

400; Bear Robe, Reuben; M; 1905-27; F; M; Head 393; Yes; Yes; Al. 6229 An. 401

401; Bear Robe (Friday Scares), Jennie; F; 1898-34; F; M; Wife 394; Yes; Yes; Al. 3389 An. 402

402; Friday Scares, Julia; F; 6/6/21-10; F; S; Stepdaughter 395; Yes; Yes; Id. U-10994 An. 403

403; Bear Robe, Raymond; M; 9/3/27-4; F; S; Son; 396; Yes; Yes; Id. U-12858 An. none

Census of the __Pine Ridge__ reservation of the __Pine Ridge, South Dakota__ jurisdiction, as of __April 1__, 19**32**, taken by __James H. McGregor__, Superintendent.

Key: Number; Surname, Given; Sex; Date of Birth-Age at Last Birthday; Tribe (Oglala Sioux, unless stated otherwise); Degree of Blood; Marital Status; Relationship to Head of Family [Last Census Roll Number]; At Jurisdiction Where Enrolled (Yes/No); (If no – Where); Ward (Yes/No, if given); Allotment, Annuity and Identification Numbers (if given).

404; Bear Robe, Wallace; M; 6/28/30-1; F; S; Son 397; Yes; Yes; Id. U-13525 An. none

405; Bear Robe, Thomas; M; 1899-33; F; M; Head 398; Yes; Yes; Al. 4829 An. 404

406; Bear Robe (Iron Heart), Hannah; F; 1901-31; plus 1/4; M; Wife 399; Yes; Yes; Al. 4106 An. 405

407; Bear Robe, Rose Victoria; F; 1/22/25-7; plus 1/4; S; Daughter 400; Yes; Yes; Id. U-12159 An. none

408; Bear Robe, Zelda A; F; 8/17/28-3; plus 1/4; S; Daughter 401; Yes; Yes; Id. U-12795 An. none

409; Bear Robe, William; M; 12/20/10-21; F; M; Head 380; Yes; Yes; Al. 6909 An. 386

410; Bear Robe (Black Bear, Mabel), Mabel; F; 9/28/12-19; F; M; Wife 639; Yes; Yes; Id. U-9165 An. 654

411; Bear Runner, Oscar; M; 4/10/13-19; F; S; Alone 402; Yes; Yes; Al. 7786 An. 409

412; Bear Saves Life, Eva; F; 1869-63; F; Wd; Head 403; Yes; Yes; Al. 6342 An. 415

413; Bear Saves Life, Jennie; F; 1902-30; plus 1/4; Wd; Head 404; Yes; Yes; Al. 2009 An. 416

414; Randall, Carl Richard; M; 3/8/23-9; plus 1/4; S; Son 405; Yes; Yes; Id. U-11687 An. none

415; Three Stars, Andrew; M; 5/23/28-3; plus 1/4; S; Son 406; Yes; Yes; Id. U-12704 An. none

416; Bear Saves Life, Paul; M; 1891-41; F; M; Head 407; Yes; Yes; Al. 6340 An. 417

417; Bear Saves Life (Brown Ear Horse, Fannie), Fannie; F; 1893-39; F; M; Wife 408; Yes; Yes; Al. 6341 An. 418

418; Bear Saves Life, Floyd; M; 10/8/17-14; F; S; Son 409; Yes; Yes; Id. U-9102 An. 420

419; Bear Saves Life, May; F; 1/9/21-11; F; S; Daughter 410; Yes; Yes; Id. U-9103 An. 421

420; Bear Saves Life, Alvina; F; 9/1/27-4; F; S; Dau 411; Yes; Yes; Id. U-12417 An. none

421; Bear Saves Life, Johnson; M; 10/7/30-1; F; S; Son 412; Yes; Yes; Id. U-13588 An. none

Census of the **Pine Ridge** reservation of the **Pine Ridge, South Dakota** jurisdiction, as of **April 1**, 19**32**, taken by **James H. McGregor**, Superintendent.

Key: Number; Surname, Given; Sex; Date of Birth-Age at Last Birthday; Tribe (Oglala Sioux, unless stated otherwise); Degree of Blood; Marital Status; Relationship to Head of Family [Last Census Roll Number]; At Jurisdiction Where Enrolled (Yes/No); (If no – Where); Ward (Yes/No, if given); Allotment, Annuity and Identification Numbers (if given).

422; Bear Shield, Nancy; F; 1862-70; F; Wd; Head 413; Yes; Yes; Al. 2571 An. 425

423; Bear Shield, John; M; 1884-48; F; M; Head 414; Yes; Yes; Al. 180 An. 424
424; Bear Shield (Medicine Boy, Mary), Mary; F; 1890-42; F; M; Wife 415; Yes; Yes; Al. 1893 An. 425
425; Bear Shield, Stella; F; 5/27/13-18; F; S; Dau; 416; Yes; Yes; Al. 7936 An. 426
426; Bear Shield, Kermit; M; 3/12/18-14; F; S; Son 417; Yes; Yes; Id. U-9104 An. 427
427; Bear Shield, Jessie; F; 3/20/23-7; F; S; Daughter 418; Yes; Yes; Id. U-11535 An. 429
428; Bear Shield, Matthew; M; 11/14/27-4; F; S; Son 419; Yes; Yes; Id. U-12455 An. none

429; Bear Shield, William; M; 1880-52; F; M; Head 421; Yes; Yes; Id. U-11535 An. 429

430; Bear Shield (Ringing Shield, Lucy), Lucy; F; 1904-28; F; M; Wife 422; Yes; Yes; Al. 2423 An. 431
431; Bear Shield, Evelyn; F; 2/11/24-8; F; S; Daughter 423; Yes; Yes; Id. U-11281 An. 432
432; Bear Shield, Lawrence; M; 11/26/28-3; F; S; Son 424; Yes; Yes; Id. U-12941 An. none
433; Bear Shield, Theresa; F; 4/10/31-11/12; F; S; Daughter ---; Yes; Yes; Id. U-213796 An. none

N.E. Bear Shirt, Arthur; M; Rosebud Sioux; F; M; Head
434; Bear Shirt (Swallow, Lucy), Lucy; F; 1906-26; F; M; Wife 425; Yes; Yes; Al. 2418 An. 6723

435; Bear Stops, Willie; M; 1885-48; F; Wd; Head 426; Yes; Yes; Al. 7380 An. 422
436; Bear Stops, Ephraim; M; 10/27/22-9; F; S; Son 427; Yes; Yes; Id. U-12045 An. 435

437; Bear Tail, William; M; 1888-44; F; Wd; Head 429; Yes; Yes; Al. 1469 An. 437
438; Bear Tail, Regina; F; 3/8/28-4; F; S; Daughter 431; Yes; Yes; Id. U-12669 An. none

439; Bear Tail, Lema[sic]; F; 8/23/12-19; F; S; Head 430; Yes; Yes; Al. 9109 An. 439

Census of the **Pine Ridge** reservation of the **Pine Ridge, South Dakota** jurisdiction, as of **April 1**, 19**32**, taken by **James H. McGregor**, Superintendent.

Key: Number; Surname, Given; Sex; Date of Birth-Age at Last Birthday; Tribe (Oglala Sioux, unless stated otherwise); Degree of Blood; Marital Status; Relationship to Head of Family [Last Census Roll Number]; At Jurisdiction Where Enrolled (Yes/No); (If no – Where); Ward (Yes/No, if given); Allotment, Annuity and Identification Numbers (if given).

~~N.E. Beauvais, Benjamin; M; Rosebud Sioux; 1/4; M; Head~~

440; Beauvais (Hawkins, Lottie), Lottie; F; 1887-45; plus 1/4; M; Wife 432; Yes; No; Al. 1112 An. 444

441; Beauvais, Mary M; F; 3/15/18-14; Sioux; plus 1/4; S; Daughter 433; Yes; Yes; Id. U-9114 An. 445

442; Beck, Alice; F; 1905-27; plus 1/4; Wd; Head 434; No; Rosebud S.D.; Yes; Al. 2694 An. 446
443; Beck, Brenhilda; F; 1/21/21-11; 1/4; S; Daughter 435; No; Sioux City, Woodbury Co, Ia; Yes; Id. U-11052 An. 447

~~N.E. Bell, Elza; M; White; Head~~

444; Bell (Twiss, Stella), Stella; F; 3/17/97-35; plus 1/4; M; Wife 436; No; Chadron, Dawes Co, Neb; Yes; Al. 2924 An. 3699
445; Bell, Harvey E; M; 7/1/26-5; -1/4; S; Son 438; No; Chadron, Dawes Co, Neb; Yes; Id. U-12918 An. none
446; Bell, Donald D; M; 10/13/27-4; -1/4; S; Son 439; No; Chadron, Dawes Co, Neb; Yes; Id. U-12917 An. none
447; Bell, Frances; F; 10/16/29-2; -1/4; S; Son 440; No; Chadron, Dawes Co, Neb; Yes; Id. U-13372 An. none
448; LaPointe, Georgene Esther; F; 7/9/17-14; -1/4; S; Stepdaughter 437; No; Chadron, Dawes Co, Neb; Yes; Id. U-9845 An. 3700

449; Belt; M; 1860-72; F; Wd; Head 441; Yes; Yes; Al. 2871 An. 446

450; Belt, Frank; M; 1881-51; F; Wd; Head 442; Yes; Yes; Al. 3274 An. 450
451; Belt, Kate; F; 10/22/12-19; F; S; Daughter 443; Yes; Yes; Al. 7578 An. 454
452; Belt, Ambrose; M; 10/11/22-9; F; S; Son 444; Yes; Yes; Id. U-12021 An. 457
453; Belt, Roland; M; 6/16/24-7; F; S; Son 445; Yes; Yes; Id. U-11548 An. 458

454; Belt, Jonas; m ; 8/15/08-23; F; S; Head 446; Yes; Yes; Al. 6249 An. 452

455; Belt, Levi; M; 1887-45; F; M; Head 447; Yes; Yes; Al. 5896 An. 459
456; Belt (Last Horse, Salina), Salina; F; 1887-45; F; M; wife 448; Yes; Yes; Al. 3864 An. 460
457; Belt, Guy; M; 5/17/317-14; F; S; Son 449; Yes; Yes; Id. U-9118 An. 463
458; Belt, Vienna; F; 1/21/20-12; F; S; Daughter 450; Yes; Yes; Id. U-9119 An. none

459; Belt, Samuel; M; 1902-32; F; M; Head 451; Yes; Yes; Al. 6248 An. 465

Census of the ___Pine Ridge___ reservation of the ___Pine Ridge, South Dakota___ jurisdiction, as of ___April 1___, 1932, taken by ___James H. McGregor___, Superintendent.

Key: Number; Surname, Given; Sex; Date of Birth-Age at Last Birthday; Tribe (Oglala Sioux, unless stated otherwise); Degree of Blood; Marital Status; Relationship to Head of Family [Last Census Roll Number]; At Jurisdiction Where Enrolled (Yes/No); (If no – Where); Ward (Yes/No, if given); Allotment, Annuity and Identification Numbers (if given).

460; Belt (Holy Rock, Emily), Emily; F; 1910-22; plus 1/4; M; Wife 452; Yes; Yes; Al. 6422 An. 3014
461; Belt, Jerry Fritz; M; 1/20/29-3; plus 1/4; S; Son 453; Yes; Yes; Id. U-12985 An. none
462; Belt, Evelyn Magdaline; F; 5/11/31-11/12; plus 1/4; S; Daughter ---; Yes; Yes; Id. U-13827 An. none

463; Bent, Alonzo; M; 1903-29; plus 1/4; S; Head 454; No; Leupp, Ariz; Yes; Al. 2470 An. 466

N.E. Bent, William; M; Arapaho; 5/8; M; Head
464; Bent (Adams, Ellen), Ellen; F; 1891-43; plus 1/4; M; Wife 455; Yes; Yes; Al. 471 An. 467
465; Bent, Lucille M; F; 6/6/26-5; Arapaho & Sioux; plus 1/4; S; Daughter 456; Yes; Yes; Id. U-11931 An. none
466; Bent, William H; M; 6/2/29-2; Arapaho & Sioux; plus 1/4; S; Son 457; Yes; Yes; Id. U-13204 An. none
467; Galligo, Kiva; g; 11/10/19-13; plus 1/4; S; Niece 458; Yes; Yes; Id. U-9551 An. 2373

468; Bergen, William; M; 1880-52; plus 1/4; M; Head 459; Yes; No; Al. 2224 An. 468
N.E. Bergen (Larvie, Maggie), Maggie; F; Rosebud Sioux; plus 1/4; M; Wife
469; Bergen, Sylvia M; F; 11/26/13-18; Sioux; plus 1/4; S; Daughter 460; Yes; Yes; Id. U-9120 An. 470
470; Bergen, Florine; F; 2/29/16-16; Sioux; plus 1/4; S; Daughter 461; Yes; Yes; Id. U-9121 An. 471
471; Bergen, Minnie E; F; 10/25/25-6; Sioux; plus 1/4; S; Daughter 462; Yes; Yes; Id. U-11744 An. none

472; Bergen, Richard; M; 6/1/07-24; plus 1/4; M; Head 463; No; Sisseton, S.D; Yes; Al. 2225 An. 469
N.E. Bergen (Schoenhut, Evelyn), Evelyn; F; Standing Rock Sioux; plus 1/4; M; Wife
473; Bergen, Richard Darrell; M; 9/10/29-2; Sioux; plus 1/4; S; Son 464; No; Sisseton, S.D; Yes; Id. U-13308 An. none
474; Bergen, Robert Vernon; M; 6/9/31-10/12; Sioux; plus 1/4; S; Son ---; No; Sisseton, S.D; [blank]; Id. U-13958

475; Berzina, Gertie; F; 3/5/14-18; plus 1/4; Wd; Head 2532; Yes; Yes; Id. U-9588 An. 2528

Census of the **Pine Ridge** reservation of the **Pine Ridge, South Dakota** jurisdiction, as of **April 1**, 19**32**, taken by **James H. McGregor**, Superintendent.

Key: Number; Surname, Given; Sex; Date of Birth-Age at Last Birthday; Tribe (Oglala Sioux, unless stated otherwise); Degree of Blood; Marital Status; Relationship to Head of Family [Last Census Roll Number]; At Jurisdiction Where Enrolled (Yes/No); (If no – Where); Ward (Yes/No, if given); Allotment, Annuity and Identification Numbers (if given).

476; Bettelyoun, Amos; M; 7/29/06-26; plus 1/4; S; Head 465; Yes; Yes; Al. 2185 An. 472

477; Bettelyoun, Earl; M; 1907-25; plus 1/4; M; Head 466; Yes; Yes; Al. 4433 An. 473

~~N.E. Bettelyoun (Dunlap, Mabel), Mabel; F; White; M; Wife~~
478; Bettelyoun, Maxine M; F; 5/18/28-3; -1/4; S; Daughter 467; Yes; Yes; Id. U-12663 An. none

479; Bettelyoun, Norval Stewart; M; 7/17/30-1; -1/4; S; Son 468; Yes; Yes; Id. U-13625 An. none

480; Bettelyoun, Edward G; M; 1884-48; plus 1/4; M; Head 469; Yes; No; Al. 4704 An. 474

481; Bettelyoun (Gleason, Pearl), Pearl; F; 1884-48; plus 1/4; M; Wife 470; Yes; No; Al. 4432 An. 475

482; Bettelyoun, Dennison; M; 11/8/11-20; plus 1/4; S; Son 471; Yes; Yes; Al. 7000 An. 477

483; Bettelyoun, Aaron; M; 3/21/13-19; plus 1/4; S; Son 472; Yes; Yes; Al. 6999 An. 478

484; Bettelyoun, Dorothy K; F; 3/21/16-16; plus 1/4; S; Daughter 473; Yes; Yes; Id. U-9122 An. 479

485; Bettelyoun, Sybil; F; 5/25/19-12; plus 1/4; S; Daughter 474; Yes; Yes; Id. U-9123 An. 480

486; Bettelyoun, Vivian; F; 6/30/23-8; plus 1/4; S; Daughter 475; Yes; Yes; Id. U-14022 An. 481

487; Bettelyoun, Glenn Chris; M; 8/17/25-6; plus 1/4; S; Son 476; Yes; Yes; Id. U-12859 An. none

488; Bettelyoun, E. G, Sr; M; 1871-61; plus 1/4; M; Head 477; Yes; No; Al. 2180 An. 482

489; Bettelyoun, Josephine; F; 1871-61; plus 1/4; M; Wife 478; Yes; No; Al. 2181 An. 483

490; Bettelyoun, E. G, Jr; M; 1902-30; plus 1/4; S; Head 479; Yes; Yes; Al. 5445 An. 484

491; Bettelyoun, Chester; M; 1895-37; plus 1/4; S; Head 480; Yes; Yes; Al. 2485 An. 485

492; Bettelyoun, Fred; M; 1881-51; plus 1/4; M; Head 481; Yes; No; Al. 2482 An. 486

493; Bettelyoun (Ruff, Lizzie), Lizzie; F; 1879-53; plus 1/4; M; Wife 482; Yes; Yes; Al. 4701 An. 487

Census of the **Pine Ridge** reservation of the **Pine Ridge, South Dakota** jurisdiction, as of **April 1**, 1932, taken by **James H. McGregor**, Superintendent.

Key: Number; Surname, Given; Sex; Date of Birth-Age at Last Birthday; Tribe (Oglala Sioux, unless stated otherwise); Degree of Blood; Marital Status; Relationship to Head of Family [Last Census Roll Number]; At Jurisdiction Where Enrolled (Yes/No); (If no – Where); Ward (Yes/No, if given); Allotment, Annuity and Identification Numbers (if given).

494; Bettelyoun, Carl C; M; 9/19/10-21; plus 1/4; S; Son 484; Yes; Yes; Al. 7105 An. 490

495; Bettelyoun, Isaac A; M; 3/9/14-18; plus 1/4; S; Son 485; Yes; Yes; Id. U-9124 An. 491

496; Bettelyoun, Harry R; M; 3/28/15-17; plus 1/4; S; Son 486; Yes; Yes; Id. U-9125 An. 492

497; Bettelyoun, Roby; M; 12/7/18-13; plus 1/4; S; Son 487; Yes; Yes; Id. U-9126 An. 493;

498; Bettelyoun, Joseph; M; 9/7/19-12; plus 1/4; S; Son 488; Yes; Yes; Id. U-9127 An. 494

499; Bettelyoun, Everett; M; 8/7/09-22; plus 1/4; S; Head 483; Yes; Yes; Al. 4703 An. 489

500; Bettelyoun, George W; M; 1/7/08-24; plus 1/4; S; Head 489; Yes; Yes; Al. 4767 An. 488

501; Bettelyoun, George; M; 1873-59; plus 1/4; M; Head 490; Yes; No; Al. 2200 An. 495

502; Bettelyoun (Richard, Angeline), Angeline; F; 1885-47; plus 1/4; M; Wife 491; Yes; Yes; Al. 2488 An. 496

503; Bettelyoun, Richard L; M; 5/17/14-17; plus 1/4; S; Son 492; Yes; Yes; Id. U-9128 An. 499

504; Bettelyoun, Ned; M; 9/4/15-16; S; Son 493; Yes; Yes; Id. U-9129 An. 500

505; Bettelyoun, Percy; M; 8/26/17-14; plus 1/4; S; Son 494; Yes; Yes; Id. U-9130 An. 501

506; Bettelyoun, Bertha; F; 9/21/19-12; plus 1/4; S; Daughter 495; Yes; Yes; Id. U-9131 An. 502

507; Bettelyoun, Frank Jayrold; M; 5/12/11-9; plus 1/4; S; Son 496; Yes; Yes; Id. U-10987 An. 503

508; Bettelyoun, Rossie Alvin; M; 6/22/24-7; plus 1/4; S; Son 497; Yes; Yes; Id. U-11561 An. 504

509; Bettelyoun, Prudie H; F; 2/16/26-5; plus 1/4; S; Daughter 498; Yes; Yes; Id. U-11904 An. none

510; Bettelyoun, Gertrude; F; 11/2/28-3; plus 1/4; S; Daughter 499; Yes; Yes; Id. U-12919 An. none

511; Bettelyoun, Dora L; F; 7/20/12-19; plus 1/4; S; Head 500; Yes; Yes; Al. 7023 An. 498

512; Bettelyoun, Isaac; M; 1893-39; plus 1/4; M; Head 501; Yes; Yes; Al. 2181 An. 506

N.E. Bettelyoun (Wabanescom, Sophia), Sophia; F; Menominee; plus 1/4; M; Wife

Census of the _____ **Pine Ridge** _____ reservation of the _**Pine Ridge, South Dakota**_
jurisdiction, as of_____ **April 1** _____, 1932, taken by _____ **James H. McGregor** _____,
Superintendent.

Key: Number; Surname, Given; Sex; Date of Birth-Age at Last Birthday; Tribe (Oglala Sioux, unless stated otherwise); Degree of Blood; Marital Status; Relationship to Head of Family [Last Census Roll Number]; At Jurisdiction Where Enrolled (Yes/No); (If no – Where); Ward (Yes/No, if given); Allotment, Annuity and Identification Numbers (if given).

513; Bettelyoun, Edith M; F; 5/14/17-14; Menominee & Sioux; plus 1/4; S; Daughter 502; Yes; Yes; Id. U-9132 An. 507

514; Bettelyoun, Howard; M; 1/26/20-12; Menominee & Sioux; plus 1/4; S; Son 503; Yes; Yes; Id. U-9133 An. 508

515; Bettelyoun, Waldron; M; 8/2/24-7; Menominee & Sioux; plus 1/4; Son 504; Yes; Yes; Id. U-12942 An. none

516; Bettelyoun, Ethel Marie; F; 12/20/26-5; Menominee & Sioux; plus 1/4; Daughter 505; Yes; Yes; Id. U-12943 An. none

517; Bettelyoun, Vance Virgil; M; 6/9/30-1; Menominee & Sioux; plus 1/4; S; Son 506; Yes; Yes; Id. U-13680 An. none

518; Bettelyoun, Lorenzo; M; 1897-35; plus 1/4; M; Head 508; Yes; Yes; Al. 2486 An. 511

N.E. Bettelyoun (Guarne, Mary), Mary; F; Rosebud Sioux; plus 1/4; Wife

519; Between Lodges, Henry; M; 1878-54; F; M; Head 908; Yes; Yes; Al. 5981 An. 516

520; Between Lodged (Sitting Up, Esther), Esther; F; 1880-52; F; M; Wife 510; Yes; Yes; Al. 1911 An. 517

521; Between Lodges, Rosa; F; 8/9/13-18; F; S; Daughter 511; Yes; Yes; Al. 7759 An. 519

522; Between Lodges, Paul; M; 10/10/19-12; F; S; Son 512; Yes; Yes; Id. U-11060 An. 520

523; Between Lodges, Julia; F; 11/17/22-9; F; S; Daughter 513; Yes; Yes; Id. U-12030 An. 521

524; Between Lodges, Agnes; F; 1/11/11-21; F; S; Head 514; Yes; Yes; Al. 5881 An. 518

525; Between Lodges, Marie Agatha; F; 5/8/30-1; F; S; Daughter 515; Yes; Yes; Id. U-13510 An. none

526; Bianas, Leo; M; 5/7/12-19; plus 1/4; S; Alone 516; Yes; Yes; Id. U-9139 An. 7818

N.E. Big Roy, Henry; M; Cheyenne River Sioux; F; M; Head

527; Big Roy (Palmier, Laura), Laura; F; 1884-48; plus 1/4; M; Wife 517; Yes; Yes; Al. 3791 An. 4876

528; Big Roy, Henry; M; 10/17/13-18; Sioux; F; S; Son 523; Yes; Yes; Al. 7214 An. 524

529; Big Roy, Augustus; M; 8/11/17-14; Sioux; F; S; Son 524; Yes; Yes; Id. U-9140 An. 525

Census of the   **Pine Ridge**   reservation of the **Pine Ridge, South Dakota**
jurisdiction, as of   **April 1**   , 19**32**, taken by   **James H. McGregor**   ,
Superintendent.

Key: Number; Surname, Given; Sex; Date of Birth-Age at Last Birthday; Tribe (Oglala Sioux, unless stated otherwise); Degree of Blood; Marital Status; Relationship to Head of Family [Last Census Roll Number]; At Jurisdiction Where Enrolled (Yes/No); (If no – Where); Ward (Yes/No, if given); Allotment, Annuity and Identification Numbers (if given).

530; Big Roy, Dora; F; 9/21/30-1; Sioux; plus 1/4; S; Daughter 525; Yes; Yes; Id. U-13635 An. none
531; Palmier, Louis; M; 4/26/12-19; plus 1/4; S; Stepson 518; Yes; Yes; Al. 7253 An. 4879
532; Palmier, Catherine; F; 11/23/16-15; plus 1/4; S; Stepdaughter 519; Yes; Yes; Id. U-10098 An. 4880
533; Palmier, Lucille; F; 4/16/19-12; plus 1/4; S; Stepdaughter 520; Yes; Yes; Id. U-10099 An. 4881
534; Palmier, Leo; M; 4/11/21-10; plus 1/4; S; Stepson 521; Id. U-11495 An. 4882
535; Palmier, Elizabeth; F; 4/13/27-4; plus 1/4; S; Stepdaughter 522; Yes; Yes; Id. 12326 An. none
536; Big Charger, Albert; M; 1891-41; F; M; Head 526; Yes; Yes; Al. 1375 An. 527
537; Big Charger (Shot To Pieces, Sadie), Sadie; F; 1901-31; F; M; Wife 527; Yes; Yes; Al. 183 An. 528
538; Big Charger, Nora; F; 12/26/23-8; F; S; Daughter 528; Yes; Yes; Id. U-11269 An. 529
539; Big Charger, William; M; 1872-60; F; M; Head 529; Yes; Yes; Al. 1720 An. 530
540; Big Charger (Long Cat, Julia), Julia; F; 1874-58; F; M; Wife 530; Yes; Yes; Al. 6881 An. 531
541; Big Cheyenne Woman, Samuel; M; 1/18/08-24; F; S; Head 531; Yes; Yes; Al. 6100 An. 5745
542; Big Crow, Raymond; M; 1892-40; plus 1/4; M; Head 532; Yes; Yes; Al. 7514 An. 532
543; Big Crow (Patton, Theresa), Theresa; F; 1884-48; plus 1/4; Yes; No; Al 2765 An. 533
544; Big Crow, Louisa; F; 9/2/13-18; plus 1/4; S; Daughter 534; Yes; Yes; Al. 7824 An. 535
545; Big Crow, Alvina; F; 12/20/15-16; plus 1/4; S; Daughter 535; Yes; Yes; Id. U-9142 An. 536
546; Big Crow, James; M; 10/18/18-13; plus 1/4; S; Son 536; Yes; Yes; Id. U-9143 An. 537
547; Big Crow, Lloyd; M; 5/4/21-10; plus 1/4; S; Son 537; Yes; Yes; Id. U-9144 An. 538
548; Big Crow, Phelma; F; 7/14/23-8; plus 1/4; S; Daughter 538; Yes; Yes; Id. U-14006 An. 538[sic]

Census of the **Pine Ridge** reservation of the **Pine Ridge, South Dakota** jurisdiction, as of **April 1**, 1932, taken by **James H. McGregor**, Superintendent.

Key: Number; Surname, Given; Sex; Date of Birth-Age at Last Birthday; Tribe (Oglala Sioux, unless stated otherwise); Degree of Blood; Marital Status; Relationship to Head of Family [Last Census Roll Number]; At Jurisdiction Where Enrolled (Yes/No); (If no – Where); Ward (Yes/No, if given); Allotment, Annuity and Identification Numbers (if given).

549; Big Crow, Francis; M; 4/23/26-5; plus 1/4; S; Son 539; Yes; Yes; Id. U-11900 An. none

550; Big Crow, Ave Marie; F; 5/15/28-3; plus 1/4; S; Daughter 540; Yes; Yes; Id. U-9980 An. none

551; Big Crow, Leatrice C; F; 8/26/31-8/12; plus 1/4; S; Daughter ---; Yes; Yes; Id. U-13882 An. none

552; Big Hawk, Peter; M; 1863-69; F; Wd; Head 541; Yes; Yes; Al. 1182 An. 540
553; Yellow Thunder, Louisa; F; 1/26/22-10; F; S; Granddaughter 542; Yes; Yes; Id. U-10898 An. 7925

554; Big Head, Brave; M; 1877-55; F; Wd; Head 543; Yes; Yes; Al. 4170 An. 543
555; Big Head, George; M; 11/8/26-5; F; S; Son 544; Yes; Yes; Id. U-12173 An. none
556; Big Head, Victoria; F; 11/8/26-5; F; S; Daughter 545; Yes; Yes; Id. U-12174 An. none

557; Big Mouth, John; M; 1855-77; F; Wd; Head 546; Yes; Yes; Al. 1088 An. 545

558; Big Owl, Thomas; M; 1890-42; F; M; Head 547; Yes; Yes; Al. 524 An. 547

559; Big Owl (Lays Bad, Helen), Helen; F; 1906-26; F; M; Wife 549; Yes; Yes; Al. 4780 An. 550
560; Big Owl, Ernest; M; 6/7/17-14; F; S; Son 548; Yes; Yes; Id. U-9145 An. 549
561; Big Owl, Effie; F; 9/10/22-9; F; S; Daughter 550; Yes; Yes; Id. U-11163 An. 551

562; Big Turnip, Luke; M; 1876-56; F; M; Head 551; Yes; No; Al. 2984 An. 552
563; Big Turnip (Runs Against, Sophia), Sophia; F; 1875-57; F; M; Wife 552; Yes; Yes; Al. 2975 An. 555

564; Big Wolf, Jessie; F; 1904-28; F; S; Head 553; Yes; Yes; Al. 2476 An. 559
565; Picket Pin, Susie Aurelia; F; 10/14/31-5/12; F; S; Daughter ---; Yes; Yes; Id. U-14047 An. none

566; Bird, Eugene H; M; 1880-52; F; M; Head 556; Yes; No; Al. 3097 An. 563
567; Bird, Jennie; F; 1874-58; plus 1/4; M; Wife 557; Yes; No; Al. 6104 An. 564
568; Bird, Samuel; M; 2/24/12-20; 1/4; S; Son 558; Yes; Yes; Al. 6106 An. 566
569; Bird, Leroy; M; 5/6/16-15; 1/4; S; Son 559; Yes; Yes; Id. U-9149 An. 567

570; Bird, Dora H; F; 11/26/07-24; plus 1/4; S; Head 560; Yes; Yes; Al. 7266 An. 4818

Census of the   **Pine Ridge**   reservation of the **Pine Ridge, South Dakota**
jurisdiction, as of   **April 1**   , 1932, taken by   **James H. McGregor** ,
Superintendent.

Key: Number; Surname, Given; Sex; Date of Birth-Age at Last Birthday; Tribe (Oglala Sioux, unless stated otherwise); Degree of Blood; Marital Status; Relationship to Head of Family [Last Census Roll Number]; At Jurisdiction Where Enrolled (Yes/No); (If no – Where); Ward (Yes/No, if given); Allotment, Annuity and Identification Numbers (if given).

571; Bird, Raymond Clark; M; 2/24/32-1/12; plus 1/4; S; Son --; Yes; Yes; Id. U-14080 An. none

572; Bird, Emma Kate; F; 1906-26; plus 1/4; M; Head 561; Yes; Yes; Al. 7266 An. 4818

573; Bird, Elmer Lloyd; M; 10/30/28-3; -1/4; S; Son 562; Yes; Yes; Id. U-13129 An. none

574; Bird, Darwin Eugene; M; 5/24/30-1; -1/4; S; Son 563; Yes; Yes; Id. U-13590 An. none

~~N.E. Bird, Harry; M; Flandreau Sioux; ?; M; Head~~

575; Bird (Turning Bear, Ollie), Ollie; F; 3/9/14-18; plus 1/4; M; Wife 201; Yes; Yes; Id. U-10201 An. 5243

576; Bird Eagle, Austin; M; 1857-75; F; M; Head 564; Yes; Yes; Al. 1166 An. 570

577; Bird Eagle (No data), Sallie; F; 1864-68; F; M; Wife 565; Yes; Yes; Al. 7599 An. 571

578; Bird Eagle, George; M; 1889-43; F; M; Head 566; Yes; Yes; Al. 1168 An. 585

~~N.E. Bird Eagle (Kills Crow, Julia), Julia; F; Standing Rock Sioux; F; M; Wife~~

579; Bird Eagle, Joseph; M; 1896-36; F; S; Head 567; Yes; Yes; Al. 1169 An. 573

580; Bird Head, Bismark; M; 1892-48; F; Wd; Head 568; Yes; Yes; Al. 489 An. 574

581; Bird Head, Julia; F; 3/6/23-9; F; S; Daughter 571; Yes; Yes; Id. U-12095 An. 579

582; Monroe, James Clifford; M; 3/8/14-18; F; S; Stepson 572; Yes; Yes; Id. U-10029 An. 577

583; Lone Hill, Tillie; F; 11/5/18-13; F; S; Stepdaughter 573; Yes; Yes; Id. U-9924 An. 578

584; Bird Head, Elk Woman; F; 1863-69; F; Wd; Head 576; Yes; Yes; Al. 5702 An. 585

585; Bird Head, Hudson; M; 1890-42; F; M; Head 572; Yes; Yes; Al. 490 An. 580

586; Bird Head (Plenty Wounds), Nellie; F; 1896-36; F; M; Wife 573; Yes; Yes; Al. 534 An. 581

587; Bird Head, Vincent; M; 1/22/19-13; F; S; Son 574; Yes; Yes; Id. U-9150 An. 582

588; Bird Head, Margrett; F; 9/28/22-9; F; S; Daughter 575; Yes; Yes; Id. U-11898 An. 583

Census of the **Pine Ridge** reservation of the **Pine Ridge, South Dakota** jurisdiction, as of **April 1**, 19**32**, taken by **James H. McGregor**, Superintendent.

Key: Number; Surname, Given; Sex; Date of Birth-Age at Last Birthday; Tribe (Oglala Sioux, unless stated otherwise); Degree of Blood; Marital Status; Relationship to Head of Family [Last Census Roll Number]; At Jurisdiction Where Enrolled (Yes/No); (If no – Where); Ward (Yes/No, if given); Allotment, Annuity and Identification Numbers (if given).

589; Bird Head, Agnes; F; 5/13/31-11/12; F; S; Daughter ---; Yes; Yes; Id. U-13828 An. none

590; Bird Head, John; M; 1902-30; F; M; Head 577; Yes; Yes; Al. 492 An. 586
591; Bird Head (Craven, Hazel), Hazel; F; 1906-26; plus 1/4; M; Wife 578; Yes; Yes; Al. 5813 An. 1695

592; Bird Head, Dolly; F; 1861-71; F; Wd; Head 579; Yes; Yes; Al. 7809 An. 589

593; Bird Necklace, Frank; M; 1876-56; plus 1/4; M; Head 580; Yes; Yes; Al. 279 An. 590
594; Bird Necklace (No data), Lula; F; 1874-58; plus 1/4; M; Wife 581; Yes; Yes; Al. 6481 An. 591
595; Bird Necklace, William; M; 3/19/13-19; plus 1/4; S; Son 583; Yes; Yes; Id. U-9151 An. 593

596; Bissonette, Andrew; M; 1891-41; plus 1/4; M; Head 584; Yes; Yes; Al. 3031 An. 596

597; Bissonette, Angelique; F; 1906-26; plus 1/4; Wd; Head 585; Yes; Yes; Al. 5895 An. 7092
598; Bissonette, Jackson Vern; M; 6/15/26-5; plus 1/4; S; Son 586; Yes; Yes; Id. U-11932 An. none
599; Bissonette, Clement E; M; 7/11/28-3; plus 1/4; S; Son 587; Yes; Yes; Id. U-12737 An. none

600; Bissonette, Chauncey; M; 1903-29; plus 1/4; S; Head 588; Yes; Yes; Al. 7312 An. 597

601; Bissonette, Dora; F; 1906-26; plus 1/4; S; Head 589; Yes; Yes; Al. 3057 An. 599

602; Bissonette, Eddie; M; 1899-33; plus 1/4; M; Head 590; Yes; Yes; Al. 2934 An. 600
603; Bissonette (Brave, Maggie), Maggie; F; 5/4/1904-28; plus 1/4; M; Wife 591; Yes; Yes; Al. 6291 An. 928
604; Bissonette, Pearl; F; 9/22/28-3; plus 1/4; S; Daughter 592; Yes; Yes; Id. U-12844 An. none
605; Bissonette, Elfreda; F; 5/10/31-11/12; plus 1/4; S; Daughter ---; Yes; Yes; Id. U-14121 An. none

606; Bissonette, Frank P; M; 1876-56; plus 1/4; Wd; Head 593; Yes; Yes; Al. 2989 An. 601

Census of the **Pine Ridge** reservation of the **Pine Ridge, South Dakota** jurisdiction, as of **April 1**, 19**32**, taken by **James H. McGregor**, Superintendent.

Key: Number; Surname, Given; Sex; Date of Birth-Age at Last Birthday; Tribe (Oglala Sioux, unless stated otherwise); Degree of Blood; Marital Status; Relationship to Head of Family [Last Census Roll Number]; At Jurisdiction Where Enrolled (Yes/No); (If no – Where); Ward (Yes/No, if given); Allotment, Annuity and Identification Numbers (if given).

607; Bissonette, Fred; M; 1886-46; plus 1/4; S; Head 594; Yes; Yes; Al. 1021 An. 602

608; Bissonette, Herbert; M; 1871-61; plus 1/4; M; Head 595; Yes; Yes; Al. 1259 An. 603

609; Bissonette (No data), Julia; F; 1874-58; plus 1/4; M; Wife 596; Yes; Yes; Al. 7313 An. 604

610; Bissonette, Percy; M; 11/19/10-21; plus 1/4; S; Son 597; Yes; Yes; Id. U-9154 An. 606

611; Bissonette, Robert; M; 1915-16; plus 1/4; S; Son 599; Yes; Yes; Id. U-9156 An. 608

612; Bissonette, Leonard; M; 6/1/07-24; plus 1/4; S; Head 600; Yes; Yes; Id. U-9153 An. 605

613; Bissonette, Hobart; M; 1897-35; plus 1/4; M; Head 601; Yes; Yes; Al. 7309 An. 609

614; Bissonette (Frog, Anna), Anna; F; 1/17/08-24; F; M; Wife 602; Yes; Yes; Al. 6227 An. 2344

615; Bissonette, Lester A; M; 5/17/21-10; plus 1/4; S; Son 603; Yes; Yes; Id. U-9447 An. 611

616; Bissonette, Melvin G; M; 3/22/25-7; plus 1/4; S; Son; 604; Yes; Yes; Id. U-11544 An. 612

617; Bissonette, Lucy; F; 4/14/26-5; plus 1/4; S; Daughter 605; Yes; Yes; Id. U-11933 An. none

618; Bissonette, Mildred K; F; 6/5/29-2; plus 1/4; S; Daughter 606; Yes; Yes; Id. U-13408 An. none

619; Bissonette, Ethel Pearl; F; 1/2/32-3/12; plus 1/4; S; Daughter 607; Yes; Yes; Id. U-14081 An. none

620; Bissonette, John J; M; 1861-71; plus 1/4; M; Head 607; Yes; Yes; Al. 3027 An. 613

621; Bissonette (No data), Julia; F; 1869-63; F; M; Wife 608; Yes; Yes; Al. 3028 An. 614

622; Bissonette, John P; M; 1871-61; plus 1/4; Wd; Head 609; Yes; Yes; Al. 2927 An. 615

623; Bissonette, Joseph; M; 1879-53; plus 1/4; M; Head 610; Yes; Yes; Al. 3094 An. 616

624; Bissonette (Lone Elk, Susie), Susie; F; 1902-30; F; M; Wife 611; Yes; Yes; Al. 903 An. 4140

Census of the **Pine Ridge** reservation of the **Pine Ridge, South Dakota** jurisdiction, as of **April 1**, 19**32**, taken by **James H. McGregor**, Superintendent.

Key: Number; Surname, Given; Sex; Date of Birth-Age at Last Birthday; Tribe (Oglala Sioux, unless stated otherwise); Degree of Blood; Marital Status; Relationship to Head of Family [Last Census Roll Number]; At Jurisdiction Where Enrolled (Yes/No); (If no – Where); Ward (Yes/No, if given); Allotment, Annuity and Identification Numbers (if given).

625; Bissonette, Louis; M; 8/9 14-17; plus 1/4; S; Son 612; Yes; Yes; Id. U-9157 An. 620

626; Bissonette, Agnes; F; 9/11/16-15; plus 1/4; S; Daughter 613; Yes; Yes; Id. U-9158 An. 621

627; Bissonette, Mattie Marie; F; 5/23/31-11/12; plus 1/4; S; Daughter ---; Yes; Yes; Id. U-13829 An. none

628; Tells His Name, Isabel; F; 4/27/27-4; F; S; Stepdaughter 614; Yes; Yes; Id. U-12372 An. none

629; Bissonette, Joseph; M; 1895-37; plus 1/4; M; Head 615; Yes; Yes; Al. 3763 An. 613

630; Bissonette (Cross, Sarah), Sarah; F; 1902-30; plus 1/4; M; Wife 616; Yes; Yes; Al. 707 An. 623

631; Bissonette, Ella; F; 6/8/13-18; plus 1/4; S; Sister 617; Yes; Yes; Al. 7402 An. 625

632; Bissonette, Richard; M; 1905-27; plus 1/4; M; Head 618; No; Chadron, Dawes Co, Nebr, Dawes Co, Neb; Yes; Al. 7314 An. 629

633; Bitters, Patrick; M; 1872-60; F; M; Head 619; Yes; Yes; Al. 2042 An. 630

634; Bitters (Black Bear, Emma), Emma; F; 1888-44; F; M; Wife 620; Yes; Yes; Al. 5143 An. 631

635; Black Bear, #2; M; 1860-62; F; M; Head 621; Yes; Yes; Al. 2298 An. 632
636; Black Bear, Emma; F; 1865-67; F; M; Wife 622; Yes; Yes; Al. 2299 An. 633

637; Black Bear, Alfred; M; 1884-48; F; M; Head 623; Yes; Yes; Al. 4331 An. 635
638; Black Bear, Eliza; F; 1882-50; F; M; Wife 624; Yes; Yes; Al. 4332 An. 636
639; Black Bear, Daniel; M; 6/13/14-17; F; S; Son 625; Yes; Yes; Al. 7568 An. 637
640; Black Bear, Washington; M; 9/27/17-11; F; S; Son 626; Yes; Yes; Id. U-9159 An. 638

641; Black Bear. Charles; M; 8/4/23-8; F; S; Son 627; Yes; Yes; Id. U-14034 An. 640

642; Black Bear, Edward; M; 1888-44; F; M; Head 628; Yes; Yes; Al. 1433 An. 641

643; Black Bear (Red Eyes, Louisa), Louisa; F; 1870-62; F; M; Wife 629; Yes; Yes; Al. 5837 An. 5464

644; Black Bear, James; M; 4/15/13-17; F; S; Son 630; Yes; Yes; Id. U-9161 An. 644

645; Black Bear, Benjamin; M; 6/12/18-13; F; S; Son 631; Yes; Yes; Id. U-9162 An. 645

Census of the **Pine Ridge** reservation of the **Pine Ridge, South Dakota** jurisdiction, as of **April 1**, 19**32**, taken by **James H. McGregor**, Superintendent.

Key: Number; Surname, Given; Sex; Date of Birth-Age at Last Birthday; Tribe (Oglala Sioux, unless stated otherwise); Degree of Blood; Marital Status; Relationship to Head of Family [Last Census Roll Number]; At Jurisdiction Where Enrolled (Yes/No); (If no – Where); Ward (Yes/No, if given); Allotment, Annuity and Identification Numbers (if given).

646; Black Bear, Edward, Jr; M; 1902-30; F; Wd; Head 632; Yes; Yes; Al. 1001 An. 646

647; Black Bear, Harry; M; 1880-52; F; Wd; Head 633; Yes; Yes; Al. 4264 An. 648

648; Black Bear, David; M; 9/12/15-16; F; S; Son 634; Yes; Yes; Id. U-9164 An. 649

649; Black Bear, Jacob; M; 1906-26; F; M; Head 635; Yes; Yes; Al. 5336 An. 650

650; Black Bear, James; M; 1880-52; F; M; Head 636; Yes; Yes; Al. 920 An. 651
651; Black Bear (Bear Shield, Annie), Annie; F; 1881-51; F; M; Wife 637; Yes; Yes; Al. 7379 An. 652

652; Black Bear, Antoine; M; 1/24/11-21; F; S; Son 638; Yes; Yes; Al. 5559 An. 653

653; Black Bear, Eugene; M; 8/18/18-13; F; S; Son 640; Yes; Yes; Id. U-9167 An. 656

654; Black Bear, Lillie; F; 9/24/24-7; F; S; Daughter 641; Yes; Yes; Id. U-11414 An. 659

655; Black Bear, Cecelia; F; 2/6/28-4; F; S; Daughter 642; Yes; Yes; Id. U-12475 An. none

656; Black Bear, John, Jr; M; 1891-41; F; M; Head 644; Yes; Yes; Al. 998 An. 660
657; Black Bear (Brave Eagle, Jessie), Jessie; F; 1901-31; F; M; Wife 645; Yes; Yes; Al. 3652 An. 661

658; Black Bear, Joseph; M; 1886-46; F; Wd; Head 646; Yes; Yes; Al. 2300 An. 663

659; Black Bear, Leo; M; 12/9/08-23; F; S; Head 643; Yes; Yes; Al. 3752 An. 652

660; Black Bear, Levi; M; 1899-33; F; S; Head 647; Yes; Yes; Al. 727 An. 664

661; Black Bear, Moses; M; 1900-32; F; S; Head 648; Yes; Yes; Al. 1000 An. 665

662; Black Bear, Nellie; F; 4/18/12-19; F; S; Head 649; Yes; Yes; Al. 7088 An. 5685

663; Black Bear, Peter; M; 1904-28; F; S; Head 651; Yes; Yes; Al. 5331 An. 669

664; Black Bear, Sallie; F; 1848-84; F; Wd; Head 652; Yes; Yes; Al. 1240 An. 670

665; Black Bear, Thomas; M; 1902-30; F; M; Head 653; Yes; Yes; Al. 1496 An. 671

Census of the **Pine Ridge** reservation of the **Pine Ridge, South Dakota** jurisdiction, as of **April 1**, 19**32**, taken by **James H. McGregor**, Superintendent.

Key: Number; Surname, Given; Sex; Date of Birth-Age at Last Birthday; Tribe (Oglala Sioux, unless stated otherwise); Degree of Blood; Marital Status; Relationship to Head of Family [Last Census Roll Number]; At Jurisdiction Where Enrolled (Yes/No); (If no – Where); Ward (Yes/No, if given); Allotment, Annuity and Identification Numbers (if given).

666; Black Bear (Spotted Owl), Fannie; F; 1906-26; F; M; Wife 654; Yes; Yes; Al. 7504 An. 657
667; Black Bear, William; M; 11/27/25-6; F; S; Son 655; Yes; Yes; Id. U-11802 An. none
668; Black Bear, Agnes; F; 2/21/29-2; F; S; Daughter 656; Yes; Yes; Id. U-13101 An. none
669; Black Bear, Aloysius; M; 12/7/31-4/12; F; S; Son ---; Yes; Yes; Id. U-13982 An. none

670; Black Bear, Thomas; M; 1904-28; F; M; Head 657; Yes; Yes; Al. 2303 An. 673
671; Black Bear (Poor Bear, Elsie), Elsie; F; 4/2/09-23; F; M; Wife 658; Yes; Yes; Al. 4322 An. 5025
672; Black Bear, Iona M; F; 2/9/32-1; F; S; Daughter 660; Yes; Yes; Id. U-13728 An. none
673; Poor Bear, Allen; M; 3/19/28-4; F; S; Stepson 659; Yes; Yes; Id. U-12713 An. none

674; Black Bear, Thomas; M; 1869-63; F; M; Head 661; Yes; Yes; Al. 726 An. 675
675; Black Bear, Emma; F; 1872-60; F; M; Wife 662; Yes; Yes; Al. 5940 An. 676

676; Black Bear, William; M; 1880-52; F; M; Head 663; Yes; Yes; Al. 1056 An. 681
677; Black Bear (Crow, Annie), Annie; F; 1895-37; F; M; Wife 664; Yes; Yes; Al. 850 An. 682
678; Black Bear, Herbert; M; 5/5/20-11; F; S; Son 665; Yes; Yes; Id. U-9171 An. 684
679; Black Bear, Esther; F; 4/2/25-6; F; S; Daughter 666; Yes; Yes; Id. U-11528 An. none
680; Black Bear, Christina; F; 12/14/29-2; F; S; Daughter 667; Yes; Yes; Id. U-13309 An. none

681; Black Bear, William; M; 1905-26; F; M: Head 668; Yes; Yes; Al. 4334 An. 685
682; Black Bear (Mousseau, Susie), Susie; F; 1894-38; Oglala; plus 1/4; M; Wife 669; Yes; Yes; Al. 701 An. 3472

683; Black Beard, Leslie; M; 1895-37; F; M; Head 670; Yes; Yes; Id. U-9172 An. 586
684; Black Beard (Don't Think, Mary), Mary; F; 1877-55; F; M; Wife 671; Yes; Yes; Al. 6641 An. 1941

685; Black Bird, Isaac; M; 1893-39; F; Wd; Head 672; Yes; Yes; Al. 2356 An. 694

Census of the **Pine Ridge** reservation of the **Pine Ridge, South Dakota** jurisdiction, as of **April 1**, 1932, taken by **James H. McGregor**, Superintendent.

Key: Number; Surname, Given; Sex; Date of Birth-Age at Last Birthday; Tribe (Oglala Sioux, unless stated otherwise); Degree of Blood; Marital Status; Relationship to Head of Family [Last Census Roll Number]; At Jurisdiction Where Enrolled (Yes/No); (If no – Where); Ward (Yes/No, if given); Allotment, Annuity and Identification Numbers (if given).

686; Black Bird, Sarah; F; 3/21/18-14; F; S; Daughter 674; Yes; Yes; Id. U-9175 An. 696
687; Black Bird, Jacob; M; 5/4/21-10; F; S; Son 675; Yes; Yes; Id. U-9176 An. 697
688; Black Bird, Martha; F; 1/28/24-8; F; S; Daughter 676; Yes; Yes; Id. U-11216 An. 698
689; Black Bird, Jessie; F; 3/10/26-6; F; S; Daughter 677; Yes; Yes; Id. U-11861 An. none
690; Black Bird, Edna;; F; 11/24/27-4; F; S; Daughter 678; Yes; Yes; Id. U-12509 An. none

691; Black Bird, Richard; M; 1896-36; F; Wd; Head 679; Yes; Yes; Al. 2357 An. 700

692; Black Bird, Thomas; M; 1898-34; F; S; Head 681; Yes; Yes; Al. 6755 An. 702

693; Black Bull, James; M; 1879-53; F; M; Head 682; Yes; No; Al. 756 An. 708
694; Black Bull (No Flesh, Emma), Emma; F; 1880-52; F; M; Wife 683; Yes; Yes; Al. 4416 An. 704
695; Black Bull, Catherine; F; 7/20/14-17; F; S; Daughter 684; Yes; Yes; Al. 7758 An. 705
696; Black Bull, Emily; F; 9/28/18-13; F; S; Daughter 685; Yes; Yes; Id. U-9177 An. 708

697; Black Bull, Thomas; M; 1863-69; F; M; Head 686; Yes; Yes; Al. 554 An. 708
698; Black Bull, Susie; F; 1860-72; F; M; Wife 687; Yes; Yes; Al. 7157 An. 709

699; Black Cat, John; M; 1886-46; F; M; Head 688; Yes; Yes; Al. 4568 An. 713
700; Black Cat (Imitates Dog, Bessie), Bessie; F; 1900-32; F; M; Wife 689; Yes; Yes; Al. 1060 An. 711
701; Black Cat, Joseph; M; 7/20/26-5; F; S; Son 690; Yes; Yes; Id. U-11985 An. none
702; Black Cat, Chris; M; 1/28/30-2; F; S; Son 691; Yes; Yes; Id. U-13317 An. none

703; Black Cat, Maggie; F; 1878-54; F; Wd; Head 692; Yes; Yes; Al. 7593 An. 714
704; Black Cat, David; M; 8/5/13-18; F; S; Son 693; Yes; Yes; Al. 7594 An. 716
705; Black Cat, Mary; F; 1/13/22-10; F; S; Daughter 695; Yes; Yes; Id. U-10888 An. 717

706; Black Crow, Amos; M; 1893-39; F; M; Head 696; Yes; Yes; Al. 2376 An. 721
707; Black Crow (Holy Eagle, Julia), Julia; F; 1889-43; F; M; Wife 697; Yes; Yes; Al. 2382 An. 722

Census of the __Pine Ridge__ reservation of the __Pine Ridge, South Dakota__ jurisdiction, as of __April 1__, 19**32**, taken by __James H. McGregor__, Superintendent.

Key: Number; Surname, Given; Sex; Date of Birth-Age at Last Birthday; Tribe (Oglala Sioux, unless stated otherwise); Degree of Blood; Marital Status; Relationship to Head of Family [Last Census Roll Number]; At Jurisdiction Where Enrolled (Yes/No); (If no – Where); Ward (Yes/No, if given); Allotment, Annuity and Identification Numbers (if given).

708; Black Crow, Louisa; F; 3/26/22-10; F; S; Daughter 698; Yes; Yes; Id. U-10951 An. 724
709; Black Crow, Sylvia; F; 4/8/24-7; F; S; Daughter 699; Yes; Yes; Id. U-11259 An. 725
710; Black Crow, Hazel; F; 3/22/27-5; F; S; Daughter 700; Yes; Yes; Id. U-12343 An. none
711; Black Crow, Cleveland; M; 5/9/29-2; F; S; Son 701; Yes; Yes; Id. U-13179 An. none

712; Black Crow, Austin; M; 1866-66; F; M; Head 702; Yes; Yes; Al. 2373 An. 726
713; Black Crow (Big White Horse, Julia), Julia; F; 1870-62; F; M; Wife 703; Yes; Yes; Al. 2374 An. 727
714; Thunder Hawk, Joseph; M; 9/5/18-13; F; S; Grand-son 704; Yes; Yes; Id. U-10569 An. 6898

715; Black Crow, Jacob; M; 1/26/09-23; F; M; Head 705; Yes; Yes; Al. 5743 An. 728
716; Black Crow (Shout At, Louisa), Louisa; F; 8/1/13-18; F; M; Wife 706; Yes; Yes; Id. U-9923 An. 6275
717; Black Crow, Frances Sallie; F; 5/17/31-11/12; F; S; Daughter ---; Yes; Yes; Id. U-13830 An. none

~~N.E. Black Crow, Samuel; M; Rosebud Sioux; Head~~
718; Black Crow (Bad Cob, Mary), Mary; F; 1898-34; F; M; Wife 707; Yes; Yes; Al. 4241 An. 729
719; Black Crow, Aaron; M; 6/4/28-3; F; S; Son 709; Yes; Yes; Id. U-12664 An. none
720; Black Crow, Milo; M; 4/24/30-1; F; S; Son 710; Yes; Yes; Id. U-13467 An. none
721; Black Crow, Catherine; F; 12/27/24-7; F; S; Daughter 708; Yes; Yes; Id. U-10769 An. 731

722; Black Deer, William; M; 1876-56; F; Wd; Head 711; Yes; Yes; Al. 2842 An. 732

723; Black Elk #2; M; 1865-67; F; M; Head 712; Yes; Yes; Al. 3021 An. 733
724; Brings White; F; 1871-61; F; M; Wife 713; Yes; Yes; Al. 5085 An. 734
725; Black Elk, Nick; M; 5/1/14-17; F; S; Son 714; Yes; Yes; Id. U-9184 An. 738

726; Black Elk, Benjamin; M; 1899-33; F; M; Head 715; Yes; Yes; Al. 3023 An. 736

Census of the __Pine Ridge__ reservation of the __Pine Ridge, South Dakota__ jurisdiction, as of __April 1__, 1932, taken by __James H. McGregor__, Superintendent.

Key: Number; Surname, Given; Sex; Date of Birth-Age at Last Birthday; Tribe (Oglala Sioux, unless stated otherwise); Degree of Blood; Marital Status; Relationship to Head of Family [Last Census Roll Number]; At Jurisdiction Where Enrolled (Yes/No); (If no – Where); Ward (Yes/No, if given); Allotment, Annuity and Identification Numbers (if given).

727; Black Elk (Bissonette, Angelina), Angelina; F; 1903-29; plus 1/4; M; Wife 716; Yes; Yes; Al. 873 An. 737
728; Black Elk, Henry L; M; 12/16/19-12; plus 1/4; S; Son 717; Yes; Yes; Id. U-9185 An. 738

729; Black Elk, Catherine; F; 1/24/22-10; 1/4[sic]; S; Daughter 718; Yes; Yes; Id. U-10900 An. 739
730; Black Elk, Esther; F; 6/11/24-7; plus 1/4; S; Daughter 719; Yes; Yes; Id. U-11292 An. 740
731; Black Elk, Olivia; F; 10/10/27-4; plus 1/4; S; Daughter 720; Yes; Yes; Id. U-12438 An. none
732; Black Elk, Deloris G; F; 7/14/30-1; plus 1/4; S; Daughter 721; Yes; Yes; Id. U-13541 An. none

733; Black Elk, Joseph; M; 1895-37; plus 1/4; M; Head 722; Yes; Yes; Al. 4944 An. 741
734; Black Elk (Bissonette, Sophia), Sophia; F; 1892-34; plus 1/4; M; Wife 723; Yes; Yes; Al. 7110 An. 610
735; Black Elk, Henry; M; 9/8/19-13; plus 1/4; S; Son 724; Yes; Yes; Id. U-9187 An. 743
736; Black Elk, Luke; M; 1/1/21-11; plus 1/4; S; Son 725; Yes; Yes; Id. U-9187 An. 744
737; Black Elk, Wilson; M; 7/26/26-5; plus 1/4; S; Son 726; Yes; Yes; Id. U-11981 An. none

738; Black Elk, Peter; M; 1883-39; plus 1/4; M; Head 727; Yes; Yes; Al. 4943 An. 748
739; Black Elk (Slow Bear, Amelia), Amelia; F; 1885-47; F; M; Wife 728; Yes; Yes; Al. 6289 An. 747
740; Black Elk, Iva; F; 1/15/24-8; plus 1/4; S; dau 730; Yes; Yes; Id. U-11220 An. 751
741; Slow Bear, Tony; M; 4/26/13-18; F; S; Stepson 729; Yes; Yes; Al. 8034 An. 749

742; Black Eyes, Adam; M; 1902-30; F; S; Head 731; Yes; Yes; Al. 5032 An. 752

743; Black Eyes, David; M; 1904-28; F; S; Head 732; Yes; Yes; Al. 5033 An. 753

744; Black Eyes, Thomas; M; 1882-50; F; M; Head 733; Yes; Yes; Al. 2175 An. 754
745; Black Eyes (Moccasin Top, Emma), Emma; F; 1881-51; F; M; Wife 734; Yes; Yes; Al. 5381 An. 755

Census of the __**Pine Ridge**__ reservation of the __**Pine Ridge, South Dakota**__ jurisdiction, as of __**April 1**__, 19**32**, taken by __**James H. McGregor**__, Superintendent.

Key: Number; Surname, Given; Sex; Date of Birth-Age at Last Birthday; Tribe (Oglala Sioux, unless stated otherwise); Degree of Blood; Marital Status; Relationship to Head of Family [Last Census Roll Number]; At Jurisdiction Where Enrolled (Yes/No); (If no – Where); Ward (Yes/No, if given); Allotment, Annuity and Identification Numbers (if given).

746; Black Eyes, William; M; 11/8/11-20; F; S; Son 735; Yes; Yes; Id. U-9189 An. 758

747; Black Eyes, Hastings; M; 3/12/13-19; F; S; Son 736; Yes; Yes; Id. U-9190 An. 759

748; Black Eyes, Noah; M; 1907-25; F; S; Head 737; Yes; Yes; Al. 5034 An. 756

749; Black Feather; M; 1860072; F; M; Head 738; Yes; Yes; Al. 2821 An. 760

750; Black Feather, Amette; F; 1863-69; plus 1/4; M; Wife 739; Yes; Yes; Al. 3017 An. 761

751; Black Feather, Geoffrey; M; 1895-37; plus 1/4; M; Head 740; Yes; Yes; Al. 3019 An. 762

752; Black Feather (Fast Wolf, Cora), Cora; F; 1905-27; plus 1/4; M; Wife 741; Yes; Yes; Al. 1985 An. 2152

753; Black Feather, Eugene; M; 6/4/16-15; plus 1/4; S; Son 742; Yes; Yes; Id. U-9191 An. 764

754; Black Feather, Leo; M; 11/17/28-3; plus 1/4; S; Son 743; Yes; Yes; Id. U-13130 An. none

755; Black Feather, Luther; M; 10/ ?/1900-32; plus 1/4; M; Head 745; Yes; Yes; Al. 3014 An. 767

756; Black Feather (Yellow Boy, Jessie), Jessie; F; 8/20/11-20; plus 1/4; M; Wife 746; Yes; Yes; Al. 7856 An. 7862

757; Black Feather, Raymond; M; 8/8/31-7/12; plus 1/4; S; Son ---; Yes; Yes; Id. U-14082 An. none

758; Black Feather, Washington; M; 1877-55; plus 1/4; Wd; Head 748; Yes; Yes; Al. 3013 An. 771

759; Black Feather, Frank; M; 6/14/10-21; plus 1/4; S; Son 749; Yes; Yes; Al. 6377 An. 773

760; Black Feather, Julia; F; 1/16/13-19; plus 1/4; S; Daughter 750; Yes; Yes; Al. 7664 An. 775

761; Black Feather, William; M; 1886-46; plus 1/4; M; Head 751; Yes; Yes; Al. 3033 An. 776

762; Black Feather (Garnier, Emma), Emma; F; 1888-44; plus 1/4; M; Wife 752; Yes; Yes; Al. 3034 An. 777

763; Black Feather, Louisa; F; 6/25/11-20; plus 1/4; S; Daughter 753; Yes; Yes; Al. 6373 An. 779

764; Black Feather, Wilbert; M; 11/25/15-16; plus 1/4; S; Son 754; Yes; Yes; Id. U-9192 An. 780

765; Black Feather, Stephen; M; 2/8/21-11; plus 1/4; S; Son 755; Yes; Yes; Id. U-9194 An. 782

Census of the **Pine Ridge** reservation of the **Pine Ridge, South Dakota** jurisdiction, as of **April 1**, 19**32**, taken by **James H. McGregor**, Superintendent.

Key: Number; Surname, Given; Sex; Date of Birth-Age at Last Birthday; Tribe (Oglala Sioux, unless stated otherwise); Degree of Blood; Marital Status; Relationship to Head of Family [Last Census Roll Number]; At Jurisdiction Where Enrolled (Yes/No); (If no – Where); Ward (Yes/No, if given); Allotment, Annuity and Identification Numbers (if given).

766; Black Feather, Alonzo; M; 10/23/23-8; plus 1/4; S; Son 756; Yes; Yes; Id. U-11695 An. none
767; Black Feather, Oliver; M; 9/19/28-3; plus 1/4; S; Son 757; Yes; Yes; Id. U-12849 An. none
768; Black Feather, Francis B; M; 5/25/30-1; plus 1/4; S; Son 758; Yes; Yes; Id. U-13681 An. none
769; Black Feather, Margaret; F; 1908-24; plus 1/4; S; Head 759; Yes; Yes; Al. 3035 An. 778

770; Black Fox, John; M; 1860-72; F; M; Head 760; Yes; Yes; Al. 2783 An. 783
771; Black Fox (Lone Hill, Sallie), Sallie; F; 1862-70; F; M; Wife 761; Yes; Yes; Al. 4101 An. 786

772; Black Hair, Joseph; M; 1858-74; F; M; Head 762; Yes; Yes; Al. 6524 An. 787
773; Black Hair, Catherine; F; 1872-60; F; M; Wife 763; Yes; Yes;Al. 6525 An. 788

774; Black Horse, Charles; M; 1857-75; F; M; Head 764; Yes; Yes; Al. 251 An. 789
775; Black Horse, Susie; F; 1886-66; F; M; Wife 765; Yes; Yes; Al. 8035 An. 790

776; Black Horse, Charles, Jr; M; 1896-36; F; Wd; Head 766; Yes; Yes; Al. 275 An. 791
777; Black Horse, Ralph; M; 10/ /20-11; plus 1/4; S; Son 767; Yes; Yes; Id. U-12442 An. none
778; Black Horse, James; M; 1855-77; F; M; Head 768; Yes; Yes; Al. 3431 An. 792
779; Black Horse, Susie; F; 1853-79; F; M; Wife 769; Yes; Yes; Al. 6154 An. 793

780; Black Road; Peter; M; 1/8/14-18; F; S; Alone 770; Yes; Yes; Al. 7476 An. 800
781; Black Road, Esther; F; 6/23/16-15; F; S; Sister 771; Yes; Yes; Id. U-9195 An. 801

~~N.E. Blacksmith, Thomas; M; Cheyenne River Sioux; F; M; Head~~
782; Blacksmith (Black Elk, Ida), Ida; F; 2/13/08-24; plus 1/4; M; Wife 772; No; Cheyenne River, SD; Yes; Id. U-9312 An. 1328

~~N.E. Blacksmith, John; M; Cheyenne River Sioux; F; M; Head~~
783; Blacksmith (Loafer Joe, Edna), Edna; F; 1902-30; F; M; Wife 773; Yes; Yes; Al. 6588 An. 4114
784; Blacksmith, Lucile; F; 5/9/30-1; F; S; Daughter 000; Yes; Yes; Id. U-13797 An. none

41

Census of the __**Pine Ridge**__ reservation of the __**Pine Ridge, South Dakota**__ jurisdiction, as of __**April 1**__, 19**32**, taken by __**James H. McGregor**__, Superintendent.

Key: Number; Surname, Given; Sex; Date of Birth-Age at Last Birthday; Tribe (Oglala Sioux, unless stated otherwise); Degree of Blood; Marital Status; Relationship to Head of Family [Last Census Roll Number]; At Jurisdiction Where Enrolled (Yes/No); (If no – Where); Ward (Yes/No, if given); Allotment, Annuity and Identification Numbers (if given).

785; Black Tail Deer, Henry; M; 1908-24; F; M; Head 777; Yes; Yes; Al. 5074 An. 805

786; Black Tail Deer (Brave, Daisy), Daisy; F; 9/4/13-18; plus 1/4; M; Wife 883; Yes; Yes; Al. 7638 An. 932

787; Black Tail Deer, Frank; M; 1891-41; F; M; Head 778; Yes; Yes; Al. 5071 An. 808

788; Black Tail Deer (Wounded, Mary), Mary; F; 1899-33; F; M; Wife 779; Yes; Yes; Al. 5053 An. 810

789; Black Tail Deer, Francis; M; 2/2/20-12; F; S; Son 780; Yes; Yes; Al. 5052 An. 811

790; Black Tail Deer, Llewellyn; M; 6/4/22-9; F; S; Son 781; Yes; Yes; Id. U-11018 An. 812

791; Black Tail Deer, Andrew; M; 8/8/25-6; F; S; Son 782; Yes; Yes; Id. U-11720 An. none

792; Black Tail Deer, Martha; F; 7/8/27-4; F; S; Daughter 783; Yes; Yes; Id. U-13439 An. none

793; Black Tail Deer, Thomas; M; 1903-29; F; S; Head 786; Yes; Yes; Al. 888 An. 813

794; Black Whirlwind, Rosa; F; 1859-73; F; Wd; Head 788; Yes; Yes; Al. 4706 An. 817

795; Blind Man, Charles; M; 1888-44; F; M; Head 789; Yes; Yes; Al. 8206 An. 829
796; Blind Man (Little Bird, Nettie), Nettie; F; 1889-43; F; M; Wife 790; Yes; Yes; Al. 3259 An. 830
797; Blind Man, Charles, Jr; M; 8/2/12-19; F; S; Son 791; Yes; Yes; Al. 6255 An. 832
798; Blind Man, Cordelia; F; 8/26/16-16; F; S; Daughter 792; Yes; Yes; Id. U-9200 An. 832
799; Blind Man, Eugene; M; 1/22/20-12; F; S; Son 793; Yes; Yes; Id. U-9201 An. 833
800; Blind Man, Moses; M; 1/21/22/-10; F; S; Son 794; Yes; Yes; Id. U-10878 An. 834

801; Blind Man, Thomas; M; 1884-48; F; M; Head 795; Yes; Yes; Al. 7539 An. 835
802; Blind Man (Big Bend, Katie), Katie; F; 1887-45; F; M; Wife 796; Yes; Yes; Al. 7538 An. 836
803; Blind Man, Stephen; M; 10/4/11-20; F; S; Son 797; Yes; Yes; Al. 6412 An. 837

Census of the __Pine Ridge__ reservation of the __Pine Ridge, South Dakota__ jurisdiction, as of __April 1__, 1932, taken by __James H. McGregor__, Superintendent.

Key: Number; Surname, Given; Sex; Date of Birth-Age at Last Birthday; Tribe (Oglala Sioux, unless stated otherwise); Degree of Blood; Marital Status; Relationship to Head of Family [Last Census Roll Number]; At Jurisdiction Where Enrolled (Yes/No); (If no – Where); Ward (Yes/No, if given); Allotment, Annuity and Identification Numbers (if given).

804; Blind Man, Lena; F; 4/23/16-15; F; S; Daughter 798; Yes; Yes; Id. U-9202 An. 838
805; Blind Man, Percy; M; 8/3/21-10; F; S; Son 799; Yes; Yes; Id. U-9204 An. 840
806; Blind Man, Bertha R; F; 4/14/26-5; F; S; Daughter 800; Yes; Yes; Id. U-11902 An. none
807; Blind Man, Helen R; F; 2/10/29-3; F; S; Daughter 801; Yes; Yes; Id. U-13102 An. none
808; Blind Man, Alfonzo; M; 8/19/31-7/12; F; S; Son ---; Yes; Yes; Id. U-13883 An. none

N.E. Blue Arm, John; M; Cheyenne River Sioux; M; Head
809; Blue Arm (Chips, Minnie), Minnie; F; 1907-25; F; M; Wife 802; Yes; Yes; Al. 3985 An. 843

810; Blue Bird, Mabel; F; 10/6/06-25; plus 1/4; Wd; Head 803; Yes; Yes; Al. 5736 An. 6068
811; Blue Bird, Beatrice Mae; F; 12/27/30-1; plus 1/4; S; Daughter 804; Yes; Yes; Id. U-13692 An. none

812; Blue Bird, James; M; 1888-44; F; M; Head 805; Yes; Yes; Al. 1286 An. 846
813; Blue Bird (Imitates Dog, Nettie), Nettie; F; 5/6/14-17; F; M; Wife 7972; Yes; Yes; Al. 7864 An. 3118
814; Blue Bird, Vivian Doris; F; 87/12; F; S; Daughter ---; Yes; Yes; Id. U-13931 An. none

815; Blue Bird, Ruth; F; 4/6/12-19; F; S; Head 806; Yes; Yes; Al. 7156 An. 852
816; Blue Bird, Philip; ,M; 1898-34; F; M; Head 807; Yes; Yes; Al. 1380 An. 853
817; Blue Bird (Fire Thunder, Lydia), Lydia; F; 1892-40; plus 1/4; M; Wife 806; Yes; Yes; Al. 1958 An. 854
818; Blue Bird, Arlene E; F; 5/9/22-9; plus 1/4; S; Daughter 809; Yes; Yes; Id. U-13018 An. none

819; Blue Bird, Thomas; M; 1890-42; F; M; Head 810; Yes; Yes; Al. 1287 An. 856
820; Blue Bird (Red Kettle, Nancy), Nancy; F; 1900-32; plus 1/4; M; Wife 811; Yes; Yes; Al. 1676 An. 857
821; Blue Bird, Margerate[sic]; F; 1/17/21-11; plus 1/4; S; Daughter 812; Yes; Yes; Id. U-9208 An. 858
822; Blue Bird, Rachel; F; 7/17/22-9; plus 1/4; S; Daughter 813; Yes; Yes; Id. U-11309 An. 859
823; Blue Bird, Elizabeth; F; 3/18/24-8; plus 1/4; S; Daughter 814; Yes; Yes; Id. U-11308 An. 860
824; Blue Bird, Chester; M; 10/18/27-4; plus 1/4; S; Son 815; Yes; Yes; Id. U-12418 An. none

Census of the __Pine Ridge__ reservation of the __Pine Ridge, South Dakota__ jurisdiction, as of __April 1__, 19**32,** taken by __James H. McGregor__, Superintendent.

Key: Number; Surname, Given; Sex; Date of Birth-Age at Last Birthday; Tribe (Oglala Sioux, unless stated otherwise); Degree of Blood; Marital Status; Relationship to Head of Family [Last Census Roll Number]; At Jurisdiction Where Enrolled (Yes/No); (If no – Where); Ward (Yes/No, if given); Allotment, Annuity and Identification Numbers (if given).

825; Blue Bird, Everett; M; 1/18/29-2; plus 1/4; S; Son 816; Yes; Yes; Id. U-13318 An. none

826; Blue Bird, Florence Emily; F; 4/19/13-11/12; plus 1/4; S; Daughter 0--[sic]; Yes; Yes; Id. U-13831 An. none

827; Blue Horse, Baldwin; M; 1857-75; F; Wd; Head 817; Yes; Yes; Al. 6021 An. 861

828; Blue Horse Owner, Arthur; M; 1889-43; F; M; Head 818; Yes; Yes; Al. 3143 An. 863

829; Blue Horse Owner (Short Bull, Katie), Katie; F; 1893-39; F; M; Wife 819; Yes; Yes; Id. U-9209 An. 865

830; Blue Horse Owner, Andrew; M; 4/25/17-14; F; S; Son 820; Yes; Yes; Id. U-9209 An. 865

831; Blue Horse Owner, Eugene; M; 5/6/21-10; F; S; Son 821; Yes; Yes; Id. U-9210 An. 866

832; Blue Horse Owner, Jonas; M; 6/25/07-24; F; S; Head 822; Yes; Yes; Al. 3161 An. 6488

833; Blue Legs; M; 1857-75; F; Wd; Head 823; Yes; Yes; Al. 1917 An. 868

834; Blue Legs, George; M; 1884-48; F; M; Head 824; Yes; Yes; Al. 1850 An. 869
835; Blue Legs (Fox Belly, Jennie), Jennie; F; 1894-38; F; M; Wife 825; Yes; Yes; Al. 7704 An. 870
836; Blue Legs, Bert; M; 11/10/17-14; F; S; Son 826; Yes; Yes; Al. 5806 An. 873
837; Blue Legs, Vesta; F; 1/14/20-12; F; S; Daughter 827; Yes; Yes; Yes; Id. U-9212 An. 874
838; Blue Legs, Gladys; F; 8/14/30-1; F; S; Daughter 829; Yes; Yes; Id. U-13563 An. none

839; Blue Legs, Thomas; M; 1886-46; F; M; Head 830; Yes; No; Al. 1851 An. 876
840; Blue Legs (Red Elk, Mattie), Mattie; F; 1904-28; F; M; Wife 832; Yes; Yes; Al. 5650 An. 2946
841; Blue Legs, Ernest; M; 11/1/18-13; F; S; Son 831; Yes; Yes; Id. U-9213 An. 877
842; Blue Legs, Emil; M; 3/26/20-2; F; S; Son 833; Yes; Yes; Id. U-13410 An. none

843; Bluffing Bear, Sophia; F; 1867-65; F; Wd; Head 835; Yes; Yes; Al. 2313 An. 879

844; Blunt Horn, Charles; M; 1900-32; F; M; Head 836; Yes; Yes; Al. 140 An. 881

Census of the __Pine Ridge__ reservation of the __Pine Ridge, South Dakota__ jurisdiction, as of __April 1__, 1932, taken by __James H. McGregor__, Superintendent.

Key: Number; Surname, Given; Sex; Date of Birth-Age at Last Birthday; Tribe (Oglala Sioux, unless stated otherwise); Degree of Blood; Marital Status; Relationship to Head of Family [Last Census Roll Number]; At Jurisdiction Where Enrolled (Yes/No); (If no – Where); Ward (Yes/No, if given); Allotment, Annuity and Identification Numbers (if given).

845; Blunt Horn (Romero, Rosa), Rosa; F; 4/21/12-19; plus 1/4; M; Wife 837; Yes; Yes; Al. 6538 An. 5791

846; Blunt Horn, Levi E; M; 3/7/28-4; plus 1/4; S; Son 838; Yes; Yes; Id. U-12666 An. none

847; Blunt Horn, George; M; 8/20/02-30; F; S; Head 839; Yes; Yes; Al. 141 An. 882

848; Blunt Horn, Nellie; F; 1863-69; F; Wd; Head 840; Yes; Yes; Al. 2496 An. 883

849; Bone Necklace #2; M; 1868-64; F; M; Head 841; Yes; Yes; Id. U-9214 An. 890

850; Booras, Emma; F; 4/1/07-25; plus 1/4; Wd; Head 842; Yes; Yes; Al. 5535 An. 4511

~~N.E. Bordeaux, Ernest; M; Rosebud Sioux; plus 1/4; Head~~

851; Bordeaux (Standing Soldier, Mary), Mary; F; 1905-27; plus 1/4; M; Wife 843; No; Rosebud, S.D; Yes; Yes; Al 1934 An. 891

852; Bordeaux, Millie; F; 1892-40; F; Wd; Head 844; Yes; Yes; Al. 7194 An. 6547

853; Standing Rock Sioux Bear, Oliver W; M; 6/8/15-16; plus 1/4; S; Son 845; Yes; Yes; Al. 8096 An. 6548

854; Bores A Hole; M; 1861-71; F; Wd; Head 846; Yes; No; Al. 2902 An. 892

855; Bores A Hole, George; M; 1890-42; F; S; Head 847; Yes; Yes; Al. 3402 An. 894

~~N.E. Bores A Hole, Jacob; M; 5/30/12-19; Cheyenne River Sioux; F; M; Head~~

856; Bores A Hole (Spotted Horse, Sarah), Sarah; F; 11/19/07-25; F; M; Wife 6532; Yes; Yes; Al. 6331 An. 3648

857; Bores A Hole, Willie; M; 1887-45; F; M; Head 848; Yes; Yes; Al. 7489 An. 895

~~N.E. Bores A Hole (Pretty Cloud, Isabelle), Isabelle; F; Cheyenne River Sioux; F; M; Wife~~

858; Bores A Hole, Winifred; F; 10-5-18-13; Sioux; F; S; Daughter 849; Yes; Yes; Id. U-9215 An. 897

859; Bores A Hole, Glen; M; 12/13;26-5; Sioux; F; S; Son 850; Yes; Yes; Id. U-12214 An. none

~~N.E. Bowdish, Fred; f[sic]; White; M; Head~~

Census of the __Pine Ridge__ reservation of the __Pine Ridge, South Dakota__ jurisdiction, as of __April 1__, 19**32**, taken by __James H. McGregor__, Superintendent.

Key: Number; Surname, Given; Sex; Date of Birth-Age at Last Birthday; Tribe (Oglala Sioux, unless stated otherwise); Degree of Blood; Marital Status; Relationship to Head of Family [Last Census Roll Number]; At Jurisdiction Where Enrolled (Yes/No); (If no – Where); Ward (Yes/No, if given); Allotment, Annuity and Identification Numbers (if given).

860; Bowdish (Peck, Dora), Dora; F; 1887-45; plus 1/4; M; Wife 851; Yes; Yes; Al. 2550 An. 4945

861; Picotte, Cecil; M; 8/13/13-18; plus 1/4; S; Son 852; Yes; Yes; Al. 8185 An. 4948

862; Bowman, Joseph; M; 1906-26; plus 1/4; S; Head 853; Yes; Yes; Al. 2590 An. 899

863; Bowman, Thomas; M; 1877-55; plus 1/4; M; Head 854; Yes; Yes; Al. 2587 An. 900

864; Bowman, Nettie; F; 1881-51; plus 1/4; M; Wife 855; Yes; Yes; Al. 5440 An. 901

865; Bowman, Wilma; F; 1/10/11-21; plus 1/4; S; Daughter 856; Yes; Yes; Al. 5476 An. 902

866; Bowman, Hazel; F; 4/19/16-15; plus 1/4; S; Daughter 857; Yes; Yes; Id. U-9216 An. 903

867; Bowman, Verna; F; 1903-29; plus 1/4; S; Head 858; Yes; Yes; Al. 2589 An. 904

868; Bowman, Victor; M; 1901-31; plus 1/4; S; Head 859; Yes; Yes; Al. 2588 An. 905

869; Boyer, John; M; 189-63; plus 1/4; M; Head 860; Yes; Yes; Al. 549 An. 906
870; Boyer (Good Voice Dog, Katie), Katie; F; 11879-53; F; M; Wife 861; Yes; Yes; Al. 7335 An. 907
871; Boyer, Lena; F; 11/3/15-16; plus 1/4; S; Daughter 862; Yes; Yes; Id. U-9217 An. 909
872; Boyer, Lucy; F; 9/10/17-14; plus 1/4; S; Daughter 863; Yes; Yes; Id. U-9218 An. 910

873; Boyer, Samuel; M; 1903-29; plus 1/4; Wd; Head 864; Yes; Yes; Al. 5655 An. 912

874; Boyer, Vetal; M; 1906-26; plus 1/4; s; Head 865; Yes; Yes; Al. 5656 An. 913

~~N.E. Brace, Luther; M; Kiowa, Okla, Indian; plus 1/4; M; Head~~
875; Brace (Hill, Esther), Esther; F; 1906-26; plus 1/4; SM; Wife 866; Yes; Yes; Al. 2768 An. 914

~~N.E. Brafford, Bert; M; White; M; Head~~
876; Brafford (Davidson, Elizabeth), Elizabeth; F; 1894-38; plus 1/4; M; Wife 867; No; Rapid City, Pennington Co, S.D; Yes; Al. 1621 An. 915

Census of the ___**Pine Ridge**___ reservation of the ___**Pine Ridge, South Dakota**___
jurisdiction, as of ___**April 1**___, 19**32**, taken by ___**James H. McGregor**___,
Superintendent.

Key: Number; Surname, Given; Sex; Date of Birth-Age at Last Birthday; Tribe (Oglala Sioux, unless stated otherwise); Degree of Blood; Marital Status; Relationship to Head of Family [Last Census Roll Number]; At Jurisdiction Where Enrolled (Yes/No); (If no – Where); Ward (Yes/No, if given); Allotment, Annuity and Identification Numbers (if given).

877; Brafford, Leona; F; 8/8/16-15; -1/4; S; Daughter 868; No; No; Rapid City, Pennington Co, S.D; Yes; Al. 8267 An. 915
878; Brafford, John WM; M; 9/14/19-12; -1/4; S; Son 869; No; Rapid City, Pennington Co, S.D; Yes; Al.
879; Brafford, Hazel; F; 7/6/22-9; -1/4; S; Daughter 870; No; Rapid City, Pennington Co, S.D; Yes; Al.

~~N.E. Brafford, Marion; M; White; Head~~
880; Brafford (Clifford, Julia), Julia; F; 1878-54; plus 1/4; M; Wife 871; Yes; Yes; Al. 1648 & 5971 An. 918
881; Brafford, Ephriam; M; 5/26/09-22; plus 1/4; S; Son 872; Yes; Yes; Al. 7439 An. 919
882; Brafford, Walter; M; 1/23/11-21; plus 1/4; S; Neph. 2869; Yes; Yes; Al. 7439 An. 921
883; Brafford, Lincoln; M; 1904-28; plus 1/4; M; Head 873; Yes; Yes; Al. 5972 An. 920
884; Brafford (Montileaux, Clara), Clara; F; 1903-29; plus 1/4; M; Wife 874; Yes; Yes; Al. 3574 An. 4555
885; Brafford, Merle L; M; 6/8/30-1; plus 1/4; S; Son 875; Yes; Yes; Id. U-13526 An. none
886; Brafford, Thelma M; F; 11/21/31-4/12; plus 1/4; S; Daughter ---; Yes; Yes; Id. U-13958 An. none

887; Brave, Charles; M; 1870-62; F; M; Head 878; Yes; Yes; Al. 5382 An. 926
888; Brave (Red Elk, Ruth), Ruth; F; 1879-53; F; M; Wife 879; Yes; Yes; Al. 2957 An. 5434
889; Red Elk, Dora; F; 12/3/22-9; F; S; Stepdaughter 880; Yes; Yes; Id. U-13038 An. 5435

890; Brave, Milton; M; 1898-34; F; M; Head 876; Yes; Yes; Al. 5389 An. 922
891; Brave (Belt, Sarah), Sarah; F; 4/15/10-21; F; M; Wife 877; Yes; Yes; Al. 6191 An. 455
892; Brave, Verne Elmer; M; 12/19/31-3/12; F; S; Son 000; Yes; Yes; Id. U-13893 An. none

893; Brave, Philip; M; 1883-49; plus 1/4; M; Head 881; Yes; Yes; Al. 6271 An. 929
894; Brave (Brings, Minnie), Minnie; F; 1877-55; F; M; Wife 882; Yes; Yes; Al. 6115 An. 1006
895; Brave, Cordelia; F; 11/22/19-12; plus 1/4; S; Dau 884; Yes; Yes; Id. U-9225 An. 924

Census of the **Pine Ridge** reservation of the **Pine Ridge, South Dakota** jurisdiction, as of **April 1**, 19**32**, taken by **James H. McGregor**, Superintendent.

Key: Number; Surname, Given; Sex; Date of Birth-Age at Last Birthday; Tribe (Oglala Sioux, unless stated otherwise); Degree of Blood; Marital Status; Relationship to Head of Family [Last Census Roll Number]; At Jurisdiction Where Enrolled (Yes/No); (If no – Where); Ward (Yes/No, if given); Allotment, Annuity and Identification Numbers (if given).

896; Brave, Gilbert; M; 3/17/22-10; plus 1/4; S; Son 885; Yes; Yes; Id. U-10937 An. 935

897; Brave, Elsie; F; 10/30/25-6; plus 1/4; S; Daughter 886; Yes; Yes; Id. U-11760 An. none

898; Brave, Reuben; M; 1890-42; F; M; Head 890; Yes; Yes; Al. 6290 An. 936

899; Brave (Black Bear, Rosa), Rosa; F; 11/1/02-30; F; M; Wife 747; Yes; Yes; Al. 4333 An. 768

900; Brave, Wilson; M; 3/1/14-18; F; S; Son 891; Yes; Yes; Al. 8012 An. 938

901; Brave, Lydia; F; 2/29/17-14; F; S; Daughter 892; Yes; Yes; Id. U-9226 An. 939

902; Between Lodges, Walter; M; 5/20/10-21; F; S; Stepson 893; Yes; Yes; Al. 5985 An. 513

903; Between Lodges, Laura; F; 12/23/18-13; F; S; Stepdaughter 894; Yes; Yes; Id. U-9135 An. none

904; Between Lodges, Esther; F; 4/13/21-10; F; S; Stepdaughter 895; Yes; Yes; Id. U-9136 An. none

905; Brave, William; M; 3/15/10-21; plus 1/4; M; Head 887; Yes; Yes; Al. 6398 An. 931

906; Brave (Good Soldier, Lena), Lena; F; 7/8/12-19; F; M; Wife 888; Yes; Yes; Al. 7645 An. 2606

907; Brave, Bessie; F; 6/8/29-2; plus 1/4; S; Daughter 889; Yes; Yes; Id. U-13201 An. none

908; Brave Eagle, Isaac; M; 1906-26; F; S; Head 896; Yes; Yes; Al. 5893 An. 944

909; Brave Eagle, Oscar; M; 1868-64; F; M; Head 897; Yes; Yes; Al. 1483 An. 947

910; Brave (Crazy Dog, Lucy), Lucy; F; 1878-54; F; M; Wife 898; Yes; Yes; Al. 1823 An. 948

N.E. ~~Brave Hawk, Jesse; M; Rosebud Sioux; F; M; Head~~

910; Brave Hawk (Menard, Ethel), Ethel; F; 1902-30; plus 1/4; M; Wife 899; No; Rosebud, S.D; Yes; Al. 5111 An. 950

N.E. Brave Hawk, Charles; M; Rosebud Sioux; F; M; Head

912; Brave Hawk (High Eagle, Alice), Alice; F; 1900-32; plus 1/4; M; Wife 900; Yes; hes[sic]; Al. 2408 An. 1524

913; Brave Heart, Charles; M; 1904-28; F; M; Head 901; Yes; Yes; Al. 802 An. 952

914; Brave Heart (Broken Leg, Rosa), Rosa; F; 1905-27; F; M; Wife 902; Yes; Yes; Al. 1867 An. 1027

Census of the **Pine Ridge** reservation of the **Pine Ridge, South Dakota** jurisdiction, as of **April 1**, 19**32**, taken by **James H. McGregor**, Superintendent.

Key: Number; Surname, Given; Sex; Date of Birth-Age at Last Birthday; Tribe (Oglala Sioux, unless stated otherwise); Degree of Blood; Marital Status; Relationship to Head of Family [Last Census Roll Number]; At Jurisdiction Where Enrolled (Yes/No); (If no – Where); Ward (Yes/No, if given); Allotment, Annuity and Identification Numbers (if given).

915; Brave Heart, Joseph; M; 12/8/27-4; F; S; Son 903; Yes; Yes; Id. U-12440 An. none

916; Brave Heart, Louis; M; 11/19/29-2; F; S; Son 904; Yes; Yes; Id. U-13285 An. none

917; Brave Heart, Lucy; F; 1/10/32-3/12; F; S; Daughter 000; Yes; Yes; Id. U-14058 An. none

918; Brave Heart, James; ; 1868-64; F; Wd; Head 905; Yes; Yes; Al. 798 An. 953

919; Brave Heart, Julia; F; 4/22/18-13; F; s; Daughter 906; Yes; Yes; Id. U-9229 An. 954

920; Brave Heart, Joseph; M; 1905-27; plus 1/4; S; Head 907; Yes; Yes; Al. 7349 An. 955

921; Brave Heart, John; M; 1880-48; F; M; Head 908; Yes; Yes; Al. 3176 An. 956

922; Brave Heart (Blue Horse Owner, Hilda), Hilda; F; 1869-63; plus 1/4; M; Wife 909; Yes; Yes; Al. 3271 An. 957

923; Brave Heart, Eliza; F; 9/7/17-14; plus 1/4; S; Daughter 910; Yes; Yes;] Id. U-9230 An. 958

924; Brave Heart, Joseph; M; 1886-46; F; M; Head 911; Yes; No; Al. 3177 An. 959

925; Brave Heart (Spotted Elk, Minnie), Minnie; F; 1884-48; F; M; Wife 916; Yes; Yes; Al. 3160 An. 6487

926; Brave Heart, Wilson; M; 2/4/10-22; F; S; Son 912; Yes; Yes; Id. U-9231 An. 960

927; Brave Heart, Andrew; M; 12/10/12-19; F; S; Son 913; Yes; Yes; Id. U-9232 An. 961

928; Brave Heart, Lilly; F; 11/1/19-12; F; S; Daughter 915; Yes; Yes; Id. U-9236 An. 964

929; Brave Heart, Moses; M; 1895-37; F; M; Head 917; Yes; Yes; Al. 799 An. 965

930; Brave Heart (Means, Ada), Ada; F; 1902-30; plus 1/4; M; Wife 918; Yes; Yes; Al. 7163 An. 966

931; Brave Heart, Bertha; F; 4/13/29-2; plus 1/4; S; Daughter 919; Yes; Yes; Id. U-13131 An. none

932; Brave Heart, Christopher; M; 3/5/32-1/12; plus 1/4; S; Son ---; Yes; Yes; Id. U-1[?]122 An. none

933; Breast, John; M; 1874-58; F; S; Head 920; Yes; Yes; Al. 4195 An. 971

934; Breast, Lucy; F; 1862-68; F; S; Head 921; Yes; Yes; Al. 4237 An. 9723

Census of the **Pine Ridge** reservation of the **Pine Ridge, South Dakota** jurisdiction, as of **April 1**, 19**32,** taken by **James H. McGregor**, Superintendent.

Key: Number; Surname, Given; Sex; Date of Birth-Age at Last Birthday; Tribe (Oglala Sioux, unless stated otherwise); Degree of Blood; Marital Status; Relationship to Head of Family [Last Census Roll Number]; At Jurisdiction Where Enrolled (Yes/No); (If no – Where); Ward (Yes/No, if given); Allotment, Annuity and Identification Numbers (if given).

935; Breast, Silas; M; 1882-50; F; M; Head 922; Yes; No; Al. 4204 An. 973
936; Breast, Elizabeth; F; 5/17/13-19; F; S; Daughter 923; Yes; Yes; Al. 7027 An. 976

937; Breast, William; M; 1876-56; F; M; Head 924; Yes; ues[sic]; Al. 4248 An. 977
~~N.E. Breast (Larvie, Rose), Rose; F; Rosebud Sioux; plus 1/4; M; Wife~~
938; Breast, Burton; M; 6/10/15-16; Sioux; plus 1/4; S; Son 925; Yes; Yes; Al. 8150 An. 978
939; Breast, Irene; F; 3/10/19-12; Sioux; plus 1/4; S; Daughter 926; ues[sic]; Yes; Id. U-9241 An. 980
940; Breast, Emma; F; 2/9/20-11; Sioux; plus 1/4; S; Daughter 927; Yes; Yes; Id. U-9449 An. 981
941; Breast, Dora; F; 1/7/23-9; Sioux; plus 1/4; S; Daughter 928; Yes; Yes; Id. U-13019 An. 982
942; Breast, John; M; 7/29/25-6; Sioux; plus 1/4; S; Son 929; Yes; Yes; Id. U-11704 An. none
943; Breast, Ollie L; F; 10/21/27-4; Sioux; plus 1/4; S; Daughter 930; Yes; Yes; Id. U-12420 An. none
944; Breast, Louise; F; 11/1/30-1; Sioux; plus 1/4; S; Daughter 931; Yes; Yes; Id. U-13729 An. none

945; Brewer, Robert; M; 1887-45; plus 1/4; M; Head 932; Yes; Yes; Al. 3964 An. 983
946; Brewer (Janis, Bessie), Bessie; F; 1890-42; plus 1/4; M; Wife 933; Yes; Yes; Al. 712 An. 984

947; Brewer, Philip; M; 1/2/11-21; plus 1/4; S; Son 934; Yes; Yes; Al. 7688 An. 985
948; Brewer, Paul; M; 8/7/14-17; plus 1/4; S; Son 935; Yes; Yes; Al. 7687 An. 987
949; Brewer, Benjamin; M; 2/11/16-16; plus 1/4; S; Son 936; Yes; Yes; Id. U-9242 An. 988
950; Brewer, Francis; M; 2/12/18-14; plus 1/4; S; Son 937; Yes; Yes; Id. U-9243 An. 989
951; Brewer, Margaret; F; 2/20/20-12; plus 1/4; S; Daughter 938; Yes; Yes; Id. U-9244 An. 990
952; Brewer, Vincent; M; 2/14/22-10; plus 1/4; S; Son 939; Yes; Yes; Id. U-10908 An. 991
953; Brewer, Katherine; F; 5/12/24-7; plus 1/4; S; Daughter 940; Yes; Yes; Id. U-11853 An. none
954; Brewer, Madeline; F; 3/1/28-4; plus 1/4; S; Daughter 941; Yes; Yes; Id. U-12543 An. none

Census of the __Pine Ridge__ reservation of the __Pine Ridge, South Dakota__ jurisdiction, as of __April 1__, 19**32**, taken by __James H. McGregor__, Superintendent.

Key: Number; Surname, Given; Sex; Date of Birth-Age at Last Birthday; Tribe (Oglala Sioux, unless stated otherwise); Degree of Blood; Marital Status; Relationship to Head of Family [Last Census Roll Number]; At Jurisdiction Where Enrolled (Yes/No); (If no – Where); Ward (Yes/No, if given); Allotment, Annuity and Identification Numbers (if given).

955; Brewer, William; M; 3/12/30-2; plus 1/4; S; Son 942; Yes; Yes; Id. U-13411 An. none

956; Brewer, Robert, Jr; M; 3/12/30-2; plus 1/4; S; Son 943; Yes; Yes; Id. U-13412 An. none

957; Brewer, Ernest W; M; 11/29/31-4/12; plus 1/4; S; Son ---; Yes; Yes; Id. U-13984 An. none

958; Brewer, William; M; 1880-52; plus 1/4; M; Head 944; Yes; No; Al. 837 An. 992

959; Brewer (Knight, Helen), Helen; F; 1880-44; plus 1/4; M; Wife 945; Yes; Yes; Al. 400 An. 993

960; Brewer, Arthur J; M; 1/15/09-23; plus 1/4; S; Son 946; Yes; Yes; Al. 7064 An. 994

961; Brewer, Louis W; M; 6/7/10-21; plus 1/4; S; Son 947; Yes; Yes; Al. 7067 An. 995

962; Brewer, Helen C; F; 9/13/11-20; plus 1/4; S; Daughter 948; Yes; Yes; Al. 7068 An. 996

963; Brewer, Frederick; M; 2/2/14-18; plus 1/4; Son 949; Yes; Yes; Id. U-9245 An. 997

964; Brewer, David C; M; 3/8/16-16; plus 1/4; S; Son 950; Yes; Yes; Id. U-9246 An. 998

965; Brewer, Clement; M; 11/10/17-14; plus 1/4; S; Son 951; Yes; Yes; Id. U-9247 An. 999

966; Brewer, Clara; F; 10/6/19-12; plus 1/4; S; Daughter 952; Yes; Yes; Id. U-9248 An. 1000

967; Brewer, Bertie W; F; 4/22/21-10; plus 1/4; S; Daughter 953; Yes; Yes; Id. U-9249 An. 1001

968; Brewer, Joseph C; M; 7/30/23-8; plus 1/4; S; Son 954; Yes; Yes; Id. U-14011 An. 1002

969; Brewer, Sylvia C; F; 5/15/26-5; plus 1/4; S; Daughter 955; Yes; Yes; Id. U-11935 An. none

970; Brewer, Fannie E; F; 2/14/29-3; plus 1/4; ; Daughter 956; Yes; Yes; Id. U-13132 An. none

971; Brewer, Leona I; F; 9/14/31-6/12; plus 1/4; S; Daughter ---; Yes; Yes; Id. U-13913 An. none

972; Brewer, Emilene G; F; 9/14/31-6/12; plus 1/4; S; Daughter ---; Yes; Yes; Id. U-13914 An. none

973; Bright Eyes; F; 1854-78; F; Wd; Head 957; Yes; Yes; Al. 4565 An. 4182

974; Brings Him Back, Henry; M; 1874-58; F; M; Head 958; Yes; Yes; Al. 3264 An. 1007

Census of the __Pine Ridge__ reservation of the __Pine Ridge, South Dakota__ jurisdiction, as of __April 1__, 19**32**, taken by __James H. McGregor__, Superintendent.

Key: Number; Surname, Given; Sex; Date of Birth-Age at Last Birthday; Tribe (Oglala Sioux, unless stated otherwise); Degree of Blood; Marital Status; Relationship to Head of Family [Last Census Roll Number]; At Jurisdiction Where Enrolled (Yes/No); (If no – Where); Ward (Yes/No, if given); Allotment, Annuity and Identification Numbers (if given).

975; Brings Him Back (Hollow Wood, Mollie), Mollie; F; 1877-55; F; M; Wife 959; Yes; Yes; Al. 3267 An. 1008

976; Brings Him Back, Ellis; M; 12/1/18-13; F; S; Son 960; Yes; Yes; Id. U-9251 An. 1010

977; Brings Him Back, Philip; M; 10/2/09-22; F; M; Head 961; Yes; Yes; Al. 6598 An. 1009

978; Brings Him Back (Yellow Bear, Ruth), Ruth; F; 8/22/11-20; F; M; Wife 962; Yes; Yes; Al. 7204 An. 7811

979; Brings Him Back, Rose Mary; F; 8/4/30-1; F; S; Daughter 963; Yes; Yes; Id. U-13591 An. none

980; Brings Plenty, Jacob; M; 11/27/11-20; F; S; Head 6317; Yes; Yes; Al. 6396 An. 6310

981; Brings Plenty, James; M; 1886-46; F; M; Head 964; Yes; Yes; Al. 7420 An. 1015

982; Brings Plenty (Big Wolf, Susie), Susie; F; 1892-40; F; M; Wife 965; Yes; Yes; Al. 2474 An. 1016

983; Brings Plenty, Philip J; M; 19-5-27; F; M; Head 964; Yes; Yes; Al. 3497 An. 1019

984; Brings Plenty (Smith, Sophia), Sophia; F; 6/1/11-20; F; M; Wife 968; Yes; Yes; Al. 7339 An. 3748

985; Brings Plenty, Leo Garfield; M; 4/17/28-3; plus 1/4; S; Son 969; Yes; Yes; Id. U-10020 An. none

986; Brings Plenty, Vincent Ansol; M; 8/13/30-1; plus 1/4; S; Son 970; Yes; Yes; Id. U-13564 An. none

987; Brings Them, David; M; 1891-41; F; M; Head 971; Yes; Yes; Al. 3508 An. 1020

N.E. ~~Brings Them (Bull or No Leaf, or Woodpecker), Nancy; F; Rosebud Sioux; F; M; Wife~~

988; Brings Yellow, James; M; 1899-33; GF; M: Head 973; Yes; Yes; Al. 3284 An. 1021

989; Brings Yellow (Little Bird, Lucy), Lucy; F; 1894-38; F; M; Wife 974; Yes; Yes; Al. 3260 An. 3878

990; Little Bird, Ambrose; M; 12/21/20-11; F; S; Stepson 975; Yes; Yes; Id. U-9889 An. 3873

991; Brings Yellow, John; M; 1901-31; F; M; Head 976; Yes; Yes; Al. 3285 An. 1022

Census of the **Pine Ridge** reservation of the **Pine Ridge, South Dakota** jurisdiction, as of **April 1**, 19**32**, taken by **James H. McGregor**, Superintendent.

Key: Number; Surname, Given; Sex; Date of Birth-Age at Last Birthday; Tribe (Oglala Sioux, unless stated otherwise); Degree of Blood; Marital Status; Relationship to Head of Family [Last Census Roll Number]; At Jurisdiction Where Enrolled (Yes/No); (If no – Where); Ward (Yes/No, if given); Allotment, Annuity and Identification Numbers (if given).

992; Brings Yellow (Afraid Of His Horses), Jennie; F; 1906-26; F; M; Wife 977; Yes; Yes; Al. 3282 An. 52
993; Brings Yellow, Theodore; M; 9/23/27-4; F; S; Son 978; Yes; Yes; Id. U-12421 An. none
994; Brings Yellow, John Chas; M; 7/31/30-1; F; S; Son 979; Yes; Yes; Id. U-13592 An. none

995; Broken Leg, Charles; M; 1895-37; F; Wd; Head 980; Yes; Yes; Al. 1864 An. 1023
996; Broken Leg, Moses; M; 2/23/23-9; F; S; Son 981; Yes; Yes; Id. U-13012 An. 1025
997; Broken Leg, Rebecca; F; 10/26/26-5; F; S; Daughter 982; Yes; Yes; Id. U-12203 An. none

998; Broken Legs, Matilda; F; 1855-77; F; S; Head 983; Yes; Yes; Al. 78 An. 1028

999; Broken Nose, Basil; M; 1893-39; F; M; Head 984; Yes; Yes; Al. 3168 An. 1029
1000; Broken Nose (Red Horse), Elizabeth; F; 1904-28; F; M; Wife 988; Yes; Yes; Al. 6353 An. 3105
1001; Broken Nose, Eleanor; F; 12/12/19-13; F; S; Daughter 985; Yes; Yes; Al[sic]. U-9253 An. 1031
1002; Broken Nose, All; M; 5/18/21-11; F; S; Son 986; Yes; Yes; Id. U-9254 An. 1032
1003; Broken Nose, Oly; M; 7/19/23-8; F; S; Son 987; Yes; Yes; Id. U-11104 An. 1033

1004; Broken Nose, Fox; F; 1871-61; F; Wd; Head 989; Yes; Yes; Al. 6529 An. 1034
1005; Broken Nose, Leon; M; 1906-26; F; M; Head 990; Yes; Yes; Al. 3169 An. 1036
1006; Broken Nose (Lays Bear), Emma; F; 8/25/11-20; F; M; Wife 991; Yes; Yes; Al. 7495 An. 7757
1007; Broken Nose, Bernard; M; 1/11/32-3/12; F; S; Son; Yes; Yes; U-14083

1008; Broken Rope, Creighton; M; 1882-50; F; M; Head 992; Yes; Yes; Al. 5031 An. 1038
1009; Broken Rope (Rough Feathers), Julia; F; 1890-42; F; M; Wife 993; Yes; Yes; Al. 311 An. 1039
1010; Tail, Mary; F; 3/19/23-9; F; S; Ward 994; Yes; Yes; Id. U-12099 An. 6781

1011; Broken Rope, Joseph; M; 1871-61; F; Wd; Head 995; Yes; Yes; Al. 3591 An. 1045

Census of the **Pine Ridge** reservation of the **Pine Ridge, South Dakota** jurisdiction, as of **April 1**, 1932, taken by **James H. McGregor**, Superintendent.

Key: Number; Surname, Given; Sex; Date of Birth-Age at Last Birthday; Tribe (Oglala Sioux, unless stated otherwise); Degree of Blood; Marital Status; Relationship to Head of Family [Last Census Roll Number]; At Jurisdiction Where Enrolled (Yes/No); (If no – Where); Ward (Yes/No, if given); Allotment, Annuity and Identification Numbers (if given).

1012; Broken Rope, Anna; F; 5/11/15-17; F; S; Daughter 996; Yes; Yes; Id. U-9256 An. 1047

1013; Broken Rope, Luke; M; 1906-26; F; M: Head 997; Yes; Yes; Al. 5387 An. 1048

1014; Broken Rope (Yellow Hawk), Nancy; F; 2/24/12-20; F; M; Wife 998; Yes; Yes; Al. 6974 An. 7891

1015; Broken Rope, Mildred; F; 2/29/28-4; F; S; Daughter 999; Yes; Yes; Id. U-12510 An. none

1016; Broken Rope, Florida; F; 3/25/29-3; F; S; Daughter 1000; Yes; Yes; Id. U-13104 An. none

1017; Broken Rope, Lucy; F; 10/16/30-1; F; S; Daughter 1001; Yes; Yes; Id. U-12593 An. none

1018; Broken Rope, Samuel; M; 1861-71; F; M; Head 1002; Yes; Yes; Al. 1461 An. 1049

~~N.E. Broken Rope (Dorian), Esther; F; Rosebud Sioux; 5/8; M; Wife~~

1019; Broken Rope, Godfrey; M; 7/29/08-23; plus 1/4; S; Son 1003; Yes; Yes; Al. 6977 An. 1050

1020; Broken Rope, Elsie R; F; 3/24/11-21; 1/4; S; Daughter 1004; Yes; Yes; Al. 6978 An. 1051

1021; Broken Rope, Carlisle; M; 11/4/16-15; 1/4; S; Son 1005; Yes; Yes; Id. U-9257 An. 1052

1022; Broken Rope, Freedom; F; 7/17/27-4; 1/4; S; Daughter 1006; Yes; Yes; Id. U-12360 An. none

1023; Broken Rope, Esther L; F; 1/22/31-1; 1/4; S; Daughter 1007; Yes; Yes; Id. U-13683 An. none

1024; Brooks, Fern; F; 1907-25; 1/4; M; Head 1008; No; Merriman, Cherry Co, Nebr; Yes; Al. 7159 An. 3824

1025; Brooks (Jumping Eagle), Alice; F; 1883-49; F; M: Wife 1010; Yes; Yes; Al. 509 An. 1057

1026; Brousseau (Carlow), Anna; F; 1894-38; 1/4; M; Head 1011; No; Rosebud, S.D; Yes; Al. 1072 Id. 1058

1027; Brousseau, Vivian; F; 4/18/13-18; -1/4; S; Daughter 1012; No; Rosebud, S.D; Yes; Al 8236 Al. 1059

1028; Brousseau, Lois; F; 2/23/15-17; -1/4; S; Daughter 1013; No; Rosebud, S.D; Yes; Yes Id. U-9259 An. 1060

Census of the __Pine Ridge__ reservation of the __Pine Ridge, South Dakota__ jurisdiction, as of __April 1__, 1932, taken by __James H. McGregor__, Superintendent.

Key: Number; Surname, Given; Sex; Date of Birth-Age at Last Birthday; Tribe (Oglala Sioux, unless stated otherwise); Degree of Blood; Marital Status; Relationship to Head of Family [Last Census Roll Number]; At Jurisdiction Where Enrolled (Yes/No); (If no – Where); Ward (Yes/No, if given); Allotment, Annuity and Identification Numbers (if given).

1029; Brown, Angeline; F; 1898-34; plus 1/4; S; Head 1014; Yes; Yes; Al. 1196 An. 1061

1030; Brown, Benjamin; M; 1884-48; F; M; Head 1015; Yes; No; Al. 4389 An. 1062
1031; Brown (No data), Anna; F; 1883-49; F; M; Wife 1016; Yes; Yes; Al. 3625 An. 1063
1032; Brown, Asay; M; 8/22/19-12; F; S; Son 1017; Yes; Yes; Id. U-9261 An. 1065

1033; Brown, Harriet; F; 7/21/27-4; F; S; Daughter 1018; Yes; Yes; Id. U-12361 An. none
1034; Brown, Louis H; M; 3/8/31-1; F; S; Son 1019; Yes; Yes; Id. U-13756 An. none
1035; Elbow Shield, Daniel; M; 10/16/22-9; F; S; Ward 1020; Yes; Yes; Id. U-12061 An. 2096

1036; Brown, Carl J; M; 1894-38; -1/4; M; Head 1021; Yes; Yes; Al. 4450 An. 1067
1037; Brown (Williams), Jennie; F; 3/16/97-35; plus 1/4; M; Wife 1022; Yes; Yes; Al. 4574 An. 7684
1038; Brown, Irma Irene; F; 8/21/24-7; -1/4; S; Daughter 1023; Yes; Yes; Id. 12610 An. none
1039; Brown, Wm Frederick; M; 9/24/26-5; -1/4; S; Son 1024; Yes; Yes; Id. U-12611 An. none
1040; Brown, Shirley Alice; F; 4/10/30-1; -1/4; S; Daughter 1025; Yes; Yes; Id. SU-13512 An. none
1041; Brown, Charlotte Mary; F; 4/10/30-1; -1/4; S; Daughter 1026; Yes; Yes; Id. U-13511 An. none

1042; Brown, Charles; M; 1902-30; plus 1/4; M; Head 1027; Yes; Yes; Al. 7768 An. 1068
1043; Brown, (Fast Wolf), Lena; F; 1902-30; 1/4; M; Wife 1028; Yes; Yes; Al. 1927 An. 1069
1044; Brown. Garfield; M; 1/26/24-8; 1/4; S; Son 1029; Yes; Yes; Id. U-11212 An. 1070
1045; Brown, Archie; M; 9/21/21-4; plus 1/4; S; Son 1030; Yes; Yes; Id. U-12441 An. none
1046; Brown, William J; M; 11/1/29-2; plus 1/4; S; Son 1031; Yes; Yes; Id. U-13307 An. none

1047; Brown, Charles; M; 1907-25; -1/4; M; Head 1032; Yes; Yes; Al. 4456 An. 1071

1048; Brown, David; M; 1879-53; F; M; Head 1033; Yes; No; Al. 4221 An. 1072

Census of the **Pine Ridge** reservation of the **Pine Ridge, South Dakota** jurisdiction, as of **April 1**, 19**32**, taken by **James H. McGregor**, Superintendent.

Key: Number; Surname, Given; Sex; Date of Birth-Age at Last Birthday; Tribe (Oglala Sioux, unless stated otherwise); Degree of Blood; Marital Status; Relationship to Head of Family [Last Census Roll Number]; At Jurisdiction Where Enrolled (Yes/No); (If no – Where); Ward (Yes/No, if given); Allotment, Annuity and Identification Numbers (if given).

1049; Brown (Goes In Center), Alice; F; 1977-55; F; M; Wife 1034; Yes; Yes; Al. 4222 An. 1073
1050; Brown, William; M; 1/19/11-21; F; S; Son 1035; Yes; Yes; Al. 6537 An. 1074
1051; Brown, Jacob; M; 3/1/17-15; F; S; Son 1036; Yes; Yes; Id. U-9262 An. 1075
1052; Brown, Garfield; M; 11/4/19-12; F; S; Son 1037; Yes; Yes; Id. U-9263 An. 1076

1053; Brown, George; M; 1894-38; plus 1/4; M; Head 1038; No; Rapid City, Pennington Co, S.D; Yes; Al. 4018 An. 1081
N.E. Brown (Cornelius), Lottie; F; Oneida; 1/2; M; Wife
1054; Brown, Genevieve; F; 3/29/15-17; -1/4; S; Daughter 1039; No; Rapid City, Pennington Co, S.D; Yes; All. 8117 An. 1083
1055; Brown, Irene; F; 4/4/17-14; -1/4; S; Daughter 1040; No; Rapid City, Pennington Co, S.D; Yes; Id. U-9266 An. 1084
1056; Brown, George R; M; 7/12/28-3; -1/4; S; Son 1041; No; Rapid City, Pennington Co, S.D; Yes; Id. U-12824 An. none
1057; Brown, Joyce A; F; 4/16/31-11/12; -1/4; S; Daughter 1042; No; Rapid City, Pennington Co, S.D; Yes; U-13798

1058; Brown, Gloretta; F; 1908-24; -1/4; S; Head 1042; No; Rapid City, Pennington Co, S.D; Yes; Al. 4025 An. 1106
1059; Brown, Dolores V; F; 5/24/31-10/12; -1/4; S; Daughter; No; Rapid City, Pennington Co, S.D; Yes; Yes; U-13959

1060; Brown, Harry; M; 1891-41; -1/4; M; Head 1043; Yes; Yes; Al. 1872 An. 1085
N.E. Brown (Larabee), Nellie; F; Rosebud Sioux; M; Wife
1061; Brown, Cleveland; M; 2/15/20-12; -1/4; S; Son 1044; Yes; Yes; Id. U-9268 An. 1089
1062; Brown, Ollie Norma; F; 3/30/25-7; 1/4[sic]; S; Daughter 1045; Yes; Yes;Id. U-11562 An. none

1063; Brown, James; M; 1891-41; -1/4; M; Head 1046; Yes; Yes; Al. 4448 An. 1090
1064; Brown, Paul Peter; M; 10/1/21-10; -1/4; S; Son 1047; Yes; Yes; Yes; Id. U-10832 An. 1091

1065; Brown, John; M; 1904-28; F; M; Head 1048; Yes; Yes; Al. 5638 An. 1093
N.E. Brown (La Plant), Delia; F; Cheyenne Sioux; 1/4; M; Wife
1066; Brown, Elsworth; M; 4/18/28-2; plus 1/4; S; Son 1049; Yes; Yes; Id. U-12668 An. none

1067; Brown, Joseph; M; 1869-63; 1/4; M; Head 1050; No; Chadron, Dawes Co, Nebr; No; Al. 4446 An. 1094

Census of the __Pine Ridge__ reservation of the __Pine Ridge, South Dakota__ jurisdiction, as of __April 1__, 19**32**, taken by __James H. McGregor__, Superintendent.

Key: Number; Surname, Given; Sex; Date of Birth-Age at Last Birthday; Tribe (Oglala Sioux, unless stated otherwise); Degree of Blood; Marital Status; Relationship to Head of Family [Last Census Roll Number]; At Jurisdiction Where Enrolled (Yes/No); (If no – Where); Ward (Yes/No, if given); Allotment, Annuity and Identification Numbers (if given).

1068; Brown (no data), Alice; F; 1870-62; -1/4; M; Wife 1051; No; Chadron, Dawes Co, Nebr; Yes; Al. 4447 An. 1095

1069; Brown, Weston; M; 3/18/11-21; -1/4; M; Head 1052; No; Chadron, Dawes Co, Nebr; Yes; Al. 5693 An. 1097

1070; Brown, Imogene; F; 1/12/32-2/12; -1/4; S; Daughter; No; Chadron, Dawes Co, Nebr; [blank]; U-14059

1071; Brown, Jessie; F; 3/27/13-19; -1/4; S; Head 1053; No; Chadron, Dawes Co, Nebr; Al. 7212 An. 1098

1072; Brown, Theodore; M; 1907-25; -1/4; S; Head 1054; No; Chadron, Dawes Co, Nebr; Yes; Al. 4457 An. 1107

1073; Brown, Thomas; M; 7/24/10-21; plus 1/4; S; Head 1055; Yes; Yes; Al. 7089 An. 1107

1074; Brown, Joseph R; M; 1897-35; 1/4; M; Head 1056; Yes; Yes; Al. 4019 An. 1099

1075; Brown (Trimble), Eloise; F; 1899-33; 1/4; M; Wife 1057; Yes; Yes; Al. 3794 An. 1100

1076; Brown, Lodine; F; 7/30/18-13; 1/4; S; Daughter 1058; Yes; Yes; Id. U-9268 An. 1101

1077; Brown, Florence; F; 6/5/20-11; 1/4; S; Daughter 1059; Yes; Yes; Id. U-9269 An. 1102

1078; Brown, Joseph L; M; 7/3/26-5; 1/4; S; Son 1060; Yes; Yes; Id. U-12239 An. none

1079; Brown, Doris J; F; 12/17/29-2; 1/4; S; Daughter 1061; Yes; Yes; Id. U-13365 An. none

1080; Brown, Louis; M; 1896-36; -1/4; M; Head 1062; Yes; Yes; Al. 4451 An. 1103

1081; Brown, Reuben; M; 1906-26; F; M; Head 1063; Yes; Yes; Al. 4224 An. 1104

~~N.E. Brown (Zimiga), Ellen; F; Cherokee; M; Wife~~

1082; Brown, William; M; 1869-63; plus 1/4; M; Head 1064; Yes; Yes; Al. 1896 An. 1109

~~N.E. Brown (Dubray Nellie), Lizzie; F; 1871-61; Rosebud Sioux; 1/4; M; Wife 1065; Yes;~~ Yes; Al. 1870 An. 1110

1083; Brown, Lema Jessie; F; 2/8/20-12; 1/4; S; Gr. daughter 1066; Yes; Yes; Id. U-9270 An. 295

1084; Mesteth, Vincent; M; 5/14/14-17; 1/4; S; Ward 1067; Yes; Yes; Id. U-10009 An. 4467

Census of the **Pine Ridge** reservation of the **Pine Ridge, South Dakota** jurisdiction, as of **April 1**, 19**32**, taken by **James H. McGregor**, Superintendent.

Key: Number; Surname, Given; Sex; Date of Birth-Age at Last Birthday; Tribe (Oglala Sioux, unless stated otherwise); Degree of Blood; Marital Status; Relationship to Head of Family [Last Census Roll Number]; At Jurisdiction Where Enrolled (Yes/No); (If no – Where); Ward (Yes/No, if given); Allotment, Annuity and Identification Numbers (if given).

1085; Mesteth, Lucille; F; 8/26/19-12; 1/4; S; Ward 1068; Yes; Yes; Id. U-10011 An. 4469

1086; Mesteth, Myrtle; F; 11/30/21-10; 1/4; S; Ward 1069; Yes; Yes; Id. U-19849 An. 4470

1087; Brown Bull, Thompson; M; 1867-65; F; M; Head 1070; Yes; Yes; Al. 1501 An. 1111

1088; Brown Bull (Morrison), Lena; F; 1891-41; plus 1/4; M; Wife 1071; Yes; Yes; Al. 5844 An. 1112

1089; Brown Bull, Sarah; F; 5/7/11-20; 1/4; S; Daughter 1072; Yes; Yes; Al. 7807 An. 1113

1090; Brown Bull, Oliver; M; 1/5/14-18; 1/4; S; Son 1073; Yes; Yes; Al. 7808 An. 1114

1091; Brown Bull, Jerome; M; 6/4/18-13; 1/4; S; Son 1074; Yes; Yes; Id. U-9271 An. 1115

1092; Brown Cloud (Red Eagle); F; 1854-78; F; Wd; Head 1076; Yes; Yes; Al. 5403 An. 1117

1093; Brown Ear Horse, George; M; 1873-59; F; M; Head 1077; Yes; Yes; Al. 6196 An. 1119

1094; Brown Ear Horse, Agnes; F; 7/19/17-14; F; S; Daughter 1078; Yes; Yes; Id. U-9272 An. 1123

1095; Brown Eyes; M; 1856-76; F; Wd; Head 1081; Yes; Yes; Al. 1657 An. 1184

1096; Brown Eyes, George; M; 1891-41; plus 1/4; M; Head 1082; Yes; Yes; Al. 574 An. 1126

1097; Brown Eyes (Yellow Boy), Lucy; F; 1896-36; 1/4; M; Wife 1083; Yes; Yes; Al. 3950 An. 1127

1098; Brown Eyes, Bernice; F; 7/20/25-6; plus 1/4; S; Niece 7119; Yes; Yes; Id. U-11680 An. none

1099; Brown Eyes, Louis; M; 1889-43; 1/4; M; Head 1084; Yes; Yes; Al. 660 An. 1130

1100; Brown Eyes (Red Wolf), Jennie; F; 1898-34; F; M; Wife 1085; Yes; Yes; Al. 1311 An. 1131

1101; Brown Eyes, Lanert; M; 11/30/19-12; plus 1/4; S; Son 1086; Yes; Yes; Id. U-9274 An. 1132

1102; Brown Eyes. Anna; F; 6/22/21-10; plus 1/4; S; Daughter 1087; Yes; Yes; Id. U-12089 An. 1133

Census of the __**Pine Ridge**__ reservation of the __**Pine Ridge, South Dakota**__ jurisdiction, as of __**April 1**__, 19**32**, taken by __**James H. McGregor**__, Superintendent.

Key: Number; Surname, Given; Sex; Date of Birth-Age at Last Birthday; Tribe (Oglala Sioux, unless stated otherwise); Degree of Blood; Marital Status; Relationship to Head of Family [Last Census Roll Number]; At Jurisdiction Where Enrolled (Yes/No); (If no – Where); Ward (Yes/No, if given); Allotment, Annuity and Identification Numbers (if given).

1103; Brown Eyes, Wanza; F; 11/23/24-7; 1/4; S; Daughter 1088; Yes; Yes; Id. U-11383 An. 1134

1104; Brown Eyes, Floyd; M; 5/24/29-2; 1/4; S; Son 1089; Yes; Yes; Id. U-13184 An. none

1105; Brown Eyes, Virginia M; F; 11/16/31-4/12; 1/4; S; Daughter; Yes; Yes; U-13960

1106; Brown Eyes, Philip; M; 1898-34; plus 1/4; S; Head 1090; Yes; Yes; Al. 5522

1107; Brown Eyes, Thomas; M; 1889-43; plus 1/4; M; Head 1091; Yes; Yes; Al. 6065 An. 1136

1108; Brown Eyes (no data), Lizzie; F; 1906-36; 1/4; F[sic]; Wife 1092; Yes; Yes; Al. 7145 An. 6764

1109; Brown Eyes, Norman; M; 6/18/17-14; 1/4; S; Son 1093; Yes; Yes; Id. U-9276 An. 1139

1110; Brown Eyes, Elizabeth; F; 6/29/22-9; 1/4; S; Daughter 1094; Yes; Yes; Id. U-11-73 An. 1140

1111; Brown Eyes, Joseph; M; 8/31/28-3; 1/4; S; Son 1095; Yes; Yes; Id. U-12796 An. none

1112; Brown Eyes, Bernard; M; 3/15/30-2; 1/4; S; Son 1096; Yes; Yes; Id. U-13413 An. none

1113; Brown Thunder, John; M; 1887-45; F; M; Head 1097; Yes; Yes; Al. 6864 An. 1142

1114; Brown Thunder (Poor Bear), Julia; F; 1887-45; F; M; Wife 1098; Yes; Yes; Al. 620 An. 5040

1115; Brown Thunder, Cecelia; F; 1/9/12-10; plus 1/4; S; Daughter 1099; Yes; Yes; Al. 6957 An. 1144

1116; Brown Thunder, Lucy; F; 6/17/13-8; 1/4; S; Daughter 1100; Yes; Yes; Al. 6956 An. 1145

1117; Brown Thunder, Delia; F; 5/10/15-16; plus 1/4; S; Daughter 1101; Yes; Yes; Al. 8100 An. 1146

1118; Brown Thunder, Leroy; M; 9/25/19-12; 1/4; S; Son 1102; Yes; Yes; Id. U-9278 An. 1147

1119; Brown Thunder, Dorine; F; 7/4/24-7; 1/4; S; Daughter 1103; Yes; Yes; Id. U-11498 An. 1148

1120; Bruce, Louis R; M; 1906-26; 1/4; S; Head 1104; No; Evans Mills, Jefferson Co, N.Y; Yes; Al. 4063 An. 1151

1121; Bruce (Rooks), Noresta; F; 1878-54; plus 1/4; M; Head 1105; No; Evans Mills, Jefferson Co, N.Y; Yes; Al. 4056, An. 1152

Census of the __**Pine Ridge**__ reservation of the __**Pine Ridge, South Dakota**__ jurisdiction, as of __**April 1**__, 19**32**, taken by __**James H. McGregor**__, Superintendent.

Key: Number; Surname, Given; Sex; Date of Birth-Age at Last Birthday; Tribe (Oglala Sioux, unless stated otherwise); Degree of Blood; Marital Status; Relationship to Head of Family [Last Census Roll Number]; At Jurisdiction Where Enrolled (Yes/No); (If no – Where); Ward (Yes/No, if given); Allotment, Annuity and Identification Numbers (if given).

1122; Bruce, Noresta; F; 1907-25; 1/4; S; Head 1106; No; Evans Mills, Jefferson Co, N.Y; Yes; Al. 4064 An. 1153

1123; Buckingham (Stirk), Mildred; F; 9/1/12-19; -1/4; M; Head 6674; Yes; [blank]; Al. 7452 An. 6644

1124; Buckingham, Wm. Darrell; M; 9/29/30-1; 1/8; S; Son; Yes; [blank]; U-13848

1125; Buckman, Benjamin; M; 1905-27; 1/4; M; Head 1107; Yes; Yes; Id. U-9279 An. 1154

1126; Buckman (Two Two), Lottie; F; 1901-31; 1/4; M; Wife 1108; Yes; Yes; Al. 267 An. 1155

1127; Buckman, Edith; F; 11/22/25-7; 1/4; S; Daughter 1109; Yes; Yes; Id. U-11457 An. 1156

1128; Buckman, Verna; F; 8/21/26-5; 1/4; S; Daughter 1110; Yes; Yes; Id. U-12544 An. none

1129; Buckman, Wilbert; M; 8/25/28-3; 1/4; S; Son 1111; Yes; Yes; Id. U-12772 An. none

1130; Buckman, James; M; 1867-65; 1/4; M; Head 1112; No; Rosebud, S.D; Yes; Al. 257 An. 1157

1131; Buckman, John; M; 1887-45; 1/4; M; Head 1113; No; Rosebud, S.D; Yes; Id. U-9280 An. 1159

1132; Buckman, George; M; 1892-40; plus 1/4; S; Head 1114; Yes; Yes; Al. 259 An. 1160

1133; Buckman, William; M; 1903-29; 1/4; S; Head 1115; Yes; Yes; Al. 8220 An. 1161

1134; Bull, ---; M; 1862-70; F; S; Head 1116; Yes; Yes; Al. 2381 An. 1163

1135; Bullard, Elizabeth; F; 1905-27; plus 1/4; S; Head 1117; Yes; Yes; Al. 2597 An. 1164

1136; Bullard, Elmus; M; 1883-49; 1/4; Head 1118; No; Hot Springs, Fall River Co, S.D; Yes; Al. 4441 An. 1165

1137; Bullard (Gresh), Susie; F; 1890-42; 1/4; M; Wife 1119; No; Hot Springs, Fall River Co, S.D; Yes; Al. 5502 An. 1146

1138; Bullard, Scott; M; 4/5/10-21; 1/4; S; Son 1120; No; Hot Springs, Fall River Co, S.D; Yes; Al. 5503 An. 1167

1139; Bullard, Bernice; F; 3/31/12-10[sic]; 1/4; S; Daughter 1121; No; Hot Springs, Fall River Co, S.D; Yes; Al. 7002 An. 1168

Census of the **Pine Ridge** reservation of the **Pine Ridge, South Dakota** jurisdiction, as of **April 1**, 1932, taken by **James H. McGregor**, Superintendent.

Key: Number; Surname, Given; Sex; Date of Birth-Age at Last Birthday; Tribe (Oglala Sioux, unless stated otherwise); Degree of Blood; Marital Status; Relationship to Head of Family [Last Census Roll Number]; At Jurisdiction Where Enrolled (Yes/No); (If no – Where); Ward (Yes/No, if given); Allotment, Annuity and Identification Numbers (if given).

1140; Bullard, Todd A; M; 4/5/14-17; 1/4; S; Son 1122; No; Hot Springs, Fall River Co, S.D; Yes; Id. U-9281 An. 1169
1141; Bullard, Mary; F; 5/2/28-13; 1/4; S; Daughter 1123; No; Hot Springs, Fall River Co, S.D; Yes; Id. U-9282 An. 1170

1142; Bullard, Frank; M; 1904-28; 1/4; M; Head 1124; Yes; Yes; Al. 2596 An. 1171
1143; Bullard, Francis W; M; 12/27/26-5; 1/4; S; Son 1125; Yes; Yes; Id. U-13133
1144; Bullard, Virginia; F; 1/28/28-4; plus 1/4; S; Daughter 1126; Yes; Yes; Id. U-13134 An. none
1145; Bullard (Gresh), Lizzie; F; 1888-44; plus 1/4; Wd; Head 1127; Yes; Yes; Al. 4724 An. 1173
1146; Bullard, Helena; F; 3/22/12-20; 1/4; S; Daughter 1128; Yes; Yes; Al. 7003 An. 1175
1147; Bullard, Martha; F; 11/26/13-18; 1/4; S; Daughter 1129; Yes; Yes; Id. 9283 An. 1176

1148; Bullard, Mary V; F; 10/31/10-21; 1/4; S; Head 1130; Yes; Yes; Al. 5495 An. 1174

1149; Bullard, Walter; M; 1881-51; 1/4; M; Head 1131; Yes; Yes; Al. 2594 An. 1178
1150; Bullard (Gresh), Nellie; F; 1885-47; 1/4; M; Wife 1132; Yes; Yes; Al. 2595 An. 1179

1151; Bullard, Messana; M; 1907-25; 1/4; S; Head 1133; Yes; Yes; Al. 2598 An. 1180

1152; Bull Bear, Amos; M; 6/23/13-18; F; S; Head 1134; Yes; Yes; Al. 7201 An. 7411

1153; Bull Bear, Henry; M; 1881-51; F; M; Head; Yes; No; Al. 1700 An. 1181
1154; Bull Bear (Feather), Mary; F; 1883-49; F; M; Wife 1136; Yes; Yes; Al. 1535
1155; Long Soldier, Levi; M; 3/23/14-8; F; S; S. Son 1137; Yes; Yes; Id. U-9945 An. 4225
1156; Long Soldier, Emily; F; 10-16/18-13; F; S; S. Daughter 1138; Yes; Yes; Id. U-9946 An. 4226
1157; Long Soldier, Lucy; F; 11/27/21-10; F; S; S. Daughter 1139; Yes; Yes; Id. U-10864 An. 4227

1158; Bull Bear, Henry; 9/10/96-35; F; M; Head 1141; Yes; Yes; Al. 1700 An. 1187
1159; Bull Bear (Not Help Him), Sallie; F; 2/4/09-33; F; M; Wife 1142; Yes; Yes; Al. 5669 An. 5290

Census of the __Pine Ridge__ reservation of the __Pine Ridge, South Dakota__ jurisdiction, as of __April 1__, 19**32**, taken by __James H. McGregor__, Superintendent.

Key: Number; Surname, Given; Sex; Date of Birth-Age at Last Birthday; Tribe (Oglala Sioux, unless stated otherwise); Degree of Blood; Marital Status; Relationship to Head of Family [Last Census Roll Number]; At Jurisdiction Where Enrolled (Yes/No); (If no – Where); Ward (Yes/No, if given); Allotment, Annuity and Identification Numbers (if given).

1160; Not Help Him, Seth; M; 11/5/25-6; F; S; S. Son 1143; Yes; Yes; Id. U-11741 An. none

1161; Bull Bear, Jacob; M; 1903-29; F; M; Head 1144; Yes; Yes; Al. 1702 An. 1188
1162; Bull Bear, Elsie M; F; 9/2/30-1; plus 1/4; S; Daughter 1145; Yes; Yes; Id. U-1359 An. none

1163; Bull Bear, Lawrence; M; 1865-67; F; M; Head 1146; Yes; Yes; Al. 1695 An. 1189
1164; Bull Bear (no data), Julia; F; 1863-69; F; M; Wife 1147; Yes; Yes; Al. 5886 An. 1190

1165; Bull Bear, Paul; M; 1891-41; F; M; Head 1148; Yes; Yes; Al. 1550 An. 1198
1166; Bull Bear (Morrison), Rosa; F; 1902-30; plus 1/4; M; Wife 1149; Yes; Yes; Al. 4254 An. 1199
1167; Bull Bear, Paulina; F; 8/13/22-9; 1/4; S; Daughter 1150; Yes; [blank]; Id. U-14045
1168; Bull Bear, Jerry; M; 12/19/23-8; plus 1/4; S; Son 1151; Yes; Yes; Id. U-11161 An. 1201
1169; Bull Bear, Mary; F; 5/19/24-7; 1/4; S; Daughter 1152; Yes; Yes; Id. U-12200 An. none
1170; Bull Bear, Nora; F; 12/2/26-5; 1/4; S; Daughter 1153; Yes; Yes; Id. U-12201 An. none
1171; Bull Bear, Theodore; M; 9/16/28-3; 1/4; S; Son 1154; Yes; Yes; Id. U-12805 An. none
1172; Bull Bear, Barbara; F; 10/22/31-5/12; 1/4; S; Daughter; Yes; Yes; U-13985

1173; Bull Bear, Peter; M; 1886-46; F; M; Head 1155; Yes; Yes; Al. 1697 An. 1202
1174; Bull Bear (no data), Edith; F; 1888-44; F; M; Wife 1156; Yes; Yes; Al. 1704 An. 1203
1175; Bull Bear, Royal; M; 12/3/11-20; F; M[sic]; Son 1157; Yes; Yes; Al. 7800 An. 1205
1176; Bull Bear, Lizzie; F; 10/3/17-14; F; M[sic]; Daughter 1158; Yes; Yes; Id. U-9290 An. 1206
1177; Bull Bear, Stephen; M; 4/7/22-9; F; M[sic]; Son 1159; Yes; Yes; Id. U-10947 An. 1207
1178; Bull Bear, Vernie; M; 3/26/28-4; F; M[sic]; Son 1160; Yes; Yes; Id. U-10774 An. none

1179; Bull Bear, Robert; M; 1899-38; F; S; Head 1161; Yes; Yes; Al. 1552 An. 1208

1180; Bull Head, Louis; M; 1877-55; F; S; Wd 1162; Yes; Yes; Al. 1318 An. 1209

Census of the __Pine Ridge__ reservation of the __Pine Ridge, South Dakota__ jurisdiction, as of __April 1__, 1932, taken by __James H. McGregor__, Superintendent.

Key: Number; Surname, Given; Sex; Date of Birth-Age at Last Birthday; Tribe (Oglala Sioux, unless stated otherwise); Degree of Blood; Marital Status; Relationship to Head of Family [Last Census Roll Number]; At Jurisdiction Where Enrolled (Yes/No); (If no – Where); Ward (Yes/No, if given); Allotment, Annuity and Identification Numbers (if given).

1181; Bull Man, Daniel; M; 1878-54; F M; Head 1163; Yes; Yes; Al. 1722 An. 1210
1182; Bull Man (no data), Sallie; F; 1881-51; F; M; Wife 1164; Yes; Yes; Al. 3674 An. 1211
1183; Bull Man, Frank; M; 9/26/12-19; F; S; Son 1165; Yes; Yes; Al. 7231 An. 1212
1184; Bull Man, Ida; F; 1/13/15-17; F; S; Daughter 1166; Yes; Yes; Al. 8199 An. 1213
1185; Bull Man, Moses; M; 6/10/17-14; F; S; Son 1167; Yes; Yes; Id. U-9292 An. 1214
1186; Bull Man, Mabel; F; 5/14/20-11; F; S; Daughter 1168; Yes; Yes; Id. U-9293 An. 1215
1187; Bull Man, Paul; M; 8/3/27-4; F; S; Son 1169; Yes; Yes; Id. U-12363 An. none

1188; Bull Man, Joseph; M; 1900-32; F; M; Head 1170; Yes; Yes; Al. 1724 An. 1216
1189; Bull Man (Chips), Emma; F; 1903-29; F; M; Wife 1171; Yes; Yes; Al. 5572 An. 1217
1190; Bull Man, Silver; M; 5/14/30-1; F; M[sic]; Son 1172; Yes; Yes; Id. U-13468 An. none

1191; Bull Man, Thomas; M; 1904-28; F; M; Head 1173; Yes; Yes; Al. 1724 An. 1219
1192; Bull Man (Black Crow), Millie; F; 1875-57; F; M; Wife 1174; Yes; Yes; Al. 4980 An. 1220
1193; Little Dog, Jessie; F; 3/14/14-18; F; M[sic]; S. Daughter 1175; Yes; Yes; Al. 7709 An. 1221
1194; Little Dog, Frank; M; 2/13/16-16; F; M; S. Son 1176; Yes; Yes; Al. 8082 An. 1222

1195; Bullock, William; M; 1864-68; 1/4; S; Head 1177; Yes; Yes; Al. 8272 An. 1222

1196; Bull-tail, James; m, 1864-68; F; M; Head 1178; Yes; Yes; Al. 589 An. 1223
1197; Bull-tail (Jealous Of Him), Alice; F; 1904-28; F; M; Wife 1179; Yes; Yes; Al. 498 An. 1225
1198; Jealous Of Him, Woodrwo[sic]; M; 4/16/22-9; F; S; S. Son 1180; Yes; Yes; Id. U-10944 An. 1226

1199; Bull Tail (Locke), Annie; F; 1907-25; F; M; Head 4148; Yes; Yes; 3953 1121

1200; Burns Prairie, Edward; M; 1894-38; F; M; Head 1181; Yes; Yes; Al. 5793 An. 1227
1201; Burns Prairie (Kills Above), Maggie; F; 1897-35; F; M; Wife 1182; Yes; Yes; Al. 1248 An. 1228

Census of the __Pine Ridge__ reservation of the __Pine Ridge, South Dakota__ jurisdiction, as of __April 1__, 1932, taken by __James H. McGregor__, Superintendent.

Key: Number; Surname, Given; Sex; Date of Birth-Age at Last Birthday; Tribe (Oglala Sioux, unless stated otherwise); Degree of Blood; Marital Status; Relationship to Head of Family [Last Census Roll Number]; At Jurisdiction Where Enrolled (Yes/No); (If no – Where); Ward (Yes/No, if given); Allotment, Annuity and Identification Numbers (if given).

1202; Burns Prairie, Edward, Jr; M; 12/3/15-15; F; S; Son 1183; Yes; Yes; Id. U-9298 An. 1229

1203; Burns Prairie, Catherine; F; 11/11/19-12; F; S; Daughter 1184; Yes; Yes; Id. U-9299 An. 1230

1204; Burns Prairie, Lizzie; F; 5/31/22-9; F; S; Daughter 1185; Yes; Yes; Id. U-11004 An. 1231

1205; Burns Prairie, Freda; F; 8/6/28-3; F; S; Daughter 1186; Yes; Yes; Id. U-12885 An. none

1206; Burns Prairie, Timothy[sic]; M; 1904-28; F; S; Son[sic] 1187; Yes; Yes; Id. U-93-- An. 1235

1207; Bush, Charles; M; 1900-32; plus 1/4; M; Head 1188; Yes; Yes; Al. 776 An. 1240

1208; Bush (Lone War), Lizzie; F; 8/ /04-27; F; M; Wife 1189; Yes; Yes; Id. U-9684 An. 1237

1209; Bush, Mary; F; 6/19/24-7; plus 1/4; S; Daughter 1190; Yes; Yes; Id. U-11521 An. 1238

1210; Bush, Clara; F; 11/28/31-4/12; 1/4; S; Daughter; Yes; Yes; U-12986

1211; Bush, Frank; M; 9/93-39; 1/4; S; Head 1193; Yes; Yes; Al. 733 An. 1240

1212; Bush, James; M; 1878-54; F; M; Head 1194; Yes; Yes; Al. 1706 An. 1241

1213; Bush (no data), Rosa; F; 1971-61; plus 1/4; M; Wife 1195; Yes; Yes; Al. 3689 An. 1242

1214; Blue Bird, Earl; M; 4/29/18-13; 1/4; S; Ward 1196; Yes; Yes; Id. U-9205 An. 7772

1215; Bush, William; M; 3/1895-37; 1/4; M; Head 1197; Yes; Yes; Al. 734 An. 1246

1216; Bush (Yankton), Grace; F; 1900-32; 1/4; M; Wife 1198; Yes; Yes; Al. 127 An. 1247

1217; Bush, Emelia; F; 2/19/21-11; 1/4; S; Daughter 1199; Yes; Yes; Id. U-9302 An. 1248

1218; Bush, Ella Agnes; F; 7/21/23-8; 1/4; S; Daughter 1200; Yes; Yes; Id. U-14041 An. 1249

1219; Bush, Maggie; F; 3/29/25-7; 1/4; S; Daughter 1201; Yes; Yes; Id. U-11508 An. 1250

1220; Bush, Vincent; M; 6/14/27-4; 1/4; S; Son 1202; Yes; Yes; Id. U-12344 An. none

1221; Bush, Percy; M; 4/19/30-1; 1/4; S; Son 1203; Yes; Yes; Id. U-13469 An. none

1222; Bush (Cuny), Laura Pearl; F; 8/31/11-20; plus 1/4; M; Head 1204; Yes; Yes; Al. 7454 An. 1799

Census of the **Pine Ridge** reservation of the **Pine Ridge, South Dakota** jurisdiction, as of **April 1**, 19**32**, taken by **James H. McGregor**, Superintendent.

Key: Number; Surname, Given; Sex; Date of Birth-Age at Last Birthday; Tribe (Oglala Sioux, unless stated otherwise); Degree of Blood; Marital Status; Relationship to Head of Family [Last Census Roll Number]; At Jurisdiction Where Enrolled (Yes/No); (If no – Where); Ward (Yes/No, if given); Allotment, Annuity and Identification Numbers (if given).

1223; Bush, Lois Jean; F; 11/17/30-1; -1/4; S; Daughter 1205; Yes; Yes; Id. U-13684 An. none

1224; Bushy Top Pine; M; 1868-64; F; Wd; Head 1206; Yes; Yes; Al. 92 An. 1251

1225; Bushy Top Pine, George; M; 1899-33; F; M; Head 1207; Yes; Yes; Al. 93 An. 1253

1226; Bushy Top Pine (Make Shine), Louisa; F; 1904-28; F; M; Wife 1208; Yes; Yes; Al. 4993 An. 1254

1227; Bushy Top Pine, Isaac; M; 5/29/25-6; F; M[sic]; Son 1209; Yes; Yes; Id. U-11837 An. none

1228; Bushy Top Pine, Louis; M; 6/27/29-2; F; M[sic]; Son 1210; Yes; Yes; Id. U-13319 An. none

1229; Bushy Top Pine, Abraham; M; 1/27/31-4/12; F; M[sic]; Son; Yes; Yes; U-13961

1230; Butcher (Amiotte), Nora; F; 1886-46; plus 1/4; M; Head 1211; No; Gillette, Campbell Co, Wyo; No; Al. 2308 An. 1255

1231; Butcher, Audrey; F; 5/27/13-18; -1/4; S; Daughter 1212; No; Gillette, Campbell Co, Wyo; Yes; Al. 7172 An. 1257

1232; Butcher, Delma; F; 12/31/10-21; -1/4; S; Head 1213; No; Gillette, Campbell Co, Wyo; Yes; Al. 5465 An. 1256

1233; Campbell, Earl; M; 1906-26; plus 1/4; S; Head 1214; No; Alliance, Box Butte Co, Nebr; Yes; Al 3229 An. 1260

1234; Cane Woman (no data); F; 1868-64; F; S; Head 1215; No; Lame Deer, Mont; Yes; Yes; Al. 5803 An. 1262

1235; Carlow, Abraham; M; 5/13/98-34; plus 1/4; M; Head 1216; No; Chadron, Dawes Co, Nebr; Yes; Al. 1074 An. 1264

1236; Carlow, Byrd S; M; 5/26/26-5; -1/4; S; Son 1217; No; Chadron, Dawes Co, Nebr; Yes; Id. U-1346 An. none

1237; Carlow, David; M; 1900-32; plus 1/4; M; Head 1218; No; Hemingford, Box Butte Co, Nebr; Yes; Al. 1076 An. 1265

1238; Carlow (Provost), Hazel; F; 1901-31; 1/4; M; Wife 1219; No; Hemingford, Box Butte Co, Nebr; Yes; Al. 2240 An. 1266

1239; Carlow, Clementine; F; 8/22/21-10; 1/4; S; Daughter 1220; No; Hemingford, Box Butte Co, Nebr; Yes; Id. U-9304 An. 1267

1240; Carlow, Marie E; F; 2/10/24-8; 1/4; S; Daughter 1221; No; Hemingford, Box Butte Co, Nebr; Yes; Id. U-11595 An. 1268

Census of the **Pine Ridge** reservation of the **Pine Ridge, South Dakota** jurisdiction, as of **April 1**, 19**32**, taken by **James H. McGregor**, Superintendent.

Key: Number; Surname, Given; Sex; Date of Birth-Age at Last Birthday; Tribe (Oglala Sioux, unless stated otherwise); Degree of Blood; Marital Status; Relationship to Head of Family [Last Census Roll Number]; At Jurisdiction Where Enrolled (Yes/No); (If no – Where); Ward (Yes/No, if given); Allotment, Annuity and Identification Numbers (if given).

1241; Carlow, David; M; 3/1/26-6; 1/4; S; Son 1222; No; Hemingford, Box Butte Co, Nebr; Yes; Id. U-11938 An. none

1242; Carlow, Margaret; F; 3/12/28-4; 1/4; S; Daughter 1223; No; Hemingford, Box Butte Co, Nebr; Yes; Id. U-12734 An. none

1243; Carlow, Theodore; M; 4/15/30-1; 1/4; S; Son 1224; No; Hemingford, Box Butte Co, Nebr; Yes; Id. U-13470 An. none

1244; Carlow, Frank; M; 1891-41; 1/4; M; Head 1225; Yes; Yes; Al. 1071 An. 1269

1245; Carlow (Little Chief), Elva; F; 1896-36; 1/4; M; Wife 1226; Yes; Yes; Al. 8024 An. 1270

1246; Carlow, Irene; F; 3/7/23-9; plus 1/4; S; Daughter 1227; Yes; Yes; Id. U-13007 An. 1271

1247; Carlow, Robert; M; 1896-36; 1/4; M; Head 1228; Yes; Yes; Al. 1073 An. 1272

1248; Carlow (Allen), Lizzie; F; 1886-46; -1/4; M; Wife 1229; Yes; Yes; Al. 1105 An. 1273

1249; Carlow, Robert J; M; 5/22/21-10; -1/4; S; Son 1230; Yes; Yes; Id. U-9306 An. 1274

1250; Carlow, Eileen V; F; 12/28/22-9; -1/4; S; Daughter 1231; Yes; Yes; Id. U-12062 An. 1275

1251; Carlow, Theodore; M; 1884-48; plus 1/4; M; Head 1232; No; Bremerton, Kitsap County, Wash; No; Al. 1069 An. 1276

1252; Carlow, Theodore H; M; 9/5/09-22; -1/4; S; Son 1233; No; Bremerton, Kitsap Co, Wash; Yes; Al. 5295 An. 1277

1253; Carlow, Alma L; F; 2/2/12-20; -1/4; S; Daughter 2345; No; Bremerton, Kitsap County, Wash; Yes; Al. 7881 An. 1278

1254; Carlow, Ruth; F; 2/1/13-19; -1/4; S; Daughter 1235; No; Bremerton, Kitsap County, Wash; Yes; Al. 7882 An. 1279

1255; Carlow, Randolph; M; 3/7/15-17; -1/4; S; Son 1236; No; Bremerton, Kitsap County, Wash; Yes; Al. 8204 An. 1280

1256; Carson, Lizzie; F; 1883-49; F; S; Head 1237; Yes; Yes; Al. 4937 An. 1283

1257; Cassidy (Davidson), Julia; F; 1854-78; plus 1/4; M; Head 1238; Yes; Yes; Al. 3823 An. 1850

1258; Catches, James; M; 1899-33; F; M; Head 1239; Yes; Yes; Al. 5777 An. 1284

1259; Catches (Star), Rosa; F; 1907-25; F; M; Wife 1240; Yes; Yes; Al. 7435 An. 6606

Census of the __Pine Ridge__ reservation of the __Pine Ridge, South Dakota__ jurisdiction, as of __April 1__, 1932, taken by __James H. McGregor__, Superintendent.

Key: Number; Surname, Given; Sex; Date of Birth-Age at Last Birthday; Tribe (Oglala Sioux, unless stated otherwise); Degree of Blood; Marital Status; Relationship to Head of Family [Last Census Roll Number]; At Jurisdiction Where Enrolled (Yes/No); (If no – Where); Ward (Yes/No, if given); Allotment, Annuity and Identification Numbers (if given).

1260; Catches, Everett; M; 2/27/25-7; F; S; Son 1241; Yes; Yes; Id. U-11770 An. none

1261; Catches, Adeline; F; 12/17/25-6; F; S; Daughter 1242; Yes; Yes; Id. U-11792 An. none

1262; Catches, Rosa; F; 6/25/28-3; F; S; Daughter 1243; Yes; Yes; Id. U-12670 An. none

1263; Catches, Caroline; F; 12/27/30-1; F; S; Daughter 1244; Yes; Yes; Id. U-13636 An. none

1264; Catches, Peter; M; 3/8/12-20; F; S; Brother 1245; Yes; Yes; Al. 7998 An. 1297

1265; Catches, Moses; M; 7/4/07-24; F; S; Head 1246; Yes; Yes; Al. 5774 An. 1286

1266; Cazeaux, Peter; M; 1858-74; plus 1/4; Wd; Head 1247; Yes; No; Al. 2045 An. 1288

1267; Cedar, James; M; 1865-67; F; M; Head 1248; Yes; Yes; Al. 508 An. 1290

1268; Cedar (no data), Mary; F; 1859-73; F; M; Wife 1249; Yes; Yes; Al. 6845 An. 1291

1269; Cedar, Philomene; F; 3/17/23-9; plus 1/4; S; Ad. Daughter 1250; Yes; Yes; Id. U-13917 An. 6542

1270; Cedar Face, Samuel; M; 1903-29; F; M; Head 1251; Yes; Yes; Al. 6432 An. 1292

1271; Cedar Face (Eagle Bird), Helen; F; 6/28/10-21; F; M; Wife 1252; Yes; Yes; Al. 6388 An. 1996

1272; Cedar Face, William; M; 1872-60; F; M; Head 1253; Yes; Yes; Al. 3044 An. 1293

1273; Cedar Face (Little Bird), Rosa; F; 1895-37; F; M; Wife 1254; Yes; Yes; Al. 5884 An. 1294

1274; Cedar Face, Christine; F; 7/23/18-13; F; S; Daughter 1255; Yes; Yes; Id. U-9307 An. 1295

1275; Cedar Face, Paul; M; 6/27/22-9; F; S; Son 1256; Yes; Yes; Id. U-12040 An. 1296

1276; Cedar Face, Annie; F; 3/30/28-4; F; S; Daughter 1257; Yes; Yes; Id. U-12876 An. none

1277; Cedar Face, Pearl; F; 3/31/30-2; F; S; Daughter 1258; Yes; Yes; Id. U-13440 An. none

1278; Cedar Woman; F; 1847-85; F; Wd; Head 1259; Yes; Yes; Al. 5039 An. 1298

1279; Center, William; M; 1890-48; F; M; Head 1260; Yes; Yes; Al. 464 An. 1300

Census of the __Pine Ridge__ reservation of the __Pine Ridge, South Dakota__ jurisdiction, as of __April 1__, 19**32**, taken by __James H. McGregor__, Superintendent.

Key: Number; Surname, Given; Sex; Date of Birth-Age at Last Birthday; Tribe (Oglala Sioux, unless stated otherwise); Degree of Blood; Marital Status; Relationship to Head of Family [Last Census Roll Number]; At Jurisdiction Where Enrolled (Yes/No); (If no – Where); Ward (Yes/No, if given); Allotment, Annuity and Identification Numbers (if given).

1280; Center (Fast Thunder), Emma; F; 1895-37; F; M: Wife 1261; Yes; Yes; Al. 5763 An. 1301

1281; Center, Floyd; M; 8/20/18-13; F; S; Son 1262; Yes; Yes; Id. U-9309 An. 1302

1282; Center, Rachel; F; 10/10/20-11; F; S; Daughter 1263; Yes; Yes; Id. U-9310 An. 1303

1283; Center, Percy; M; 2/15/15-5; F; S; Son 1264; Yes; Yes; Id. U-12240

~~N.E. Chapman, Francis; M; Eastern Cherokee; Wd; Head; Chey & Arapaho; Okla.~~

1284; Chapman, Francis E; M; 3/28/14-18; plus 1/4; S; Ward 1265; No; Chey & Arapaho; yes; Al. 7762 An. 1306

1285; Chapman, Jennie; F; 12/14/15-16; 1/4; S; Ward 1266; No; Chey & Arapaho; Yes; Yes; Al. 8228 An. 1307

~~N.E. Chapman, Joseph W; M; Santee Sioux; M; Head~~

1286; Chapman (Yellow Horse), Eva; F; 9/28/11-20; plus 1/4; M; Wife 7984; Yes; [blank]; Al. 6796 An. 7900

1287; Charges Enemy, James; M; 1871-61; F; M; Head 1267; Yes; No; Al. 6393 An. 1308

1288; Charges Enemy (no data), Jennie; F; 1881-51; F; M; Wife 1268; Yes; Yes; Al. 6650 An. 1309

1289; Charging, David; M; 1886-45; plus 1/4; M; Head 1269; Yes; Yes; Al. 8143 An. 1313

1290; Charging (Gray Blanket), Lizzie; F; 1891-41; F; M; Wife 1270; Yes; Yes; Al. 332 An. 1314

1291; Charging, Flora; F; 2/14/14-18; plus 1/4; S; Daughter 1271; Yes; Yes; Id. U-9311 An. 1315

1292; Charging, Martha; F; 8/4/17-14; 1/4; S; Daughter 1272; Yes; Yes; Id. U-9312 An. 1316

1293; Charging, Theodore; M; 10/25/19-12; 1/4; S; Son 1273; Yes; Yes; Id. U-9313 An. 1317

1294; Charging, Rempzer; M; 11/17/21-10; 1/4; S; Son 1274; Yes; Yes; Id. U-10869 An. 1318

1295; Charging, George; M; 1861-71; F; M; Head 1275; Yes; Yes; Al. 5100 An. 1319

1296; Charging (Badger), Alice; F; 1851-81; F; M; Wife 1276; Yes; Yes; Al. 6736 An. 1320

1297; Charging Crow, Jacob; M; 1847-85; F; M; Head 1277; Yes; Yes; Al. 2134 An. 1329

Census of the __Pine Ridge__ reservation of the __Pine Ridge, South Dakota__ jurisdiction, as of __April 1__, 19**32**, taken by __James H. McGregor__, Superintendent.

Key: Number; Surname, Given; Sex; Date of Birth-Age at Last Birthday; Tribe (Oglala Sioux, unless stated otherwise); Degree of Blood; Marital Status; Relationship to Head of Family [Last Census Roll Number]; At Jurisdiction Where Enrolled (Yes/No); (If no – Where); Ward (Yes/No, if given); Allotment, Annuity and Identification Numbers (if given).

1298; Charging Crow (Iron Road); F; 1858-74; F; M; Wife 1278; Yes; Yes; Al. 2135 An. 1330

1299; Charging Crow, Samuel; M; 1896-36; F; M; Head 1279; Yes; Yes; Al. 5283 An. 1331

1300; Charging Crow (Strikes Enemy), Lizzie; F; 1899-33; F; M; Wife 1280; Yes; Yes; Al. 2447 An. 1332

1301; Charging Crow, Andrew; M; 2/17/23-9; F; S; Son 1281; Yes; Yes; Id. U-12075 An. 1334

1302; Charging Crow, Eva; F; 1/27/26-6; F; S; Daughter 1282; Yes; Yes; Id. U-11818 An. none

1303; Charging Crow, James; M; 8/16/27-4; F; S; Son 1283; Yes; Yes; Id. U-12382 An. none

1304; Charging Crow, Roy; M; 2/8/29-3; F; S; Son 1284; Yes; Yes; Id. U-12897 An. none

1305; Charging Crow, Everett I; M; 12/11/30-1; F; S; Son 1285; Yes; Yes; Id. U-13638 An. none

1306; Charging Crow, Wallace; M; 1883-49; F; M; Head 1286; Yes; Yes; Al. 7030 An. 1335

1307; Charging Crow (Walks Fast), Rosa; F; 1882-50; F; M; Wife 1287; Yes; Yes; Al. 1801 An. 1336

1308; Charging Crow, Orlando; M; 6/2/18-13; F; S; Son 1288; Yes; Yes; Id. U-9315

1309; Charging Crow, William; M; 1870-62; F; M; Head 1289; Yes; Yes; Al. 2091 An. 1339

1310; Charging Crow (no data), Nancy; F; 1875-57; F; M; Wife 1290; Yes; Yes; Al. 2092 An. 1240

1311; Charging Thunder; ---; M; 1869-63; F; M; Head 1291; Yes; No; Al. 23 An. 1341

1312; Charging Thunder (Loafer), Adaline; F; 1882-51; F; M; Wife 1292; Yes; Yes; Al. 2019 An. 1342

1313; Charging Thunder, Daniel; M; 12/7/14-17; F; S; Son 1293; Yes; Yes; Al. 6688 An. 1343

1314; Charging Thunder, Cecelia; F; 8/31/18-13; F; S; Daughter 1284; Yes; Yes; Al. 7316 An. 1344

1315; Charging Thunder, Moses; M; 2/14/21-11; F; S; Son 1295; Yes; Yes; Id. U-9317 An. 1345

1316; Fast Horse, Lucinda; F; 6/3/25-6; F; S; Ward 1296; Yes; Yes; Id. U-11655 An. none

Census of the **Pine Ridge** reservation of the **Pine Ridge, South Dakota** jurisdiction, as of **April 1**, 1932, taken by **James H. McGregor**, Superintendent.

Key: Number; Surname, Given; Sex; Date of Birth-Age at Last Birthday; Tribe (Oglala Sioux, unless stated otherwise); Degree of Blood; Marital Status; Relationship to Head of Family [Last Census Roll Number]; At Jurisdiction Where Enrolled (Yes/No); (If no – Where); Ward (Yes/No, if given); Allotment, Annuity and Identification Numbers (if given).

1317; Charging Thunder (Yankton Woman), Bird; F; 1873-59; F; Wd; Head 1297; Yes; Yes; Al. 4739 An. 1347

1318; Eagle Shirt, Mary; F; 1/18/17-15; F; S; Daughter 1298; Yes; Yes; Id. U 9319 An. 1349

1319; Charging Thunder, Peter; M; 1/2/09-23; F; M; Head 1299; Yes; Yes; Al. 4741 An. 1348

1320; Charging Thunder (Black Fox), Hannah; F; 11/18/10-21; F; M; Wife 1300; Yes; Yes; Al. 6821 An. 784

1321; Charging Thunder, John W; M; 10/28/29-2; F; S; Son 1301; Yes; Yes; Id. U-13261 An. none

1322; Chase Alone, Martin; M; 1903-29; F; M; Head 1303; Yes; Yes; Al. 6638 An. 1352

1323; Chase Alone (Black Bear), Lizzie; F; 1904-28; F; M; Wife 1303; Yes; Yes; Al. 3750 An. 1353

1324; Chase Alone, Agnes; F; 10/17/25-6; F; S; Daughter 1305; Yes; Yes; Id. U-11787 An. none

1325; Chase Alone, Pearl; F; 2/8/28-4; F; S; Daughter 1306; Yes; Yes; Id. U-12542 An. none

1326; Chase Alone, Anna; F; 2/11/30-2; F; S; Daughter 1307; Yes; Yes; Id. U-13414 An. none

1327; Chase-in-Morning, James; M; 1888-44; F; M; Head 1308; Yes; Yes; Al. 912 An. 1369

1328; Chase-in-Morning (White Whirlwind), Ellen; F; 1893-39; F; M; Wife 1309; Yes; Yes; Al. 6048 An. 1370

1329; Chase-in-Morning, William; M; 9/24/15-16; F; S; Son 1310; Yes; Yes; Id. U-9320 An. 1371

1330; Chase-in-Morning, Annie; F; 3/29/19-12; F; S; Daughter 1311; Yes; Yes; Id. U-9321 An. 1372

1331; Chase-in-Morning, Elizabeth; F; 9/27/29-2; F; S; Daughter 1312; Yes; Yes; Id. U-13283 An. none

1332; Chase-in-Morning, Stanley; M; 1871-61; F; M; Head 1313; Yes; Yes; Al. 911 An. 1374

1333; Chase-in-Morning (Yellow Horse Woman), F; 1863-69; F; M; Wife 1314; Yes; Yes; Al. 2987 An. 1375

1334; Chase-in-Winter; M; 78; F; Wd; Head 1315; Yes; Yes; Al. 3542 An. 1356

1335; Chase-in-Winter, Frederick; M; 9/4/16-15; F; S; Son 1316; Yes; Yes; Id. U-9323

Census of the **Pine Ridge** reservation of the **Pine Ridge, South Dakota** jurisdiction, as of **April 1**, 19**32**, taken by **James H. McGregor**, Superintendent.

Key: Number; Surname, Given; Sex; Date of Birth-Age at Last Birthday; Tribe (Oglala Sioux, unless stated otherwise); Degree of Blood; Marital Status; Relationship to Head of Family [Last Census Roll Number]; At Jurisdiction Where Enrolled (Yes/No); (If no – Where); Ward (Yes/No, if given); Allotment, Annuity and Identification Numbers (if given).

1336; Chase-in-Winter, William; M; 1883-49; F; M; Head 1317; Yes; Yes; Al. 3545 An. 1361
1337; Chase-in-Winter (Weasel Bear), Cora; F; 189-42; F; M; Wife 1318; Yes; Yes; Al. 6138 An. 1362
1338; Chase-in-Winter, Sidney; M; 10/10/13-18; F; S; Son 1319; Yes; Yes; Al. 7571 An. 1366
1339; Chase-in-Winter, Jennie; F; 6/3/21-10; F; S; Daughter 1320; Yes; Yes; Id. U-11003 An. 1367
1340; Chase-in-Winter, Arthur; M; 4/21/24-7; F; S; Son 1321; Yes; Yes; Id. U-11301 An. 1369
1341; Chase-in-Winter, Wm. Webster; M; 8/15/27-4; F; S; Son 1322; Yes; Yes; Id. U-12380 An. none
1342; Chase-in-Winter, Alfred; M; 7/11/31-8/12; F; S; Son; Yes; Yes; U-13887

1343; Chase-in-Winter, Nancy; F; 8/8/10-21; F; M; Head 1323; Yes; Yes; Al. 6172 An. 1364
1344; Mesteth, Aloysius; M; 6/25/30-1; plus 1/4; S; Son 1324; Yes; Yes; Id. U-13701 An. none

1345; Cherry Eye (no data); F; 1862-70; F; Wd; Head 1325; Yes; Yes; Al. 5136 An. 4976

1346; Cheyenne, Thomas; M; 1905-27; F; M; Head 1326; Yes; Yes; Al. 3377 An. 1380
1347; Cheyenne (Kindle), Emma; F; 3/1/07-25; F; M; Wife 1327; Yes; Yes; Al. 3157 An. 3562
1347; Cheyenne, Zona; F; 7/27/27-4; F; S; Daughter 1328; Yes; Yes; Id. U-12400 An. none

1349; Chief, Benjamin; M; 1899-33; plus 1/4; M; Head 1329; Yes; Yes; Al. 6486 An. 1381
1350; Chief (Morrisette), Sophia; F; 1880-52; F; M; Wife 1330; Yes; Yes; Al. 617 An. 1382
1351; Chief, Lucy; F; 7/25/22-9; 1/4; S; Daughter 1331; Yes; Yes; Id. U-11129 An. 1386
1352; Morrisette, Zoey; F; 11/20/17-14; 1/4; S; S. Daughter 1332; Yes; Yes; Id. U-9327 An. 1385

1353; Chief, Elbert; M; 1892-40; F; M; Head 1333; Yes; Yes; Al. 2943 An. 1387
1354; Chief (Fills the Pipe), Hattie; F; 1894-38; F; M; Wife 1334; Yes; Yes; Al. 3446 An. 1388
1355; Chief, William; M; 12/27/21-10; F; S; Son 1335; Yes; Yes; Id. U-10843 An. 1390

Census of the___**Pine Ridge**___reservation of the___**Pine Ridge, South Dakota**
jurisdiction, as of___**April 1**___, 19**32**, taken by___**James H. McGregor**___,
Superintendent.

Key: Number; Surname, Given; Sex; Date of Birth-Age at Last Birthday; Tribe (Oglala Sioux, unless stated otherwise); Degree of Blood; Marital Status; Relationship to Head of Family [Last Census Roll Number]; At Jurisdiction Where Enrolled (Yes/No); (If no – Where); Ward (Yes/No, if given); Allotment, Annuity and Identification Numbers (if given).

1356; Chief, Douglas; M; 12/2/25-7; F; S; Son 1336; Yes; Yes; Id. U-11763 An. none
1357; Chief, Bluche; M; 7/16/28-3; F; S; Son 1337; Yes; Yes; Id. U-12825 An. none
1358; Chief, Yakima; M; 6/25/30-1; F; S; Son 1338; Yes; Yes; Id. U-13595 An. none

1359; Chief, James; M; 1876-56; plus 1/4; M; Head 1339; Yes; Yes; Al. 226 An. 1391
1360; Chief (Allman), Myrtle; F; 1896-36; F; M; Wife 1340; Yes; Yes; Al. 211 An. 1391[sic]
1361; Chief, Raymond; M; 7/24/16-15; plus 1/4; S; Son 1341; Yes; Yes; Id. U-9330 An. 1393

1362; Chief, Amelia; F; 2/19/20-12; 1/4; S; Daughter 1342; Yes; Yes; Id. U-9331 An. 1394
1363; Chief, Roy; M; 6/3/27-4; 1/4; S; Son 1343; Yes; Yes; Id. U-12860 An. none

1364; Chief, John; M; 1898-34; plus 1/4; M; Head 1344; Yes; Yes; Al. 3931 An. 1395
1365; Chief (Weir), Katie; F; 1/20/99-33; 1/4; M; Wife 1345; Yes; Yes; Al. 7703 An. 1396
1366; Chief, Corrine; F; 6/18/20-11; 1/4; S; Daughter 1346; Yes; Yes; Id. U-9332 An. 1397
1367; Chief, Myrtle; F; 6/15/25-6; 1/4; S; Daughter 1347; Yes; Yes; Id. U-11745 An. none
1368; Chief, William; M; 7/11/30-1; 1/4; S; Son 1348; Yes; Yes; Id. U-13542 An. none

1369; Chief Bear, Joseph; M; 1895-37; F; Wd; Head 1349; Yes; Yes; Al. 2003 An. 1398

1370; Chief Bear, William; M; 1865-68; F; M; Head 1350; Yes; Yes; Al. 2001 An. 1402
1371; Chief Bear (no data), Susie; F; 1870-62; F; M; Wife 1351; Yes; Yes; Al. 2002 An. 1403
1372; Chief Bear, Fannie; F; 8/24/10-21; F; S; dau 1352; Yes; Yes; Al. 6923 An. 1404

1373; Chief Eagle, Philip; M; 10/5/08-23; F; S; Head 1354; Yes; Yes; Al. 6382 An. 1407
1374; Chief Eagle, Eugene; M; 11/20/14-17; F; S; Brother 1355; Yes; Yes; Al. 7890 An. 1408
1375; Chief Eagle, Albert; M; 7/18/16-15; F; S; Brother 1356; Yes; Yes; Id. U-9335 An. 1409

Census of the   **Pine Ridge**   reservation of the **Pine Ridge, South Dakota**
jurisdiction, as of   **April 1**   , 19**32**, taken by   **James H. McGregor**   ,
Superintendent.

Key: Number; Surname, Given; Sex; Date of Birth-Age at Last Birthday; Tribe (Oglala Sioux, unless stated otherwise); Degree of Blood; Marital Status; Relationship to Head of Family [Last Census Roll Number]; At Jurisdiction Where Enrolled (Yes/No); (If no – Where); Ward (Yes/No, if given); Allotment, Annuity and Identification Numbers (if given).

1376; Chief Eagle, George; M; 1906-26; F; M; Head 1357; Yes; Yes; Al. 6381 An. 1412
1377; Chief Eagle (Kills Warrior), Ella; F; 3/3/08-24; F; M; Wife 1358; Yes; Yes; Al. 6227 An. 3550
1378; Chief Eagle, Martha W; F; 10/1/31-6/12; F; S; Dau; Yes; [blank]; U-14084

1379; Chief Eagle, Otto; M; 1872-60; F; Wd; Head 1359; Yes; Yes; Al. 1787 An. 1413

~~N.E. Childers, Clarence; M; Creek; plus 1/4; M; Head~~
1380; Childers (Babby), Grace; F; 5/11/08-23; -1/4; M; Wife 1360; Yes; Yes; Al. 4611 An. 2351
1381; Childers, Daniel W; M; 12/10/25-5; Oglala Sioux & Creek; 1/4; S; Son 1361; Yes; Yes; Id. I-12797 An. none
1382; Childers, Clarice G; F; 7/7/29-3; Oglala Sioux & Creek; 1/4; S; Daughter 1362; Yes; Yes; Id. U-13242 An. none
1383; Childers, Harold C; M; 1/5/32-2/12; Oglala Sioux & Creek; 1/4; S; Son; Yes; [blank]; U-14060

1384; Chips, James; M; 1902-30; F; M; Head 1363; Yes; Yes; Al. 5600 An. 1421
1385; Chips, Dallas; M; 4/30/25-6; F; S; Son 1364; Yes; Yes; Id. U-11609 An. none
1386; Chips, Vivian; F; 8/12/27-4; F; S; Daughter 1365; Yes; Yes; Id. U-12383 An. none

1387; Chips, Ellis; M; 10/4/09-22; F; M; Head 1366; Yes; Yes; Al. 5566 An. 3031
1388; Chips (Hawk Wing), Alice; F; 1905-27; plus 1/4; M; Wife 1367; Yes; Yes; Al. 4299 An. 2785
1389; Chips, Vincent; M; 8/8/26-5; plus 1/4; S; Son 1368; Yes; Yes; Id. U-11991 An. none
1390; Chips, Bessie; F; 3/27/30-3; 1/4; S; Daughter 1369; Yes; Yes; Id. U-13415 An. none

1391; Chips, Oliver; M; 1898-34; F; Wd; Head 1370; Yes; Yes; Al. 5570 An. 1422
1392; Chips, Ruby; F; 9/16/28-3; F; S; Dau 1372; Yes; Yes; Id. U-12798 An. none
1393; Chips, Leona; F; 11/20/30-1; F; S; Daughter 1373; Yes; Yes; Id. U-13637 An. none

1394; Christensen (Bettelyoun), Ruby L; F; 12/23/08-23; plus 1/4; M; Head 1374; Yes; Yes; Al. 4434 An. 476
1395; Christensen, Vern A; M; 10.10/27-4; -1/4; S; Son 1375; Yes; Yes; Id. U-12671 An. none
1396; Christensen, Gene S; M; 11/22/29-2; -1/4; S; Son 1376; Yes; Yes; Id. U-13321 An. none

Census of the____**Pine Ridge**_____reservation of the__**Pine Ridge, South Dakota**
jurisdiction, as of____**April 1**_____, 19**32,** taken by__**James H. McGregor**____,
Superintendent.

Key: Number; Surname, Given; Sex; Date of Birth-Age at Last Birthday; Tribe (Oglala Sioux, unless stated otherwise); Degree of Blood; Marital Status; Relationship to Head of Family [Last Census Roll Number]; At Jurisdiction Where Enrolled (Yes/No); (If no – Where); Ward (Yes/No, if given); Allotment, Annuity and Identification Numbers (if given).

1397; Clark (Robinson), Dorothy; F; 1901-31; plus 1/4; M; Head 1377; No; Browning, Teton Co, Mont; Yes; Al. 7357 An. 5749

~~N.E. Clark, Thomas; M; Walapai [Hualapai]; F; M; Head~~
1398; Clark (Amiotte), Delma; F; 1899-33; 1/4; M; Wife 1378; Yes; Yes; Al. 2585 An. 1426

1399; Clark (no data), Susan Sears; F; 1855-77; 1/4; M; Head 1379; Yes; Yes; Al. 375 An. 1427
1400; Frazier, Maxine; F; 4/1/16-16; 1/4; S; Ward 1380; Yes; Yes; Id. U-9542 An. 2333
1401; Clement (Hat), Lucy N; F; 1900-32; F; M; Head 1382; Yes; Yes; Al. 2868 An. 1430
1402; Clement, Dorothy; F; 9/26/27-4; plus 1/4; S; Daughter 1383; Yes; Yes; Id. U-12422 An. none
1403; Clement, Rosemary; F; 7/20/29-2; 1/4; S; Daughter 1384; Yes; Yes; Id. U-13222 An. none
1404; Clement, Alfred; M; 10/7/31-5/12; 1/4; S; Son; Yes; Yes; U-14085

1405; Clifford, Arthur; M; 10/21/99-32; plus 1/4; M; Head 1385; Yes; Yes; Al. 4475 An. 1432
1406; Clifford (Brown), Susie I; F; 12/18/04-27; -1/4; M; Wife 1386; Yes; Yes; Al. 4455 An. 1108
1407; Clifford, Lovella A; F; 8/25/25-6; -1/4; S; Daughter 1387; Yes; Yes; Id. U-11810 An. none
1408; Clifford, Floyde[sic]; M; 8/5/26-5; -1/4; S; Son 1388; Yes; Yes; Id. U-12236 An. none

1409; Clifford, Charles, Sr; M; 1867-65; plus 1/4; M; Head 1389; Yes; No; Al. 1637 An. 1433
1410; Clifford (Saunders), Julia; F; 1867-65; 1/4; M; Wife 1390; Yes; No; Al. 5974 An. 1434

1411; Clifford, Charles, Jr; M; 1891-41; 1/4; M; Head 1391; Yes; Yes; Al. 1639
1412; Clifford (Mills), Annie; F; 1895-37; 1/4; M; Wife 1392; Yes; Yes; Al. 1200 An. 1436
1413; Clifford, Margaret; F; 12/3/15-16; plus 1/4; S; Daughter 1393; Yes; Yes Id. U-9339 An. 1437
1414; Clifford, Abner; M; 6/17/18-13; 1/4; S; Son 1394; Yes; Yes; Id. U-9340 An. 1438
1415; Clifford, Dewey J; M; 3/12/21-11; 1/4; S; Son 1395; Yes; Yes; Id. U-9341 An. 1439

Census of the __**Pine Ridge**__ reservation of the __**Pine Ridge, South Dakota**__ jurisdiction, as of __**April 1**__, 1932, taken by __**James H. McGregor**__, Superintendent.

Key: Number; Surname, Given; Sex; Date of Birth-Age at Last Birthday; Tribe (Oglala Sioux, unless stated otherwise); Degree of Blood; Marital Status; Relationship to Head of Family [Last Census Roll Number]; At Jurisdiction Where Enrolled (Yes/No); (If no – Where); Ward (Yes/No, if given); Allotment, Annuity and Identification Numbers (if given).

1416; Clifford, Leslie; M; 10/13/23-8; 1/4; S; Son 1396; Yes; Yes; Id. U-11180 An. 1440

1417; Clifford, Owen S; M; 6/12/26-5; 1/4; S; Son 1397; Yes; Yes; Id. U-11973 An. none

1418; Clifford, Daniel; M; 1907-25; 1/4; S; Son 1398; Yes; Yes; Al. 5976 An. 1441

1419; Clifford, George; M; 1874-58; plus 1/4; M; Head 1399; Yes; No; Al. 2753 An. 1444

1420; Clifford (White), Emma; F; 1885-47; 1/4; M; Wife 1400; Yes; No; Al. 2754 An. 1445

1421; Clifford, Marion; M; 1/10/13-19; 1/4; S; Son 1401; Yes; Yes; Al. 7689 An. 1447

1422; Clifford, George, Jr; M; 1896-36; 1/4; M; Head 1403; Yes; Yes; Al. 2756 An. 1448

N.E. Clifford (Catchall), Florence; F; Rosebud Sioux; 1/4; M; Wife; Yes

1423; Clifford, Leroy; M; 7/1/21-10; 1/4; S; Son 1404; Yes; Yes; Id. U-11778 An. none

1424; Clifford, Thomas; M; 12/2/24-7; 1/4; S; Son 1405; Yes; Yes; Id. U-11779 An. none

1425; Clifford, Henry; M; 2/3/98-32; 1/4; M; Head 1406; Yes; Yes; Al. 2757 An. 1450

1426; Clifford (Hornbeck), Viola; F; 11/13/09-22; 1/4; M; Wife 1407; Yes; Yes; Al. 7345 An. 3027

1427; Clifford, Reuben C; M; 8/1/29-2; 1/4; S; Son 1408; Yes; Yes; Id. U-13263 An. none

1428; Clifford, Herbert; M; 1905-27; 1/4; S; Head 1409; Yes; Yes; Al. 7302 An. 1451

1429; Clifford, James; M; 1883-49; plus 1/4; M; Head 1410; Yes; Yes; Al. 1487 An. 1452

N.E. Clifford (Wilson), Ellen; F; Skagit; 1/4; M; Wife; Yes

1430; Clifford, Frederick; M; 11/26/12-19; Oglala Sioux & Skagit; 1/4; S; Son 1411; Yes; Yes; Al. 7306 An. 1454

1431; Clifford, Edith; F; 12/4/14-17; Oglala Sioux & Skagit; 1/4; S; Daughter 1412; Yes; Yes; Al. 7900 An. 1455

1432; Clifford, Frances M; F; 7/11/20-11; Oglala Sioux & Skagit; 1/4; S; Daughter 1413; Yes; Yes; Id. U-12077 An. 1456

1433; Clifford, Sybil; F; 7/9/08-24; 1/4; S; Head 1414; Yes; Yes; Al. 7305 An. 1453

Census of the **Pine Ridge** reservation of the **Pine Ridge, South Dakota** jurisdiction, as of **April 1**, 19**32**, taken by **James H. McGregor**, Superintendent.

Key: Number; Surname, Given; Sex; Date of Birth-Age at Last Birthday; Tribe (Oglala Sioux, unless stated otherwise); Degree of Blood; Marital Status; Relationship to Head of Family [Last Census Roll Number]; At Jurisdiction Where Enrolled (Yes/No); (If no – Where); Ward (Yes/No, if given); Allotment, Annuity and Identification Numbers (if given).

1434; Clifford, John H; M; 1871-61; 1/4; M; Head 1415; Yes; No; Al. 2672 An. 1457

1435; Clifford (Ruben), Hattie; F; 1879-53; 1/4; M; Wife 1416; Yes; No; Al. 2673 An. 1458

1436; Clifford, Joseph L; M; 1/31/10-22; 1/4; S; Son 1417; Yes; Yes; Al. 7363 An. 1460

1437; Clifford, Edith; F; 12/10/14-17; 1/4; S; Daughter 1419; Yes; Yes; Al. 7949 An. 1462

1438; Clifford, Paul S; M; 12/8/19-12; 1/4; S; Son 1420; Yes; Yes; Id. U-9344 An. 1464

1439; Clifford, Lemah; F; 8/3/17-14; 1/4; S; Daughter 1421; Yes; Yes; Id. U-9343 An. 1463

1440; Clifford, Eugene; M; 9/15/22-9; 1/4; S; Son 1422; Yes; Yes; Id. U-13051 An. 1465

1441; Clifford, Benjamin; M; 1908-24; 1/4; S; Head 1423; Yes; Yes; Al. 2758 An. 1459

1442; Clifford, John M; M; 1880-52; plus 1/4 1/4; M; Head 1424; Yes; No; Al. 2749 An. 1466

1443; Clifford (Martinez), Emma; F; 1882-50; 1/4; M; Wife 1425; Yes; Yes; Al. 2750 An. 1467

1444; Clifford, Clarence; M; 9/26/10-21; 1/4; S; Son 1426; Yes; Yes; Al. 7299 An. 1469

1445; Clifford, Matilda J; F; 4/14/12-19; 1/4; S; Daughter 1427; Yes; Yes; Al. 7300 An. 1470

1446; Clifford, Martha; F; 4/23/16-15; 1/4; S; Daughter 1428; Yes; Yes; Id. U-9345 An. 1471

1447; Clifford, Bethel; M; 8/22/18-13; 1/4; S; Son 1429; Yes; Yes; Id. U-9346 An. 1472

1448; Clifford, Frances; F; 4/6/21-10; 1/4; S; Daughter 1430; Yes; Yes; Id. U-10906 An. 1473

1449; Clifford, Veronica; F; 12/18/23-8; 1/4; S; Daughter 1431; Yes; Yes; Id. U-11270 An. 1474

1450; Clifford, Isabelle; F; 8/22/26-5; 1/4; S; Daughter 1432; Yes; Yes; Id. U-12673 An. none

1451; Clifford, Alvina; F; 1/7/09-23; plus 1/4; S; Head 1433; Yes; Yes; Al. 7298 An. [blank]

1452; Clifford, Julia; F; 1851-81; 1/4; S; Head 1434; Yes; Yes; Al. 1585 An. 1475

Census of the __**Pine Ridge**__ reservation of the __**Pine Ridge, South Dakota**__
jurisdiction, as of __**April 1**__, 19**32**, taken by __**James H. McGregor**__,
Superintendent.

Key: Number; Surname, Given; Sex; Date of Birth-Age at Last Birthday; Tribe (Oglala Sioux, unless stated otherwise); Degree of Blood; Marital Status; Relationship to Head of Family [Last Census Roll Number]; At Jurisdiction Where Enrolled (Yes/No); (If no – Where); Ward (Yes/No, if given); Allotment, Annuity and Identification Numbers (if given).

1453; Clifford, Mary; F; 1885-47; 1/4; S; Head 1436; No; Canton Hospital; Yes; Al. 1586 An. 1477

1454; Clifford, Louis; F; 1901-31; 1/4; S; Head 1435; Yes; Yes; Al. 7700 An. 1476

1455; Clifford, Mortimer; M; 1893-39; plus 1/4; M; Head 1437; Yes; Yes; Al. 1589 An. 1479

1456; Clifford (Hernandez), Catalina; F; 1895-37; 1/4; M; Wife 1438; Yes; Yes; Al. 1413 An. 1480

1457; Clifford, Agnes; F; 2/12/13-19; 1/4; S; Daughter 1439; Yes; Yes; Al. 7285 An. 1481

1458; Clifford, Mortimer, Jr; M; 3/2/15-17; 1/4; S; Son 1440; Yes; Yes; Al. 8069 An. 1482

1459; Clifford, Evelyn; F; 6/1/17-14; 1/4; S; Daughter 1441; Yes; Yes; Id. U-9347 An. 1482[sic]

1460; Clifford, Calvin H; M; 10/4/18-13; 1/4; S; Son 1442; Yes; Yes; Id. U-9348 An. 1483

1461; Clifford, Sidney; M; 2/18/21-11; 1/4; S; Son 1443; Yes; Yes; Id. U-9349 An. 1485

1462; Clifford, Jennett G; F; 12/19/25-6; 1/4; S; Daughter 1444; Yes; Yes; Id. U-11865 An. none

1463; Clifford, Orlando; M; 1873-59; 1/4; M; Head 1445; Yes; No; Al. 4438 An. 1486

1464; Clifford (Riff), Alice; F; 1875-57; 1/4; M; Wife 1446; Yes; No; Al. 4439 An. 1487

1465; Clifford, Robert; M; 6/21/98-34; 1/4; M; Head 1447; No; Busby, Big Horn Co, Mont; Yes; Yes; Al. 1642 An. 1489

1466; Clifford (Swallow), Geraldine; F; 3/10/10-22; -1/4; M; Wife 1448; No; Busby, Big Horn Co, Mont; Yes; Al. 7628 An. 6741

1467; Clifford, Esther H; F; 6/3/31-9/12; -1/4; S; Daughter; No; Busby, Big Horn Co, Mont; Yes; U-13852

1468; Clifford (Waite), Susie; F; 1892-40; plus 1/4; Wd; Head 1449; Yes; Yes; Al. 2740 An. 1490

1469; Clifford, Nathaniel; M; 12/29/16-16; 1/4; S; Son 1451; Yes; Yes; Al. 8121 An. 1492

1470; Clifford, William; M; 1897-35; plus 1/4; S; Head 1452; Yes; Yes; Al. 1640 An. 1495

Census of the __Pine Ridge__ reservation of the __Pine Ridge, South Dakota__ jurisdiction, as of __April 1__, 19**32**, taken by __James H. McGregor__, Superintendent.

Key: Number; Surname, Given; Sex; Date of Birth-Age at Last Birthday; Tribe (Oglala Sioux, unless stated otherwise); Degree of Blood; Marital Status; Relationship to Head of Family [Last Census Roll Number]; At Jurisdiction Where Enrolled (Yes/No); (If no – Where); Ward (Yes/No, if given); Allotment, Annuity and Identification Numbers (if given).

1471; Clincher, Calvin; M; 1881-51; F; Wd; Head 1453; Yes; No; Al. 4363 An. 1496
1472; Clincher, Joseph; M; 7/29/21-10; F; S; Son 1455; Yes; Yes; Id. U-9451 An. 2171

1473; Clincher, Frank; M; 1898-34; F; M; Head 1456; Yes; Yes; Al. 5273 An. 1501
1474; Clincher (Long Bull), Marguerite; F; 1905-27; F; M; Wife 1457; Yes; Yes; Al. 4567 An. 1502
1475; Clincher, Zouis[sic]; F; 10/22/21-10; F; S; Daughter 1458; Yes; Yes; Id. U-1302 An. 1503
1476; Clincher, Benjamin; M; 6/19/23-8; F; S; Son 1459; Yes; Yes; Id. U-14015 An. 1504
1477; Clincher, Floyd; M; 8/24/27-4; F; S; Son 1450; Yes; Yes; Id. U-12401 An. none
1478; Clincher, George J; M; 10/10/31-5/12; F; S; Son; Yes; Yes; U-13933

1479; Clincher, George; M; 1787-54; F; M; Head 1461; Yes; Yes; Al. 4365 An. 1505
1480; Clincher (no data), Lizzie; F; 1877-55; F; M; Wife 1462; Yes; Yes; Al. 4366 An. 1506
1481; Clincher, Louisa; F; 1/1/20-12; F; S; Daughter 1463; Yes; Yes; Id. U-9354 An. 1507
1482; Clincher, Silas; M; 12/7/21-10; F; S; Son 1464; Yes; Yes; Id. U-10848 An. 1508

1483; Close (no data), Feather; F; 1865-67; F; Wd; Head 1465; Yes; Yes; Al. 5933 An. 2171

1484; Close, George; M; 1875-57; F; Wd; Head 1466; Yes; Yes; Al. 5199 An. 1515
1485; Close, Lizzie; F; 1/3/13-19; F; S; Daughter 1467; Yes; Yes; Id. U-9356 An. 1518
1486; Close, Charles; M; 4/8/10-21; F; S; Son 1468; Yes; Yes; Id. U-9355 An. 1517

1487; Close, Silas; M; 10/4/07-24; F; S; Head 1469; Yes; Yes; Al. 7794 An. 1516

1488; Cloud (no data); F; 1849-83; F; Wd; Head 1470; Yes; Yes; Al. 6649 An. 1377

1489; Cloud Chief (Black Horse), Emma; F; 1898-34; F; Wd; Head 1471; No; Chey & Arapahoe Okla; Yes; Yes; Al. 276 An. 1519
1490; Cloud Chief, Victoria; F; 4/30/15-16; F; S; Daughter 1472; No; Chey & Arapahoe Okla; Yes; Id. U-9357 An. 1520
1491; Tasso, Sidney; M; 7/28/18-13; F; S; Son 1473; No; Chey & Arapahoe Okla; Yes; Yes; Id. U-9358 An. 1521

Census of the **Pine Ridge** reservation of the **Pine Ridge, South Dakota** jurisdiction, as of **April 1**, 19**32**, taken by **James H. McGregor**, Superintendent.

Key: Number; Surname, Given; Sex; Date of Birth-Age at Last Birthday; Tribe (Oglala Sioux, unless stated otherwise); Degree of Blood; Marital Status; Relationship to Head of Family [Last Census Roll Number]; At Jurisdiction Where Enrolled (Yes/No); (If no – Where); Ward (Yes/No, if given); Allotment, Annuity and Identification Numbers (if given).

1492; Tasso, John; M; 7/28/18-13; F; S; Son 1474; No; Chey & Arapahoe Okla; Yes; Yes; Id. U-9359 An. 1522

1493; Black Horse, Clifford; M; 11/1/26-5; F; S; Son 1475; No; Chey & Arapahoe Okla; Yes; U-12160

1494; Cloud Shield, Henry; M; 1889-43; F; M; Head 1476; Yes; Yes; Id. U-9360 An. 1526

1495; Cloud Shield (Fire Thunder), Dorothy; F; 2/25/09-23; F; M; Wife 1477; Yes; Yes; Al. 5107 6038

1496; Fire Thunder, Ambrose; M; 3/30/26-6; F; S; S. Son 1478; Yes; Yes; Id. U-11896 An. none

1497; Clown Horse, Bennie; M; 1898-34; F; Wd; Head 1479; No; Belle Fourche, Butte Co, S.D; Yes; Al. 8104 An. 1527

1498; Clown Horse (Dirt Kettle), Julia; F; 1899-33; F; Wd; Head 1489; Yes; Yes; Al. 1236 An. 1528

1499; Clown Horse, Scholastic; F; 1/2/24-8; F; S; Daughter 1481; Yes; Yes; Id. U-11225 An. 1530

1500; Dirt Kettle, Marie; F; 8/15/27-4; F; S; Daughter 1482; Yes; Yes; Id. U-12515 An. none

1501; Clown Horse (no data), Edna; F; 1847-85; F; Wd; Head 1483; Yes; Yes; Al. 5952 An. 1531

1502; Clown Horse, Frank; M; 1878-54; F; M; Head 1484; Yes; Yes; Al. 3072 An. 1552

1503; Clown Horse (Chase-in-Winter), Theresa; F; 1884-48; F; M; Wife 1485; Yes; Yes; Al. 5029 An. 1553

1504; Clown Horse, Edison; M; 8/18/25-6; F; S; Nephew 1486; Yes; Yes; Id. U-12513 An. none

1505; Coats (Cummings), Jennie; F; 3/6/98-34; -1/4; M; Head 1487; No; Merriman, Cherry Co, Nebr; Yes; Al. 2153 An. 1533

1506; Coats, Verda; F; 9/5/17-14; -1/4; S; Daughter 1488; No; Merriman, Cherry Co, Nebr; Yes; Id. U-9361 An. 1534

1507; Coats, Robert L; M; 12/22/19-12; -1/4; S; Son 1489; No; Merriman, Cherry Co, Nebr; Yes; Id. U-9362 An. 1535

1508; Coats, Darwin L; M; 3/24/23-9; -1/4; S; Son 1490; No; Merriman, Cherry Co, Nebr; Yes; Id. U-11417 An. 1536

1509; Coats, George M; M; 3/14/25-7; -1/4; S; Son 1491; No; Merriman, Cherry Co, Nebr; Yes; Id. U-11821 An. none

Census of the **Pine Ridge** reservation of the **Pine Ridge, South Dakota** jurisdiction, as of **April 1**, 19**32**, taken by **James H. McGregor**, Superintendent.

Key: Number; Surname, Given; Sex; Date of Birth-Age at Last Birthday; Tribe (Oglala Sioux, unless stated otherwise); Degree of Blood; Marital Status; Relationship to Head of Family [Last Census Roll Number]; At Jurisdiction Where Enrolled (Yes/No); (If no – Where); Ward (Yes/No, if given); Allotment, Annuity and Identification Numbers (if given).

1510; Coats, Clyde; M; 10/22/28-3; -1/4; S; Son 1492; No; Merriman, Cherry Co, Nebr; Yes; Id. U-12913 An. none

1511; Coats, Hazel Ione; F; 11/1/29-2; -1/4; S; Daughter 1493; No; Merriman, Cherry Co, Nebr; Yes; U-13565 An. none

1512; Coats, Eulala E; F; 7/4/31-8/12; -1/4; S; Daughter; No; Merriman, Cherry Co, Nebr; Yes; U-13888

1513; Cold Water (no data); ---; F; 1864-68; F; Wd; Head 1494; Yes; Yes; Al. 4239 An. 252

1514; Colhoff, Frederick; M; 1902-30; plus 1/4; M; Head 1495; No; Rapid City, Pennington Co, S.D; Yes; Al. 290 An. 1537

1515; Colhoff (Janis), Dorotha[sic]; F; 1905-27; 1/4; M; Wife 1495; No; Rapid City, Pennington Co, S.D; Yes; Al. 361 An. 1538

1516; Colhoff, Frederick M; M; 1/16/27-5; 1/4; S; Son 1497; No; Rapid City, Pennington Co, S.D; Id. U-12384 An. none

1517; Colhoff, Bernard L; M; 12/17/28-3; 1/4; S; Son 1498; No; Rapid City, Pennington Co, S.D; Yes; Id. U-12966 An. none

1518; Colhoff, Luella R; F; 8/20/30-1; 1/4; S; Daughter 1499; No; Rapid City, Pennington Co, S.D; Yes; Id. U-13598 An. none

1519; Colhoff, George; M; 1884-48; 1/4; M; Head 1500; Yes; Yes; Al. 337 An. 1539

1520; Colhoff (Stirk), Louisa; F; 1887-45; 1/4; M; Wife 1500; Yes; Yes; Al. 2668 An. 1540

1521; Colhoff, Estella; F; 11/11/13-18; 1/4; S; Daughter 1502; Yes; Yes; Al. 7457 An. 1543

1522; Colhoff, Adelaide; F; 4/19/16-15; 1/4; S; Daughter 1503; Yes; Yes; Id. U-9363 An. 1544

1523; Colhoff, Georgia L; F; 11/4/17-14; 1/4; S; Daughter 1504; Yes; Id. U-9364 An. 1545

1524; Colhoff, Vernon; M; 10/18/20-11; 1/4; S; Son 1505; Yes; Yes; Id. U-9365 An. 1546

1525; Colhoff, Richard; M; 12/8/28-3; 1/4; S; Son 1506; Yes; Yes; Id. U-13205 An. none

1526; Colhoff, Geraldine; F; 8/1/08-23; plus; S; Head 1507; No; Rapid City, Pennington Co, S.D; Yes; Al. 5978 An. 1541

1527; Colhoff, Marcella; F; 5/4/10-21; 1/4; S; Head 1508; No; Rapid City, Pennington Co, S.D; Yes; Al. 5879 An. 1542

1528; Colhoff, James; M; 1900-32; plus 1/4; M; Head 1509; Yes; Yes; Al. 292 An. 1547

Census of the **Pine Ridge** reservation of the **Pine Ridge, South Dakota** jurisdiction, as of **April 1**, 19**32**, taken by **James H. McGregor**, Superintendent.

Key: Number; Surname, Given; Sex; Date of Birth-Age at Last Birthday; Tribe (Oglala Sioux, unless stated otherwise); Degree of Blood; Marital Status; Relationship to Head of Family [Last Census Roll Number]; At Jurisdiction Where Enrolled (Yes/No); (If no – Where); Ward (Yes/No, if given); Allotment, Annuity and Identification Numbers (if given).

1529; Colhoff (Mesteth), Annie; F; 1901-31; 1/4; M; Wife 1510; Yes; Yes; Al. 7273 An. 1548

1530; Colhoff, Vestana; F; 4/2/23-8; 1/4; S; Daughter 1511; Yes; Yes; Id. U-1302 An. 1549

1531; Colhoff, Ira James; M; 11/6/24-7; 1/4; S; Son 1512; Yes; Yes; Id. U-11374 An. 1550

1532; Colhoff, Norma; F; 4/5/28-3; 1/4; S; Daughter 1513; Yes; Yes; Id. U-11132 An. none

1533; Colhoff, Herbert; M; 12/27/29-2; 1/4; S; Son 1514; Yes; Yes; Id. U-13322 An. none

1534; Colhoff, Virgil; M; 3/25/32-1/12; 1/4; S; Son; Yes; Yes; U-14123

1535; Colhoff, John; M; 1880-52; 1/4; Wd; Head 1515; Yes; No; Al. 291 An. 1551

1536; Colhoff, Norma; F; 8/30/15-16; 1/4; S; Daughter 1516; Yes; Yes; Al. 8216 An. 1554

1537; Colhoff, Norbert; M; 2/19/08-24; 1/4; S; Head 1517; Yes; Yes; Al. 3919 An. 1553

1538; Colhoff, Louis; M; 1899-33; plus 1/4; M; Head 1518; Yes; Yes; Al. 289 An. 1555

1539; Colhoff (Janis), Cecelia; F; 11/28/11-20; 1/4; S; Wife 1519; Yes; Yes; Al. 7330 An. 3341

1540; Colhoff, Phyllis L; F; 9/16/31-6/12; 1/4; S; Daughter; Yes; [blank]; U-13916

1541; Colhoff, William; M; 1890-42; 1/4; Wd; Head 1520; Yes; Yes; Al. 288 An. 1556

~~N.E. Colhoff (Rowland), Emma; F; Cheyenne; plus 1/4; M; Wife~~

1542; Colhoff, Melvin; M; 4/8/31-11/12; 1/4; S; Son; Yes; Yes; U-13799

1543; Combs (Amiotte), Belle; F; 7/5/08-23; 1/4; M; Head 1521; Yes; Yes; Al. 4753 An. 148

1544; Combs, Vance; M; 11/9/29-2; -1/4; S; Son 1522; Yes; Yes; Id. U-13376 An. none

1545; Comes Again, James; M; 1870-62; F; M; Head 1523; Yes; Yes; Al. 3455 An. 1557

1546; Comes Again (no data), Nancy; F; 1875-57; F; M; Wife 1524; Yes; Yes; Al. 3481 An. 1558

1547; Comes Again, Joseph; M; 1891-41; F; M; Head 1525; Yes; Yes; Al. 1374 An. 1559

Census of the **Pine Ridge** reservation of the **Pine Ridge, South Dakota** jurisdiction, as of **April 1**, 19**32**, taken by **James H. McGregor**, Superintendent.

Key: Number; Surname, Given; Sex; Date of Birth-Age at Last Birthday; Tribe (Oglala Sioux, unless stated otherwise); Degree of Blood; Marital Status; Relationship to Head of Family [Last Census Roll Number]; At Jurisdiction Where Enrolled (Yes/No); (If no – Where); Ward (Yes/No, if given); Allotment, Annuity and Identification Numbers (if given).

1548; Comes Again (Plenty Bear), Mabel; F; 2883-49; F; M; Wife 1526; Yes; Yes; Al. 5187 An. 4977

1549; Comes Again, Leo; M; 9/28/26-5; F; S; Son 1527; Yes; Yes; Id. U-12132 An. none

1550; Comes From Among Them, Donald; M; 1868-64; F; M; Head 1528; Yes; Yes; Al. 3160 An. 1563

1551; Comes From Among Them (no data), Annie; F; 1866-66; plus 1/4; M; Wife 1529; Yes; Yes; 3141 An. 1564

1552; Comes From Among Them, Jenette; F; 10/31/09-22; plus 1/4; S; Head 1530; Yes; Yes; Al. 8253 An. 1565

1553; Comes Killing, Aaron; M; 1877-55; F; Wd; Head 1531; Yes; Yes; Al. 349 An. 1566

1554; Comes Killing Amelia; F; 8/9/12-19; F; S; Daughter 1532; Yes; Yes; Al. 7098 An. 1568

1555; Comes Killing, Julia; F; 1/23/17-15; F; S; Daughter 1533; Yes; Yes; Id. U-9367 An. 1569

1556; Comes Killing, Jessie; F; 9/3/07-24; F; S; Head 1534; Yes; Yes; Al. 4382 An. none

1557; Comes Last, Robert; M; 1902-30; F; M; Head 1535; Yes; Yes; Al. 4860 An. 1570

1558; Comes Last (Yellow Thunder), Amelia; F; 1907-25; F; M; Wife 1536; Yes; Yes; Al. 8122 An. 7917

1559; Comes Out (no data); F; 1863-69; F; Wd; Head 1537; Yes; Yes; Al. 4371 An. 1571

1560; Comes Out Whirlwind, Richard; M; 1899-33; F; M; Head 1538; No; Standing Rock; Yes; Yes; Al. 2952 An. 1574

1561; Condelario, Bernard; M; 1900-32; plus 1/4; S; Head 1539; Yes; Yes; Al. 2102 An. 1575

1562; Condelario, Joseph; M; 3/5/16-16; plus 1/4; Wd; Head 1540; Yes; Yes; Al. 8181 An. 1576

1563; Condelario, Peter; M; 1878-54; plus 1/4; M; Head 1541; Yes; No; Al. 2100 An. 1580

Census of the **Pine Ridge** reservation of the **Pine Ridge, South Dakota** jurisdiction, as of **April 1**, 19**32**, taken by **James H. McGregor**, Superintendent.

Key: Number; Surname, Given; Sex; Date of Birth-Age at Last Birthday; Tribe (Oglala Sioux, unless stated otherwise); Degree of Blood; Marital Status; Relationship to Head of Family [Last Census Roll Number]; At Jurisdiction Where Enrolled (Yes/No); (If no – Where); Ward (Yes/No, if given); Allotment, Annuity and Identification Numbers (if given).

1564; Condelario (Moran), Nancy; F; 1879-53; 1/4; M; Wife 1542; Yes; Yes; Al. 2101 An. 1581

1565; Condelario, Peter; M; 1/11/11-21; 1/4; S; Son 1543; Yes; Yes; Al. 5504 Al. 1584

1566; Condelario, Richard; M; 3/25/13-19; S; Son 1544; Yes; Yes; Al. 8181 An. 1585

1567; Condelario, Joseph; M; 3/5/16-16; 1/4; S; Son 1545; Yes; Yes; Al. 8183 An. 1586

1568; Condelario, Alberta; F; 2/3/19-13; 1/4; S; Daughter 1545; Yes; Yes; Id. U-9368 An. 1587

1569; Condelario, Vincent; M; 6/8/20-11; 1/4; s; Son 1547; Yes; Yes; Id. U-9369 An. 1588

1570; Conquering Bear, Abe; M; 1872-60; F; M; Head 1548; Yes; Yes; Al. 1014 An. 1589

1571; Conquering Bear (Yellow Hawk), Susie; F; 1879-53; F; M; Wife 1549; Yes; Yes; Al. 5244 An. 1590

1572; Conquering Bear, Matthew; M; 4/30/10-21; F; S; Son 1550; Yes; Yes; Al. 5251 An. 1592

1573; Conquering Bear, Thomas; M; 11/29/16-15; F; S; Son 1551; Yes; Yes; Id. U-9370 An. 1495

1574; Conquering Bear, William; M; 4/29/20-11; F; S; Son 1552; Yes; Yes; Id. U-9371 An. 1595

1575; Conquering Bear, Benjamin; M; 11/17/07-24; F; S; Head 1553; Yes; Yes; Al. 5838 An. 1591

1576; Conquering Bear, Amos; M; 1876-56; F; M; Head 1564; Yes; Yes; Al. 5242 An. 1596

1577; Conquering Bear (Plenty Haranger), Jennie; F; 1883-49; F; M; Wife 1555; Yes; Yes; Al. 5242 An. 1597

1578; Conquering Bear (no data), Goldie; F; 1905-27; F; S; Head 1556; Yes; Yes; Al. 5250 An. 1598

1579; Conquering Bear, Ray; M; 10/18/26-5; F; S; Son 1557; Yes; Yes; Id. U-12192 An. none

1580; Turning Holy, Kenneth; M; 2/17/31-1; F; S; Son 1558; Yes; Yes; Id. U-13749 An. none

1581; Conquering Bear, Herman; M; 1879-53; F; Wd; Head 1559; Yes; Yes; Al. 5224 An. 1599

Census of the___**Pine Ridge**___reservation of the___**Pine Ridge, South Dakota** jurisdiction, as of___**April 1**___, 19**32**, taken by___**James H. McGregor**___, Superintendent.

Key: Number; Surname, Given; Sex; Date of Birth-Age at Last Birthday; Tribe (Oglala Sioux, unless stated otherwise); Degree of Blood; Marital Status; Relationship to Head of Family [Last Census Roll Number]; At Jurisdiction Where Enrolled (Yes/No); (If no – Where); Ward (Yes/No, if given); Allotment, Annuity and Identification Numbers (if given).

1582; Conquering Bear, Martin; M; 1880-52; F; M; Head 1560; Yes; Yes; Al. 5241 An. 1600

1583; Conquering Bear, Joshua; M; 5/15/11-20; F; M; Head 1562; Yes; Yes; Al. 5826 An. 1601

1584; Conquering Bear (Nelson), Grace; F; 11/22/12-19; plus 1/4; M; Wife 1563; Yes; Yes; Id. U-10059 An. 4718

1585; Conquering Bear, Mary; F; 1905-27; F; S; Head 1564; Yes; Yes; Al. 5249 An. 1602

1586; Conquering Bear, Casy[sic]; M; 5/19/22-5; F; S; Son 1565; Yes; Yes; Id. U-1099 An. 1603

1587; Conquering Bear, Dawson; M; 3/30/25-6; F S; Son 1566; Yes; Yes; Id. U-11866 An. none

1588; Conquering Bear, Stephen; M; 4/11/20-2; F; S; Son 1567; Yes; Yes; Id. U-13206 An. none

1589; Conquering Bear, Oliver; M; 1907-25; F; S; Head 1568; Yes; Yes; Al. 5239 An. 2524

1590; Conroy, Benjamin; M; 1886-46; plus 1/4; M; Head 1570; Yes; Yes; Al. 357 An. 1606

1591; Conroy (Cottier), Esther; F; 1894-38; 1/4; M; Wife 1571; Yes; Yes; Al. 989 An. 1609

1592; Conroy, Delbert; M; 5/12/17-14; 1/4; S; Son 1573; Yes; Yes; Id. U-9374 An. 1608

1593; Conroy, Norma; F; 7/5/25-6; 1/4; S; Daughter 1574; Yes; Yes; Id. U-11685 An. none

1594; Conroy, Melvin; M; 7/7/28-3; 1/4; S; Son 1575; Yes; Yes; Id. U-12736 An. none

1595; Conroy, Doris A; F; 7/17/30-1; 1/4; S; Daughter 1576; Yes; Yes; Id. U-13566 An. none

1596; Conroy, Orville J; M; 1/23/32-2/12; 1/4; S; Son; Yes; Yes; U-14086

1598; Conroy, Sophia; F; 5/11/15-16; 1/4; S; Head 1572; Yes; Yes; Id. U-9373 An. 1607

1599; Cottier, Wm. Jr; M; 3/30/31-1; 1/4; S; Son; Yes; Yes; U-13962

1600; Conroy, Frank; M; 1865-67; plus 1/4; M; Head 1577; Yes; Yes; Al. 4584 An. 1612

1601; Conroy (no data), Victoria; F; 1866-66; 1/4; M; Wife 1578; Yes; Yes; Al. 4585 An. 1613

Census of the **Pine Ridge** reservation of the **Pine Ridge, South Dakota** jurisdiction, as of **April 1**, 1932, taken by **James H. McGregor**, Superintendent.

Key: Number; Surname, Given; Sex; Date of Birth-Age at Last Birthday; Tribe (Oglala Sioux, unless stated otherwise); Degree of Blood; Marital Status; Relationship to Head of Family [Last Census Roll Number]; At Jurisdiction Where Enrolled (Yes/No); (If no – Where); Ward (Yes/No, if given); Allotment, Annuity and Identification Numbers (if given).

1602; Conroy, Harry; M; 1894-38; plus 1/4; M; Head 1579; Yes; Yes; Al. 4587 An. 1614

1603; Conroy (Fire Thunder), Bertha; F; 1898-34; 1/4; M; Wife 1580; Yes; Yes; Al. 5270 An. 2238

1604; Conroy, Virginia; F; 1/31/30-2; 1/4; S; Daughter 1581; Yes; Yes; Id. U-13441 An. none

1605; Conroy, John R; M; 7/13/97-34; 1/4; M; Head 1582; Yes; Yes; Al. 361 An. 1615

~~N.E Conroy (Lamar), Margorie; F; Wichita; M; Wife~~

1606; Conroy, Freda; F; 6/15/24-7; Oglala Sioux-Wichita; -1/4; S; Daughter 1583; Yes; Yes; Id. U-11906 An. none

1607; Conroy, Vivian; F; 11/22/25-6; Oglala Sioux-Wichita; -1/4; S; Daughter 1584; Yes; Yes; Id. U-12682 An. none

1608; Conroy, John, Sr; M; 1861-71; plus 1/4; M; Head 1585; Yes; Yes; Al. 355 An. 1616

1609; Conroy (Gerry), Lucy; F; 1869-63; 1/4; M; Wife 1586; Yes; Yes; Al. 4581 An. 1617

1610; Conroy, Thomas; M; 3/20/11-21; 1/4; S; Son 1587; Yes; Yes; Al. 7899 An. 1618

1611; Conroy, Gerry; M; 3/5/13-19; 1/4; S; Son 1588; Yes; Yes; Al. 7860 An. 1619

1612; Conroy, Lucy; F; 1901-31; 1/4; S; Head 1589; Yes; Yes; Al. 363 An. 1620

1613; Conroy, Pearl; F; 1903-29; 1/4; S; Head 1590; Yes; Yes; Al. 266 An. 1622

1614; Conroy, Sarah; F; 1899-33; 1/4; ; Head 1591; Yes; Yes; Al. 363 An. 1623

1615; Conroy, Taylor; M; 1893-39; plus 1/4; M; Head 1592; Yes; Yes; Al. 360 An. 1624

1616; Conroy (Charging Bear), Alice; F; 1898-34; 1/4; M; Wife 1593; Yes; Yes; Al. 5280 An. 1625

1617; Conroy, Eli J; M; 10/23/18-13; 1/4; S; Son 1594; Yes; Yes; Id. U-9375 An. 1626

1618; Conroy, Sarah; F; 9-27-22-9; 1/4; S; Daughter 1595; Yes; Yes; Id. U-12038 An. 1627

1619; Conroy, Mercy; F; 1/14/25-7; 1/4; S; Daughter 1596; Yes; Yes; Id. U-11707 An. 1628

1620; Conroy, Norman; M; 12/25/29-2; 1/4; S; Son 1597; Yes; Yes; Id. U-13323 An. none

1621; Conroy, Walter; M; 1896-36; 1/4; S; Head 1598; Yes; Yes; Al. 4588 An. 1629

Census of the **Pine Ridge** reservation of the **Pine Ridge, South Dakota** jurisdiction, as of **April 1**, 19**32**, taken by **James H. McGregor**, Superintendent.

Key: Number; Surname, Given; Sex; Date of Birth-Age at Last Birthday; Tribe (Oglala Sioux, unless stated otherwise); Degree of Blood; Marital Status; Relationship to Head of Family [Last Census Roll Number]; At Jurisdiction Where Enrolled (Yes/No); (If no – Where); Ward (Yes/No, if given); Allotment, Annuity and Identification Numbers (if given).

1622; Cook (Herman), Winifred; F; 1886-36; 1/4; M; Head 1599; No; Lame Deer, Mont; No; Al. 2675 An. 1630

1623; Cook, Vernie; M; 5/27/12-19; 1/4; S; Son 1600; Yes; Yes; Al. 7352 An. 1632

1624; Cook, Lamont; M; 10/18/16-7-14; 1/4; S; Son 1602; No; Lame Deer, Mont; Yes; Id. U-9377 An. 1634

1625; Cook, Ernest; M; 9/18/23-8; 1/4; S; Son 1603; No; Lame Deer; Yes; Id. U-11574 An. 1635

1626; Cook, Stanley; M; 3/18/26-6; 1/4; S; Son 1604; No; Lame Deer; Yes; Id. U-12657 An. none

1627; Coryell (Tway), Emma; F; 1890-42; -1/4; M; Head 1605; No; Long Pine, Brown Co, Nebr; Yes; Al. 4838 An. 1637

1628; Coryell, Lester L; M; 7/16/12-19; -1/4; S; Son 1606; No; Long Pine, Brown Co, Nebr; Yes; Al. 7913 An. 1638

1629; Coryell, Mary G; F; 12/12/18-13; -1/4; S; Daughter 1607; No; Long Pine, Brown Co, Nebr; Yes; Yes; Id. U-9378 An. 1639

1630; Coryell, William L; M; 2/10/22-10; -1/4; Son 1608; No; Long Pine, Brown Co, Nebr; Yes; Id. U-11724 An. 1640

1631; Coryell, Paul E; M; 2/27/28-4; -1/4; S; Son 1609; No; Long Pine, Brown Co, Nebr; Yes; Id. U-11934 An. none

1632; Cottier, Bennie; M; 1900-32; plus 1/4; M; Head 1610; No; Nemo, Custer Co, S.D; Yes; Al. 4662 An. 1641

1633; Cottier (Irvings[sic]), Ollie; F; 4/15/09-22; 1/4; M; Wife 3218; Yes; Yes; Al. 4719 An. 3233

1634; Cottier, Mary Jane; F; 2/2/25-7; 1/4; S; Daughter 1611; No; Tulsa, Tulsa Co, Okla; Yes; Id. U-11974 An. none

1635; Cottier, Charles; M; 1888-44; 1/4; M; Head 1612; No; Chadron, Dawes Co, Nebr; No; Al. 980 An. 1642

1636; Cottier (Livermont), Hazel; F; 1896-36; -1/4; M; Wife 1613; No; Chadron, Dawes Co, Nebr; Yes; Al. 2542 An. 1643

1637; Cottier, Charles; M; 8/1/15-16; -1/4; S; Son 1614; No; Chadron, Dawes Co, Nebr; Yes; Id. U-9379 An. 1644

1638; Cottier, Florence; F; 6/16/17-14; -1/4; S; Daughter 1615; No; Chadron, Dawes Co, Nebr; Yes; Id. U-9380 An. 1645

1639; Cottier, Eddie; M; 1896-36; plus 1/4; M; Head 1616; Yes; Yes; Al. 990 An. 1646

1640; Cottier (Morrison), Helena; F; 5/23/04-27; -1/4; M; Wife 1617; Yes; Yes; Al. 1127 An. 1647

Census of the **Pine Ridge** reservation of the **Pine Ridge, South Dakota** jurisdiction, as of **April 1** , 19**32**, taken by **James H. McGregor** , Superintendent.

Key: Number; Surname, Given; Sex; Date of Birth-Age at Last Birthday; Tribe (Oglala Sioux, unless stated otherwise); Degree of Blood; Marital Status; Relationship to Head of Family [Last Census Roll Number]; At Jurisdiction Where Enrolled (Yes/No); (If no – Where); Ward (Yes/No, if given); Allotment, Annuity and Identification Numbers (if given).

1641; Cottier, Carmen R; F; 5/6/29-2; 1/4; S; Daughter 1618; Yes; Yes; Id. U-13181 An. none

1642; Cottier (no data), Emma; F; 1885-47; plus 1/4; Wd; Head 1619; Yes; Yes; Al. 1565 An. 1648

1643; Cottier, Frances; F; 8/27/11-20; 1/4; S; Daughter 1620; Yes; Yes; Al. 6927 An. 1649

1644; Cottier, Henry C; M; 4/5/16-15; 1/4; S; Son 1621; Yes; Yes; Id. U-9381 An. 1650

1645; Cottier, Gilbert; M; 1891-41; 1/4; M; Head 1622; Yes; Yes; Al. 991 An. 1652
1646; Cottier (Slow Dog), Helen; F; 1897-35; F; M; Wife 1623; Yes; Yes; Al. 5827 An. 1653
1647; Cottier, Victor; M; 11/21/14-17; plus 1/4; S; Son 1624; Yes; Yes; Id. U-9382 An. 1654
1648; Cottier, Rachel; F; 4/3/22-9; 1/4; S; Daughter 1625; Yes; Yes; Id. U-10922 An. 1656
1649; Cottier, Rebecca; F; 4/3/22-9; 1/4; S; Daughter 1626; Yes; Yes; Id. U-10927 An. 1657
1650; Cottier, Vivian; F; 10/23/24-7; 1/4; S; Daughter 1627; Yes; Yes; Id. U-9429 An. 1658

1651; Cottier, Henry; M; 1877-55; 1/4; M; Head 1628; Yes; Yes; Al. 984 An. 1659
1652; Cottier (Babby), Minnie; F; 3/7/77-55; -1/4; M; Wife 1629; Yes; Yes; Al. 4660 An. 1660
1653; Randall, Opal; F; 1/15/19-13; -1/4; S; Gr. Daughter 1630; Yes; Yes; Id. U-10191 An. 5297

1654; Cottier, John; M; 1865-67; plus 1/4; M; Head 1631; Yes; Yes; Al. 986 An. 1661
1655; Cottier (no data), Susie; F; 1865-67; 1/4; M; Wife 1632; Yes; Yes; Al. 5328 An. 1662

1656; Cottier, John, Jr; M; 1889-43; plus 1/4; M; Head 1633; Yes; Yes; Al. 988 An. 1663
1657; Cottier (Janis), Aggie; F; 1894-38; 1/4; M; Wife 1634; Yes; Yes; Al. 713 An. 1664
1658; Cottier, Isabella; F; 9/1/13-18; 1/4; S; Daughter 1635; Yes; Yes; Al. 7754 An. 1665
1659; Cottier, Lucy; F; 10/27/14-17; 1/4; S; Daughter 1636; Yes; Yes; Id. U-9385 An. 1666
1660; Cottier, Louis; M; 7/16/16-15; 1/4; S; Son 1637; Yes; Yes; Id. U-9386 An. 1667

Census of the **Pine Ridge** reservation of the **Pine Ridge, South Dakota** jurisdiction, as of **April 1**, 19**32**, taken by **James H. McGregor**, Superintendent.

Key: Number; Surname, Given; Sex; Date of Birth-Age at Last Birthday; Tribe (Oglala Sioux, unless stated otherwise); Degree of Blood; Marital Status; Relationship to Head of Family [Last Census Roll Number]; At Jurisdiction Where Enrolled (Yes/No); (If no – Where); Ward (Yes/No, if given); Allotment, Annuity and Identification Numbers (if given).

1661; Cottier, Bert Roy; M; 1/27/18-14; 1/4; S; Son 1638; Yes; Yes; Id. U-9387 An. 1668

1662; Cottier, Margaret; F; 6/23/20-11; 1/4; S; Daughter 1639; Yes; Yes; Id. U-9288 An. 1669

1663; Cottier, Leo F; M; 3/11/22-10; 1/4; S; Son 1640; Yes; Yes; Id. U-11649 An. 1670

1664; Cottier, Eleanor; F; 3/27/25-7; 1/4; S; Daughter 1641; Yes; Yes; Id. U-11672 An. none

1665; Cottier, Kenneth; M; 5/5/28-3; 1/4; S; Son 1642; Yes; Yes; Id. U-12614 An. none

1666; Cottier, Robert; M; 9/27/26-5; 1/4; S; Son 1643; Yes; Yes; Id. U-12216 An. none

1667; Cottier, John H; M; 5/29/13-10/12; 1/4; S; Son; Yes; Yes; U-13832

1668; Cottier, Samuel; M; 1890-42; 1/4; S; Head 1646; Yes; Yes; Al. 981 An. 1676

1669; Cottier, Walter; M; 1894-38; plus; M; Head 1647; Yes; Yes; Al. 992 An. 1676[sic]

1670; Cottier (Ruleau), Louisa; F; 1896-36; 1/4; M; Wife 1648; Yes; Yes; Al. 2145 An. 1677

1671; Cottier, Esther; F; 8/17/15-16; 1/4; S; Daughter 1649; Yes; Yes; Id. U-9389 An. 1678

1672; Cottier, Katherine; F; 2/8/17-15; 1/4; S; Daughter 1650; Yes; Yes; Id. U-9390 An. 1679

1673; Cottier, Pearl; F; 12/9/18-13; 1/4; S; Daughter 1651; Yes; Yes; Id. U-9391 An. 1680

1674; Cottier, William; M; 1903-29; 1/4; M; Head 1652; Yes; Yes; Al. 4663 An. 1681

1675; Cottier (Deon), Mary; F; 1903-29; 1/4; M; Wife 1653; No; Cheyenne, Laramie Co, Wyo; Yes; Al. 7430 An. 1869

1676; Couch (Kocer), Johanna; F; 1892-40; 1/4; M; Head 1654; No; Seattle, King Co, Wash; No; Al. 420 An. 3603

1677; Coulombe (Allen-Boyer), Augusta; F; 10/16/09-22; -1/4; M; Head; Yes; Yes; Al. 4666 An. 79

1678; Cow Horn (no data); F; 1850-82; F; S; Head 1655; Yes; Yes; Al. 2660 An. 1682

1679; Crane (Craven), Jessie; F; 1898-34; -1/4; M; Head 1656; Yes; Yes; Al. 3819 An. 1697

Census of the **Pine Ridge** reservation of the **Pine Ridge, South Dakota** jurisdiction, as of **April 1**, **1932**, taken by **James H. McGregor**, Superintendent.

Key: Number; Surname, Given; Sex; Date of Birth-Age at Last Birthday; Tribe (Oglala Sioux, unless stated otherwise); Degree of Blood; Marital Status; Relationship to Head of Family [Last Census Roll Number]; At Jurisdiction Where Enrolled (Yes/No); (If no – Where); Ward (Yes/No, if given); Allotment, Annuity and Identification Numbers (if given).

1680; Crane, Carolyn; F; 12/18/27-4; -1/4; S; Dau 1657; Yes; Yes; Id. U-12890 An. none

1681; Crane, Kenneth; M; 12/6/29-2; -1/4; S; Son; Yes; Yes; U-13800

1682; Crane, Nail; M; 12/6/29-2; -1/4; S; Son 1[sic]; Yes; Yes; U-13824

1683; Craven, Benjamin; M; 1901-31; -1/4; S; Head 1658; Yes; Yes; Al. 3856 An. 1683

1684; Craven, Cornelius; M; 1885-47; -1/4; M; Head 1659; Yes; Yes; Al. 3810 An. 1684

1685; Craven, Cecil; M; 1/23-16-16; -1/4; S; Son 1660; Yes; Yes; Al. 8131 1685

1686; Craven, Theda; F; 2/24/17-15; -1/4; S; Daughter 1661; Yes; Yes; Id. U-9392 An. 1686

1687; Craven, Cornelius; M; 6/17/18-13; -1/4; S; Son 1662; Yes; Yes; Id. U-9393 An. 1687

1688; Craven, Frances y[sic]; F; 7/30/24-7; -1/4; S; Daughter 1663; Yes; Yes; Id. U-11867 An. none

1689; Craven, George; M; 1879-53; -1/4; M; Head 1664; Yes; Yes; Al. 1852 An. 1688

1690; Craven (no data), Alice; F; 1876-56; plus 1/4; M; Wife 1665; Yes; Yes; Al. 1853 An. 1689

1691; Craven, Nellis; F; 4/24/12-19; 1/4; S; Daughter 1666; Yes; Yes; Id. U-9395 An. 1692

1692; Craven, Jess W; M; 3/28/16-16; 1/4; S; Son 1667; Yes; Yes; Id. U-9397 An. 1694

1693; Craven, Emma; F; 11/1/10-21; 1/4; S; Head 1668; Yes; Yes; Id. U-9394 An. 1691

1694; Crave (no data), Jessie; F; 1865-67; 1/4; Wd; Head 1669; Yes; Yes; Al. 3809 An. 1696

1695; Craven, John; M; 1884-48; -1/4; Wd; Head 1670; Yes; Yes; Al. 3899 An. 1698

1696; Crawford (O'Rourke), Agnes; F; 1903-29; plus 1/4; SM; Head 1671; Yes; Yes; Al. 1610 An. 4664

1697; Crawford, Merna D; F; 8/25/29-2; -1/4; S; Daughter; Yes; Yes; U-13366

1698; Crawford, Wm. T; M; 8/3/31-7/12; -1/4; S; Son; Yes; Yes; U-13948

Census of the **Pine Ridge** reservation of the **Pine Ridge, South Dakota** jurisdiction, as of **April 1**, 19**32,** taken by **James H. McGregor**, Superintendent.

Key: Number; Surname, Given; Sex; Date of Birth-Age at Last Birthday; Tribe (Oglala Sioux, unless stated otherwise); Degree of Blood; Marital Status; Relationship to Head of Family [Last Census Roll Number]; At Jurisdiction Where Enrolled (Yes/No); (If no – Where); Ward (Yes/No, if given); Allotment, Annuity and Identification Numbers (if given).

1699; Crazy Bear, Albert; M; 1906-26; F; S; Head 1672; Yes; Yes; Al. 4897 An. 7257

1700; Crazy Dog, Zoey; F; 1903-29; F; S; Head 1673; Yes; Yes; Al. 1661 An. 1701

1701; Crazy Ghost, Frank; M; 1881-51; F Wd; Head 1674; Yes; Yes; Al. 4157 An. 1704

1702; Crazy Ghost, Samuel; M; 6/23/16-15; F; S; Son 1676; Yes; Yes; Id. U-9398 An. 1706

1703; Crazy Ghost, Frank C; M; 9/19/17-13; F; S; Son 1677; Yes; Yes; Id. U-9399 An. 1707

1704; Crazy Ghost, Lucille; F; 4/18/21-10; F; S; Daughter 1678; Yes; Yes; Id. U-9400 An. 1708

1705; Crazy Ghost, Alice; F; 9/1/23-8; F; S; Daughter 1679; Yes; Yes; Id. U-11206 An. 1708

1706; Crazy Ghost, Lillian; F; 7/17/29-2; F; S; Daughter 1680; Yes; Yes; Id. U-13223 An. none

1707; Crazy Horse; M; 1854-78; F; Wd; Head 1681; Yes; Yes; Al. 6807 An. 1711

1708; Crazy Horse, Richard; M; 1894-38; plus 1/4; Wd; Head 1683; Yes; Yes; Al. 5491 An. 1714

1709; Crazy Horse, Lizzie; F; 7/11/20-11; 1/4; S; Daughter 1685; Yes; Yes; Id. U-9402 An. 1721

1710; Crazy Thunder (no data), Julia; F; 1866-66; F; Wd; Head 1685; Yes; Yes; Al. 2642 An. 1723

1711; Crazy Thunder, Joseph; M; 1895-37; F; M; Head 1686; Yes; Yes; Al. 7094 An. 1724

1712; Crazy Thunder (Janis), Rose; F; 1895-37; plus 1/4; M; Wife 1687; Yes; Yes; Al. 69 An. 1725

1713; Crazy Thunder, Nicholas J; M; 5/9/21-10; 1/4; S; Son 1688; Yes; Yes; Id. U-9404 An. 1726

1714; Crazy Thunder, Clement; M; 6/19/22-9; 1/4; S; Son 1689; Yes; Yes; Id. U-11099 An. 1727

1715; Crazy Thunder, David; M; 10/10/23-8; 1/4; S; Son 1690; Yes; Yes; Id. U-11545 An. 1728

1716; Crazy Thunder, Irene; F; 6/28/25-6; 1/4; S; Daughter 1691; Yes; Yes; Id. U-11838 An. none

1717; Crazy Thunder, Emma; F; 12/21/27-4; 1/4; S; Dau 1692; Yes; Yes; Id. U-12066 An. none

Census of the **Pine Ridge** reservation of the **Pine Ridge, South Dakota** jurisdiction, as of **April 1**, 19**32**, taken by **James H. McGregor**, Superintendent.

Key: Number; Surname, Given; Sex; Date of Birth-Age at Last Birthday; Tribe (Oglala Sioux, unless stated otherwise); Degree of Blood; Marital Status; Relationship to Head of Family [Last Census Roll Number]; At Jurisdiction Where Enrolled (Yes/No); (If no – Where); Ward (Yes/No, if given); Allotment, Annuity and Identification Numbers (if given).

1718; Crazy Thunder, Allen; F; 2/6/29-3; 1/4; S; Daughter 1693; Yes; Yes; Id. U-13278 An. none

1719; Crazy Thunder, Louis; M; 1907-25; F; S; Head 1694; Yes; Yes; Al. 2644 An. 1729

1720; Crazy Thunder, Robert; M; 1886-46; F; M; Head 1695; Yes; Yes; Al. 7113 An. 1730

1721; Crazy Thunder (Center), Maggie; F; 1873-59; F; M; Wife 1695; Yes; Yes; Al. 463 An. 1731

1722; Kills In Water, Eugene; M; 1/18/11-21; F; S; Son 1697; Yes; Yes; Al. 5715 An. 1733

1723; Crier, Paul; M; 1864-68; F; M; Head 1698; Yes; No; Al. 4208 An. 1734

1724; Crier (Short Bull), Jessie; F; 1859-73; F; M; Wife 6226; Yes; Yes; Al. 4347 An. 5217

1725; Crier, Peter; M; 1887-45; F; M; Head 1700; Yes; Yes; Al. 4235 An. 1736

1726; Crier (Kicking Bear), Mary; F; 1882-50; F; M; Wife 1701; Yes; Yes; Al. 2941 An. 1737

1727; Crooked Eyes; M; 1866-66; F; Wd; Head 1702; Yes; Yes; Al. 2314 An. 1738

1728; Crooked Eyes, Elias; M; 3/15/13-19; F; S; Gr. Son 1703; Yes; Yes; Id. U-9405 An. 1740

1729; Crooked Eyes, Samuel; M; 1890-42; F; M; Head 1704; Yes; Yes; Al. 6871 An. 1741

1730; Crooked Eyes (Bear Shield), Alice; F; 1894-38; F; M; Wife 1705; Yes; Yes; Al. 109 An. 1742

1731; Crooked Eyes, Dorothy; F; 5/1/18-13; F; S; Dau 1706; Yes; Yes; Id. U-9406 An. 1743

1732; Crooked Eyes, Florence; F; 2/19/21-11; F; S; Dau 1707; Yes; Yes; Id. U-9407 An. 1744

1733; Crooked Eyes, Aloysius; M; 5/27/23-8; F; S; Son 1708; Yes; Yes; Id. U-12913 An. none

1734; Crooked Eyes, Malinda; F; 6/26/26-5; F; S; Daughter 1709; Yes; Yes; Id. U-1261 An. none

1735; Cross, Frank; M; 2/21/11-21; plus 1/4; S; Head 1711; No; U.S. Navy; Yes; Al. 7061 An. 619

1736; Cross, Lawrence; M; 1900-32; plus 1/4; M; Head 1712; Yes; Yes; Al. 706 An. 1745

Census of the **Pine Ridge** reservation of the **Pine Ridge, South Dakota** jurisdiction, as of **April 1**, 19**32,** taken by **James H. McGregor**, Superintendent.

Key: Number; Surname, Given; Sex; Date of Birth-Age at Last Birthday; Tribe (Oglala Sioux, unless stated otherwise); Degree of Blood; Marital Status; Relationship to Head of Family [Last Census Roll Number]; At Jurisdiction Where Enrolled (Yes/No); (If no – Where); Ward (Yes/No, if given); Allotment, Annuity and Identification Numbers (if given).

1737; Cross (Red Bear), Emma; F; 1892-40; F; M; Wife 1713; Yes; Yes; Al. 4428 An. 1746
1738; Cross, Stephen; M; 8/22/15-16; F; S; S. Son 1714; Yes; Yes; Id. U-10208 An. 1747
1739; Cross, Lawrence O; M; 9/21/20-11; plus 1/4; S; Son 1715; Yes; Yes; Id. U-10930 An. 1748
1740; Cross, James P; M; 6/17/22-9; 1/4; S; Son 1716; Yes; Yes; Id. U-11845 An. 1749
1741; Cross, Robert H; M; 2/25/28-4; 1/4; S; Son 1717; Yes; Yes; Id. U-11294 An. 1750

1742; Cross, Thomas; 1905-27; 1/4; M; Head 1718; Yes; Yes; Al. 7059 An. 1751
1743; Cross (Red Eyes), Susie; F; 1908-24; F; M; Wife 5477; Yes; Yes; Al. 4189 An. 5454

1744; Cross Dog, John; M; 1874-58; F; M; Head 1719; Yes; Yes; Al. 328 An. 1752
1745; Cross Dog (Black Whilrwind[sic]), Susie; F; 1889-43; F; M; Wife 1720; Yes; Yes; Al. 99 An. 4807
1746; Cross Dog, Lincoln; M; 2/12/28-4; F; S; Son 1721; Yes; Yes; Id. U-12514 An. none
1747; American Horse, Albert; M; 10/2/17-14; F; S; S. Son 1722; Yes; Yes; Id. U-9029 An. 118
1748; American Horse, Leonard; M; 11/18/20-11; F; S; S. Son 1723; Yes; Yes; Id. U-9030 An. 119

1749; Crow, Henry, Sr; M; 1866-66; F; M; Head 1724; Yes; Yes; Al. 2640 An. 1754
1750; Crow (White Butterfly), Ellen; F; 1869-63; F; M; Wife 1725; Yes; Yes; Al. 3003 An. 1755
1751; Crow, Samuel; M; 7/14/09-23; F; S; Son 1726; Yes; Yes; Al. 7511 An. 1756

1752; Crow, Henry, Jr; M; 1901-31; F; M: Head 1727; Yes; Yes; Al. 7497 An. 1757
1753; Crow (Kills At Lodge), Jessie; F; 10/1/06-25; F; M; Wife 1728; Yes; Yes; Al. 7574 An. 3469
1754; Crow, Nelson; M; 11/29/26-5; F; S; Son 1729; Yes; Yes; Id. U-12179 An. none
1755; Crow, Russell; M; 10/2/29-2; F; S; Son 1730; Yes; Yes; Id. U-13264 An. none

1756; Crow, James; M; 1892-40; F; Wd; Head 1731; Yes; Yes; Al. 851 An. 1758
1757; Crow, Rachel; F; 2/27/27-5; F; S; Daughter; Yes; Yes; U-14087

1758; Crow (Strikes Enemy), Susie; F; 1909-23; F; Wd; Head 1732; Yes; Yes; Id. U-10082 An. 4807

Census of the __Pine Ridge__ reservation of the __Pine Ridge, South Dakota__ jurisdiction, as of __April 1__, 1932, taken by __James H. McGregor__, Superintendent.

Key: Number; Surname, Given; Sex; Date of Birth-Age at Last Birthday; Tribe (Oglala Sioux, unless stated otherwise); Degree of Blood; Marital Status; Relationship to Head of Family [Last Census Roll Number]; At Jurisdiction Where Enrolled (Yes/No); (If no – Where); Ward (Yes/No, if given); Allotment, Annuity and Identification Numbers (if given).

1759; Crow, Elsie; F; 3/23/28-4; F; S; Daughter 1733; Yes; Yes; Id. U-12217 An. none

1760; Broken Leg, Jessie; F; 10/2/31-5/12; F; S; Daughter; Yes; Yes; U-13932

1761; Crow, Peter; M; 1903-29; F; M; Head 1734; Yes; Yes; Al. 7510 An. 1760

1762; Crow (High Eagle), Mary; F; 1897-35; F; M; Wife 1735; Yes; Yes; Al. 3485 An. 1761

1763; Crow, Thelma; F; 11/2/23-8; F; S; Daughter 1736; Yes; Yes; Id. U-11138 An. 1762

1764; Crow; Alvina; F; 5/2/27-4; F; S; Daughter 1737; Yes; Yes; Id. U-12304 An. none

1765; Crow, Owen; M; 3/13/31-1; F; S; Son 1738; Yes; Yes; Id. U-13777 An. none

1766; Crow, Schuyler; M; 1906-26; F; M; Head 1739; No; Riverside, Riverside Co, Cal; Yes; Yes; Al. 4902 An. 1763

N.E. Crow (Serawop), Emma; F; Uncompahgre Ute; M; Wife

N.E. Crow Eagle, George; M; North. Cheyenne; F; M; Head

1767; Crow Eagle (Fire Thunder), Annie; F; 1908-32; plus 1/4; M; Wife 1740; Yes; Yes; Al. 1948 An. 1764

1768; Crow Eagle, Virginia; F; 8/29/23-8; 1/4; S; Daughter 1741; Yes; Yes; Id. U-11608 An. 1765

1769; Cummings, Frank M; M; 1902-30; -1/4; S; Head 1742; Yes; Yes; Al. 2155 An. 1768

1770; Cummings, Leroy; M; 1904-28; -1/4; M; Head 1743; No; Rapid City, Pennington, S.D; Yes; Al. 2156 A. 1769

N.E. Cummings (Smith), Marion; F; Rosebud Sioux; -1/4; M; Wife

1771; Cummings, Joyce; F; 4/10/27-4; -1/4; S; Daughter 1744; No; Rapid City, Pennington Co, S.D; Yes; Id. U-12618 An. none

1772; Cummings, Geraldine; F; 12/31/28-3; -1/4; S; Daughter 1745; No; Rapid City, Pennington Co, S.D; Yes; Id. U-13324 An. none

1773; Cummings, Newton; M; 1902-30; -1/4; S; Head 1746; Yes; Yes; Al. 2154 An. 1770

1774; Cummings, Peter M; M; 1894-38; -1/4; M; Head 1747; Yes; Yes; Al. 2151 An. 1771

1775; Cummings (Graham), Ollie; F; 1895-37; plus 1/4; M Wife 1748; Yes; Yes; Al. 2198 An. 2648

1776; Graham, Florence A; F; 10/12/20-11; 1/4; S; Niece 1749; Yes; Yes; Id. U-9619 An. 2648

Census of the **Pine Ridge** reservation of the **Pine Ridge, South Dakota** jurisdiction, as of **April 1**, 19**32**, taken by **James H. McGregor**, Superintendent.

Key: Number; Surname, Given; Sex; Date of Birth-Age at Last Birthday; Tribe (Oglala Sioux, unless stated otherwise); Degree of Blood; Marital Status; Relationship to Head of Family [Last Census Roll Number]; At Jurisdiction Where Enrolled (Yes/No); (If no – Where); Ward (Yes/No, if given); Allotment, Annuity and Identification Numbers (if given).

1777; Cuny, Adolph; M; 1897-35; plus 1/4; M; Head 1750; Yes; Yes; Al. 2912 An. 1773

1778; Cuny (Pourier), Mary L; F; 10/6/04-27; 1/4; M; Wife 1761; Yes; Yes; Al. 2615 An. 1774

1779; Cuny, Vernon J; M; 10/25/24-7; 1/4; S; Son 1752; Yes; Yes; Id. U-11552 An. 1775

1780; Cuny, Doris; F; 9/10/26-5; 1/4; S; Daughter 1753; Yes; Yes; Id. U-12103 An. none

1781; Cuny, Elnora; F; 9/13/28-3; 1/4; S; Daughter 1754; Yes; Yes; Id. U-12846 An. none

1782; Cuny, Loretta; F; 10/3/30-1; 1/4; S; Daughter 1755; Yes; Yes; Id. U-13731 An. none

1783; Cuny, Charles, Jr[sic]; M; 1862-70; 1/4; M; Head 1756; Yes; Yes; Al. 2907 An. 1776

1784; Cuny, Richard; M; 11/14/16-15; 1/4; S; Son 1757; Yes; Yes; Id. U-9410 An. 1777

1785; Cuny, Mildred; F; 7/9/18-13; 1/4; S; Daughter 1758; Yes; Yes; Id. U-9411 An. 1778

1786; Cuny, Ernest; M; 2/19/21-11; 1/4; S; Son 1759; Yes; Yes; Id. U-9412 An. 1779

1787; Cuny, Patrick; M; 11/29/23-8; 1/4; S; Son 1760; Yes; Yes; Id. U-11229 An. 1780

1788; Cuny, Charles, Jr; M; 1889-43; 1/4; M; Head 1761; Yes; Yes; Al. 2909 Al. 1781

1789; Cuny, Hester; F; 3/3/18-14; 1/4; S; Daughter 1762; Yes; Yes; Id. U-9413 An. 1782

1790; Cuny, Sidney; M; 11/28/19-12; 1/4; S; Son 1763; Yes; Yes; Id. U-9414 An. 1783

1791; Cuny, Jess V; M; 4/23/23-8; 1/4; S; Son 1764; Yes; Yes; Id. U-11134 An. 1784

1792; Cuny, Alta; F; 4-6-27-4; -1/4; S; Daughter 1765; Yes; Yes; Id. U-12305 An. none

1793; Cuny, Wm Joseph; M; 3/25/31-1; -1/4; S; Son 1766; Yes; Yes; Id. U-13757 An. none

1794; Cuny, Eddie; M; 1886-46; plus 1/4; M; Head 1767; Yes; Yes; Id. 2908 An. 1785

1795; Cuny (Fire Thunder), Angelique; F; 1885-47; F; M; Wife 1768; Yes; Yes; Al. 2915 An. 1786

1796; Cuny, Elton; M; 7/17/14-17; 1/4; S; Son 1770; Yes; Yes; Al. 7708 An. 1790

Census of the **Pine Ridge** reservation of the **Pine Ridge, South Dakota** jurisdiction, as of **April 1**, 19**32**, taken by **James H. McGregor**, Superintendent.

Key: Number; Surname, Given; Sex; Date of Birth-Age at Last Birthday; Tribe (Oglala Sioux, unless stated otherwise); Degree of Blood; Marital Status; Relationship to Head of Family [Last Census Roll Number]; At Jurisdiction Where Enrolled (Yes/No); (If no – Where); Ward (Yes/No, if given); Allotment, Annuity and Identification Numbers (if given).

1797; Cuny, Rebecca; F; 8/4/17-14; 1/4; S; Dau 1771; Yes; Yes; Id. U-9415 An. 1791
1798; Cuny, Woodrow; M; 12/25/19-12; 1/4; S; Son 1772; Yes; Yes; Id. U-9416 An. 1792
1799; Cuny, Elaine M; F; 5/31/21-10; 1/4; S; Daughter 1773; Yes; Yes; Id. U-10935 An. 1793
1800; Cuny, Thomas; M; 12/4/23-8; 1/4; S; Son 1774; Yes; Yes; Id. U-11222 An. 1794

1801; Cuny (no data), Josephine; F; 1835-97; 1/4; Wd; Head 1775; Yes; Yes; Al. 2906 An. 1795

1802; Cuny, Jule; M; 1876-58; 1/4; M; Head 1776; Yes; Yes; Al. 2759 An. 1796
1803; Cuny (no data), Prudy; F; 1883-49; 1/4; M; Wife 1777; Yes; Yes; Al. 2760 An. 1800
1804; Cuny, Leslie; M; 4/11/13-18; 1/4; S; Son 1778; Yes; Yes; Al. 7455 An. 1800[sic]

1805; Cuny, Myrle; F; 3/19/17-15; 1/4; S; Daughter 1779; Yes; Yes; Id. U-9417 An. 1801
1806; Cuny, Delphine; F; 11/28/23-8; 1/4; S; Daughter 1780; Yes; Yes; Id. U-11611 An. 1802

1807; Cuny, Carlos; M; 7/7/08-23; 1/4; S; Head 1781; Yes; Yes; Al. 2993 An. 1798

1808; Cuny, Lawrence; M; 1901-31; 1/4; M; Head 1782; Yes; Yes; Al. 2914 An. 1803
1809; Cuny, Beulah; F; 10/12/24-7; -1/4; S; Daughter 1783; Yes; Yes; Id. U-11411 An. 1804
1810; Cuny, Evelyn; F; 8/5/26-5; -1/4; S; Daughter 1784; Yes; Yes; Id. U-12104 An. none
1811; Cuny, Norma; F; 8/29/28-3; -1/4; S; Daughter 1785; Yes; Yes; Id. U-12845 An. none

1812; Cuny, Leroy; M; 1891-41; plus 1/4; M; Head 1786; Yes; Yes; Al. 3910 An. 1805
1813; Cuny, Louis; M; 5/3/15-16; 1/4; S; Son 1787; Yes; Yes; Id. U-9419 An. 1807
1814; Cuny, Francis I; F; 12/1/19-12; 1/4; S; Dau 1788; Yes; Yes; Id. U-9420 An. 1808

1815; Cuny, Grace; F; 6/1/13-18; 1/4; S; Head 1789; Yes; Yes; Al. 7520 N. 1806

Census of the **Pine Ridge** reservation of the **Pine Ridge, South Dakota** jurisdiction, as of **April 1**, 19**32,** taken by **James H. McGregor**, Superintendent.

Key: Number; Surname, Given; Sex; Date of Birth-Age at Last Birthday; Tribe (Oglala Sioux, unless stated otherwise); Degree of Blood; Marital Status; Relationship to Head of Family [Last Census Roll Number]; At Jurisdiction Where Enrolled (Yes/No); (If no – Where); Ward (Yes/No, if given); Allotment, Annuity and Identification Numbers (if given).

1816; Cottier, Sadie L; F; 6/3/30-1; 1/4; S; Daughter 1790; Yes; Yes; Id. U-13544 An. none

1817; Cuny, Wilson; M; 1893-39; plus 1/4; M; Head 1791; Yes; Yes; Al. 2911 An. 1810

1818; Cuny (Twiss), Florence; F; 1893-39; 1/4; M; Wife 1792; Yes; Yes; Al. 818 An. 1811

1819; Cuny, Elizabeth; F; 1/20/15-17; 1/4; S; Daughter 1793; Yes; Yes; Al. 7963 An. 1812

1820; Cuny, Alfonzo; M; 3/19/16-16; 1/4; S; Son 1794; Yes; Yes; Id. U-9421 An. 1813

1821; Cuny, Pearl; F; 6/1/18-13; 1/4; S; Daughter 1795; Yes; Yes; Id. U-9422 An. 1814

1822; Cuny, Louisa; F; 11/12/19-12; 1/4; S; Daughter 1796; Yes; Yes; Id. U-9423 An. 1815

1823; Cuny, Orvall; M; 5/9/21-10; 1/4; S; Son 1797; Yes; Yes; Id. U-10863 An. 1816

1824; Cuny, Robert; M; 11/20/25-6; 1/4; S; Son 1798; Yes; Yes; Id. U-11939 An. none

1825; Cuny, Willard; M; 11/18/27-4; 1/4; S; Son 1799; Yes; Yes; Id. U-12896 An. none

1826; Cuny, Elvin; M; 4/5/29-2; 1/4; S; Son 1800; Yes; Yes; Id. U-13242 An. none
1827; Cuny, Pansy; F; 7/16/30-1; 1/4; S; Daughter 1801; Yes; Yes; Id. U-13597 An. none

1828; Cuny, Mary Jane; F; 1/11/32-2/12; 1/4; S; Daughter; Yes; Yes; U-14088

1829; Curington (Daniels), Ruth; F; 1901-31; 1/4; M; Head 1802; No; Kadoka, Jackson Co, S.D; Yes; Al. 4061 An. 1817

1830; Curington, Joyce; F; 6/19/22-9; -1/4; S; Daughter 1803; No; Kadoka, Jackson Co, S.D; Yes; Id. U-13004 An. 1818

1831; Curington, Russell R; M; 8/25/23-8; -1/4; S; Son 1804; No; Kadoka, Jackson Co, S.D; Id. U-11572 An. 1819

1832; Curington, Norma Jean; F; 1/22/25-7; -1/4; S; Dau 1805; No; Kadoka, Jackson Co, S.D; Yes; Id. U-11571 An. 1820

1833; Currey (Cornett), Olive; F; 1902-30; plus 1/4; Wd; Head 1806; No; Chadron, Dawes Co, Nebr; Yes; Al. 3781 An. 1821

1834; Currey, Claude; M; 7/15/21-10; 1/4; S; Son 1807; No; Chadron, Dawes Co, Nebr; Yes; Id. U-10912 An. 1822

1835; Currey, Percy; M; 7/17/23-8; 1/4; S; Son 1808; No; Chadron, Dawes Co, Nebr; Yes; Id. U-11221 An. 1823

1836; Rios, Delores; F; 7/22/28-3; 1/4; S; Daughter 1809; No; Chadron, Dawes Co, Nebr; Yes; Id. U-12852 An. none

Census of the __Pine Ridge__ reservation of the __Pine Ridge, South Dakota__ jurisdiction, as of __April 1__, 1932, taken by __James H. McGregor__, Superintendent.

Key: Number; Surname, Given; Sex; Date of Birth-Age at Last Birthday; Tribe (Oglala Sioux, unless stated otherwise); Degree of Blood; Marital Status; Relationship to Head of Family [Last Census Roll Number]; At Jurisdiction Where Enrolled (Yes/No); (If no – Where); Ward (Yes/No, if given); Allotment, Annuity and Identification Numbers (if given).

1837; Rios, Francis; M; 2/6/30-2; 1/4; S; Son 1810; No; Chadron, Dawes Co, Nebr; Yes; Id. U-13424 An. none

1838; Curtis (Bettelyoun), Lillie; F; 1892-40; plus 1/4; M; Head 1811; Yes; Yes; Al. 2484 An. 1824
1839; Curtis, Elsie M; F; 11/15/18-13; -1/4; S; Daughter 1812; Yes; Yes; Id. U-9425 An. 1825
1840; Curtis, Edward C; M; 8/26/20-11; -1/4; S; Son 1813; Yes; Yes; Id. U-9426 An. 1827
1841; Curtis, Deloris F; F; 1/11/23-9; -1/4; S; Daughter 1814; Yes; Yes; Id. U-13000 An. 1828
1842; Curtis, Alice E; F; 11/13/24-7; -1/4; S; Daughter 1815; Yes; Yes; Id. U-11399 An. 1829
1843; Curtis, Verna M; F; 8/12; -1/4; S; Daughter; Yes; Yes; U-13866

1844; Cut, Ellis; M; 1883-49; F; Wd; Head 1816; Yes; Yes; Al. 6520 An. 1830

1845; Cut, Raymond; M; 1888-44; F; M; Head 1817; Yes; Yes; Al. 5646 An. 1832

1846; Cut (Holy Hock), Julia; F; 1892-40; F; M; Wife 1818; Yes; Yes; Al. 4267 An. 1833
1847; Cut, Isabel; F; 7/20/19-12; F; S; Daughter 1819; Yes; Yes; Id. U-9427 An. 1835
1848; Cut, Isaac; M; 5/20/24-7; F; S; Son 1820; Yes; Yes; Id. U-11319 An. none
1849; Cut, Martha; F; 3/14/29-3; F; S; Daughter 1821; Yes; Yes; Id. U-13136 An. none
1850; Cut, Julia E; F; 1/14/31-1; F; S; Daughter 1822; Yes; Yes; Id. U-13732 An. none

1851; Cut Grass, Fred; M; 1881-51; F; M; Head 1823; Yes; Yes; Al. 443 An. 1839
1852; Cut Grass (Long Soldier), Bessie; F; 1893-39; F; M; Wife 1824; Yes; Yes; Al. 506 An. 1840
1853; Cut Grass, Lydia; F; 9/21/21-10; F; S; Daughter 1825; Yes; Yes; Id. U-9452 An. 1841
1854; Cut Grass, Eddie; M; 1/22/24-8; F; S; Son 1826; Yes; Yes; Id. U-11177 An. 1842
1855; Cut Grass, Dora; F; 7/21/26-5; F; S; Daughter 1827; Yes; Yes; Id. U-11983 An. none

1856; Cut Off (no data); F; 1849-93; F; Wd; Head 1828; Yes; Yes; Al. 4955 An. 1844

~~N.E.   Cutnose, Theodore; M; 1899-33; Cheyenne; F; M; Head; Chey & Araphoe[sic]~~

Census of the **Pine Ridge** reservation of the **Pine Ridge, South Dakota** jurisdiction, as of **April 1**, 19**32,** taken by **James H. McGregor**, Superintendent.

Key: Number; Surname, Given; Sex; Date of Birth-Age at Last Birthday; Tribe (Oglala Sioux, unless stated otherwise); Degree of Blood; Marital Status; Relationship to Head of Family [Last Census Roll Number]; At Jurisdiction Where Enrolled (Yes/No); (If no – Where); Ward (Yes/No, if given); Allotment, Annuity and Identification Numbers (if given).

1857; Cutnose (High Eagle), Pearl; F; 11/19/02-29; plus 1/4; M; Wife 1829; No; Geary, Blaine Co, Okla; Al. 610 An. 2891

1858; Cutnose, Imogene; F; 8/4/24-7; Oglala Sioux-Cheyenne; S; Daughter 1830; No; Geary, Blaine Co, Okla; Id. U-12308 An. none

1859; Cutnose, Pendelton[sic]; M; 7/15/27-4; -1/4; S; Son 1831; No; Geary, Blaine Co, Okla; Yes; Id. U-12367 An. none

1860; Cutnose, Flora Ann; F; 8/31/29-2; -1/4; S; Daughter 1832; No; Geary, Blaine Co, Okla; Yes; Id. U-13265 An. none

1861; Darling, Henry; M; 4/21/08-23; plus 1/4; M; Head 1833; Yes; Yes; Id. U-9798 An. 6178

1862; Davidson, David; M; 1896-36; 1/4; S; Head 1834; Yes; Yes; Al. 1622 An. 1845

1863; Davidson, Edward; M; 1886-46; 1/4; S; Head 1835; Yes; Yes; Al. 1619 An. 1846

1864; Davidson (no data), Julia; F; 1854-78; 1/4; Wd; Head 1836; Yes; Yes; Al. 1616 An. 1848

1865; Davidson, William; M; 1880-52; 1/4; Wd; Head 1837; Yes; Yes; Al. 1618 An. 1849

1866; Day, David; M; 1880-52; 1/4; M; Head 1838; Yes; Yes; Al. 3833 An. 1851
1867; Day (Means), Josephine; F; 1872-60; 1/4; M; Wife 1839; Yes; Yes; Al. 7164 An. 1852

1868; Deaf and Dumb #1; F; 1867-65; F; S; Head 1840; Yes; Yes; Al. 6571 An. 1854

1869; Deaf and Dumb #2; M; 1867-65; F; Wd; Head 1841; Yes; Yes; Al. 3407 An. 1856

1870; Dearly; M; 1870-62; F; M; Head 1842; Yes; No; Al. 3317 An. 1856
1871; Dearly (no data), Virginia; F; 1867-65; F; M; Wife 1843; Yes; Yes; Al. 3318 An. 1857

1872; Dearly, Jimson; M; 1900-32; F; S; Head 1844; Yes; Yes; Al. 8211 An. 1858

1873; Dearly, Lucy; F; 11/18/02-29; F; S; Head 1845; Yes; Yes; Al. 8207 An. 1859

1874; Debredo, Evelyn; F; 7/27/14-17; F; S; Head 1846; No; Chilocco School, Oklahoma; Yes; Id. U-9710 An. 1861

Census of the __Pine Ridge__ reservation of the __Pine Ridge, South Dakota__ jurisdiction, as of __April 1__, 19**32**, taken by __James H. McGregor__, Superintendent.

Key: Number; Surname, Given; Sex; Date of Birth-Age at Last Birthday; Tribe (Oglala Sioux, unless stated otherwise); Degree of Blood; Marital Status; Relationship to Head of Family [Last Census Roll Number]; At Jurisdiction Where Enrolled (Yes/No); (If no – Where); Ward (Yes/No, if given); Allotment, Annuity and Identification Numbers (if given).

~~N.E. DeCory, George D; M; Rosebud Sioux; plus 1/4; M; Head~~
1875; DeCory (Swain), Lillian; F; 6/14/09-22; 1/4; M; Wife 1847; Yes; Yes; Al. 4071 An. 2107

~~N.E. DeMarsche, Joseph J; M; Rosebud Sioux; M; Head~~
1876; DeMarsche (Brown), Jennie; F; 1895-37; 1/4; M; Wife 1848; No; Lead, Lawrence Co, S.D; Yes; Al. 4020 An. 1092

1877; Deon, Gilbert; M; 1905-27; 1/4; S; Head 1849; No; Kansas City, Jackson Co, Mo; Yes; Al. 7431 An. 1862

1878; Deon, Louis, Jr; M; 1897-35; 1/4; Wd; Head 1850; No; Chadron, Dawes Co, Nebr; Al. 8235 An. 1863
1879; Deon, Nancy J; F; 5/25/28-3; -1/4; S; Daughter 1851; No; Rushville, Sheridan Co, Nebr; Yes; Id. U-13137 An. none

1880; Deon, Louis, Sr; M; 1870-62; plus 1/4; M; Head 1852; Yes; Yes; Al. 5001 An. 1864

1881; Deon (no data), Julia; F; 1876-56; 1/4; M; Wife 1853; Yes; Yes; Al. 5002 An. 1865
1882; Deon, Earl P; M; 11/17/08-23; 1/4; S; Son 1854; Yes; Yes; Al. 7432 An. 1866
1883; Deon, Ray; M; 2/25/10-22; 1/4; S; Son 1855; Yes; Yes; Al. 7433 An. 1867
1884; Deon, Evaline; F; 2/11/12-20; 1/4; S; Daughter 1856; Yes; Yes; Al. 7434 An. 1868
1885; Deon, Marie; F; 3/20/20-13; 1/4; S; Gr. Daughter 1857; No; Sac & Fox Sanatorium; ~~Toledo, Ohio;~~ Yes; Id. U-9432 An. 1878

1886; Deon, Richard; M; 1905-27; 1/4; M; Head 1858; Yes; Yes; Al. 6218 An. 1870

1887; Deon, Ross; M; 1899-33; 1/4; S; Head 1859; No; Unknown; Yes; Al. 6217An. 1871

1888; Deon, Samuel; M; 1872-60; F; M; Head 1860; Yes; Yes; Al. 4888 An. 1872
1889; Deon (no data), Alice; F; 1870-62; plus 1/4; M; Wife 1861; Yes; Yes; Al. 2246 An. 1873
1890; Janis, Eugene; M; 4/25/16-15; 1/4; S; Gr. Son 1862; Yes; Yes; Id. U-9766 An. 1876
1891; Janis, Frank L; M; 3/10/19-13; 1/4; S; Gr. Son 1863; Yes; Yes; Id. U-9767 An. 1877

1892; Deon, William; M; 1873-59; 1/4; M; Head 1864; Yes; Yes; Al. 5591 An. 1879
~~N.E. Deon (Good Walking); F; Ft. Peck; M; Wife~~

Census of the____**Pine Ridge**_____reservation of the___**Pine Ridge, South Dakota**
jurisdiction, as of____**April 1**_____, 19**32**, taken by____**James H. McGregor**____,
Superintendent.

Key: Number; Surname, Given; Sex; Date of Birth-Age at Last Birthday; Tribe (Oglala Sioux, unless stated otherwise); Degree of Blood; Marital Status; Relationship to Head of Family [Last Census Roll Number]; At Jurisdiction Where Enrolled (Yes/No); (If no – Where); Ward (Yes/No, if given); Allotment, Annuity and Identification Numbers (if given).

1893; Deon, Ward; M; 1895-37; -1/4; M; Head 1874; No; Scottsbluff; Scottsbluff Co, Neb; Yes; 6667 Ab, 1877

1894; Deon, Daniel D; M; 11/30/26-5; -1/4; S; Son 1875; No; Scottsbluff, Scottsbluff Co, Neb; Yes; Id. U-13207 An. none

1895; Deon, Donna L; F; 2/1/29-3; -1/4; S; Daughter 1876; No; Scottsbluff, Scottsbluff Co, Neb; Yes; Id. U-13208 An. none

~~N.E. DeSera, Alex; M; Rosebud Sioux; plus 1/4; M; Head~~
1896; DeSera (Turning Holy), Angelique; F; 1907-25; F; M; Wife 1877; Yes; Yes; Al. 2127 An. 6993

1897; Turning Holy, Tony; M; 4/22/24-7; F; S; S Son 1878; Yes; Yes; Id. U-11272 An. 6994

1898; DeSera, Bernice; F; 9/27/28-3; plus 1/4; S; Daughter 1879; Yes; Yes; Id. U-12809 An. none

~~N.E. Desera, Louis; M; Rosebud Sioux; plus 1/4; M; Head~~
1899; Desera (Stover), Laura; F; 1892-40; 1/4; M; Wife 1880; No; Rapid City, Pennington Co, S.D; Yes; Al. 1115 An. 1881

~~N.E. Desera, Leo W; M; Rosebud Sioux; 1/4; M; Head~~
1900; Desera (Rowland), Pearl; F; 1899-33; plus 1/4; M; Wife 5886; No; Rapid City, Pennington Co, S.D; Yes; Al. 1646 An. 5857

~~N.E. DeShequette, Jasper L; M; Lower Brule Sioux; plus 1/4; M; Head; Crow Creek Agency, S.D.~~
1901; DeShequette (Fog), Pearl; F; 1903-29; 1/4; M; Wife 1881; No; Crow Creek Agency, S.D; Yes; Al. 5879 An. 1882

1902; DeShequette, Gerald; M; 6/24/30-1; 1/4; S; Son 1883; No; Crow Creek Agency, S.D; Yes; Id. U-13687 An. none

1903; DeShequette, Irene; F; 5/31/27-4; 1/4; S; Daughter 1882; No; Crow Creek Agency, S.D; Yes; Id. U-13686 An. none

1904; DeWolf (Sears), Cora; F; 1894-38; plus 1/4; M; Head 1865; Yes; No; Al. 379 An. 6194

1905; Shields, Gerald; M; 7/4/12-19; -1/4; S; Son 1866; Yes; Yes; Al. 7421 An. 6195

1906; Shields, Cora E; F; 7/28/12-18; -1/4; S; Daughter 1867; Yes; Yes; Al. 7422 An. 6196

1907; Shields, Dora J; F; 8/19/16-15; -1/4; S; Daughter 1868; Yes; Yes; Id. U-10401 An. 6197

1908; Shields, Wendell; M; 10/17/19-12; -1/4; S; Son 1869; Yes; Yes; Id. U-10402 An. 6198

Census of the **Pine Ridge** reservation of the **Pine Ridge, South Dakota** jurisdiction, as of **April 1**, 19**32**, taken by **James H. McGregor**, Superintendent.

Key: Number; Surname, Given; Sex; Date of Birth-Age at Last Birthday; Tribe (Oglala Sioux, unless stated otherwise); Degree of Blood; Marital Status; Relationship to Head of Family [Last Census Roll Number]; At Jurisdiction Where Enrolled (Yes/No); (If no – Where); Ward (Yes/No, if given); Allotment, Annuity and Identification Numbers (if given).

1909; DeWolf, Helen; F; 10/5/26-5; -1/4; S; Daughter 1870; Yes; Yes; Id. U-12281 An. none

1910; DeWolf, Margaret; F; 4/8/24-7; -1/4; S; Daughter 1871; Yes; Yes; Id. U-12282 An. none

1911; DeWolf, Vera J;; F; 6/1/27-4; -1/4; S; Daughter 1872; Yes; Yes; Id. U-12752 An. none

1912; DeWolf, James H; M; 12/22/28-3; -1/4; S; Son 1873; Yes; Yes; Id. U-13688 An. none

1913; DeWolf, Alice M; F; 3/2/31-1; -1/4; S; Daughter; Yes; Yes; U-13801

1914; DeWolf, Frances E; F; 3/2/31-1; -1/4; S; Daughter; Yes; Yes; U-13802

~~N.E. Dial, Lawton; M; Osage; -1/4; M; Head~~

1915; Dial (Sears), Ollie; F; 1902-30; 1/4; M; Wife 1884; No; Arkansas City, Cowley Co, Kan; Yes; Al. 4757 An. 1883

1916; Dial, Dora; F; 2/25/21-11; Oglala Sioux-Osage; S; Daughter 1885; No; Arkansas City, Cowley Co, Kan; Yes; U-Id. U-12944 An. none

1917; Dial, Maxine; F; 4/30/24-7; Oglala Sioux-Osage; S; Daughter 1886; No; Arkansas City, Cowley Co, Kan; Yes; Id. U-12945 An. none

1918; Dial, Lawton M; M; 2/26/28-4; Oglala Sioux-Osage; S; Son 1887; No; Arkansas City, Cowley Co, Kan; Yes; Yes; Id. U-12946 An. none

1919; Dickinson (Lamb), Edith; F; 1899-33; -1/4; M; Head 1888; Yes; Yes; Al. 2581 An. 1884

1920; Dickinson, Dorothy; F; 3/14/21-11; -1/4; S; Daughter 1889; Yes; Yes; Id. U-11305 An. 1885

1921; Dickinson, Donald; M; 9/25/24-7; -1/4; S; Don 1890; Yes; Yes; said. U-11871 An. none

1922; Dillon, John; M; 1879-53; plus 1/4; S; Head 1891; No; Unknown; No; Al. 4727 An. 1886

1923; Dillon, Peter; M; 1880-52; 1/4; M; Head 1892; Yes; Yes; Al. 4509 An. 1887

1924; Dillon (no data), Emily; F; 1870-62; 1/4; M; Wife 1893; Yes; Yes; Al. 4511 An. 1888

1925; Dillon, Robert M; M; 4/23/09-22; 1/4; S; Son 1894; No; Chicago, Cook Co, Ill; Yes; Yes; Al 4540 An. 1890

1926; Dillon, Julia; F; 8/21/11-20; 1/4; S; Daughter 1895; Yes; Yes; Al. 7198 An. 1891

1927; Dillon, Rienzie; M; 1901-31; 1/4; M; Head 1896; Yes; Yes; Al. 4510 An. 1892

~~N.E. Dillon (Larvie), Susie; F; Rosebud Sioux; plus 1/4; M; Wife~~

Census of the **Pine Ridge** reservation of the **Pine Ridge, South Dakota** jurisdiction, as of **April 1**, 19**32,** taken by **James H. McGregor**, Superintendent.

Key: Number; Surname, Given; Sex; Date of Birth-Age at Last Birthday; Tribe (Oglala Sioux, unless stated otherwise); Degree of Blood; Marital Status; Relationship to Head of Family [Last Census Roll Number]; At Jurisdiction Where Enrolled (Yes/No); (If no – Where); Ward (Yes/No, if given); Allotment, Annuity and Identification Numbers (if given).

1928; Dillon, Purle; F; 11/26/21-10; 1/4; S; Daughter 1897; Yes; Yes; Id. U-9453 An. 1893

1929; Dillon, Tinnie; F; 1907-25; 1/4; S; Head 1898; Yes; Yes; Al. 4512 An. 1889

1930; Dismounts Thrice, Albert; M; 9/95-36; F; S; Head 1899; Yes; Yes; Al. 1770 An. 1896

1931; Dismounts Thrice, Edward; M; 1892-40; F; M; Head 1900; Yes; Yes; Al. 1769 An. 1897

1932; Dismounts Thrice, Edward, Jr; M; 3/19/19-13; F; S; Son 1901; Yes; Yes; Id; U-9434 An. 1899

1933; Dismounts Thrice, James; M; 1867-65; F; M; Head 1902; Yes; No; Al. 1440 An. 1900

1934; Distribution #2; M; 1873-59; F; M; Head 1903; Yes; Yes; Al. 4857 An. 1902
1935; Distribution (no data), Katie; F; 1877-55; F; M; Wife 1904; Yes; Yes; Id. U-9436 An. 1903
1936; Distribution, Nellie; F; 7/26/14-17; F; S; Daughter 1905; Yes; Yes; Id. U-9437 An. 1904
1937; Distribution, George; M; 7/2/25-6; F; S; Son 1906; Yes; Yes; Id. U-11652 An. none

1938; Distribution, Dewey; M; 1856-76; F; Wd; Head 1907; Yes; Yes; Al. 4214 An. 1905

1939; Dixon, Charles; M; 1906-26; plus 1/4; S; Head 1908; Yes; Yes; Al. 5457 An. 1909

1940; Dixon (no data), Elizabeth; F; 1870-62; 1/4; Wd; Head 1909; Yes; Yes; Al. 4[?]6 An. 1910
1941; Dixon, Evert D; M; 8/9/10-21; 1/4; S; Son 1910; Yes; Yes; Al. 5458 An. 1914

1942; Dixon, George; M; 11/98-33; plus 1/4; M; Head 1911; Yes; Yes; Al. 411 An. 1912
1943; Dixon, Georgia; F; 8/1/18-13; -1/4; S; Daughter 1912; Yes; Yes; Id. U-9441 An. 1913
1944; Dixon, Thomas; M; 5/26/19-12; -1/4; S; Son 1913; Yes; Yes; Id. U-9442 An. 1914

1945; Dixon, James G; M; 1892-40; plus 1/4; M; Head 1914; Yes; Yes; Al. 408 An. 1915

Census of the __**Pine Ridge**__ reservation of the __**Pine Ridge, South Dakota**__ jurisdiction, as of __**April 1**__, 19**32**, taken by __**James H. McGregor**__, Superintendent.

Key: Number; Surname, Given; Sex; Date of Birth-Age at Last Birthday; Tribe (Oglala Sioux, unless stated otherwise); Degree of Blood; Marital Status; Relationship to Head of Family [Last Census Roll Number]; At Jurisdiction Where Enrolled (Yes/No); (If no – Where); Ward (Yes/No, if given); Allotment, Annuity and Identification Numbers (if given).

1946; Dixon (Twiss), Lillian; F; 1898-34; 1/4; M; Wife 1915; Yes; Yes; Al. 830 An. 7037
1947; Dixon, Jesse; M; 2/22/24-8; 1/4; S; Son 1916; Yes; Yes; Id. U-11379 An. 7039
1948; Dixon, Doris; F; 10/11/27-4; 1/4; S; Daughter 1917; Yes; Yes; Id. U-13474 An. None

1949; Dixon, John Y; M; 1895-37; 1/4; M; Head 1918; Yes; Yes; Al. 410 An. 1921
1950; Dixon (Twiss-Knight), Clara; F; 1896-36; plus 1/4; M; Wife 3593; Yes; Yes; Al. 819 An. 3583
1951; Knight, Oliver; M; 11/5/15-16; 1/4; S; S Son 3594; Yes; Yes; Id-U-9821 An. 3584
1952; Knight, Helen; F; 10/11/18-13; 1/4; S; S Daughter 3595; Yes; Yes; Id. U-9822 An. 3585
1953; Dixon, Catherine; F; 7/25/23-8; 1/4; S; Daughter 1919; Yes; Yes; Id. U-12817 An. none
1954; Dixon, Mildred; F; 10/28/24-7; 1/4; S; Daughter 1920; Yes; Yes; Id. U-12818 An. none
1955; Dixon, Frederick; M; 5/28/30-1; 1/4; S; Son; Yes; Yes; U-14124
1956; Dixon, Raymond; M; 10/20/26-5; 1/4; S; Son; Yes; Yes; U-14125

1957; Dixon, William H; M; 1890-42; 1/4; M; Head 1921; Yes; No; Al. 407 An. 1923
1958; Dixon (Sears), Susan; 1888-44; 1/4; M; Wife 1922; Yes; Yes; Al. 378 An. 1924
1959; Dixon, Kenneth; M; 8/7/14-17; 1/4; S; Son 1923; Yes; Yes; Al. 7879 An. 1925
1960; Dixon, Lawrence; M; 4/14/16-15; plus 1/4; S; Son 1924; Yes; Yes; Al. 8266 An. 1926
1961; Dixon, Elizabeth; F; 11/14/18-13; 1/4; S; Daughter 1925; Yes; Yes; Id. U-9443 An. 1927
1962; Dixon, Grace L; F; 5/8/20-11; 1/4; S; Daughter 1926; Yes; Yes; Id. U-9444 An. 1928
1963; Dixon, Leona; F; 10/24/21-10; 1/4; S; Daughter 1927; Yes; Yes; Id. U-11092 An. 1929
1964; Dixon, William R; M; 9/14/23-9; 1/4; S; Son 1928; Yes; Yes; Id. U-11199 An. 1930
1965; Dixon, Vesla; F; 12/9/24-7; 1/4; S; Daughter 1929; Yes; Yes; Id. U-11409 An. 1931
1966; Dixon, Benjamin; M; 1/21/27-5; 1/4; S; Son 1930; Yes; Yes; Id. U-12242 An. none
1967; Dixon, Harold R; M; 11/15/28-3; 1/4; S; Son 1931; Yes; Yes; Id. U-12920 An. none

Census of the **Pine Ridge** reservation of the **Pine Ridge, South Dakota** jurisdiction, as of **April 1**, 19**32**, taken by **James H. McGregor**, Superintendent.

Key: Number; Surname, Given; Sex; Date of Birth-Age at Last Birthday; Tribe (Oglala Sioux, unless stated otherwise); Degree of Blood; Marital Status; Relationship to Head of Family [Last Census Roll Number]; At Jurisdiction Where Enrolled (Yes/No); (If no – Where); Ward (Yes/No, if given); Allotment, Annuity and Identification Numbers (if given).

1968; Dog, William; M; 1894-38; F; M; Head 1932; Yes; Yes; Al. 753 An. 1932
1969; Dog (White Lance), Lucy; F; 1904-28; F; M; Wife 1934; Yes; Yes; Al. 1546 An. 826
1970; Dog, Winadel; F; 11/17/24-7; F; S; Daughter 1933; Yes; Yes; Id. U-11376 An. 1936
1971; Dog, Daniel; M; 11/11/29-2; F; S; Son 1935; Yes; Yes; Id. U-13286 An. none
1972; Dog, Doris; F; 1/26/32-2/12; F; S; Daughter; Yes; Yes; U-14061

1973; Dog Chief, Joseph; M; 1871-61; F; M; Head 1936; Yes; Yes; Al. 930 An. 1937
1974; Dog Chief (no data), Mary; F; 1866-66; F; M; Wife 1937; Yes; Yes; Al. 6661 An. 1938

N.E. Dog Trail, Bert; M; Rosebud Sioux; M; Head
1975; Dog Trail (Mousseau), Mary; F; 1901-31; plus 1/4; M; Wife 1938; Yes; Yes; Al. 2210 An. 264

1976; Dopson (Ryan), Rose; F; 1885-47; 1/4; M; Head 1939; No; Oakland, Alameda Co, Cal; Yes; Al. 4279 An. 1943

1977; Dreamer, Aaron; M; 1891-41; F; M; Head 1940; Yes; Yes; Al. 6163 An. 1944
1978; Dreamer (Gillispie), Maggie; F; 1891-41; plus 1/4; M; Wife 1941; Yes; Yes; Al. 3251 An. 2489

1979; Dreamer, George; M; 1895-37; F; Wd; Head 1942; Yes; Yes; Al. 4035 An. 1946
1980; Dreamer, Juline; F; 12/28/26-5; F; S; Daughter 1943; Yes; Yes; Id. U-12234 An. none

1981; Dreaming Bear, Herbert; M; 1901-31; F; M; Head 1944; Yes; Yes; Al. 6153 An. 1947
1982; Dreaming Bear (Brown Ear Horse), Mary; F; 1/15/10-22; F; M; Wife 1945; Yes; Yes; Al. 6197 An. 1121
1983; Dreaming Bear, Doris; F; 3/26/28-4; F; S; Daughter 1946; Yes; Yes; Id. U-12679 An. none
1984; Dreaming Bear, Victor; M; 2/4/31-1; F; S; Son 1947; Yes; Yes; Id. U-13733 An. none

1985; Dreaming Bear (Cheyenne), Effie; F; 1865-67; F; Wd; Head 1948; Yes; Yes; Al. 3064 An. 1949

1986: Dripping, Jacob; M; 5/4/09-23; plus 1/4; S; Head; 1949; Yes; Yes; Al. 6113 An. 6751

Census of the **Pine Ridge** reservation of the **Pine Ridge, South Dakota** jurisdiction, as of **April 1**, 19**32**, taken by **James H. McGregor**, Superintendent.

Key: Number; Surname, Given; Sex; Date of Birth-Age at Last Birthday; Tribe (Oglala Sioux, unless stated otherwise); Degree of Blood; Marital Status; Relationship to Head of Family [Last Census Roll Number]; At Jurisdiction Where Enrolled (Yes/No); (If no – Where); Ward (Yes/No, if given); Allotment, Annuity and Identification Numbers (if given).

1987: Dripping, James; M; 1905-27; 1/4; S; Head; 1950; Yes; Yes; Al. 7606 An. 1951

1988: Dripping, Mark; M; 1892-40; F; M; Head; 1952; Yes; Yes; Al. 7601 An. 1954

1989: Dripping (Iron Wing), Maggie; F; 1869-63; F; M; Wife; 1953; Yes; Yes; Al. 3400 An. 1955

1990: Dripping, Philip; M; 1884-48; F; Wd.; Head; 1954; Yes; Yes; Al. 8097 An. 1956

1991: Dubray, Baptiste; M; 1889-46; plus 1/4; M; Head; 1955; Yes; Yes; Al. 4497 An. 1957

1992: Dubray (Cottier), Pearl; F; 1897-35; 1/4; M; Wife; 1956; Yes; Yes; Al. 994 An. 1958

1993; Dubray, John; M; 8/8/12-19; 1/4; S; Son 1957; Yes; Yes; Id. Al.-6932 An. 1959

1994; Dubray, Rose; F; 12/18/13-18; 1/4; S; Daughter 1958; Yes; Yes; Id. U-9458 An. 1960

1995: Dubray, Charles Sr.; M; 1873-59; plus 1/4; M; Head; 1959; Yes; Yes; Al. 4485 An. 1962

1996: Dubray (Cribb), Elizabeth; F; 1878-54; 1/4; M; Wife; 1960; Yes; Yes; Al. 4486 An. 1963

1997; Dubray, Louisa; F; 10/18/14-17; 1/4; S; Daughter 1961; Yes; Yes; Id. U-9459 An. 1965

1998; Dubray, Cynthia; F; 6/3/17-14; 1/4; S; Daughter 1962; Yes; Yes; Id. U-9460 An. 1966

1999: Dubray, Charles Jr.; M; 1906-26; 1/4; S; Head; 1963; Yes; Yes; Al. 4491 An. 1961

2000: Dubray, Cleveland; M; 1902-30; 1/4; M; Head; 1964; Yes; Yes; Al. 4489 An. 1967

2001: Dubray (Wilde), Edna; F; 1905-27; 1/4; M; Wife; 1965; Yes; Yes; Al. 3761 An. 1968

2002; Dubray, Grace; F; 4/11/24-7; 1/4; S; Daughter 1966; Yes; Yes; Id. U-11265 An. 1969

2003: Dubray, Eugene; M; 1896-36; 1/4; M; Head; 1967; Yes; Yes; Al. 4487 An. 1970

2004: Dubray (Hawkins), Eva; F; 1905-27; 1/4; M; Wife; 1968; Yes; Yes; Al. 4626 An. 1971

Census of the **Pine Ridge** reservation of the **Pine Ridge, South Dakota** jurisdiction, as of **April 1**, 19**32,** taken by **James H. McGregor**, Superintendent.

Key: Number; Surname, Given; Sex; Date of Birth-Age at Last Birthday; Tribe (Oglala Sioux, unless stated otherwise); Degree of Blood; Marital Status; Relationship to Head of Family [Last Census Roll Number]; At Jurisdiction Where Enrolled (Yes/No); (If no – Where); Ward (Yes/No, if given); Allotment, Annuity and Identification Numbers (if given).

2005; Dubray, James C; M; 6/16/25-6; 1/4; S; Son 1969; Yes; Yes; Id. U.-11678 An. none

2006; Dubray, Dave; M; 8/20/26-5; 1/4; S; Son 1970; Yes; Yes; Id. U.-12134 An. none

2007; Dubray, Everett; M; 11/10/27-4; 1/4; S; Son 1971; Yes; Yes; Id. U.-12368 An. none

2008; Dubray, Amelia; F; 4/4/29-2; 1/4; S; Daughter 1972; Yes; Yes; Id. U-13209 An. none

2009; Dubray, Ora Jennie; F; 11/27/30-1; 1/4; S; Daughter 1973; Yes; Yes; Id. U-13660 An. none

2010: Dubray, George; M; 1900-32; plus 1/4; M; Head; 1974; Yes; Yes; Al. 4488 An. 1972

2011: Dubray (Richard), Ollie; F; 1899-33; F; M; Wife; 1975; Yes; Yes; Al. 2343 An. 5722

2012; Dubray, Leo; M; 5/26/27-4; Plus 1/4; S; Son 1976; Yes; Yes; Id. U.-12680 An. none

2013; Dubray, Gordon; M; 9/12/29-2; 1/4; S; Son 1977; Yes; Yes; Id. U.-13368 An. none

2014; Dubray, Annie M; F; 5/6/31-10/12; plus 1/4; S; Daughter ---; Yes; Yes; U-13867

2015: Dull Knife, George; M; 1875-57; F; M; Head; 1978; Yes; Yes; Al. 1884 An. 1975

2016: Dull Knife (Red Rabbit), Mary; F; 1876-56; F; M; Wife; 1979; Yes; Yes; Al. 2116 An. 1976

2017: Dull Knife, Geoffrey; M; 4/6/12-19; F; S; Son 1980; Yes; Yes; Id. Al. 7032 An. 1978

2018: Dull Knife, Eunice; F; 1/9/14-18; F; S; Daughter 1981; Yes; Yes; Id. U-9461 An. 1979

2019: Dull Knife, Daniel; M; 6/2/21-10; F; S; Son 1982; Yes; Yes; Id. Al. U-9464 An. 1982

2020: Dull Knife, Guy; M; 1899-33; F; M; Head; 1983; Yes; Yes; Al. 2137 An. 1983
2021: Dull Knife (Bull Bear), Rosa; F; 1907-25; F; M; Wife; 1984; Yes; Yes; Al. 5853 An. 1204

2022: Dunbar (Pourier), Ella; F; 1886-46; F; M; Head; 1985; Yes; Yes; Al. 4472 An. 5069

2023: Eagle, (no data); ---; F; 1853-79; F; Wd.; Head; 1986; Yes; Yes; Al. 6648 An. 1984

Census of the **Pine Ridge** reservation of the **Pine Ridge, South Dakota** jurisdiction, as of **April 1**, 19**32**, taken by **James H. McGregor**, Superintendent.

Key: Number; Surname, Given; Sex; Date of Birth-Age at Last Birthday; Tribe (Oglala Sioux, unless stated otherwise); Degree of Blood; Marital Status; Relationship to Head of Family [Last Census Roll Number]; At Jurisdiction Where Enrolled (Yes/No); (If no – Where); Ward (Yes/No, if given); Allotment, Annuity and Identification Numbers (if given).

2024: Eagle Bear; ---; F; 1858-74; F; Wd.; Head; 1987; Yes; Yes; Al. 613 An. 1985

2025: Eagle Bear, James; M; 1878-54; F; M; Head; 1988; Yes; Yes; Al. 130 An. 1986

2026: Eagle Bear (Bull Tail), Stella; F; 1897-35; F; M; Wife; 1989; Yes; Yes; Al. 603 An. 1987

2027; Eagle Bear, Lydia; F; 5/2/18-13; F; S; Daughter 1990; Yes; Yes; Id. U-9467 An. 1988

2028; Eagle Bear, Esther; F; 2/11/22-10; F; S; Daughter 1991; Yes; Yes; Id. U-10952 An. 1989

2029; Eagle Bear, Ephraim; M; 2/11/22-10; F; S; Son 1992; Yes; Yes; Id. U-10953 An. 1990

2030; Eagle Bear, Zona; F; 5/5/28-3; F; S; Daughter 1993; Yes; Yes; Id. U-12793 An. None

2031; Eagle Bear, Bertha; F; 5/6/24-7; F; S; Daughter 1994; Yes; Yes; Id. U-12921 An. None

2032; Eagle Bear, Wilfred; M; 12/10/31-3/12; F; S; Son ---; Yes; Yes; U-14089

2033: Eagle Bird, William; M; 1877-55; F; M; Head; 1996; Yes; Yes; Al. 2819 An. 1992

2034: Eagle Bird (Good Weasel), Etta; F; 1872-60; F; M; Wife; 1997; Yes; Yes; Al. 6356 An. 1993

2035; Eagle Bird, David; M; 3/4/14-18; F; S; S.Son 1998; Yes; Yes; Id. 7669 An. 1995

2036; Thunder Tail, Edith; F; 1/13/27-5; F; S; Ward 1999; Yes; Yes; Id. U-12270 An. None

2037: Eagle Bull, Henry; M; 1877-55; F; M; Head; 2000; Yes; Yes; Al. 1289 An. 2006

2038: Eagle Bull (Parts His Hair), Emma; F; 1885-47; F; M; Wife; 2001; Yes; Yes; Al. 1388 An. 2007

2039; Eagle Bull, Cecelia; F; 11/3/31-10; F; S; Daughter 2002; Yes; Yes; Id. U-10899 An. 2010

2040; Eagle Bull, Emma; F; 6/24/23-8; F; S; Daughter 2003; Yes; Yes; Id. U-14804 An. 2011

2041; Eagle Bull, Mercy; F; 3/15/25-7; F; S; Daughter 2004; Yes; Yes; Id. U-11604 An. 2012

2042: Eagle Bull, John J; M; 1900-32; F; M; Head; 2005; Yes; Yes; Al. 1392 An. 2013

2043: Eagle Bull (Make Shine), Jessie; F; 1907-25; F; M; Wife; 2006; Yes; Yes; Al. 4994 An. 2014

Census of the **Pine Ridge** reservation of the **Pine Ridge, South Dakota** jurisdiction, as of **April 1**, 19**32**, taken by **James H. McGregor**, Superintendent.

Key: Number; Surname, Given; Sex; Date of Birth-Age at Last Birthday; Tribe (Oglala Sioux, unless stated otherwise); Degree of Blood; Marital Status; Relationship to Head of Family [Last Census Roll Number]; At Jurisdiction Where Enrolled (Yes/No); (If no – Where); Ward (Yes/No, if given); Allotment, Annuity and Identification Numbers (if given).

2044; Eagle Bull, Chester; M; 12/25/29-2; F; S; Son 2008; Yes; Yes; Id. U-13377 An. none

2045; Eagle Bull, William Jr.; M; 2/4/31-1; F; S; Son 2009; Yes; Yes; Id. U-13734 An. none

2046: Eagle Bull, William; M; 4/30/03-28; F; S; Head; 2010; Yes; Yes; Al. 1391 An. 2015

2047: Eagle Elk; M; 1851-81; F; M; Head; 2011; Yes; Yes; Al. 6051 An. 2016

2048: Eagle Elk (Red Ring); F; 1860-72; F; M; Wife; 2012; Yes; Yes; Al. 6489 An. 2017

2049: Eagle Elk, #1; M; 1859-73; F; Wd.; Head; 2013; Yes; Yes; Al. 3498 An. 2019

2050: Eagle Elk, Alexander; M; 1904-28; F; M; Head; 2014; Yes; Yes; Al. 501 An. 2020

2051: Eagle Elk (War Bonnet), Jennie; F; 1906-26; F; M; Wife; 2015; Yes; Yes; Al. 6953 An. 7305

2052; Eagle Elk, Morris E; M; 6/19/30-1; F; S; Son 2016; Yes; Yes; U-13527 An. none

2053: Eagle Elk, George; M; 1896-36; F; M; Head; 2017; Yes; Yes; Al. 6632 An. 2021

2054: Eagle Elk (High Crane), Nancy; F; 1902-30; F; M; Wife; 2018; Yes; Yes; Al. 7418 An. 2022

2055; Eagle Elk, Clara; F; 2/9/22-10; F; S; Daughter 2019; Yes; Yes; Id. U-1086 An. 2023

2056; Eagle Elk, Pearl; F; 7/16/27-4; F; S; Daughter 2020; Yes; Yes; Id. U-12364 An. none

2057: Eagle Fox, (no data), Mary; F; 1877-55; F; Wd.; Head; 2022; Yes; Yes; Al. 4337 An. 2028

2058: Eagle Fox, Thomas; M; 1898-34; F; M; Head; 2023; Yes; Yes; Al. 766 An. 2029

2059: Eagle Fox (Yellow Thunder), Julia; F; 1901-31; F; M; Wife; 2024; Yes; Yes; Al. 1365 An. 2030

2060; Eagle Fox, Grace; F; 10/15/23-8; F; S; Daughter 2025; Yes; Yes; Id. U-11144 An. 2032

2061; Eagle Fox, Josephine; F; 10/8/27-4; F; S; Daughter 2026; Yes; Yes; Id. U-12402 An. none

Census of the ____Pine Ridge____ reservation of the __Pine Ridge, South Dakota__ jurisdiction, as of ____April 1____, 1932, taken by ____James H. McGregor____, Superintendent.

Key: Number; Surname, Given; Sex; Date of Birth-Age at Last Birthday; Tribe (Oglala Sioux, unless stated otherwise); Degree of Blood; Marital Status; Relationship to Head of Family [Last Census Roll Number]; At Jurisdiction Where Enrolled (Yes/No); (If no – Where); Ward (Yes/No, if given); Allotment, Annuity and Identification Numbers (if given).

2062: Eagle Hand, (No Data); F; 1848-84; F; Wd.; Head; 2027; Yes; Yes; Al. 5709 An. 2033

2063: Eagle Hawk, Joseph; M; 1869-63; F; M; Head; 2028; Yes; Yes; Al. 3107 An. 2034

2064: Eagle Hawk, (no data), Agnes; F; 1872-60; F; M; Wife; 2029; Yes; Yes; Al. 7614 An. 2035

~~N.E.: Eagle Hawk, Raymond; M; ------; Rosebud Sioux; F; M; Head;~~

2065: Eagle Hawk (Cut Grass), Louisa; F; 1891-31; F; M; Wife; 2030; Yes; Yes; Al. 444 An. 1843

2066: Eagle Hawk, Samuel; M; 1892-40; F; M; Head; 2031; Yes; Yes; Al. 6144 An. 2036

2067: Eagle Hawk (Brown Dog), Eva; F; 1883-49; F; M; Wife; 2032; Yes; Yes; Al. 3115 An. 2037

2068: Eagle Hawk, Nelson; M; 3/11/10-22; F; S; S. Son 2033; Yes; Yes; Al. 6145 An. 2038

2069: Eagle Hawk, Tibbits; M; 9/29/22-9; F; S; S. Son 2035; Yes; Yes; Id.. U-11090 An. 2041

2070: Eagle Hawk, Lester; M; 2/27/29-3; F; S; Son 2037; Yes; Yes; Id. U-13105 An. none

2071: Eagle Hawk, Joseph; M; 9/12/20-11; F; S; Son 2034; Yes; Yes; Id. U-9477 An. 2040

2072: Eagle Heart; M; 1867-65; F; M; Head; 2038; Yes; Yes; Al. 1429 An. 2044

2073: Eagle Heart (Pretty Woman), Bessie; F; 1875-57; F; M; Wife; 2039; Yes; Yes; Al. 1451 An. 2045

2074: Eagle Heart, Noah; M; 4/19/10-21; F; S; Head; 2040; Yes; Yes; Al. 5954 An. 2047

2075: Eagle Heart, Matthew; M; 1906-26; F; M; Head; 2041; Yes; Yes; Al. 6873 An. 2049

2076: Eagle Heart (Thunder Bull), Mabel; F; 1906-26; plus 1/4; M; Wife; 2042; Yes; Yes; Al. 5371 An. 6884

2077; Eagle Heart, Victoria; F; 3/28/26-6; 1/4; S; Daughter 2043; Yes; Yes; Id. U-11940 An. none

2078; Eagle Heart, Eddie; M; 5/23/28-3; 1/4; S; Son 2044; Yes; Yes; Id. U-12620 An. none

2079: Eagle Hand (no data), Agnes; F; 1852-80; F; Wd.; Head; 2045; Yes; Yes; Al. 6862 An. 2051

Census of the ___Pine Ridge___ reservation of the ___Pine Ridge, South Dakota___ jurisdiction, as of ___April 1___, 19**32,** taken by ___James H. McGregor___, Superintendent.

Key: Number; Surname, Given; Sex; Date of Birth-Age at Last Birthday; Tribe (Oglala Sioux, unless stated otherwise); Degree of Blood; Marital Status; Relationship to Head of Family [Last Census Roll Number]; At Jurisdiction Where Enrolled (Yes/No); (If no – Where); Ward (Yes/No, if given); Allotment, Annuity and Identification Numbers (if given).

2080: Eagle Horse, John, Jr.; M; 1880-52; F; M; Head; 2046; Yes; Yes; Al. 277 An. 2052

2081: Eagle Horse (Yankton), Sallie; F; 1863-69; F; M; Wife; 2047; Yes; Yes; Al. 1159 An. 2053

2082; Calligo, Catherine; F; 7/6/22-9; plus 1/4; S; Ward 2048; Yes; Yes; Id. U-12004 An. 2375

2083: Eagle Louse, Charles; M; 1884-48; F; M; Head; 2049; Yes; Yes; Al. 6568 An. 2054

2084: Eagle Louse (Little Soldier), Sallie; F; 1886-46; F; M; Wife; 2050; Yes; Yes; Al. 3385 An. 2055

2085; Eagle Louse, Adolph; M; 10/11/16-15; F; S; Son 2051; Yes; Yes; Id. U-9480 An. 2056

2086; Eagle Louse, Sylvia; F; 3/7/21-11; F; S; Daughter 2052; Yes; Yes; Id. U-9481 An. none

2087; Eagle Louse, Charles Jr; M; 1/12/29-3; F; S; Son 2053; Yes; Yes; Id. U-12968 An. none

2088: Eagle Louse, John; M; 1882-50; F; Wd.; Head; 2054; Yes; Yes; Al. 3411 An. 2058

N.E.: Eagle Man, Alfred; M; ------; Rosebud Sioux; F; M; Head;

2089: Eagle Man (Red Tomahawk), Julia; F; 1897-35; F; M; Wife; 5600; Yes; Yes; Al. 4828 An. 5590

2090: Eagle Pipe, Charles; M; 1856-76; F; M; Head; 2055; Yes; Yes; Al. 601 An. 2061

2091: Eagle Man (Red Crow), Maggie; F; 1857-75; F; M; Wife; 2056; Yes; Yes; Al. 6905 An. 5389

2092; Thunder Hawk, Francis; M; 8/12/21-10; plus 1/4; S; Ward 2057; Yes; Yes; Id. U-12090 An. 6904

2093; Thunder Hawk, Vincent; M; 1/23/23-9; 1/4; S; Ward 2058; Yes; Yes; Id. U-12091 An. 6905

N.E.: Eagle Road, Charles; M; ------; Rosebud Sioux; F; M; Head;

2094: Eagle Man (Red Fish), Lizzie; F; 1903-29; F; M; Wife; 2059; Yes; Yes; Al. 2398 An. 2064

2095: Eagle Shirt, William; M; 1873-59; F; M; Head; 2061; Yes; Yes; Al. 5998 An. 2067

2096: Eagle Shirt (Good Lance), Emma; F; 1873-59; F; M; Wife; 2062; Yes; Yes; Al. 7215 An. 2068

Census of the **Pine Ridge** reservation of the **Pine Ridge, South Dakota** jurisdiction, as of **April 1**, 1932, taken by **James H. McGregor**, Superintendent.

Key: Number; Surname, Given; Sex; Date of Birth-Age at Last Birthday; Tribe (Oglala Sioux, unless stated otherwise); Degree of Blood; Marital Status; Relationship to Head of Family [Last Census Roll Number]; At Jurisdiction Where Enrolled (Yes/No); (If no – Where); Ward (Yes/No, if given); Allotment, Annuity and Identification Numbers (if given).

2097: Eagle Tail Feather (no data), Stella; F; 1876-66; F; Wd.; Head; 2063; Yes; Yes; Al. 842 An. 2070

N.E.: Eagle Thunder, Nicholas; M; ------; Rosebud Sioux; F; M; Head;
2098: Eagle Thunder (Little Elk), Viola; F; 1911-21; F; M; Wife; 2064; Yes; Yes; Al. 10636 An. 3311

2099: Eagle Woman (no data); ---; F; 1863-69; F; Wd.; Head; 2065; Yes; Yes; Al. 6056 An. 1895

N.E.: Eastman, Rufus; M; ------; Rosebud Sioux; --; M; Head; --; Yes; Yes;
2100: Eagle Thunder (Young), Lottie; F; 1904-28; plus 1/4; M; Wife; 2066; No; Rosebud, S.D.; Yes; Al. 2520 An. 7985
2101; Young, Louise; F; 7/7/27-4; 1/4; S; S.Daughter 2067; No; Rosebud, S.D.; Yes; Id. U-9483 An. none

2102: Ecoffey, Albert Sr.; M; 1884-48; 1/4; M; Head; 2068; Yes; Yes; Al. 5614 An. 2072
2103; Ecoffey, Joseph; M; 4/30/18-13; 1/4; S; Son 2070; Yes; Yes; Id. U-9483 An. 2077
2104; Ecoffey, John; M; 3/2/23-9; 1/4; S; Son 2071; Yes; Yes; Id. U-12092 An. 2078

2105: Ecoffey, Rosamond; F; 12/19/11-20; 1/4; S; Head; 2072; Yes; Yes; Al. 61719 An. 2075
2106; Ecoffey, Kenneth; M; 9/4/30-1; 1/4; S; Son 2073; Yes; Yes; Id. U-13599 An. none

2107: Ecoffey, Albert Jr.; M; 3/22/08-24; 1/4; S; Head; 2068; No; Miles City, town Custer, Mont.; Yes; Al. 5616 An. 2074

2108: Ecoffeym[sic], Evelyn; F; 1908-24; plus 1/4; S; Head; 2075; Yes; Yes; Al. 5494 An. 2085

2109: Ecoffey, Frankey; M; 1901-31; 1/4; M; Head; 2076; No; Gordon, town Sheridan, Nebr.; Yes; Al. 1362 An. 2080
2110; Ecoffey, Betty Lou; F; 2/10/22-10; 1/4; S; Daughter 2077; No; Same; Yes; Id. U-10918 An. 2081
2111; Ecoffey, Catherine; F; 1/19/24-8; 1/4; S; Daughter 2078; No; Same; Yes; Id. U-11330 An. 2082
2112; Ecoffey, Frank; M; 2/8/26-6; 1/4; S; Son 2079; No; Same; Yes; Id. U-11941 An. none

Census of the **Pine Ridge** reservation of the **Pine Ridge, South Dakota** jurisdiction, as of **April 1**, 19**32,** taken by **James H. McGregor**, Superintendent.

Key: Number; Surname, Given; Sex; Date of Birth-Age at Last Birthday; Tribe (Oglala Sioux, unless stated otherwise); Degree of Blood; Marital Status; Relationship to Head of Family [Last Census Roll Number]; At Jurisdiction Where Enrolled (Yes/No); (If no – Where); Ward (Yes/No, if given); Allotment, Annuity and Identification Numbers (if given).

2113: Ecoffey, Joseph; M; 1877-55; 1/4; M; Head; 2080; Yes; Yes; Al. 1360 An. 2083

2114; Ecoffey, (no data), Rosa; F; 1880-52; 1/4; M; Wife 2081; Yes; Yes; Al. 4634 An. 2084

2115; Ecoffey, Ed Ross; M; 7/4/13-12; 1/4; S; Son 2082; Yes; Yes; Al. 7791 An. 2087

2116; Ecoffey, Lawrence; M; 10/18/15-16; 1/4; S; Son 2083; Yes; Yes; Id. U-9482 An. 2088

2117; McDaniels, Paul A; M; 9/12/27-4; 1/4; S; Gr. Son 2084; Yes; Yes; Id. U-12462 An. none

2118: Ecoffey, Jules Sr.; M; 1874-58; 1/4; M; Head; 2085; Yes; Yes; Al. 1358 An. 2089

2119: Ecoffey (Yellow Bird), Alice; F; 1875-57; 1/4; M; Wife; 2086; Yes; Yes; Al. 5451 An. 2090

2120: Ecoffey, Jule Jr.; M; 1895-37; 1/4; S; Head; 2087; Yes; Yes; Al. 1359 An. 2091

2121: Ecoffey, Jules; M; 1906-26; plus 1/4; S; Head; 2088; Yes; Yes; Al. 5615 An. 2092

2122: Eisenbraun (Thompson), Hazel; F; 12/22/08-23; -1/4; M; Head; 2089; Yes; Yes; Al. 6678 An. 6854

2123; Eisenbraun, John M; M; 3/15/28-4; -1/4; S; Son 2090; Yes; Yes; Id. U-12992 An. none

2124; Eisenbraun, Theo M; M; 11/27/29-2; -1/4; S; Son 2091; Yes; Yes; Id. U-13378 An. none

2125; Eisenbraun, Donald; M; 6/1/31-10/12; -1/4; S; Son 2090; Yes; Yes; U-12992

2126: Elk Boy, Joseph; M; 1883-49; F; M; Head; 2092; Yes; Yes; Al. 4418 An. 2099

2127: Elk Boy, Ira; M; 12/4/12-19; F; M; Head; 4177; Yes; Yes; Al. 7498 An. 2102

2128: Elk Boy, (Hard Heart), Helen; F; 11/17/10-21; F; M; Wife; 2742; Yes; Yes; Al. 5525 An. 2729

2129: Elrod, (Swain), Eva; F; 1884-48; plus 1/4; Wd.; Head; 2094; Yes; Yes; Al. 4068 An. 2104

N.E.: Emery, Vital; M; -------; Rosebud Sioux; 1/4; M; Head;

Census of the __Pine Ridge__ reservation of the __Pine Ridge, South Dakota__ jurisdiction, as of __April 1__, 1932, taken by __James H. McGregor__, Superintendent.

Key: Number; Surname, Given; Sex; Date of Birth-Age at Last Birthday; Tribe (Oglala Sioux, unless stated otherwise); Degree of Blood; Marital Status; Relationship to Head of Family [Last Census Roll Number]; At Jurisdiction Where Enrolled (Yes/No); (If no – Where); Ward (Yes/No, if given); Allotment, Annuity and Identification Numbers (if given).

2130: Emery, (Young), Florence; F; 1899-33; 1/4; M; Wife; 2742; No; Rosebud, S.D.; Yes; Al. 1792 An. 2108

N.E.: Emery, Clarence; M; ---- ---; Rosebud Sioux; plus 1/4; M; Head;
2131: Emery, (Young), Nellie; F; 1906-26; 1/4; M; Wife; 2096; No; Rosebud, S.D.; Yes; Al. 2521 An. 7987

2132: Evans, (Peck), Julia; F; 1857-75; 1/4; M; Head; 2097; Yes; Yes; Al. 2254 An. 2109

2133: Evans, (Sickler), Ruby; F; 1903-29; plus 1/4; M; Head; 2098; Yes; Yes; Al. 3845 An. 2110
2134: Evans, Mildred; F; 7/10/23-8; 1/4; S; Daughter; 2099; Yes; Yes; Al. U-14029 An. 2111
2135: Evans, Myrtle; F; 10/26/24-7; 1/4; S; Daughter; 2100; Yes; Yes; Al. U-11391 An. 2112
2136: Evans, Norman; M; 8/15/26-5; 1/4; S; Son; 2101; Yes; Yes; Al. U-12106 An. none
2137: Evans, Ralph; M; 7/9/28-3; 1/4; S; Son; 2102; Yes; Yes; Al. U-12738 An. none

2138: Farnham, (no data), Ellen; F; 1855-77; F; M; Head; 2103; No; Interior, town, Jackson, S.D.; Yes; Al. 3786 An. 2113

2139: Fast, ---; M; 1839-93; F; M; Head; 2104; Yes; Yes; Al. 3316 An. 2114
2140: Fast (notdata[sic]), Mattie; F; 1864-68; F; M; Wife; 2105; Yes; Yes; Al. 6243 An. 2115

2141: Fast, Lottie; F; 1889-43; F; S; Head; 2106; Yes; Yes; Al. 6244 An. 2116

2142: Fast, Samuel; M; 1887-45; F; M; Head; 2107; Yes; Yes; Al. 6620 An. 2117
2143: Fast (Iron Bull), Eva; F; 1883-49; F; M; Wife; 2108; Yes; Yes; Al. 3211 An. 3143
2144: Iron Bull, Olive; F; 12/7/14-17; F; S; S.Daughter; 2109; Yes; Yes; Al. 8015 An. 3144
2145: Iron Bull, Daniel; M; 1/19/17-15; F; S; S.Son; 2110; Yes; Yes; Id. U-9728 An. 3145
2146: Fast, Joseph; M; 4/21/31-11/12; F; S; Son; ---; Yes; Yes; U-13803

2147: Fast, Thomas; M; 6/6/09-22; F; M; Head; 2111; Yes; Yes; Al. 7014 An. 2118
2148: Fast (Bear Nose), Susie; F; 4/1/07-25; F; M; Wife; 2112; Yes; Yes; Id. U-9071 An. 361

Census of the **Pine Ridge** reservation of the **Pine Ridge, South Dakota** jurisdiction, as of **April 1**, 19**32**, taken by **James H. McGregor**, Superintendent.

Key: Number; Surname, Given; Sex; Date of Birth-Age at Last Birthday; Tribe (Oglala Sioux, unless stated otherwise); Degree of Blood; Marital Status; Relationship to Head of Family [Last Census Roll Number]; At Jurisdiction Where Enrolled (Yes/No); (If no – Where); Ward (Yes/No, if given); Allotment, Annuity and Identification Numbers (if given).

2149: Fast, Gabriel; M; 6/17/30-1; F; S; Son; 2113; Yes; Yes; Id. U-13528 An. none

2150: Fast Horse, Alfred; M; 1882-50; F; M; Head; 2114; Yes; Yes; Al. 1519 An. 2125

2151: Fast Horse (Long Cat), Bessie; F; 1881-51; F; M; Wife; 2115; Yes; Yes; Al. 2126 An. 2126

2152: Fast Horse, Amos; M; 1883-49; F; M; Head; 2116; Yes; Yes; Al. 4 An. 2127

2153: Fast Horse (Erving), Elizabeth; F; 1885-47; plus 1/4; M; Wife; 2117; Yes; Yes; Al. 19 An. 2128

2154: Fast Horse, Levi; M; 3/22/14-18; 1/4; S; Son; 2118; Yes; Yes; Id. U-9494 An. 2129

2155: Fast Horse, Vincent; M; 5/10/18-13; 1/4; S; Son; 2119; Yes; Yes; Id. U-9495 An. 2130

2156: Fast Horse, Frank; M; 1/21/21-11; 1/4; S; Son; 2120; Yes; Yes; Id. U-9496 An. 2131

2157: Fast Horse, Peter; M; 4/20/26-5; 1/4; S; Son; 2121; Yes; Yes; Id. U-11942 An. Noen[sic]

2158: Fast Horse, Antoine; M; 1900-32; 1/4; M; Head; 2122; Yes; Yes; Al. 8 An. 2135

2159: Fast Horse (Mesteth), Mary; F; 1900-32; 1/4; M; Wife; 4474; Yes; Yes; Al. 7272 An. 4472

2160: Fast Horse, Patrick; M; 2/20/22-10; 1/4; S; Son; 2123; Yes; Yes; Id. U-10933 An. 2137

2161: Fast Horse, Lawrence; M; 7/24/24-7; 1/4; S; Son; 2124; Yes; Yes; Id. U-11601 An. 2138

2162: Keith, Jess G.; M; 2/21/22-10; 1/4; S; S.Son; 4475; Yes; Yes; Id. U-12036 An. 4473

2163: Fast Horse, Robert; M; 1898-34; 1/4; M; Head; 2125; Yes; Yes; Al. 7 An. 2140

2164: Fast Horse (Spotted Bear), Stella; F; 1898-34; 1/4; M; Wife; 2126; Yes; Yes; Al. 2283 An. 2141

2165: Fast Horse, Vandell; M; 12/24/20-11; 1/4; S; Son; 2127; Yes; Yes; Id. U-9493 An. 2142

2166: Fast Horse, Thomas; M; 1882-50; F; M; Head; 2128; Yes; Yes; Al. 3 An. 2143

2167: Fast Horse (Breaks Land), Mollie; F; 1884-48; F; M; Wife; 2129; Yes; Yes; Al. 647 An. 2144

Census of the **Pine Ridge** reservation of the **Pine Ridge, South Dakota** jurisdiction, as of **April 1**, 19**32,** taken by **James H. McGregor**, Superintendent.

Key: Number; Surname, Given; Sex; Date of Birth-Age at Last Birthday; Tribe (Oglala Sioux, unless stated otherwise); Degree of Blood; Marital Status; Relationship to Head of Family [Last Census Roll Number]; At Jurisdiction Where Enrolled (Yes/No); (If no – Where); Ward (Yes/No, if given); Allotment, Annuity and Identification Numbers (if given).

2168: Fast Horse, Joseph Jr.; M; 9/21/14-17; F; S; Son; 2130; Yes; Yes; Al. 7896 An. 2146

2169: Fast Horse, Emma; F; 1907-25; plus 1/4; S; Head; 2131; Yes; Yes; Al. 6706 An. 2145

2170: Fast Horse, William Jr; M; 1905-27; 1/4; M; Head; 2132; Yes; Yes; Al. 1615 An. 2147

2171: Fast Horse (Spotted Bear), Elizabeth; F; 1903-29; 1/4; M; Wife; 2133; Yes; Yes; Al. 2285 An. 2148

2172: Fast Horse, Nicholas; M; 4/16/24-7; 1/4; S; Son; 2134; Yes; Yes; Id. U-11388 An. 2149

2173: Fast Horse, Alton; M; 11/29/26-5; 1/4; S; Son; 2135; Yes; Yes; Id. U-12564 An. none

2174: Fast Horse, Beatrice; F; 7/22/28-3; 1/4; S; Daughter; 2136; Yes; Yes; Id. U-12869 An. none

2175: Fast Horse, Annie E; F; 3/14/30-2; 1/4; S; Daughter; 2137; Yes; Yes; Id. U-13452 An. none

2176: Fast Whirlwind, ---; M; 1850-82; F; Wd; Head; 2138; Yes; Yes; Al. 3049 An. 2150

2177: Fast Wolf, John; M; 1872-60; plus 1/4; M; Head; 2139; Yes; Yes; Al. 1981 An. 2153

2178: Fast Wolf (no data), Jessie; F; 1867-65; F; M; Wife; 2140; Yes; Yes; Al. 1982 An. 2154

2179: Fast Wolf, Cecelia; F; 12/30/12-19; plus 1/4; S; Daughter; 2141; Yes; Yes; Al. 8243 An. 2155

2180: Fast Wolf, Rosa; F; 10/27/16-15; plus 1/4; S; Daughter; 2142; Yes; Yes; Id. U-9498 An. 2156

2181: Fast Wolf, Frank; M; 10/26/19-12; 1/4; S; Son; 2143; Yes; Yes; Id. U-9499 An. 2157

2182: Fast Wolf, Moses; M; 1900-32; 1/4; M; Head; 5339; Yes; Yes; Al. 5221 An. 1716

2183: Fast Wolf (Spotted Bear), Rosa; F; 2/21/11-21; 1/4; M; Wife; 5340; Yes; Yes; Al. 5753 An. 6455

2184: Fast Wolf, Mary; F; 4/17/31-11/12; 1/4; S; Daughter; --; Yes; Yes; U-13833

2185: Fast Wolf, Philip; M; 1879-53; 1/4; Wd; Head; 2144; Yes; Yes; Al. 5137 An. 2158

Census of the   **Pine Ridge**   reservation of the **Pine Ridge, South Dakota** jurisdiction, as of   **April 1**   , 19**32**, taken by   **James H. McGregor**   , Superintendent.

Key: Number; Surname, Given; Sex; Date of Birth-Age at Last Birthday; Tribe (Oglala Sioux, unless stated otherwise); Degree of Blood; Marital Status; Relationship to Head of Family [Last Census Roll Number]; At Jurisdiction Where Enrolled (Yes/No); (If no – Where); Ward (Yes/No, if given); Allotment, Annuity and Identification Numbers (if given).

2186: Fast Wolf, Reuben; M; 1896-36; 1/4; S; Head; 2145; Yes; Yes; Al. 1983 An. 2160

2187: Fast Wolf, Thomas; M; 1881-51; 1/4; M; Head; 2146; Yes; Yes; Al. 1925 An. 2161
2188: Fast Wolf (Short Bear), Jennie; F; 1881-51; 1/4; M; Wife; 2147; Yes; Yes; Al. 1926 An. 2162
2189: Fast Wolf, Susie; F; 4/13/14-17; 1/4; S; Daughter; 2148; Yes; Yes; Al. 7730 An. 2165
2190: Fast Wolf, Peter; M; 7/9/17-14; 1/4; S; Son; 2149; Yes; Yes; Id. U-9500 An. 2166
2191: Fast Wolf, Charles; M; 12/19/19-12; 1/4; S; Son; 2150; Yes; Yes; Id. U-9501 An. 2167

2192: Fast Wolf, Todd; M; 1902-30; 1/4; M; Head; 2151; Yes; Yes; Al. 1984 An. 2168
2193: Fast Wolf (Two Bulls), Dora; F; 1905-27; 1/4; M; Wife; 2152; Yes; Yes; Al. 3478 An. 7070
2194: Fast Wolf, Thomas; M; 9/11/28-3; 1/4; S; Son; 2153; Yes; Yes; Id. U-12778 An. none
2195: Fast Wolf, James; M; 1/3/32-2/12; 1/4; S; Son; --; Yes; Yes; Id. U-14090

2196: Fast Wolf, William; M; 1905-27; 1/4; M; Head; 2155; Yes; Yes; Al. 1928 An. 2169
2197: Fast Wolf (Tail) (Jennie), Sarah; F; 12/26/12-19; F; M; Wife; 2156; Yes; Yes; Al. 6848 An. 6786

2198: Feather, John; M; 1886-46; F; M; Head; 2157; Yes; Yes; Al. 1536 An. 2172
2199: Fast Wolf (Iron Crow), Rosa; F; 1903-29; F; M; Wife; 2158; Yes; Yes; Al. 5399 An. 3172

2200: Feather, William; M; 1906-26; F; S; Head; 2159; Yes; Yes; Al. 5934 An. 2174

2201: Featherman, Daniel; M; 1880-52; F; M; Head; 2160; Yes; Yes; Al. 3846 An. 2175
N.E.:   ~~Featherman (Standing Buffalo), Emma; F; -------; Rosebud Sioux; plus F; M; Wife;~~
2202: Featherman, Isabelle; F; 3/26/28-4; F; S; Daughter; 2161; Yes; Yes; Id. U-12727 An. none
2203: Featherman, Gladys; F; 1/14/31-1; F; S; Daughter; 2162; Yes; Yes; Id. U-13689 An. none

Census of the __Pine Ridge__ reservation of the __Pine Ridge, South Dakota__ jurisdiction, as of __April 1__, 1932, taken by __James H. McGregor__, Superintendent.

Key: Number; Surname, Given; Sex; Date of Birth-Age at Last Birthday; Tribe (Oglala Sioux, unless stated otherwise); Degree of Blood; Marital Status; Relationship to Head of Family [Last Census Roll Number]; At Jurisdiction Where Enrolled (Yes/No); (If no – Where); Ward (Yes/No, if given); Allotment, Annuity and Identification Numbers (if given).

2204: Featherman, John; M; 1904-28; F; M; Head; 2163; Yes; Yes; Al. 3847 An. 2177

2205: Featherman (Black Bear), Stella; F; 1906-26; F; M; Wife; 2164; Yes; Yes; Al. 5332 An. 2178

2206: Featherman, John; M; 1884-48; F; M; Head; 2166; Yes; Yes; Al. 1330 An. 2180

2207: Featherman (Stabber), May M; F; 1879-53; F; M; Wife; 2167; Yes; Yes; Al. 7239 An. 2181

2208: Featherman, Moses; M; 2/24/17-15; F; S; Son; 2168; Yes; Yes; Al. 9502 An. 2183

2209: Featherman, Lila; F; 5/29/19-12; F; S; Daughter; 2169; Yes; Yes; Id. U-9504 An. 2184

2210: Featherman, Zona; F; 5/6/25-6; F; S; Daughter; 2170; Yes; Yes; Id. U-11641 An. none

2211: Featherman, Louis; M; 1878-54; F; M; Head; 2171; Yes; Yes; Al. 3634 An. 2186

2212: Featherman, Fannie; F; 5/1919-12; F; S; Daughter; 2172; Yes; Yes; Id. U-9503 An. 2189

2213: FeatherOnhead, William; M; 1878-54; F; M; Head; 2173; Yes; Yes; Al. 6713 An. 2191

2214: FeatherOnhead (Running Shield), Nora; F; 1884-48; plus 1/4; M; Wife; 2174; Yes; Yes; Al. 2510 An. 2192

2215: FeatherOnhead, Emiley; F; 2/4/19-13; 1/4; S; Daughter; 2175; Yes; Yes; Id. U-9506 An. 2196

2216: FeatherOnhead, Sarah; F; 3/7/21-11; 1/4; S; Daughter; 2176; Yes; Yes; Id. U-9507 An. 2197

2217: FeatherOnhead, Ledia; F; 3/28/23-9; 1/4; S; Daughter; 2177; Yes; Yes; Id. U-13043 An. 2198

2218: FeatherOnhead, Amelia; F; 10/5/28-3; 1/4; S; Daughter; 2178; Yes; Yes; Id. U-12850 An. none

2219: Furgusion (Clifford), Alice; F; 1907-25; plus 1/4; M; Head; 2179; Yes; Yes; Al. 7304 An. 1442

2220: Furgusion, Carolyn; F; 7/9/27-4; 1/4; S; Daughter; 2180; Yes; Yes; Id. U-12774 An. none

2221: Furgusion, Ethelyn; F; 1/17/29-3; 1/4; S; Daughter; 2181; Yes; Yes; Id. U-12989 An. none

2222: Furgusion, Thomas; M; 1906-26; 1/4; M; Head; 2182; No; Sanborn, town, Niagra[sic], N.Y.; Yes; Al. 2129 An. 2199

Census of the __**Pine Ridge**__ reservation of the __**Pine Ridge, South Dakota**__ jurisdiction, as of __**April 1**__, 19**32**, taken by __**James H. McGregor**__, Superintendent.

Key: Number; Surname, Given; Sex; Date of Birth-Age at Last Birthday; Tribe (Oglala Sioux, unless stated otherwise); Degree of Blood; Marital Status; Relationship to Head of Family [Last Census Roll Number]; At Jurisdiction Where Enrolled (Yes/No); (If no – Where); Ward (Yes/No, if given); Allotment, Annuity and Identification Numbers (if given).

2223: Few Tails, John; M; 5/13/13-18; F; S; Head; 2183; Yes; Yes; Al. 7256 An. 2201

2224: Fight (no data), Julia; F; 1884-48; F; Wd.; Head; 2184; Yes; Yes; Al. 161 An. 2203

2225: Fight, Lena; F; 11/26/13-18; F; S; Daughter; 2185; Yes; Yes; Id. U-9509 An. 2204

2226: Fights Bear, ---; M; 1858-74; F; M; Head; 2186; Yes; Yes; Al. 178 An. 2206

2227: Fights Bear (Rainbow), ---; F; 1855-77; F; M; Wife; 2187; Yes; Yes; Al. 2451 An. 2207

2228: Eagle Bull, Stuart; M; 12/1/16-15; F; S; Ward; 2188; Yes; Yes; Id. U- 9471 An. 2009

2229: Eagle Bull, Ella; F; 7/6/18-13; F; S; Ward; 2189; Yes; Yes; Id. U- 9472 An. 2009

2230: Fights Bear, John; M; 1888-44; F; M; Head; 2190; Yes; Yes; Al. 176 An. 2108

2231: Fights Bear (Sleeps), Ruth; F; 1885-47; F; M; Wife; 2191; Yes; Yes; Al. 6087 An. 2209

2232: Fights Bear, Dora; F; 3/22/16-16; F; S; Daughter; 2192; Yes; Yes; Id. U-9513 An. 2212

2233: Fights Bear, Nelson; M; 12/17/17-14; F; S; Son; 2193; Yes; Yes; Id. U-9514 An. 2213

2234: Fights Bear, Bertha; F; 12/3/21-10; F; S; Daughter; 2194; Yes; Yes; Id. U-10877 An. 2214

2235: Fights Bear, Nellie; F; 9/1/24-7; F; S; Daughter; 2195; Yes; Yes; Id. U-11337 An. 2215

2236: Fights Bear, Emma; F; 8/20/29-2; F; S; Daughter; 2196; Yes; Yes; Id. U-13326 An. none

2237: Fights Bear, Lena; F; 12/7/14-17; F; S; Head; 2197; Yes; Yes; Id. U-9512 An. 2211

2238: Fights Over, Edward; M; 1898-34; F; M; Head; 2199; Yes; Yes; Al. 3382 An. 2216

2239: Fights Over (no data), Fannie; F; 1893-39; F; M; Wife; 2200; Yes; Yes; Al. 3504 An. 4630

2240: Fights Over, Matthew; M; 11/16/30-1; F; S; Son; 2201; Yes; Yes; Id. U-13690 An. none

2241: Fights Over, Wilson; M; 1897-35; F; S; Head; 2202; Yes; Yes; Al. 3381 An. 2217

Census of the **Pine Ridge** reservation of the **Pine Ridge, South Dakota** jurisdiction, as of **April 1**, 19**32**, taken by **James H. McGregor**, Superintendent.

Key: Number; Surname, Given; Sex; Date of Birth-Age at Last Birthday; Tribe (Oglala Sioux, unless stated otherwise); Degree of Blood; Marital Status; Relationship to Head of Family [Last Census Roll Number]; At Jurisdiction Where Enrolled (Yes/No); (If no – Where); Ward (Yes/No, if given); Allotment, Annuity and Identification Numbers (if given).

2242: Fills The Pipe, Silas; M; 1857-75; F; M; Head; 2203; Yes; Yes; Al. 3444 An. 2218

2243: Fills The Pipe (no data), Sophia; F; 1857-75; F; M; Wife; 2204; Yes; Yes; Al. 3445 An. 2219

2244: Fills The Pipe, Paul; M; 3/3/10-22; F; M; Head; 2205; Yes; Yes; Al. 7546 An. 2222

2245: Fills The Pipe (Mesteth), Jennie; F; 9/8/09-22; plus 1/4; M; Wife; 2206; Yes; Yes; Al. 6362 An. 4435

2246: Fills The Pipe, Isaac P; M; 8/12/31-7/12; plus 1/4; S; Son; --; Yes; Yes; U-13889

2247: Fills The Pipe, William; M; 1880-52; F; M; Head; 2207; Yes; Yes; Al. 3524 An. 2220

2248: Fills The Pipe (no data), Sarah; F; 1882-50; F; M; Wife; 2208; Yes; Yes; Al. 3525 An. 2221

2249: Fills The Pipe, Peter; M; 6/13/12-19; F; S; Son; 2209; Yes; Yes; Al. 7574 An. 2223

2250: Fills The Pipe, Noah; M; 12/18/17-14; F; S; Son; 2210; Yes; Yes; Id. U-9517 An. 2224

2251: Fills The Pipe, David; M; 12/23/20-11; F; S; Son; 2211; Yes; Yes; Id. U-9518 An. 2225

2252: Fills The Pipe, Andrew; M; 3/10/24-8; F; S; Son; 2212; Yes; Yes; Id. U-11275 An. 2226

2253: Finnegan (no data), Fannie; F; 1880-52; plus 1/4; Wd; Head; 2213; No; Miami, city, Dade, Fla; No; Al. 4087 An. 2227

2254: Fire Place, Dallas; M; 1897-35; F; M; Head; 2214; Yes; Yes; Al. 4129 An. 2230

2255: Fire Place (Two Lance), Christine; F; 1906-26; F; M; Wife; 2215; Yes; Yes; Al. 6693 An. 7145

2256: Fire Place, William; M; 1864-68; F; M; Head; 2216; Yes; Yes; Al. 4128 An. 2233

2257: Fire Place (Yellow Bear), Mary; F; 1868-64; F; M; Wife; 2217; Yes; Yes; Al. 1043 An. 7819

2258: Fire Place, Ida; F; 8/16/16-15; F; S; S.Daughter; 2218; Yes; Yes; Id. U-10780 An. 7820

2259: Fire Thunder, ---; M; 1848-84; F; Wd; Head; 2219; Yes; Yes; Al. 3025 An. 2235

Census of the **Pine Ridge** reservation of the **Pine Ridge, South Dakota** jurisdiction, as of **April 1**, 1932, taken by **James H. McGregor**, Superintendent.

Key: Number; Surname, Given; Sex; Date of Birth-Age at Last Birthday; Tribe (Oglala Sioux, unless stated otherwise); Degree of Blood; Marital Status; Relationship to Head of Family [Last Census Roll Number]; At Jurisdiction Where Enrolled (Yes/No); (If no – Where); Ward (Yes/No, if given); Allotment, Annuity and Identification Numbers (if given).

2260: Fire Thunder, Angelique; F; 1889-43; F; S; Head; 2220; Yes; Yes; Al. 1957 An. 2237

2261: Fire Thunder, Charles; M; 1890-42; F; M; Head; 2221; Yes; Yes; Al. 6652 An. 2239

2262: Fire Thunder (White Coyote), Sophia; F; 1902-30; F; M; Wife; 2223; Yes; Yes; Al. 6808 An. 7520

2263: Fire Thunder, Angelique; F; 11/27/15-16; F; S; Daughter; 2222; Yes; Yes; Id. U-9521 An. 2341

2264: Fire Thunder, Mark; M; 10/10/28-3; F; S; Son; 2224; Yes; Yes; Id. U-12864 An. none

2265: Fire Thunder, Ederson; M; 6/8/21-10; F; S; Son; 2225; Yes; Yes; Id. U-9523 An. 2242

2266: Fire Thunder, Edgar; M; 1860-72; plus 1/4; M; Head; 2226; Yes; Yes; Al. 1955 An. 2243

2267: Fire Thunder (Weasel Bear), Susie; F; 1868-64; 1/4; M; Wife; 2227; Yes; Yes; Al. 1956 An. 2244

2268: Hand Soldier, Etta M; F; 8/8/13-18; F; S; Ward; 2228; Yes; Yes; Al. 7080 An. 2346

2269: Fire Thunder, Rebecca; F; 9/2/09-22; plus 1/4; S; Head; 2229; Yes; Yes; Al. 5108 An. 2245

2270: Fire Thunder (no data), Mary; F; 1865-67; 1/4; Wd.; Head; 2230; Yes; Yes; Al. 1944 An. 2248

2271: Fire Thunder, George G; M; 1893-39; plus 1/4; M; Head; 2231; Yes; Yes; Al. 1946 An. 2249

2272: Fire Thunder (Blue Bird), Sarah; F; 1893-39; 1/4; M; Wife; 2232; Yes; Yes; Al. 1288 An. 2250

2273: Fire Thunder, Benjamin; M; 4/10/14-17; 1/4; S; Son; 2233; Yes; Yes; Al. 7323 An. 2251

2274: Fire Thunder, Emery; M; 9/17/16-15; 1/4; S; Son; 2234; Yes; Yes; Al. 8160 An. 2252

2275: Fire Thunder, Leo; M; 4/21/21-10; 1/4; S; Son; 2235; Yes; Yes; Id. U-9525 An. 2253

2276: Fire Thunder, Floyd; M; 3/1/23-9; 1/4; S; Son; 2236; Yes; Yes; Id. U-13060 An. 2254

2277: Fire Thunder, Joseph; M; 1903-29; 1/4; M; Head; 2238; Yes; Yes; Al. 1019 An. 2255

Census of the **Pine Ridge** reservation of the **Pine Ridge, South Dakota** jurisdiction, as of **April 1**, 1932, taken by **James H. McGregor**, Superintendent.

Key: Number; Surname, Given; Sex; Date of Birth-Age at Last Birthday; Tribe (Oglala Sioux, unless stated otherwise); Degree of Blood; Marital Status; Relationship to Head of Family [Last Census Roll Number]; At Jurisdiction Where Enrolled (Yes/No); (If no – Where); Ward (Yes/No, if given); Allotment, Annuity and Identification Numbers (if given).

2278: Fire Thunder (Ladeaux), Dora; F; 1908-24; 1/4; M; Wife; 2239; Yes; Yes; Al. 5705 An. 3633

2279: Fire Thunder, Leona; F; 6/23/26-5; 1/4; S; Daughter; 2240; Yes; Yes; Id. U-11968 An. none

2280: Fire Thunder, Mary C; F; 3/15/29-3; 1/4; S; Daughter; 2241; Yes; Yes; Id. U-13138 An. none

2281: Fire Thunder, Jasper; M; 1898-34; 1/4; M; Head; 2242; Yes; Yes; Al. 1947 An. 2256

2282: Fire Thunder (Randall), Pearl; F; 3/14/1909-23; 1/4; M; Wife; 2243; Yes; Yes; Al. 4599 An. 5305

2283: Fire Thunder, Chris; M; 11/25/30-1; 1/4; S; Son; 2244; Yes; Yes; Id. U-13691 An. none

2284: Fire Thunder, Joshua; M; 1904-28; plus 1/4; S; Head; 2245; Yes; Yes; Al. 1953 An. 2257

2285: Fire Thunder, Noah A; M; 1905-27; F; M; Head; 2246; Yes; Yes; Al. 6428 An. 2258

2286: Fire Thunder (Iron Boy), Lottie; F; 1902-30; F; M; Wife; 2247; Yes; Yes; Al. 6633 An. 3137

2287: Fire Thunder, Lillian; F; 1/28/28-4; F; S; Daughter; 2248; Yes; Yes; Id. U-12681 An. none

2288: Fire Thunder, Alice; F; 8/12/19-2; F; S; Daughter; 2249; Yes; Yes; Id. U-13327 An. none

2289: Fire Thunder, Stephen; M; 3/12/32-1/12; F; S; Son; --; Yes; Yes; U-14127

2290: Fire Thunder, Peter; M; 1900-32; plus 1/4; M; Head; 2250; Yes; Yes; Al. 1960 An. 2257

2291: Fire Thunder (Six Feathers), Sallie; F; 1903-29; 1/4; M; Wife; 2251; Yes; Yes; Al. 5176 An. 2260

2292: Fire Thunder, Agnes; F; 1/24/22-10; 1/4; S; Daughter; 2252; Yes; Yes; Id. U-10981 An. 2261

2293: Fire Thunder, Josephine; F; 12/7/23-8; 1/4; S; Daughter; 2253; Yes; Yes; Id. U-11145 An. 2262

2294: Fire Thunder, William; M; 1894-38; 1/4; M; Head; 2254; Yes; Yes; Al. 1959 An. 2263

N.E.: Fire Thunder (Humphrey), Maud; F; ——; Crow; plus 1/4; M; Wife;

2295: Fire Thunder, William; M; 1902-30; 1/4; M; Head; 2255; Yes; Yes; Al. 1018 An. 2264

Census of the _____ **Pine Ridge** _____ reservation of the _**Pine Ridge, South Dakota**_ jurisdiction, as of _____ **April 1** _____, 19**32**, taken by _____ **James H. McGregor** _____, Superintendent.

Key: Number; Surname, Given; Sex; Date of Birth-Age at Last Birthday; Tribe (Oglala Sioux, unless stated otherwise); Degree of Blood; Marital Status; Relationship to Head of Family [Last Census Roll Number]; At Jurisdiction Where Enrolled (Yes/No); (If no – Where); Ward (Yes/No, if given); Allotment, Annuity and Identification Numbers (if given).

2296: Fire Thunder (Salway), Cecelia; F; 11/15/11-20; 1/4; M; Wife; 2256; Yes; Yes; Al. 7945 An. 6012

2297: Fire Thunder, William; M; 1872-60; F; M; Head; 2257; Yes; Yes; Al. 943 An. 2265

2298: Fire Thunder (Gray Grass), Mary; F; 1871-61; F; M; Wife; 2258; Yes; Yes; Al. 6427 An. 2266

2299: Fisher, Albert; M; 46; plus 1/4; M; Head; 2259; No; Unknown; No; Al. 3766 An. 2267

2300: Fisher, Alberta; F; 8/7/15-16; -1/4; S; Daughter; 2260; Yes; Yes; Al. 8083 An. 2268

2301: Fisher, Elinor; F; 8/17/17-14; -1/4; S; Daughter; 2261; Yes; Yes; Id. U-9526 An. 2269

2302: Fisher, Earl; M; 1896-36; plus 1/4; M; Head; 2262; No; Unknown; Yes; Al. 3768 An. 2270

N.E.: Fisher (Johnston), Florence; F; ------; Athabaska Ind.; -1/4; M; Wife;

2303: Fisher, Marjory; F; 12/24/17-14; -1/4; S; Daughter; 2263; No; Athabaska, town Foreign, Alberta; Yes; Id. U-9527 An. 2271

2304: Fisher, James; M; 8/17/19-12; -1/4; S; Son; 2264; No; Same; Yes; Id. U-9528 An. 2272

2305: Fisher, Stella; F; 1899-33; plus 1/4; S; Head; 2265; No; Rapid City, city Pennington S.D.; Yes; Al. 3869 An. 2273

2306: Flesh, George; M; 1890-42; F; M; Head; 2266; Yes; Yes; Al. 4664 An. 2274

2307: Flesh, Seth; M; 1/6/17-15; plus 1/4; S; Son; 2267; Yes; Yes; Id. U-9530 An. 2275

2308: Flesh, Donald O; M; 2/12/22-10; 1/4; S; Son; 2268; Yes; Yes; Id. U-10866 An. 2276

2309: Fisher, Cecelia; F; 11/28/24-7; -1/4; S; Daughter; 2269; Yes; Yes; Id. U-11375 An. 2277

2310: Bushy Top Pine, Owenn; M; 5/7/27-4; F; S; Ward; 2270; Yes; Yes; Id. U-12613 An. none

2311: Flies Above, (David); M; 1855-77; F; Wd.; Head; 2271; Yes; Yes; Al. 2837 An. 2278

2312: Flies Above (Little Boy), Cecelia; F; 1870-63; F; Wd.; Head; 2272; Yes; Yes; Al. 7968 An. 2876

Census of the __**Pine Ridge**__ reservation of the **Pine Ridge, South Dakota** jurisdiction, as of __**April 1**__, 19**32**, taken by **James H. McGregor**, Superintendent.

Key: Number; Surname, Given; Sex; Date of Birth-Age at Last Birthday; Tribe (Oglala Sioux, unless stated otherwise); Degree of Blood; Marital Status; Relationship to Head of Family [Last Census Roll Number]; At Jurisdiction Where Enrolled (Yes/No); (If no – Where); Ward (Yes/No, if given); Allotment, Annuity and Identification Numbers (if given).

2313: Flying Hawk, David; M; 1903-29; plus 1/4; M; Head; 2274; Yes; Yes; Al. 2771 An. 2281

2314: Flying Hawk (Kills Enemy), Cecelia; F; 5/1/12-19; F; M; Wife; 2275; Yes; Yes; Al. 9806 An. 3498

2315: Flying Hawk, Lizzie; F; 3/17/30-2; F; S; Daughter; 2276; Yes; Yes; Id. U-13417 An. none

2316: Flying Hawk, Madeline J.; F; 11/7/31-4/12; F; S; Daughter; --; Yes; Yes; U-13417

2317: Flying Hawk, Philip; M; 1881-51; 1/4; M; Head; 2277; Yes; Yes; Al. 2769 An. 2282

2318: Flying Hawk (Ten Fingers), Lucy; F; 1885-47; F; M; Wife; 2278; Yes; Yes; Al. 7475 An. 2283

2319: Flying Hawk, Esther; F; 12/18/13-18; plus 1/4; S; Daughter; 2279; Yes; Yes; Al. 7533 An. 2285

2320: Flying Hawk, Louisa; F; 2/10/19-13; 1/4; S; Daughter; 2280; Yes; Yes; Id. U-9537 An. 2286

2321: Flying Hawk, Andrew; M; 9/12/21-10; 1/4; S; Son; 2281; Yes; Yes; Id. U-11027 An. 2287

2322: Flying Hawk, Albert; M; 1/28/23-9; 1/4; S; Son; 2282; Yes; Yes; Id. U-12071 An. 2288

2323: Flying Hawk, Nancy; F; 12/17/24-7; 1/4; S; Daughter; 2283; Yes; Yes; Id. U-9856 An. 2289

2324: Flying Hawk, Earnest; M; 11/3/26-5; 1/4; S; Son; 2284; Yes; Yes; Id. U-12135 An. none

2325: Flying Hawk, Stella; F; 4/19/29-2; 1/4; S; Daughter; 2285; Yes; Yes; Id. U-13163 An. none

2326: Flying Horse, ---; M; 1878-54; F; M; Head; 2286; Yes; Yes; Al. 5048 An. 2290

2327: Flying Horse (Whirlwind Horse), Agnes; F; 1888-44; F; M; Wife; 2287; Yes; Yes; Al. 4959 An. 2291

2328: Flying Horse, Levi; M; 4/28/12-19; F; S; S.Son; 2288; Yes; Yes; Id. U-10708 An. 2292

2329: Whirlwind Horse, Christine; F; 6/26/24-7; F; S; S.Daughter; 2289; Yes; Yes; Id. U-12722 An. none

2330: Flying Horse, Paul; M; 1872-60; F; M; Head; 2290; Yes; Yes; Al. 895 An. 2295

2331: Flying Horse (Surrounded), Grace; F; 1867-65; F; M; Wife; 2291; Yes; Yes; Al. 6983 An. 2296

N.E.: ~~Flying Horse, Henry; M; -------; Rosebud Sioux; M; Head;~~

Census of the **Pine Ridge** reservation of the **Pine Ridge, South Dakota** jurisdiction, as of **April 1**, 19**32**, taken by **James H. McGregor**, Superintendent.

Key: Number; Surname, Given; Sex; Date of Birth-Age at Last Birthday; Tribe (Oglala Sioux, unless stated otherwise); Degree of Blood; Marital Status; Relationship to Head of Family [Last Census Roll Number]; At Jurisdiction Where Enrolled (Yes/No); (If no – Where); Ward (Yes/No, if given); Allotment, Annuity and Identification Numbers (if given).

2332: Flying Horse (High Eagle), Sophia; F; 1877-55; plus 1/4; M; Wife; 2292; Yes; Yes; Al. 2406 An. 2892

N.E.: Flying Walking,---; M; ------; Rosebud Sioux; F; M; Head;
2333: Flying Horse (Yellow Boy), Mabel; F; 1870-62; F; M; Wife; 2293; No; Rosebud; Yes; Id. U-10793 An. 7864

N.E.: Fog, Frank; M; ------; Crow; M; Head;
2334: Fog (no data), Emma; F; 1875-57; plus 1/4; M; Wife; 2294; No; Crow Creek; Yes; Al. 5877 An. 2297
2335: Fog, Patrick; M; 3/17/19-13; 1/4; S; Son; 2295; No; Crow Creek; Yes; Id. U-9538 An. 2299
2336: Fog, Zora; F; 6/27/21-10; 1/4; S; Daughter; 2296; No; Crow Creek; Yes; Id. U-11624 An. 2300

2337: Fog, Henry; M; 1899-33; 1/4; S; Head; 2299; No; Crow Creek; Yes; Al. 5859 An. 2302

2338: Fog, Louis; M; 1901-31; 1/4; M; Head; 2300; No; Crow Creek; Yes; Al. 5860 An. 2303
N.E.: Fog (Ross), Edna; F; ------; Crow; M; Wife;
2339: Fog, Rozalia; F; 11/29/23-8; 1/4; S; Daughter; 2301; No; Crow Creek; Yes; Id. U-13182 An. none
2340: Fog, Louis Jr.; M; 7/21/25-6; 1/4; S; Son; 2302; No; Crow Creek; Yes; Id. U-13183 An. none
2341: Fog, Bertha; F; 3/25/27-5; 1/4; S; Daughter; 2303; No; Crow Creek; Yes; Id. U-13224 An. none
2342: Fog, Emma; F; 7/29/28-3; 1/4; S; Daughter; 2304; No; Crow Creek; Yes; Id. U-13225 An. none
2343: Fog, Henry; M; 3/12/30-2; 1/4; S; Son; --; No; Crow Creek; Yes; U-13804

2344: Follows Prairie, Fire; F; 1842-90; F; Wd.; Head; 2305; Yes; Yes; Al. 1439 An. 2304

2345: Fool Crow, ---; M; 1866-66; F; M; Head; 2306; Yes; Yes; Al. 1435 An. 2305
2346: Fool Crow (no data), Emily; F; 1868-64; F; M; Wife; 2307; Yes; Yes; Al. 4300 An. 2307

2347: Fool Crow, Frank; M; 1898-34; F; M; Head; 2308; Yes; Yes; Al. 1436 An. 2308
2348: Fool Crow (Afraid of Hawk), Fannie; F; 1894-38; F; M; Wife; 2309; Yes; Yes; Al. 6003 An. 2309

Census of the __Pine Ridge__ reservation of the __Pine Ridge, South Dakota__ jurisdiction, as of __April 1__, 19**32**, taken by __James H. McGregor__, Superintendent.

Key: Number; Surname, Given; Sex; Date of Birth-Age at Last Birthday; Tribe (Oglala Sioux, unless stated otherwise); Degree of Blood; Marital Status; Relationship to Head of Family [Last Census Roll Number]; At Jurisdiction Where Enrolled (Yes/No); (If no – Where); Ward (Yes/No, if given); Allotment, Annuity and Identification Numbers (if given).

2349: Fool Crow, Mary; F; 5/20/25-6; F; S; Daughter; 2310; Yes; Yes; Id. U-11635 An. none

2350: Fool Head, Frank; M; 1862-70; F; M; Head; 2311; Yes; Yes; Al. 1436 An. 2310

2351: Fool Head (White Elk), Susie; F; 1893-39; F; M; Wife; 2312; Yes; Yes; Al. 5986 An. 2311

2352: White Elk, Hanna; F; 4/30/15-16; F; S; S.Daughter; 2313; Yes; Yes; Al. 7972 An. 2312

2353: White Elk, Emma; F; 8/10/17-14; F; S; S.Daughter; 2314; Yes; Yes; Id. U-9540 An. 2313

2354: Fool Head, Alvena; F; 10/15/20-11; F; S; Daughter; 2315; Yes; Yes; Id. U-9541 An. 2316

2355: Fool Head, Myrtle; F; 9/26/27-4; F; S; Daughter; 2316; Yes; Yes; Id. U-12385 An. none

2356: Fool Head, Hattie; F; 1/12/32-2/12; F; S; Daughter; ---; Yes; Yes; U-14062

2357: Fool Head, John; M; 1868-64; F; M; Head; 2317; Yes; Yes; Al. 6009 An. 2317

2358: Fool Head (no data), Julia; F; 1873-59; F; M; Wife; 2318; Yes; Yes; Al. 6010 An. 2318

2359: Foolish Woman, Leonard; M; 1886-46; F; Wd; Head; 2319; Yes; Yes; Al. 2854 An. 2319

2360: Foot, ---; M; 1855-77; F; Wd; Head; 2320; Yes; Yes; Al. 2389 An. 2321

N.E.: ~~Forgets Nothing, George; M; -------; Rosebud Sioux; F; M; Head;~~
2361: Forgets Nothing (Standing Bear), Angelina; F; 1872-60; plus 1/4; M; Wife; 6547; Yes; Yes; Al. 4004 An. 6530

2362: Fox Belly, John; M; 1833-49; F; Wd; Head; 2321; Yes; Yes; Al. 1827 An. 23255

N.E.: ~~Frazier, Benjamin; M; -------; Santee Sioux; plus 1/4; Wd.; Head;~~
2363: Frazier, Calvin; M; 7/3/25-6; plus 1/4; S; Son; 2322; Yes; Yes; Id. U-11697 An. none

N.E.: ~~Frazier, Robert; M; -------; Santee Sioux; plus 1/4; M; Head;~~
2364: Frazier (Conroy), Lena; F; 1899-33; plus 1/4; M; Wife; 2323; Yes; Yes; Al. 4589 An. 2328

Census of the **Pine Ridge** reservation of the **Pine Ridge, South Dakota** jurisdiction, as of **April 1**, 19**32,** taken by **James H. McGregor**, Superintendent.

Key: Number; Surname, Given; Sex; Date of Birth-Age at Last Birthday; Tribe (Oglala Sioux, unless stated otherwise); Degree of Blood; Marital Status; Relationship to Head of Family [Last Census Roll Number]; At Jurisdiction Where Enrolled (Yes/No); (If no – Where); Ward (Yes/No, if given); Allotment, Annuity and Identification Numbers (if given).

2365: Frazier, Vivian; F; 6/1/22-9; 1/4; S; Daughter; 2324; Yes; Yes; Id. U-11273 An. 2329

2366: Frazier, Victoria; F; 4/17/24-7; 1/4; S; Daughter; 2325; Yes; Yes; Id. U-11274 An. 2330

2367: Frazier, Harold; M; 8/25/26-5; 1/4; S; Son; 2326; Yes; Yes; Id. U-12219 An. none

2368: Frazier, Lloyd C; M; 8/27/28-3; 1/4; S; Son; 2327; Yes; Yes; Id. U-12788 An. none

2369: Frazier, Jewel S; F; 7/10/30-1; 1/4; S; Daughter; 2328; Yes; Yes; Id. U-13621 An. none

2370: Frazier (Sears), Pearl; F; 1896-36; 1/4; M; Head; 2329; Yes; Yes; Al. 380 An. 2331

2371: Frazier, Robert; M; 10/17/17-14; -1/4; S; Son; 2331; Yes; Yes; Id. U-9544 An. 2334

2372: Frazier, Charles; M; 5/30/19-12; -1/4; S; Son; 2332; Yes; Yes; Id. U-9545 An. 2335

2373: Frazier, Bert; M; 3/7/21-11; -1/4; S; Son; 2333; Yes; Yes; Id. U-9546 An. 2336

2374: Freeman (Picotte), Kathryn; F; 5/20/09-22; plus 1/4; M; Head; 2334; Yes; Yes; Al. 5479 An. 4946

2375: Friday, Scares; M; 1877-55; F; M; Head; 2335; Yes; Yes; Al. 2894 An. 2337

2376: Friday Scares (no data), Susan; F; 1879-53; F; M; Wife; 2336; Yes; Yes; Al. 2895 An. 2338

2377: Friday Scares, Obed; M; 3/21/09-23; F; S; Son; 2337; Yes; Yes; Al. 6161 An. 2339

2378: Friday Scares, Mary; F; 12/15/18-13; F; S; Daughter; 2338; Yes; Yes; Id. U-9547 An. 2341

2379: Fritsch (Ruleau), Leta; F; 1877-55; -1/4; M; Head; 2339; No; Rapid City, city, Pennington, S.D.; No; Al. 2144 An. 5888

2380: Frog, Alfred; M; 1868-64; F; M; Head; 2340; Yes; Yes; Al. 3186 An. 2342

2381: Frog (no data), Julia; F; 1878-54; F; M; Wife; 2341; Yes; Yes; Al. 3187 An. 2343

2382: Frog, Sophine; F; 1/2/16-16; F; S; Daughter; 2342; Yes; Yes; Id. U-9548 An. 2345

2383: Frog, Joshua; M; 1/26/10-22; F; S; Son; 2343; Yes; Yes; Al. 9549 An. 2346

2384: Frog, Felix; M; 1899-33; F; M; Head; 2344; Yes; Yes; Al. 3188 An. 2347

2385: Frog (Martin), Mattie; F; 1899-33; F; M; Wife; 2345; Yes; Yes; Al. 1130 An. 2348

Census of the __Pine Ridge__ reservation of the __Pine Ridge, South Dakota__ jurisdiction, as of __April 1__, 1932, taken by __James H. McGregor__, Superintendent.

Key: Number; Surname, Given; Sex; Date of Birth-Age at Last Birthday; Tribe (Oglala Sioux, unless stated otherwise); Degree of Blood; Marital Status; Relationship to Head of Family [Last Census Roll Number]; At Jurisdiction Where Enrolled (Yes/No); (If no – Where); Ward (Yes/No, if given); Allotment, Annuity and Identification Numbers (if given).

2386: Frog, Minnie; F; 4/26/26-5; F; S; Daughter; 2346; Yes; Yes; Id. U-11943 An. none
2387: Frog, Bernice; F; 3/19/28-4; F; S; Daughter; 2347; Yes; Yes; Id. U-12545 An. none
2388: Frog, Victor; M; 7/30/30-1; F; S; Son; 2348; Yes; Yes; Id. U-13546 An. none

2389: Frog, Luke; M; 1901-31; F; M; Head; 2349; Yes; Yes; Al. 3189 An. 2349
2390: Frog (Little Soldier), Nellie; F; 1904-28; F; M; Wife; 2350; Yes; Yes; Al. 7653 An. 2350
2391: Frog, Edith; F; 11/5/24-7; F; S; Daughter; 2351; Yes; Yes; Id. U-11381 An. 2351
2392: Frog, Ephraim; M; 9/9/26-5; F; S; Son; 2352; Yes; Yes; Id. U-12177 An. none
2393: Frog, Thomas; M; 8/5/29-2; F; S; Son; 2353; Yes; Yes; Id. U-13240 An. none

2394: Frog, Oliver; M; 1903-29; F; S; Head; 2354; Yes; Yes; Al. 3190 An. 2354

2395: Gallagher, Paul; M; 1898-34; plus 1/4; S; Head; 2355; No; Alliance, town, Box Butte, Nebr.; Yes Al. 4042 An. 2355

2396: Galligo (no data), Julia; F; 1868-64; 1/4; Wd; Head; 2356; Yes; Yes; Al. 2786 An. 2357

2397: Galligo, Lawrence; M; 12/25/08-23; 1/4; S; Head; 2357; Yes; Yes; Al. 8250 An. 2358

2398: Galligo, Jay; M; 1900-32; 1/4; M; Head; 2358; Yes; Yes; Al. 1179 An. 2364
2399: Galligo (Shangreau), Myrtle; F; 1897-35; 1/4; M; Wife; 2359; Yes; Yes; Al. 1210 An. 2365
2400: Galligo, Liona; F; 6/15/24-7; 1/4; S; Daughter; 2361; Yes; Yes; Id. U-11340 An. 2367
2401: Galligo, Louis J; M; 3/21/27-5; 1/4; S; Son; 2362; Yes; Yes; Id. U-12283 An. none
2402: Galligo, John W.; M; 12/20/29-2; 1/4; S; Son; 2363; Yes; Yes; Id. U-13328 An. none

2403: Galligo, John Sr.; M; 1877-55; 1/4; M; Head; 2364; Yes; Yes; Al. 1178 An. 2368
2404: Galligo (Walking), Clarinda; F; 1876-56; 1/4; M; Wife; 2366; Yes; Yes; Id. U-10145 An. 7263

Census of the __Pine Ridge__ reservation of the __Pine Ridge, South Dakota__ jurisdiction, as of __April 1__, 19**32**, taken by __James H. McGregor__, Superintendent.

Key: Number; Surname, Given; Sex; Date of Birth-Age at Last Birthday; Tribe (Oglala Sioux, unless stated otherwise); Degree of Blood; Marital Status; Relationship to Head of Family [Last Census Roll Number]; At Jurisdiction Where Enrolled (Yes/No); (If no – Where); Ward (Yes/No, if given); Allotment, Annuity and Identification Numbers (if given).

2405: Galligo, Laura; F; 3/29/13-19; 1/4; S; Daughter; 2365; Yes; Yes; Id. Al. 7181 An. 2371

2406: Walking, Annie; F; 4/22/18-13; 1/4; S; S.Daughter; 2367; Yes; Yes; Id. U-10672 An. 7266

2407: Walking, Katie; F; 6/22/20-11; 1/4; S; S.Daughter; 2368; Yes; Yes; Id. U-10673 An. 7267

2408: Galligo, Jessie; F; 1/8/15-17; 1/4; S; Daughter; 2369; Yes; Yes; Id. Al. 7975 An. 2372

2409: Galligo, Zohy; M; 6/8/09-22; 1/4; S; Head; 2370; Yes; Yes; Al. 7180 An. 2370

2410: Galligo, Joseph; M; 1906-26; 1/4; S; Head; 2371; Yes; Yes; Al. 7182 An. 2376

2411: Galligo, Peter; M; 1899-33; 1/4; M; Head; 2372; Yes; Yes; Al. 2791 An. 2377

2412: Galligo (Pablo), Agnes; F; 7/26/11-20; plus 1/4; M; Wife; 4866; Yes; Yes; Al. 6662 An. 4847

2413: Galligo, May; F; 11/11/31-4/12; 1/4; S; Daughter; ---; Yes; Yes; U-14063

2414: Garcia, Thomas; M; 1887-45; 1/4; M; Head; 2373; Yes; Yes; Al. 7917 An. 2378

2415: Garcia (Lee), Vienna; F; 1890-42; 1/4; M; Wife; 2374; Yes; Yes; Al. 2379 An. 64

2416: Lee, Jessie; F; 2/12/17-15; 1/4; S; S.Daughter; 2375; Yes; Yes; Id. U-0553 An. 2381

2417: Garcia, Helena; F; 3/9/22-10; 1/4; S; Daughter; 2376; Yes; Yes; Id. U-10908 An. 2383

2418: Garcia, Leo; M; 4/22/28-3; 1/4; S; Son; 2377; Yes; Yes; Id. U-12566 An. none

2419: Garnett, Charles; M; 1876-56; 1/4; M; Head; 2378; No; Chadron, town, Dawes, Nebr.; Yes; Al. 3734 An. 2386

2420: Garnett (no data), Alice; F; 1881-51; 1/4; M; Wife; 2379; No; Chadron, town, Dawes, Nebr.; Yes; Al. 3735 An. 2387

2421: Garnett, Alice; F; 2/28/14-18; 1/4; M; Daughter; 2380; No; Same; Yes; Al. 7874 An. 2388

2422: Garnett, Charles; M; 3/17/21-11; 1/4; S; Son; 2381; No; Same; Yes; Id. U-11009 An. 2390

2423: Garnett, Susie; F; 1879-53; 1/4; S; Head; 2382; Yes; Yes; Al. 286 An. 2393

2424: Garnett (Janis), Filla; F; 1856-76; 1/4; Wd; Head; 2383; Yes; Yes; Al. 1830 An. 2395

Census of the **Pine Ridge** reservation of the **Pine Ridge, South Dakota** jurisdiction, as of **April 1**, 19**32**, taken by **James H. McGregor**, Superintendent.

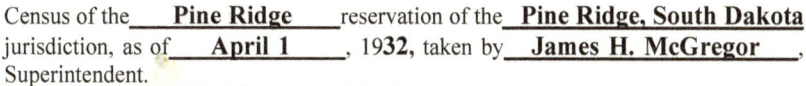

Key: Number; Surname, Given; Sex; Date of Birth-Age at Last Birthday; Tribe (Oglala Sioux, unless stated otherwise); Degree of Blood; Marital Status; Relationship to Head of Family [Last Census Roll Number]; At Jurisdiction Where Enrolled (Yes/No); (If no – Where); Ward (Yes/No, if given); Allotment, Annuity and Identification Numbers (if given).

2425: Garnett, Henry; M; 2/25/09-23; 1/4; M; Head; 2384; Yes; Yes; Al. 2667 An. 2396
2426: Garnett (Ciago), Grace; F; 4/18/12-19; 1/4; M; Wife; 2385; Yes; Yes; Id. U-9571 An. 2465
2427: Garnett, Anna; F; 7/3/31-8/12; 1/4; S; Daughter; ---; Yes; Yes; U-13868

2428: Garnier, Baptiste; M; 1904-28; 1/4; M; Head; 2386; Yes; Yes; Al. 6129 An. 2397
2429: Garnier (Siers), Julia; F; 1906-26; 1/4; M; Wife; 2387; Yes; Yes; Al. 4050 An. 6301
2430: Garnier, Gladys; F; 7/12/27-4; 1/4; S; Daughter; 2388; Yes; Yes; Id. U-12386 An. none
2431: Garnier, Sarah; F; 12/22/29-2; 1/4; S; Daughter; 2389; Yes; Yes; Id. U-13329 An. none
2432: Garnier, John; M; 10/24/31-5/12; 1/4; S; Son; ---; Yes; Yes; U-14092

2433: Garnier, David; M; 9/29/02-29; 1/4; Wd; Head; 2390; Yes; Yes; Al. 6128 An. 2398
2434: Garnier, Effie; F; 4/26/30-1; 1/4; S; Daughter; 2391; Yes; Yes; Id. U-13513 An. none

2435: Garnier, John; M; 1881-51; plus 1/4; M; Head; 2392; Yes; Yes; Al. 6127 An. 2399
2436: Garnier (Gillespie), Lizzie; F; 1879-53; 1/4; M; Wife; 2393; Yes; Yes; Al. 5162 An. 2400

2437: Garnier, Oliver; M; 4/4/08-23; 1/4; M; Head; 2394; Yes; Yes; Al. 6130 An. 2401
2438: Garnier (Red Shirt), Varia; F; 8/3/11-20; F; M; Wife; 5773; Yes; Yes; Al. 6514 An. 5558
2439: Garnier, Bertha; F; 9/14/31-5/12; plus 1/4; S; Daughter; ---; Yes; Yes; U-13924

2440: Garter, ---; M; 1859-73; F; M; Head; 2395; Yes; Yes; Al. 2782 An. 2403
2441: Garnier (pine[sic] Leaf), ---; F; 1857-75; F; M; Wife; 2396; Yes; Yes; Al. 5799 An. 2404

2442: Gay, Daisy; F; 1907-25; plus 1/4; S; Head; 2397; Yes; Yes; Al. 4182 An. 2405
2443: Witt, Wilbur F; M; 2/2/31-1; 1/4; S; Son; 2398; Yes; Yes; Id. U-13753 An. none

2444: Gay, Stephen; M; 1900-32; 1/4; M; Head; 2399; Yes; Yes; Al. 4180 An. 2407

Census of the **Pine Ridge** reservation of the **Pine Ridge, South Dakota** jurisdiction, as of **April 1**, 19**32**, taken by **James H. McGregor**, Superintendent.

Key: Number; Surname, Given; Sex; Date of Birth-Age at Last Birthday; Tribe (Oglala Sioux, unless stated otherwise); Degree of Blood; Marital Status; Relationship to Head of Family [Last Census Roll Number]; At Jurisdiction Where Enrolled (Yes/No); (If no – Where); Ward (Yes/No, if given); Allotment, Annuity and Identification Numbers (if given).

2445: Gay (Shot to Pieces), Dora; F; 1899-33; F; M; Wife; 2400; Yes; Yes; Al. 182 An. 2408

2446: Gay, Martha; F; 4/27/22-9; plus 1/4; S; Daughter; 2401; Yes; Yes; Id. U-11010 An. 2409

2447: Gay, Christine; F; 12/2/26-5; 1/4; S; Daughter; 2402; Yes; Yes; Id. U-12178 An. none

2448: Gay, Daisy; F; 8/23/29-2; 1/4; S; Daughter; 2403; Yes; Yes; Id. U-13252 An. none

2449: Gay, Lavina; F; 12/19/31-3/12; 1/4; S; Daughter; ---; Yes; Yes; Id. U-13989

2450: Gay, William; M; 1868-64; plus 1/4; M; Head; 2404; Yes; Yes; Al. 1321 An. 2410

2451: Gay (Cloud Horse), Nancy; F; 1881-51; F; M; Wife; 2405; Yes; Yes; Al. 4179 An. 2411

2452: Gay, Alexander; M; 1/12/14-18; plus 1/4 1/4; S; Son; 2406; Yes; Yes; Id. U-9558 An. 2414

2453: Gay, Wilson; M; 2/24/16-15; 1/4; S; Son; 2407; Yes; Yes; Id. U-9559 An. 2415

2454: Gay, Adam; M; 5/18/1-12; 1/4; S; Son; 2408; Yes; Yes; Id. U-9560 An. 2416

2455: Gay, Joshua; M; 11/4/21-10; 1/4; S; Son; 2409; Yes; Yes; Id. U-9561 An. 2417

2456: Gay, Leon; M; 12/12/08-23; 1/4; S; Head; 2410; Yes; Yes; Al. 4183 An. 2412

2457: Gay, Agnes; F; 3/17/11-21; 1/4; S; Head; 2411; Yes; Yes; Al. 7167 An. 2413

2458: Gerry, David; M; 1907-25; 1/4; M; Head; 2412; Yes; Yes; Al. 2365 An. 2419
N.E.: ~~Gerry (Bull Tail), Lizzie; F; 1909-23; Rosebud Sioux; F; M; Wife;~~
2459: Gerry, Benjamin; M; 9/9/27-4; 1/4; S; Son; 2413; Yes; Yes; Id. U-13423 An. none

2460: Gerry, Edward; M; 1883-49; 1/4; M; Head; 2414; No; Rapid City, city, Pennington, S.D.; Yes; Al. 2455 An. 2420
N.E.: ~~Gerry (Larvia), Helena; F; 1889-43; Rosebud Sioux; plus 1/4; M; Wife;~~
2461: Gerry, John H.; M; 6/2/12-19; 1/4; S; Son; 2405; No; Rapid City, city, Pennington, S.D.; Yes; Al. 6844 An. 2421

2462: Gerry, Elbridge; M; 1893-39; plus 1/4; S; Head; 2416; No; Merriman, town, Cherry, Nebr.; Yes; Al. 4495 An. 2422

2463: Gerry, John; M; 1874-58; 1/4; S; Head; 2417; Yes; Yes; Al. 4190 An. 2423

Census of the __Pine Ridge__ reservation of the __Pine Ridge, South Dakota__ jurisdiction, as of __April 1__, 19**32,** taken by __James H. McGregor__, Superintendent.

Key: Number; Surname, Given; Sex; Date of Birth-Age at Last Birthday; Tribe (Oglala Sioux, unless stated otherwise); Degree of Blood; Marital Status; Relationship to Head of Family [Last Census Roll Number]; At Jurisdiction Where Enrolled (Yes/No); (If no – Where); Ward (Yes/No, if given); Allotment, Annuity and Identification Numbers (if given).

2464: Gets There First, David; M; 1872-60; F; M; Head; 2418; Yes; Yes; Al. 1490 An. 2425

2465: Gets There First (no data), Susan; F; 1864-68; F; M; Wife; 2419; Yes; Yes; Al. 7946 An. 2426

2466: Gets There First, Herbert; M; 1904-28; F; S; Head; 2420; Yes; Yes; Al. 1493 An. 2427

2467: Ghost, Frank; M; 1888-44; F; M; Head; 2424; Yes; Yes; Al. 6783 An. 2431

2468: Ghost (Jones), Julia; F; 1898-34; F; M; Wife; 2425; Yes; Yes; Al. 6769 An. 2432

2469: Ghost, Alvina; F; 8/26/15-16; F; S; Daughter; 2426; Yes; Yes; Id. U-9562 An. 2433

2470: Ghost, Mayrose; F; 3/28/17-15; F; S; Daughter; 2427; Yes; Yes; Id. U-9563 An. 2434

2471: Ghost, Flora; F; 2/19/19-13; F; S; Daughter; 2428; Yes; Yes; Id. U-9564 An. 2435

2472: Ghost, Vance; M; 2/28/21-11; F; S; Son; 2429; Yes; Yes; Id. U-9565 An. 2436

2473: Ghost, Curtis H.; M; 12/19/24-7; F; S; Son; 2430; Yes; Yes; Id. U-11421 An. 2437

2474: Ghost, Keva; F; 6/4/27-4; F; S; Daughter; 2431; Yes; Yes; Id. U-12877 An. none

2475: Ghost, Malvin P; M; 6/19/30-1; F; S; Son; 2432; Yes; Yes; Id. U-13547 An. none

2476: Ghost Bear, Charles; M; 1882-50; F; M; Head; 2434; Yes; Yes; Al. 306 An. 2439

2477: Ghost Bear (Crazy Horse), Jennie; F; 1889-43; plus 1/4; M; Wife; 2436; Yes; Yes; Al. 5144 An. 1715

2478: Ghost Bear, Thomas; M; 4/10/24-8; 1/4; S; Son; 2435; Yes; Yes; Id. U-11390 An. 2443

2479: Randall, Thomas; M; 10/30/11-20; 1/4; S; S.Son; 2437; Yes; Yes; Id. U-9401 An. 1717

2480: Ghost Bear, Rudy; M; 7/1/30-1; 1/4; S; Son; 2438; Yes; Yes; Id. U-13575 An. none

2481: Ghost Bear, Charles; M; 12/25/08-23; F; S; Head; 2439; Yes; Yes; Al. 5738 An. 2440

2482: Ghost, ---; M; 1855-77; F; M; Head; 2421; Yes; Yes; Al. 2949 An. 2428

2483: Ghost (no data), Emma; F; 1858-74; F; M; Wife; 2422; Yes; Yes; Al. 2967 An. 2429

Census of the **Pine Ridge** reservation of the **Pine Ridge, South Dakota** jurisdiction, as of **April 1**, 19**32,** taken by **James H. McGregor**, Superintendent.

Key: Number; Surname, Given; Sex; Date of Birth-Age at Last Birthday; Tribe (Oglala Sioux, unless stated otherwise); Degree of Blood; Marital Status; Relationship to Head of Family [Last Census Roll Number]; At Jurisdiction Where Enrolled (Yes/No); (If no – Where); Ward (Yes/No, if given); Allotment, Annuity and Identification Numbers (if given).

2484: Ghost, Edison; M; 6/5/18-13; F; S; Gr. Son; 2423; Yes; Yes; Al. 187 An. 2438

2485: Ghost Bear, Benjamin; M; 1893-39; F; S; Head; 2433; Yes; Yes; Al. 187 An. 2438

2486: Ghost Bear, Charles; M; 6/4/15-16; F; S; Alone; 2440; Yes; Yes; Al. 8148 An. 4980

2487: Ghost Bear, Charles; M; 1897-35; F; M; Head; 2441; Yes; Yes; Al. 475 An. 2453

2488: Ghost Bear (Eagle Bull), Jennie; F; 1883-49; plus 1/4; M; Wife; 2442; Yes; Yes; Al. 6696 An. 2001

2489: Eagle Bull, Lloyd; M; 8/2/16-15; 1/4; S; S.Son; 2444; Yes; Yes; Id. U-9474 An. 2004

2490: Eagle Bull, Bertha; F; 3/14/22-10; 1/4; S; S.Daughter; 2445; Yes; Yes; Id. U-10920 An. 2005

2491: Ghost Bear (Chief), Lillie; F; 1900-32; plus 1/4; Wd; Head; 2446; No; Rosebud; Yes; Al. 6487 An. 2445

2492: Ghost Bear, John; M; 1855-77; F; M; Head; 2447; Yes; Yes; Al. 22 An. 2451

2493: Ghost Bear (no data), Alice; F; 1856-76; F; M; Wife; 2448; Yes; Yes; Al. 5611 An. 2452

2494: Ghost, George; M; 6/16/12-19; F; S; Gr. Son; 2449; Yes; Yes; Al. 6714 An. 2448

2495: Ghost, Theodore; M; 7/26/14-17; F; S; Gr. Son; 2450; Yes; Yes; Id. U-9568 An. 2449

2496: Ghost, Wilbert; M; 3/14/16-16; F; S; Gr. Son; 2451; Yes; Yes; Id. U-9569 An. 2450

2497: Ghost Bear, William; M; 1877-55; F; M; Head; 2452; Yes; Yes; Al. 30 An. 2453

2498: Ghost Bear, Isaac; M; 10/24/15-16; F; S; Son; 2453; Yes; Yes; Id. U-9570 An. 2456

2499: Ghost Dog, William; M; 1898-34; F; M; Head; 2455; Yes; Yes; Al. 191 An. 2457

2500: Ghost Dog (Old Shield), Susie; F; 1896-36; F; M; Wife; 2456; Yes; Yes; Al. 2172 An. 2458

2501: Ghost Dog, Ralph; M; 4/5/22-9; F; S; Son; 2457; Yes; Yes; Id. U-10958 An. 2459

Census of the ___Pine Ridge___ reservation of the ___Pine Ridge, South Dakota___ jurisdiction, as of ___April 1___, 19**32**, taken by ___James H. McGregor___, Superintendent.

Key: Number; Surname, Given; Sex; Date of Birth-Age at Last Birthday; Tribe (Oglala Sioux, unless stated otherwise); Degree of Blood; Marital Status; Relationship to Head of Family [Last Census Roll Number]; At Jurisdiction Where Enrolled (Yes/No); (If no – Where); Ward (Yes/No, if given); Allotment, Annuity and Identification Numbers (if given).

2502: Ghost Dog, Theophila; F; 3/9/25-7; F; S; Daughter; 2458; Yes; Yes; Id. U-11551 An. 2450

2503: Ghost Dog, George W.; M; 11/13/26-5; F; S; Son; 2459; Yes; Yes; Id. U-12165 An. none

2504: Giago, Joseph; M; 9/27/00-31; plus 1/4; S; Head; 2460; Yes; Yes; Al. 1423 An. 2461

2505: Giago (no data), Sophia; F; 1870-62; 1/4; Wd; Head; 2461; Yes; Yes; Al. 1419 An. 2463

2506: Giago, Timothy; M; 1895-37; 1/4; M; Head; 2462; Yes; Yes; Al. 1421 An. 2466

2507: Giago, Mary; F; 11/15/22-9; 1/4; S; Daughter; 2463; Yes; Yes; Id. U-9820 An. 2467

2508: Giago, Sophia; F; 6/28/25-6; 1/4; S; Daughter; 2464; Yes; Yes; Id. U-11693 An. none

2509: Giago, Antoine; M; 12/22/27-4; 1/4; S; Son; 2465; Yes; Yes; Id. U-12847 An. none

2510: Giago, Ethel; F; 2/9/30-2; 1/4; S; Daughter; 2466; Yes; Yes; Id. U-13400 An. none

2511: Giago, Lillian; F; 12/19/31-3/12; 1/4; S; Daughter; ---; Yes; Yes; U-13988

2512: Gibbons, Agnes; F; 1890-42; 1/4; S; Head; 2467; Yes; Yes; Al. 2697 An. 2468

2513: Gibbons, William; M; 1889-43; plus 1/4; M; Head; 2468; Yes; Yes; Al. 2678 An. 2470

2514: Gibbons (Long Cat), Elsie; F; 1904-28; F; M; Wife; 2472; Yes; Yes; Al. 2495 An. 2474

2515: Gibbons, Madaline; F; 8/15/14-17; 1/4; S; Daughter; 2469; Yes; Yes; Al. 7691 An. 2471

2516: Gibbons, Martin; M; 1/28/16-16; 1/4; S; Son; 2470; Yes; Yes; Id. U-9572 An. 2472

2517: Gibbons, Clement; M; 9/21/19-12; 1/4; S; Son; 2471; Yes; Yes; Id. U-9574 An. 2473

2518: Gibbons, Charles; M; 7/13/25-6; plus 1/4; S; Son; 2473; Yes; Yes; Id. U-11717 An. none

2519: Gibbons, Antoine; M; 3/18/28-4; 1/4; S; Son; 2474; Yes; Yes; Id. U-12567 An. none

2520: Gibbons, Orval; M; 8/20/30-1; 1/4; S; Son; 2475; Yes; Yes; Id. U-12568 An. none

Census of the __Pine Ridge__ reservation of the __Pine Ridge, South Dakota__ jurisdiction, as of __April 1__, 19**32**, taken by __James H. McGregor__, Superintendent.

Key: Number; Surname, Given; Sex; Date of Birth-Age at Last Birthday; Tribe (Oglala Sioux, unless stated otherwise); Degree of Blood; Marital Status; Relationship to Head of Family [Last Census Roll Number]; At Jurisdiction Where Enrolled (Yes/No); (If no – Where); Ward (Yes/No, if given); Allotment, Annuity and Identification Numbers (if given).

2521: Gibbons, Winfield; M; 1893-39; 1/4; M; Head; 2476; Yes; Yes; Al. 2680 An. 2473

2522: Gibbons (Palmier), Ida; F; 1901-31; 1/4; M; Wife; 2477; Yes; Yes; Al. 2714 An. 2476

2523: Gibbons, Lawrence; M; 8/1/22-9; 1/4; S; Son; 2478; Yes; Yes; Id. U-13039 An. 2477

2524: Gibbons, Pauline; F; 4/8/19-12; 1/4; S; Daughter; 2479; Yes; Yes; Al. 11317 An. 2478

2525: Gibbons, Eugene; M; 2/5/27-5; 1/4; S; Son; 2480; Yes; Yes; Id. U-12284 An. none

2526: Gibbons, Jerome; M; 6/8/31-9/12; 1/4; S; Son; ---; Yes; Yes; U-13934

2527: Gillispie, George; M; 1882-50; 1/4; M; Head; 2481; Yes; Yes; Al. 3246 An. 2480

N.E.: ~~Gillispie (Parker), May; F; -------; Cheyenne; 1/4; M; Wife;~~

2528: Gillispie, Benjamin; M; 10/30/11-20; Oglala Sioux-Cheyenne; 1/4; S; Son; 2482; Yes; Yes; Al. 7631 An. 2482

2529: Gillispie, Tom; M; 2/14/14-18; Oglala Sioux-Cheyenne; 1/4; S; Son; 2483; Yes; Yes; Id. U-9577 An. 2483

2530: Gillispie, John; M; 1/20/16-16; Oglala Sioux-Cheyenne; 1/4; S; Son; 2484; Yes; Yes; Id. U-9578 An. 2484

2531: Gillispie, Emma; F; 10/10/20-11; Oglala Sioux-Cheyenne; 1/4; S; Daughter; 2486; Yes; Yes; Id. U-9580 An. 2486

2532: Gillispie, Henry; M; 6/24/23-8; Oglala Sioux-Cheyenne; 1/4; S; Son; 2487; Yes; Yes; Id. U-11103 An. 2487

2533: Gillispie, Betty; F; 1/03/26-6; Oglala Sioux-Cheyenne; 1/4; S; Daughter; 2488; Yes; Yes; Id. U-11971 An. none

2534: Gillispie, Marion; M; 9/2/28-3; Oglala Sioux-Cheyenne; 1/4; S; Son; 2489; Yes; Yes; Id. U-12826 An. none

2535: Gillispie, Robert; M; 1884-48; 1/4; M; Head; 2490; Yes; Yes; Al. 3250 An. 2490

2536: Gillispie (Janis), Alice; F; 1897-35; 1/4; M; Wife; 2491; Yes; Yes; Al. 1158 An. 2491

2537: Gillispie, Robert, Jr.; M; 7/1/18-13; 1/4; S; Son; 2492; Yes; Yes; Id. U-9575 An. 2492

2538: Gillispie, David T; M; 4/18/21-10; 1/4; S; Son; 2493; Yes; Yes; Id. U-9576 An. 2493

2539: Gillispie, George; M; 3/23/24-8; 1/4; S; Son; 2494; Yes; Yes; Id. U-11684 An. none

2540: Gillispie, William; M; 9/21/27-4; 1/4; S; Son; 2495; Yes; Yes; Id. U-12403 An. none

Census of the **Pine Ridge** reservation of the **Pine Ridge, South Dakota** jurisdiction, as of **April 1**, 19**32**, taken by **James H. McGregor**, Superintendent.

Key: Number; Surname, Given; Sex; Date of Birth-Age at Last Birthday; Tribe (Oglala Sioux, unless stated otherwise); Degree of Blood; Marital Status; Relationship to Head of Family [Last Census Roll Number]; At Jurisdiction Where Enrolled (Yes/No); (If no – Where); Ward (Yes/No, if given); Allotment, Annuity and Identification Numbers (if given).

2541: Gillispie, Jennie; F; 12/31/30-1; 1/4; S; Daughter; 2496; Yes; Yes; Id. U-13692 An. none

2542: Girard, Bell N.; M; 1893-39; -1/4; S; Head; 2497; No; Seattle, City, King, Wash; Yes; Al. 2164 An. 2495

2543: Girard, Ethel; F; 1894-38; -1/4; S; Head; 2498; No; Wenatchee, town, Chelan, Wash; Yes; Al. 2165 An. 2496

2544: Girard, Joseph; M; 1899-33; -1/4; S; Head; 2499; No; Winthrop, town, Okanogan, Wash; Yes; Al. 2166 An. 2497

2545: Girard (no data), Louisa; F; 1872-60; -1/4; M; Head; 2500; No; Seattle, city, King, Wash; Yes; Al. 2163 An. 2498

2546: Girard, Millie; F; 1905-27; -1/4; S; Head; 2501; No; Seattle, City, King, Wash; Yes; Al. 2168 An. 2499

2547: Girard, Robert; M; 1903-29; -1/4; S; Head; 2502; No; Seattle, City, King, Wash; Yes; Al. 2167 An. 2500

2548: Glenn, Edison; M; 1894-38; plus 1/4; M; Head; 2503; Yes; Yes; Al. 5845 An. 2502

2549: Glenn (Gay), Lizzie; F; 1905-27; 1/4; M; Wife; 2507; Yes; Yes; Al. 4181 An. 2406

2550: Glenn, Robert; M; 2/18/16-16; plus 1/4; S; Son; 2504; Yes; Yes; Al. 8094 An. 2503

2551: Glenn, Rollo; M; 2/14/19-13; 1/4; S; Son; 2505; Yes; Yes; Id. U-9581 An. 2504

2552: Glenn, Margaret; F; 6/11/20-11; 1/4; S; Daughter; 2506; Yes; Yes; Id. U-9582 An. 2505

2553: Glenn, Ruby; F; 7/27/26-5; 1/4; S; Daughter; 2508; Yes; Yes; Id. U-12220 An. none

2554: Glenn, Cecell; F; 8/23/28-3; 1/4; S; Daughter; 2509; Yes; Yes; Id. U-12773 An. none

2555: Glenn, Donald; M; 3/16/31-1; 1/4; S; Son; 2510; Yes; Yes; Id. U-13779 An. none

2556: Glenn, James; M; 6/5/97-34; plus 1/4; M; Head; 2511; Yes; Yes; Al. 5846 An. 2506

2557: Glenn (Lone Wolf), Marion; F; 1906-26; 1/4; M; Wife; 2512; Yes; Yes; Al. 4687 An. 4164

Census of the **Pine Ridge** reservation of the **Pine Ridge, South Dakota** jurisdiction, as of **April 1**, 19**32**, taken by **James H. McGregor**, Superintendent.

Key: Number; Surname, Given; Sex; Date of Birth-Age at Last Birthday; Tribe (Oglala Sioux, unless stated otherwise); Degree of Blood; Marital Status; Relationship to Head of Family [Last Census Roll Number]; At Jurisdiction Where Enrolled (Yes/No); (If no – Where); Ward (Yes/No, if given); Allotment, Annuity and Identification Numbers (if given).

2558: Glenn, Viola; F; 9/26/28-3; 1/4; S; Daughter; 2513; Yes; Yes; Id. U-12806 An. none

2559: Glenn, Flora; F; 3/28/31-1; 1/4; S; Daughter; 2514; Yes; Yes; Id. U-13780 An. none

2560: Glick, Otis; M; 1906-26; -1/4; S; Head; 2515; No; Unknown; Yes; Al. 2969 An. 2507

2561: Glick, William; M; 1904-28; -1/4; S; Head; 2516; No; Milwaukee, city, Milwaukee, Wis; Yes; Al. 3968 An. 2508

2562: Godfrey, Arthur; M; 1906-26; -1/4; S; Head; 2517; No; Hot Springs, town, Fall River, S.D.; Yes; Al. 2960 An. 2509

2563: Godfrey (no data), Mattie; F; 1868-64; plus 1/4; Wd.; Head; 2518; No; Hot Springs, town, Fall River, S.D.; Yes; Al. 2687 An. 2510

2564: Goes in Center, John; M; 1876-56; F; M; Head; 2519; Yes; Yes; Al. 5768 An. 2513

2565: Goes in Center (Lip), Katie; F; 1883-49; F; M; Wife; 2520; Yes; Yes; Al. 3936 An. 2514

2566: Goes in Center, Abraham; M; 9/1/10-21; F; S; Son; 2521; Yes; Yes; Al. 5771 An. 2515

2567: Goes in Center, Martha; F; 7/20/12-19; F; S; Daughter; 2522; Yes; Yes; Al. 7855 An. 2516

2568: Goes in Center, Maggie; F; 8/13/14-17; F; S; Daughter; 2523; Yes; Yes; Id. U-8128 An. 2517

2569: Goes in Center, Lucy; F; 12/17/16-15; F; S; Daughter; 2524; Yes; Yes; Id. U-9584 An. 2518

2570: Goes in Center, Veronica; F; 3/25/28-4; F; S; Daughter; 2525; Yes; Yes; Id. U-12547 An. none

2571: Goes in Center, Amos; M; 2/27/31-1; F; S; Son; 2526; Yes; Yes; Id. U-13758 An. none

2572: Goes in Center, Oliver; M; 6/28/05-26; F; M; Head; 2527; Yes; Yes; Al. 3937 An. 2522

2573: Goes in Center (Romero), Mabel; F; 2/ /07-25; plus 1/4; M; Wife; 2528; Yes; Yes; Al. 1921 An. 5785

2574: Goings (no data), Blanche; F; 1876-56; plus 1/4; S; Head; 2530; Yes; Yes; Al. 2222 An. 2526

2575: Goings, Oliver; M; 3/14/11-21; 1/4; S; Son; 2531; Yes; Yes; Id. U-9587 An. 2527

Census of the **Pine Ridge** reservation of the **Pine Ridge, South Dakota** jurisdiction, as of **April 1**, 19**32**, taken by **James H. McGregor**, Superintendent.

Key: Number; Surname, Given; Sex; Date of Birth-Age at Last Birthday; Tribe (Oglala Sioux, unless stated otherwise); Degree of Blood; Marital Status; Relationship to Head of Family [Last Census Roll Number]; At Jurisdiction Where Enrolled (Yes/No); (If no – Where); Ward (Yes/No, if given); Allotment, Annuity and Identification Numbers (if given).

2576: Goings, Ione; F; 2/26/18-14; 1/4; S; Daughter; 2533; Yes; Yes; Id. U-9589 An. 2529

2577: Goings, Earl; M; 1894-38; 1/4; S; Head; 2534; Yes; Yes; Al. 3702 An. 2530

2578: Goings, Frank; M; 1872-60; plus 1/4; M; Head; 2535; Yes; no; Al. 2591 An. 2531

2579: Goings (no data), Julia; F; 1872-60; F; M; Wife; 2536; Yes; no; Al. 5460 An. 2532

2580: Goings, Roland; M; 11/3/14-17; 1/4; S; Son; 2537; Yes; Yes; Al. 7919 An. 2533

2581: Goings, Quintard; M; 4/26/18-13; 1/4; S; Son; 2538; Yes; Yes; Id. U-9590 An. 2534

2582: Goings, Garnet; M; 1896-36; 1/4; M; Head; 2539; Yes; Yes; Al. 3743 An. 2535

2583: Goings (Little Crow), Ellen; F; 1900-32; 1/4; M; Wife; 2540; Yes; Yes; Al. 6454 An. 2536

2584: Goings, Lloyd; M; 4/6/23-8; 1/4; S; Son; 2541; Yes; Yes; Id. U-13031 An. 2537

2585: Goings, Vincent; M; 7/28/27-4; 1/4; S; Son; 2542; Yes; Yes; Id. U-12376 An. none

2586: Goings, Joseph; M; 3/19/29-3; 1/4; S; Son; 2543; Yes; Yes; Id. U-13108 An. none

2587: Goings, Hobson; M; 1899-33; 1/4; M; Head; 2544; Yes; Yes; Al. 5462 An. 2556

2588: Goings (Chief), Mary; F; 1896-36; 1/4; M; Wife; 2545; Yes; Yes; Al. 3930 An. 2539

2589: Allman, Frank; M; 6/7/18-13; 1/4; S; S.Son; 2546; Yes; Yes; Id. U-9022 An. 2540

2590: Goings, Lloyd; M; 9/9/20-11; 1/4; S; Son; 2547; Yes; Yes; Id. U-9780 An. 2541

2591: Goings, Cecil; M; 7/5/23-8; 1/4; S; Son; 2548; Yes; Yes; Id. U-11102 An. 2542

2592: Goings, Lessanes; F; 4/6/25-6; 1/4; S; Daughter; 2549; Yes; Yes; Id. U-11560 An. none

2593: Goings, Katherine; F; 4/22/27-4; plus 1/4; S; Daughter; 2550; Yes; Yes; Id. U-12285 An. none

2594: Goings, Angelique; F; 3/7/27-1/12; 1/4; S; Daughter; ---; Yes; Yes; U-14128

2595: Goings, John H; M; 1896-36; 1/4; M; Head; 2552; Yes; Yes; Al. 3744 An. 2543

Census of the ___**Pine Ridge**___ reservation of the **Pine Ridge, South Dakota** jurisdiction, as of ___**April 1**___, 19**32**, taken by ___**James H. McGregor**___, Superintendent.

Key: Number; Surname, Given; Sex; Date of Birth-Age at Last Birthday; Tribe (Oglala Sioux, unless stated otherwise); Degree of Blood; Marital Status; Relationship to Head of Family [Last Census Roll Number]; At Jurisdiction Where Enrolled (Yes/No); (If no – Where); Ward (Yes/No, if given); Allotment, Annuity and Identification Numbers (if given).

2596: Goings (Janis), Kiva; F; 1896-36; 1/4; M; Wife; 2553; Yes; Yes; Al. 3607 An. 2544

2597: Goings, Florine; F; 4/26/17-14; 1/4; S; Daughter; 2554; Yes; Yes; Id. U-9591 An. 2545

2598: Goings, Lenora; F; 2/3/23-9; 1/4; S; Daughter; 2555; Yes; Yes; Id. U-13008 An. 2547

2599: Goings, Louis; M; 1874-58; 1/4; M; Head; 2556; No; Flandreau, town, Moody, S.D.; Yes; Al. 5728 An. 2549

N.E.: ~~Goings (Henderson), Florence; F; ------; Santee Sioux; plus 1/4; M; Wife; Ft. Peck Agency, Poplar, Mont.;~~

2600: Goings, Francis; M; 5/10/19-22; 1/4; S; Head; 2557; No; Flandreau, town, Moody, S.D.; Yes; Al. 5731 An. 2550

2601: Goings, Louise; F; 6/22/04-27; 1/4; S; Head; 2558; Yes; Yes; Al. 5729 An. 2553

2602: Goings, Luke; M; 1905-27; 1/4; S; Head; 2559; Yes; Yes; Al. 6922 An. 2554

2603: Goings, Nettie; F; 1906-26; 1/4; S; Head; 2560; Yes; Yes; Al. 5730 An. 2555
2604: Goings, William; M; 1903-29; plus 1/4; S; Head; 2561; Yes; Yes; Al. 4562 An. 2556

2605: Good, ---; F; 1858-74; F; Wd.; Head; 2562; Yes; Yes; Al. 3514 An. 2557
2606: High Pine, Reynold; M; 11/26/11-10; F; S; Gr. Son; 2563; Yes; Yes; Al. 6745 An. 2559

N.E.: ~~Good, Baptiste E; M; -------; Rosebud Sioux; F; M; Head;~~

2607: Good (Swallow), Ellen; F; 1904-28; F; M; Wife; 2564; Yes; Yes; Al. 2417 An. 6736

2608: Good Buffalo, Charles; M; 1891-41; F; M; Head; 2565; Yes; Yes; Al. 7675 An. 2560
2609: Good Buffalo (Spotted Buffalo), Hilda; F; 1893-39; F; M; Wife; 2566; Yes; Yes; Al. 4196 An. 2561
2610: Good Buffalo, Elizabeth; F; 6/27/16-15; F; S; Daughter; 2567; Yes; Yes; Id. U-9597 An. 2562
2611: Good Buffalo, Comer; M; 11/19/19-12; F; S; Son; 2568; Yes; Yes; Id. U-9599 An. 2563
2612: Good Buffalo, Peter; M; 4/24/27-4; F; S; Son; 2570; Yes; Yes; Id. U-12310 An. none
2613: Good Buffalo, Charles Jr.; M; 7/17/29-2; F; S; Son; 2571; Yes; Yes; Id. U-13227 An. none

Census of the __Pine Ridge__ reservation of the __Pine Ridge, South Dakota__ jurisdiction, as of __April 1__, 1932, taken by __James H. McGregor__, Superintendent.

Key: Number; Surname, Given; Sex; Date of Birth-Age at Last Birthday; Tribe (Oglala Sioux, unless stated otherwise); Degree of Blood; Marital Status; Relationship to Head of Family [Last Census Roll Number]; At Jurisdiction Where Enrolled (Yes/No); (If no – Where); Ward (Yes/No, if given); Allotment, Annuity and Identification Numbers (if given).

2614: Good Buffalo, Minnie; F; 6/5/31-9/12; F; S; Daughter; ---; Yes; Yes; U-13869

2615: Good Buffalo, Frank; M; 1888-44; F; M; Head; 2572; Yes; Yes; Id. U-5945 An. 2564

2616: Good Buffalo (Runs Close To Lodge), Annie; F; 1882-50; F; M; Wife; 2577; Yes; Yes; Al. 5820 An. 5971

2617: Good Buffalo, Henry; M; 3/31/11-21; F; S; Son; 2573; Yes; Yes; Al. 7375 An. 2566

2618: Good Buffalo, Oliver; M; 6/9/13-18; F; S; Son; 2574; Yes; Yes; Al. 7376 An. 2567

2619: Good Buffalo, Amelia; F; 3/11/16-16; F; S; Daughter; 2575; Yes; Yes; Id. U-9595 An. 2568

2620: Good Buffalo, Daniel; M; 5/21/22-9; F; S; Son; 2576; Yes; Yes; Id. U-11046 An. 2569

2621: Runs Close To Lodge, Peter; M; 11/17/15-16; F; S; S.Son; 2578; Yes; Yes; Id. U-10351 An. 5973

2622: Good Crow, Levi; M; 1/31/10-22; F; M; Head; 966; Yes; Yes; Al. 6741 An. 558

2623: Good Crow (Cuny), Viola; F; 12/8/12-19; plus 1/4; M; Wife; 1769; Yes; Yes; Al. 7503 An. 1789

2624: Good Crow, Levi E.; M; 4/30/31-11/12; 1/4; S; Son; ---; Yes; Yes; U-13935

2625: Good Crow, Felix; M; 2/19/09-23; F; M; Head; 2579; Yes; Yes; Al. 6426 An. 2578

2626: Good Crow (Eagle Bull), Eva; F; 11/14/05-26; F; M; Wife; 2580; Yes; Yes; Al. 6689 An. 1999

2627: Good Crow, Mildred; F; 7/11/28-3; F; S; Daughter; 2581; Yes; Yes; Id. U-12757 An. none

2628: Good Horse, ---; F; 1863-69; F; S; Head; 2582; Yes; Yes; Al. 6168 An. 2580

2629: Good Horse, Bob; M; 1887-45; F; S; Head; 2583; Yes; Yes; Al. 9010 An. 2583

2630: Good Lance, Frank; M; 1879-53; F; Wd.; Head; 2584; Yes; Yes; Al. 111 An. 2584

N.E.: ~~Good Lance (Scout), Cecelia; F; ------; Rosebud Sioux; M; Wife;~~

2631: Good Lance, Peter; M; 1904-28; F; Wd.; Head; 2585; Yes; Yes; Al. 5708 An. 2586

Census of the **Pine Ridge** reservation of the **Pine Ridge, South Dakota** jurisdiction, as of **April 1**, 19**32**, taken by **James H. McGregor**, Superintendent.

Key: Number; Surname, Given; Sex; Date of Birth-Age at Last Birthday; Tribe (Oglala Sioux, unless stated otherwise); Degree of Blood; Marital Status; Relationship to Head of Family [Last Census Roll Number]; At Jurisdiction Where Enrolled (Yes/No); (If no – Where); Ward (Yes/No, if given); Allotment, Annuity and Identification Numbers (if given).

2632: Good Lance (Spotted Crow), Lucy; F; 4/16/08-23; F; Wd.; Head; 2586; Yes; Yes; Al. 7719 An. 6464

2633: Good Lance, Lena; F; 9/11/28-3; F; S; Daughter; 2587; Yes; Yes; Id. U-12863 An. none

2634: Good Medicine, Louis; M; 1897-35; plus 1/4; M; Head; 2588; Yes; Yes; Al. 6764 An. 2588

2635: Good Medicine (Pretty Bull), Katie; F; 1905-27; 1/4; M; Wife; 2589; Yes; Yes; Al. 6834 An. 2589

2636: Good Medicine, Sallie; F; 1/21/26-6; 1/4; S; Daughter; 2590; Yes; Yes; Id. U-11816 An. none

2637: Good Medicine, Vivian; F; 8/26/28-3; 1/4; S; Daughter; 2591; Yes; Yes; Id. U-12878 An. none

2638: Good Medicine, Lena; F; 8/27/30-1; 1/4; S; Daughter; 2592; Yes; Yes; Id. U-13601 An. none

2639: Good Medicine, Velma; F; 2/6/32-1/12; 1/4; S; Daughter; ---; Yes; Yes; U-14093

2640: Good Plume, Louis; M; 1863-69; F; M; Head; 2593; Yes; Yes; Al. 527 An. 2590

2641: Good Plume, Lucy; F; 11/23/17-14; F; S; Daughter; 2595; Yes; Yes; Id. U-11107 An. 2592

2642: Good Plume, Mamie; F; 12/14/22-9; F; S; Daughter; 2596; Yes; Yes; Id. U-12093 An. none

2643: Good Plume, Jennie; F; 2/8/26-6; F; S; Daughter; 2597; Yes; Yes; Id. U-11827 An. none

2644: Good Plume, Carver; M; 11/27/29-2; F; S; Son; 2598; Yes; Yes; Id. U-13288 An. none

2645: Good Shell, Jesse; F; 1849-83; F; Wd; Head; 2599; Yes; Yes; Al. 6758 An. 2594

N.E.: ~~Good Shield, Jesse; M; ------; Rosebud Sioux; M; Head;~~

2646: Good Shield (Bald Eagle), Jessie; F; 1904-28; F; M; Wife; 2600; Yes; Yes; Al. 954 An. 3859

N.E.: ~~Good Shield, Edwin; M; ------; Rosebud Sioux; F; M; Head;~~

2647: Good Shield (Her Horses), Maggie; F; 1904-28; F; M; Wife; 2601; Yes; Yes; Al. 1881 An. 2595

2648: Good Shield, Theresa; F; 4/4/25-6; F; S; Daughter; 2602; Yes; Yes; Id. U-11518 An. 2596

2649: Good Shield, Jeanette; F; 4/30/28-3; F; S; Daughter; 2603; Yes; Yes; Id. U-12622 An. none

Census of the **Pine Ridge** reservation of the **Pine Ridge, South Dakota** jurisdiction, as of **April 1**, 1932, taken by **James H. McGregor**, Superintendent.

Key: Number; Surname, Given; Sex; Date of Birth-Age at Last Birthday; Tribe (Oglala Sioux, unless stated otherwise); Degree of Blood; Marital Status; Relationship to Head of Family [Last Census Roll Number]; At Jurisdiction Where Enrolled (Yes/No); (If no – Where); Ward (Yes/No, if given); Allotment, Annuity and Identification Numbers (if given).

2650: Good Shield, Grace; F; 8/16/31-7/12; F; S; Daughter; ---; Yes; Yes; U-13890

2651: Good Shield, Oliver; M; 1862-70; F; M; Head; 2604; Yes; Yes; Al. 742 An. 2597

2652: Good Shield (no data), Mary; F; 1856-76; F; M; Wife; 2605; Yes; Yes; Al. 7332 An. 2598

2653: Good Shield, Philip; M; 1900-32; F; M; Head; 2606; Yes; Yes; Al. 7442 An. 2599

2654: Good Shield (Eagle Bear), Helen; F; 1900-32; F; M; Wife; 2607; Yes; Yes; Al. 750 An. 2600

2655: Good Shield, Carolina; F; 6/5/21-10; F; S; Daughter; 2608; Yes; Yes; Id. U-10870 An. 2601

2656: Good Shield, Matthew; M; 7/30/24-7; F; S; Son; 2609; Yes; Yes; Id. U-12895 An. none

2657: Good Shield, Alfonzo; M; 10/23/29-2; F; S; Son; 2610; Yes; Yes; Id. U-13289 An. none

2658: Good Shot, Jacob; M; 1894-38; F; S; Head; 2611; No; Cincinnati, Hamilton, Ohio; Yes; Al. 580 An. 2602

2659: Good Shot, Oscar; M; 1897-35; F; S; Head; 2612; Yes; Yes; Al. 581 An. 2603

2660: Good Soldier, Richard; M; 1869-63; F; M: Head; 2613; Yes; Yes; Al. 2869 An. 2604

2661: Good Soldier (no data), Cora; F; 1874-58; F; M; Wife; 2614; Yes; Yes; Al. 2870 An. 2605

2662: Good Soldier, Keva; F; 3/2/16-16; F; S; Daughter; 2615; Yes; Yes; Id. U-9605 An. 2607

2663: Good Soldier, Stephen; M; 1893-39; F; M: Head; 2616; Yes; Yes; Al. 3392 An. 2608

2664: Good Voice Crow, ---; M; 1859-73; F; M: Head; 2617; Yes; Yes; Al. 3633 An. 2609

2665: Owns the Mule, ---; F; 1845-87; F; M; Wife; 2618; Yes; Yes; Al. 5398 An. 2610

2666: Good Voice Elk, Samuel; M; 1897-35; F; M: Head; 2619; Yes; Yes; Al. 1040 An. 2616

2667: Good Voice Elk (Sitting Eagle), Winnie; F; 1905-27; F; M; Wife; 2620; Yes; Yes; Al. 6863 An. 6325

2668: Good Voice Elk, Vienna; F; 11/2/27-4; F; S; Daughter; 2621; Yes; Yes; Id. U-12424 An. none

Census of the **Pine Ridge** reservation of the **Pine Ridge, South Dakota** jurisdiction, as of **April 1**, 19**32**, taken by **James H. McGregor**, Superintendent.

Key: Number; Surname, Given; Sex; Date of Birth-Age at Last Birthday; Tribe (Oglala Sioux, unless stated otherwise); Degree of Blood; Marital Status; Relationship to Head of Family [Last Census Roll Number]; At Jurisdiction Where Enrolled (Yes/No); (If no – Where); Ward (Yes/No, if given); Allotment, Annuity and Identification Numbers (if given).

2669: Good Voice Elk, Jeannette; F; 7/1/29-2; F; S; Daughter; 2622; Yes; Yes; Id. U-13226 An. none
2670: Good Voice Elk, William; M; 9/18/31-6/12; F; S; Son; ---; Yes; Yes; U-13964

2671: Good Voice Elk, Frank; M; 1895-37; F; M; Head; 2623; Yes; Yes; Al. 1039 An. 2612
2672: Good Voice Elk (Fox Belly), Eva; F; 7/29/09-22; F; M; Wife; 2624; Yes; Yes; Al. 5906 An. 2326
2673: Good Voice Elk, May; F; 5/30/31-10/12; F; S; Daughter; ---; Yes; Yes; U-13854

2674: Good Voice Flute, Austin; M; 1885-47; F; M; Head; 2625; Yes; Yes; Al. 3181 An. 2619
2675: Good Voice Flute (Chase In Winter), Clara; F; 1886-46; F; M; Wife; 2626; Yes; Yes; Al. 6169 An. 2620
2676: Good Voice Flute, Victoria; F; 5/7/14-17; F; S; Daughter; 2627; Yes; Yes; Al. 7572 An. 2622
2677: Good Voice Flute, Mark; M; 9/26/16-15; F; S; Son; 2628; Yes; Yes; Id. U-9609 An. 2623
2678: Good Voice Flute, Alexander; M; 8/8/24-7; F; S; Son; 2629; Yes; Yes; Id. U-11513 An. 2625
2679: Good Voice Flute, Wilson; M; 6/23/27-4; F; S; Son; 2630; Yes; Yes; Id. U-12404 An. none
2680: Good Voice Flute, Andrew; M; 2/9/22-10; F; S; Son; 2631; Yes; Yes; Id. U-10889 An. 2624

2681: Good Voice Flute (no data), Dinah; F; 1854-78; F; Wd.; Head; 2632; Yes; Yes; Al. 6223 An. 2618

2682: Good Voice Flute, Guy; M; 1890-42; F; M; Head; 2634; Yes; Yes; Al. 3210 An. 2625
2683: Good Voice Flute, Levi; M; 7/27/13-18; F; S; Son; 2635; Yes; Yes; Al. 7644 An. 2628
2684: Good Voice Flute, Guy Jr.; M; 11/30/16-15; F; S; Son; 2636; Yes; Yes; Id. U-9610 An. 2629
2685: Good Voice Flute, Eugene; M; 11/11/19-12; F; S; Son; 2637; Yes; Yes; Id. U-9611 An. 2630
2686: Good Voice Flute, Martha; F; 12/3/21-10; F; S; Daughter; 2638; Yes; Yes; Al. 9612 An. 2631
2687: Good Voice Flute, Joseph; M; 10/16/27-4; F; S; Son; 2639; Yes; Yes; Id. U-12425 An. none

Census of the __**Pine Ridge**__ reservation of the __**Pine Ridge, South Dakota**__ jurisdiction, as of __**April 1**__, 19**32**, taken by __**James H. McGregor**__, Superintendent.

Key: Number; Surname, Given; Sex; Date of Birth-Age at Last Birthday; Tribe (Oglala Sioux, unless stated otherwise); Degree of Blood; Marital Status; Relationship to Head of Family [Last Census Roll Number]; At Jurisdiction Where Enrolled (Yes/No); (If no – Where); Ward (Yes/No, if given); Allotment, Annuity and Identification Numbers (if given).

2688: Good Voice Iron, Charles; M; 1872-60; F; M: Head; 2640; Yes; Yes; Al. 7854 An. 2633

2689: Good Weasel, Joseph; M; 1900-32; F; M: Head; 2641; Yes; Yes; Al. 6424 An. 2634

2690: Good Weasel (Crow), Mary; F; 1899-33; F; M; Wife; 2642; Yes; Yes; Al. 7509 An. 2635

2691: Good Weasel, Simon; M; 2/4/26-6; F; S; Son; 2643; Yes; Yes; Id. U-11825 An. none

2692: Good Weasel, Lavern; M; 2/25/30-2; F; S; Son; 2644; Yes; Yes; Id. U-11380 An. none

2693: Good Weasel, Lizzie; F; 1907-25; F; S; Head; 2645; Yes; Yes; Al. 6425 An. 1994

2694: Chase Alone, Margaret; F; 6/4/29-2; F; S; Daughter; 2646; Yes; Yes; Id. U-13320 An. none

2695: Chase Alone, Rowland; M; 7/28/31-8/12; F; S; Son; ---; Yes; Yes; U-13886

~~N.E.: Grabbing Bear, Bernard; M; ------; Rosebud Sioux; M; Head;~~
2696: Grabbing Bear (Uses Bow), Julia; F; 1869-63; F; M; Wife; 2647; Yes; Yes; Al. 2312 An. 2637

~~N.E.: Grabbing Bear, Baptiste; M; ------; Rosebud Sioux; F; M; Head;~~
2697: Grabbing Bear (Hornbeck), Julia; F; 1898-34; F; M; Wife; 2648; Yes; Yes; Al. 854 An. 2638

2698: Grabbing Bear, Howard; M; 10/16/18-13; plus 1/4; S; Son; 2649; Yes; Yes; Id. U-9613 An. 2639

2699: Grabbing Bear, Dorothy; F; 3/26/21-11; 1/4; S; Daughter; 2650; Yes; Yes; Id. U-9614 An. 2640

2700: Grabbing Bear, Edna; F; 3/16/23-9; 1/4; S; Daughter; 2651; Yes; Yes; Id. U-13079 An. 2641

2701: Grabbing Bear, Theresa; F; 1/28/29-3; plus 1/4; S; Daughter; 2652; Yes; Yes; Id. U-13106 An. none

2702: Grabbing Bear, Emily; F; 1/14/31-1; 1/4; S; Daughter; 2653; Yes; Yes; Id. U-13693 An. none

2703: Graham, Howard; M; 1888-44; 1/4; M: Head; 2654; Yes; Yes; Al. 4169 An. 2643

2704: Graham (Galligo), Alvina; F; 1888-44; 1/4; M; Wife; 2655; Yes; Yes; Al. 2787 An. 2644

2705: Graham, Francis; M; 11/4/16-15; 1/4; S; Son; 2656; Yes; Yes; Id. U-9616 An. 2645

Census of the **Pine Ridge** reservation of the **Pine Ridge, South Dakota** jurisdiction, as of **April 1**, 1932, taken by **James H. McGregor**, Superintendent.

Key: Number; Surname, Given; Sex; Date of Birth-Age at Last Birthday; Tribe (Oglala Sioux, unless stated otherwise); Degree of Blood; Marital Status; Relationship to Head of Family [Last Census Roll Number]; At Jurisdiction Where Enrolled (Yes/No); (If no – Where); Ward (Yes/No, if given); Allotment, Annuity and Identification Numbers (if given).

2706: Graham, Bennie; M; 10/1/17-14; 1/4; S; Son; 2657; Yes; Yes; Id. U-9617 An. 2646
2707: Graham, Hobart; M; 3/5/19-13; 1/4; S; Son; 2658; Yes; Yes; Id. U-9618 An. 2647
2708: Graham, John; M; 2/25/22-10; 1/4; S; Son; 2659; Yes; Yes; Id. U-12023 An. 2649
2709: Graham, Ollie A; F; 3/3/21-8; 1/4; S; Daughter; 2660; Yes; Yes; Id. U-11250 An. 2650
2710: Graham, Gloria; F; 2/15/28-4; 1/4; S; Daughter; 2661; Yes; Yes; Id. U-12623 An. none
2711: Graham, Mary B; F; 1/11/30-2; 1/4; S; Daughter; 2662; Yes; Yes; Id. U-13416 An. none

2712: Graham, Ernest; M; 1905-27; 1/4; S: Head; 2663; Yes; Yes; Al. 2196 An. 2651

2713: Graham, John; M; 1898-34; 1/4; S: Head; 2664; Yes; Yes; Al. 2199 An. 2652

2714: Graham (no data), Lizzie; F; 1864-68; plus 1/4; Wd; Head; 2665; Yes; Yes; Al. 2195 An. 2653
2715: Grainger (Janis-Sears), Josephine; F; 1879-53; 1/4; M: Head; 2666; No; Poplar, town, Sheridan, Mont.; Yes; Al. 4551 An. 2654
2716: Grainger, Earl; M; 5/15/18-13; 1/4; S; Son; 2667; No; Same; Yes; Id. U-9620 An. 2655
2717: Grainger, Ruth; F; 5/31/21-10; 1/4; S; Daughter; 2668; No; same; Yes; Id. U-9621 An. 2656

2718: Grass, Edward; M; 1889-43; F; M: Head; 2669; Yes; Yes; Al. 5542 An. 2657
2719: Grass (War Bonnet), Lizzie; F; 1894-38; F; M; Wife; 2670; Yes; Yes; Al. 447 An. 2658
2720: Grass, Sarah; F; 7/5/15-16; F; S; Daughter; 2671; Yes; Yes; Id. U-9624 An. 2659
2721: Grass, Dora; F; 8/23/18-13; F; S; Daughter; 2672; Yes; Yes; Id. U-9625 An. 2660
2722: Grass, Duffy; M; 2/19/21-11; F; S; Son; 2673; Yes; Yes; Id. U-9626 An. 2661

2723: Grass, James Sr.; M; 1865-67; F; M: Head; 2674; Yes; Yes; Al. 690 An. 2663
2724: Grass (Rabbit-Good Horse), Jennie; F; 1872-60; F; M; Wife; 2675; Yes; Yes; Al. 5007 An. 2582

2725: Grass, James Jr.; M; 1895-37; F; M: Head; 2676; Yes; Yes; Al. 688 An. 2666
N.E.: Grass (Red Bird), Lucy; F; ------; Rosebud Sioux; F; M; Wife;

Census of the __**Pine Ridge**__ reservation of the __**Pine Ridge, South Dakota**__ jurisdiction, as of __**April 1**__, 19**32**, taken by __**James H. McGregor**__, Superintendent.

Key: Number; Surname, Given; Sex; Date of Birth-Age at Last Birthday; Tribe (Oglala Sioux, unless stated otherwise); Degree of Blood; Marital Status; Relationship to Head of Family [Last Census Roll Number]; At Jurisdiction Where Enrolled (Yes/No); (If no – Where); Ward (Yes/No, if given); Allotment, Annuity and Identification Numbers (if given).

2726: Grass, John; M; 1897-35; F; M: Head; 2678; Yes; Yes; Al. 5543 An. 2667

~~N.E.: Grass (Weston), Etta C; F; ------; Flandreau Sioux; F; M; Wife;~~

2727: Grass, Christine; F; 4/9/25-6; F; S; Daughter; 2679; Yes; Yes; Id. U-11700 An. none

2728: Grass, Kenneth; M; 2/24/27-5; F; S; Son; 2680; Yes; Yes; Id. U-12311 An. none

2729: Grass, Velma; F; 8/7/29-2; F; S; Daughter; 2681; Yes; Yes; Id. U-13291 An. none

2730: Grass, Newman; M; 4/30-29; plus 1/4; S: Head; 2682; Yes; Yes; Al. 4259 An. 2668

2731: Grass, Thomas; M; 1858-74; F; Wd.: Head; 2683; Yes; Yes; Al. 687 An. 2669

2732: Grass, Joseph; M; 4/13/09-22; F; M: Head; 2684; Yes; Yes; Al. 5541 An. 2670

2733: Grass (Romero), Sussie; F; 8/23/07-24; 1/4; M; Wife; 5817; Yes; Yes; Al. 3895 An. 5790

2734: Romero, Leo H; M; 1/7/27-5; 1/4; S; S.Son; 5818; Yes; Yes; Id. U-12210 An. none

2735: Romero, Edward; M; 5/31/29-2; 1/4; S; S.Son; 5819; Yes; Yes; Id. U-13193 An. none

2736: Grass, Carmen; M; 12/27/31-3/12; plus 1/4; S; Son; ---; Yes; Yes; U-13990 An. none

~~N.E.: Grass Rope, Joseph; M; ------; Lower Brule Sioux; F; M; Head;~~

2737: Grass Rope (Brave Eagle), Bessie; M; 1897-35; F; M: Head; 2685; Yes; Yes; Al. 1487 An. 2671

~~N.E.: Gray (Eagle Tail), Paul; M; ------; Rosebud Sioux; F; M; Head;~~

2738: Gray (Monroe), Lena; F; 1902-30; plus 1/4; M; Wife; 2686; Yes; Yes; Al. 2324 An. 4522

2739: Gray Blanket, John; M; 1897-35; F; S: Head; 2687; No; Canton Hospital, S.D.; Yes; Al. 333 An. 2672

2740: Gray Cow Eagle, John; M; 1883-49; F; S: Head; 2688; Yes; Yes; Al. 3015 An. 2674

2741: Gray Grass, Charles; M; 1893-39; F; M: Head; 2689; Yes; Yes; Al. 942 An. 2675

2742: Gray Grass (Pretty Bull), Carrie; F; 1896-36; F; M; Wife; 2690; Yes; Yes; Al. 494 An. 2676

Census of the __Pine Ridge__ reservation of the __Pine Ridge, South Dakota__ jurisdiction, as of __April 1__, 19**32**, taken by __James H. McGregor__, Superintendent.

Key: Number; Surname, Given; Sex; Date of Birth-Age at Last Birthday; Tribe (Oglala Sioux, unless stated otherwise); Degree of Blood; Marital Status; Relationship to Head of Family [Last Census Roll Number]; At Jurisdiction Where Enrolled (Yes/No); (If no – Where); Ward (Yes/No, if given); Allotment, Annuity and Identification Numbers (if given).

2743: Gray Grass, Blair; M; 2/18/18-14; F; S; Son; 2691; Yes; Yes; U-9628 An. 2677

2744: Grass Gray, Martha; F; 2/7/28-4; F; S; Daughter; 2692; Yes; Yes; Id. U-12516 An. none

2745: Gray Grass, Kenneth; M; 9/18/30-1; F; S; Son; 2693; Yes; Yes; U-13640 An. none

2746: Green, Estella; F; 1906-26; plus 1/4; S: Head; 2693; No; Interior, town, Jackson, S.D.; Yes; Al. 3887 An. 2679

2747: Green, George; M; 9/18/08-23; 1/4; S: Head; 2695; No; Interior, town, Jackson, S.D.; Yes; Al. 3888 An. 2682

2748: Green (no data), Lucy; F; 1879-53; 1/4; Wd: Head; 2696; No; Interior, town, Jackson, S.D.; No; Al. 3886 An. 2681

2749: Green, Douglas; M; 12/9/14-17; 1/4; S: Son; 2697; No; Same; Yes; Al. 8091 An. 2684

2750 Green (Ecoffey), Inez; F; 12/14/13-18; 1/4; M; Head; 2698; Yes; Yes; Al. 7914 An. 2076

2751: Green, Geraldine; F; 9/9/31-6/12; -1/4; S; Daughter; ---; Yes; Yes; U-13917

2752: Green, Myrtle; F; 10/12/11-20; 1/4; S: Head; 2693; No; Interior, town, Jackson, S.D.; Yes; Al. 7752 An. 2683

2753: Green, Alma; F; 12/22/19-12; -1/4; S: Alone; 2700; No; Omaha, city, Douglas, Nebr.; Yes; Id. U-10852 An. 2686

2754: Green (no data), Susie; F; 1863-69; plus 1/4; Wd: Head; 2701; No; Merriman, town, Cherry, Nebr.; Yes; Al. 5453 An. 2687

2755: Gresh, John; M; 1896-36; 1/4; M: Head; 2702; Yes; Yes; Al. 5496 An. 2688

2756: Gresh (Clifford), Myrtle; F; 1907-25; 1/4; M; Wife; 2703; Yes; Yes; Al. 5496 An. 2688

2757: Gresh, Margaret; F; 12/17/28-3; 1/4; S; Daughter; 2704; Yes; Yes; Id. U-13139 An. none

2758: Gresh, John O.; M; 7/19/30-1; 1/4; S; Son; 2705; Yes; Yes; Id. U-13641 An. none

2759: Gresh, Todd; M; 1893-39; 1/4; S; Head; 2706; Yes; Yes; Al. 4798 An. 2689

2760: Griffith (Craven), Hattie; F; 1881-51; -1/4; M; Head; 2707; Yes; Yes; Al. 3900 An. 2690

Census of the   **Pine Ridge**   reservation of the **Pine Ridge, South Dakota** jurisdiction, as of   **April 1**   , 19**32**, taken by   **James H. McGregor**   , Superintendent.

Key: Number; Surname, Given; Sex; Date of Birth-Age at Last Birthday; Tribe (Oglala Sioux, unless stated otherwise); Degree of Blood; Marital Status; Relationship to Head of Family [Last Census Roll Number]; At Jurisdiction Where Enrolled (Yes/No); (If no – Where); Ward (Yes/No, if given); Allotment, Annuity and Identification Numbers (if given).

2761: Griffith, Miriam; (Hand Note: Counted as Male), M; 12/12/12-19; -1/4; S; Son; 2708; Yes; Yes; Al. 7205 An. 2693

2762: Griffith, Frances; F; 1/16/15-17; -1/4; S; Daughter; 2709; Yes; Yes Al. 8142 An. 2694

2763: Groaning Bear, Henry; M; 1889-43; F; Wd.; Head; 2710; Yes; Yes; Al. 2696 An. 7835

2764: Groshong (Provost), Julia; F; 1904-28; 1/4; M; Head; 1644; Yes; Yes; Al. 4484 An. 1671

2765: Cottier, Allen; M; 3/3/22-10; 1/4; S; Son; 1645; Yes; Yes; Id. U-11509 An. 1672

2766: Ground Spider, Jonah; M; 1897-35; F; M: Head; 2711; Yes; Yes; Al. 6561 An. 2697

2767: Ground Spider (Red Breath Bear), Mildred; F; 1893-39; F; M; Wife; 2712; Yes; Yes; Al. 6430 An. 2698

2768: Red Breath Bear, Ella; F; 6/17/17-14; F; S; S.Daughter; 2713; Yes; Yes; Id. U-9631 An. 2699

2769: Ground Spider, Elinan; F; 10/23/20-11; F; S; Daughter; 2714; Yes; Yes; Id. U-9630 An. 2700

2770: Ground Spider, Cyril; M; 9/14/22-9; F; S; Son; 2715; Yes; Yes; Id. U-12000 An. 2701

2771: Ground Spider, Allen J.; M; 1901-31; F; M: Head; 2716; Yes; Yes; Al. 7431 An. 2702

2772: Ground Spider (Iron Heart), Elizabeth; F; 1904-28; F; M; Wife; 4104; Yes; Yes; Al. 6430 An. 2703

2773: Ground Spider, Vincent; M; 5/10/28-3; F; S; Son; 2718; Yes; Yes; Id. U-12568 An. none

2774: Ground Spider, Mary E.; F; 9/25/30-1; F; S; Daughter; 2719; Yes; Yes; Id. U-13627 An. none

2775: Grunting, ---; F; 1847-85; F; Wd; Head; 2720; Yes; Yes; Al. 2114 An. 2705

2776: Guerrier, Rosa; F; 6/16/19-12; Oglala Sioux; plus 1/4; S; Alone; 2721; No; Chey. & Arapahoe; Yes; Id. U-9632 An. 2708

N.E.:   Haikey, Clarence; M; ---- --; Creek Indian; F; M; Head;
2777: Haikey (Young), Freda; F; 4/27/09-22; plus 1/4; M; Wife; 2722; No; Broken Arrow, town, Tulsa, Okla.; Yes; Al. 4868 An. 7971

Census of the **Pine Ridge** reservation of the **Pine Ridge, South Dakota** jurisdiction, as of **April 1**, 19**32,** taken by **James H. McGregor**, Superintendent.

Key: Number; Surname, Given; Sex; Date of Birth-Age at Last Birthday; Tribe (Oglala Sioux, unless stated otherwise); Degree of Blood; Marital Status; Relationship to Head of Family [Last Census Roll Number]; At Jurisdiction Where Enrolled (Yes/No); (If no – Where); Ward (Yes/No, if given); Allotment, Annuity and Identification Numbers (if given).

2778: Hairy Bird, Jonas; M; 1908-24; F; S: Head; 2723; Yes; Yes; Al. 4093 An. 7277

2779: Hall, Alfred; M; 1907-25; -1/4; S: Head; 2724; No; Cody, town, Cherry, Nebr.; Yes; Al. 2577 An. 2710

2780: Hall, Alice E; F; 6/15/10-21; -1/4; S: Head; 2725; No; Chicago, city, Cook, Ill.; Yes; Al. 5441 An. 2711

2781: Hall, James H.; M; 11/10/11-20; -1/4; S: Head; 2726; No; Waukegan, town, Lake, Ill.; Yes; Al. 7190 An. 2712

2782: Hall, Nellie; F; 1908-24; -1/4; S: Head; 2727; Yes; Yes; Al. 4766 An. 2713

2783: Hall (Fisher), Hattie; F; 1883-49; -1/4; M; Head; 2728; No; Rapid City, city, Pennington, S.D.; Yes; Al. 3765 An. 2714

2784: Hall, Charles; M; 11/8/16-15; -1/4; S: Son; 2729; No; Same; Yes; Id. U-9633 An. 2715

2785: Hall, Stephen; M; 1900-32; -1/4; S: Head; 2730; No; Cody, town, Cherry, Nebr.; Yes; Al. 2574 An. 2716

2786: Hall, Walter; M; 1901-31; -1/4; S: Head; 2731; Yes; Yes; Al. 2575 An. 2717

2787: Hall, William A; M; 1905-27; -1/4; S: Head; 2732; No; Litchfield, town, Sherman, Nebr.; Yes; Al. 2756 An. 2720

2788: Hamernick (Provost), Josephine; F; 1/12/10-22; 1/4; M; Head; 2734; Yes; Yes; Al. 6698 An. 5190

2789: Hamernick, Mary L.; F; 9/7/29-2; -1/4; S; Daughter; 2735; Yes; Yes; Id. U-13245 An. none

2790: Hamernick, Louisa; F; 10/5/31-5/12; -1/4; S; Daughter; ---; Yes; Yes; U-13936

2791: Hamilton, Mary; F; 4/14/23-8; plus 1/4; S; Alone; 2735; No; Sanborn, town, Niagara, N.Y.; Yes; Id. U-11134 An. 2719

2792: Hand, Joseph; M; 1895-37; F; M: Head; 2736; Yes; Yes; Al. 1257 An. 2721

2793: Hand (Chief Eagle), Susanna; F; 1891-41; F; M; Wife; 2737; Yes; Yes; Id. U-9634 An. 2722

2794: Hall, Floyd; M; 1/11/18-14; F; S: Son; 2738; No; Same; Yes; Id. U-9635 An. 2723

2795: Handsome Elk (Chips), Avena; F; 12/24/12-19; F; M; Head; 5307; Yes; Yes; Al. 7054 An. 1419

Census of the **Pine Ridge** reservation of the **Pine Ridge, South Dakota** jurisdiction, as of **April 1**, 19**32**, taken by **James H. McGregor**, Superintendent.

Key: Number; Surname, Given; Sex; Date of Birth-Age at Last Birthday; Tribe (Oglala Sioux, unless stated otherwise); Degree of Blood; Marital Status; Relationship to Head of Family [Last Census Roll Number]; At Jurisdiction Where Enrolled (Yes/No); (If no – Where); Ward (Yes/No, if given); Allotment, Annuity and Identification Numbers (if given).

2796: Hansen (Rooks), Catherine; F; 4/30/98-33; plus 1/4; M; Head; 2741; Yes; Yes; Al. 4060 An. 5793

2797: Hard Heart, Johnson; M; 1883-49; F; Wd.: Head; 2743; Yes; Yes; Al. 5120 An. 2728

2798: Hard Heart, Edward; M; 1906-26; F; M: Head; 2744; Yes; Yes; Al. 5124 An. 2730

2799: Hard Heart (Kills Well), Ida; F; 2/23/13-19; F; M; Wife; 2745; Yes; Yes Al. 7029 An. 3557

2800: Hard Heart, Leona; F; 2/22/32-1/12; F; S; Daughter; ---; Yes; Yes; U-149094

2801: Hard to Hit, Edward; M; 1874-58; F; M: Head; 2746; Yes; Yes; Al. 1716 An. 2731

2802: Hard to Hit (Bear Stops-Shot), Nellie; F; 1899-33; F; M; Wife; 428; Yes; Yes; Al. 197 An. 434

2803: Harvey, Emma; F; 1902-30; plus 1/4; S; Head; 2747; Yes; Yes; Al. 2726 An. 2733

2804: Harvey, Edward H; M; 1907-25; 1/4; S; Head; 2748; Yes; Yes; Al. 2727 An. 2735

2805: Harvey, Jacob; M; 1891-41; 1/4; S; Head; 2749; Yes; Yes; Al. 2722 An. 2736

2806: Harvey, John; M; 1888-44; 1/4; M; Head; 2750; Yes; Yes; Al. 2721 An. 2737

2807: Harvey (Conroy), Millie; F; 1891-41; 1/4; M; Wife; 2751; Yes; Yes; Al. 358 An. 1621

2808: Harvey, Wilbert; M; 8/19/25-6; 1/4; S; Son; 2752; Yes; Yes; Id. U-12286 An. none

2809: Harvey, Zella; F; 1/29/27-5; 1/4; S; Daughter; 2753; Yes; Yes; Id. U-12312 An. none

2810: Harvey, George Jr.; M; 10/13/29-2; 1/4; S; Son; 2754; Yes; Yes; Id. U-13694 An. none

2811: Harvey, Joseph; M; 1896-36; plus 1/4; S; Head; 2755; Yes; Yes; Al. 2724 An. 2738

2812: Has No Horses, Morris; M; 1903-29; F; M; Head; 2756; Yes; Yes; Al. 1029 An. 2739

2813: Has No Horses (Chips), Ethel; F; 1908-24; F; M; Wife; 2757; Yes; Yes; Al. 3987 An. 7938

2814: Has No Horses, Arthur; M; 1/28/29-3; F; S; Son; 2758; Yes; Yes; Id. U-13210 An. none

Census of the __Pine Ridge__ reservation of the __Pine Ridge, South Dakota__ jurisdiction, as of __April 1__, 19**32**, taken by __James H. McGregor__, Superintendent.

Key: Number; Surname, Given; Sex; Date of Birth-Age at Last Birthday; Tribe (Oglala Sioux, unless stated otherwise); Degree of Blood; Marital Status; Relationship to Head of Family [Last Census Roll Number]; At Jurisdiction Where Enrolled (Yes/No); (If no – Where); Ward (Yes/No, if given); Allotment, Annuity and Identification Numbers (if given).

2815: Has No Horses, Ramona; F; 10/2/30-1; F; S; Daughter; 2759; Yes; Yes; Id. U-13667 An. none

2816: Hat, James; M; 1897-35; F; M; Head; 2760; Yes; Yes; Al. 2867 An. 2740
2817: Hat (Kills Enemy), Sallie; F; 1901-31; F; M; Wife; 2761; Yes; Yes; Id. U-9805 An. 2742
2818: Hat, Febie; F; 8/21/20-11; F; S; Daughter; 2762; Yes; Yes; Id. U-9638 An. 2741
2819: Hat, Rosie; F; 5/8/24-7; F; S; Daughter; 2763; Yes; Yes; Id. U-11313 An. 2743
2820: Hat, Mary E; F; 9/29/26-6; F; S; Daughter; 2764; Yes; Yes; Id. U-11874 An. none
2821: Hat, Rapheal; M; 1/18/28-4; F; S; Son; 2765; Yes; Yes; Id. U-12517 An. none
2822: Hat, Annie; F; 1/26/30-2; F; S; Daughter; 2766; Yes; Yes; Id. U-13331 An. none

2823: Hat, Lambert; M; 1867-65; F; M; Head; 2767; Yes; Yes; Al. 2865 An. 2745
2824: Hat (no date), Sallie; F; 1872-60; F; M; Wife; 2768; Yes; Yes; Al. 2866 An. 2746
2825: Hat, Stephen; M; 2/9/12-20; F; S; Son; 2769; Yes; Yes; Al. 6405 An. 2748

2826: Hauff (Brown), Leona; F; 1903-29; plus 1/4; M; Head; 2770; Yes; Yes; Al. 4023 An. 2749
2827: Hauff, William; M; 10/26/25-6; -1/4; S; Son; 2771; Yes; Yes; Id. U-12158 An. none
2828: Hauff, Richard; M; 1/13/28-4; -1/4; S; Son; 2772; Yes; Yes; Id. U-12569 An. none
2829: Hauff, Sylvia; F; 11/28/29-2; -1/4; S; Daughter; 2773; Yes; Yes; Id. U-13332 An. none

2830: Hawk, ---; M; 1862-70; F; M; Head; 2774; Yes; Yes; Al. 3253 An. 2750
2831: Plenty Horses, ---; F; 1873-59; F; M; Wife; 2775; Yes; Yes; Al. 3283 An. 2751
2832: Hawk, Betty; F; 1912-20; F; S; Daughter; 2776; Yes; Yes; Id. U-9639 An. 2754

2833: Hawk, Marjory; F; 7/10/10-21; F; S; Head; 2777; Yes; Yes; Al. 6136 An. 2753

2834: Hawk, Robert; M; 11/7/08-23; F; S; Head; 2778; Yes; Yes; Al. 6135 An. 2752

2835: Hawk, Fal; M; 1906-26; F; M; Head; 2779; Yes; Yes; Al. 3286 An. 2751

Census of the __Pine Ridge__ reservation of the __Pine Ridge, South Dakota__ jurisdiction, as of __April 1__, 19**32**, taken by __James H. McGregor__, Superintendent.

Key: Number; Surname, Given; Sex; Date of Birth-Age at Last Birthday; Tribe (Oglala Sioux, unless stated otherwise); Degree of Blood; Marital Status; Relationship to Head of Family [Last Census Roll Number]; At Jurisdiction Where Enrolled (Yes/No); (If no – Where); Ward (Yes/No, if given); Allotment, Annuity and Identification Numbers (if given).

2836: Hawk (Hat), Jennie; F; 1906-26; F; M; Wife; 2780; Yes; Yes; Al. 2880 An. 2744
2837: Hawk, Michael J; M; 11/19/31-4/12; F; S; Son; ---; Yes; Yes; U-14095

2838: Hawk, Louis; M; 1902-30; F; M; Head; 2781; Yes; Yes; Al. 185 An. 2757
2839: Hawk (Provost), Julia; F; 1904-28; plus 1/4; M; Wife; 2782; Yes; Yes; Al. 49 An. 5187
2840: Hawk, Rosaline; F; 10/7/26-5; 1/4; S; Daughter; 2783; Yes; Yes; Id. U-12111 An. none
2841: Hawk, Ramona; F; 12/1/28-3; 1/4; S; Daughter; 2784; Yes; Yes; Id. U-13108 An. none

2842: Hawkins, Benjamin; M; 1901-31; 1/4; S; Head; 2785; Yes; Yes; Al. 4651 An. 2761

2843: Hawkins, James Sr.; M; 1860-72; 1/4; M; Head; 2786; Yes; Yes; Al. 4612 An. 2762
2844: Hawkins (Ladeau), Emma; F; 1876-56; 1/4; M; Wife; 2787; Yes; Yes; Al. 4613 An. 2763
2845: Hawkins, Grace; F; 8/13/13-18; 1/4; S; Daughter; 2789; Yes; Yes; Id. U-9644 An. 2766
2846: Hawkins, Emma Marie; F; 11/2/19-12; 1/4; S; Daughter; 2790; Yes; Yes; Id. U-9645 An. 2767

2847: Hawkins, Posie; M; 12/4/10-21; 1/4; M; Head; 2788; Yes; Yes; Al. 5812 An. 2765
2848: Hawkins (Randall), Gertrude; F; 12/12/09-22; plus 1/4; M; Wife; 5356; Yes; Yes; Al. 5674 An. 5313

2849: Hawkins, James Jr.; M; 1882-50; 1/4; M; Head; 2791; Yes; Yes; Al. 4624 An. 2768
2850: Hawkins (Owl Bull), Mabel; F; 1883-49; F; M; Wife; 2792; Yes; Yes; Al. 4625 An. 2769
2851: Hawkins, Lawrence; M; 6/27/16-15; plus 1/4; S; Son; 2793; Yes; Yes; Id. U-9646 An. 2771

2852: Hawkins, Roy; M; 1908-24; 1/4; M; Head; 2794; Yes; Yes; Al. 2642 An. 2768
N.E.: ~~Hawkins (Quick Bear), Eve; F; ------; Rosebud Sioux; F; M; Wife;~~
2853: Hawkins, Rena; F; 4/9/30-1; plus 1/4; S; Daughter; ---; Yes; Yes; U-13792

2854: Hawkins, Joseph; M; 1884-48; plus 1/4; M; Head; 2795; Yes; Yes; Al. 1110 An. 2772

Census of the **Pine Ridge** reservation of the **Pine Ridge, South Dakota** jurisdiction, as of **April 1**, 19**32**, taken by **James H. McGregor**, Superintendent.

Key: Number; Surname, Given; Sex; Date of Birth-Age at Last Birthday; Tribe (Oglala Sioux, unless stated otherwise); Degree of Blood; Marital Status; Relationship to Head of Family [Last Census Roll Number]; At Jurisdiction Where Enrolled (Yes/No); (If no – Where); Ward (Yes/No, if given); Allotment, Annuity and Identification Numbers (if given).

2855: Hawkins (Richard), Julia; F; 1891-41; 1/4; M; Wife; 2796; Yes; Yes; Al. 2034 An. 2773

2856: Charging, Lavon; F; 6/14/23-8; 1/4; S; Ward; 2797; Yes; Yes; Id. U-11333 An. 1324

2857: Hawkins, Louis; M; 1858-74; 1/4; Wd.; Head; 2798; Yes; Yes; Al. 1108 An. 2774

2858: Hawkins, William; M; 1891-41; 1/4; M; Head; 2799; No; Yankton Agency, S.D.; Yes; Al. 1111 An. 2776

N.E.: Hawkins (Cournoyer), Agnes; F; ------; Yankton Sioux; plus 1/4; M; Wife;

2859: Hawkins, Henry; M; 2/28/16-16; 1/4; S; Son; 2800; No; Yankton Agency, S.D.; Yes; Id. U-9640 An. 2777

2860: Hawkins, William M; M; 10/4/17-14; 1/4; S; Son; 2801; No; Yankton Agency, S.D.; Yes; Id. U-9641 An. 2778

2861: Hawkins, Archibald; M; 4/24/19-13; 1/4; S; Son; 2802; No; Yankton Agency, S.D.; Yes; Id. U-9642 An. 2779

2862: Hawkins, Louise; F; 11/27/20-11; 1/4; S; Daughter; 2803; No; Yankton Agency, S.D.; Yes; Id. U-9643 An. 2780

2863: Hawkins, Joseph; M; 5/19/29-2; 1/4; S; Son; 2804; No; Yankton Agency, S.D.; Yes; Id. U-13333 An. none

2864: Hawkins, Benedict; M; 7/22/30-1; 1/4; S; Son; 2805; No; Yankton Agency, S.D.; Yes; Id. U-13549 An. none

2865: Hawk Man, ---; M; 1855-77; F; M; Head; 2806; Yes; Yes; Al. 1276 An. 2781

2866: Hawk Man (Horn Chips), Rosa; F; 1874-58; F; M; Wife; 2807; Yes; Yes; Al. 5112 An. 2782

2867: Hawk Wing, ---; M; 1850-82; plus 1/4; Wd; Head; 2808; Yes; Yes; Al. 5526 An. 2305

2868: Hawk Wing, Garfield; M; 5/14/18-13; 1/4; S; Gr. Son; 2809; Yes; Yes; Id. U-9650 An. 2787

2869: Hawk Wing, James; M; 1886-46; 1/4; M; Head; 2810; Yes; Yes; Al. 2158 An. 2786

N.E.: Hawk Wing (Comes From War), Lucy; F; ------; Rosebud Sioux; M; Wife;

2870: Hawk Wing, Peter; M; 2/29/30-2; 1/4; S; Son; 2811; Yes; Yes; Id. U-13453 An. none

2871: Hawk Wing, Luke; M; 1885-47; 1/4; M; Head; 2812; Yes; Yes; Al. 2162 An. 2788

2872: Hawk Wing (Wolf On Hill), Alice; F; 1890-42; F; M; Wife; 2813; Yes; Yes; Al. 5527 An. 2789

Census of the __**Pine Ridge**__ reservation of the __**Pine Ridge, South Dakota**__ jurisdiction, as of __**April 1**__, 19**32**, taken by __**James H. McGregor**__, Superintendent.

Key: Number; Surname, Given; Sex; Date of Birth-Age at Last Birthday; Tribe (Oglala Sioux, unless stated otherwise); Degree of Blood; Marital Status; Relationship to Head of Family [Last Census Roll Number]; At Jurisdiction Where Enrolled (Yes/No); (If no – Where); Ward (Yes/No, if given); Allotment, Annuity and Identification Numbers (if given).

2873: Hawk Wing, Nicholas; M; 4/10/11-20; plus 1/4; S; Son; 2814; Yes; Yes; Al. 5528 An. 2790

2874: Hawk Wing, Foster; M; 2/6/16-16; 1/4; S; Son; 2815; Yes; Yes; Al. 7863 An. 2792

2875: Hawk Wing, Greely; M; 3/29/20-12; 1/4; S; Son; 2816; Yes; Yes; Id. U-9648 An. 2793

2876: Hawk Wing, Ollie; F; 9/30/22-9; 1/4; S; Daughter; 2817; Yes; Yes; Id. U-9649 An. 2794

2877: Hawk Wing, Owen; M; 8/30/24-7; 1/4; S; Son; 2818; Yes; Yes; Id. U-12007 An. 2795

2878: Hawk Wing, Elsie; F; 1/18/27-5; 1/4; S; Daughter; 2819; Yes; Yes; Id. U-12213 An. none

2879: Hawk Wing, George; M; 3/30/29-3; 1/4; S; Son; 2820; Yes; Yes; Id. U-13140 An. none

2880: Hay Leg, ---; M; 1854-78; F; Wd.; Head; 2821; Yes; Yes; Al. 7206 An. 2796

2881: Heart Man, Thomas; M; 1880-52; F; S; Head; 2822; Yes; Yes; Al. 3497 An. 2800

2882: He Crow, Jackson; M; 1881-51; F; M; Head; 2823; Yes; Yes; Al. 3067 An. 2801

2883: He Crow (Chase In Winter), Winola; F; 1881-51; F; M; Wife; 2824; Yes; Yes; Al. 3068 An. 2802

2884: He Crow, Stephen; M; 12/3/11-20; F; S; Son; 2825; Yes; Yes; Al. 6080 An. 2804

2885: He Crow, Robert; M; 5/18/21-10; F; S; Son; 2826; Yes; Yes; Id. U-11628 An. 2805

2886: He Crow, Moses; M; 10/2/07-24; F; M; Head; 2827; Yes; Yes; Al. 3069 An. 2803

2887: He Crow (Pumpkin Seed), Eva; F; 5/16/10-21; F; M; Wife; 2828; Yes; Yes; Al. 7386 An. 5233

2888: He Crow, Jefferson; M; 3/29/27-5; F; S; Son; 2829; Yes; Yes; Id. U-12313 An. none

2889: He Crow, Herman; M; 9/12/28-3; F; S; Son; 2830; Yes; Yes; Id. U-12828 An. none

2890: He Crow, Francis; M; 7/15/30-1; F; S; Son; 2831; Yes; Yes; Id. U-13602 An. none

2891: He Dog, ---; M; 1837-95; F; Wd.; Head; 2832; Yes; Yes; Al. 6157 An. 2806

2892: He Dog (Cloud Man), Lucy; F; 1856-76; F; Wd; Head; 2833; Yes; Yes; Al. 3105 An. 2807

Census of the **Pine Ridge** reservation of the **Pine Ridge, South Dakota** jurisdiction, as of **April 1**, 19**32**, taken by **James H. McGregor**, Superintendent.

Key: Number; Surname, Given; Sex; Date of Birth-Age at Last Birthday; Tribe (Oglala Sioux, unless stated otherwise); Degree of Blood; Marital Status; Relationship to Head of Family [Last Census Roll Number]; At Jurisdiction Where Enrolled (Yes/No); (If no – Where); Ward (Yes/No, if given); Allotment, Annuity and Identification Numbers (if given).

2893: Helm (O'Rourke), Georgianna; F; 1859-73; plus 1/4; M; Head; 2834; Yes; Yes; Al. 1116 An. 2808

2894: Helm, William Jr.; M; 1904-28; Plus 1/4; Wd.; Head; 2835; Yes; Yes; Al. 1614 An. 2809

2895: Helper, Simon; M; 1876-56; F; Wd.; Head; 2836; Yes; Yes; Al. 3328 An. 2812

2896: Helper, Peter; M; 11/14/09-22; F; S; Son; 2838; Yes; Yes; Al. 6343 An. 2814

2897: Helper, Jacob; M; 3/16/12-20; F; S; Son; 2839; Yes; Yes; Al. 6344 An. 2815

2898: Helper, Sadie; F; 3/28/19-13; F; S; Daughter; 2840; Yes; Yes; Id. U-9651 An. 2816

2899: Heminger (Montileaux), Julia; F; 1876-56; plus 1/4; Wd; Head; 2841; No; Rapid City, city, Pennington, S.D.; No; Al. 3615 An. 2817

2900: Henderson (no data), Louisa; F; 1870-62; 1/4; M; Head; 2842; No; Hay Springs, town, Sheridan, Nebr.; No; Al. 1349 An. 2818

N.E.: Henry, Alex; M; ---- --; Yankton Sioux; F; M; Head;

2901: Henry (Thunder Bear), Alice; F; 1880-52; F; M; Wife; 2843; Yes; Yes; Al. 4372 An. 7776

2902: Henry, Thomas; M; 1862-70; F; M; Head; 2844; Yes; Yes; Al. 1398 An. 2819

2903: Henry (Pawnee Leggins), Lizzie; F; 1873-59; F; M; Wife; 2845; Yes; Yes; Al. 5892 An. 2820

2904: Henry, Wallace; M; 1893-39; F; M; Head; 2846; Yes; Yes; Al. 1399 An. 2821

2905: Henry (Bear Robe), Annie; F; 1880-52; F; M; Wife; 2847; Yes; Yes; Al. 8014 An. 2822

2906: Henry, Ross; M; 5/4/23-8; F; S; Son; 2848; Yes; Yes; Id. U-13087 An. 2826

2907: Hercher (Trimble), Ellen; F; 1899-33; plus 1/4; M; Head; 2849; No; Interior, town, Jackson, S.D.; Yes; Al. 3795 An. 2827

2908: Hercher, Ellen G.; F; 5/2/20-11; -1/4; S; Daughter; 2850; No; Same; Yes; Id. U-9653 An. 2828

2909: Hercher, William H; M; 1/13/23-9; -1/4; S; Son; 2851; No; Same; Yes; Id. U-14020 An. 2829

2910: Hercher, John A; M; 8/16/25-6; -1/4; S; Son; 2852; No; Same; Yes; Id. U-11839 An. none

2911: Her Deer, ---; F; 1854-78; F; Wd; Head; 2853; Yes; Yes; Al. 3831 An. 2830

Census of the ____**Pine Ridge**____ reservation of the ____**Pine Ridge, South Dakota**____ jurisdiction, as of ____**April 1**____, 19**32**, taken by ____**James H. McGregor**____, Superintendent.

Key: Number; Surname, Given; Sex; Date of Birth-Age at Last Birthday; Tribe (Oglala Sioux, unless stated otherwise); Degree of Blood; Marital Status; Relationship to Head of Family [Last Census Roll Number]; At Jurisdiction Where Enrolled (Yes/No); (If no – Where); Ward (Yes/No, if given); Allotment, Annuity and Identification Numbers (if given).

2912:   Her Good Horse, ---; F; 1857-75; F; Wd.; Head; 2854; Yes; Yes; Al. 3686 An. 2831

2913:   Her Holy Blanket, ---; F; 1846-86; F; Wd.; Head; 2855; Yes; Yes; Al. 4429 An. 2833

2914:   Her Horses, #2; M; 1872-60; F; M; Head; 2856; Yes; Yes; Al. 1879 An. 2834

2915:   Herley (Fisher), Grace; F; 1884-48; plus 1/4; M; Head; 2860; No; Stanfield, town, Umatilla, Ore; Yes; Al. 3824 An. 2839

2916;   Herley, Loretta; F; 8/22/11-20; -1/4; S; Daughter; 2861; No; Same; Yes; Al. 7778 An. 2841

2917;   Herley, Adelia; F; 12/22/15-16; -1/4; S; Daughter; 2862; No; Stanfield, town, Umatilla, Ore.; Yes; Al. 8075 An. 2842

2918;   Herley, Lawrence; M; 12/26/20-11; -1/4; S; Son; 2863; No; Same; Yes; Id. U-9654 An. 2843

2919;   Herley, Henry; M; 1907-25; -1/4; S; Head; 2864; No; Portland, city, Multnomah, Ore.; Yes; Al. 3825 An. 2840

2920;   Herman, Jacob; M; 1892-40; plus 1/4; M; Head; 2865; Yes; No; Al. 5926 An. 2844

2921;   Herman (Janis), Alice; F; 1901-31; 1/4; M; Wife; 2866; Yes; Yes; Al. 3582 An. 2845

2922;   Herman, Jacob T; M; 9/5/25-6; 1/4; S; Son; 2867; Yes; Yes; Id. U-11807 An. none

2923;   Herman, Paul J; M; 5/4/27-4; 1/4; S; Son; 2868; Yes; Yes; Id. U-12314 An. none

2924;   Her Many Horses, Samuel; M; 1886-46; F; M; Head; 2870; Yes; Yes; Al. 745 An. 2848

2925;   Her Many Horses (Mathews), Susie; F; 1886-46; plus 1/4; M; Wife; 2871; Yes; Yes; Al. 142 An. 2853

2926;   Her Many Horses, Josephine; F; 1/11/13-19; 1/4; S; Daughter; 2872; Yes; Yes; Al. 7092 An. 2851

2927;   Her Many Horses, David; M; 6/3/15-16; 1/4; S; Son; 2873; Yes; Yes; Id. U-9658 An. 2852

2928;   Mathews, Vina; F; 11/19/12-19; 1/4; S; S. Daughter; 2874; Yes; Yes; Al. 6695 An. 2855

2929;   Mathews, Aloysius; M; 6/21/15-16; 1/4; S; S. Son; 2875; Yes; Yes; Id. U-9656 An. 2856

2930;   Mathews, Gilbert; M; 5/19/17-14; 1/4; S; S. Son; 2876; Yes; Yes; Id. U-9655 An. 2857

Census of the __Pine Ridge__ reservation of the __Pine Ridge, South Dakota__ jurisdiction, as of __April 1__, 19**32,** taken by __James H. McGregor__, Superintendent.

Key: Number; Surname, Given; Sex; Date of Birth-Age at Last Birthday; Tribe (Oglala Sioux, unless stated otherwise); Degree of Blood; Marital Status; Relationship to Head of Family [Last Census Roll Number]; At Jurisdiction Where Enrolled (Yes/No); (If no – Where); Ward (Yes/No, if given); Allotment, Annuity and Identification Numbers (if given).

2931; Matthews, Julia; F; 6/3/19-12; 1/4; S; S. Daughter; 2877; Yes; Yes; Id. U-9657 An. 2858

2932; Her Many Horses, Daniel T.; M; 12/28/08-23; 1/4; M; Head; 2878; Yes; Yes; Al. 6860 An. 2850

2933; Her Many Horses (Matthews), Emily; F; 4/15/11-20; 1/4; M; Wife; 2879; Yes; Yes; Al. 6694 An. 2854

2934; Her Many Horses, Louis; M; 10/2/30-1; 1/4; S; Son; 2880; Yes; Yes; Id. U-13642 An. none

2935; Her Many Horses, Antoine; M; 4/30/11-20; 1/4; S; Head; 2881; Yes; Yes; Al. 7091 An. 2849

2936; Hernandez, Florenco; M; 1881-51; 1/4; M; Head; 2882; Yes; Yes; Al. 1591 An. 2859

2937; Hernandez (no data), Lillie; F; 1887-45; 1/4; M; Wife; 2883; Yes; No; Al. 1590 An. 2860

2938; Hernandez, Mortimer; M; 4/7/09-23; plus 1/4; S; Son; 2884; Yes; Yes; Al. 7283 An. 2861

2939; Hernandez, Ambrose; M; 11/2/12-19; 1/4; S; Son; 2885; Yes; Yes; Al. 7284 An. 2862

2940; Hernandez, Floyd F; M; 1/28/15-17; 1/4; S; Son; 2886; Yes; Yes; Al. 8069 An. 2863

2941; Hernandez, Annie; F; 4/14/17-14; 1/4; S; Daughter; 2887; Yes; Yes; Id. U-9662 An. 2864

2942; Hernandez, Chancy; M; 5/7/26-5; 1/4; S; Son; 2888; Yes; Yes; Id. U-11913 An. none

2943; Hernandez, Reys; M; 1887-45; 1/4; M; Head; 2889; Yes; No; Al. 1410 An. 2865

2944; Hernandez (Mousseau), Sophia; F; 1887-45; 1/4; M; Wife; 2890; Yes; Yes; Al. 698 An. 2866

2945; Hernandez, Joseph; M; 5/28/13-18; 1/4; S; Son; 2891; Yes; Yes; Al. 7282 An.2868

2946; Hernandez, Alice; F; 4/22/16-16; 1/4; S; Daughter; 2892; Yes; Yes; Al. 7943 An.2869

2947; Hernandez, Alexander; M; 4/27/17-14; 1/4; S; Son; 2893; Yes; Yes; Id. U-9660 An. 2870

2948; Hernandez, Louis; M; 9/21/19-12; 1/4; S; Son; 2894; Yes; Yes; Id. U-9661 An. 2871

2949; Hernandez, Raymond; M; 3/19/22-10; 1/4; S; Son; 2895; Yes; Yes; Id. U-10910 An. 2872

Census of the __Pine Ridge__ reservation of the __Pine Ridge, South Dakota__ jurisdiction, as of __April 1__, 19**32**, taken by __James H. McGregor__, Superintendent.

Key: Number; Surname; Given; Sex; Date of Birth-Age at Last Birthday; Tribe (Oglala Sioux, unless stated otherwise); Degree of Blood; Marital Status; Relationship to Head of Family [Last Census Roll Number]; At Jurisdiction Where Enrolled (Yes/No); (If no – Where); Ward (Yes/No, if given); Allotment, Annuity and Identification Numbers (if given).

2950; Hernandez, Katherine; F; 2/7/24-8; 1/4; S; Daughter; 2896; Yes; Yes; Id. U-11208 An. 2873

2951; Hernandez, Alfonzo; M; 6/17/26-5; 1/4; S; Son; 2897; Yes; Yes; Id. U-11945 An. none

2952; Hernandez, Cecelia; F; 11/2/10-21; 1/4; S; Head; 2898; Yes; Yes; Al. 7281 An.2867

2953; Hernandez, Valentine; M; 1889-43; plus 1/4; M; Head; 2899; Yes; No; Al. 1411 An. 2874

2954; Hernandez (Cross), Daisy; F; 1908-24; 1/4; M; Wife; 2900; Yes; Yes; Al. 7060 An. 618

2955; Hernandez, Regina; F; 4/9/28-3; 1/4; S; Daughter; 2901; Yes; Yes; Id. U-12570 An. none

2956; Hernandez, Anna M; F; 5/21/31-10/12; 1/4; S; Daughter; ---; Yes; Yes; U-13834

2957; Her Road, ---; F; 1860-72; F; Wd; Head; 2902; Yes; Yes; Al. 5173 An. 2877

2958; High Bull, Charles; M; 1899-33; F; M; Head; 2903; Yes; Yes; Al. 94 An. 2878

N.E.: ~~High Bull (Arrow Side), Annie; F; ------; Rosebud Sioux;F; M; Wife;~~

2959; Hill Bull, Charles Jr.; M; 6/3/31-9/12; F; S; Son; ---; Yes; Yes; U-13855

2960; High Cat, Leo; M; 1874-58; F; M; Head; 2904; Yes; Yes; Al. 6532 An. 2881
2961; High Cat (no data), Alice; F; 1873-59; F; M; Wife; 2905; Yes; Yes; Al. 6351 An. 2882

2962; High Cat, Sarah; F; 2/25/09-23; F; S; Head; 2906; Yes; Yes; Al. 6352 An. 2883

2963; High Chief, Charles; M; 1903-29; F; M; Head; 2907; Yes; Yes; Al. 4903 An. 2885

N.E.: ~~High Chief (Grouse[sic]), Alice; F; ------; Cheyenne; F; M; Wife;~~

2964; High Chief, Clara; F; 1896-36; F; S; Head; 2908; Yes; Yes; Al. 4730 An. 2886

2965; High Crane, Otto; M; 1899-33; F; M; Head; 2909; Yes; Yes; Al. 2979 An. 2887
2966; High Crane (Charging), Tillie; F; 12/3/04-27; plus 1/4; M; Wife; 2910; Yes; Yes; Al. 5192 An. 1321

Census of the **Pine Ridge** reservation of the **Pine Ridge, South Dakota** jurisdiction, as of **April 1**, 19**32,** taken by **James H. McGregor**, Superintendent.

Key: Number; Surname, Given; Sex; Date of Birth-Age at Last Birthday; Tribe (Oglala Sioux, unless stated otherwise); Degree of Blood; Marital Status; Relationship to Head of Family [Last Census Roll Number]; At Jurisdiction Where Enrolled (Yes/No); (If no – Where); Ward (Yes/No, if given); Allotment, Annuity and Identification Numbers (if given).

2967; High Crane, Frank; M; 5/22/29-2; 1/4; S; Son; 2911; Yes; Yes; Id. U-13185 An. none

2968; High Eagle (Brown Eyes), Fannie; F; 1852-80; F; Wd.; Head; 2912; Yes; Yes; Al. 4814 An. 2888

2969; High Eagle, Joseph; M; 1862-70; F; Wd.; Head; 2913; Yes; Yes; Al. 3454 An. 2889

2970; High Eagle (Ecoffey), Nora; F; 12/11/10-21; plus 1/4; Wd.; Head; 2914; Yes; Yes; Al. 5435 An. 2086

2971; High Heron, ---; M; 1872-60; F; Wd.; Head; 2915; Yes; Yes; Al. 5087 An. 2893

N.E.: High Horse, Paul; M; -------; Rosebud Sioux; F; M; Head;
2972; High Horse (Whirlwind), Anna; F; 1888-44; F; M; Wife; 2916; Yes; Yes; Al. 5746 An. 2894

2973; High Pine, Mathew; M; 1906-26; F; Wd.; Head; 2918; Yes; Yes; Al. 4404 An. 2897

2974; High Pine, Mollie; F; 12/9/09-22; F; S; Head; 2919; Yes; Yes; Al. 6671 An. 2558

2975; High Pine, Thomas; M; 1882-50; F; Wd.; Head; 2920; Yes; Yes; Al. 6670 An. 2899

N.E.: High Pipe, David; M; -------; Rosebud Sioux; F; M; Head;
2976; High Pipe (Fox), Susie; F; 1888-44; F; M; Wife; 2921; Yes; Yes; Al. 4177 An. 2900

2977; High Shield, Karl; M; 5/26/09-22; F; S; Head; 2922; Yes; Yes; Al. 5023 An. 2902

2978; High White Man, Grant; M; 1877-55; F; M; Head; 2923; Yes; Yes; Al. 3108 An. 2903
2979; High White Man (Warrior), Dora; F; 1882-50; F; M; Wife; 2924; Yes; Yes; Al. 3114 An. 2904
2980; High White Man, Edgar; M; 6/7/09-22; F; S; Son; 2925; Yes; Yes; Al. 6179 An. 2905
2981; High White Man, Angelique; F; 6/25/13-18; F; S; Daughter; 2926; Yes; Yes; Al. 7264 An. 2906

Census of the __Pine Ridge__ reservation of the __Pine Ridge, South Dakota__ jurisdiction, as of __April 1__, 19**32**, taken by __James H. McGregor__, Superintendent.

Key: Number; Surname, Given; Sex; Date of Birth-Age at Last Birthday; Tribe (Oglala Sioux, unless stated otherwise); Degree of Blood; Marital Status; Relationship to Head of Family [Last Census Roll Number]; At Jurisdiction Where Enrolled (Yes/No); (If no – Where); Ward (Yes/No, if given); Allotment, Annuity and Identification Numbers (if given).

2982; High White Man, Zacharias; M; 1/14/17-15; F; S; Son; 2927; Yes; Yes; Id. U-9667 An. 2907

2983; High White Man, Ida; F; 8/9/20-11; F; S; Daughter; 2928; Yes; Yes; Al. 9668 An. 2908

2984; High White Man, Oscar; M; 4/3/24-7; F; S; Son; 2929; Yes; Yes; Id. U-11302 An. 2909

2985; High Wolf, Clayton; M; 1873-59; F; M; Head; 2930; Yes; Yes; Al. 476 An. 2910

2986; High Wolf (Scraper), Lizzie; F; 1879-53; F; M; Wife; 2931; Yes; Yes; Al. 5061 An. 2911

2987; High Wolf, Jessie L; F; 9/23/23-8; F; S; Daughter; 2932; Yes; Yes; Id. U-11738 An. 2913

2988; Tail, Leo; M; 8/11/18-13; F; S; Ward; 2933; Yes; Yes; Id. U-10532 An. 8773

2989; High Wolf, Raymond; M; 9/6/09-22; F; M; Head; 2934; Yes; Yes; Al. 5062 An. 2912

2990; High Wolf (Goings), Leta; F; 10/17/06-25; plus 1/4; M; Wife; 2935; Yes; Yes; Al. 5463 An. 2548

2991; High Wolf, Geraldine; F; 5/28/28-3; 1/4; S; Daughtre[sic]; 2936; Yes; Yes; Id. U-12717 An. none

2992; High Wolf, Leonard; M; 5/28/30-1; 1/4; S; Son; 2937; Yes; Yes; Id. U-13514 An. none

2993; Hill, George E.; M; 1/25/05-27; 1/4; S; Head; 2938; No; Ft. Totten, N.D.; Yes; Al. 2767 An. 2914

2994; Hill, Eveyline; M; 9/15/11-20; 1/4; S; Head; 2938; no; Ft. Totten; Yes; Id. U-9672 An. 2916

N.E.:   Hill, George W.; M; ------; Oneida Indian; plus 1/4; M; Head;

2995; Hill (no data), Lizzie; F; 1882-50; 1/4; M; Wife; 2940; No; Ft. Totten; Yes; Al. 2766 An. 2915

2996; Hill, Annie; F; 2/19/14-18; Oglala Sioux-Oneida 1/4; S; Daughter; 2941; No; Ft. Totten; Yes; Id. U-9673 An. 2917

2997; Hill, Rowland; M; 12/25/16-15; Oglala Sioux-Oneida 1/4; S; Son; 2942; No; Ft. Totten; Yes; Id. U-9674 An. 2918

2998; Hill, Virginia; F; 3/7/22-10; Oglala Sioux-Oneida 1/4; S; Daughter; 2943; No; Ft. Totten; Yes; Id. U-11069 An. 2919

2999; Hill, Frank; M; 11/5/25-6; Oglala Sioux-Oneida 1/4; S; Son; 2944; No; Ft. Totten; Yes; Id. U-11777 An. none

Census of the __Pine Ridge__ reservation of the **Pine Ridge, South Dakota** jurisdiction, as of __April 1__, 1932, taken by **James H. McGregor**, Superintendent.

Key: Number; Surname, Given; Sex; Date of Birth-Age at Last Birthday; Tribe (Oglala Sioux, unless stated otherwise); Degree of Blood; Marital Status; Relationship to Head of Family [Last Census Roll Number]; At Jurisdiction Where Enrolled (Yes/No); (If no – Where); Ward (Yes/No, if given); Allotment, Annuity and Identification Numbers (if given).

3000; Hill, Robert L.; M; 1904-28; 1/4; M; Head; 2945; No; Ft. Totten, N.D.; Yes; Al. 2457 An. 2920

N.E.: Hill (Kinkade), Rose; F; ------; Rosebud Sioux; 1/4; M; Wife;

3001; Hill (Bettelyoun), Martha E; F; 1889-43; 1/4; M; Head; 2946; Yes; Yes; Al. 2483 An. 2921

3002; Hill, Lorenzo; M; 10/10/11-20; 1/4; S; Son; 2947; Yes; Yes; Id. U-9134 An. 2922

3003; Hill, Sarah; F; 9/15/15-16; -1/4; S; Daughter; 2948; Yes; Yes; Id. U-9676 An. 2923

3004; Hill, Lloyd M; M; 10/1/17-14; -1/4; S; Son; 2949; Yes; Yes; Id. U-9677 An. 2924

3005; Hill, Harriet; F; 10/29/21-10; -1/4; S; Daughter; 2950; Yes; Yes; Id. U-10841 An. 2925

3006; Hill, Evelyn M; F; 9/18/24-7; -1/4; S; Daughter; 2951; Yes; Yes; Id. U-11378 An. 2926

3007; Hill, Kenneth L; M; 1/14/27-5; -1/4; S; Son; 2952; Yes; Yes; Id. U-12206 An. none

3008; Hill, Venus; F; 1/14/31-1; -1/4; S; Daughter; 2953; Yes; Yes; Id. U-13695 An. none

3009; Hill, Robert; M; 1877-55; plus 1/4; M; Head; 2954; Yes; Yes; Al. 2456 An. 2927

N.E.: Hill (Bardeaux), Lulu; F; ------; Rosebud Sioux; plus 1/4; M; Wife;

3010; Hill, Louis J.; M; 4/26/18-13; 1/4; S; Son; 2955; Yes; Yes; Id. U-9670 An. 2929

3011; Hill, Leah; F; 8/10/21-10; 1/4; S; Daughter; 2956; Yes; Yes; Id. U-9671 An. 2930

3012; Hillman (Gerry), Cynthia; F; 1884-48; plus 1/4; M; Head; 2957; No; Merriman, town, Cherry, Nebr.; No; Al. 4494 An. 2931

3013; Hillman, Mildred; F; 6/25/19-12; -1/4; S; Daughter; 2958; No; Same; Yes; Id. U-9679 An. 2932

3014; His Roan Horse, ---; M; 1855-77; F; Wd.; Head; 2959; Yes; Yes; Al. 636 An. 2933

3015; Hit The Arm, ---; F; 1852-80; F; Wd.; Head; 2960; Yes; Yes; Al. 3384 An. 2935

3016; Hodge (Midkiff), Goldie; F; 1901-31; -1/4; M; Head; 2961; Yes; Yes; Al. 3923 An. 2936

3017; Hodge, Marvel; F; 9/15/17-14; -1/4; S; Daughter; 2962; Yes; Yes; Id. U-9680 An. 2937

Census of the **Pine Ridge** reservation of the **Pine Ridge, South Dakota** jurisdiction, as of **April 1**, 19**32**, taken by **James H. McGregor**, Superintendent.

Key: Number; Surname, Given; Sex; Date of Birth-Age at Last Birthday; Tribe (Oglala Sioux, unless stated otherwise); Degree of Blood; Marital Status; Relationship to Head of Family [Last Census Roll Number]; At Jurisdiction Where Enrolled (Yes/No); (If no – Where); Ward (Yes/No, if given); Allotment, Annuity and Identification Numbers (if given).

3018; Hodge, Flossie; F; 1/28/25-7; -1/4; S; Daughter; 2964; Yes; Yes; Id. U-11711 An. none

3019; Hodge, Guindalyne; F; 3/2/27-5; -1/4; S; Daughter; 2965; Yes; Yes; Id. U-12345 An. none

3020; Hodgkinson (Means), Lorene; F; 7/6/05-26; plus 1/4; M; Head; 2966; No; San Francisco, San Francisco, Cal.; Yes; Al. 5338 An. 4402

3021; Hodgkinson, Frederick; M; 3/24/29-3; -1/4; S; Son; 2967; No; Same Yes; Id. U-13401 An. none

3022; Hodgkinson, Rae L; F; 2/2/31-1; -1/4; S; Daughter; 2968; No; Same Yes; Id. U-13781 An. none

3023; Hoke (Vierling), Myrle[sic]; F; 10/27/08-23; -1/4; M; Head; 7304; Yes; Yes; Al. 4641 An. 7253

3024; Hollow Head, Jobson; M; 1877-55; F; M; Head; 2969; Yes; Yes; Al. 1747 An. 2943

3025; Hollow Head (no data), Fannie; F; 1876-56; F; M; Wife; 2970; Yes; Yes; Al. 3815 An. 2944

3026; Hollow Head, Martha; F; 12/25/20-11; F; S; Gr. Daughter; 2971; Yes; Yes; Id. U-11007 An. 2942

3027; Hollow Head, Thomas; M; 1884-48; F; M; Head; 2972; Yes; Yes; Al. 7768 An. 2947

3028; Hollow Head (Two Tail), Emma; F; 1877-55; F; M; Wife; 2973; Yes; Yes; Al. 3834 An. 2948

3029; Hollow Head, Ellen; F; 2/7/14-18; F; S; Daughter; 2974; Yes; Yes; Al. 7785 An. 2950

3030; Hollow Head, Annie; F; 12/26/15-16; F; S; Daughter; 2975; Yes; Yes; Al. 8175 An. 2951

3031; Hollow Head, Fannie; F; 3/13/19-13; F; S; Daughter; 2976; Yes; Yes; Id. U-9683 An. 2952

3032; Hollow Horn, ---; F; 1850-82; F; Wd.; Wife; 2977; Yes; Yes; Al. 6747 An. 2953

3033; Hollow Horn, #1; M; 1859-73; F; M; Head; 2978; Yes; Yes; Al. 7556 An. 2954

3034; Hollow Horn (Yellow Hair), Mary; F; 1866-66; F; M; Wife; 2979; Yes; Yes; Al. 4751 An. 2955

3035; Hollow Horn, Norris; M; 10/30/10-21; F; S; Son; 2980; Yes; Yes; Al. 7196 An. 2954

Census of the __Pine Ridge__ reservation of the __Pine Ridge, South Dakota__ jurisdiction, as of __April 1__, 19**32**, taken by __James H. McGregor__, Superintendent.

Key: Number; Surname, Given; Sex; Date of Birth-Age at Last Birthday; Tribe (Oglala Sioux, unless stated otherwise); Degree of Blood; Marital Status; Relationship to Head of Family [Last Census Roll Number]; At Jurisdiction Where Enrolled (Yes/No); (If no – Where); Ward (Yes/No, if given); Allotment, Annuity and Identification Numbers (if given).

3036; Hollow Horn, #2; M; 1867-65; F; M; Head; 2981; Yes; Yes; Al. 904 An. 2957

3037; Hollow Horn (Looking Horse), Rosa; F; 1867-65; F; M; Wife; 2982; Yes; Yes; Al. 3458 An. 2958

3038; Hollow Horn, Jonas; M; 1904-28; F; M; Head; 2983; Yes; Yes; Al. 7560 An. 2960

3039; Hollow Horn (Walks Under the Ground), Sarah; F; 7/7/08-23; F; M; Wife; 2984; Yes; Yes; Al. 7483 An. 7287

3040; Hollow Horn, Murdy; M; 5/14/29-2; F; S; Son; 2985; Yes; Yes; Id. U-13186 An. none

3041; Hollow Horn, Martha; F; 10/01-30; F; M; Head; 2986; Yes; Yes; Al. 7559 An. 2966

3042; Hollow Horn, Thomas; M; 1885-47; F; M; Head; 2987; Yes; Yes; Al. 7557 An. 2967

3043; Hollow Horn (Plenty Wolf), Emma; F; 1893-39; F; M; Wife; 2988; Yes; Yes; Al. 4387 An. 2968

3044; Hollow Horn, Lawrence; M; 5/30/11-20; F; S; Son; 2989; Yes; Yes; Al. 8042 An. 2969

3045; Hollow Horn, Irene; F; 3/19/13-19; F; S; Daughter; 2990; Yes; Yes; Id. U-9688 An. 2970

3046; Hollow Horn, Raymond; M; 9/15/15-16; F; S; Son; 2991; Yes; Yes; Id. U-9689 An. 2971

3047; Hollow Horn, Lydia; F; 1/18/20-12; F; S; Daughter; 2992; Yes; Yes; Id. U-9691 An. 2972

3048; Hollow Horn, Agnes; F; 12/22/27-4; F; S; Daughter; 2993; Yes; Yes; Id. U-12457 An. none

3049; Hollow Horn, George; M; 5/16/31-10/12; F; S; Son; ---; Yes; Yes; U-13891

3050; Holy Bear, Lucy; F; 1875-57; F; Wd.; Head; 2994; Yes; Yes; Al. 5216 An. 2975

3051; Holy Bear, Thomas; M; 1895-37; F; M; Head; 2995; Yes; Yes; Al. 537 An. 2978

3052; Holy Bear (Blunt Horn), Lucy; F; 1897-35; F; M; Wife; 2996; Yes; Yes; Al. 4523 An. 2979

3053; Hollow Bear, Elizabeth; F; 3/24/18-14; F; S; Daughter; 2997; Yes; Yes; Id. U-9692 An. 2976

3054; Holy Cloud, Andrew; M; 4/29/12-19; F; Wd; Head; 2998; Yes; Yes; Id. U-9060 An. 239

Census of the **Pine Ridge** reservation of the **Pine Ridge, South Dakota** jurisdiction, as of **April 1**, 19**32**, taken by **James H. McGregor**, Superintendent.

Key: Number; Surname, Given; Sex; Date of Birth-Age at Last Birthday; Tribe (Oglala Sioux, unless stated otherwise); Degree of Blood; Marital Status; Relationship to Head of Family [Last Census Roll Number]; At Jurisdiction Where Enrolled (Yes/No); (If no – Where); Ward (Yes/No, if given); Allotment, Annuity and Identification Numbers (if given).

3055; Holy Dance, Rex; M; 1892-40; F; M; Head; 3000; Yes; Yes; Al. 7592 An. 2982
3056; Holy Dance (Pretty Face), Antonia; F; 1891-41; plus 1/4; M; Wife; 3001; Yes; Yes; Al. 1195 An. 2983
3057; Pretty Face, Peter; M; 10/7/13-18; 1/4; S; S. Son; 3002; Yes; Yes; Id. U-9694 An. 2985
3058; Holy Dance, Rita; F; 5/25/25-6; 1/4; S; Daughter; 3003; Yes; Yes; Id. U-11657 An. none
3059; Holy Dance, Beatrice; F; 5/12/27-4; 1/4; S; Daughter; 3004; Yes; Yes; Id. U-12337 An. none
3060; Holy Dance, Rex, Jr.; M; 10/26/29-2; 1/4; S; Son; 3005; Yes; Yes; Id. U-13292 An. none

3061; Holy Eagle, ---; M; 1864-68; F; M; Head; 3006; Yes; Yes; Al. 2399 An. 2989
3062; Holy Eagle (no data), Alice; F; 1869-63; F; M; Wife; 3007; Yes; Yes; Al. 2490 An. 2990

3063; Holy Eagle, Moses; M; 11/13/08-23; F; Wd.; Head; 3008; Yes; Yes; Al. 5515 An. 2991
3064; Holy Eagle (Owns Many Horses), Rosa, F; 7/9/11-20; F; M; Wife; ~~3009~~4863; Yes; Yes; Al. 4842 An. 6588

3065; Holy Eagle nee(Good Elk), Lucy, F; 19044[sic]-28; F; Wd.; Head; 3009; Yes; Yes; Al. 5125 An. 2579

3066; Holy Eagle, James; M; 1889-43; F; M; Head; 3010; Yes; Yes; Al. 2401 An. 2992
3067; Holy Eagle (Turning Holy), Eliza; F; 1899-33; F; M; Wife; 3011; Yes; Yes; Al. 5291 An. 2993
3068; Holy Eagle, Elijah; M; 10/13/24-8; F; S; Son; 3012; Yes; Yes; Id. U-11353 An. 2994
3069; Holy Eagle, LeRoy; M; 9/4/28-3; F; S; Son; 3013; Yes; Yes; Id. U-12923 An. none

3070; Holy Elk, Herbert; M; 1891-41; F; Wd; Head; 3014; Yes; Yes; Al. 1909 An. 2995
3071; Holy Elk, Alice; F; 6/3/21-10; F; S; Daughter; 3015; Yes; Yes; Id. U-9698 An. 2998
3072; Holy Elk, Nancy; F; 1/20/23-9; F; S; Daughter; 3016; Yes; Yes; Id. U-12050 An. 2999

3073; Holy Hand, ---; M; 1867-65; F; S; Head; 3017; Yes; Yes; Al. 1463 An. 3001

Census of the __**Pine Ridge**__ reservation of the __**Pine Ridge, South Dakota**__ jurisdiction, as of __**April 1**__, 19**32**, taken by __**James H. McGregor**__, Superintendent.

Key: Number; Surname, Given; Sex; Date of Birth-Age at Last Birthday; Tribe (Oglala Sioux, unless stated otherwise); Degree of Blood; Marital Status; Relationship to Head of Family [Last Census Roll Number]; At Jurisdiction Where Enrolled (Yes/No); (If no – Where); Ward (Yes/No, if given); Allotment, Annuity and Identification Numbers (if given).

3074; Holy Horse, ---; M; 1862-70; F; Wd.; Head; 3018; Yes; Yes; Al. 5086 An. 3002

3075; Holy Pipe, Laban; M; 1879-53; F; M; Head; 3019; Yes; Yes; Al. 7619 An. 3006

3076; Holy Pipe (Bear Stops), Mary; F; 1888-44; F; M; Wife; 3020; Yes; Yes; Al. 6337 An. 3007

3077; Holy Pipe, Charles; M; 5/5/23-8; F; S; Son; 3021; Yes; Yes; Id. U-13062 An. 3008

3078; Holy Pipe, Jennie; F; 8/25/31-7/12; F; S; Daughter; ---; Yes; Yes; U-13892

3079; Holy Rock, Frank; M; 1901-31; plus 1/4; M; Head; 3022; Yes; Yes; Al. 6419 An. 3010

N.E.: Holy Rock (LaBeau), Adelia; F; ------; Cheyenne Sioux; plus 1/4; M; Wife;

3080; Holy Rock, Cecil; M; 11/9/27-4; 1/4; S; Son; 3023; Yes; Yes; Id. U-12427 An. none

3081; Holy Rock, Morris; M; 5/19/30-1; 1/4; S; Son; 3024; Yes; Yes; Id. U-13478 An. none

3082; Holy Rock, Jonas; M; 1865-67; F; M; Head; 3025; Yes; Yes; Al. 6416 An. 3011

3083; Holy Rock (no data), Polly; F; 1878-54; plus 1/4; M; Wife; 3026; Yes; Yes; Al. 6417 An. 3012

3084; Holy Rock, Zona; F; 4/6/13-18; 1/4; S; Daughter; 3027; Yes; Yes; Id. U-7377 An. 3015

3085; Holy Rock, Mildred; F; 10/14/16-16; 1/4; S; Daughter; 3028; Yes; Yes; Id. U-9699 An. 3016

3086; Holy Rock, Johnson; M; 9/7/18-13; 1/4; S; Son; 3029; Yes; Yes; Id. U-9700 An. 3017

3087; Holy Skin (Lays Bear), Clara; F; 1849-83; F; Wd.; Head; 3030; Yes; Yes; Al. 6005 An. 3020

N.E.: Hopkins, Peter; M; ------; Lower Brule Sioux; M; Head;

3088; Hopkins (Fog), Fannie; F; 3/22/06-26; plus 1/4; M; Wife; 2298; Yes; Yes; Al. 5880 An. 2301

3089; Hornbeck, Joseph; M; 1879-53; plus 1/4; M; Head; 3036; Yes; Yes; Al. 835 An. 3025

3090; Hornbeck (Gibbons), Annie; F; 1882-50; 1/4; M; Wife; 3037; Yes; Yes; Al. 2677 An. 3026

Census of the __Pine Ridge__ reservation of the __Pine Ridge, South Dakota__ jurisdiction, as of __April 1__, 19**32**, taken by __James H. McGregor__, Superintendent.

Key: Number; Surname, Given; Sex; Date of Birth-Age at Last Birthday; Tribe (Oglala Sioux, unless stated otherwise); Degree of Blood; Marital Status; Relationship to Head of Family [Last Census Roll Number]; At Jurisdiction Where Enrolled (Yes/No); (If no – Where); Ward (Yes/No, if given); Allotment, Annuity and Identification Numbers (if given).

3091; Hornbeck, Winfield; M; 7/6/17-14; 1/4; S; Son; 3038; Yes; Yes; Id. U-9702 An. 3028

3092; Horn Chips, ---; M; 1873-59; F; M; Head; 3039; Yes; Yes; Al. 1975 An. 3030

3093; Horn Cloud, William; M; 1907-25; F; M; Head; 3040; Yes; Yes; Al. 3854 An. 3034
3094; Horn Cloud, Joseph; M; 7/12/12-19; F; S; Ward; 3041; Yes; Yes; Al. 7764 An. 3035

3095; Horse, Henry; M; 1881-51; F; M; Head; 3042; Yes; Yes; Al. 7063 An. 3037
3096; Horse (no data), Bessie; F; 1883-49; F; M; Wife; 3043; Yes; Yes; Al. 3045 An. 3038
3097; Horse, Ramson; M; 4/2/15-16; F; S; Son; 3044; Yes; Yes; Al. 7980 An. 3042
3098; Horse, Mary; F; 9/7/25-6; F; S; Daughter; 3045; Yes; Yes; Id. U-11721 An. none
3099; Horse, Nancy; F; 3/3/31-1; F; S; Daughter; 3046; Yes; Yes; Id. U-13759 An. none

3100; Horse, Joseph; M; 1899-33; F; M; Head; 3047; Yes; Yes; Al. 7330 An. 3044
3101; Horse (Clifford), Irene; F; 6/14/12-19; plus 1/4; M; Wife; 1418; Yes; Yes; Al. 7364 An. 1461

3102; Horse, Noah; M; 3/10/04-28; F; M; Head; 3048; Yes; Yes; Al. 7173 An. 3046
3103; Horse (Kills Ree), Carrie; F; 1905-27; F; M; Wife; 3049; Yes; Yes; Al. 4967 An. 3047
3104; Horse, Daisy; F; 6/10/26-5; F; S; Daughter; 3050; Yes; Yes; Id. U-11946 An. none
3105; Horse, Douglas; M; 4/23/28-4; F; S; Son; 3051; Yes; Yes; Id. U-12571 An. none
3106; Horse, Tex; M; 7/5/30-1; F; M; Son; 3052; Yes; Yes; Id. U-13550 An. none

3107; Horse, Robert; M; 1873-59; F; M; Head; 3053; Yes; Yes; Al. 4998 An. 3048
3108; Horse (Two Dogs), Helen; F; 1880-52; F; M; Wife; 3054; Yes; Yes; Al. 3715 An. 3051
3109; Horse, Brooks; M; 11/23/13-18; F; S; Son; 3055; Yes; Yes; Id. U-9704 An. 3049
3110; Two Dogs, Asay; M; 1/6/11-21; F; S; S. Son; 3056; Yes; Yes; Id. U-10632 An. 3054
3111; Two Dogs, Edith; F; 11/17/12-19; F; S; S. Daughter; 3057; Yes; Yes; Id. U-10633 An. 3055
3112; Two Dogs, John; M; 9/11/14-17; F; S; S. Son; 3058; Yes; Yes; Id. U-10634 An. 3056

Census of the **Pine Ridge** reservation of the **Pine Ridge, South Dakota** jurisdiction, as of **April 1**, 19**32**, taken by **James H. McGregor**, Superintendent.

Key: Number; Surname, Given; Sex; Date of Birth-Age at Last Birthday; Tribe (Oglala Sioux, unless stated otherwise); Degree of Blood; Marital Status; Relationship to Head of Family [Last Census Roll Number]; At Jurisdiction Where Enrolled (Yes/No); (If no – Where); Ward (Yes/No, if given); Allotment, Annuity and Identification Numbers (if given).

3113; Two Dogs, Margaret; F; 12/22/16-15; F; S; S. Daughter; 3059; Yes; Yes; Id. U-10629 An. 3057

3114; Two Dogs, Joe; M; 6/12/19-12; F; S; S. Son; 3060; Yes; Yes; Id. U-10630 An. 3058

3115; Horse Stands In Sight, Charles; M; 1890-42; F; M; Head; 3061; Yes; Yes; Al. 780 An. 3060

3116; Horse Stands In Sight, Clarence; M; 6/16/18-13; F; S; Son; 3062; Yes; Yes; Id. U-9706 An. 3061

3117; Horse Stands In Sight, Robert; M; 1895-37; F; S; Head; 3063; Yes; Yes; Al. 781 An. 3063

N.E.: Howe, John; M; ------; Ponca Indian; M; Head;

3118; Howe (Ross), Angelique; F; 7/7/86-45; plus 1/4; M; Wife; 3064; Yes; Yes; Al. 7044 An. 3065

3119; Howe, Percy; M; 12/17/13-18; Oglala Sioux-Ponca; 1/4; S; Son; 3065; Yes; Yes; AI. 7902 An. 3066

3120; Howe, Raymond; M; 9/4/16-15; Oglala Sioux-Ponca; 1/4; S; Son; 3066; Yes; Yes; Id. U-9707 An. 3066

3121; Howe, Ross G; M; 8/24/18-13; Oglala Sioux-Ponca; 1/4; S; Son; 3067; Yes; Yes; Id. U-9708 An. 3068

3122; Howe, Irene; F; 12/11/20-11; Oglala Sioux-Ponca; 1/4; S; Daughter; 3068; Yes; Yes; Id. U-9709 An. 3069

3123; Howe, Velma; F; 9/9/23-8; Oglala Sioux-Ponca; 1/4; S; Daughter; 3069; Yes; Yes; Id. U-11184 An. 3070

3124; Hoyle (Ten Fingers), Ellene; F; 1901-31; F; M; Head; 5288; Yes; Yes; Al. 7044 An. 3065

3125; Quinn, Thomasena; F; 10/3/27-4; plus 1/4; S; Daughter; 5289; Yes; Yes; Id. U-12726 An. none

3126; Hudspeth, Oliver; M; 1885-47; plus 1/4; M; Head; 3070; Yes; Yes; Al. 3363 An. 3072

3127; Hudspeth (Many Horses), Lillie; F; 1880-52; 1/4; M; Wife; 3071; Yes; Yes; Al. 3364 An. 3073

3128; Hudspeth, William J; M; 3/2/11-21; 1/4; S; Son; 3072; Yes; Yes; AI. 6368 An. 3075

3129; Hudspeth, Alice; F; 12/13/12-19; 1/4; S; Daughter; 3073; Yes; Yes; AI. 7566 An. 3077

3130; Hudspeth, Oliver Jr.; M; 10/9/14-17; 1/4; S; Son; 3074; Yes; Yes; Id. U-9711 An. 3078

Census of the   **Pine Ridge**   reservation of the **Pine Ridge, South Dakota** jurisdiction, as of   **April 1**   , 19**32**, taken by   **James H. McGregor**   , Superintendent.

Key: Number; Surname, Given; Sex; Date of Birth-Age at Last Birthday; Tribe (Oglala Sioux, unless stated otherwise); Degree of Blood; Marital Status; Relationship to Head of Family [Last Census Roll Number]; At Jurisdiction Where Enrolled (Yes/No); (If no – Where); Ward (Yes/No, if given); Allotment, Annuity and Identification Numbers (if given).

3131; Hudspeth, Henry; M; 12/25/22-9; 1/4; S; Son; 3075; Yes; Yes; Id. U-13041 An. 3079

3132; Hudspeth, Lela M; F; 11/14/24-7; 1/4; S; Daughter; 3076; Yes; Yes; Id. U-12247 An. none

3133; Hudspeth, Mary; F; 3/24/10-22; 1/4; S; Head; 3078; Yes; Yes; AI. 6367 An. 3076

3134; Hudspeth (Goings), Vergie; F; 1884-48; 1/4; Wd; Head; 3079; Yes; Yes; Al. 5727 An. 3080

3135; Hudspeth, Zona; F; 1907-25; 1/4; S; Head; 3080; No; Omaha, City, Douglas, Nebr.; Yes; Al. 3367 An. 3081

3136; Huebner, Charlotte; F; 1887-45; Plus 1/4; M; Head; 3081; Yes; Yes; Al. 3037 An. 3082

3137; Huebner, Floyd; M; 7/20/12-19; -1/4; S; Son; 3082; Yes; Yes; Al. 6370 An. 3084

3138; Huebner, Iris; F; 4/14/14-17; -1/4; S; Daughter; 3083; Yes; Yes; Al. 7531 An. 3085

3139; Huebner, Leslie; M; 6/14/17-14; -1/4; S; Son; 3084; Yes; Yes; Id. U-9712 An. 3086

3140; Huebner, Wm G.; M; 7/17/22-9; -1/4; S; Son; 3085; Yes; Yes; Id. U-11065 An. 3087

3141; Huebner, Edward; M; 5/3/27-4; -1/4; S; Son; 3086; Yes; Yes; Id. U-12315 An. none

3142; Huebner, Bertha; F; 4/2/09-22; -1/4; S; Head; 3087; Yes; Yes; Al. 6369 An. 3083

3143; Hume (Whitcomb), Mary; F; 1871-62; plus 1/4; S; Head; 3088; Yes; Yes; Al. 6984 An. 3089

3144; Hunter, John; M; 1883-49; 1/4; M; Head; 3089; Yes; Yes; Al. 3679 An. 3090
3145; Hunter (Gibbons), Maggie; F; 1894-38; 1/4; M; Wife; 3090; Yes; Yes; Al. 2681 An. 3091
3146; Hunter, Stephen; M; 3/30/20-12; 1/4; S; Son; 3091; Yes; Yes; Id. U-9713 An. 3092
3147; Hunter, Carolina; F; 4/30/21-10; 1/4; S; Daughter; 3092; Yes; Yes; Id. U-9714 An. 3093
3148; Hunter, Vivian; F; 11/28/22-9; 1/4; S; Daughter; 3093; Yes; Yes; Id. U-12068 An. 3094

Census of the **Pine Ridge** reservation of the **Pine Ridge, South Dakota** jurisdiction, as of **April 1**, 19**32,** taken by **James H. McGregor**, Superintendent.

Key: Number; Surname, Given; Sex; Date of Birth-Age at Last Birthday; Tribe (Oglala Sioux, unless stated otherwise); Degree of Blood; Marital Status; Relationship to Head of Family [Last Census Roll Number]; At Jurisdiction Where Enrolled (Yes/No); (If no – Where); Ward (Yes/No, if given); Allotment, Annuity and Identification Numbers (if given).

3149; Hunter, Aloysius; M; 6/20/24-7; 1/4; S; Son; 3094; Yes; Yes; Id. U-11321 An. 3095

3150; Hunter, Rebecca; F; 3/1/26-6; 1/4; S; Daughter; 3095; Yes; Yes; Id. U-12316 An. none

3151; Hunter, Ambrose; M; 3/1/28-4; 1/4; S; Son; 3096; Yes; Yes; Id. U-12725 An. none

3152; Hunter, Babe; M; 3/19/30-2; 1/4; S; Son; 3097; Yes; Yes; Id. U-13760 An. none

3153; Hunter, Olive; F; 1878-54; 1/4; Wd.; Head; 3098; Yes; Yes; Al. 3655 An. 3096

3154; Hunter, Richard; M; 1905-27; 1/4; S; Head; 3099; Yes; Yes; Al. 3659 An. 3098

3155; Hunts Horses, John; M; 1891-41; F; M; Head; 3102; Yes; Yes; Al. 203 An. 3108

3156; Hunts Horses (Running Shield), Anna; F; 1895-37; F; M; Wife; 3103; Yes; Yes; Al. 235 An. 3110

3157; Hunts Horses, Vincetn[sic]; M; 4/26/23-8; F; S; Son; 3104; Yes; Yes; Id. U-13063 An. 3111

3158; Ice, ---; M; 1859-73; F; Wd.; Head; 3105; Yes; Yes; Al. 395 An. 3111

3159; Ice, Alex; M; 1902-30; F; M; Head; 3106; Yes; Yes; Al. 403 An. 3113

3160; Ice (Runs Against), Mabel; F; 1904-28; F; M; Wife; 3107; Yes; Yes; Al. 2977 An. 3114

3161; Ice, Bernard; M; 5/26/25-6; F; S; Son; 3108; Yes; Yes; Id. U-11646 An. none

3162; Ice, Frances R; F; 9/5/28-3; F; S; Daughter; 3109; Yes; Yes; Id. U-12811 An. none

3163; Ice, Ellen; M; 9/10/30-1; F; S; Daughter; 3110; Yes; Yes; Id. U-13603 An. none

3164; Iron Bear, Alex; M; 1886-46; F; M; Head; 3114; Yes; Yes; Al. 677 An. 3123

3165; Iron Bear (Arapahoe), Lucy; F; 1873-59; F; M; Wife; 3115; Yes; Yes; Al. 5145 An. 3124

3166; Iron Bear, Vernice; M; 3/8/17-15; F; S; Daughter; 3116; Yes; Yes; Id. U-9721 An. 3126

3167; Iron Bear, James; M; 1891-41; F; Wd.; Head; 3117; Yes; Yes; Al. 2040 An. 3128

Census of the __Pine Ridge__ reservation of the __Pine Ridge, South Dakota__ jurisdiction, as of __April 1__, 1932, taken by __James H. McGregor__, Superintendent.

Key: Number; Surname, Given; Sex; Date of Birth-Age at Last Birthday; Tribe (Oglala Sioux, unless stated otherwise); Degree of Blood; Marital Status; Relationship to Head of Family [Last Census Roll Number]; At Jurisdiction Where Enrolled (Yes/No); (If no – Where); Ward (Yes/No, if given); Allotment, Annuity and Identification Numbers (if given).

3168; Iron Bear, Fred; M; 1895-37; F; M; Head; 3118; Yes; Yes; Al. 2041 An. 3127

3169; Iron Bear (Runs Along The Edge), Alice; F; 1902-30; plus 1/4; M; Wife; 5828; Yes; Yes; Al. 1099 An. 5803

3170; Rooks, Timothy; M; 11/23/24-7; 1/4; S; S. Son; 5829; Yes; Yes; Id. U-11555 An. 5805

3171; Iron Bear, Beatrice; F; 10/20/25-6; 1/4; S; Daughter; 5830; Yes; Yes; Id. U-11875 An. none

3172; Iron Bear, Lincoln; M; 2/12/29-3; 1/4; S; Son; 5831; Yes; Yes; Id. U-13141 An. none

3173; Iron Bear, Madeline; F; 3/30/31-1; 1/4; S; Daughter; ---; Yes; Yes; U-13870

3174; Iron Bear (no data), Julia; F; 1852-80; F; Wd.; Head; 3119; Yes; Yes; Al. 2039 An. 3130

3175; Iron Bear, Mathew; M; 10/5/18-13; F; S; Gr. Son; 3120; Yes; Yes; Id. U-9725 An. 3129

3176; Iron Boy, Jacob; M; 1875-57; F; M; Head; 3121; Yes; Yes; Al. 2981 An. 3131
3177; Iron Boy (no data), Mabel; F; 1877-55; F; M; Wife; 3122; Yes; Yes; Al. 5804 An. 3132
3178; Iron Boy, Quintin; M; 8/15/15-16; F; S; Son; 3123; Yes; Yes; Id. U-9726 An. 3134
3179; Iron Boy, James; M; 3/28/18-14; F; S; Son; 3124; Yes; Yes; Id. U-9727 An. 3135
3180; Iron Boy, Mary; F; 4/4/22-9; F; S; Daughter; 3125; Yes; Yes; Id. U-10925 An. 3136

3181; Iron Bull, Jacob; M; 1864-68; F; M; Head; 3127; Yes; Yes; Al. 747 An. 3140

3182; Iron Bull, Wallace; M; 2/12/09-23; F; M; Head; 3128; Yes; Yes; Al. 7656 An. 2823

3183; Iron Cedar, ---; F; 1863-69; F; Wd.; Head; 3129; Yes; Yes; Al. 3857 An. 3147

3184; Iron Cloud, Edward; M; 1881-51; F; M; Head; 3130; Yes; Yes; Al. 541 An. 3148
3185; Iron Cloud (Bad Wound), Emily; F; 1887-55; F; M; Wife; 3131; Yes; Yes; Al. 5185 An. 3149
3186; Iron Cloud, Isaac; M; 10/2/12-19; F; S; Son; 3132; Yes; Yes; Al. 7942 An. 3150
3187; Iron Cloud, Eddy; M; 7/25/18-13; F; S; Son; 3133; Yes; Yes; Id. U-7931 An. 3151

Census of the **Pine Ridge** reservation of the **Pine Ridge, South Dakota** jurisdiction, as of **April 1**, 19**32**, taken by **James H. McGregor**, Superintendent.

Key: Number; Surname, Given; Sex; Date of Birth-Age at Last Birthday; Tribe (Oglala Sioux, unless stated otherwise); Degree of Blood; Marital Status; Relationship to Head of Family [Last Census Roll Number]; At Jurisdiction Where Enrolled (Yes/No); (If no – Where); Ward (Yes/No, if given); Allotment, Annuity and Identification Numbers (if given).

3188; Iron Cloud, Lillian; F; 2/17/23-9; F; S; Daughter; 3134; Yes; Yes; Id. U-12087 An. 3153

3189; Iron Cloud, Daniel; M; 9/12/26-5; F; S; Son; 3135; Yes; Yes; Id. U-12112 An. none

3190; Iron Cloud, Martha; F; 4/12/31-11/12; F; S; Daughter; ---; Yes; Yes; U-13805

3191; Iron Cloud, George; M; 1900-32; F; M; Head; 3136; Yes; Yes; Al. 547 An. 3154

3192; Iron Cloud (Janis Twiss), Pearl; F; 7/17/97-35; plus 1/4; M; Wife; 3137; Yes; Yes; Al. 714 An. 7029

3193; Iron Cloud, Corbett; M; 12/27/30-1; 1/4; S; Son; 3138; Yes; Yes; Id. U-13696 An. none

3194; Twiss, Clara; F; 11/11/20-11; 1/4; S; S. Daughter; 3139; Yes; Yes; Id. U-10611 An. 7030

3195; Iron Cloud (Moose), Mary; F; 1908-24; F; Wd.; Head; 3140; Yes; Yes; Al. 6951 An. 4577

3196; Iron Cloud, Lavern; F; 4/13/26-5; F; S; Daughter; 3141; Yes; Yes; Id. U-11899 An. none

3197; Iron Cloud, Cleveland; M; 2/5/29-3; F; S; Son; 3142; Yes; Yes; ld. U-12991 An. none

3198; Iron Cloud, James; M; 1895-37; F; M; Head; 3143; Yes; Yes; Al. 546 An. 3157

3199; Iron Cloud (Janis), Ellen; F; 1904-28; plus 1/4; M; Wife; 3144; Yes; Yes; Al. 4134 An. 3287

3200; Iron Cloud, Philip; M; 8/28/18-13; F; S; Son; 3145; Yes; Yes; ld. U-9736 An. 3159

3201; Iron Cloud (Young Wolf Ears), Annie; F; 1894-38; F; Wd; Head; 3147; Yes; Yes; Al. 1243 An. 3163

3202; Iron Cloud, Esther; F; 4/19/24-8; F; S; Daughter; 3148; Yes; Yes; Id. U-12255 An. 3166

3203; Iron Cloud, Alice; F; 12/30/30-1; F; S; Daughter; 3149; Yes; Yes; Id. U-13643 An. none

3204; Iron Crow, Rock; M; 1885-47; F; Wd.; Head; 3150; Yes; Yes; Al.1522 An. 3167

3205; Iron Crow, Thomas; M; 1895-37; F; M; Head; 3151; Yes; Yes; Al.6637 An. 3171

3206; Iron Crow (Plenty Stars), Fannie; F; 1874-58; F; M; Wife; 5000; Yes; Yes; Al. 3518 An. 4992

Census of the __Pine Ridge__ reservation of the __Pine Ridge, South Dakota__ jurisdiction, as of __April 1__ , 19**32**, taken by __James H. McGregor__ , Superintendent.

Key: Number; Surname, Given; Sex; Date of Birth-Age at Last Birthday; Tribe (Oglala Sioux, unless stated otherwise); Degree of Blood; Marital Status; Relationship to Head of Family [Last Census Roll Number]; At Jurisdiction Where Enrolled (Yes/No); (If no – Where); Ward (Yes/No, if given); Allotment, Annuity and Identification Numbers (if given).

3207; Iron Crow, Rosa; F; 1902-30; F; S; Head; 3152; Yes; Yes; Al. 5399 An. 3172

3208; Iron Crow, Ida; F; --/--/-- -3; F; S; Daughter; 3153; Yes; Yes; Id. U-12625 An. none

3209; Iron Crow (no data), Grace; F; 1865-67; F; Wd.; Head; 3154; Yes; Yes; Al. 6907 An. 3174

3210; White, Ernest; M; 5/13/19-12; F; S; Ward; 3155; Yes; Yes; Id. U-10716 An. 5978

N.E.: ~~Iron Deer, Vincent; M; ------; Rosebud Sioux; F; M; Head;~~

3211; Iron Deer (White Bird), Emma; F; 1879-53; F; M; Wife; 3156; Yes; Yes; Al. 6083 An. 3797

3212; Left Hand, Adam; M; 8/28/11-20; F; S; S. Son; 3157; Yes; Yes; Al. 6553 An. 3798

3213; Left Hand, Jacob; M; 1/5/17-15; F; S; S. Son; 3158; Yes; Yes; Id. U-9873 An. 3799

3214; Left Hand, Julia; F; 10/21/19-12; F; S; S. Daughter; 3159; Yes; Yes; Id. U-9873 An. 3800

3215; Iron Elk, Moses; M; 1902-30; F; M; Head; 3160; Yes; Yes; Al.6644 An. 3181

3216; Iron Elk (Red Ear Horse), Bessie; F; 1901-31; F; M; Wife; 3161; Yes; Yes; Id. U-9089 An. 5425

3217; Red Ear Horse, Eva; F; 10/4/24-7; F; S; S. Daughter; 3162; Yes; Yes; Id. U-11352 An. 5426

3218; Iron Hawk, Moses; M; 1860-72; F; Wd.; Head; 3165; Yes; Yes; Al.6645 An. 3183

3219; Iron Hawk, Frank; M; 1893-39; F; M; Head; 3166; Yes; Yes; Al.6832 An. 3185

3220; Iron Hawk (No Braid), Lizzie; F; 1898-34; F; M; Wife; 3167; Yes; Yes; Al. 5695 An. 3186

3221; Iron Hawk, Lizzie; F; 1/13/18-14; F; S; Daughter; 3168; Yes; Yes; Id. U-9738 An. 3187

3222; Iron Hawk, Calvin; M; 11/12/26-5; F; S; Son; 3169; Yes; Yes; Id. U-12136 An. none

3223; Iron Hawk, Rebecca; F; 3/31/29-3; F; S; Daughter; 3170; Yes; Yes; Id. U-12142 An. none

3224; Iron Hawk, Homer; M; 1864-68; F; Wd.; Head; 3171; Yes; Yes; Al.6533 An. 3188

Census of the __**Pine Ridge**__ reservation of the __**Pine Ridge, South Dakota**__ jurisdiction, as of __**April 1**__, 19**32,** taken by __**James H. McGregor**__, Superintendent.

Key: Number; Surname, Given; Sex; Date of Birth-Age at Last Birthday; Tribe (Oglala Sioux, unless stated otherwise); Degree of Blood; Marital Status; Relationship to Head of Family [Last Census Roll Number]; At Jurisdiction Where Enrolled (Yes/No); (If no – Where); Ward (Yes/No, if given); Allotment, Annuity and Identification Numbers (if given).

3225; Iron Hawk, Louis; M; 1901-31; F; M; Head; 3172; Yes; Yes; Al.6823 An. 3189

3226; Iron Hawk (Horse), Jessie; F; 4/10/09-22; F; M; Wife; 3173; Yes; Yes; Al. 7175 An. 3040

3227; Iron Hawk, Lawson; M; 5/5/28-3; F; S; Son; 3174; Yes; Yes; Id. U-12572 An. none

3228; Iron Hawk, Clardia; F; 3/30/30-2; F; S; Daughter; 3175; Yes; Yes; Id. U-13442 An. none

3229; Iron Heart, George; M; 1879-53; plus 1/4; M; Head; 3176; Yes; Yes; Al. 4103 An. 3190

3230; Iron Heart (no date), Josephine; F; 1882-50; F; M; Wife; 3177; Yes; Yes; Al. 5135 An. 3191

3231; Iron Heart, Lucy; F; 12/27/12-19; plus 1/4; S; Daughter; 3178; Yes; Yes; Al. 7976 An. 3192

3232; Iron Heart, Carrie; F; 7/6/15-16; 1/4; S; Daughter; 3179; Yes; Yes; Al. 8097 An. 3193

3233; Iron Heart, Grace; F; 3/30/20-12; 1/4; S; Daughter; 3180; Yes; Yes; Al. 8270 An. 3194

3234; Iron Heart, Calvin; M; 9/7/24-7; 1/4; S; Son; 3181; Yes; Yes; Id. U-11372 An. 3195

3235; Iron Horse, Amos; M; 1898-34; F; M; Head; 3183; Yes; Yes; Al. 5740 An. 3198

3236; Iron Horse (Steals Horse), Susanna; F; 8/15/05-26; F; M; Wife; 3184; Yes; Yes; Al. 5929 An. 3199

3237; Iron Horse, Sallie; F; 11/28/26-5; F; S; Daughter; 3185; Yes; Yes; Id. U-12161 An. none

3238; Iron Horse, Ernest; M; 11/2/28-3; F; S; Son; 3186; Yes; Yes; Id. U-12947 An. none

3239; Iron Rope, John; M; 1894-38; F; M; Head; 3187; Yes; Yes; Al. 2000 An. 3202
3240; Iron Rope (Fool Head), Jennie; F; 1899-33; F; M; Wife; 3188; Yes; Yes; Al. 6011 An. 3203
3241; Iron Rope, Martin; M; 11/1/22-9; F; S; Son; 3189; Yes; Yes; Id. U-12027 An. 3204
3242; Iron Rope, Ambrose; M; 12/1/24-8; F; S; Son; 3190; Yes; Yes; Id. U-11400 An. 3205
3243; Iron Rope, Marie; F; 4/24/27-4; F; S; Daughter; 3191; Yes; Yes; Id. U-12318 An. none
3244; Iron Rope, Sophia; F; 6/12/29-2; F; S; Daughter; 3192; Yes; Yes; Id. U-13247 An. none
3245; Iron Rope, Freda; F; 12/8/31-3/12; F; S; Daughter; ---; Yes; Yes; U-13992

Census of the **Pine Ridge** reservation of the **Pine Ridge, South Dakota** jurisdiction, as of **April 1**, 19**32**, taken by **James H. McGregor**, Superintendent.

Key: Number; Surname, Given; Sex; Date of Birth-Age at Last Birthday; Tribe (Oglala Sioux, unless stated otherwise); Degree of Blood; Marital Status; Relationship to Head of Family [Last Census Roll Number]; At Jurisdiction Where Enrolled (Yes/No); (If no – Where); Ward (Yes/No, if given); Allotment, Annuity and Identification Numbers (if given).

3246; Iron Rope, Paul; M; 1888-44; F; M; Head; 3193; Yes; Yes; Al. 1998 An. 3206
3247; Iron Rope (Chips), Susie; F; 1899-33; F; M; Wife; 3194; Yes; Yes; Al. 5567 An. 3207

3248; Iron Rope, Peter; M; 1888-44; F; M; Head; 3195; Yes; Yes; Al. 1997 An. 3209
3249; Iron Rope (Lone Bear), Susie; F; ---- -38; F; M; Wife; 3196; Yes; Yes; Al. 2388 An. 3210
3250; Iron Rope, Darline; F; 4/3/22-9; F; S; Daughter; 3197; Yes; Yes; Id. U-10954 An. 3212
3251; Iron Rope, Peter Jr.; M; 1/10/24-8; F; S; Son; 3198; Yes; Yes; Id. U-11217 An. 3213
3252; Iron Rope, Abel; M; 4/1/28-4; F; S; Son; 3199; Yes; Yes; Id. U-12573 An. none
3253; Iron Rope, Eugene; M; 3/5/31-1; F; S; Son; 3200; Yes; Yes; Id. U-13761 An. none

3254; Iron Shell, ---; M; 1846-86; F; M; Head; 3201; Yes; Yes; Al. 3728 An. 3214
3255; Iron Shell (no data), Lizzie; F; 1857-75; F; M; Wife; 3202; Yes; Yes; Al. 3729 An. 3216

3256; Iron Teeth, George; M; 1891-31; plus 1/4; S; Head; 3203; Yes; Yes; Al. 2730 An. 3219

3257; Iron Teeth, Theodore; M; 9/18/10-21; 1/4; S; Head; 3204; Yes; Yes; Al. 7369 An. 3221
3257; Iron Teeth, Theodore; M; 9/18/10-21; 1/4; S; Head; 3204; Yes; Yes; Al. 7369 An. 3221
3258; Iron Teeth, Timothy; M; 1/24/14-18; 1/4; S; Brother; 3205; Yes; Yes; Al. 7370 An. 3222

3259; Iron White Man, James Alex; M; 1896-36; F; S; Head; 3206; Yes; Yes; Al. 6055 An. 3225
3260; Iron White Man (Deon), Florence; F; 10/11/10-21; plus 1/4; M; Wife; 3207; Yes; Yes; Al. 6938 An. 1875
3261; Iron White Man, Leroy C.; M; 2/9/26-6; 1/4; S; Son; 3208; Yes; Id. U-11840 An. none
3262; Iron White Man, Cleveland; M; 12/22/28-3; 1/4; S; Son; 3209; Yes; Yes; Id. U-12973 An. none

3263; Iron White Man (no data), Cora; F; 1865-67; F; Wd.; Head; 3210; Yes; Yes; Al. 6468 An. 3230

Census of the **Pine Ridge** reservation of the **Pine Ridge, South Dakota** jurisdiction, as of **April 1**, 19**32**, taken by **James H. McGregor**, Superintendent.

Key: Number; Surname, Given; Sex; Date of Birth-Age at Last Birthday; Tribe (Oglala Sioux, unless stated otherwise); Degree of Blood; Marital Status; Relationship to Head of Family [Last Census Roll Number]; At Jurisdiction Where Enrolled (Yes/No); (If no – Where); Ward (Yes/No, if given); Allotment, Annuity and Identification Numbers (if given).

3264; Irving, Benjamin; M; 1880-53; plus 1/4; M; Head; 3211; Yes; Yes; Al. 18 An. 3231

3265; Irving (no data), Nancy; F; 1884-48; 1/4; M; Wife; 3212; Yes; Yes; Al. 479 An. 3232

3266; Irving, Arta; F; 1/25/13-19; 1/4; S; Daughter; 3213; Yes; Yes; Al. 6929 An. 3234

3267; Irving, Bernice; F; 3/13/18-14; 1/4; S; Daughter; 3214; Yes; Yes; Id. U-9745 An. 3235

3268; Irving, Zelda; F; 3/18/22-10; 1/4; S; Daughter; 3215; Yes; Yes; Id. U-11048 An. 3236

3269; Irving, Chester; M; 12/27/09-22; 1/4; M; Head; 3216; Yes; Yes; Al. 8205 An. 3240

3270; Irving (White Crow), Susie; F; 5/15/10-21; 1/4; M; Wife; 3217; Yes; Yes; Al. 5825 An. 7523

3271; Irving, William; M; 7/30/31-8/12; 1/4; S; Son; ---; Yes; Yes; U-13918

----; ~~Irving, Ollie; F; 4/15/09-21; 1/4; S; Head; 3218; Yes;~~ Duplication; Yes; Al. 4719 An. 3233

3272; Irving, Webster; M; 2/2/10-22; 1/4; M; Head; 3228; Yes; Yes; U-9553 An. 2380

N.E.: ~~Irving (Brandon), Wilma; F; ------; Rosebud Sioux; M; Wife;~~

N.E.: ~~Jack, Oliver; M; ------; Rosebud Sioux; F; M; Head;~~

3273; Jack (Chips), Alice; F; 1888-44; F; M; Wife; 3229; Yes; Yes; Al. 5569 An. 3248

3274; Jack, Isadore; M; 4/17/19-12; F; S; Son; 3230; Yes; Yes; Id. U-9750 An. 3249

3275; Jack, Irene; F; 2/25/27-5; F; S; Daughter; 3232; Yes; Yes; Id. U-12472 An. none

3276; Jacobs, Belma; F; 9/29/11-20; plus 1/4; S; Head; 3233; Yes; Yes; Al. 5968 An. 1920

3277; Jacobs, Caroline; F; 10/17/08-23; 1/4; S; Head; 3234; Yes; Yes; Al. 3624 An. 1918

3278; Jacobs, Charles; M; 1904-28; 1/4; S; Head; 3235; Yes; Yes; Al. 3622 An. 3251

3279; Jacobs, Francis; M; 1901-31; 1/4; S; Head; 3236; Yes; Yes; Al. 3620 An. 3252

3280; Jacobs, Harry; M; 1907-25; 1/4; S; Head; 3237; Yes; Yes; Al. 3623 An. 1917

Census of the __Pine Ridge__ reservation of the __Pine Ridge, South Dakota__ jurisdiction, as of __April 1__, 19**32**, taken by __James H. McGregor__, Superintendent.

Key: Number; Surname, Given; Sex; Date of Birth-Age at Last Birthday; Tribe (Oglala Sioux, unless stated otherwise); Degree of Blood; Marital Status; Relationship to Head of Family [Last Census Roll Number]; At Jurisdiction Where Enrolled (Yes/No); (If no – Where); Ward (Yes/No, if given); Allotment, Annuity and Identification Numbers (if given).

3281; Jacobs, Isaac; M; 3/31/10-22; 1/4; S; Head; 3238; Yes; Yes; Al. 5967 An. 1919

3282; Jacobs, William; M; 9/1900-31; plus 1/4; M; Head; 3239; Yes; Yes; Al. 3619 An. 3253

3283; Jacobs (Montileaux), Lottie; F; 1901-31; 1/4; M; Wife; 3240; Yes; Yes; Al. 3573 An. 3254

3284; Jacobs, Julia L.; F; 8/22/21-10; 1/4; S; Daughter; 3241; Yes; Yes; Id. U-11267 An. 3255

3285; Jacobs, Joseph; M; 10/13/22-9; 1/4; S; Son; 3242; Yes; Yes; Id. U-11268 An. 3256

3286; Jacobs, Earl; M; 12/26/24-7; 1/4; S; Son; 3243; Yes; Yes; Id. U-11558 An. 3257

3287; Jacobs, Ethelyn; F; 4/3/29-2; 1/4; S; Daughter; 3244; Yes; Yes; Id. U-13165 An. none

3288; Jacobs, Caroline; F; 8/15/31-7/12; 1/4; S; Daughter; ---; Yes; Yes; U-13937

N.E.: ~~Jackson, Henry; M; ------; Cheyenne Sioux; F; M; Head;~~

3289; Jackson (Little Elk), Lizzie; F; 1889-43; F; M; Wife; 3245; Yes; Yes; Al. 667 An. 3258

3290; Janis (Goodman), Fannie; F; 1863-69; plus 1/4; Wd.; Head; 3246; Yes; Yes; Id. U-9760 An. 3260

3291; Janis, Antoine; M; 1902-30; 1/4; S; Head; 3247; Yes; Yes; Al. 71 An. 3262

3292; Janis, Benjamin; M; 1864-68; 1/4; Wd.; Head; 3248; Yes; Yes; Al. 709 An. 3263

3293; Janis, Benjamin Jr.; M; 1895-37; 1/4; M; Head; 3249; Yes; Yes; Al. 711 An. 265

3294; Janis (Pourier), Josephine; F; 1893-39; -1/4; M; Wife; 3250; Yes; Yes; Al. 718 An. 3266

3295; Janis, Myrtle; F; 9/15/22-9; plus 1/4; S; Daughter; 3251; Yes; Yes; Id. U-11082 An. 3267

3296; Janis, Ralph E; M; 9/23/24-7; 1/4; S; Son; 3252; Yes; Yes; Id. U-11358 An. 3268

3297; Janis, Emmit; M; 11/5/26-5; 1/4; S; Son; 3253; Yes; Yes; Id. U-12180 An. none

3298; Janis, Cecelia; F; 6/6/29-2; 1/4; S; Daughter; 3254; Yes; Yes; Id. U-13266 An. none

3299; Janis, Benjamin; M; 1886-46; 1/4; M; Head; 3255; Yes; Yes; Al. 1630 An. 3269

Census of the **Pine Ridge** reservation of the **Pine Ridge, South Dakota** jurisdiction, as of **April 1**, 19**32**, taken by **James H. McGregor**, Superintendent.

Key: Number; Surname, Given; Sex; Date of Birth-Age at Last Birthday; Tribe (Oglala Sioux, unless stated otherwise); Degree of Blood; Marital Status; Relationship to Head of Family [Last Census Roll Number]; At Jurisdiction Where Enrolled (Yes/No); (If no – Where); Ward (Yes/No, if given); Allotment, Annuity and Identification Numbers (if given).

3300; Janis (Two Bulls), Julia; F; 1892-40; F; M; Wife; 7132; Yes; Yes; Al. 6002 An. 7088
3301; Janis, Emily; F; 2/2/15-17; 1/4; S; Daughter; 3256; Yes; Yes; Al. 8101 An. 3271
3302; Janis, Chester; M; 7/24/17-14; 1/4; S; Son; 3257; Yes; Yes; Id. U-9777 An. 3272
3303; Janis, Norman; M; 4/10/19-12; 1/4; S; Son; 3258; Yes; Yes; Id. U-9778 An. 3273
3304; Janis, Leonard; M; 2/5/21-11; 1/4; S; Son; 3259; Yes; Yes; Id. U-9779 An. 3274
3305; Janis, Cleveland; M; 3/26/23-9; 1/4; S; Son; 3260; Yes; Yes; Id. U-11603 An. 3275
3306; Janis, Dwyer; M; 8/8/28-3; 1/4; S; Son; 3261; Yes; Yes; Id. U-12758 An. none
3307; Janis, Annabel; F; 11/18/31-4/12; 1/4; S; Daughter; ---; Yes; Yes; U-13993

3308; Janis, Bernard; M; 1899-33; 1/4; M; Head; 3262; Yes; Yes; Al. 3608 An. 3276
3309; Janis (Hunter), Cornelia; F; 1903-29; 1/4; M; Wife; 3263; Yes; Yes; Al. 3658 An. 3277
3310; Janis, Olive; MF; 7/16/29-2; 1/4; S; Daughter; 3264; Yes; Yes; Id. U-13253 An. none

3311; Janis, Charles; M; 1897-35; plus 1/4; M; Head; 3265; Yes; Yes; Al. 70 An. 3278
3312; Janis (Bluffing Bear), Dora; F; 12/20/10-21; F; M; Wife; 3266; Yes; Yes; Al. 6750 An. 880
3313; Janis, Kenneth; M; 1/7/31-1; plus 1/4; S; Son; 3267; Yes; Yes; Id. U-13668 An. none

3314; Janis, Edward; M; 1897-35; 1/4; M; Head; 3268; Yes; Yes; Al. 3681 An. 3279
N.E.: Janis (Rouse), Ellen; F; ------; Yankton Sioux; 1/4; M; Wife;
3315; Janis, Edw. Jr.; M; 4/28/18-13; 1/4; S; Son; 3269; Yes; Yes; Al. 8271 An. 3280
3316; Janis, Harry; M; 9/28/19-12; 1/4; S; Son; 3270; Yes; Yes; Id. U-9775 An. 3281
3317; Janis, Edna; F; 4/22/21-10; 1/4; S; Daughter; 3271; Yes; Yes; Id. U-9776 An. 3282
3318; Janis, Richard; M; 12/17/22-9; 1/4; S; Son; 3272; Yes; Yes; Id. U-14032 An. 3283
3319; Janis, James H.; M; 9/5/24-7; 1/4; S; Son; 3273; Yes; Yes; Id. U-11364 An. 3284

Census of the **Pine Ridge** reservation of the **Pine Ridge, South Dakota** jurisdiction, as of **April 1**, 19**32**, taken by **James H. McGregor**, Superintendent.

Key: Number; Surname, Given; Sex; Date of Birth-Age at Last Birthday; Tribe (Oglala Sioux, unless stated otherwise); Degree of Blood; Marital Status; Relationship to Head of Family [Last Census Roll Number]; At Jurisdiction Where Enrolled (Yes/No); (If no – Where); Ward (Yes/No, if given); Allotment, Annuity and Identification Numbers (if given).

3320; Janis, Dorothy; F; 3/25/26-6; 1/4; S; Daughter; 3274; Yes; Yes; Id. U-12319 An. none
3321; Janis, Otto; M; 1/3/28-4; 1/4; S; Son; 3275; Yes; Yes; Id. U-12479 An. none
3322; Janis, Theresa; F; 9/24/29-2; 1/4; S; Daughter; 3276; Yes; Yes; Id. U-13335 An. none
3323; Janis, Aurea; F; 8/14/31-7/12; 1/4; S; Daughter; ---; Yes; Yes; U-13938

3324; Janis, Elizabeth; F; 1893-39; 1/4; M; Head; 3277; Yes; Yes; Al. 3614 An. 3285
3325; Janis, Norman E; M; 4/8/20-11; 1/4; S; Son; 3278; Yes; Yes; Id. U-9754 An. 3286
3326; Schrader, Frances; F; 2/26/24-8; 1/4; S; Daughter; 3279; Yes; Yes; Id. U-12862 An. none
3327; Ear Ring, Leon; M; 7/2/29-2; 1/4; S; Son; 3280; Yes; Yes; Id. U-13782 An. none

3328; Janis, Francis; M; 8/7/98-33; plus 1/4; M; Head; 3281; Yes; Yes; Al. 715 An. 3288
3329; Janis (Birdnecklace), Ida; F; 1902-30; 1/4; M; Wife; 3282; Yes; Yes; Al. 281 An. 3289
3330; Janis, Clarence; M; 8/17/22-9; 1/4; S; Son; 3283; Yes; Yes; Id. U-12033 An. 3290
3331; Janis, Ival; M; 3/24/24-8; 1/4; S; Son; 3284; Yes; Yes; Id. U-11230 An. 3291
3332; Janis, Guy; M; 12/1/25-6; 1/4; S; Son; 3285; Yes; Yes; Id. U-11812 An. none
3333; Janis, Curtis; M; 6/16/28-3; 1/4; S; Son; 3286; Yes; Yes; Id. U-12684 An. none

3334; Janis, Henry; M; 1894-38; 1/4; M; Head; 3287; Yes; Yes; Al. 1156 An. 3292
3335; Janis (Hawk Wing), Zona; F; 9/4/10-21; 1/4; M; Wife; 3288; Yes; Yes; Al. 5303 An. 4984
3336; Janis, Cecelia; F; 11/30/17-14; 1/4; S; Daughter; 3289; Yes; Yes; Id. U-9752 An. 3295
3337; Janis, Viannie R; F; 8/9/30-1; 1/4; S; Daughter; 3290; Yes; Yes; Id. U-13604 An. none
3338; Janis, Godfrey; M; 12/26/31-3/12; 1/4; S; Son; ---; Yes; Yes; U-14096

3339; Janis, Clara I; F; 5/22/15-16; 1/4; S; Head; 3291; Yes; Yes; Id. U-9751 An. 3294
3340; Janis, Mildred G; F; 2/1/31-1; 1/4; S; Daughter; ---; Yes; Yes; U-13835

3341; Janis, James; M; 1893-39; 1/4; M; Head; 3301; Yes; Yes; Al. 5662 An. 3310

Census of the __Pine Ridge__ reservation of the __Pine Ridge, South Dakota__ jurisdiction, as of __April 1__, 19**32**, taken by __James H. McGregor__, Superintendent.

Key: Number; Surname, Given; Sex; Date of Birth-Age at Last Birthday; Tribe (Oglala Sioux, unless stated otherwise); Degree of Blood; Marital Status; Relationship to Head of Family [Last Census Roll Number]; At Jurisdiction Where Enrolled (Yes/No); (If no – Where); Ward (Yes/No, if given); Allotment, Annuity and Identification Numbers (if given).

3342; Janis (Runs Along The Edge), Julia; F; 1897-35; 1/4; M; Wife; 3302; Yes; Yes; Al. 1100 An. 3311

3343; Janis, Lillie; F; 11/15/21-10; 1/4; S; Daughter; 3303; Yes; Yes; Id. U-10885 An. 3313

3344; Janis, Enoch; M; 8/6/23-8; 1/4; S; Son; 3304; Yes; Yes; Id. U-14027 An. 3314

3345; Janis, Levi; M; 12/26/27-4; 1/4; S; Son; 3305; Yes; Yes; Id. U-12444 An. none

3346; Janis, Joe; M; 1898-34; 1/4; S; Head; 3306; Yes; Yes; Al. 303 An. 3315

3347; Janis, Herbert; M; ---- -42; 1/4; M; Head; 3307; Yes; Yes; Al. 300 An. 3299

3348; Janis, Redwing; F; 3/1/14-18; plus 1/4; S; Daughter; 3308; No; Gordon, town, Sheridan, Nebr.; Yes; Id. U-9761 An. 3301

3349; Janis, James; M; 1889-43; plus 1/4; M; Head; 3294; Yes; Yes; Al. 710 An. 3303

3350; Janis (Cottier), Lucy; F; 1888-44; 1/4; M; Wife; 3295; Yes; Yes; Al. 987 An. 3304

3351; Janis, David W; M; 1/2[sic]/14/12-19; 1/4; S; Son; 3296; Yes; Yes; Al. 7753 An. 3305

3352; Janis, James I.; M; 4/2/15-17; 1/4; S; Son; 3297; Yes; Yes; Al. 7964 An. 3306

3353; Janis, Theodore; M; 4/28/17-14; 1/4; S; Son; 3298; Yes; Yes; Id. U-9768 An. 3307

3354; Janis, Benjamin; M; 2/6/19-13; 1/4; S; Son; 3299; Yes; Yes; Id. U-9769 An. 3308

3355; Janis, Susanna; F; 1/30/21-11; 1/4; S; Daughter; 3300; Yes; Yes; Id. U-9770 An. 3309

3356; Kills Small, Mary A; F; 1/23/31-1; F; S; Ward; ---; Yes; Yes; U-13980

3357; Janis, Evelyn; F; 2/11/19-13; 1/4; S; Daughter; 3309; No; Gordon, town, Sheridan, Nebr.; Yes; Id. U-9763 An. 3302

3358; Janis, Ruth; F; 10/8/25-6; 1/4; S; Daughter; 3310; No; Same; Yes; Id. U-11746 An. none

3359; Janis, Herbert Jr.; M; 10/12/28-3; 1/4; S; Son; 3311; No; Same; Yes; Id. U-12868 An. none

3360; Janis, Bertha; F; 1/7/12-19; 1/4; S; Head; 3312; No; Gordon, town, Sheridan, Nebr.; Yes; Al. 7855 An. 3300

3361; Janis, Joseph (George); M; 1891-41; 1/4; M; Head; 3313; Yes; Yes; Al. 65 An. 3316

Census of the **Pine Ridge** reservation of the **Pine Ridge, South Dakota** jurisdiction, as of **April 1**, 19**32**, taken by **James H. McGregor**, Superintendent.

Key: Number; Surname, Given; Sex; Date of Birth-Age at Last Birthday; Tribe (Oglala Sioux, unless stated otherwise); Degree of Blood; Marital Status; Relationship to Head of Family [Last Census Roll Number]; At Jurisdiction Where Enrolled (Yes/No); (If no – Where); Ward (Yes/No, if given); Allotment, Annuity and Identification Numbers (if given).

3362; Janis (Siers), Josephine; F; 1906-36; 1/4; M; Wife; 3314; Yes; Yes; Al. 4845 An. 3317
3363; Janis, Lydia; F; 4/10/17-14; 1/4; S; Daughter; 3315; Yes; Yes; Id. U-9764 An. 3318
3364; Janis, Emma; F; 1/16/22-10; 1/4; S; Daughter; 3316; Yes; Yes; Id. U-10902 An. 3319
3365; Janis, Geraldine; F; 3/8/25-7; 1/4; S; Daughter; 3317; Yes; Yes; Id. U-11580 An. 3320
3366; Janis, Willard; M; 3/18/28-4; 1/4; S; Son; 3318; Yes; Yes; Id. U-12714 An. none
3367; Janis, John; M; 3/15/31-1; 1/4; S; Son; 3319; Yes; Yes; Id. U-13762 An. none

3368; Janis (Beauvois), Mollie; F; 1865-67; 1/4; Wd.; Head; 3320; Yes; Yes; Al. 1783 An. 3322
3369; Janis, John Lee; M; 1904-28; plus 1/4; M; Head; 3321; Yes; Yes; Al. 1785 An. 3777
3370; Janis (Nelson), Madge; F; 1902-30; 1/4; M; Wife; 3322; Yes; Yes; Al. 2223 An. 3315
3371; Janis, John G.; M; 1/3/31-1; 1/4; S; Son; 3323; Yes; Yes; Id. U-13669 An. none
3372; Trotterschaud, Vernon; M; 8/24/23-8; 1/4; S; S. Son; 3324; Yes; Yes; Id. U-11105 An. 7217

3373; Janis, Peter; M; 1/11/02-30; 1/4; Wd; Head; 3325; Yes; Yes; Al. 1636 An. 3324

3374; Janis, Peter; M; 1894-38; 1/4; M; Head; 3326; Yes; Yes; Al. 301 An. 3325
3375; Janis (Garnier), Sophia; F; 1889-43; 1/4; M; Wife; 3327; Yes; Yes; Al. 5787 An. 3326
3376; Janis, Oliver; FM; 11/9/13-18; 1/4; S; Son; 3328; Yes; Yes; Al. 7920 An. 3327
3377; Janis, Russel; M; 12/28/14-17; 1/4; S; Son; 3329; Yes; Yes; Id. U-9755 An. 3328
3378; Janis, Hobert; M; 9/1/16-15; 1/4; S; Son; 3330; Yes; Yes; Id. U-9756 An. 3329
3379; Janis, Catherine; F; 7/24/21-10; 1/4; S; Daughter; 3331; Yes; Yes; Id. U-10883 An. 3330
3380; Janis, Baptiste; M; 1/30/23-9; 1/4; S; Son; 3332; Yes; Yes; Id. U-12096 An. 3331
3381; Janis, Ray; M; 7/5/25-6; 1/4; S; Son; 3333; Yes; Yes; Id. U-11679 An. none
3382; Janis, Norbert; M; 5/31/27-4; 1/4; S; Son; 3334; Yes; Yes; Id. U-12406 An. 3331

Census of the **Pine Ridge** reservation of the **Pine Ridge, South Dakota** jurisdiction, as of **April 1**, 19**32**, taken by **James H. McGregor**, Superintendent.

Key: Number; Surname, Given; Sex; Date of Birth-Age at Last Birthday; Tribe (Oglala Sioux, unless stated otherwise); Degree of Blood; Marital Status; Relationship to Head of Family [Last Census Roll Number]; At Jurisdiction Where Enrolled (Yes/No); (If no – Where); Ward (Yes/No, if given); Allotment, Annuity and Identification Numbers (if given).

3383; Janis, Hilda; F; 12/21/28-3; 1/4; S; Daughter; 3335; Yes; Yes; Id. U-12948 An. 3330

3384; Janis, Lillian; F; 1/2/31-1; 1/4; S; Daughter; 3336; Yes; Yes; Id. U-13670 An. 3330

3385; Janis, Raymond; M; 1901-31; plus 1/4; M; Head; 3337; Yes; Yes; Al. 716 An. 3332

N.E.: Janis (Keith), Marie; F; ---- ---; Yankton Sioux; 1/4; M; Wife;

3386; Janis, Mildred; F; 4/13/22-9; 1/4; S; Daughter; 3338; Yes; Yes; Id. U-11618 An. 3333

3387; Janis, Irene; F; 3/13/24-8; 1/4; S; Daughter; 3339; Yes; Yes; Id. U-11708 An. none

3388; Janis, Raymond; M; 5/16/26-5; 1/4; S; Son; 3340; Yes; Yes; Id. U-11969 An. none

3389; Janis, James D; M; 2/25/28-4; 1/4; S; Son; 3341; Yes; Yes; Id. U-12658 An. none

3390; Janis, Roy; M; 1901-31; 1/4; M; Head; 3342; Yes; Yes; Al. 3609 An. 3334

3391; Janis (Palmier), Josephine; F; 1905-27; 1/4; M; Wife; 3343; Yes; Yes; Al. 2709 An. 3335

3392; Janis, Lenora; F; 10/24/23-8; 1/4; S; Daughter; 3344; Yes; Yes; Id. U-11323 An. 3336

3393; Janis, Leora; F; 7/12/25-6; 1/4; S; Daughter; 3345; Yes; Yes; Id. U-11730 An. none

3394; Janis, Leroy; M; 2/20/27-5; 1/4; S; Son; 3346; Yes; Yes; Id. U-12289 An. none

3395; Janis, Marian; F; 4/28/29-3; 1/4; S; Daughter; 3347; Yes; Yes; Id. U-13166 An. none

3396; Janis, Donald R; M; 4/2/31-1; 1/4; S; Son; ---; Yes; Yes; U-13806

3397; Janis, Stanley; M; 1907-25; 1/4; Wd.; Head; 3348; Yes; Yes; Al. 9759 An. 5261

3398; Janis, Thomas; M; 1888-44; 1/4; M; Head; 3349; Yes; Yes; Al. 1629 An. 3338

3399; Janis (no data), Rose; F; 1871-61; 1/4; M; Wife; 3350; Yes; Yes; Al. 3606 An. 3339

3400; Janis, Eunice; F; 9/14/14-17; 1/4; S; Daughter; 3351; Yes; Yes; Al. 7894 An. 3342

3401; Janis, Vincent; M; 1908-24; 1/4; S; Head; 3352; Yes; Yes; Al. 3611 An. 3340

3402; Janis, William; M; 1888-44; 1/4; M; Head; 3353; Yes; Yes; Al. 1022 An. 3343

N.E.: Janis (Wood Ring), Edith; F; ---- ---; Rosebud Sioux; F; M; Wife;

Census of the **Pine Ridge** reservation of the **Pine Ridge, South Dakota** jurisdiction, as of **April 1**, 19**32**, taken by **James H. McGregor**, Superintendent.

Key: Number; Surname, Given; Sex; Date of Birth-Age at Last Birthday; Tribe (Oglala Sioux, unless stated otherwise); Degree of Blood; Marital Status; Relationship to Head of Family [Last Census Roll Number]; At Jurisdiction Where Enrolled (Yes/No); (If no – Where); Ward (Yes/No, if given); Allotment, Annuity and Identification Numbers (if given).

3403; Janis, Intha; F; 4/9/30-11; 1/4; S; Daughter; 3354; Yes; Yes; Id. U-13735 An. none

3404; Janis (No Flesh), Mable; F; 1870-62; 1/4; Wd; Wife; 3356; Yes; NO.; Al. 3802 An. 3345

3405; Janis, Wilson; M; 1894-38; 1/4; M; Head; 3357; Yes; Yes; Al. 1564 An. 2346
3406; Janis (Fool Head), Alice; F; 1894-38; 1/4; M; Wife; 3358; Yes; Yes; Al. 6804 An. 3347
3407; Janis, Louisa; F; 3/26/17-15; 1/4; S; Daughter; 3359; Yes; Yes; Id. U-9771 An. 3348
3408; Janis, Isabelle; F; 10/27/21-10; 1/4; S; Daughter; 3360; Yes; Yes; Id. U-9773 An. 3350
3409; Janis, Evelyn; F; 1/9/24-8; 1/4; S; Daughter; 3361; Yes; Yes; Id. U-11179 An. 3351
3410; Janis, Wilson; M; 3/9/27-5; 1/4; S; Son; 3362; Yes; Yes; Id. U-12248 An. none
3411; Janis, Ora; F; 10/9/29-2; 1/4; S; Daughter; 3363; Yes; Yes; Id. U-13293 An. none

3412; Jarvis, Grace; F; 1853-79; F; Wd; Head; 3364; Yes; Yes; Al. 6501 An. 3352

3413; Jarvis, Giles; M; 1908-24; plus 1/4; S; Head; 3365; Yes; Yes; Al. 6503 An. 3353

3414; Jarvis, Michael; M; 1880-52; 1/4; M; Head; 3366; Yes; Yes; Al. 5011 An. 3355
3415; Jarvis (Two Bulls), Lucy; F; 1895-37; 1/4; M; Wife; 3367; Yes; Yes; Al. 3474 An. 3356

3416; Jarvis, Joseph; M; 1879-53; 1/4; S; Head; 3369; No; Unknown; No; Al. 7346 An. 3354

3417; Jealous Of Him, Ofliver[sic]; M; 1902-30; 1/4; M; Head; 3370; Yes; Yes; Al. 34 An. 3359
3418; Jealous Of Him (Little Boy), Mary; F; 1903-29; 1/4; M; Wife; 3371; Yes; Yes; Al. 598 An. 3360
3419; Jealous Of Him, Roy; M; 6/7/24-7; 1/4; S; Son; 3372; Yes; Yes; Id. U-11282 An. 3361
3420; Jealous Of Him, Lucy; F; 11/27/27-4; 1/4; S; Daughter; 3373; Yes; Yes; Id. U-12138 An. none

Census of the **Pine Ridge** reservation of the **Pine Ridge, South Dakota** jurisdiction, as of **April 1**, 19**32**, taken by **James H. McGregor**, Superintendent.

Key: Number; Surname, Given; Sex; Date of Birth-Age at Last Birthday; Tribe (Oglala Sioux, unless stated otherwise); Degree of Blood; Marital Status; Relationship to Head of Family [Last Census Roll Number]; At Jurisdiction Where Enrolled (Yes/No); (If no – Where); Ward (Yes/No, if given); Allotment, Annuity and Identification Numbers (if given).

3421; Jealous Of Him, Mary C; F; 2/16/30-2; 1/4; S; Daughter; 3374; Yes; Yes; Id. U-13381 An. none

3422; Jealous Of Him, Oscar; M; 1865-67; plus 1/4; M; Head; 3375; Yes; Yes; Al. 32 An. 3362

3423; Jealous Of Him (Holy Track), ---; F; 1857-75; F; M; Wife; 3376; Yes; Yes; Al. 4884 An. 3363

3424; Jealous Of Him, Frank; M; 1/29/09-23; 1/4; M; Head; 3377; Yes; Yes; Al. 6686 An. 3364

3425; Jealous Of Him (White Face), Agnes; F; 1908-24; F; M; Wife; 3378; Yes; Yes; Al. 4940 An. 7575

3426; Jealous Of Him, Oscar Jr.; M; 1/27/31-1; plus 1/4; S; Son; 3379; Yes; Yes; Id. U-13697 An. none

3427; Jenkins (Grist), Ramona; F; 1897-35; -1/4; M; Head; 3380; Yes; Yes; Al. 3966 An. 3365

3428; Jenkins, Annete; F; 9/23/17-14; -1/4; S; Daughter; 3381; Yes; Yes; Id. U-9781 An. 3366

3429; Jenkins, Lloyd; M; 2/2/19-13; -1/4; S; Son; 3382; Yes; Yes; Id. U-9782 An. 3367

3430; Jenkins, Billie; M; 7/7/20-11; -1/4; S; Son; 3383; Yes; Yes; Id. U-10928 An. 3368

3431; Jensen, Antoine; M; 1907-25; plus 1/4; S; Head; 3384; Yes; Yes; Id. U-2695 An. 3369

3432; Jensen, Benjamin; M; 1901-31; 1/4; S; Head; 3385; Yes; Yes; Id. U-2693 An. 3370

3433; Jensen, George; M; 6/17/99-32; 1/4; S; Head; 3386; Yes; Yes; Id. U-2692 An. 3371

3434; (Jensen) (no data), Ramona; F; 1878-54; plus 1/4; M; Head; 3387; Yes; Yes; Al. 3966 An. 3365

3435; Jensen, Thelma; F; 9/5/16-16; 1/4; S; Daughter; 3388; Yes; Yes; Id. U-9785 An. 3376

3436; Jensen, Mildred; F; 6/18/19-12; 1/4; S; Daughter; 3389; Yes; Yes; Id. U-9786 An. 3377

3437; Jensen, Albert; M; 4/7/22-9; 1/4; S; Son; 3390; Yes; Yes; Id. U-11096 An. 3378

Census of the **Pine Ridge** reservation of the **Pine Ridge, South Dakota** jurisdiction, as of **April 1**, 19**32**, taken by **James H. McGregor**, Superintendent.

Key: Number; Surname, Given; Sex; Date of Birth-Age at Last Birthday; Tribe (Oglala Sioux, unless stated otherwise); Degree of Blood; Marital Status; Relationship to Head of Family [Last Census Roll Number]; At Jurisdiction Where Enrolled (Yes/No); (If no – Where); Ward (Yes/No, if given); Allotment, Annuity and Identification Numbers (if given).

3438; Jensen, John; M; 2/7/09-23; 1/4; S; Head; 3391; Yes; Yes; Al. 5970 An. 3373

3439; Jensen (Wilson), May Belle; F; 1904-28; -1/4; M; Head; 3392; Yes; Yes; Al. 8247 An. 7712

3440; Jewett, Samuel; M; 1858-74; plus 1/4; S; Head; 3393; Yes; Yes; Id. U-5432 An. 3379

3441; Johnson, May Anna M; F; 5/21/16-16; -1/4; S; Head; 3394; No; Rushville, town, Sheridan, Nebr.; Yes; Al. 7956 An. none

3442; Johnson (Livermont), Mary Ivy; F; 1886-46; -1/4; M; Head; 3395; No; Gordon, town, Sheridan, Nebr.; Yes; Al. 2549 An. 3380

3443; Johnson, Clara; F; 6/6/14-17; -1/4; S; Daughter; 3396; No; Same; Yes; Al. 8208 An. 3381

3444; Johnson, Pearl; F; 11/29/15-16; -1/4; S; Daughter; 3397; No; Same; Yes; Al. 8209 An. 3382

3445; Johnson, Samuel L; M; 8/22/20-11; -1/4; S; Son; 3398; No; Same; Yes; Id. U-10859 An. 3383

3446; Johnson, Opal L; F; 7/7/23-8; -1/4; S; Daughter; 3399; No; Gordon, town, Sheridan, Nebr.; Id. U-12949 An. none

3447; Johnson (Ruff), Edna; F; 1890-42; plus 1/4; M; Head; 3400; No; Rapid City, city, Pennington, S.D.; No; Al. 4507 An. 3384

3448; Johnson, George C; M; 10/6/15-16; 1/4; S; Son; 3401; No; Same; Yes; Id. U-9787 An. 3385

3449; Johnson, Riner M; M; 1/4/18-14; 1/4; S; Son; 3402; No; Same; Yes; Id. U-9788 An. 3386

3450; Johnson (Lang), Myra; F; 10/31/97-34; -1/4; M; Head; 3403; No; Rapid City, city, Pennington, S.D.; Yes; Al. 3706 An. 3684

3451; Johnson, Georgianna; F; 4/27/23-8; -1/4; S; Daughter; 3404; No; Same; Yes; Id. U-12791 An. none

3452; Johnson, Robert L; M; 5/27/24-7; -1/4; S; Son; 3405; No; Same; Yes; Id. U-12792 An. none

N.E.: ~~Johnston, Douglas; M; ------; Chickasha[sic]; -1/4; M; Head;~~

3453; Johnston (Sears), Bernice; F; 12/1/08-23; plus 1/4; M; Wife; 3406; No; Arkansas City, city, Cowley, Kan.; Yes; Al. 4951 An. 6089

3454; Jones, Asa; M; 9/30/08-23; F; M; Head; 3407; Yes; Yes; Al. 4272 An. 7001

N.E.: ~~Jones (Crazy Bear), Forine; F; ------; Rosebud Sioux; F; M; Wife;~~

Census of the __**Pine Ridge**__ reservation of the __**Pine Ridge, South Dakota**__ jurisdiction, as of __**April 1**__, 19**32**, taken by __**James H. McGregor**__, Superintendent.

Key: Number; Surname, Given; Sex; Date of Birth-Age at Last Birthday; Tribe (Oglala Sioux, unless stated otherwise); Degree of Blood; Marital Status; Relationship to Head of Family [Last Census Roll Number]; At Jurisdiction Where Enrolled (Yes/No); (If no – Where); Ward (Yes/No, if given); Allotment, Annuity and Identification Numbers (if given).

3455; Jones, Charles Jr.; M; 1901-31; plus 1/4; M; Head; 3408; Yes; Yes; Al. 2701 An. 3389

3456; Jones, Emma; F; 1904-28; 1/4; M; Wife; 3409; Yes; Yes; Al. 9342 An. 3390

3457; Jones, Lorine; F; 2/3/22-10; 1/4; S; Daughter; 3410; Yes; Yes; Id. U-13050 An. 3391

3458; Jones, Bernadine; F; 11/17/23-8; 1/4; S; Daughter; 3411; Yes; Yes; Id. U-11540 An. 3392

3459; Jones, Laren; F; 2/3/25-7; 1/4; S; Daughter; 3412; Yes; Yes; Id. U-11541 An. 3393

3460; Jones, Anthony; M; 1/28/27-5; 1/4; S; Son; 3413; Yes; Yes; Id. U-12320 An. none

3461; Jones, Grace M; F; 10/17/30-1; 1/4; S; Daughter; 3414; Yes; Yes; Id. U-13645 An. none

3462; Jones, Charles Sr.; M; 1871-61; 1/4; M; Head; 3415; Yes; Yes; Al. 2696 An. 3394

3463; Jones, Joseph; M; 4/8/0922; 1/4; S; Son; 3416; Yes; Yes; Al. 7324 An. 3397

3464; Jones, Earl; M; 11/11/13-18; 1/4; S; Son; 3417; Yes; Yes; Al. 7325 An. 3398

3465; Jones, Ollie; F; 1/25/17-15; 1/4; S; Daughter; 3418; Yes; Yes; Id. U-9789 An. 3399

~~N.E.: Jones, Seymour; M; ------; Rosebud Sioux; F; M; Head;~~

3466; Jones (Young), May Flora; F; 10/12/08-23; 1/4; M; Wife; 3419; No; Rosebud, S.D.; Yes; Al. 5442 An. 7996

3467; Jones, Agnes; F; 3/1/12-20; F; M; Wife; 3420; Yes; Yes; Id. U-9790 An. 3402

3468; Jones, Christopher; M; 4/15/31-11/12; F; S; Son; ---; Yes; Yes; U-13807

3469; Jones, Annabelle; F; 3/8/23-9; plus 1/4; S; Alone; 3421; No; Rosebud, S.D,; Yes; Id. U-14017 An. none

3470; Jones, John; M; 1904-28; 1/4; S; Head; 3422; Yes; Yes; Al. 2703 An. 3404

3471; Jones, John; M; 1882-50; F; Wd; Head; 3423; Yes; Yes; Al. 3747 An. 3403

3472; Jones, Laurene; F; 1895-37; 1/4; S; Head; 3424; Yes; Yes; Al. 2698 An. 3405

3473; Jones, Mary; F; 1904-28; plus 1/4; S; Head; 3425; No; Alliance, town, Box Butte, Nebr.; Yes; Al. 2702 An. 3406

3474; Jones (Crow Woman), Nancy; F; 1868-64; F; Wd; Head; 3426; Yes; Yes; Al. 1907 An. 3401

Census of the **Pine Ridge** reservation of the **Pine Ridge, South Dakota** jurisdiction, as of **April 1**, 19**32**, taken by **James H. McGregor**, Superintendent.

Key: Number; Surname, Given; Sex; Date of Birth-Age at Last Birthday; Tribe (Oglala Sioux, unless stated otherwise); Degree of Blood; Marital Status; Relationship to Head of Family [Last Census Roll Number]; At Jurisdiction Where Enrolled (Yes/No); (If no – Where); Ward (Yes/No, if given); Allotment, Annuity and Identification Numbers (if given).

3475; Jones, William; M; 1899-33; 1/4; Wd; Head; 3427; Yes; Yes; Al. 2700 An. 3407

3476; Jones (Stirk), Pearl; F; 1902-30; 1/4; Wd; Head; 3428; Yes; Yes; Al. 2963 An. 3408

3477; Jones, Edward A; M; 3/15/26-6; 1/4; S; Son; 3429; Yes; Yes; Id. U-12114 An. none

3478; Jumping Bull, Harry; M; 1898-34; plus 1/4; M; Head; 3430; Yes; Yes; Al. 6612 An. 3409

3479; Jumping Bull (Running Hawk), Cecelia; F; 1902-30; 1/4; M; Wife; 3431; Yes; Yes; Al. 5294 An. 3410

3480; Jumping Bull, Ida; F; 4/14/22-9; 1/4; S; Daughter; 3432; Yes; Yes; Id. U-11023 An. 3411

3481; Jumping Bull, Chris; M; 1/18/25-7; 1/4; S; Son; 3433; Yes; Yes; Id. U-11512 An. 3412

3482; Jumping Bull, Karl; M; 4/10/27-4; 1/4; S; Son; 3434; Yes; Yes; Id. U-12548 An. none

3483; Jumping Bull, Calvin; M; 11/9/29-2; 1/4; S; Son; 3435; Yes; Yes; Id. U-13336 An. none

3484; Jumping Bull, Roselyn; F; 11/18/31-4/12; 1/4; S; Daughter; ---; Yes; Yes; U-13965

3485; Jumping Bull, Louis; M; 1871-61; F; M; Head; 3436; Yes; Yes; Al. 6403 An. 3414

3486; Jumping Bull (Kills Right), Lizzie; F; 1876-56; F; M; Wife; 3437; Yes; Yes; Al. 5641 An. 3415

3487; Jumping Bull, Melvin; M; 7/1/13-18; F; S; Son; 3438; Yes; Yes; Al. 7583 An. 3417

3488; Jumping Bull, Mercy; F; 1/4/11-21; F; S; Head; 3439; Yes; Yes; Al. 6575 An. 3416

3489; Jumping Bull, Silas; M; 1907-25; F; S; Head; 3440; Yes; Yes; Al. 5629 An. 3418

3490; Jumping Eagle, Henry; M; 1907-25; 1/4; S; Head; 3452; No; Flandreau, town, Moody, S.D.; Yes; Al. 6911 An. 13421

3491; Jumping Eagle, Oliver; M; 1882-50; F; M; Head; 3441; Yes; Yes; Al. 511 An. 3419

3492; Jumping Eagle (Rocky Bear), Mamie; F; 1884-48; plus 1/4; M; Wife; 3442; Yes; Yes; Al. 762 An. 3420

Census of the __**Pine Ridge**__ reservation of the __**Pine Ridge, South Dakota**__ jurisdiction, as of __**April 1**__, 19**32**, taken by __**James H. McGregor**__, Superintendent.

Key: Number; Surname, Given; Sex; Date of Birth-Age at Last Birthday; Tribe (Oglala Sioux, unless stated otherwise); Degree of Blood; Marital Status; Relationship to Head of Family [Last Census Roll Number]; At Jurisdiction Where Enrolled (Yes/No); (If no – Where); Ward (Yes/No, if given); Allotment, Annuity and Identification Numbers (if given).

3493; Jumping Eagle, Delmus; M; 5/13/09-22; 1/4; S; Son; 3443; Yes; Yes; Al. 6912 An. 3422

3494; Jumping Eagle, Jessie; F; 5/15/12-19; 1/4; S; Daughter; 3444; Yes; Yes; Al. 6914 An. 3424

3495; Jumping Eagle, Josephine; F; 1/8/14-18; 1/4; S; Daughter; 3445; Yes; Yes; Al. 7998 An. 3425

3496; Jumping Eagle, Irving; M; 3/23/15-17; 1/4; S; Son; 3446; Yes; Yes; Al. 7999 An. 3426

3497; Jumping Eagle, Alice; F; 1/19/17-15; 1/4; S; Daughter; 3447; Yes; Yes; Id. U-9791 An. 3427

3498; Jumping Eagle, Oliver Jr.; M; 8/8/19-12; 1/4; S; Son; 3448; Yes; Yes; Id. U-9792 An. 3428

3499; Jumping Eagle, Catherine; F; 4/14/22-9; 1/4; S; Daughter; 3449; Yes; Yes; Id. U-10965 An. 3429

3500; Jumping Eagle, Irene; F; 2/28/27-5; 1/4; S; Daughter; 3450; Yes; Yes; Id. U-12249 An. none

3501; Jumping Eagle, Robert E.; M; 12/3/28-3; 1/4; S; Son; 3451; Yes; Yes; Id. U-13382 An. none

3502; Keester (Harvey), Susie; F; 1893-39; Plus 1/4; M; Head; 3453; Yes; Yes; Al. 2723 An. 3431

3503; Keester, Bernice; F; 7/8/22-9; 1/4; S; Daughter; 3454; Yes; Yes; Id. U-14023 An. 3432

3504; Keester, Katherine; F; 2/14/24-8; 1/4; S; Daughter; 3455; Yes; Yes; Id. U-11479 An. 3433

3505; Keester, Gilbert; M; 2/24/25-7; 1/4; S; Son; 3456; Yes; Yes; Id. U-12887 An. none

3506; Keester, Henry; M; 1/~~22~~30/27-4; 1/4; S; Son; 3457; Yes; Yes; Id. U-12888 An. none

3507; Keester, Arthur; M; 12/12/29-2; 1/4; S; Son; 3458; Yes; Yes; Id. U-13383 An. none

~~N.E.: Keith, Hobart; M; ------; Yankton Sioux; 1/4; M; Head;~~

3508; Keith (Ecoffey), Louisa; F; 1899-33; -1/4; M; Wife; 3459; Yes; Yes; Al. 1361 An. 3434

3509; Keith, Rosa M; F; 3/16/21-11; 1/4; S; Daughter; 3460; Yes; Yes; Id. U-9793 An. 3435

3510; Keith, Hobart E; M; 3/8/22-10; 1/4; S; Son; 3461; Yes; Yes; Id. U-10909 An. 3436

3511; Keith, Ethel M; F; 2/19/25-7; 1/4; S; Daughter; 3462; Yes; Yes; Id. U-11510 An. 3437

3512; Keith, Joseph; M; 9/7/27-4; 1/4; S; Son; 3463; Yes; Yes; Id. U-12387 An. none

Census of the___**Pine Ridge**___reservation of the___**Pine Ridge, South Dakota**
jurisdiction, as of___**April 1**___, 19**32,** taken by___**James H. McGregor**___,
Superintendent.

Key: Number; Surname, Given; Sex; Date of Birth-Age at Last Birthday; Tribe (Oglala Sioux, unless stated otherwise); Degree of Blood; Marital Status; Relationship to Head of Family [Last Census Roll Number]; At Jurisdiction Where Enrolled (Yes/No); (If no – Where); Ward (Yes/No, if given); Allotment, Annuity and Identification Numbers (if given).

3513; Keith, Mary E; F; 7/15/29-2; 1/4; S; Daughter; 3464; Yes; Yes; Id. U-13257 An. none

3514; Kelly, Benjamin; M; 1868-64; 1/4; M; Head; 3465; No; Unknown; No; Al. 4139 An. 3438

3515; Kelly, Cora; F; 1878-54; 1/4; S; Head; 3466; No; Ft. Collins, town Larimer, Colo; No; Al. 3631 An. 3439

3516; Kelly, Frank B; M; 1865-67; plus 1/4; Wd; Head; 3467; No; Unknown; No; Al. 4138 An. 3441

3517; Kelly, John A; M; 1872-60; 1/4; S; Head; 3468; No; Portland, city, Multnomah, Ore.; No; Al. 3630 An. 3442

3518; Kelly, William H; M; 1873-59; 1/4; S; Head; 3469; No; Denver, city, Denver, Colo; No; Al. 4140 An. 3443

N.E.:   Kennedy, Howard T; M; ----- --; Lower Brule Sioux; plus 1/4; M; Head;
3519; Keith (Fog), Mary A; F; 3/24/09-23; plus 1/4; M; Wife; 2297; Yes; Yes; Al. 7905 An. 2298

3520; Kicking Bear, Frank; M; 1887-45; F; M; Head; 3470; Yes; Yes; Al. 6639 An. 3444
3521; Kicking Bear (Sitting Bull), Nancy; F; 1903-29; F; M; Wife; 6654; Yes; Yes; Al. 5556 An. 6627
3522; Stewart, Emerson; M; 4/13/25-6; F; S; S. Son; 6655; Yes; Yes; Id. U-11750 An. none
3523; Stewart, Sifrey; M; 6/13/29-2; F; S; S. Son; 6656; Yes; Yes; Id. U-13216 An. none
3524; Kills Above, ---; M; 1865-67; F; M; Head; 3471; Yes; Yes; Al. 1246 An. 3447
3525; Kicking Bear (Charges At), ---; F; 1862-70; F; M; Wife; 3472; Yes; Yes; Al. 6060 An. 3448

3526; Kills Ahead, Charles; M; 1887-45; F; M; Head; 3473; No; Cheyenne River, S.D.; No; Al. 1216 An. 3456

3527; Kills A Hundred (Bear Nose), Julia; F; 1877-55; plus 1/4; Wd; Head; 3475; Yes; Yes; Al. 6232 An. 368

Census of the **Pine Ridge** reservation of the **Pine Ridge, South Dakota** jurisdiction, as of **April 1**, 19**32**, taken by **James H. McGregor**, Superintendent.

Key: Number; Surname, Given; Sex; Date of Birth-Age at Last Birthday; Tribe (Oglala Sioux, unless stated otherwise); Degree of Blood; Marital Status; Relationship to Head of Family [Last Census Roll Number]; At Jurisdiction Where Enrolled (Yes/No); (If no – Where); Ward (Yes/No, if given); Allotment, Annuity and Identification Numbers (if given).

3528; Kills A Hundred (Hudspeth), Myrtle; F; 1888-44; 1/4; Wd; Head; 3476; Yes; Yes; Al. 3370 An. 6177

3529; Kills A Hundred (no data), Susie; F; 1860-72; F; Wd.; Head; 3477; Yes; Yes; Al. 3492 An. 3459

3530; Kills Alone, ---; M; 1867-65; F; Wd; Head; 3478; Yes; Yes; Al. 3326 An. 3462

3531; Kills At Lodge, ---; M; 1865-67; F; Wd.; Head; 3479; Yes; Yes; Al. 3420 An. 3466

3532; Kills At Lodge (Brings It), Bertha; F; 1867-65; F; Wd.; Head; 3480; Yes; Yes; Al. 3421 An. 3467

3533; Kills Back, George; M; 1899-33; F; M; Head; 3481; Yes; Yes; Al. 570 An. 3471

3534; Kills Back (Bear Runner), Julia; F; 1906-26; F; M; Wife; 3482; Yes; Yes; Al. 5847 An. 410

3535; Kills Back, Mowis E; M; 12/8/31-3/12; F; S; Son; ---; Yes; Yes; U-13996

3536; Kills Bad, Pugh; M; 1893-39; F; Wd.; Head; 3483; Yes; Yes; Al. 107 An. 3473

3537; Kills Brave, Fred; M; 1897-35; F; S; Head; 3484; Yes; Yes; Al. 7403 An. 3475

3538; Kills Brave, Samuel; M; 1865-67; F; M; Head; 3485; Yes; Yes; Al. 4522 An. 3476

3539; Kills Close To Lodge, Bert; M; 1868-64; F; M; Head; 3487; Yes; Yes; Al. 5049 An. 3478

3540; Kills Close To Lodge (no data), Mollie; F; 1881-51; F; M; Wife; 3488; Yes; Yes; Al. 5050 An. 3479

3541; Kills Crow Indian, Bert; M; 1872-60; F; M; Head; 3489; Yes; Yes; Al. 789 An. 3480

3542; Kills Crow Indian (no data), Rosa; F; 1874-58; F; M; Wife; 3490; Yes; Yes; Al. 7122 An. 3481

3542[sic]; Kills Crow Indian, William; M; 11/8/12-19; F; S; Son; 3491; Yes; Yes; Al. 8127 An. 3482

3544; Kills Crow Indian, Abraham; M; 8/17/19-12; F; S; Son; 3492; Yes; Yes; Id. U-9801 An. 3483

Census of the **Pine Ridge** reservation of the **Pine Ridge, South Dakota** jurisdiction, as of **April 1**, 19**32**, taken by **James H. McGregor**, Superintendent.

Key: Number; Surname, Given; Sex; Date of Birth-Age at Last Birthday; Tribe (Oglala Sioux, unless stated otherwise); Degree of Blood; Marital Status; Relationship to Head of Family [Last Census Roll Number]; At Jurisdiction Where Enrolled (Yes/No); (If no – Where); Ward (Yes/No, if given); Allotment, Annuity and Identification Numbers (if given).

3545; Kills Crow Indian, Asa; M; 1906-26; F; S; Head; 3493; Yes; Yes; Al. 7126 An. 3484

3546; Kills Crow Indian, Jacob; M; 1904-28; F; M; Head; 3494; Yes; Yes; Al. 7125 An. 3485

3547; Kills Crow Indian (Eagle Elk), Jessie; F; 1899-33; F; M; Wife; 3495; Yes; Yes; Al. 500 An. 5787

3548; Kills Crow Indian, Jackson; M; 1901-31; F; M; Head; 3496; Yes; Yes; Al. 7184 An. 3486

3549; Kills Crow Indian, Geraldine; F; 11/15/29-2; F; S; Daughter; 3498; Yes; Yes; Id. U-13294 An. none

3550; Kills Crow Indian, Samuel; M; 1894-38; F; M; Head; 3499; Yes; Yes; Al. 7121 An. 3487

3551; Kills Crow Indian (Old Shield), Jessie; F; 1899-33; F; M; Wife; 3500; Yes; Yes; Al. 2173 An. 3488

3552; Kills Crow Indian, Virginia; F; 5/9/17-14; F; S; Daughter; 3501; Yes; Yes; Id. U-9802 An. 3489

3553; Kills Crow Indian, Aloysius; M; 4/26/19-13; F; S; Son; 3502; Yes; Yes; Id. U-9803 An. 3490

3554; Kills Crow Indian, Viola; F; 1/22/25-7; F; S; Daughter; 3503; Yes; Yes; Id. U-10801 An. 3492

3555; Kills Crow Indian, Tessie; F; 6/11/29-2; F; S; Daughter; 3504; Yes; Yes; Id. U-13187 An. none

3556; Kills Crow Indian, Rufus; M; 6/11/31-9/12; F; S; Son; ---; Yes; Yes; U-13856

3557; Kills Enemy, ---; M; 1864-68; F; M; Head; 3505; Yes; Yes; Al. 6028 An. 3493

3558; Kills Enemy (Runs Between), ---; F; 1866-66; F; M; Wife; 3506; Yes; Yes; Al. 6029 An. 3494

3559; Kills Enemy, Charles; M; 1866-66; F; M; Head; 3507; Yes; Yes; Al. 951 An. 3496

3560; Kills Enemy (no data), Rosa; F; 1869-63; F; M; Wife; 3508; Yes; Yes; Al. 5093 An. 3497

3561; Kills Enemy, Frank; M; 1893-39; F; M; Head; 3509; Yes; Yes; Al. 6825 An. 3499

3562; Kills Enemy (Little Chief), Lucy; F; 1900-32; F; M; Wife; 3510; Yes; Yes; Al. 1574 An. 3500

3563; Kills Enemy, Edward; M; 4/2/27-4; F; S; Son; 3511; Yes; Yes; Id. U-12879 An. none

Census of the **Pine Ridge** reservation of the **Pine Ridge, South Dakota** jurisdiction, as of **April 1**, 19**32**, taken by **James H. McGregor**, Superintendent.

Key: Number; Surname, Given; Sex; Date of Birth-Age at Last Birthday; Tribe (Oglala Sioux, unless stated otherwise); Degree of Blood; Marital Status; Relationship to Head of Family [Last Census Roll Number]; At Jurisdiction Where Enrolled (Yes/No); (If no – Where); Ward (Yes/No, if given); Allotment, Annuity and Identification Numbers (if given).

3564; Kills Enemy, George; M; 1902-30; F; S; Head; 3512; Yes; Yes; Al. 5095 An. 3502

3565; Kills Enemy At Night (Two-Two), Helena; F; 1861-71; plus 1/4; Wd; Head; 3513; Yes; Yes; Al. 8032 An. 3504

3566; Kills Enemy At Night, Norbert; M; 4/20/12-19; 1/4; S; Gr. Son; 3514; Yes; Yes; Id. Al. 8051 An. 3505

3567; Kills Enemy At Night, Noah; M; 1907-25; F; S; Head; 3515; Yes; Yes; Id. Al. 3439 An. 3506

3568; Kills First, Benjamin; M; 1900-32; F; M; Head; 3516; No; Apache, town, Daddo, Okla; Yes; Id. Al. 4861 An. 3507

~~N.E.: Kills First (Mulkehay), Della; F; ------; Apache Indian; F; M; Wife;~~

3569; Kills First, John; M; 1884-48; F; Wd; Head; 3517; Yes; Yes; Id. Al. 7378 An. 3508

3570; Kills In Timber; ---; M; 1864-68; F; Wd; Head; 3518; No; Chey & Arapahoe Okla.; Yes; Id. Al. 4904 An. 3510
(no data)

3571; Kills In Timber, Thomas; M; 1855-77; F; Wd; Head; 3519; Yes; Yes; Id. Al. 108 An. 3512

3572; Kills In the Water, Samuel; M; 1886-46; F; M; Head; 3520; Yes; Yes; Id. Al. 234 An. 3514

3573; Kills In the Water (Dog Chief), Nellie; F; 1898-34; F; M; Wife; 3521; Yes; Yes; Al. 933 An. 3515

3574; Kills In the Water, Clara; F; 7/13/16-15; F; S; Daughter; 3522; Yes; Yes; Id. U-9808 An. 3516

3575; Kills In the Water, James; M; 10/9/20-11; F; S; Son; 3523; Yes; Yes; Id. U-9809 An. 3517

3576; Kills In the Water, Elane; F; 12/15/25-6; F; S; Daughter; 3524; Yes; Yes; Id. U-11758 An. none

3577; Kills In Water, Samuel; M; 1901-31; F; M; Head; 3525; Yes; Yes; Id. Al. 7389 An. 3518

3578; Kills In Water (Black Bear), Lucy; F; 1908-24; F; M; Wife; 3526; Yes; Yes; Al. 3731 An. 643

3579; Kills In Water, Bertha; F; 2/19/28-4; F; S; Daughter; 3527; Yes; Yes; Id. U-12480 An. none

3580; Kills In Water, Willard; M; 11/30/29-2; F; S; Son; 3528; Yes; Yes; Id. U-13310 An. none

Census of the **Pine Ridge** reservation of the **Pine Ridge, South Dakota** jurisdiction, as of **April 1**, 19**32**, taken by **James H. McGregor**, Superintendent.

Key: Number; Surname, Given; Sex; Date of Birth-Age at Last Birthday; Tribe (Oglala Sioux, unless stated otherwise); Degree of Blood; Marital Status; Relationship to Head of Family [Last Census Roll Number]; At Jurisdiction Where Enrolled (Yes/No); (If no – Where); Ward (Yes/No, if given); Allotment, Annuity and Identification Numbers (if given).

3581; Kills In Water, Bernard; M; 10/20/31-5/12; F; S; Son; ---; Yes; Yes; U-13939

3582; Kills On Horseback, James; M; 1875-57; F; M; Head; 3529; Yes; Yes; Id. Al. 2775 An. 3519

3583; Kills On Horseback (Bissonette), Eliza; F; 1886-46; plus 1/4; M; Wife; 3530; Yes; Yes; Al. 3029 An. 3520

3584; Kills On Horseback, Hannah; F; 12/1/12-19; 1/4; S; Daughter; 3531; Yes; Yes; Al. 7667 An. 3522

3585; Kills On Horseback, Enoch; M; 3/18/15-17; 1/4; S; Son; 3532; Yes; Yes; Al. 7995 An. 3523

3586; Kills On Horseback, Andrew; M; 2/13/25-7; 1/4; S; Son; 3533; Yes; Yes; Id. U-11581 An. 3533

3587; Kills On Horseback, Eva; F; 9/7/11-20; 1/4; S; Head; 3534; Yes; Yes; Al. 6391 An. 3521

3588; Kills Plenty, ---; F; 1871-61; F; S; Head; 3535; Yes; Yes; Al. 1513 An. 3526

3589; Kills Ree, John; M; 1873-59; F; M; Head; 3536; Yes; Yes; Id. Al. 3522 An. 3527

3590; Kills Ree (Location), ---; F; 1872-60; F; M; Wife; 3537; Yes; Yes; Al. 3521 An. 3528

3591; Kills Ree, Charles; M; 2/26/13-19; F; S; Son; 3538; Yes; Yes; Al. 7112 An. 3536

3592; Kills Right, Britton; M; 10/24/13-18; F; S; Head; 3539; Yes; Yes; Id. U-9811 An. 4955

3593; Kills Right, Frank; M; 1898-34; F; M; Head; 3540; Yes; Yes; Al. 520 An. 3531

3594; Kills Right (Red Eyes), Maggie; F; 1902-30; F; M; Wife; 3541; Yes; Yes; Al. 295 An. 3532

3595; Kills Right, Evis; F; 10/18/21-10; F; S; Daughter; 3542; Yes; Yes; Id. U-12002 An. 3533

3596; Kills Right, Rufus; M; 2/8/23-9; F; S; Son; 3543; Yes; Yes; Id. U-12098 An. 3534

3597; Kills Right, Neoma; F; 3/12/28-4; F; S; Daughter; 3544; Yes; Yes; Id. U-12549 An. none

3598; Kills Right, Ivan S; M; 9/7/30-1; F; S; Son; 3545; Yes; Yes; Id. U-13576 An. none

Census of the __Pine Ridge__ reservation of the __Pine Ridge, South Dakota__ jurisdiction, as of __April 1__, 19**32**, taken by __James H. McGregor__, Superintendent.

Key: Number; Surname, Given; Sex; Date of Birth-Age at Last Birthday; Tribe (Oglala Sioux, unless stated otherwise); Degree of Blood; Marital Status; Relationship to Head of Family [Last Census Roll Number]; At Jurisdiction Where Enrolled (Yes/No); (If no – Where); Ward (Yes/No, if given); Allotment, Annuity and Identification Numbers (if given).

3599; Kills Right, Joseph; M; 1902-30; F; M; Head; 3546; Yes; Yes; Al. 522 An. 3535

N.E.: Kills Right (Blue Cloud), Elsie; F; ---- - --; Sisseton Sioux; F; M; Wife;

3600; Kills Right, Marie B; F; 4/7/31-11/12; F; S; Daughter; ---; Yes; Yes; U-13940

3601; Kills Small, Jerome; M; 4/29/21-10; F; S; Alone; 3547; Yes; Yes; Id. U- 9812 An. 3539

3602; Kills Small, Loran; M; 12/27/24-7; F; S; Alone; 3548; Yes; Yes; Id. U- 9857 An. 3540

3603; Kills Small, Sam; M; 12/17/28-3; F; S; Alone; 3549; Yes; Yes; Id. U- 13167 An. none

3604; Kills Small, Samuel; M; 1900-32; F; S; Head; 3550; Yes; Yes; Al. 4328 An. 3541

3605; Kills The Chief, Jack; M; 1873-59; F; M; Head; 3551; Yes; Yes; Al. 6016 An. 3542

3606; Kills The Chief (no data), Julia; F; 1863-69; F; M; Wife; 3552; Yes; Yes; Al. 7612 An. 3543

3607; Kills Two, ---; M; 1873-59; F; M; Head; 3553; Yes; Yes; Al. 1595 An. 3544

3608; Kills Two (Brave Eagle), Mary; F; 1868-64; F; M; Wife; 3554; Yes; Yes; Al. 3649 An. 3545

3609; Kills Two, Lydia; F; 12/19/13-18; F; S; Daughter; 3555; Yes; Yes; Al. 7500 An. 3546

3610; Kills Two, Victoria; F; 1/19/16-16; F; S; Daughter; 3556; Yes; Yes; U- 9813 An. 3547

3611; Kills Warrior, Henry; M; 1877-55; F; M; Head; 3557; Yes; Yes; Al. 3182 An. 3548

3612; Kills Warrior (no data), Elma; F; 1879-53; F; M; Wife; 3558; Yes; Yes; Al. 3183 An. 3549

3613; Kills Warrior, Ralph; M; 1900-32; F; M; Head; 3559; Yes; Yes; Al. 3184 An. 3551

3614; Kills Warrior (High Cat), Julia; F; 1901-31; F; M; Wife; 3560; Yes; Yes; Al. 6622 An. 3552

3515; Kills Warrior, Louis; M; 9/13/23-8; F; S; Son; 3561; Yes; Yes; Id. U-10199 An. 3553

3616; Kills Warrior, Grace; F; 5/14/29-2; F; S; Daughter; 3562; Yes; Yes; U- 13169 An. none

Census of the____**Pine Ridge**____reservation of the__**Pine Ridge, South Dakota**
jurisdiction, as of____**April 1**____, 19**32**, taken by__**James H. McGregor**____,
Superintendent.

Key: Number; Surname, Given; Sex; Date of Birth-Age at Last Birthday; Tribe (Oglala Sioux, unless stated otherwise); Degree of Blood; Marital Status; Relationship to Head of Family [Last Census Roll Number]; At Jurisdiction Where Enrolled (Yes/No); (If no – Where); Ward (Yes/No, if given); Allotment, Annuity and Identification Numbers (if given).

3617; Kills Warrior, Willie P; M; 1903-29; F; M; Head; 3563; Yes; Yes; Al. 3185 An. 3554
3618; Kills Warrior (Lone Wolf), Emma; F; 1894-38; F; M; Wife; 3564; Yes; Yes; Al. 3312 An. 1945
3619; Kills Warrior, Bertha; F; 4/17/29-2; F; S; Daughter; 3565; Yes; Yes; Id. U-13168 An. none

3620; Kills Well, ---; M; 1872-60; F; M; Head; 3566; Yes; Yes; Al. 4148 An. 3555
3621; Kills Well (no data), Sallie; F; 1878-54; F; M; Wife; 3567; Yes; Yes; Al. 4149 An. 3556
3622; Kills Well, Hattie; F; 4/1/21-11; F; S; Daughter; 3568; Yes; Yes; Id. U-9814 An. 3558

3623; Kills Well, Edgar; M; 12/04-27; F; M; Head; 3569; Yes; Yes; Al. 4151 An. 3559
3624; Kills Well (Last Horse), Mary; F; 8/2/06-25; F; M; Wife; 3570; Yes; Yes; Al. 2229 An. 3753

3625; Kindle, Ben; M; 1877-55; F; M; Head; 3571; Yes; Yes; Al. 3150 An. 3560
3626; Kindle (Blue Horse Owner), Martha; F; 1881-51; F; M; Wife; 3572; Yes; Yes; Al. 3151 An. 3561
3627; Kindle, Stephen; M; 10/9/14-17; F; S; Son; 3573; Yes; Yes; Al. 3156 An. 3564
3628; Kindle, Bessie; F; 3/4/19-13; F; S; Daughter; 3574; Yes; Yes; Id. U- 9817 An. 3565

3629; Kindle, Lucy; F; 5/22/11-20; F; S; Head; 3575; Yes; Yes; Al. 6193 An. 3563

3630; Kindle, King; M; 1892-40; F; M; Head; 3576; Yes; Yes; Al. 3134 An. 3566
3631; Kindle (Poor Elk), Rosie; F; 1890-42; F; M; Wife; 3577; Yes; Yes; Al. 6194 An. 3567
3632; Kindle, Mark; M; 1/19/21-11; F; S; Son; 3578; Yes; Yes; Id. U- 9816 An. 3570
3633; Kindle, Patrick; M; 10/23/23-8; F; S; Son; 3579; Yes; Yes; Id. U- 11122 An. 3571
3634; Kindle, Katherine; F; 9/1/29-2; F; S; Daughter; 3580; Yes; Yes; Id. U- 13237 An. none

3635; Kindle, Pauline; F; 1/8/12-20; F; S; Head; 3581; Yes; Yes; Al. 6192 An. 3568

N.E.: ~~King, Thomas; M; ---- - --; Sisseton Sioux; M; Head;~~
3636; King (Last Horse), Jennie; F; 1907-25; plus 1/4; M; Wife; 3582; Yes; Yes; Al. 2057 An. 3734

Census of the **Pine Ridge** reservation of the **Pine Ridge, South Dakota** jurisdiction, as of **April 1**, 19**32,** taken by **James H. McGregor**, Superintendent.

Key: Number; Surname, Given; Sex; Date of Birth-Age at Last Birthday; Tribe (Oglala Sioux, unless stated otherwise); Degree of Blood; Marital Status; Relationship to Head of Family [Last Census Roll Number]; At Jurisdiction Where Enrolled (Yes/No); (If no – Where); Ward (Yes/No, if given); Allotment, Annuity and Identification Numbers (if given).

3637; King (no data), Mary; F; 1879-53; F; Wd; Wife; 3583; Yes; Yes; Al. 2648 An. 3573

3638; King, Stephen; M; 1878-54; F; M; Head; 3584; Yes; Yes; Al. 927 An. 3574
3639; King (Tyon), Susan; F; 1889-43; plus 1/4; M; Wife; 3585; Yes; Yes; Al. 3417 An. 3575
3640; Runs Along The Edge, Christine; F; 9/30/19-12; 1/4; S; Ward; 3586; Yes; Yes; Id. U- 9819 An. 3576
3641; King, Charles; M; 5/24/24-7; 1/4; S; Son; 3587; Yes; Yes; Id. U- 11288 An. 3577
3642; King, Timothy; M; 3/9/28-4; 1/4; S; Son; 3588; Yes; Yes; Id. U- 12574 An. none

3643; Knee, Wilson; M; 1878-54; F; M; Head; 3589; Yes; Yes; Al. 3476 An. 3578
3644; Knee (Long Commander), Carrie; F; 1876-56; F; M; Wife; 3590; Yes; Yes; Al. 3467 An. 3579

3645; Knife, Andrew; M; 1873-59; F; M; Head; 3591; Yes; Yes; Al. 4032 An. 3580
3646; Knife (no data), Lucy; F; 1883-49; F; M; Wife; 3592; Yes; Yes; Al. 4033 An. 3581

3647; Knight (Craven), Edith; F; 1890-42; -1/4; M; Head; 3596; Yes; Yes; Al. 3821 An. 3586
3648; Knight, Harry S; M; 11/29/18-13; -1/4; S; Son; 3597; Yes; Yes; Id. U- 9823 An. 3587
3649; Knight, Edith M; F; 11/24/19-12; -1/4; S; Daughter; 3598; Yes; Yes; Id. U- 9824 An. 3588
3650; Knight, Robert C; M; 10/1/21-10; -1/4; S; Son; 3599; Yes; Yes; Id. U- 11058 An. 3589
3651; Knight, Richard L; M; 11/8/28-3; -1/4; S; Son; 3600; Yes; Yes; Id. U- 12950 An. none

3652; Knight, Joseph Sr.; M; 1859-73; plus 1/4; M; Head; 3601; Yes; Yes; Al. 399 An. 3590
3653; Knight (no data), Lizzie; F; 1870-62; 1/4; M; Wife; 3602; Yes; Yes; Al. 7066 An. 3591

3654; Kocer, Frank; M; 1882-50; 1/4; M; Head; 3603; No; Hot Springs, town, Fall River, S.D.; No; Al. 417 An. 3592
3655; Kocer, Clifford; M; 2/11/12-20; -1/4; S; Son; 3604; No; Same; Yes; Al. 7487 An. 3594
3656; Kocer, Donald; M; 4/2/16-15; -1/4; S; Son; 3605; No; Same; Yes; Id. U- 9826 An. 3595

Census of the **Pine Ridge** reservation of the **Pine Ridge, South Dakota** jurisdiction, as of **April 1**, 19**32**, taken by **James H. McGregor**, Superintendent.

Key: Number; Surname, Given; Sex; Date of Birth-Age at Last Birthday; Tribe (Oglala Sioux, unless stated otherwise); Degree of Blood; Marital Status; Relationship to Head of Family [Last Census Roll Number]; At Jurisdiction Where Enrolled (Yes/No); (If no – Where); Ward (Yes/No, if given); Allotment, Annuity and Identification Numbers (if given).

3657; Kocer, Francella; F; 8/25/17-14; -1/4; S; Daughter; 3606; No; Same; Yes; Id. U- 9827 An. 3596

3658; Kocer, Frank Jr.; M; 4/30/21-10; -1/4; S; Son; 3607; No; Same; Yes; Id. U-9828 An. 3597

3659; Kocer, Zora; F; 3/8/10-22; -1/4; S; Head; 3608; No; Berkley, city, Alameda, Cal.; Yes; Al. 4657 An. 3593

3660; Kocer, Hobart; M; 1883-49; plus 1/4; M; Head; 3609; Yes; No; Al. 418 An. 3598

3661; Kocer (Stirk), Ellen; F; 1885-47; 1/4; M; Wife; 3610; Yes; No; Al. 2666 An. 3599

3662; Kocer, Clancy; M; 9/11/13-18; 1/4; S; Son; 3612; Yes; Yes; Al. 7471 An. 3601

3663; Kocer, Arline; F; 2/8/19-13; 1/4; S; Daughter; 3613; Yes; Yes; Id. U-9825 An. 3602

3664; Kocer, Kenneth; M; 5/29/12-19; 1/4; M; Head; 3611; Yes; Yes; Al. 7470 An. 3600

3665; Kocer (Cook), Dorothy; F; 11/9/14-17; 1/4; M; Wife; 1601; Yes; Yes; Al. 8066 An. 1633

3666; Kocer (no data), Julia; F; 1855-77; 1/4; Wd.; Head; 3614; No; Gordon, town, Sheridan, Nebr.; No; Al. 415 An. 3604

N.E.: LaBelle, Stephen; M; ———; Sisseton Sioux; M; Head;
3667; LaBelle (Cottier), Mabel; F; 1895-37; plus 1/4; M; Wife; 1615; Yes; Yes; Al. 1993 An. 1673

3668; La Buff, Alex; M; 1862-70; 1/4; Wd; Head; 3616; Yes; Yes; Al. 2260 An. 3605

3669; La Buff, Godfrey; M; 10/03-28; 1/4; S; Son; 3617; Yes; Yes; Al. 2265 An. 3609

3670; La Buff, Lucy; F; 3/1/12-20; 1/4; S; Daughter; 3618; Yes; Yes; Al. 7104 An. 3607

N.E.: LaClair, Charlie; M; ———; Sioux and Pottawatomie; -1/4; M; Head;
3671; LaClair (Waln-Hill), Lucille; F; 1908-24; 1/4; M; Wife; 3619; Yes; Yes; Al. 2876 An. 2928

3672; LaClair, Letoy; F; 12/28/30-1; 1/4; S; Daughter; ---; Yes; Yes; U-13837

3673; Ladeaux, Peter; M; 1897-35; 1/4; S; Head; 3620; Yes; Yes; Al. 1805 An. 3630

Census of the **Pine Ridge** reservation of the **Pine Ridge, South Dakota** jurisdiction, as of **April 1**, 19**32**, taken by **James H. McGregor**, Superintendent.

Key: Number; Surname, Given; Sex; Date of Birth-Age at Last Birthday; Tribe (Oglala Sioux, unless stated otherwise); Degree of Blood; Marital Status; Relationship to Head of Family [Last Census Roll Number]; At Jurisdiction Where Enrolled (Yes/No); (If no – Where); Ward (Yes/No, if given); Allotment, Annuity and Identification Numbers (if given).

3674; Ladeaux, Samuel Sr.; M; 1872-60; 1/4; M; Head; 3621; Yes; Yes; Al. 2625 An. 3631
3675; Ladeaux (no data), Katie; F; 1873-59; 1/4; M; Wife; 3622; Yes; Yes; Al. 2624 An. 3632
3676; Ladeaux, George; M; 1909-23; 1/4; S; Son; 3623; Yes; Same; Yes; Id. U-9831 An. 3633

3677; Ladeaux, Bennie; M; 1902-30; 1/4; M; Head; 3624; Yes; Yes; Al. 6786 An. 3635
3678; Ladeaux (Kills Small), Bessie; F; 1906-26; 1/4; M; Wife; 3625; Yes; Yes; Al. 4330 An. 3636
3679; Ladeaux, Abraham; M; 5/18/27-4; 1/4; S; Son; 3626; Yes; Yes; Id. U-12685 An. none
3680; Ladeaux, Pearl; F; 2/23/30-2; 1/4; S; Daughter; 3627; Yes; Yes; Id. U-13402 An. none
3681; Ladeaux, Grace; F; 12/5/31-3/12; 1/4; S; Daughter; ---; Yes; Yes; U-13997

3682; Ladeaux, Antoine; M; 1899-33; plus 1/4; M; Head; 3628; Yes; Yes; Al. 3587 An. 3615
N.E.: Ladeaux (McDonald), Edna; F; -------; Cherokee; plus 1/4; M; Wife;
3683; Ladeaux, George; M; 10/5/21-10; Oglala Sioux-Cherokee; 1/4; S; Son; 3629; Yes; Same; Yes; Id. U-9835 An. 3616
3684; Ladeaux, Donald; M; 2/2/23-9; Oglala Sioux-Cherokee; 1/4; S; Son; 3630; Yes; Same; Yes; Id. U-13005 An. 3617
3685; Ladeaux, Thomas; M; 10/1/24-4; Oglala Sioux-Cherokee; 1/4; S; Son; 3631; Yes; Same; Yes; Id. U-11395 An. 3618

3686; Ladeaux (High Crane), Ella; F; 1875-57; F; Wd; Head; 3632; Yes; Yes; Al. 2978 An. 3620
3687; Ladeaux, Moses; M; 5/14/09-22; plus 1/4; S; Son; 3633; Yes; Yes; Al. 6437 An. 3622
3688; Ladeaux, Lillie; F; 5/25/15-16; 1/4; S; Daughter; 3634; Yes; Yes; Id. U-9832 An. 3623
3689; Ladeaux, Louisa; F; 10/18/17-14; 1/4; S; Daughter; 3635; Yes; Yes; Id. U-9833 An. 3624

3690; Ladeaux, Emanuel; M; 1907-25; 1/4; M; Head; 3636; Yes; Yes; Al. 6772 An. 3621
3691; Ladeaux (Plenty Wolf), Mary; F; 9/8/12-19; F; M; Wife; 3637; Yes; Yes; Al. 7552 An. 4996
3692; Ladeaux, Mary; F; 3/21/32-1/12; F; S; Daughter; ---; Yes; Yes; U-14129

Census of the ___**Pine Ridge**___ reservation of the ___**Pine Ridge, South Dakota**___ jurisdiction, as of ___**April 1**___, 19**32**, taken by ___**James H. McGregor**___, Superintendent.

Key: Number; Surname, Given; Sex; Date of Birth-Age at Last Birthday; Tribe (Oglala Sioux, unless stated otherwise); Degree of Blood; Marital Status; Relationship to Head of Family [Last Census Roll Number]; At Jurisdiction Where Enrolled (Yes/No); (If no – Where); Ward (Yes/No, if given); Allotment, Annuity and Identification Numbers (if given).

3693; Ladeaux, John Jr.; M; 1874-58; plus 1/4; S; Head; 3638; Yes; Yes; Al. 1215 An. 3626

3694; Ladeaux, John; M; 1884-48; 1/4; M; Head; 3639; Yes; Yes; Al. 5016 An. 3627
3695; Ladeaux (Good Weasel), Nellie; F; 1898-34; 1/4F; M; Wife; 3640; Yes; Yes; Al. 7038 An. 6915
3696; Ladeaux, Zona; F; 4/10/30-1; 1/4; S; Daughter; 3641; Yes; Yes; Id. U-13647 An. none

3697; Ladeaux, William; M; 5/22/00-31; plus 1/4; M; Head; 3642; Yes; Yes; Al. 6779 An. 3634
3698; Ladeaux (Shield), Sallie; F; 1/14/06-26; F; M; Wife; 3643; Yes; Yes; Al. 3978 An. 6187
3699; Ladeaux, Albertson; M; 8/16/28-3; 1/4; S; Son; 3645; Yes; Yes; Id. U-12760 An. none
3700; Ladeaux, Winfred; M; 7/15/30-1; 1/4; S; Son; 3646; Yes; Yes; Id. U-13551 An. none
3701; Ladeaux, Viola; F; 3/14/32-1/12; 1/4; S; Daughter; ---; Yes; Yes; U-14130

N.E.: Lafferty Gilbert; M; --------; Cheyenne Sioux; 1/4; M; Head;
3702; Lafferty (Richard), Mary; F; 1899-33; 1/4; M; Wife; 3647; Yes; Yes; Al. 4744 An. 3635

3703; Lakota, Alexander; M; 1880-52; F; M; Head; 3648; Yes; Yes; Al. 3016 An. 3636
3704; Lakota (Sitting Holy), Mary; F; 1884-48; F; M; Wife; 3649; Yes; Yes; Al. 7436 An. 6341
3705; Sitting Holy, George; M; 6/6/10-21; F; S; S. Son; 3650; Yes; Yes; Al. 5737 An. 6342

3706; Lakota, Harry; M; 4/13/06-25; F; S[sic]; Head; 3651; Yes; Yes; Al. 7075 An. 3637
3707; Lakota (Weasel Bear), Nancy; F; 4/6/11-20; F; S[sic]; Wife; 7411; Yes; Yes; Al. 6142 An. 7344

3708; Lakota (White Butterfly), Julia; F; 1879-53; F; Wd; Head; 3652; Yes; Yes; Al. 6132 An. 3640

3709; Lakota, Leon; M; 3/25/04-28; F; M; Head; 3653; Yes; Yes; Al. 6601 An. 3640
3710; Lakota (Water), Ida; F; 1905-27; plus 1/4; M; Wife; 3654; Yes; Yes; Al. 5226 An. 7333

Census of the **Pine Ridge** reservation of the **Pine Ridge, South Dakota** jurisdiction, as of **April 1**, 19**32**, taken by **James H. McGregor**, Superintendent.

Key: Number; Surname, Given; Sex; Date of Birth-Age at Last Birthday; Tribe (Oglala Sioux, unless stated otherwise); Degree of Blood; Marital Status; Relationship to Head of Family [Last Census Roll Number]; At Jurisdiction Where Enrolled (Yes/No); (If no – Where); Ward (Yes/No, if given); Allotment, Annuity and Identification Numbers (if given).

3711; Lakota, Walter; M; 1/2/09-23; F; M; Head; 3655; Yes; Yes; Al. 7074 An. 3641

3712; Lakota (Baggage), Mary; F; 1906-26; plus 1/4; M; Wife; 3656; Yes; Yes; Al. 6037 An. 307

3713; Lakota, Marylin; F; 4/29/31-11/12; 1/4; S; Daughter; ---; Yes; Yes; U-13836

3714; Lamb, Anna; F; 1901-31; -1/4; S; Head; 3657; No; Cody, town, Cherry, Nebr.; Yes; Al. 5439 An. 3645

3715; Wartensleben, Bettie; F; 1/27/28-4; -1/4; S; Daughter; 3658; No; Same; Yes; Id. U-12960 An. none

3716; Lamb, Jule; M; 1895-37; -1/4; S; Head; 3659; Yes; Yes; Al. 2570 An. 3646

3717; Lamb, Kenneth; M; 4/24/21-10; -1/4; S; Alone; 3660; No; Sheridan, town, Sheridan, Wyo; Yes; Id. U-11172 An. 3643

3718; Lamb, Adolph; M; 11/21/22-9; -1/4; S; Alone; 3661; No; Same; Yes; Id. U-11173 An. 3644

3719; Lamb, Marlin; F; 8/9/28-3; -1/4; S; Alone; 3662; No; Same; Yes; Id. U-12924 An. none

3720; Lamb, Susie; F; 1870-62; plus 1/4; Wd; Alone; 3663; Yes; Yes; Al. 2578 An. 3647

3721; Lame, John; M; 1901-31; F; M; Head; 3664; Yes; Yes; Al. 6600 An. 2648
3722; Lame (Little Spotted Horse), Fannie; F; 1906-30; F; M; Wife; 3665; Yes; Yes; Al. 3424 An. 4016
3723; Lame, Leroy; M; 4/12/26-5; F; S; Son; 3666; Yes; Yes; Id. U-11903 An. none
3724; Lame, Charles; M; 7/30/27-4; F; S; Son; 3667; Yes; Yes; Id. U-12481 An. none
3725; Lame, Wilbert; M; 10/18/28-3; F; S; Son; 3668; Yes; Yes; Id. U-12889 An. none
3726; Lame, Flora; F; 10/25/30-1; F; S; Daughter; 3669; Yes; Yes; Id. U-13628 An. none
3727; Lame, Matilda; F; 12/20/31-3/12; F; S; Daughter; ---; Yes; Yes; U-14097

3728; Lame, Ned; M; 1858-74; F; M; Head; 3670; Yes; Yes; Al. 3042 An. 3649
3729; Lame (no data), Edna; F; 1872-60; F; M; Wife; 3671; Yes; Yes; Al. 3043 An. 3650

3730; Lame-Dog (no data), Grace; F; 1857-75; F; Wd; Head; 3672; Yes; Yes; Al. 3710 An. 3653

Census of the __Pine Ridge__ reservation of the __Pine Ridge, South Dakota__ jurisdiction, as of __April 1__, 19**32,** taken by __James H. McGregor__, Superintendent.

Key: Number; Surname, Given; Sex; Date of Birth-Age at Last Birthday; Tribe (Oglala Sioux, unless stated otherwise); Degree of Blood; Marital Status; Relationship to Head of Family [Last Census Roll Number]; At Jurisdiction Where Enrolled (Yes/No); (If no – Where); Ward (Yes/No, if given); Allotment, Annuity and Identification Numbers (if given).

3731; Lame Dog, William; M; 1882-50; F; M; Head; 3673; Yes; Yes; Al. 7117 An. 5654

3732; Lame Dog (Bear Eagle), Mary; F; 1899-33; F; M; Wife; 3674; Yes; Yes; Al. 186 An. 2962

3733; Hollow Horn, Albert; M; 3/25/18-14; F; S; S. Son; 3675; Yes; Yes; Id. U-9685 An. 2963

3734; Hollow Horn, Adolph; M; 10/21/19-12; F; S; S. Son; 3676; Yes; Yes; Id. U-9686 An. 2964

3735; Hollow Horn, Stanley; M; 9/12/26-5; F; S; S. Son; 3677; Yes; Yes; Id. U-12287 An. none

3736; Lame Dog, Elmer; M; 12/14/30-1; F; S; Son; 3678; Yes; Yes; Id. U-13628 An. none

3737; Lamont, Francis; M; 1886-46; plus 1/4; M; Head; 3679; Yes; Yes; Al. 5148 An. 3055

3738; Lamont (Last Horse), Millie; F; 1880-52; F; M; Wife; 3680; Yes; Yes; Al. 2471 An. 3656

3739; Lamont, Hazel; F; 12/8/14-17; plus 1/4; S; Daughter; 3682; Yes; Yes; Al. 8242 An. 3658

3740; Lamont, Olive; F; 11/19/17-14; 1/4; S; Daughter; 3683; Yes; Yes; Id. U-9840 An. 3659

3741; Lamont, Ruby; F; 4/12/19-12; 1/4; S; Daughter; 3684; Yes; Yes; Id. U-9841 An. 3660

3742; Lamont, Eugene; M; 1/14/25-7; 1/4; S; Son; 3685; Yes; Yes; Id. U-11525 An. 5662

3743; Lamont, George F; M; 1883-49; 1/4; M; Head; 3686; Yes; Yes; Al. 5149 An. 3663

3744; Lamont (Apple), Jennie; F; 1887-45; F; M; Wife; 3687; Yes; Yes; Al. 5139 An. 3664

3745; Lamont, Vincent; M; 8/10/11-20; 1/4; S; Son; 3688; Yes; Yes; Al. 7776 An. 3666

3746; Lamont, Gilbert; M; 4/20/13-18; 1/4; S; Son; 3689; Yes; Yes; Al. 7777 An. 3667

3747; Lamont, Viola; F; 8/1/15-16; 1/4; S; Daughter; 3690; Yes; Yes; Id. U-9838 An. 3668

3748; Lamont, Winena; F; 10/21/19-12; 1/4; S; Daughter; 3691; Yes; Yes; Id. U-9839 An. 3669

3749; Lamont, Jay; M; 3/22/22-10; 1/4; S; Son; 3692; Yes; Yes; Id. U-10977 An. 3670

3750; Lamont, Earl H; M; 3/12/24-8; 1/4; S; Son; 3693; Yes; Yes; Id. U-11523 An. 3671

Census of the __Pine Ridge__ reservation of the __Pine Ridge, South Dakota__ jurisdiction, as of __April 1__, 19**32**, taken by __James H. McGregor__, Superintendent.

Key: Number; Surname, Given; Sex; Date of Birth-Age at Last Birthday; Tribe (Oglala Sioux, unless stated otherwise); Degree of Blood; Marital Status; Relationship to Head of Family [Last Census Roll Number]; At Jurisdiction Where Enrolled (Yes/No); (If no – Where); Ward (Yes/No, if given); Allotment, Annuity and Identification Numbers (if given).

3751; Lamont, John; M; 1906-26; plus 1/4; M; Head; 3694; Yes; Yes; Al. 3150 An. 3672

3752; Lamont (Dubray), Mollie; F; 1904-28; 1/4; M; Wife; 3695; Yes; Yes; Al. 4490 An. 1974

3753; Lamont, John; M; 1890-42; 1/4; M; Head; 3696; Yes; No; Al. 3141 An. 3673

3754; Lamont (Fast Horse), Cecelia; F; 1895-37; F; M; Wife; 3697; Yes; Yes; Al. 2 An. 3674

3755; Fast Horse, Wilbur; M; 7/10/13-18; plus 1/4; S; S. Son; 3698; Yes; Yes; Al. 7893 An. 3675

3756; Lamont, Angelique; F; 3/2/18-14; 1/4; S; Daughter; 3699; Yes; Yes; Id. U-9836 An. 3676

3757; Lamont, Marie; F; 2/7/20-12; 1/4; S; Daughter; 3700; Yes; Yes; Id. U-9837 An. 3677

3758; Lamont, Rebecca; F; 2/23/22-10; 1/4; S; Daughter; 3701; Yes; Yes; Id. U-10967 An. 3678

3759; Lamont, Florence; F; 8/28/25-6; 1/4; S; Daughter; 3702; Yes; Yes; Id. U-11877 An. none

3760; Lamont, Florine; F; 5/14/28-3; 1/4; S; Daughter; 3703; Yes; Yes; Id. U-12775 An. none

3761; Lamont, Alice; F; 5/8/30-1; 1/4; S; Daughter; 3704; Yes; Yes; Id. U-13515 An. none

3762; Lamont, Lawrence; M; 3/7/08-24; 1/4; M; Head; 3705; Yes; Yes; Al. 5391 An. 3665

N.E.: ~~Lamont (White Buffalo Chief), Nada; F; ------; Rosebud Sioux; F; M; Wife;~~

3763; Lamont, Florentine; F; 7/19/27-4; 1/4; S; Daughter; 3706; Yes; Yes; Id. U-12721 An. none

3764; Lamont, Verna; F; 12/12/29-2; 1/4; S; Daughter; 3707; Yes; Yes; Id. U-13418 An. none

3765; Lang, Georgianna; F; 12/21/10-21; -1/4; S; Head; 3708; No; Blackhawk, town, Meade, S.D.; Yes; Al. 7238 An. 3680

3766; Lang, Willard; M; 9/8/14-17; -1/4; S; Brother; 3709; No; Same; Yes; Al. 8080 An. 3681

3767; Lang, Albert; M; 10/24/16-15; -1/4; S; Brother; 3710; No; Same; Yes; U-9843 An. 3682

3768; Lang, George; M; 7/13/19-12; -1/4; S; Brother; 3711; No; Same; Yes; U-9844 An. 3683

3769; Lang, Ray; M; 10/30/97-34; -1/4; M; Head; ---; No; Blackhawk, town, Meade, S.D.; No; Al. 3704 An. 3685

Census of the __Pine Ridge__ reservation of the __Pine Ridge, South Dakota__ jurisdiction, as of __April 1__, 19**32,** taken by __James H. McGregor__, Superintendent.

Key: Number; Surname, Given; Sex; Date of Birth-Age at Last Birthday; Tribe (Oglala Sioux, unless stated otherwise); Degree of Blood; Marital Status; Relationship to Head of Family [Last Census Roll Number]; At Jurisdiction Where Enrolled (Yes/No); (If no – Where); Ward (Yes/No, if given); Allotment, Annuity and Identification Numbers (if given).

3770; Lang, Lucille; F; 10/12/22-9; -1/4; S; Daughter; 3713; No; Same; Yes; Id. U-12831 An. none

3771; Lang, Dorothy; F; 4/22/24-7; -1/4; S; Daughter; 3714; No; Same; Yes; Id. U-12832 An. none

3772; Lang, Charles; M; 3/20/27-5; -1/4; S; Son; 3715; No; Same; Yes; Id. U-12833 An. none

3773; Lapoint, Bennie; M; 1900-32; plus 1/4; M; Head; 3716; Yes; Yes; Al. 4678 An. 3687

N.E.: Lapoint (Whirlwind Soldier), Rachinda; F; ------; Rosebud Sioux; M; Wife;

3774; Lapoint, Claude; M; 1898-34; 1/4; M; Head; 3717; Yes; Yes; Al. 6515 An. 3688

3775; Lapoint (Nelson), Mary; F; 1900-32; 1/4; M; Wife; 3718; Yes; Yes; Al. 1147 An. 3689

3776; Lapoint, Benson; M; 4/4/19-12; 1/4; S; Son; 3719; Yes; Yes; Id. U-9846 An. 3690

3777; Lapoint, Delphine; F; 3/18/21-11; 1/4; S; Daughter; 3720; Yes; Yes; Id. U-9847 An. 3691

3778; Lapoint, Cynthia; F; 7/17/27-4; plus 1/4; S; Daughter; 3721; Yes; Yes; Id. U-12365 An. none

3779; Lapoint, Robert; M; 6/11/23-8; 1/4; S; Son; 3722; Yes; Yes; Id. U-11559 An. 3692

3780; Lapoint, Zeralda; F; 9/20/30-1; 1/4; S; Daughter; 3723; Yes; Yes; Id. U-13605 An. none

3781; Lapoint, Jacob; M; 1875-57; 1/4; M; Head; 3724; Yes; Yes; Al. 4675 An. 3694

3782; Lapoint, Burton; M; 5/30/10-21; 1/4; S; Son; 3725; Yes; Yes; Al. 4682 An. 3696

3783; Lapoint, Jennie; F; 3/19/11-21; 1/4; S; Head; 3726; Yes; Yes; Al. 6897 An. 3695

3784; Lapoint (no data), Jennie; F; 1848-84; 1/4; Wd.; Head; 3727; Yes; Yes; Al. 4519 An. 3701

3785; Lapoint, James; M; 1893-39; 1/4; M; Head; 3728; Yes; Yes; Al. 5395 An. 3698

3786; Lapoint (no data), Myrle; F; 3/10/03-29; 1/4; M; Wife; 3729; Yes; Yes; Al. 1126 An. 4621

3787; Lapoint, James M; M; 7/15/24-7; 1/4; S; Son; 3730; Yes; Yes; Id. U-11365 An. 4622

Census of the **Pine Ridge** reservation of the **Pine Ridge, South Dakota** jurisdiction, as of **April 1**, 19**32**, taken by **James H. McGregor**, Superintendent.

Key: Number; Surname, Given; Sex; Date of Birth-Age at Last Birthday; Tribe (Oglala Sioux, unless stated otherwise); Degree of Blood; Marital Status; Relationship to Head of Family [Last Census Roll Number]; At Jurisdiction Where Enrolled (Yes/No); (If no – Where); Ward (Yes/No, if given); Allotment, Annuity and Identification Numbers (if given).

3788; Lapoint, Yvonne; F; 9/29/26-5; 1/4; S; Daughter; 3731; Yes; Yes; Id. U-11964 An. none

3789; Lapoint, Richard; M; 11/20/27-4; 1/4; S; Son; 3732; Yes; Yes; Id. U-12488 An. 4622

3790; Lapoint, Jacqueline; F; 10/6/30-1; 1/4; S; Daughter; 3733; Yes; Yes; Id. U-13649 An. none

3791; Lapoint, Joseph; M; 1878-54; plus 1/4; M; Head; 3734; Yes; No; Al. 4515 An. 3702

3792; Lapoint (White), Rosalie; F; 1882-50; 1/4; M; Wife; 3735; Yes; No; Al. 4516 An. 3703

3793; Lapoint, Maggie; F; 5/11/15-16; 1/4; S; Daughter; 3736; Yes; Yes; Al. 8118 An. 3707

3794; Lapoint, Narcisse; M; 11/14/08-23; 1/4; S; Head; 3737; Yes; Yes; Al. 4518 An. 3704

3795; Lapoint, Eunice; F; 1/27/12-20; 1/4; S; Head; 3738; Yes; Yes; Al. 6980 An. 3706

3796; Lapoint, Oliver; M; 1889-43; plus 1/4; M; Head; 3739; Yes; Yes; Al. 4520 An. 3708

3797; Lapoint (Giroux), Lucy; F; 1883-49; 1/4; M; Wife; 3740; Yes; No; Al. 5544 An. 3709

3798; Lapoint, Vera; F; 2/11/24-8; 1/4; S; Daughter; 3741; Yes; Yes; Id. U-11224 An. 3710

3799; Lapoint, Stanislaus; M; 1905-27; 1/4; S; Head; 3742; Yes; Yes; Al. 4680 An. 3711

3800; Larabee, Louis; M; 1889-43; 1/4; M; Head; 3743; Yes; No; Al. 481 An. 3712
3801; Larabee (Ruff), Grace; F; 1886-46; 1/4; M; Wife; 3744; Yes; No; Al. 4505 An. 3715
3802; Larabee, William; M; 6/11-20; 1/4; S; Son; 3745; Yes; Yes; Al. 7025 An. 3714
3803; Larabee, Alice; F; 12/1/15-16; plus 1/4; S; Daughter; 3746; Yes; Yes; Id. U-9850 An. 3715
3804; Larabee, Donald; M; 10/2/17-14; 1/4; S; Son; 3747; Yes; Yes; Id. U-9851 An. 3716
3805; Larabee, Alvina; F; 2/6/26-66; 1/4; S; Daughter; 3748; Yes; Yes; Id. U-11878 An. none

3806; Larabee, Samuel; M; 1887-45; 1/4; M; Head; 3749; Yes; No; Al. 480 An. 3717
3807; Larabee (Cottier), Ollie; F; 1882-50; 1/4; M; Wife; 3750; Yes; No; Al. 978 An. 3718

Census of the **Pine Ridge** reservation of the **Pine Ridge, South Dakota** jurisdiction, as of **April 1**, 19**32**, taken by **James H. McGregor**, Superintendent.

Key: Number; Surname, Given; Sex; Date of Birth-Age at Last Birthday; Tribe (Oglala Sioux, unless stated otherwise); Degree of Blood; Marital Status; Relationship to Head of Family [Last Census Roll Number]; At Jurisdiction Where Enrolled (Yes/No); (If no – Where); Ward (Yes/No, if given); Allotment, Annuity and Identification Numbers (if given).

3808; Larabee, Ernest; M; 2/6/12-20; 1/4; S; Son; 3751; Yes; Yes; Al. 6930 An. 3720

3809; Larabee, Joseph; M; 9/25/13-18; 1/4; S; Son; 3752; Yes; Yes; Al. 7862 An. 3721

3810; Larabee, Edison; M; 9/23/15-16; 1/4; S; Son; 3753; Yes; Yes; Id. U-9848 An. 3722

3811; Larabee, Pearl; F; 8/4/24-7; plus 1/4; S; Daughter; 3754; Yes; Yes; Id. U-11357 An. 3723

3812; Larabee, William; M; 1860-72; 1/4; M; Head; 3755; Yes; No; Al. 478 An. 3724

3813; Larabee (no data), Alice; F; 1863-69; 1/4; M; Wife; 3756; Yes; Yes; Al. 4658 An. 3725

N.E.: Laravie Joseph; M; ------; Rosebud Sioux; plus 1/4; M; Head;
3814; Laravie (Brown), Alice; F; 1889-43; 1/4; M; Wife; 3757; Yes; Yes; Al. 1871 An. 3727

3815; Last Horse, Allen; M; 1882-50; F; M; Head; 3758; Yes; Yes; Al. 2226 An. 3728

3816; Last Horse, Owen; M; 10/13/14-17; F; S; Son; 3759; Yes; Yes; Id. U-9852 An. 3729

3817; Last Horse, James; M; 1901-31; F; S; Head; 3760; Yes; Yes; Al. 5278 An. 3731

3818; Last Horse, Joseph; M; 1875-57; F; M; Head; 3761; Yes; Yes; Al. 3732 An. 2053

3819; Last Horse (Flood), Elizabeth; FM; 1863-69; plus 1/4; M; Wife; 3762; Yes; Yes; Al. 2054 An. 3733

3820; Last Horse, Samuel Jr.; M; 1875-57; F; M; Head; 3763; Yes; Yes; Al. 2201 An. 3736

3821; Last Horse (Chasing Hawk), Mattie; F; 1879-53; F; M; Wife; 3764; Yes; Yes; Al. 2202 An. 3737

3822; Last Horse, Johnson; M; 12/26/11-20; F; S; Son; 3765; Yes; Yes; Al. 6870 An. 3738

3823; Last Horse, Emil; M; 11/8/15-16; F; S; Son; 3766; Yes; Yes; Id. U-9854 An. 3740

N.E.: Lawrence Joseph; M; ------; Standing Rock Sioux; F; M; Head;
3824; Lawrence (Thunder Bear), Victoria; F; 1896-36; F; M; Wife; 3767; Yes; Yes; Al. 162 An. 3743

Census of the __**Pine Ridge**__ reservation of the __**Pine Ridge, South Dakota**__ jurisdiction, as of __**April 1**__, 19**32**, taken by __**James H. McGregor**__, Superintendent.

Key: Number; Surname, Given; Sex; Date of Birth-Age at Last Birthday; Tribe (Oglala Sioux, unless stated otherwise); Degree of Blood; Marital Status; Relationship to Head of Family [Last Census Roll Number]; At Jurisdiction Where Enrolled (Yes/No); (If no – Where); Ward (Yes/No, if given); Allotment, Annuity and Identification Numbers (if given).

N.E.: Lawyer Corbett; M; -------; Nez Perce; F; M; Head;
3825; Lawyer (Allman), Lillian; F; 1880-52; plus 1/4; M; Wife; 3768; No; Lapwai, Idaho; No; Al. 208 An. 3744
3826; Lawyer, Millie; F; 3/24/12-20; 1/4; S; Daughter; 3769; No; Lapwai, Idaho; Yes; Al. 6123 An. 3745

3827; Lays Bad, James; M; 1896-36; F; M; Head; 3770; Yes; Yes; Al. 562 An. 3750
3828; Lays Bad (Walks Under Ground), Millie; F; 1901-31; F; M; Wife; 3771; Yes; Yes; Al. 6836 An. 3751
3829; Lays Bad, Sadie; F; 6/8/19-12; F; S; Daughter; 3772; Yes; Yes; Id. U-9859 An. 3752
3830; Lays Bad, Agnes; F; 4/13/24-7; F; S; Daughter; 3773; Yes; Yes; Id. U-11332 An. 3754
3831; Lays Bad, Ramsey; M; 7/12/27-4; F; S; Son; 3774; Yes; Yes; Id. U-12842 An. none
3832; Lays Bad, Francis; M; 4/9/29-2; F; S; Son~~Daughter~~; 3775; Yes; Yes; Id. U-13211 An. none
3833; Lays Bad, Pauline; F; 7/14/31-9/12; F; S; Daughter; ---; Yes; Yes; U-13893

3834; Lays Bad, George; M; 8/7/11-20; F; S; Head; 3776; Yes; Yes; Id. U-9858 An. 3749

3835; Lays Bad, Thomas; M; 1904-28; F; M; Head; 3777; Yes; Yes; Al. 564 An. 3755
3836; Lays Bad (Brings Plenty), Alice; F; 1887-45; F; M; Wife; 3778; Yes; Yes; Al. 3946 An. 1018

3837; Lays Bad (Charging), Mary; F; 1899-33; plus 1/4; Wd; Head; 3779; Yes; Yes; Al. 5191 An. 1322
3838; Lays Bad, Stanley; M; 2/16/25-7; 1/4; S; Son; 3780; Yes; Yes; Id. U-11475 An. 1325
3839; Lays Bad, Skinner, Benjamin; M; 1/28/29-3; 1/4; S; Son; 3781; Yes; Yes; Id. U-13149 An. none
3840; Lays Bad, Nellie; F; 11/3/30-1; 1/4; S; Daughter; 3782; Yes; Yes; Id. U-13763 An. none

3841; Lays Hard, Frank; M; 1869-63; F; M; Head; 3783; Yes; Yes; Al. 1523 An. 3756
3842; Lays Hard (no data), Millie; F; 1867-65; F; M; Wife; 3784; Yes; Yes; Al. 5930 An. 3757

3843; Lays Hard, Thomas; M; 1882-50; F; M; Head; 3785; Yes; Yes; Al. 4823 An. 3763

Census of the __Pine Ridge__ reservation of the __Pine Ridge, South Dakota__ jurisdiction, as of __April 1__, 19**32**, taken by __James H. McGregor__, Superintendent.

Key: Number; Surname, Given; Sex; Date of Birth-Age at Last Birthday; Tribe (Oglala Sioux, unless stated otherwise); Degree of Blood; Marital Status; Relationship to Head of Family [Last Census Roll Number]; At Jurisdiction Where Enrolled (Yes/No); (If no – Where); Ward (Yes/No, if given); Allotment, Annuity and Identification Numbers (if given).

3844; Lays Hard (no data), Louisa; F; 1881-51; Plus 1/4; M; Wife; 3786; Yes; Yes; Al. 4824 An. 3759
3845; Lays Bad, Cora; F; 1/22/18-14; 1/4; S; Daughter; 3787; Yes; Yes; Id. U-9864 An. 3761

3846; Lays Hard, Thomas; M; 1898-34; F; M; Head; 3788; Yes; Yes; Al. 1525 An. 3763
3847; Lays Hard (Kills Indian Crow), Jennie; F; 1898-34; F; M; Wife; 3789; Yes; Yes; Al. 7123 An. 3764
3848; Lays Hard, Pershing; M; 11/28/19-12; F; S; Son; 3790; Yes; Yes; Id. U-12009 An. 3765
3849; Lays Hard, Noah; M; 9/16/22-9; F; S; Son; 3791; Yes; Yes; Id. U-11076 An. 3766
3850; Lays Hard, Stella; F; 1/15/28-4; F; S; Daughter; 3792; Yes; Yes; Id. U-12459 An. none

3851; Leading Buffalo, ---; F; 1881-51; F; S; Head; 3793; Yes; Yes; Al. 6628 An. 3768

3852; LeClaire (Richard), Josephine; F; 1889-43; plus 1/4; M; Head; 3794; Yes; Yes; Al. 4465 An. 2360
3853; Walters, Susie; F; 6/14/13-18; 1/4; S; Daughter; 3795; Yes; Yes; Id. U-11106 An. 2362
3854; Galligo, Felmoor; M; 7/16/23-8; 1/4; S; Son; 3796; Yes; Yes; Id. U-11593 An. 2363

3855; Lee, Albert; M; 1905-27; 1/4; M; Head; 3797; Yes; Yes; Al. 2268 An. 3769
3856; Lee (Brewer), Elizabeth; F; 7/27/12-19; 1/4; M; Wife; 3798; Yes; Yes; Al. 7699 An. 986
3857; Lee, Yvonne; F; 3/8/31-1; 1/4; S; Daughter; 3799; Yes; Yes; Id. U-13764 An. none
3858; Lee, Evelyn; F; 1/31/32-2/12; 1/4; S; Daughter; ---; Yes; Yes; U-14064

3859; Lee, James; M; 1889-43; 1/4; M; Head; 3800; Yes; Yes; Al. 55 An. 3770
N.E.: ~~Lee (Keith), Grace; F; ---- --; Yankton Sioux; 1/4; M; Wife;~~
3860; Lee, Lawson; M; 4/22/10-21; 1/4; S; Son; 3801; Yes; Yes; Al. 5532 An. 3771
3861; Lee, Gladys; F; 4/5/13-18; 1/4; S; Daughter; 3802; Yes; Yes; Al. 6682 An. 3773
3862; Lee, Emil; M; 3/14/15-17; 1/4; S; Son; 3803; Yes; Yes; Al. 8002 An. 3774
3863; Lee, Kenneth; M; 3/5/18-14; 1/4; S; Son; 3804; Yes; Yes; Id. U-9867 An. 3775
3864; Lee, Delbert; M; 8/25/22-9; 1/4; S; Son; 3805; Yes; Yes; Id. U-11891 An. 3776

Census of the **Pine Ridge** reservation of the **Pine Ridge, South Dakota** jurisdiction, as of **April 1**, 19**32**, taken by **James H. McGregor**, Superintendent.

Key: Number; Surname, Given; Sex; Date of Birth-Age at Last Birthday; Tribe (Oglala Sioux, unless stated otherwise); Degree of Blood; Marital Status; Relationship to Head of Family [Last Census Roll Number]; At Jurisdiction Where Enrolled (Yes/No); (If no – Where); Ward (Yes/No, if given); Allotment, Annuity and Identification Numbers (if given).

3865; Lee, Emma M; F; 10/17/11-20; 1/4; S; Head; 3806; Yes; Yes; Al. 6681 An. 3772

3866; Lee, Florence; F; 6/10/12-19; 1/4; S; Head; 3807; Yes; Yes; Al. 6665 An. 3781

3867; Lee, William; M; 3/11/14-18; 1/4; S; Brother; 3808; Yes; Yes; Al. 7973 An. 3782

3868; Lee, Annie; F; 5/6/16-15; 1/4; S; Sister; 3809; Yes; Yes; Id. U-9868 An. 3783

3869; Lee, Alice; F; 8/22/18-14; 1/4; S; Sister; 3810; Yes; Yes; Id. U-9869 An. 3784

3870; Lee, Hobert; M; 6/2/20-11; 1/4; S; Brother; 3811; Yes; Yes; Id. U-9870 An. 3785

3871; Lee, Walter; M; 5/17/23-8; 1/4; S; Brother; 3812; Yes; Yes; Id. U-13073 An. 3786

3872; Lee, Mary; F; 5/10/25-6; 1/4; S; Sister; 3813; Yes; Yes; Id. U-11661 An. none

3873; Lee, Vincent; M; 5/30/10-21; 1/4; M; Head; 3814; Yes; Yes; Al. 3664 An. 3780

3874; Lee (Allman), Myrtle; F; 7/10/09-22; 1/4; M; Wife; 3815; Yes; Yes; Al. 5714 An. 92

3875; Lee, Phyllis; F; 6/23/29-2; 1/4; S; Daughter; 3816; Yes; Yes; Id. U-13267 An. none

3876; Lee, Doris; F; 9/17/30-1; 1/4; S; Daughter; ---; Yes; Yes; U-13698

N.E.: Lee, George T.; M; -------; Cherokee Ind.; M; Head;

3877; Lee (Betteiyoun), Mary M.; F; 1901-31; 1/4; M; Wife; 3817; No; Lead, town, Lawrence, S.D.; Yes; Al. 4073 An. 3787

3878; Lee, Kenneth R; M; 5/14/22-9; Oglala Sioux-Cherokee; 1/4; S; Son; 3818; No; Same; Yes; Id. U-11072 An. 3788

3879; Lee, Maxine; F; 8/8/28-3; Oglala Sioux-Cherokee; 1/4; S; Daughter; 3819; No; Same; Yes; Id. U-12880 An. none

3880; Left Hand, ---; M; 1858-74; F; M; Head; 3820; Yes; Yes; Al. 1512 An. 3789

3881; Left Hand (Wounded Head), Bessie; F; 1861-71; F; M; Wife; 3821; Yes; Yes; Al. 3942 An. 3790

3882; Left Hand, ---; M; 1863-69; F; M; Head; 3822; Yes; Yes; Al. 374 An. 3791

3883; Left Hand (no data), Jessie; F; 1865-67; F; M; Wife; 3823; Yes; Yes; Al. 5013 An. 3792

Census of the____Pine Ridge____reservation of the_Pine Ridge, South Dakota jurisdiction, as of____April 1____, 19**32**, taken by____**James H. McGregor**____, Superintendent.

Key: Number; Surname, Given; Sex; Date of Birth-Age at Last Birthday; Tribe (Oglala Sioux, unless stated otherwise); Degree of Blood; Marital Status; Relationship to Head of Family [Last Census Roll Number]; At Jurisdiction Where Enrolled (Yes/No); (If no – Where); Ward (Yes/No, if given); Allotment, Annuity and Identification Numbers (if given).

3884; Left Hand, Andrew; M; 1900-32; F; M; Head; 3824; Yes; Yes; Al. 6520 An. 3794

3885; Left Hand (Marrow Bone), Jessie; F; 1906-26; Plus 1/4; M; Wife; 3825; Yes; Yes; Al. 6478 An. 4327

3886; Left Hand, Eugene; M; 2/13/29-3; 1/4; S; Son; 3826; Yes; Yes; Id. U-12992 An. none

3887; Left Hand, Theresa; F; 8/3/31-7/12; 1/4; S; Daughter; ---; Yes; Yes; U-13894

3888; Left Hand, Charles; M; 1906-26; F; M; Head; 3827; Yes; Yes; Al. 6946 An. 3795

N.E.: Left Hand (Big Crow), Alvina; F; ------; Rosebud Sioux; F; M; Wife;

3889; Left Hand, Orpha; F; 2/24/31-1; F; S; Daughter; ---; Yes; Yes; U-13941

3890; Left Hand Bear, ---; M; 1862-70; F; Wd; Head; 3828; Yes; Yes; Al. 1250 An. 3795

3891; Left Heron, ---; M; 1849-83; F; Wd; Head; 3829; Yes; Yes; Al. 1062 An. 3804

3892; Left Heron, Oliver; M; 1890-42; plus 1/4; M; Head; 3830; Yes; Yes; Al. 1063 An. 3805

3893; Left Heron (Black Bear), Susie; F; 1897-35; 1/4; M; Wife; 5696; Yes; Yes; Al. 1067 An. 5684

3894; Leonard (Hoop), Alice; F; 1893-39; F; M; Head; 3831; Yes; Yes; Al. 4544 An. 3807

3895; Langdeau, Mary A; F; 12/26/22-9; plus 1/4; S; Niece; 3832; Yes; Yes; Id. U-13736 An. none

3896; Lessert, Benjamin; M; 1889-43; plus 1/4; M; Head; 3833; Yes; Yes; Al. 964 An. 3808

3897; Lessert (Bent), Jessie; F; 1883-49; 1/4; M; Wife; 3834; Yes; Yes; Al. 2477 An. 3809

3898; Lessert, David; M; 1886-46; 1/4; M; Head; 3835; Yes; Yes; Al. 971 An. 3810

3899; Lessert, Egan; M; 1894-38; 1/4; M; Head; 3836; Yes; Yes; Al. 974 An. 3811
3900; Lessert (Stirk), Nellie; F; 1894-38; 1/4; M; Wife; 3837; Yes; Yes; Al. 2670 An. 3812
3901; Lessert, Vivian; F; 6/14/16-15; 1/4; S; Daughter; 3838; Yes; Yes; Id. U-9874 An. 3813
3902; Lessert, Benjamin; M; 2/8/18-14; 1/4; S; Son; 3839; Yes; Yes; Id. U-9875 An. 3814

Census of the __Pine Ridge__ reservation of the __Pine Ridge, South Dakota__ jurisdiction, as of __April 1__, 19**32**, taken by __James H. McGregor__, Superintendent.

Key: Number; Surname, Given; Sex; Date of Birth-Age at Last Birthday; Tribe (Oglala Sioux, unless stated otherwise); Degree of Blood; Marital Status; Relationship to Head of Family [Last Census Roll Number]; At Jurisdiction Where Enrolled (Yes/No); (If no – Where); Ward (Yes/No, if given); Allotment, Annuity and Identification Numbers (if given).

3903; Lessert, Edward; M; 1891-41; 1/4; M; Head; 3840; Yes; Yes; Al. 965 An. 3815

N.E.: Lessert (Robertson), Minnie; F; ------; Sisseton Sioux; 1/4; M; Wife;

3904; Lessert, Dorothy; F; 11/14/13-18; -1/4; S; Daughter; 3841; Yes; Yes; Id. U-9876 An. 3816

3905; Lessert, Garfield; M; 1891-41; plus 1/4; M; Head; 3842; Yes; Yes; Al. 973 An. 3817

3906; Lessert (Skalander), Edith; F; 1890-42; -1/4; M; Wife; 3843; Yes; Yes; Al. 4501 An. 3818

3907; Lessert, Lois; F; 11/4/14-17; -1/4; S; Daughter; 3844; Yes; Yes; Id. U-9877 An. 3819

3908; Lessert, Waldren; M; 11/11/18-13; -1/4; S; Son; 3845; Yes; Yes; Id. U-9878 An. 3820

3909; Lessert, Joseph; M; 1886-46; plus 1/4; M; Head; 3846; Yes; Yes; Al. 963 An. 3821

3910; Lessert (Valandry), Minnie; F; 1885-47; 1/4; M; Wife; 3847; Yes; Yes; Al. 969 An. 3822

3911; Lessert, Ruth C; F; 1/3/13-19; 1/4; S; Daughter; 3848; Yes; Yes; Al. 6981 An. 3823

3912; Lessert, Samuel; M; 11/1/15-16; 1/4; S; Son; 3849; Yes; Yes; Id. U-9883 An. 3824

3913; Lessert, Doloris; F; 3/14/19-13; 1/4; S; Daughter; 3850; Yes; Yes; Id. U-9881 An. 3825

3914; Lessert, Maxine; F; 4/4/21-10; 1/4; S; Daughter; 3851; Yes; Yes; Id. U-9882 An. 3826

3915; Lessert (Cottier), Lucy; F; 1869-63; 1/4; Wd.; Head; 3852; Yes; Yes; Al. 3654 An. 3827

3916; Lessert, Richard; M; 1889-43; 1/4; M; Head; 3853; Yes; Yes; Al. 972 An. 3828

3917; Lessert, Lawrence; M; 8/26/11-20; 1/4; S; Son; 3854; Yes; Yes; Al. 7792 An. 3829

3918; Lessert (Valanry[sic]), Mary; F; 1868-64; 1/4; Wd; Head; 3855; No; Flandreau, town, Moody, S.D.; Yes; Al. 4655 An. 3831

3919; Lessert, Samuel Jr.; M; 1896-34; 1/4; M; Head; 3856; Yes; Yes; Al. 967 An. 3832

3920; Lessert (Collins), Vina; F; 1892-40; 1/4; M; Wife; 3857; Yes; Yes; Al. 4508 An. 3833

Census of the **Pine Ridge** reservation of the **Pine Ridge, South Dakota** jurisdiction, as of **April 1**, 1932, taken by **James H. McGregor**, Superintendent.

Key: Number; Surname, Given; Sex; Date of Birth-Age at Last Birthday; Tribe (Oglala Sioux, unless stated otherwise); Degree of Blood; Marital Status; Relationship to Head of Family [Last Census Roll Number]; At Jurisdiction Where Enrolled (Yes/No); (If no – Where); Ward (Yes/No, if given); Allotment, Annuity and Identification Numbers (if given).

3921; Lessert, Horace G; M; 10/3/22-9; 1/4; S; Son; 3858; Yes; Yes; Id. U-12010 An. 3834

N.E.: Lessert, Charles Augustus; M; -------; Oklahoma Ind.; M; Head;
3922; Lessert (McWilliams), Belle; F; 1884-48; -1/4; M; Wife; 3859; No; Ponca City, town, Kay, Okla.; Yes; Al. 1346 An. 4695

N.E.: Lewis, Albert; M; -------; Cherokee; plus 1/4; M; Head;
3923; Lewis (Ross), Alice; F; 4/4/06-25; plus 1/4; M; Wife; 3860; Yes; Yes; Al. 4982 An. 5830
3924; Lewis, Regina; F; 2/17/31-1; Oglala Sioux-Cherokee; 1/4; S; Daughter; 3861; Yes; Yes; Id. U-13737 An. none
3925; Lintt (Shangreau), Eldine; F; 1907-25; -1/4; M; Head; 3862; No; Cody, town, Cherry, Nebr.; Yes; Al. 2565 An. 6113

3926; Lip, George; M; 1876-56; F; M; Head; 3863; Yes; Yes; Al. 3906 An. 3836
3927; Lip (Charging Crow), Hattie; F; 1886-46; F; M; Wife; 3864; Yes; Yes; Al. 2090 An. 3837
3928; Lip, Cora; F; 1/29/13-19; F; S; Daughter; 3865; Yes; Yes; Al. 7189 An. 3860
3929; Lip, Joshua; M; 1/26/15-17; F; S; Son; 3866; Yes; Yes; Al. 8129 An. 3840
3930; Lip, Owen; M; 1/5/18-14; F; S; Son; 3867; Yes; Yes; Id. U-9884 An. 3841
3931; Lip, Bessie; F; 5/10/20-11; F; S; Daughter; 3868; Yes; Yes; Id. U-9885 An. 3842
3932; Lip, Annie; F; 9/6/25-6; F; S; Daughter; 3869; Yes; Yes; Id. U-11715 An. none

3933; Lip, Richard; M; 1872-60; F; M; Head; 3870; Yes; Yes; Al. 3932 An. 3843

3934; Little, ---; M; 1850-82; F; M; Head; 3871; Yes; Yes; Al. 7633 An. 3845
3935; Little (no data), Maude; F; 1867-65; F; M; Wife; 3872; Yes; Yes; Al. 7633 An. 3846

3936; Little, Miles; M; 1882-50; F; M; Head; 3873; Yes; Yes; Al. 6569 An. 3850
3937; Little (Wounded Horse), Julia; F; 1875-57; F; M; Wife; 3875; Yes; Yes; Al. 3899 An. 7779
3938; Little, William; M; 2/2/11-21; F; S; Son; 3874; Yes; Yes; Al. 6623 An. 3851
3939; Little, Thomas; M; 11/23/21-10; F; S; Son; 3876; Yes; Yes; Id. U-10948 An. 7781

3940; Little, Wallace; M; 1902-30; plus 1/4; M; Head; 3877; Yes; Yes; Al. 4765 An. 3853
3941; Little (Cuny), Millie; F; 1/13/11-21; 1/4; M; Wife; 3878; Yes; Yes; Al. 7502 An. 1788

Census of the **Pine Ridge** reservation of the **Pine Ridge, South Dakota** jurisdiction, as of **April 1**, 19**32**, taken by **James H. McGregor**, Superintendent.

Key: Number; Surname, Given; Sex; Date of Birth-Age at Last Birthday; Tribe (Oglala Sioux, unless stated otherwise); Degree of Blood; Marital Status; Relationship to Head of Family [Last Census Roll Number]; At Jurisdiction Where Enrolled (Yes/No); (If no – Where); Ward (Yes/No, if given); Allotment, Annuity and Identification Numbers (if given).

3942; Little, Orville; M; 8/7/22-9; 1/4; S; Son; 3879; Yes; Yes; Id. U-11070 An. 3835

3943; Little, Nadine; F; 10/15/24-7; 1/4; S; Daughter; 3880; Yes; Yes; Id. U-11373 An. 3856

3944; Little, Edsel; M; 8/20/26-5; 1/4; S; Son; 3881; Yes; Yes; Id. U-12115 An. none

3945; Little, Leroy; M; 4/27/31-11/12; 1/4; S; Son; ---; Yes; Yes; U-13808

N.E.: Little, Amos; M; -------; Cheyenne Sioux; F; M; Head;

3946; Little (No Water), Mary; F; 1898-34; F; M; Wife; 3882; Yes; Yes; Al. 6401 An. 6160

3947; She Elk Voice Walking, William; M; 7/6/21-10; F; S; Son; 3883; Yes; Yes; Id. U-13035 An. 6161

3948; She Elk Voice Walking, Ora; F; 4/15/23-8; F; S; Daughter; 3884; Yes; Yes; Id. U-11630 An. 6162

3949; Little, Ernest; M; 12/3/29-2; F; S; Son; 3885; Yes; Yes; Id. U-13337 An. none

3950; Little Bald Eagle, Felix; M; 1876-56; F; M; Head; 3886; Yes; Yes; Al. 953 An. 3857

3951; Little Bald Eagle (Ghost), Ellen; F; 1883-49; F; M; Wife; 3887; Yes; Yes; Al. 2947 An. 5430

3952; Red Elk, George; M; 8/4/17-14; F; S; S. Son; 3888; Yes; Yes; Id. U-10230 An. 5431

3953; Little Bald Eagle, Alice; F; 1/10/22-9; F; S; Daughter; 3889 9; Yes; Yes; Id. U-11038 An. 5432

3954; Little Bear, James; M; 1882-50; plus 1/4; M; Head; 3890; Yes; Yes; Al. 1173 An. 3860

3955; Little Bear (no data), Lucy; F; 1881-51; 1/4; M; Wife; 3891; Yes; Yes; Al. 6017 An. 3861

3956; Little Bear, Eugene; M; 10/7/09-22; 1/4; S; Son; 3892; Yes; Yes; Al. 6018 An. 3862

3957; Little Bear, Carrie; F; 4/12/12-19; 1/4; S; Daughter; 3893; Yes; Yes; Al. 6019 An. 3863

3958; Little Bear, Dorothy; F; 10/21/22-9; 1/4; S; Daughter; 3894; Yes; Yes; Id. U-12020 An. 3865

3959; Little Bear, Jennie; F; 1879-53; F; M; Head; 3895; Yes; Yes; Al. 8215 An. 3866

3960; Little Bear, Henry Y.S; M; 1868-64; F; M; Head; 3896; Yes; Yes; Al. 73 An. 3867

Census of the _____ **Pine Ridge** _____ reservation of the _**Pine Ridge, South Dakota**_ jurisdiction, as of _____ **April 1** _____, 1932, taken by _____ **James H. McGregor** _____, Superintendent.

Key: Number; Surname, Given; Sex; Date of Birth-Age at Last Birthday; Tribe (Oglala Sioux, unless stated otherwise); Degree of Blood; Marital Status; Relationship to Head of Family [Last Census Roll Number]; At Jurisdiction Where Enrolled (Yes/No); (If no – Where); Ward (Yes/No, if given); Allotment, Annuity and Identification Numbers (if given).

3961; Little Bear (Yellow Shield), Grace; F; 1870-62; F; M; Wife; 3897; Yes; Yes; Al. 4715 An. 3868
3962; Little Bear, Dora; F; 6/10/18-13; F; S; Daughter; 3898; Yes; Yes; Id. U-9887 An. 3870

3963; Little Bear, Nicholas; M; 4/11/04-27; plus 1/4; M; Head; 3899; Yes; Yes; Al. 1174 An. 3871
3964; Little Bear (Garnet), Edith; F; 6/27/04-27; 1/4; M; Wife; 3900; Yes; Yes; Al. 3782 An. 2392
3965; Little Bear, Robert; M; 18/18/26-5; 1/4; S; Son; 3901; Yes; Yes; Id. U-12163 An. none
3966; Little Bear, Evelyn; F; 9/23/28-3; 1/4; S; Daughter; 3902; Yes; Yes; Id. U-12800 An. none
3967; Little Bear, Charles; M; 6/3/30-1; 1/4; S; Son; 3903; Yes; Yes; Id. U-13570 An. none
3968; Little Bear, Royal; M; 11/29/31-4/12; 1/4; S; Son; ---; Yes; Yes; U-13967

3969; Little Boy (no data), Rachael; F; 1859-73; F; Wd; Head; 3904; Yes; Yes; Al. 3992 An. 3877

3970; Little Boy, Louis; M; 1892-40; F; M; Head; 3905; Yes; Yes; Al. 596 An. 3881
3971; Little Boy (Takes Away From Them), Bessie; F; 1888-44; F; M; Wife; 3906; Yes; Yes; Al. 6328 An. 3882
3972; Little Boy, Pearl; F; 12/9/23-8; F; S; Daughter; 3907; Yes; Yes; Id. U-11202 An. 3884
3973; Little Boy, Stanley; M; 4/2/22-9; F; S; Son; 3908; Yes; Yes; Id. U-11602 An. 3885
3974; Little Boy, Louisa; F; 12/20/27-4; F; S; Daughter; 3909; Yes; Yes; Id. U-12951 An. none

3975; Little Boy, Thomas; M; 1890-42; F; M; Head; 3911; Yes; Yes; Al. 595 An. 3886
3976; Little Boy (Boyer), Maggie; F; 4/15/09-22; plus 1/4; M; Wife; 3912; Yes; Yes; Al. 4898 An. 908
3977; Little Boy, Helen S; F; 12/20/28-3; 1/4; S; Daughter; 3913; Yes; Yes; Id. U-13109 An. none
3978; Little Boy, Joseph; M; 10/13/31-5/12; 1/4; S; Son; ---; Yes; Yes; U-13942

3979; Little Bull (no data), Clara; F; 1850-82; F; Wd; Head; 3914; Yes; Yes; Al. 6558 An. 3890

3980; Little Bull, David; M; 1907-25; F; M; Head; 3915; Yes; Yes; Al. 3641 An. 3891

Census of the **Pine Ridge** reservation of the **Pine Ridge, South Dakota** jurisdiction, as of **April 1**, 19**32**, taken by **James H. McGregor**, Superintendent.

Key: Number; Surname, Given; Sex; Date of Birth-Age at Last Birthday; Tribe (Oglala Sioux, unless stated otherwise); Degree of Blood; Marital Status; Relationship to Head of Family [Last Census Roll Number]; At Jurisdiction Where Enrolled (Yes/No); (If no – Where); Ward (Yes/No, if given); Allotment, Annuity and Identification Numbers (if given).

3981; Little Bull (Imitates Dog), Jettie; F; 3/6/12-20; F; M; Wife; 3916; Yes; Yes; Al. 7084 An. 3117

3982; Little Bull, Rebecca; F; 1/27/31-1; F; S; Daughter; ---; Yes; Yes; U-14065

3983; Little Bull, Henry; M; 1877-55; F; M; Head; 3917; Yes; Yes; Al. 3638 An. 3892

3984; Little Bull (no data), Maggie; F; 1882-50; F; M; Wife; 3918; Yes; Yes; Al. 3639 An. 3893

3985; Little Bull, Joseph; M; 1/30/10-22; F; M; Head; 3919; Yes; Yes; Al. 5420 An. 3894

3986; Little Bull (Kills In Water), Martha; F; 1907-25; F; M; Wife; 3920; Yes; Yes; Al. 3834 An. 1732

3987; Little Bull, Samuel; M; 1861-61; F; Wd; Head; 3921; Yes; Yes; Al. 857 An. 3898

3988; Little Bull (Her Good Horse), Fannie; F; 1861-61; F; Wd; Head; 3922; Yes; Yes; Al. 2971 An. 3902

3989; Little Chief, Joseph; M; 1858-74; F; M; Head; 3923; Yes; Yes; Al. 1570 An. 3904

3990; Little Chief (Hair Woman), Josephine; F; 1862-70; F; M; Wife; 3924; Yes; Yes; Al. 3665 An. 3905

3991; Little Cloud, Mollie; F; 1862-70; F; Wd.; Head; 3926; Yes; Yes; Al. 4124 An. 3908

3992; Little Cloud, Samuel; M; 7/6/10-21; F; S; Son; 3927; Yes; Yes; Al. 8004 An. 3909

3993; Little Cloud, Charles; M; 1901-31; F; S; Head; 3928; Yes; Yes; Al. 4127 An. 3910

3994; Little Cloud, Loomis; M; 1897-35; F; M; Head; 3929; Yes; Yes; Al. 4125 An. 3911

N.E.: Little Cloud (Hungry), Lucy; F; -------; Rosebud Sioux; F; M; Wife;

3995; Little Cloud, Herbert; M; 8/3/31-7/12; F; S; Son; ---; Yes; Yes; U-13968

3996; Little Cloud, Mercy; F; 1/22/22-10; F; S; Daughter; 3930; Yes; Yes; Id. U-11260 An. 3912

3997; Little Cloud, Charles; M; 1862-70; F; M; Head; 3932; Yes; Yes; Al. 382 An. 3914

Census of the __Pine Ridge__ reservation of the __Pine Ridge, South Dakota__ jurisdiction, as of __April 1__, 19**32**, taken by __James H. McGregor__, Superintendent.

Key: Number; Surname, Given; Sex; Date of Birth-Age at Last Birthday; Tribe (Oglala Sioux, unless stated otherwise); Degree of Blood; Marital Status; Relationship to Head of Family [Last Census Roll Number]; At Jurisdiction Where Enrolled (Yes/No); (If no – Where); Ward (Yes/No, if given); Allotment, Annuity and Identification Numbers (if given).

3998; Little Chief (Two Elk), Jennie; F; 1864-68; F; M; Wife; 3933; Yes; Yes; Al. 7279 An. 3915

3999; Lays Hard, Dora; F; 8/3/13-18; F; S; Daughter; 3934; Yes; Yes; Id. U-9862 An. 3916

4000; Little Commander, ---; M; 1870-61; F; M; Head; 3935; Yes; Yes; Al. 25 An. 3917

4001; Little Commander (no data), Cecelia; F; 1872-60; F; M; Wife; 3936; Yes; Yes; Al. 5516 An. 3918

4002; Little Commander, Aloysius; M; 10/17/11-20; F; S; Son; 3937; Yes; Yes; Al. 6687 An. 3919

4003; Little Commander, Ellis; M; 10/12/15-16; F; S; Son; 3938; Yes; Yes; Id. U-9892 An. 3920

4004; Little Commander, Esther; F; 1906-26; F; S; Head; 3939; Yes; Yes; Al. 5393 An. 3921

4005; Little Crow, ---; M; 1858-74; F; M; Head; 3940; Yes; Yes; Al. 1006 An. 3922
4006; Many Camps, ---; F; 1865-67; F; M; Wife; 3941; Yes; Yes; Al. 5246 An. 3923

4007; Little Crow, John; M; 1881-41; F; M; Head; 3942; Yes; Yes; Al. 5197 An. 3924

4008; Little Crow (Trouble Front), Anna; F; 1902-30; F; M; Wife; 3943; Yes; Yes; Al. 5642 An. 3925

4009; Little Crow, Louis; M; 7/22/20-11; F; S; Son; 3944; Yes; Yes; Id. U-9893 An. 3926

4010; Little Crow, Martha; F; 10/4/22-9; F; S; Daughter; 3945; Yes; Yes; Id. U-13049 An. 3927

4011; Little Crow, Ruth; F; 2/5/32-1/12; F; S; Daughter; ---; Yes; Yes; U-14098

4012; Little Crow, Sidney; M; 1907-28; F; M; Head; 3946; Yes; Yes; Al. 6572 An. 3929

4013; Little Crow (Long Bull), Lydia; F; 1904-28; Plus 1/4; M; Head; 3947; Yes; Yes; Al. 5288 An. 4187

4014; Little Dog, (Adam); M; 1853-79; F; M; Head; 3948; Yes; Yes; Al. 6150 An. 3930

4015; Little Dog (Leaf No Neck), Mary; F; 1854-78; F; M; Wife; 3949; Yes; Yes; Al. 7372 An. 4759

4016; Little Dog, Robert; M; 1879-53; F; M; Head; 3950; Yes; Yes; Al. 2956 An. 3933

Census of the **Pine Ridge** reservation of the **Pine Ridge, South Dakota** jurisdiction, as of **April 1**, 19**32**, taken by **James H. McGregor**, Superintendent.

Key: Number; Surname, Given; Sex; Date of Birth-Age at Last Birthday; Tribe (Oglala Sioux, unless stated otherwise); Degree of Blood; Marital Status; Relationship to Head of Family [Last Census Roll Number]; At Jurisdiction Where Enrolled (Yes/No); (If no – Where); Ward (Yes/No, if given); Allotment, Annuity and Identification Numbers (if given).

4017; Little Dog (Red Shirt), Sarah; F; 1896-36; F; M; Wife; 3951; Yes; Yes; Al. 6777 An. 3934

4018; Little Dog, William; M; 10/7/11-20; F; S; Son; 3952; Yes; Yes; Id. U-9894 An. 3935

4019; Little Dog, Moses; M; 3/1926-6; F; S; Son; 3953; Yes; Yes; Id. U-11879 An. none

4020; Little Dog, Peter; M; 4/27/30-1; F; S; Son; 3954; Yes; Yes; Id. U-13483 An. none

4021; Red Shirt, Evangeline; F; 2/28/18-14; F; S; S. Daughter; 3955; Yes; Yes; Id. U-9897 An. 3937

4022; Red Shirt, Rosa G; F; 5/17/19-12; F; S; S. Daughter; 3956; Yes; Yes; Id. U-9898 An. 3938

4023; Little Elk, Jerome; M; 1871-61; F; M; Head; 3957; Yes; Yes; Al. 2831 An. 3940

4024; Red Shirt, Emily; F; 12/28/13-18; F; S; Daughter; 3958; Yes; Yes; Al. 7447 An. 3942

4025; Little Elk, John; M; 1881-51; F; M; Head; 3959; Yes; Yes; Al. 668 An. 3943

4026; Little Elk (no data), Lucy; F; 1882-50; F; M; Wife; 3960; Yes; Yes; Al. 8006 An. 3944

4027; Little Finger, John; M; 1873-59; F; M; Head; 3961; Yes; Yes; Al. 2849 An. 3947

4028; Little Finger (no data), Jennie; F; 1871-61; F; M; Wife; 3962; Yes; Yes; Al. 2850 An. 3948

4029; Little Finger, Cain; M; 12/20/14-17; F; S; Son; 3963; Yes; Yes; Al. 6592 An. 3849

4030; Little Finger, Wallace; M; 1901-31; F; M; Head; 3964; Yes; Yes; Al. 6584 An. 3950

4031; Little Finger (Horn Cloud), Pearl; F; 1905-27; F; M; Wife; 3965; Yes; Yes; Al. 3670 An. 3033

4032; Little Finger, Sarah; F; 5/28/28-3; F; S; Daughter; 3966; Yes; Yes; Id. U-12630 An. none

4033; Little Finger, Lathel G; F; 2/24/31-1; F; S; Daughter; 3967; Yes; Yes; Id. U-13738 An. none

4034; Little Hawk, Charles; M; 1895-37; F; M; Head; 3968; Yes; No; Al. 917 An. 3951

4035; Little Hawk (Sierro), Hellaria; F; 1899-33; plus 1/4; M; Wife; 3969; Yes; No; Al. 1197 An. 3952

Census of the ___**Pine Ridge**___ reservation of the ___**Pine Ridge, South Dakota**___ jurisdiction, as of ___**April 1**___, 19**32**, taken by ___**James H. McGregor**___, Superintendent.

Key: Number; Surname, Given; Sex; Date of Birth-Age at Last Birthday; Tribe (Oglala Sioux, unless stated otherwise); Degree of Blood; Marital Status; Relationship to Head of Family [Last Census Roll Number]; At Jurisdiction Where Enrolled (Yes/No); (If no – Where); Ward (Yes/No, if given); Allotment, Annuity and Identification Numbers (if given).

4036; Little Hawk, Herman; M; 12/8/19-12; 1/4; S; Son; 3970; Yes; Yes; Id. U-9903 An. 3953
4037; Little Hawk, Peter A; M; 1/23/24-8; 1/4; S; Son; 3971; Yes; Yes; Id. U-11190 An. 3955
4038; Little Hawk, Richard; M; 9/17/26-5; 1/4; S; Son; 3972; Yes; Yes; Id. U-12715 An. none
4039; Little Hawk, Cecil; M; 9/27/28-3; 1/4; S; Son; 3973; Yes; Yes; Id. U-12801 An. none
4040; Little Hawk, M. Stanley; M; 12/19/30-1; 1/4; S; Son; 3974; Yes; Yes; Id. U-13699 An. none

4041; Little Hawk (Big Crow), Lucy; F; 1877-55; F; Wd.; Head; 3975; Yes; Yes; Al. 278 An. 3944

4042; Little Hoop, Charles; M; 1867-65; F; M; Head; 3976; Yes; Yes; Al. 4542 An. 3960
4043; Little Hoop (Conquering Bear), Jennie; F; 1894-38; plus 1/4; M; Wife; 3977; Yes; Yes; Al. 1031 An. 1605

4044; Little Hoop, Joseph; M; 4/26/32-23; F; M; Head; 3978; Yes; Yes; Al. 5523 An. 3962

4045; Little Hoop, Samuel; M; 1907-25; F; M; Head; 3979; Yes; Yes; Al. 4547 An. 3961
4046; Little Hoop (Red Shirt), Ollie; F; 6/12/09-22; F; M; Wife; 650; Yes; Yes; Al. 5695 An. 5575

4047; Little Hoop, George; M; 1902-30; F; M; Head; 3980; Yes; Yes; Al. 4546 An. 3963
4048; Little Hoop (Condelario), Alice; F; 1904-28; plus 1/4; M; Wife; 3981; Yes; Yes; Al. 1090 An. 1577

4049; Little Horse (Goodwin), Julia; F; 1875-57; plus 1/4; Wd.; Head; 3983; Yes; Yes; Al. 4084 An. 3966

4050; Little Horse, ---; M; 1875-57; F; M; Head; 3984; Yes; Yes; Al. 632 An. 3968
4051; Little Horse (Quick-Hawk), Lucy; F; 1866-66; F; M; Wife; 3985; Yes; Yes; Al. 7488 An. 3969

4052; Little Horse, Oliver; M; 1905-27; F; M; Head; 3986; Yes; Yes; Al. 4405 An. 3971
4053; Little Horse (Salway), Anna Christine; F; 11/24/08-23; plus 1/4; M; Wife; 6031; Yes; Yes; Al. 5238 An. 6003

Census of the **Pine Ridge** reservation of the **Pine Ridge, South Dakota** jurisdiction, as of **April 1**, 19**32**, taken by **James H. McGregor**, Superintendent.

Key: Number; Surname, Given; Sex; Date of Birth-Age at Last Birthday; Tribe (Oglala Sioux, unless stated otherwise); Degree of Blood; Marital Status; Relationship to Head of Family [Last Census Roll Number]; At Jurisdiction Where Enrolled (Yes/No); (If no – Where); Ward (Yes/No, if given); Allotment, Annuity and Identification Numbers (if given).

4054; Little Iron, Mary; F; 1905-27; F; S; Head; 3987; Yes; Yes; Al. 4832 An. 3972

4055; Little Iron, William; M; 1860-72; F; M; Head; 3988; Yes; Yes; Al. 4831 An. 3973

4056; Brings White, ---; F; 1869-63; F; M; Wife; 3989; Yes; Yes; Al. 897 An. 3974

4057; Little Killer, William; M; 1849-83; F; Wd; Head; 3990; Yes; Yes; Al. 7293 An. 3975

4058; Little Killer, John; M; 1879-53; F; Wd; Head; 3991; Yes; Yes; Al. 7270 An. 3976

4059; Little Killer, Leon; M; 4/9/12-19; F; M; Head; 5305; Yes; Yes; Al. 7043 An. 5263

4060; Little Killer (Randall), Hazel; F; 6/12/12-19; plus 1/4; M; Wife; 5326; Yes; Yes; Al. 7202 An. 5282

4061; Little Killer, Philip; M; 1900-32; F; M; Head; 3992; Yes; Yes; Al. 4197 An. 3979

4062; Little Killer (Center), Fannie; F; 1900-32; F; M; Wife; 3993; Yes; Yes; Al. 466 An. 3980

4063; Little Killer, Solomon; M; 1892-40; F; M; Head; 3994; Yes; Yes; Al. 5015 An. 3982

4064; Little Killer (Had Yellow Hair), Mary; F; 1884-48; F; M; Wife; 3995; Yes; Yes; Id. U-9715 An. 3102

4065; Hunts Enemy, Mollie; F; 12/14-17; F; M; S Daughter; 3100; Yes; Yes; Id. U-9716 An. 3103

4066; Hunts Enemy, Mamie; F; 11/16/21-10; F; M; S Daughter; 3101; Yes; Yes; Id. U-9717 An. 3104

4067; Little Leader, (John); M; 1862-70; F; Wd; Head; 3996; Yes; Yes; Al. 2047 An. 3983

4068; Little Moon, James; M; 1894-38; F; M; Head; 3997; Yes; Yes; Al. 6726 An. 3986

4069; Little Moon (Iron Teeth), Rosa; F; 1902-30; plus 1/4; M; Wife; 3998; Yes; Yes; Al. 2731 An. 3987

4070; Little Moon, Susie; F; 1/15/24-8; 1/4; S; Daughter; 3999; Yes; Yes; Id. U-11254 An. 3988

4071; Little Moon, Gilbert; M; 12/13/27-4; 1/4; S; Son; 4000; Yes; Yes; Id. U-12484 An. none

Census of the __Pine Ridge__ reservation of the __Pine Ridge, South Dakota__ jurisdiction, as of __April 1__, 19**32**, taken by __James H. McGregor__, Superintendent.

Key: Number; Surname, Given; Sex; Date of Birth-Age at Last Birthday; Tribe (Oglala Sioux, unless stated otherwise); Degree of Blood; Marital Status; Relationship to Head of Family [Last Census Roll Number]; At Jurisdiction Where Enrolled (Yes/No); (If no – Where); Ward (Yes/No, if given); Allotment, Annuity and Identification Numbers (if given).

4072; Little Moon, Pauline; F; 10/31/29-2; 1/4; S; Daughter; 4001; Yes; Yes; Id. U-;3295[sic] An. none

4073; Little Moon (Catches), Lucy; F; 1893-39; F; Wd; Head; 4002; Yes; Yes; Al. 6726 An. 3986

4074; Little Moon, Theresa; F; 11/13/17-14; F; S; Daughter; 4003; Yes; Yes; Id. U-13369 An. none

4075; Catches, Vincent; M; 3/14/23-9; plus 1/4; S; Son; 4004; Yes; Yes; Id. U-11392 An. 3991

4076; Catches, Everett; M; 6/12/24-7; 1/4; S; Son; 4005; Yes; Yes; Id. U-11393 An. 3992

4077; Catches, Eugene; M; 3/29/27-5; 1/4; S; Son; 4006; Yes; Yes; Id. U-12303 An. none

4078; Catches, Ramona; F; 8/17/29-2; 1/4; S; Daughter; 4007; Yes; Yes; Id. U-13375 An. none

N.E.: Little Shield, Thomas; M; -------; Cheyenne Sioux; F; M; Head;

4079; Little Shield (Lame), Mary; F; 12/21/09-22; F; M; Wife; 4008; Yes; Yes; Al. 7468 An. 3651

4080; Little Soldier, (Hernry)[sic]; M; 1867-65; F; Wd; Head; 4009; Yes; Yes; Al. 6203 An. 3994

4081; Little Soldier, Charles B; M; 1908-24; F; S; Head; 4010; Yes; Yes; Al. 6305 An. 3995

4082; Little Soldier, Charles; M; 1903-29; F; S; Head; 4011; Yes; Yes; Al. 6304 An. 3996

4083; Little Soldier, Harry; M; 1871-61; F; Wd; Head; 4012; Yes; Yes; Al. 6384 An. 3997

4084; Little Soldier, James; M; 1878-54; F; M; Head; 4015; Yes; Yes; Al. 900 An. 2000

4085; Little Soldier (Turning Bear), Amelia; F; 1876-56; F; M; Wife; 4016; Yes; Yes; Al. 6595 An. 4001

4086; Little Soldier, John; M; 1889-43; F; M; Head; 4017; Yes; Yes; Al. 7068 An. 4002

4087; Little Soldier (Parts His Hair), Ada; F; 1888-44; F; M; Wife; 4018; Yes; Yes; Al. 1389 An. 4003

4088; Little Soldier, Dawson; M; 5/14/17-14; F; S; Son; 4019; Yes; Yes; Id. U-9906 An. 4004

Census of the **Pine Ridge** reservation of the **Pine Ridge, South Dakota** jurisdiction, as of **April 1**, 1**932,** taken by **James H. McGregor**, Superintendent.

Key: Number; Surname, Given; Sex; Date of Birth-Age at Last Birthday; Tribe (Oglala Sioux, unless stated otherwise); Degree of Blood; Marital Status; Relationship to Head of Family [Last Census Roll Number]; At Jurisdiction Where Enrolled (Yes/No); (If no – Where); Ward (Yes/No, if given); Allotment, Annuity and Identification Numbers (if given).

4089; Little Soldier, Rebecca; F; 3/30/28-4; F; S; Daughter; 4020; Yes; Yes; Id. U-12729 An. none

4090; Little Soldier (no data), Nancy; F; 1864-68; F; Wd.; Head; 4021; Yes; Yes; Al. 4294 An. 4006

4091; Little Soldier, Samuel; M; 1902-30; F; S; Head; 4022; Yes; Yes; Al. 841 An. 4008

4092; Little Soldier, Samuel; M; 1904-28; F; M; Head; 4023; Yes; Yes; Al. 910 An. 4009

4093; Little Soldier (White Calf), Ella; F; 2/7/09-23; F; M; Wife; 4024; Yes; Yes; Al. 7463 An. 7506

4094; Little Soldier, Beatrice; F; 9/19/28-3; F; S; Daughter; 4025; Yes; Yes; Id. U-12802 An. none

4095; Little Soldier, Vivian; F; 10/7/29-2; F; S; Daughter; 4026; Yes; Yes; Id. U-13268 An. none

4096; Little Spotted Horse, Allison; M; 1900-32; F; M; Head; 4027; Yes; Yes; Al. 3223 An. 4010

4097; Little Spotted Horse (Spotted Horse), Angelique; F; 1904-28; F; M; Wife; 4028; Yes; Yes; Id. U-9199 An. 4011

4098; Little Spotted Horse, Grace; F; 2/21/26-6; F; S; Son[sic]; 4029; Yes; Yes; Id. U-11880 An. none

4099; Little Spotted Horse, Eleanor; F; 2/17/28-4; F; S; Daughter; 4030; Yes; Yes; Id. U-12577 An. none

4100; Little Spotted Horse, Lydia; F; 3/12/30-2; F; S; Daughter; 4031; Yes; Yes; Id. U-13455 An. none

4101; Little Spotted Horse, David; M; 1863-69; F; M; Head; 4032; Yes; Yes; Al. 3218 An. 4012

4102; Little Spotted Horse (no data), Eliza; F; 1862-70; F; M; Wife; 4033; Yes; Yes; Al. 6158 An. 4013

4103; Little Spotted Horse, David; M; 8/5/14-17; F; S; Son; 4034; Yes; Yes; Id. U-9912 An. 4015

4104; Little Spotted Horse (no data), Ella; F; 8/5/07-24; F; S; Head; 4035; Yes; Yes; Al. 3255 An. 4014

4105; Little Spotted Horse, Hobart; M; 1898-34; F; S; Head; 4036; Yes; Yes; Al. 3222 An. 4017

Census of the   **Pine Ridge**   reservation of the **Pine Ridge, South Dakota** jurisdiction, as of   **April 1**   , 19**32**, taken by   **James H. McGregor**   , Superintendent.

Key: Number; Surname, Given; Sex; Date of Birth-Age at Last Birthday; Tribe (Oglala Sioux, unless stated otherwise); Degree of Blood; Marital Status; Relationship to Head of Family [Last Census Roll Number]; At Jurisdiction Where Enrolled (Yes/No); (If no – Where); Ward (Yes/No, if given); Allotment, Annuity and Identification Numbers (if given).

4106; Little Spotted Horse (Bird Eagle), Mary; F; 1888-44; F; Wd; Head; 4037; Yes; Yes; Al. 1167 An. 4019

4107; Little Spotted Horse, Paul; M; 6/6/13-18; F; S; Son; 4038; Yes; Yes; Id. U-9908 An. 4020

4108; Little Spotted Horse, Louisa; F; 8/22/16-15; F; S; Daughter; 4039; Yes; Yes; Id. U-9909 An. 4021

4109; Little Thunder, Joseph; M; 1882-50; F; M; Head; 4040; Yes; Yes; Al. 2395 An. 4022

4110; Little Thunder (Living Out Side), Ida; F; 1889-43; F; M; Wife; 4041; Yes; Yes; Al. 3325 An. 4023

4111; Little Thunder, Jacob; M; 10/24/12-19; F; S; Son; 4042; Yes; Yes; Al. 6924 An. 4024

4112; Little Thunder, John; M; 12/18/19-12; F; S; Son; 4043; Yes; Yes; Id. U-9913 An. 4025

4113; Little Thunder, Gilbert; M; 5/21/22-9; F; S; Son; 4044; Yes; Yes; Id. U-9913 An. 4026

4114; Little Thunder, Mattie; F; 8/15/25-6; F; S; Daughter; 4045; Yes; Yes; Id. U-11705 An. none

4115; Little Thunder, Stephen; M; 12/17/30-1; F; S; Son; 4046; Yes; Yes; Id. U-13650 An. none

4116; Little War Bonnet, Jessie; M; 1877-55; F; M; Head; 4047; Yes; Yes; Al. 6528 An. 4028

4117; Little War Bonnet (Little Spotted Horse), Mary; F; 1890-42; F; M; Wife; 4048; Yes; Yes; Al. 3320 An. 4029

4118; Little War Bonnet, Susie; F; 8/30/19-12; F; S; Daughter; 4049; Yes; Yes; Id. U-9914 An. 4031

4119; Little War Bonnet, Zona; F; 12/11/21-10; F; S; Daughter; 4050; Yes; Yes; Id. U-10834 An. 4032

4120; Little War Bonnet, Lucille; F; 2/11/26-6; F; S; Daughter; 4051; Yes; Yes; Id. U-11881 An. none

4121; Little War Bonnet, Eliza; F; 11/11/29-2; F; S; Daughter; 4052; Yes; Yes; Id. U-13339 An. none

4122; Little War Bonnet, Peter; M; 1880-52; F; S; Head; 4053; Yes; Yes; Al. 6517 An. 4033

4123; Little Warrior, ---; M; 1871-61; F; M; Head; 4054; Yes; Yes; Al. 4037 An. 4034

4124; Little Warrior (no data), Ella; F; 1887-54; F; M; Wife; 4055; Yes; Yes; Al. 4083 An. 4035

Census of the **Pine Ridge** reservation of the **Pine Ridge, South Dakota** jurisdiction, as of **April 1**, 19**32**, taken by **James H. McGregor**, Superintendent.

Key: Number; Surname, Given; Sex; Date of Birth-Age at Last Birthday; Tribe (Oglala Sioux, unless stated otherwise); Degree of Blood; Marital Status; Relationship to Head of Family [Last Census Roll Number]; At Jurisdiction Where Enrolled (Yes/No); (If no – Where); Ward (Yes/No, if given); Allotment, Annuity and Identification Numbers (if given).

4125; Little White Man, ---; M; 1872-60; F; Wd; Head; 4056; Yes; Yes; Al. 1899 An. 4039

4126; Little White Man, Louis; M; 1898-34; F; M; Head; 4058; Yes; Yes; Al. 1902 An. 4044

4127; Little White Man (Morrison), Bettie; F; 1903-29; plus 1/4; M; Wife; 4059; Yes; Yes; Al. 4534 An. 4045

4128; Little White Man, Aloecis[sic]; M; 6/20/25-6; 1/4; S; Son; 4060; Yes; Yes; Id. U-11663 An. none

4129; Little White Man, Bernard; M; 9/4/28-3; 1/4; S; Son; 4061; Yes; Yes; Id. U-12776 An. none

4130; Little White Man, Willard; M; 4/8/30-1; 1/4; S; Son; 4062; Yes; Yes; Id. U-13484 An. none

4131; Little Wolf, Thomas; M; 1880-52; F; M; Head; 4064; Yes; Yes; Al. 2610 An. 4047

4132; Little Wolf (White Thunder), Bessie; F; 1882-50; F; M; Wife; 4065; Yes; Yes; Al. 2620 An. 4048

4133; Little Wolf, Charles; M; 10/3/14-17; F; S; Son; 4066; Yes; Yes; Al. 7883 An. 4050

4134; Little Wolf, Thomas Jr.; M; 7/28/09-22; F; M; Head; 4067; Yes; Yes; Al. 5690 An. 4049

4135; Little Wolf (Frog), Nora; F; 1906-26; F; M; Wife; 4068; Yes; Yes; Al. 6236 An. 2353

4136; Frog, Febie; F; 4/25/27-4; F; S; S. Daughter; 4069; Yes; Yes; Id. U-12309 An. none

4137; Little Wolf, Cecil; M; 8/25/31-7/12; F; S; Son; ---; Yes; Yes; U-13895

4138; Little Wound, George; M; 1868-64; F; M; Head; 4070; Yes; Yes; Al. 1684 An. 4051

4139; Little Wolf (Bissonette), Sallie; F; 1870-62; F; M; Wife; 4071; Yes; Yes; Al. 2349 An. 4052

4140; Livermont, Alexander; M; 7/15/1880-52; -1/4; M; Head; 4072; Yes; Yes; Al. 2538 An. 4053

4141; Livermont (Williams), Charlotte; F; 1886-46; -1/4; M; Wife; 4073; Yes; Yes; Al. 4736 An. 4054

4142; Livermont, Delmar; M; 8/31/13-18; -1/4; S; Son; 4074; Yes; Yes; Al. 7861 An. 4057

4143; Livermont, Oliver; M; 3/17/14-17; -1/4; S; Son; 4075; Yes; Yes; Al. 8140 An. 4058

Census of the __**Pine Ridge**__ reservation of the **Pine Ridge, South Dakota** jurisdiction, as of__**April 1**__, 19**32**, taken by__**James H. McGregor**__, Superintendent.

Key: Number; Surname, Given; Sex; Date of Birth-Age at Last Birthday; Tribe (Oglala Sioux, unless stated otherwise); Degree of Blood; Marital Status; Relationship to Head of Family [Last Census Roll Number]; At Jurisdiction Where Enrolled (Yes/No); (If no – Where); Ward (Yes/No, if given); Allotment, Annuity and Identification Numbers (if given).

4144; Livermont, Evelyn; F; 2/13/17-15; -1/4; S; Daughter; 4076; Yes; Yes; Id. U-9918 An. 4059

4145; Livermont, Viola; F; 3/5/11-21; -1/4; S; Head; 4077; Yes; Yes; Al. 5486 An. 4055

4146; Livermont, Charles; M; 1885-47; -1/4; M; Head; 4078; Yes; ~~Yes~~No; Al. 2169 An. 4060

4147; Livermont (Rooks), Rebecca; F; 1894-38; plus 1/4; M; Wife; 4079; Yes; Yes; Al. 4058 An. 4061

4148; Livermont, Delia; F; 5/21/15-16; -1/4; S; Daughter; 4080; Yes; Yes; Al. 8138 An. 4062

4149; Livermont, Charles W; M; 4/26/17-14; -1/4; S; Son; 4081; Yes; Yes; Id. U-9919 An. 4063

4150; Livermont, Edith L; F; 12/17/23-8; -1/4; S; Daughter; 4082; Yes; Yes; Id. U-11266 An. 4064

4151; Livermont, Stella; F; 2/16/24-8; -1/4; S; Daughter; 4083; Yes; Yes; Id. U-11800 An. none

4152; Livermont, Lewis; M; 4/2/28-4; -1/4; S; Son; 4084; Yes; Yes; Id. U-12732 An. none

4153; Livermont, Clarence; M; 1880-52; 1/4; S; Head; 4085; Yes; No; Al. 310 An. 4055

4154; Livermont, Edward; M; 1853-79; Plus 1/4; M; Head; 4086; Yes; No; Al. 309 An. 4066

4155; Livermont, Edward Jr.; M; 1887-45; 1/4; M; Head; 4087; Yes; No; Al. 468 An. 4067

4156; Livermont (Dubray), Irene; F; 1890-42; 1/4; M; Wife; 4088; Yes; Yes; Al. 4579 An. 4068

4157; Livermont, Mamie; F; 4/19/30-1; 1/4; S; Daughter; 4089; Yes; Yes; Id. U-13496 An. none

4158; Livermont, Charlotte; F; 1908-24; -1/4; S; Head; 4090; Yes; Yes; Al. 4796 An. 4072

4159; Livermont, Frank E; M; 1868-64; -1/4; M; Head; 4091; Yes; No; Al. 2544 An. 4070

4160; Livermont (Peck), Lottie; F; 1878-55; plus 1/4; M; Wife; 4092; Yes; No; Al. 2545 An. 4071

Census of the **Pine Ridge** reservation of the **Pine Ridge, South Dakota** jurisdiction, as of **April 1**, 19**32**, taken by **James H. McGregor**, Superintendent.

Key: Number; Surname, Given; Sex; Date of Birth-Age at Last Birthday; Tribe (Oglala Sioux, unless stated otherwise); Degree of Blood; Marital Status; Relationship to Head of Family [Last Census Roll Number]; At Jurisdiction Where Enrolled (Yes/No); (If no – Where); Ward (Yes/No, if given); Allotment, Annuity and Identification Numbers (if given).

4161; Livermont, Agnes; F; 3/2/10-22; -1/4; S; Head; 4093; Yes; Yes; Al. 4738 An. 4073

4162; Livermont, Elsie; F; 3/2/10-22; -1/4; S; Head; 4094; Yes; Yes; Al. 4737 An. 4074

4163; Livermont, Frank W; M; 1898-34; -1/4; M; Head; 4095; Yes; ~~Yes~~No; Al. 2546 An. 4075

~~N.E.: Livermont (Wilkie), Rose; F; ------; Chippewa; 1/4; M; Wife;~~

4164; Livermont, Myrtle; F; 4/13/20-11; plus 1/4; S; Daughter; 4096; Yes; Yes; Id. U-9922 An. 4076

4165; Livermont, Lawrence; M; 4/3/22-9; 1/4; S; Son; 4097; Yes; Yes; Id. U-13077 An. 4077

4166; Livermont, Lorraine; F; 6/13/25-6; 1/4; S; Daughter; 4098; Yes; Yes; Id. U-11716 An. none

4167; Livermont, Joseph Jr.; M; 1905-27; -1/4; M; Head; 4099; Yes; Yes; Al. 2535 An. 4078

4168; Livermont, Jewel; F; 10/1/31-5/12; -1/4; S; Daughter; ---; Yes; Yes; U-13943

4169; Livermont, Joseph Sr.; M; 1866-66; -1/4; M; Head; 4100; Yes; Yes; Al. 2531 An. 4079

4170; Livermont (no data), Martha; F; 1884-48; -1/4; M; Wife; 4101; Yes; Yes; Al. 2532 An. 4080

4171; Livermont, Jennie; F; 4/23/13-18; -1/4; S; Daughter; 4102; Yes; Yes; Al. 7146 An. 4083

4172; Livermont, Alfred; M; 4/1/15-17; -1/4; S; Son; 4103; Yes; Yes; Al. 8136 An. 4084

4173; Livermont, James A; M; 5/1/18-13; -1/4; S; Son; 4104; Yes; Yes; Id. U-9920 An. 4085

4174; Livermont, Eileen; F; 1/20/21-11; -1/4; S; Daughter; 4105; Yes; Yes; Id. U-9921 An. 4086

4175; Livermont, Lawrence; M; 2/22/23-9; -1/4; S; Son; 4106; Yes; Yes; Id. U-13067 An. 4087

4176; Livermont, John; M; 5/7/26-5; -1/4; S; Son; 4107; Yes; Yes; Id. U-12925 An. none

4177; Livermont, Henry; M; 9/11/08-23; -1/4; S; Head; 4108; Yes; Yes; Al. 4768 An. 4081

4178; Livermont, Martha; F; 12/10-21; -1/4; S; Head; 4109; Yes; Yes; Al. 6893 An. 4083

Census of the   **Pine Ridge**   reservation of the **Pine Ridge, South Dakota** jurisdiction, as of   **April 1**   , 19**32**, taken by   **James H. McGregor**   , Superintendent.

Key: Number; Surname, Given; Sex; Date of Birth-Age at Last Birthday; Tribe (Oglala Sioux, unless stated otherwise); Degree of Blood; Marital Status; Relationship to Head of Family [Last Census Roll Number]; At Jurisdiction Where Enrolled (Yes/No); (If no – Where); Ward (Yes/No, if given); Allotment, Annuity and Identification Numbers (if given).

4179; Livermont, Leonard; M; 1905-27; -1/4; M; Head; 4110; Yes; Yes; Al. 4795 An. 4088

N.E.:   Livermont (Chase), Hilda; F; -------; Chippewa; 1/4; M; Wife;

4180; Livermont, Juanita; F; 5/20/25-6; -1/4; S; Daughter; 4111; Yes; Yes; Id. U-12579 An. none

4181; Livermont, Frank; M; 6/8/27-4; -1/4; S; Son; 4112; Yes; Yes; Id. U-12580 An. none

4182; Livermont, Leonard; M; 8/2/31-7/12; -1/4; S; Son; ---; Yes; Yes; U-13919

4183; Livermont, Mary; F; 1886-46; -1/4; S; Head; 4113; Yes; Yes; Al. 311 An. 4089

4184; Livermont, Oliver; M; 1901-31; -1/4; Wd; Head; 4114; Yes; Yes; Al. 2547 An. 4090

4185; Livermont (Mc Gresh), Maggie; F; 1901-31; plus 1/4; Wd; Head; 4115; Yes; Yes; Al. 4800 An. 4091

4186; Livermont, Bernard; M; 9/18/22-9; -1/4; S; Son; 4116; Yes; Yes; Id. U-14009 An. 4092

4187; Livermont, Elizabeth; F; 11/8/23-8; -1/4; S; Daughter; 4117; Yes; Yes; Id. U-11530 An. 4093

4188; Livermont, Marian; F; 1/2/26-6; -1/4; S; Daughter; 4118; Yes; Yes; Id. U-12139 An. none

4189; Livermont, Robert; M; 1/15/29-3; -1/4; S; Son; 4119; Yes; Yes; Id. U-13296 An. none

4190; Livermont, Paul; M; 1907-25; -1/4; S; Head; 4120; Yes; Yes; Al. 2536 An. 4094

4191; Livermont, Peter O; M; 1903-29; -1/4; S; Head; 4121; Yes; Yes; Al. 2548 An. 4100

4192; Livermont, Peter A; M; 1873-59; -1/4; M; Head; 4122; Yes; No; Al. 2540 An. 4095

4193; Livermont (Fisher), Anna; F; 1880-52; plus 1/4; M; Wife; 4123; Yes; No; Al. 2541 An. 4096

4194; Living Bear, Sallie; F; 1908-24; F; S; Head; 4124; Yes; Yes; Al. 4856 An. 6274

4195; Living Outside (no data), Isabelle; F; 1855-77; F; Wd; Head; 4125; Yes; Yes; Al. 2882 An. 4106

Census of the __**Pine Ridge**__ reservation of the **Pine Ridge, South Dakota** jurisdiction, as of __**April 1**__, 19**32,** taken by __**James H. McGregor**__, Superintendent.

Key: Number; Surname, Given; Sex; Date of Birth-Age at Last Birthday; Tribe (Oglala Sioux, unless stated otherwise); Degree of Blood; Marital Status; Relationship to Head of Family [Last Census Roll Number]; At Jurisdiction Where Enrolled (Yes/No); (If no – Where); Ward (Yes/No, if given); Allotment, Annuity and Identification Numbers (if given).

4196; Living Outside, Nat; M; 1892-40; F; M; Head; 4126; Yes; Yes; Al. 3309 An. 4107

4197; Living Outside (Arrow Wound), Sallie; F; 1898-34; F; M; Wife; 4127; Yes; Yes; Al. 7563 An. 4108

4198; Living Outside, Magdalen; F; 6/5/25-6; F; S; Daughter; 4128; Yes; Yes; Id. U-11662 An. none

4199; Living Outside, Garfield; M; 11/12/26-5; F; S; Son; 4129; Yes; Yes; Id. U-12169 An. none

4200; Living Outside, Carl T.; M; 2/10/29-3; F; S; Son; 4130; Yes; Yes; Id. U-13110 An. none

~~N.E.: Loader, James; M; ------; Rosebud Sioux; M; Head;~~

4201; Loader (High Eagle), Emily; F; 1903-29; plus 1/4; M; Wife; 4131; Yes; Yes; Al. 2407 An. 647

4202; Loafer, William; M; 1879-53; F; M; Head; 4132; Yes; Yes; Al. 5000 An. 4109

4203; Loafer (Little White Man), Katie; F; 1895-37; F; M; Wife; 4133; Yes; Yes; Al. 1901 An. 4111

4204; Loafer, Francis; M; 7/10/25-6; F; S; Son; 4134; Yes; Yes; Id. U-11692 An. none

4205; Loafer, Alice; F; 1/2/27-5; F; S; Daughter; 4135; Yes; Yes; Id. U-12208 An. none

4206; Loafer, Chauncey; M; 12/11/31-3/12; F; S; Son; ---; Yes; Yes; U-13995

4207; Loafer Joe (no data), Bessie; F; 1866-66; F; Wd; Head; 4138; Yes; Yes; Al. 6178 An. 4113

4208; Loafer Joe, Frank; M; 1898-34; F; M; Head; 4139; Yes; Yes; Al. 6309 An. 4116

4209; Loafer Joe (Cheyenne), Essie; F; 1901-31; F; M; Wife; 4140; Yes; Yes; Al. 3375 An. 4117

4210; Loafer Joe, Annie; F; 9/29/28-3; F; S; Daughter; 4141; Yes; Yes; Id. U-12835 An. none

4211; Loafer Joe, Mollie; F; 2/3/31-1; F; S; Daughter; ---; Yes; Yes; U-13809

4212; Locke, James; M; 1881-51; F; M; Head; 4142; Yes; Yes; Al. 3951 An. 4119

4213; Locke (Good Pipe), Hail; F; 1887-45; F; M; Wife; 4143; Yes; Yes; Al. 3952 An. 4120

4214; Locke, Wilbur; M; 1/7/13-19; F; S; Son; 4144; Yes; Yes; Al. 6849 An. 4123

4215; Locke, Percy; M; 4/8/17-14; F; S; Son; 4145; Yes; Yes; Id. U-9925 An. 4124

4216; Locke, James F; M; 8/13/21-10; F; S; Son; 4146; Yes; Yes; Id. U-9926 An. 4125

Census of the __**Pine Ridge**__ reservation of the __**Pine Ridge, South Dakota**__ jurisdiction, as of __**April 1**__, 19**32,** taken by __**James H. McGregor**__, Superintendent.

Key: Number; Surname, Given; Sex; Date of Birth-Age at Last Birthday; Tribe (Oglala Sioux, unless stated otherwise); Degree of Blood; Marital Status; Relationship to Head of Family [Last Census Roll Number]; At Jurisdiction Where Enrolled (Yes/No); (If no – Where); Ward (Yes/No, if given); Allotment, Annuity and Identification Numbers (if given).

4217; Locke, Mary M; F; 5/9/24-7; F; S; Daughter; 4147; Yes; Yes; Id. U-11283 An. 4126

4218; Locke, Winnie; F; 9/5/09-22; F; S; Head; 4149; Yes; Yes; Al. 5341 An. 4122

4219; Lone Bear, Samuel; M; 1879-53; F; M; Head; 4150; ~~Yes~~No; Unkown[sic]Yes; Al. 2386 An. 4127

~~N.E.: Lone Bear (Sirewap), Ella; F; -------; Uncompahgre-Ute; M; Wife;~~

4220; Lone Dog, John; M; 1883-49; F; M; Head; 4151; Yes; Yes; Al. 788 An. 4130

4221; Lone Dog (Richard), Annie; F; 1888-44; plus 1/4; M; Wife; 4152; Yes; Yes; Al. 2340 An. 5851

4222; Young, Louis; M; ---- -19; 1/4; S; S. Son; 4153; Yes; Yes; Al. 6884 An. 5852

4223; Lone Elk, Adolph; M; 1872-60; F; Wd; Head; 4154; Yes; Yes; Al. 6819 An. 4132

4224; Lone Elk, Caesar; M; 1874-58; F; M; Head; 4155; Yes; Yes; Al. 901 An. 4134

4225; Lone Elk (no data), Mattie; F; 1872-60; F; M; Wife; 4156; Yes; Yes; Al. 8011 An. 4135

4226; Lone Elk, Evaline; F; 8/8/17-14; F; S; Daughter; 4157; Yes; Yes; Id. U-9929 An. 4137

4227; Lone Elk, Frank; M; 1/25/09-23; F; M; Head; 4158; Yes; Yes; Al. 7320 An. 4136

4228; Lone Elk (Bush), Agnes; F; 4/26/10-21; plus 1/4; M; Wife; 7592; Yes; Yes; Al. 7682 An. 7526

4229; Lone Elk, James; M; 1899-33; F; M; Head; 4159; Yes; Yes; Al. 902 An. 4138

4230; Lone Elk, Paul; M; 1904-28; F; M; Head; 4160; Yes; Yes; Al. 6539 An. 4139

4231; Lone Elk (Bush), Lillie; F; 1906-26; plus 1/4; M; Wife; 4161; Yes; Yes; Al. 4413 An. 1244

4232; Lone Goose, John; M; 1887-45; F; S; Head; 4162; Yes; Yes; Al. 7024 An. 4141

4233; Lone Hill, Lester; M; 1895-37; Plus 1/4; M; Head; 4163; Yes; Yes; Al. 6846 An. 4143

4234; Lone Hill (White Thunder), Eva; F; 1898-34; F; M; Wife; 4164; Yes; Yes; Al. 504 An. 4144

4235; Lone Hill, Anna; F; 7/11/18-13; plus 1/4; S; Daughter; 4165; Yes; Yes; Id. U-9930 An. 4145

Census of the __Pine Ridge__ reservation of the __Pine Ridge, South Dakota__ jurisdiction, as of __April 1__ , 19__32,__ taken by __James H. McGregor__ , Superintendent.

Key: Number; Surname, Given; Sex; Date of Birth-Age at Last Birthday; Tribe (Oglala Sioux, unless stated otherwise); Degree of Blood; Marital Status; Relationship to Head of Family [Last Census Roll Number]; At Jurisdiction Where Enrolled (Yes/No); (If no – Where); Ward (Yes/No, if given); Allotment, Annuity and Identification Numbers (if given).

4236; Lone Hill, Christian; M; 12/25/19-12; 1/4; S; Son; 4166; Yes; Yes; Id. U-9931 An. 4146

4237; Lone Hill, Amos; M; 1/27/22-10; 1/4; S; Son; 4167; Yes; Yes; Id. U-10897 An. 4147

4238; Lone Hill, Mamie; F; 1/14/28-4; plus 1/4; S; Daughter; 4168; Yes; Yes; Id. U-12485 An. none

4239; Lone Hill, Malcolm; M; 6/12/30-1; 1/4; S; Son; 4169; Yes; Yes; Id. U-13530 An. none

4240; Lone Hill, Sidney; M; 1892-40; 1/4; M; Head; 4170; Yes; Yes; Al. 6842 An. 4149

4241; Lone Hill (Elk Boy), Mary; F; 1887-45; F; M; Wife; 4176; Yes; Yes; Al. 4419 An. 2100

4242; Lone Hill, Brennan; M; 11/18/15-16; 1/4; S; Son; 4172; Yes; Yes; Al. 8251 An. 4154

4243; Lone Hill, Hellen; F; 3/11/22-10; 1/4; S; Daughter; 4173; Yes; Yes; Id. U-10895 An. 4155

4244; Lone Hill, Llewellyn; M; 6/27/17-14; 1/4; S; Son; 4174; Yes; Yes; Id. U-12428 An. none

4245; Lone Hill, Florence; F; 12/19/23-8; 1/4; S; Daughter; 4175; Yes; Yes; Id. U-12870 An. none

4246; Elk Boy, Richard; M; 3/24/17-15; F; S; S. Son; 4178; Yes; Yes; Id. U-9485 An. 2102

4247; Elk Boy, Nelson; M; 2/8/24-8; F; S; S. Son; 2093; Yes; Yes; Id. U-11206 An. 2104

4248; Lone Hill, Hobert; M; 3/29/11-21; 1/4; M; Head; 4171; Yes; Yes; Al. 7143 An. 4150

4249; Lone Hill (Eagle Bull), Mary E.; F; 7/29/13-18; plus 1/4; M; Wife; 2443; Yes; Yes; Al. 7143 An. 2003

4250; Lone Man, ---; M; 1850-82; F; Wd; Head; 4179; Yes; Yes; Al. 2841 An. 4156

4251; Lone Wolf, Felix; M; 1894-38; F; M; Head; 4180; Yes; Yes; Al. 2208 An. 4159

4252; Lone Wolf (Nelson), Jennie; F; 1897-35; plus 1/4; M; Wife; 4181; Yes; Yes; Al. 5218 An. 4160

4253; Lone Wolf, Julia; F; 9/26/14-17; 1/4; S; Daughter; 4182; Yes; Yes; Id. U-9937 An. 4161

4254; Lone Wolf, Katherine; F; 2/26/17-15; 1/4; S; Daughter; 4183; Yes; Yes; Id. U-9938 An. 4162

4255; Lone Wolf, Cora; F; 10/27/20-11; 1/4; S; Daughter; 4184; Yes; Yes; Id. U-9939 An. 4163

Census of the **Pine Ridge** reservation of the **Pine Ridge, South Dakota** jurisdiction, as of **April 1**, 19**32**, taken by **James H. McGregor**, Superintendent.

Key: Number; Surname, Given; Sex; Date of Birth-Age at Last Birthday; Tribe (Oglala Sioux, unless stated otherwise); Degree of Blood; Marital Status; Relationship to Head of Family [Last Census Roll Number]; At Jurisdiction Where Enrolled (Yes/No); (If no – Where); Ward (Yes/No, if given); Allotment, Annuity and Identification Numbers (if given).

4256; Lone Wolf, George; M; 4/30/25-6; 1/4; S; Son; 4185; Yes; Yes; Id. U-11637 An. none

4257; Lone Wolf, Dorothy; F; 1/30/31-1; 1/4; S; Daughter; 4186; Yes; Yes; Id. U-13700 An. none

4258; Lone Wolf, Mary; F; 3/1848-84; plus 1/4; Wd.; Head; 4187; Yes; Yes; Al. 5659 An. none

4259; Lone Wolf, Nathan; M; 1880-52; F; M; Head; 4188; Yes; Yes; Al. 3851 An. 4165

4260; Lone Wolf (Red Elk), Millie; F; 1864-68; F; M; Wife; 4189; Yes; Yes; Al. 1665 An. 4166

4261; Wound Head, Joshua; M; 4/20/11-20; F; S; S. Son; 4190; Yes; Yes; Al. 7765 An. 4168

4262; Red Elk, Augusta; F; 4/4/18-13; F; S; S. Daughter; 4191; Yes; Yes; Id. U-10223 An. 4169

4263; Lone Wolf, Oliver; M; 1895-37; F; M; Head; 4192; Yes; Yes; Al. 2901 An. 4170

4264; Lone Wolf (Iron Bull), Cora; F; 1896-36; F; M; Wife; 4193; Yes; Yes; Al. 3538 An. 4171

4265; Lone Wolf, Thelma; F; 5/6/20-11; F; S; Daughter; 4194; Yes; Yes; Id. U-9936 An. 4172

4266; Lone Wolf, Wilbert; M; 9/19/30-1; F; S; Son; 4196; Yes; Yes; Id. U-13606 An. none

4267; Lone Woman, ---; F; 1871-61; F; Wd; Head; 4197; Yes; Yes; Al. 2647 An. 4176

4268; Lone Woman, ---; F; 1853-79; F; Wd; Head; 4198; Yes; Yes; Al. 6061 An. 4175

4269; Long Bear (no data), Constance; F; 1869-63; F; Wd; Head; 4199; Yes; Yes; Al. 4933 An. 4177

4270; Long Bull, John; M; 1858-74; F; Wd; Head; 4200; Yes; Yes; Al. 5082 An. 4183

4271; Long Bull, Levi; M; 1873-59; F; M; Head; 4201; Yes; Yes; Al. 4548 An. 4184

4272; Long Bull (no data), Mary; F; 1875-57; plus 1/4; M; Wife; 4202; Yes; Yes; Al. 4549 An. 4185

Census of the **Pine Ridge** reservation of the **Pine Ridge, South Dakota** jurisdiction, as of **April 1**, 19**32**, taken by **James H. McGregor**, Superintendent.

Key: Number; Surname, Given; Sex; Date of Birth-Age at Last Birthday; Tribe (Oglala Sioux, unless stated otherwise); Degree of Blood; Marital Status; Relationship to Head of Family [Last Census Roll Number]; At Jurisdiction Where Enrolled (Yes/No); (If no – Where); Ward (Yes/No, if given); Allotment, Annuity and Identification Numbers (if given).

4273; Long Bull, Theodore; M; 4/29/13-18; 1/4; S; Son; 4203; Yes; Yes; Id. U-9940 An. 4186

4274; Long Cat (no data), Ellen; F; 1854-78; F; Wd; Head; 4204; Yes; Yes; Al. 6731 An. 4188

4275; Long Commander, John; M; 1869-63; F; M; Head; 4205; Yes; Yes; Al. 4345 An. 4189

4276; Comes Back Hard, ---; M; 1871-61; F; M; Wife; 4206; Yes; Yes; Al. 3984 An. 4190

4277; Long Dog, Neville; M; 6/2/13-18; F; S; Head; 4207; Yes; Yes; Id. U-9941 An. 4192

4278; Long Horn, ---; M; 1864-68; F; Wd; Head; 4208; Yes; Yes; Al. 4339 An. 4194
4279; Long Horn, Sallie; F; 1908-24; F; S; Head; 4210; Yes; Yes; Al. 4343 An. 4196

4280; Long Man, Charles; M; 1877-55; F; M; Head; 4211; Yes; Yes; Al. 2089 An. 4200
4281; Long Man (Charging Crow), Cecelia; F; 1892-40; F; M; Wife; 4212; Yes; Yes; Al. 5285 An. 4201
4282; Long Man, Adam; M; 6/19/11-20; F; S; Son; 4213; Yes; Yes; Id. U-9942 An. 4202
4283; Long Man, Winnie; F; 10/19/17-14; F; S; Daughter; 4214; Yes; Yes; Id. U-9943 An. 4203
4284; Long Man, Edison; M; 6/19/21-10; F; S; Son; 4215; Yes; Yes; Id. U-10830 An. 4204
4285; Long Man, Vernon; M; 2/28/24-8; F; S; Son; 4216; Yes; Yes; Id. U-11207 An. 4205
4286; Long Man, Stacy; M; 11/7/27-4; F; S; Son; 4217; Yes; Yes; Id. U-12735 An. none

N.E.: Long Pumpkin, Albert; M; ------; Rosebud Sioux; Plus 1/4; M; Head;
4287; Long Pumpkin (Siers), Frances; F; 1900-32; plus 1/4; M; Wife; 4218; Yes; Yes; Al. 4847 An. 4206

4288; Long Skunk, ---; M; 1871-61; F; M; Head; 4219; Yes; Yes; Al. 1969 An. 4207
4289; Long Skunk (no data), Millie; F; 1870-62; F; M; Wife; 4220; Yes; Yes; Al. 1970 An. 4208
4290; Iron Cloud, David; M; 8/27/20-11; F; S; Gr. Son; 4221; Yes; Yes; Id. U-9737 An. 3160

Census of the **Pine Ridge** reservation of the **Pine Ridge, South Dakota** jurisdiction, as of **April 1**, 1932, taken by **James H. McGregor**, Superintendent.

Key: Number; Surname, Given; Sex; Date of Birth-Age at Last Birthday; Tribe (Oglala Sioux, unless stated otherwise); Degree of Blood; Marital Status; Relationship to Head of Family [Last Census Roll Number]; At Jurisdiction Where Enrolled (Yes/No); (If no – Where); Ward (Yes/No, if given); Allotment, Annuity and Identification Numbers (if given).

4291; Iron Cloud, Ora; F; 9/5/23-8; F; S; Gr. Daughter; 4222; Yes; Yes; Id. U-14040 An. 3161

4292; Long Skunk, Emma; F; 1903-29; F; S; Head; 4223; Yes; Yes; Al. 1988 An. 4210

4293; Long Soldier, Antoine; M; 1892-40; F; M; Head; 4224; Yes; Yes; Al. 1772 An. 4228
4294; Long Soldier (Randall), Lizzie; F; 1906-26; F; M; Wife; 4225; Yes; Yes; Al. 3889 An. 4214
4295; Long Soldier, Francis; M; 1/29/26-6; F; S; Son; 4226; Yes; Yes; Id. U-11820 An. none
4296; Long Soldier, Albert; M; 7/11/30-1; F; S; Son; 4227; Yes; Yes; Id. U-13552 An. none

4297; Long Soldier, Albert; M; 1870-62; F; M; Head; 4228; Yes; Yes; Al. 1771 An. 4215
4298; Long Soldier (no data), Millie; F; 1865-67; F; M; Wife; 4229; Yes; Yes; Al. 3828 An. 4216
4299; Long Soldier, Clarence; M; 2/16/16-1; F; S; Son; 4230; Yes; Yes; Al. 8134 An. 4218

4300; Long Soldier, Levi; M; 1906-26; F; M; Head; 4231; Yes; Yes; Al. 2839 An. 4220
4301; Long Soldier (Randall), Mollie; F; 1907-25; plus 1/4; M; Wife; 4232; Yes; Yes; Al. 1994 An. 5301
4302; Long Soldier, Audrey; F; 6/16/30-1; 1/4; S; Daughter; 4233; Yes; Yes; Id. U-13607 An. none

4303; Long Soldier, Silas; M; 1900-32; F; M; Head; 4234; Yes; Yes; Al. 1773 An. 4228
4304; Long Soldier (Rooks), Susie; F; 8/20/12-19; 1/4; M; Wife; 5842; Yes; Yes; Id. U-10321 An. 5814

4305; Long Wolf, Amos; M; 1881-51; F; M; Head; 4235; Yes; Yes; Al. 996 An. 4229
4306; Long Wolf (White Dress), Lizzie; F; 1881-51; F; M; Wife; 4236; Yes; Yes; Al. 4082 An. 4230
4307; Long Wolf, Daniel; M; 12/20/15-17; F; S; Son; 4237; Yes; Yes; Id. U-9948 An. 4231
4308; Long Wolf, Lawrence; M; 4/18/18-13; F; S; Son; 4238; Yes; Yes; Id. U-9949 An. 4232

Census of the **Pine Ridge** reservation of the **Pine Ridge, South Dakota** jurisdiction, as of **April 1**, 19**32,** taken by **James H. McGregor**, Superintendent.

Key: Number; Surname, Given; Sex; Date of Birth-Age at Last Birthday; Tribe (Oglala Sioux, unless stated otherwise); Degree of Blood; Marital Status; Relationship to Head of Family [Last Census Roll Number]; At Jurisdiction Where Enrolled (Yes/No); (If no – Where); Ward (Yes/No, if given); Allotment, Annuity and Identification Numbers (if given).

4309; Long Wolf, Antoine; M; 11/29/20-11; F; S; Son; 4239; Yes; Yes; Id. U-9950 An. 4233

4310; Long Wolf, Dana; M; 1867-65; F; M; Head; 4240; Yes; Yes; Al. 4889 An. 4234

4311; Long Woman, Arthur; M; 1895-37; F; M; Head; 4242; Yes; Yes; Al. 7277 An. 4238

4312; Long Woman (Chief Eagle), Jessie; F; 1899-33; F; M; Wife; 4243; Yes; Yes; Al. 6380 An. 4239

4313; Long Woman, George; M; 12/2/18-13; F; S; Son; 4244; Yes; Yes; Id. U-9952 An. 4240

4314; Long Woman, Lillie; F; 5/31/21-10; F; S; Daughter; 4245; Yes; Yes; Id. U-9953 An. 4241

4315; Long Woman, Emerson; M; 1/18/23-9; F; S; Son; 4246; Yes; Yes; Id. U-12065 An. 4242

4316; Long Woman, Clara; F; 11/12/27-4; F; S; Daughter; 4247; Yes; Yes; Id. U-12460 An. none

4317; Long Woman, Josephine; F; 4/30/30-1; F; S; Daughter; 4248; Yes; Yes; Id. U-13486 An. none

4318; Looking Cloud, John; M; 1892-40; F; M; Head; 4249; Yes; Yes; Al. 5830 An. 4244

4319; Looking Cloud (Black Crow), Katie; F; 1894-38; F; M; Wife; 4250; Yes; Yes; Al. 4946 An. 4245

4320; Looking Cloud, John Jr.; M; 6/27/20-11; F; S; Son; 4251; Yes; Yes; Id. U-9964 An. 4246

4321; Looking Cloud, Martha; F; 9/16/25-6; F; S; Daughter; 4252; Yes; Yes; Id. U-11751 An. none

4322; Looking Cloud, Claude; M; 10/21/29-2; F; S; Son; 4253; Yes; Yes; Id. U-13311 An. none

4323; Looking Elk, Talbert; M; 1897-35; F; M; Head; 4254; Yes; Yes; Al. 3120 An. 4248

4324; Looking Elk (Holy Rock), Victoria; F; 1905-27; Plus 1/4; M; Wife; 4255; Yes; Yes; Al. 6420 An. 3018

4325; Gibbons, Myrtle; F; 2/10/24-8; 1/4; S; S. Daughter; 4256; Yes; Yes; Id. U-11311 An. 3019

4326; Looking Elk, Stanley; M; 8/10/29-2; plus 1/4; S; Son; 4257; Yes; Yes; Id. U-13454 An. none

4327; Looking Elk (no data), Sylvia; 1859-73; F; Wd; Head; 4258; Yes; Yes; Al. 3153 An. 4253

Census of the **Pine Ridge** reservation of the **Pine Ridge, South Dakota** jurisdiction, as of **April 1**, 19**32,** taken by **James H. McGregor**, Superintendent.

Key: Number; Surname, Given; Sex; Date of Birth-Age at Last Birthday; Tribe (Oglala Sioux, unless stated otherwise); Degree of Blood; Marital Status; Relationship to Head of Family [Last Census Roll Number]; At Jurisdiction Where Enrolled (Yes/No); (If no – Where); Ward (Yes/No, if given); Allotment, Annuity and Identification Numbers (if given).

4328; Looking Horse, Lincoln; M; 1882-50; F; M; Head; 4259; Yes; Yes; Al. 147 An. 4254

4329; Looking Horse (Good Medicine), Mattie; F; 1894-38; plus 1/4; M; Wife; 4260; Yes; Yes; Al. 6672 An. 4255

4330; Looks Twice, Reuben; M; 1905-27; F; M; Head; 4261; Yes; Yes; Al. 6651 An. 4250

4331; Looks Twice, Angelina; F; 3/21/27-5; F; S; Daughter; 4263; Yes; Yes; Id. U-12250 An. none

4332; Looks Twice, Rose; F; 1/14/30-2; F; S; Daughter; 4264; Yes; Yes; Id. U-13340 An. none

4333; Looks Twice, William; M; 1882-50; F; M; Head; 4265; Yes; Yes; Al. 3053 An. 4261

4334; Looking Twice (Spider), Lucy; F; 1886-46; F; M; Wife; 4266; Yes; Yes; Al. 3054 An. 4262

4335; Looks Twice, Roy; M; 5/23/14-17; F; S; Son; 4267; Yes; Yes; Id. U-9957 An. 4264

4336; Looks Twice, Flora; F; 12/16/18-13; F; S; Daughter; 4268; Yes; Yes; Id. U-9959 An. 4265

4337; Looks Twice, Rebecca; F; 2/16/26-6; F; S; Daughter; 4269; Yes; Yes; Id. U-11834 An. none

4338; Looks Twice, Leo; M; 12/19/08-23; F; M; Head; 4270; Yes; Yes; Al. 6654 An. 4263

4339; Looks Twice (Black Elk), Lucy; F; 1907-25; F; M; Wife; 4271; Yes; Yes; Al. 3024 An. 745

4340; Looks Twice, Thomasine; F; 3/31/30-2; F; S; Daughter; 4272; Yes; Yes; Id. U-13443 An. none

4341; Loud Voice Hawk (no data), Mary; 1875-57; F; Wd; Head; 4273; Yes; Yes; Al. 6527 An. 4268

4342; Loves War, Glenn; M; 1893-39; F; S; Head; 4274; Yes; Yes; Al. 5001 An. 4270

4343; Loves War, Samuel; M; 1882-50; F; M; Head; 4275; Yes; Yes; Al. 6000 An. 4273

4344; Loves War, Samuel Jr.; M; 6/26/21-10; F; S; Son; 4276; Yes; Yes; Id. U-9964 An. 4276

4345; Loves War, Margaret; F; 10/9/23-8; F; S; Daughter; 4277; Yes; Yes; Id. U-11482 An. 4277

Census of the **Pine Ridge** reservation of the **Pine Ridge, South Dakota** jurisdiction, as of **April 1**, 19**32**, taken by **James H. McGregor**, Superintendent.

Key: Number; Surname, Given; Sex; Date of Birth-Age at Last Birthday; Tribe (Oglala Sioux, unless stated otherwise); Degree of Blood; Marital Status; Relationship to Head of Family [Last Census Roll Number]; At Jurisdiction Where Enrolled (Yes/No); (If no – Where); Ward (Yes/No, if given); Allotment, Annuity and Identification Numbers (if given).

4346; Lovelady (Thompson), Florence; F; 1909-23; -1/4; M; Head; 4278; Yes; Yes; Al. 6679 An. 6855

4347; Lovelady, Kenneth; M; 8/14/29-2; -1/4; S; Son; 4279; Yes; Yes; Id. U-13248 An. none

4348; Lovelady, George T; M; 9/18/30-1; -1/4; S; Son; 4280; Yes; Yes; Id. U-13577 An. none

N.E.: Lowry, John; M; ------; Winnebago; F; M; Head;

4349; Lowry (Mousseau), Lucy; F; 1902-30; plus 1/4; M; Wife; 4281; Yes; Yes; Al. 704 An. 4278

4350; Lowry, Vanson; M; 7/2/20-11; 1/4; S; Son; 4282; Yes; Yes; Id. U-9965 An. 4279

4351; Lowry, Martin; M; 1/4/23-9; 1/4; S; Son; 4283; Yes; Yes; Id. U-12057 An. 4280

4352; Lowry, Regina; F; 5/16/25-6; 1/4; S; Daughter; 4284; Yes; Yes; Id. U-11649 An. none

4353; Makes Enemy, John; M; 1896-36; F; M; Head; 4285; Yes; Yes; Al. 6134 An. 4282

4354; Makes Enemy (Brings), Lucy; F; 5/19/08-23; F; M; Wife; 4286; Yes; Yes; Al. 6064 An. 7729

4355; Makes Enemy, Thomas; M; 12/12/30-1; F; S; Son; 4287; Yes; Yes; Id. U-13651 An. none

4356; Makes Enemy, Jeanette; F; 1/28/28-4; F; S; Daughter; 4288; Yes; Yes; Id. U-12486 An. none

N.E.: Makes It Long, Jonas; M; ------; Cheyenne Sioux; M; Head;

4357; Makes It Long (Bissonette), Lavina; F; 1902-30; plus 1/4; M; Wife; 4289; No; Rapid City, city, Pennington, S.D.; Yes; Al. 3051 An. 627

4358; Makes It Long, Junata; F; 11/6/18-13; 1/4; S; Daughter; 4290; No; Same; Yes; Id. U-11925 An. none

4359; Desera, Rosa; F; 6/17/23-8; 1/4; S; Daughter; 4291; No; Same; Yes; Id. U-11929 An. noen[sic]

4360; Makes Good, Joseph; M; 1886-46; F; M; Head; 4292; Yes; Yes; Al. 1974 An. 4285

4361; Makes Good (Red Horse), Mary; F; 1889-43; F; M; Wife; 4293; Yes; Yes; Al. 2023 An. 4286

4362; Makes Good, Antoine; M; 10/14/11-20; F; S; Son; 4294; Yes; Yes; Al. 7740 An. 4287

4363; Makes Good, Annie; F; 3/25/23-9; F; S; Daughter; 4295; Yes; Yes; Id. U-13015 An. 4290

Census of the **Pine Ridge** reservation of the **Pine Ridge, South Dakota** jurisdiction, as of **April 1**, 19**32**, taken by **James H. McGregor**, Superintendent.

Key: Number; Surname, Given; Sex; Date of Birth-Age at Last Birthday; Tribe (Oglala Sioux, unless stated otherwise); Degree of Blood; Marital Status; Relationship to Head of Family [Last Census Roll Number]; At Jurisdiction Where Enrolled (Yes/No); (If no – Where); Ward (Yes/No, if given); Allotment, Annuity and Identification Numbers (if given).

4364; Makes Good, Lucy; F; 4/26/27-4; F; S; Daughter; 4296; Yes; Yes; Id. U-12322 An. none

4365; Makes Good, Joseph M; M; 6/24/31-9/12; F; S; Son; ---; Yes; Yes; U-13896

4366; Makes Shine, Henry; M; 1895-37; F; M; Head; 4298; Yes; Yes; Al. 4991 An. 4293

4367; Makes Shine (Morrisette), Madeline; F; 1899-33; plus 1/4; M; Wife; 4299; Yes; Yes; Al. 1176 An. 5854

4368; Morrisette, Bernard; M; 5/25/24-7; 1/4; S; S. Son; 4300; Yes; Yes; Id. U-11371 An. none

4369; Makes Shine, Oletha; F; 3/17/31-1; 1/4; S; Daughter; ---; Yes; Yes; U-13810

4370; Make Shine, John; M; 1892-40; F; M; Head; 4301; Yes; Yes; Al. 7318 An. 4295

4371; Make Shine (Y.S. Little Bear), Mary; F; 1894-38; F; M; Wife; 4302; Yes; Yes; Al. 74 An. 4296

4372; Makes Shine, Ida; F; 7/18/28-3; F; S; Daughter; 4304; Yes; Yes; Id. U-12741 An. none

4373; Make Shine, Oliver; M; 1868-64; F; M; Head; 4305; Yes; Yes; Al. 256 An. 4302

4374; Make Shine (Garnier), Julia; F; 1864-68; plus 1/4; M; Wife; 4306; Yes; Yes; Al. 3668 An. 4303

4375; Makes Over, ---; F; 1843-89; F; Wd; Head; 4307; Yes; Yes; Al. 2823 An. 4304

4376; Make Above, Samuel; M; 1878-54; F; M; Head; 4308; Yes; Yes; Al. 1903 An. 4307

4377; Make Shine (Brown), Julia; F; 1880-52; F; M; Wife; 4309; Yes; Yes; Al. 2293 An. 1078

4378; Brown, Harry; M; 1/23/17-15; F; S; S. Son; 4310; Yes; Yes; Id. U-9264 An. 1079

4379; Brown, Henry; M; 1/3/23-9; F; S; S. Son; 4311; Yes; Yes; Id. U-12047 An. 1080

4380; Many Cartridges (Slow), Beulah; F; 1883-49; F; Wd; Head; 4312; Yes; Yes; Al. 3933 An. 4311

4381; Many Cartridges, William; M; 7/18/19-12; F; S; Son; 4313; Yes; Yes; Id. U-9975 An. 4315

4382; Many Cartridges, Beulah; F; 1/18/09-23; F; S; Head; 4314; Yes; Yes; Al. 4966 An. 4312

Census of the __**Pine Ridge**__ reservation of the __**Pine Ridge, South Dakota**__ jurisdiction, as of __**April 1**__, 19**32**, taken by __**James H. McGregor**__, Superintendent.

Key: Number; Surname, Given; Sex; Date of Birth-Age at Last Birthday; Tribe (Oglala Sioux, unless stated otherwise); Degree of Blood; Marital Status; Relationship to Head of Family [Last Census Roll Number]; At Jurisdiction Where Enrolled (Yes/No); (If no – Where); Ward (Yes/No, if given); Allotment, Annuity and Identification Numbers (if given).

4383; Maple, Lizzie; F; 1880-52; 1/4; M; Head; 4316; Yes; Yes; Al. 4618 An. 4318
4384; Maple, Chester; M; 2/6/12-20; -1/4; S; Son; 4317; Yes; Yes; Id. U-6989 An. 4320

4385; Marrow Bone, Henry; M; 1891-41; F; S; Head; 4318; Yes; Yes; Al. 6476 An. 4326

4386; Marrow Bone, Benjamin; M; 1889-43; F; M; Head; 4319; Yes; Yes; Al. 6475 An. 4321

N.E.: Marrow Bone (Rowland), Jessie; F; ------; Cheyenne Sioux; M; Wife;
4387; Marrow Bone, Virginia; F; 9/26/20-11; F; S; Daughter; 4320; Yes; Yes; Id. U-9976 An. 4323
4388; Marrow Bone, Emma; F; 12/30/23-8; F; S; Daughter; 4321; Yes; Yes; Id. U-11187 An. 4325
4389; Marrow Bone, Benedict; M; 1/5/29-3; F; S; Son; 4322; Yes; Yes; Id. U-12976 An. none
4390; Marrow Bone, Rufus; M; 9/29/30-1; F; S; Son; 4323; Yes; Yes; Id. U-13652 An. none

4391; Marrow Bone, Nellie; F; 1879-53; plus 1/4; Wd; Head; 4324; No; Chadron, town, Dawes, Nebr.; Yes; Al. 319 An. 1282

4392; Marshall, Charles; M; 1889-43; 1/4; S; Head; 4325; Yes; Yes; Al. 4528 An. 4328

4393; Marshall, Daniel; M; 1892-40; 1/4; M; Head; 4326; Yes; Yes; Al. 1664 An. 4329
4394; Marshall (Walks Under Ground), Maggie; F; 1907-25; F; M; Wife; 7344; Yes; Yes; Al. 5916 An. 7299
4395; Marshall, Vivian; F; 7/23/26-5; plus 1/4; S; Daughter; 7345; Yes; Yes; Id. U-12952 An. none
4396; Marshall, Antoine; M; 10/29/28-3; 1/4; S; Son; 7346; Yes; Yes; Id. U-12953 An. none
4397; Marshall, Hazel L; F; 3/1/31-1; 1/4; S; Daughter; 7347; Yes; Yes; Id. U-12765 An. none

4398; Marshall, Edward; M; 1904-28; 1/4; S; Head; 4327; Yes; Yes; Al. 4606 An. 4330

4399; Marshall, Hobart; M; 10/24/10-21; 1/4; S; Head; 4328; Yes; Yes; Al. 7022 An. 4333

Census of the **Pine Ridge** reservation of the **Pine Ridge, South Dakota** jurisdiction, as of **April 1**, 19**32**, taken by **James H. McGregor**, Superintendent.

Key: Number; Surname, Given; Sex; Date of Birth-Age at Last Birthday; Tribe (Oglala Sioux, unless stated otherwise); Degree of Blood; Marital Status; Relationship to Head of Family [Last Census Roll Number]; At Jurisdiction Where Enrolled (Yes/No); (If no -- Where); Ward (Yes/No, if given); Allotment, Annuity and Identification Numbers (if given).

4400; Marshall, Bennie; M; 3/6/10-22; 1/4; S; Head; 4330; Yes; Yes; Al. 4594 An. 4336

4401; Marshall (Yellow Hair), Esther; F; 1907-25; 1/4; Wd; Head; 4331; Yes; Yes; Al. 4593 An. 4335

4402; Marshall, Louisa; F; 12/14/27-4; 1/4; S; Daughter; 4332; Yes; Yes; Id. U-12487 An. none

4403; Marshall, Thomas R; M; 3/15/29-3; 1/4; S; Son; 4333; Yes; Yes; Id. U-13143 An. none

4404; Marshall, Louis; M; 1903-29; plus1/4; S; Head; 4334; Yes; Yes; Al. 4605 An. 4338

4405; Marshall, Peter; M; 1900-32; 1/4; S; Head; 4335; Yes; Yes; Al. 4604 An. 4339

4406; Marshall, Philip; M; 1881-51; 1/4; S; Head; 4336; Yes; Yes; Al. 4527 An. 4340

4407; Marshall, Samuel; M; 1898-34; 1/4; S; Head; 4337; Yes; Yes; Al. 4539 An. 4341

4408; Marshall, Stephen; M; 1892-40; 1/4; M; Head; 4338; Yes; Yes; Al. 4603 An. 4342

4409; Marshall (Cut), Lucinda; F; 1894-38; F; M; Wife; 4342; Yes; Yes; Al. 5647 An. 1719

4410; Marshall, Conrad; M; 10/19/16-15; 1/4; S; Son; 4339; Yes; Yes; Id. U-9978 An. 4343

4411; Marshall, Jacob; M; 10/8/18-13; 1/4; S; Son; 4340; Yes; Yes; Id. U-9979 An. 4344

4412; Marshall, Edith; F; 4/22/27-4; 1/4; S; Daughter; 4341; Yes; Yes; Id. U-12521 An. none

4413; Marshall, Francis; M; 5/15/26-5; plus 1/4; S; Son; 4344; Yes; Yes; Id. U-11949 An. none

4414; Marshall, Joy E; M; 1/19/29-3; 1/4; S; Son; 4345; Yes; Yes; Id. U-13111 An. none

4415; Hatchet, Hazel; F; 2/1/15-17; F; S; S. Daughter; 4346; Yes; Yes; Al. 8197 An. 1720

4416; Martin, Joseph A; M; 1903-29; plus 1/4; S; Head; 4354; Yes; Yes; Al. 1132 An. 4355

4417; Martin, Eva; F; 2/22/09-23; 1/4; S; Head; 4351; Yes; Yes; Al. 7588 An. 4347

Census of the __Pine Ridge__ reservation of the __Pine Ridge, South Dakota__ jurisdiction, as of __April 1__, 19**32**, taken by __James H. McGregor__, Superintendent.

Key: Number; Surname, Given; Sex; Date of Birth-Age at Last Birthday; Tribe (Oglala Sioux, unless stated otherwise); Degree of Blood; Marital Status; Relationship to Head of Family [Last Census Roll Number]; At Jurisdiction Where Enrolled (Yes/No); (If no – Where); Ward (Yes/No, if given); Allotment, Annuity and Identification Numbers (if given).

4418; Martin, Louis Sr.; M; 11/73-58; F; M; Head; 4352; Yes; Yes; Al. 1129 An. 4353

4419; Martin (no data), Mary; F; 1862-70; F; M; Wife; 4353; Yes; Yes; Al. 3745 An. 4354

4420; Martin, Louis Jr.; M; 1902-30; F; S; Head; 4355; Yes; Yes; Al. 1131 An. 4356

4421; Martin, William; M; 9/20/04-27; Plus 1/4; M; Head; 4356; Yes; Yes; Al. 6702 An. 4357

N.E.: Martin (Bouillard), Lucy; F; ------; Santee Sioux; 1/4; M; Wife;
4422; Martin, William W; M; 9/17/26-5; 1/4; S; Son; 4357; Yes; Yes; Id. U-12140 An. none

4423; Martin, Robert; M; 5/20/29-2; 1/4; S; Son; 4358; Yes; Yes; Id. U-13190 An. none

4424; Martin, Samuel; M; 7/10/12-19; 1/4; S; Alone; 4348; Yes; Yes; Al. 7589 An. 4348

4425; Martin, Roy; M; 10/7/14-17; 1/4; S; Alone; 4349; Yes; Yes; Id. U-9983 An. 4349

4426; Martin, Elma; F; 6/15/20-11; 1/4; S; Alone; 4350; Yes; Yes; Id. U-9984 An. 4350

4427; Martin, Rauline; M; 8/24/09-22; 1/4; S; Head; 4359; Yes; Yes; Al. 6704 An. 2002

4428; Martinez, Comes Out Whirlwind; F; 1869-63; F; M; Head; 4360; Yes; Yes; Al. 2951 An. 1572

4429; Martinez, Carlo; M; 1896-36; plus 1/4; M; Head; 4361; Yes; Yes; Al. 1952 An. 4358

4430; Martinez (Fire Thunder), Martha; F; 1899-33; 1/4; M; Wife; 4362; Yes; Yes; Al. 1952 An. 4359

4431; Martinez, Philomene; F; 1/19/18-14; 1/4; S; Daughter; 4363; Yes; Yes; Id. U-9985 An. 4360

4432; Martinez, Carlos Jr.; M; 10/8/19-12; 1/4; S; Son; 4364; Yes; Yes; Id. U-9986 An. 4361

4433; Martinez, Joshua; M; 2/4/21-11; 1/4; S; Son; 4365; Yes; Yes; Id. U-9987 An. 4362

4434; Martinez, Geraldine; F; 6/26/24-7; 1/4; S; Daughter; 4367; Yes; Yes; Id. U-11456 An. 4364

4435; Martinez, Martin; M; 7/11/30-1; 1/4; S; Son; 4369; Yes; Yes; Id. U-13653 An. none

Census of the __Pine Ridge__ reservation of the __Pine Ridge, South Dakota__ jurisdiction, as of __April 1__, 19**32**, taken by __James H. McGregor__, Superintendent.

Key: Number; Surname, Given; Sex; Date of Birth-Age at Last Birthday; Tribe (Oglala Sioux, unless stated otherwise); Degree of Blood; Marital Status; Relationship to Head of Family [Last Census Roll Number]; At Jurisdiction Where Enrolled (Yes/No); (If no – Where); Ward (Yes/No, if given); Allotment, Annuity and Identification Numbers (if given).

4436; Martinez, James; M; 6/27/07-24; plus 1/4; M; Head; 4370; Yes; Yes; Al. 2953 An. 1573

4437; Martinez, Joseph; M; 1890-42; 1/4; M; Head; 4371; Yes; Yes; Al. 833 An. 4365

4438; Martinez (Harvey), Julia; F; 1885-47; 1/4; M; Wife; 4372; Yes; Yes; Al. 2720 An. 4366

4439; Martinez, Eva; F; 3/22/14-18; 1/4; S; Daughter; 4373; Yes; Yes; Al. 7367 An. 4367

4440; Martinez, Walter; M; 10/25/15-16; 1/4; S; Son; 4374; Yes; Yes; Id. U-9988 An. 4368

4441; Martinez, Seth; M; 6/6/17-17; 1/4; S; Son; 4375; Yes; Yes; Id. U-9989 An. 4369

4442; Martinez, Raymond; M; 1/9/19-13; 1/4; S; Son; 4376; Yes; Yes; Id. U-9990 An. 4370

4443; Martinez, Dora; F; 10/5/20-11; 1/4; S; Daughter; 4377; Yes; Yes; Id. U-9991 An. 4371

4444; Martinez, May; F; 10/28/22-9; 1/4; S; Daughter; 4378; Yes; Yes; Id. U-12064 An. 4372

4445; Martinez, Melby; M; 1/10/25-7; 1/4; S; Son; 4379; Yes; Yes; Id. U-11441 An. 4373

4446; Martinez, Antoine; M; 11/27/27-4; 1/4; S; Son; 4380; Yes; Yes; Id. U-12659 An. none

4447; Martinez, Philip; M; 1887-45; 1/4; S; Head; 4381; Yes; Yes; Al. 832 An. 4374

4448; Maxwell (Allman), Lydia; F; 1906-26; 1/4; M; Head; 4382; No; Lapwai, Idaho; Yes; Al. 6119 An. 99

4449; Means, Bert; M; 1892-40; plus 1/4; S; Head; 4383; Yes; No; Al. 1046 An. 4375

4450; Means, Edward; M; 1899-33; 1/4; M; Head; 4384; Yes; Yes; Al. 1278 An. 4376

4451; Means (Brave Heart), Rosa; F; 1901-31; F; M; Wife; 4385; Yes; Yes; Al. 801 An. 4377

4452; Means, Wilbert; M; 5/12/21-10; plus 1/4; S; Son; 4386; Yes; Yes; Id. U-9992 An. 4378

4453; Means, Carrie; F; 5/28/24-7; 1/4; S; Daughter; 4387; Yes; Yes; Id. U-11350 An. 4379

4454; Means, Lavina; F; 2/23/26-6; 1/4; S; Daughter; 4388; Yes; Yes; Id. U-12954 An. none

Census of the __Pine Ridge__ reservation of the __Pine Ridge, South Dakota__ jurisdiction, as of __April 1__, 19**32**, taken by __James H. McGregor__, Superintendent.

Key: Number; Surname, Given; Sex; Date of Birth-Age at Last Birthday; Tribe (Oglala Sioux, unless stated otherwise); Degree of Blood; Marital Status; Relationship to Head of Family [Last Census Roll Number]; At Jurisdiction Where Enrolled (Yes/No); (If no – Where); Ward (Yes/No, if given); Allotment, Annuity and Identification Numbers (if given).

4455; Means, Josephine; F; 12/8/27-4; 1/4; S; Daughter; 4389; Yes; Yes; Id. U-12687 An. none

4456; Means, Walter; M; 9/11/29-2; 1/4; S; Son; 4390; Yes; Yes; Id. U-13269 An. none

4457; Means, Dorothy; F; 1/21/32-2/12; 1/4; S; Daughter; ---; Yes; Yes; U-14099

4458; Means, Eugene; M; 1874-58; 1/4; Wd; Head; 4391; Yes; Yes; Al. 1048 An. 4381

4459; Means, Eugene; M; 1899-32; 1/4; S; Head; 4392; Yes; Yes; Al. 2249 An. 4380

4460; Means (no data), Nellie; F; 1875-57; -1/4; Wd; Head; 4393; Yes; Yes; Al. 5334 An. 4382

4461; Means, Robert A; M; 8/30/1-20; plus1/4; S; Son; 4394; Yes; Yes; Al. 7130 An. 4384

4462; Means, Walter F; M; 4/1/15-17; 1/4; S; Son; 4395; Yes; Yes; Al. 7927 An. 4385

4463; Means, Charles; M; 4/1/15-17; 1/4; S; Son; 4396; Yes; Yes; Al. 7926 An. 4386

4464; Means, Quentin; M; 4/3/19-12; 1/4; S; Son; 4397; Yes; Yes; Id. U-9993 An. 4387

4465; Means, Austin; M; 8/4/09-22; 1/4; M; Head; 4398; No; Rosebush, town, Isabella, Mich.; Yes; Al. 7129 An. 4383

N.E.: Means (Jackson), Agnes; F; -----; Chippewa; F; M; Wife;
4466; Means, Austin E.; M; 7/20/30-1; 1/4; S; Son; 4399; No; Rosebush, town, Isabella, Mich.; Yes; Id. U-13608 An. none

4467; Means, Frank; M; 1887-45; 1/4; S; Head; 4400; Yes; Yes; Al. 1045 An. 4388

4468; Means, Hobart; M; 1903-29; 1/4; S; Head; 4401; Yes; Yes; Al. 1050 An. 4389

4469; Means, George W; M; 1871-61; 1/4; M; Head; 4402; Yes; Yes; Al. 3959 An. 4390

4470; Means (Fast Thunder), Fannie; F; 1871-61; F; M; Wife; 4403; Yes; Yes; Al. 4078 An. 4392

4471; Means, Theodore; M; 8/23/08-23; plus 1/4; S; Son; 4404; Yes; Yes Al. 7132 An. 4392

4472; Means, John; M; 1895-37; 1/4; M; Head; 4405; No; Ft. Belnap[sic], Wyo.; Yes; Al. 1047 An. 4396

Census of the **Pine Ridge** reservation of the **Pine Ridge, South Dakota** jurisdiction, as of **April 1**, 19**32**, taken by **James H. McGregor**, Superintendent.

Key: Number; Surname, Given; Sex; Date of Birth-Age at Last Birthday; Tribe (Oglala Sioux, unless stated otherwise); Degree of Blood; Marital Status; Relationship to Head of Family [Last Census Roll Number]; At Jurisdiction Where Enrolled (Yes/No); (If no – Where); Ward (Yes/No, if given); Allotment, Annuity and Identification Numbers (if given).

4473; Means (Smith), Myrtle; F; 4/2/98-34; 1/4; M; Wife; 4406; Yes; Yes; Al. 2239 An. 4397

4474; Means, John H.; M; 11/26/19-12; 1/4; S; Son; 4407; Yes; Yes; Id. U-9994 An. 4398

4475; Means, Bert A; M; 5/1/18-13; 1/4; S; Son; 4408; Yes; Yes; Id. U-9995 An. 4399

4476; Means, Robert B; M; 11/21/21-10; 1/4; S; Son; 4409; Yes; Yes; Id. U-10959 An. 4400

4477; Means, Walton J; M; 2/1/24-8; 1/4; S; Son; 4410; Yes; Yes; Id. U-11506 An. 4401

4478; Means, Thomas D; M; 11/16/27-4; 1/4; S; Son; 4411; Yes; Yes; Id. U-12632 An. none

4479; Means, William M; M; 1901-31; 1/4; S; Head; 4412; Yes; Yes; Al. 1049 An. 4403

4480; Meat, George; M; 1899-33; F; M; Head; 4413; Yes; Yes; Al. 2013 An. 4406
4481; Meat (Logan), Nancy; F; 1897-35; F; M; Wife; 4414; Yes; Yes; Al. 5633 An. 4407
4482; Meat, Melissa; F; 10/30/21-10; F; S; Daughter; 4415; Yes; Yes; Id. U-9928 An. 4408
4483; Meat, Myrtle; F; 2/27/27-5; F; S; Daughter; 4416; Yes; Yes; Id. U-12290 An. none

4484; Meat (Randall), Mollie; F; 1872-60; F; Wd; Head; 4417; Yes; Yes; Al. 2006 An. 4411
4485; Swift Eagle, Mary; F; 3/16/17-15; plus 1/4; S; Gr. Daughter; 4418; Yes; Yes; Id. U-9996 An. 4412

4486; Medicine, Claude; M; 1889-43; F; M; Head; 4419; Yes; Yes; Al. 3111 An. 4414
4487; Medicine (Black Sheep), Bessie; F; 1890-42; F; M; Wife; 4420; Yes; Yes; Al. 6572 An. 4415
4488; Medicine, Rosie; F; 5/23/27-4; F; S; Daughter; 4422; Yes; Yes; Id. U-12323 An. none
4489; Medicine, Lulu; F; 8/8/31-7/12; F; S; Daughter; ---; Yes; Yes; U-13920

4490; Mejia (red[sic] Hawk), Lucy; F; 6/6/12-19; F; M; Head; 4422; No; Minitare, town, Box Butte, Nebr.; Yes; Id. U-10249 An. 6290

4491; Menard, Lizzie; F; 6/2/08-23; plus 1/4; S; Head; 4424; Yes; Yes; Al. 5353 An. 4421

Census of the___**Pine Ridge**___reservation of the___**Pine Ridge, South Dakota** jurisdiction, as of___**April 1**___, 19**32**, taken by___**James H. McGregor**___, Superintendent.

Key: Number; Surname, Given; Sex; Date of Birth-Age at Last Birthday; Tribe (Oglala Sioux, unless stated otherwise); Degree of Blood; Marital Status; Relationship to Head of Family [Last Census Roll Number]; At Jurisdiction Where Enrolled (Yes/No); (If no – Where); Ward (Yes/No, if given); Allotment, Annuity and Identification Numbers (if given).

4492; Mendenhall (Fisher), Laura; F; 1892-40; 1/4; M; Head; 4425; Yes; Yes; Al. 3767 An. 4423

4493; Mendenhall, Frencheon; F; 5/7/12-19; -1/4; S; Daughter; 4426; Yes; Yes; Al. 7197 An. 4424

4494; Mendenhall, Wilba; F; 1/21/15-17; -1/4; S; Daughter; 4427; Yes; Yes; Al. 8081 An. 4425

4495; Mendenhall, Arlene; F; 12/17/19-18; -1/4; S; Daughter; 4428; Yes; Yes; Id. U-9998 An. 4426

4496; Mendenhall, Walter; M; 3/13/22-10; -1/4; S; Son; 4429; Yes; Yes; Id. U-10905 An. 4427

4497; Mendenhall, Howard; M; 9/15/24-7; -1/4; S; Son; 4430; Yes; Yes; Id. U-11710 An. none

4498; Mendenhall, Laura N.; F; 1/15/28-4; -1/4; S; Daughter; 4431; Yes; Yes; Id. U-12857 An. none

4499; Merdanian (Swallow), Ida; F; 1880-52; plus 1/4; M; Head; 4434; Yes; No; Al. 3562 An. 4428

4500; Merdanian (Campbell), Ida V; F; 1903-29; plus 1/4; M; Head; 4432; No; Smithwick, town, Fall River, S.D.; Yes; Al. 3228 An. 1261

4501; Merdanian, Roy E Jr.; M; 5/10/30-1; -1/4; S; Son; 4433; No ; Same; Yes; Id. U-13571 An. none

4502; Merrivall (Nelson), Ellen; F; 1902-30; 1/4; Wd; Head; 4435; Yes; Yes; Al. 2221 An. 4431

4503; Merrival (Woods), Susie; F; 1871-61; 1/4; Wd; Head; 4436; Yes; Yes; Al. 3592 An. 4429

4504; Merrivall, Hermas; M; 1896-36; 1/4; M; Head; 4437; Yes; No; Al. 315 An. 4430

4505; Merrivall (Martin), Edith; F; 1907-25; 1/4; M; Wife; 4438; Yes; Yes; Al. 6703 An. 4351

4506; Merrivall, Doris; F; 7/22/26-5; 1/4; S; Daughter; 4439; Yes; Yes; Id. U-12164 An. none

4507; Merrivall, Donroy; M; 9/13/28-3; 1/4; S; Son; 4440; Yes; Yes; Id. U-12843 An. none

4508; Merrival, Pedro; M; 1904-28; 1/4; M; Head; 4441; Yes; No; Al. 348 An. 4432

4509; Merrival (Ecoffey), Ethel; F; 1906-26; 1/4; M; Wife; 4442; Yes; Yes; Al. 4761 An. 2079

4510; Merrival, Dolores; F; 6/2/30-1; 1/4; S; Daughter; 4443; Yes; Yes; Id. U-13531 An. none

Census of the __Pine Ridge__ reservation of the __Pine Ridge, South Dakota__ jurisdiction, as of __April 1__, 19**32,** taken by __James H. McGregor__, Superintendent.

Key: Number; Surname, Given; Sex; Date of Birth-Age at Last Birthday; Tribe (Oglala Sioux, unless stated otherwise); Degree of Blood; Marital Status; Relationship to Head of Family [Last Census Roll Number]; At Jurisdiction Where Enrolled (Yes/No); (If no – Where); Ward (Yes/No, if given); Allotment, Annuity and Identification Numbers (if given).

4511; Merrival, Barton S; M; 10/24/31-5/12; 1/4; S; Son; ---; Yes; Yes; U-13998

4512; Mesteth, David; M; 1886-46; 1/4; M; Head; 4444; Yes; No; Al. 6357 An. 4438

4513; Mesteth (Talks About Her), Mabel; F; 1888-44; F; M; Wife; 4445; Yes; Yes; Al. 6245 An. 4434

4514; Mesteth, Gilbert; M; 2/23/11-3; Plus 1/4; S; Son; 4446; Yes; Yes; Al. 6246 An. 4436

4515; Mesteth, Daniel; M; 3/20/14-18; Plus 1/4; S; Son; 4447; Yes; Yes; Al. 7652 An. 4437

4516; Mesteth, Pearl; F; 11/30/18-13; 1/4; S; Daughter; 4448; Yes; Yes; Id. U-10013 An. 4438

4517; Mesteth, Nancy D; F; 9/1/27-4; 1/4; S; Daughter; 4449; Yes; Yes; Id. U-12407 An. none

4518; Mesteth, James; M; 4/19/29-2; 1/4; S; Son; 4450; Yes; Yes; Id. U-13170 An. none

4519; Mesteth, Alvina; F; 7/22/31-8/12; 1/4; S; Daughter; ---; Yes; Yes; U-13898

4520; Mesteth, Frank; M; 1896-36; 1/4; Wd; Head; 4451; Yes; No; Al. 2645 An. 4439

4521; Mesteth (Two Bonnets), Christina; F; 1898-34; 1/4; Wd; Head; 4452; Yes; Yes; Al. 939 An. 4445

4522; Mesteth, Lloyde; M; 10/25/22-9; 1/4; S; Son; 4453; Yes; Yes; Id. U-12012 An. 4449

4523; Mesteth, Olive; F; 1/18/25-7; 1/4; S; Daughter; 4454; Yes; Yes; Id. U-11410 An. 4450

4524; Mesteth, John M; M; 1/2/27-5; 1/4; S; Son; 4455; Yes; Yes; Id. U-12209 An. none

4525; Mesteth, Theresa; F; 6/24/29-2; 1/4; S; Daughter; 4456; Yes; Yes; Id. U-13341 An. none

4526; Mesteth, Jacob; M; 5/19/05-26; 1/4; M; Head; 4457; Yes; No; Al. 7274 An. 4451

4527; Mesteth (Little Dog), Rosa; F; 11/13/06-25; F; M; Wife; 4458; Yes; Yes; Al. 2959 An. 3929

4528; Mesteth, Mathew; M; 11/16/26-5; plus 1/4; S; Son; 4459; Yes; Yes; Id. U-12141 An. none

4529; Mesteth, Eva; F; 10/20/28-3; plus 1/4; S; Daughter; 4460; Yes; Yes; Id. U-12955 An. none

4530; Mesteth, Madaline; F; 10/20/30-1; 1/4; S; Daughter; 4461; Yes; Yes; Id. U-13629 An. none

Census of the __Pine Ridge__ reservation of the __Pine Ridge, South Dakota__ jurisdiction, as of __April 1__, 19**32**, taken by __James H. McGregor__, Superintendent.

Key: Number; Surname, Given; Sex; Date of Birth-Age at Last Birthday; Tribe (Oglala Sioux, unless stated otherwise); Degree of Blood; Marital Status; Relationship to Head of Family [Last Census Roll Number]; At Jurisdiction Where Enrolled (Yes/No); (If no – Where); Ward (Yes/No, if given); Allotment, Annuity and Identification Numbers (if given).

4531; Mesteth, James; M; 1882-50; 1/4; M; Head; 4462; Yes; No; Al. 2650 An. 4452

4532; Mesteth (Bissonette), Susie; F; 1889-43; 1/4; M; Wife; 4463; Yes; Yes; Al. 2651 An. 4453

4533; Mesteth, Lloyd; M; 2/7/09-23; 1/4; S; Son; 4464; Yes; Yes; Al. 7353 An. 4454

4534; Mesteth, Fred; M; 5/18/11-20; 1/4; S; Son; 4465; Yes; Yes; Al. 7354 An. 4455

4535; Mesteth, Ruben; M; 10/24/14-17; 1/4; S; Son; 4466; Yes; Yes; Al. 7884 An. 4456

4536; Mesteth, Bennie; M; 4/17/16-15; 1/4; S; Son; 4467; Yes; Yes; Id. U-10006 An. 4457

4537; Mesteth, Pearl; F; 4/4/18-13; 1/4; S; Daughter; 4468; Yes; Yes; Id. U-10007 An. 4458

4538; Mesteth, Dora; F; 7/21/22-9; 1/4; S; Daughter; 4469; Yes; Yes; Id. U-11322 An. 4459

4539; Mesteth (Little Chief), Jennie; F; 1872-60; F; Wd; Head; 4470; Yes; Yes; Al. 6915 An. 4460

4540; Mesteth, Levi; M; 5/1/12-19; plus 1/4; S; Son; 4471; Yes; Yes; Al. 6918 An. 4461

4541; Mesteth, John; M; 1875-57; 1/4; Wd; Head; 4472; Yes; Yes; Al. 868 An. 4462

4542; Mesteth, Joseph; M; 1884-48; plus 1/4; M; Head; 4473; Yes; No; Al. 7823 An. 4465

4543; Mesteth (Plenty Wounds), Eva; F; 3/31/13-19; F; M; Wife; 5021; Yes; Yes; Id. U-10135 An. 5011

4544; Mesteth, Peter; M; 1890-42; 1/4; M; Head; 4476; Yes; No; Al. 2646 An. 4474

4545; Mesteth (Irving), Julia; F; 1896-36; 1/4; M; Wife; 4477; Yes; No; Al. 4718 An. 4475

4546; Mesteth, Lillian; F; 5/1/16-15; 1/4; S; Daughter; 4478; Yes; Yes; Id. U-10000 An. 4476

4547; Mesteth, Inez; F; 2/23/22-10; 1/4; S; Daughter; 4479; Yes; Yes; Id. U-10881 An. 4477

4548; Mesteth, Philip; M; 1889-43; 1/4; M; Head; 4480; Yes; No; Al. 7390 An. 4478

4549; Mesteth (McMillan), May; F; 1899-33; 1/4; M; Wife; 4713; Yes; Yes; Al. 6795 An. 4692

4550; Mesteth, Lorene; F; 4/28/19-12; 1/4; S; Daughter; 4481; Yes; Yes; Id. U-10004 An. 4480

4551; Mesteth, Ethel; F; 6/3/22-9; 1/4; S; Daughter; 4482; Yes; Yes; Id. U-11021 An. 4481

Census of the **Pine Ridge** reservation of the **Pine Ridge, South Dakota** jurisdiction, as of **April 1**, 1932, taken by **James H. McGregor**, Superintendent.

Key: Number; Surname, Given; Sex; Date of Birth-Age at Last Birthday; Tribe (Oglala Sioux, unless stated otherwise); Degree of Blood; Marital Status; Relationship to Head of Family [Last Census Roll Number]; At Jurisdiction Where Enrolled (Yes/No); (If no – Where); Ward (Yes/No, if given); Allotment, Annuity and Identification Numbers (if given).

4552; Mesteth, Francis; M; 10/3/27-4; 1/4; S; Son; 4483; Yes; Yes; Id. U-12446 An. none

4553; McMillan, Mary J.; F; 6/20/23-8; -1/4; S; S. Daughter; 4714; Yes; Yes; Id. U-11619 An. 4693

4554; Little, Harson; M; 3/23/28-4; plus 1/4; S; S. Son; 4715; Yes; Yes; Id. U-12830 An. none

4555; Mesteth, William; M; 1880-52; 1/4; S; Head; 4474; Yes; Yes; Al. 2632 An. 4482

4556; Mesteth, Gabriel; M; 9/22/09-22; plus 1/4; M; Head; 4485; Yes; Yes; Al. 5855 An. 7095

4557; Mesteth (Her Horse), Sarah; F; 1907-25; F; M; Wife; 4486; Yes; Yes; Al. 5818 An. 2838

4558; Mexican, Ambrose; M; 1861-71; F; Wd; Head; 4489; Yes; Yes; Al. 2801 An. 4483

4559; Mexican, Willie; M; 1894-38; F; M; Head; 4490; Yes; Yes; Al. 2804 An. 4485

4560; Mexican (Goes After), Bessie; F; 1901-31; F; M; Wife; 4491; Yes; Yes; Al. 7427 An. 4486

4561; Mexican, Vera; F; 8/17/18-13; F; S; Daughter; 4492; Yes; Yes; Id. U-10015 An. 4487

4562; Mexican, Charles; M; 9/10/20-11; F; S; Son; 4493; Yes; Yes; Id. U-10016 An. 4488

4563; Mexican, Pearl; F; 11/2/23-8; F; S; Daughter; 4494; Yes; Yes; Id. U-11166 An. 4489

4564; Mexican, Sarah; F; 12/21/26-5; F; S; Daughter; 4495; Yes; Yes; Id. U-12223 An. none

4565; Midkiff, Clifford; M; 1902-30; -1/4; S; Head; 4496; No; Willow Springs, town, Howell, Mo.; Yes; Al. 3924 An. 4490

4566; Midkiff (no data), Belilah; F; 1871-61; 1/4; M; Head; 4497; No; Willow Springs, town, Howell, Mo.; No; Al. 3920 An. 4491

4567; Midkiff, Harley; M; 3/18/14-18; -1/4; S; Son; 4498; Yes; Yes; Al. 8241 An. 4492

4568; Midkiff, Reuben; M; 1899-33; -1/4; M; Head; 4499; Yes; Yes; Al. 3922 An. 4493

4569; Midkiff, Calvin; M; 8/31/23-8; -1/4; S; Son; 4500; Yes; Yes; Id. U-11863 An. none

Census of the **Pine Ridge** reservation of the **Pine Ridge, South Dakota** jurisdiction, as of **April 1**, 19**32**, taken by **James H. McGregor**, Superintendent.

Key: Number; Surname, Given; Sex; Date of Birth-Age at Last Birthday; Tribe (Oglala Sioux, unless stated otherwise); Degree of Blood; Marital Status; Relationship to Head of Family [Last Census Roll Number]; At Jurisdiction Where Enrolled (Yes/No); (If no – Where); Ward (Yes/No, if given); Allotment, Annuity and Identification Numbers (if given).

4570; Milk, ---; M; 1853-79; F; Wd; Head; 4501; Yes; Yes; Al. 4553 An. 4494

4571; Milk, John; M; 1883-49; F; M; Head; 4502; Yes; Yes; Al. 4173 An. 4496
4572; Milk (Long Horn), Hattie; F; 1883-49; F; M; Wife; 4503; Yes; Yes; Al. 4454 An. 4497
4573; Milk, Benjamin; M; 8/27/09-22; F; S; Son; 4504; Yes; Yes; Al. 4559 An. 4499
4574; Milk, John Jr.; M; 9/5/18-13; F; S; Son; 4505; Yes; Yes; Id. U-10018 An. 4513
4575; Milk, Sophia; F; 12/31/21-10; F; S; Daughter; 4506; Yes; Yes; Id. U-10892 An. 4504
4576; Milk, Jasper; M; 3/27/24-8; F; S; Son; 4507; Yes; Yes; Id. U-12251 An. none

4577; Milk, Oscar; M; 1908-24; F; M; Head; 4510; Yes; Yes; Al. 4558 An. 4498
4578; Milk (Her Horses), Julia; F; 1907-25; F; M; Wife; 2859; Yes; Yes; Al. 2817 An. 2837
4579; Milk, Susan; F; 4/21/31-11/12; F; S; Daughter; ---; Yes; Yes; U-13838

4580; Milk, Alice; F; 12/27/10-21; F; S; Head; 4511; Yes; Yes; Al. 7077 An. 4500

N.E.: Miller, Grant; M; -------; Oklahoma Indian; M; Head;
4581; Miller (Brown), Florence; F; 1906-26; plus 1/4; M; Wife; 4512; Yes; Yes; Al. 4024 An. 4507
4582; Miller, Leroy; M; 2/22/24-8; 1/4; S; Son; 4513; Yes; Yes; Id. U-11307 An. 4508
4583; Miller, Alberta; F; 12/23/25-6; 1/4; S; Daughter; 4514; Yes; Yes; Id. U-11785 An. none

4584; Mills, Benjamin; M; 1871-61; 1/4; M; Head; 4515; Yes; Yes; Al. 340 An. 4509
4585; Mills (no data), Susie; F; 1882-50; F; M; Wife; 4516; Yes; Yes; Al. 5533 An. 4510
4586; Mills, Lula; F; 12/4/12-19; plus 1/4; S; Daughter; 4517; Yes; Yes; Al. 6844 An. 4513
4587; Mills, Raymond; M; 1/23/15-17; 1/4; S; Son; 4518; Yes; Yes; Al. 8126 An. 4514
4588; Mills, Chester; M; 11/27/16-15; 1/4; S; Son; 4519; Yes; Yes; Id. U-10020 An. 4515
4589; Mills, Ethel; F; 7/28/24-7; 1/4; S; Daughter; 4520; Yes; Yes; Id. U-11435 An. 4517

4590; Mills, Henry; M; 2/6/09-23; 1/4; M; Head; 4521; Yes; Yes; Al. 5536 An. 4512

Census of the **Pine Ridge** reservation of the **Pine Ridge, South Dakota** jurisdiction, as of **April 1**, 19**32**, taken by **James H. McGregor**, Superintendent.

Key: Number; Surname, Given; Sex; Date of Birth-Age at Last Birthday; Tribe (Oglala Sioux, unless stated otherwise); Degree of Blood; Marital Status; Relationship to Head of Family [Last Census Roll Number]; At Jurisdiction Where Enrolled (Yes/No); (If no – Where); Ward (Yes/No, if given); Allotment, Annuity and Identification Numbers (if given).

4591; Mills (Van Wert), Josephine; F; 7/16/13-18; 1/4; M; Wife; 4522; Yes; Yes; Al. 7695 An. 7240

4592; Mills, Glessnor; F; 5/21/30-1; 1/4; S; Daughter; 4523; Yes; Yes; Id. U-13516 An. none

4593; Mills, Henrietta; F; 8/19/31-7/12; 1/4; S; Daughter; ---; Yes; Yes; U-13899

4594; Mills, David; M; 1898-34; Plus 1/4; M; Head; 4524; Yes; Yes; Al. 341 An. 4537

4595; Mills (Morrison), Elizabeth; F; 1882-50; 1/4; M; Wife; 4529; Yes; Yes; Al. 1125 An. 4599

4596; Mills, Benjamin Jr.; M; 8/26/18-13; 1/4; S; Son; 4525; Yes; Yes; Id. U-10022 An. 4520

4597; Mills, Geraldine; F; 2/28/20-12; 1/4; S; Daughter; 4526; Yes; Yes; Id. U-10023 An. 4521

4598; Mills, Roy; M; 5/26/23-8; 1/4; S; Son; 4527; Yes; Yes; Id. U-13076 An. 4522

4599; Mills, Marilyn; F; 8/3/25-6; 1/4; S; Daughter; 4528; Yes; Yes; Id. U-11855 An. none

4600; Morrison, Robert E; M; 2/17/10-22; 1/4; S; S. Son; 4530; Yes; Yes; Al. 4930 An. 4601

4601; Morrison, Mabel; F; 1/28/12-20; 1/4; S; S. Daughter; 4531; Yes; Yes; Al. 7458 An. 4602

4602; Morrison, Edith; F; 10/25/13-18; 1/4; S; S. Daughter; 4532; Yes; Yes; Al. 7459 An. 4603

4603; Morrison, Frank Jr.; M; 11/28/15-16; 1/4; S; S. Son; 4533; Yes; Yes; Al. 8212 An. 4604

4604; Mills, James; M; 1902-30; 1/4; M; Head; 4534; Yes; Yes; Al. 1203 An. 4524

4605; Mills (H.Bird), Jessie; F; 1905-27; 1/4; M; Wife; 4535; Yes; Yes; Al. 7696 An. 569

4606; Mills, Benjamin; M; 7/9/28-3; 1/4; S; Son; 4536; Yes; Yes; Id. U-12742 An. none

4607; Mills, Calvin; M; 11/12/29-2; 1/4; S; Son; 4537; Yes; Yes; Id. U-13297 An. none

4608; Mills, Elizabeth; F; 12/21/31-3/12; 1/4; S; Daughter; ---; Yes; Yes; U-14100

4609; Mills (LaPointe), Vera; F~~M~~; 1896-36; 1/4; Wd; Head; 4538; Yes; Yes; Al. 6885 An. 4526

4610; Mills, Sidney; M; 1902-30; plus 1/4; M; Head; 4539; Yes; Yes; Al. 343 An. 4527

4611; Mills (Allman), Grace; F; 1905-27; 1/4; M; Wife; 4540; Yes; Yes; Al. 5711 An. 4528

Census of the **Pine Ridge** reservation of the **Pine Ridge, South Dakota** jurisdiction, as of **April 1**, 19**32**, taken by **James H. McGregor**, Superintendent.

Key: Number; Surname, Given; Sex; Date of Birth-Age at Last Birthday; Tribe (Oglala Sioux, unless stated otherwise); Degree of Blood; Marital Status; Relationship to Head of Family [Last Census Roll Number]; At Jurisdiction Where Enrolled (Yes/No); (If no – Where); Ward (Yes/No, if given); Allotment, Annuity and Identification Numbers (if given).

4612; Mills, Estella; F; 7/2/24-7; 1/4; S; Daughter; 4541; Yes; Yes; Id. U-11436 An. 4529

4613; Mills, Sidney L.; M; 12/5/25-6; 1/4; S; Son; 4542; Yes; Yes; Id. U-11819 An. none

4614; Mills, Emma; F; 11/20/27-4; 1/4; S; Daughter; 4543; Yes; Yes; Id. U-12581 An. none

4615; Mills, Lucy; F; 7/21/10-21; 1/4; S; Head; 4544; Yes; Yes; Al. 6008 An. 4531

4616; Mills, Julia; F; 1/10/13-19; 1/4; S; Head; 4545; Yes; Yes; Al. 7331 An. 4532

4617; Mills (Red Bear), Alice; F; 1899-34; plus 1/4; Wd; Head; 4546; Yes; Yes; Al. 89 An. 4534

4618; Mills, Freda; F; 2/22/23-9; 1/4; S; Daughter; 4547; Yes; Yes; Id. U-11227 An. 4535

4619; Mills, Norma; F; 2/24/28-4; 1/4; S; Daughter; 4548; Yes; Yes; Id. U-12582 An. none

4620; Water, Georgette; F; 5/12/31-10/12; 1/4; S; Daughter; ---; Yes; Yes; U-14112

4621; Mills, Walter; M; 1903-29; 1/4; M; Head; 4549; Yes; Yes; Al. 344 An. 4537

4622; Mills (Robideaux), Gertrude; F; 1907-25; 1/4; M; Wife; 4551; Yes; Yes; Al. 4772 An. 5841

4623; Mills, Marcella; F; 7/1/23-9; 1/4; S; Daughter; 4550; Yes; Yes; Id. U-14042 An. 4539

4624; Mills (Standing Bear), Ora; F; 1904-28; plus 1/4; Wd; Head; 4552; No; Cheyenne, city, Laramie, Wyo.; Yes; Al. 5059 An. 4538

4625; Millspaugh (Moore), Evaline; F; 1906-26; plus 1/4; M; Head; 4576; Yes; Yes; Al. 2504 An. 4566

4626; Moccasin Top, Job; M; 1896-36; F; M; Head; 4553; Yes; Yes; Al. 7822 An. 4540

4627; Moccasin Top (Iron Bull), Louisa; F; 1885-47; F; M; Wife; 4554; Yes; Yes; Al. 3536 An. 7390

4628; Moccasin Top (no data), Nellie; F; 1852-80; F; Wd; Head; 4555; Yes; Yes; Al. 7811 An. 4541

4629; Moccasin Top, Oscar; M; 1887-45; F; S; Head; 4556; Yes; Yes; Al. 5406 An. 4542

Census of the **Pine Ridge** reservation of the **Pine Ridge, South Dakota** jurisdiction, as of **April 1**, 19**32**, taken by **James H. McGregor**, Superintendent.

Key: Number; Surname, Given; Sex; Date of Birth-Age at Last Birthday; Tribe (Oglala Sioux, unless stated otherwise); Degree of Blood; Marital Status; Relationship to Head of Family [Last Census Roll Number]; At Jurisdiction Where Enrolled (Yes/No); (If no – Where); Ward (Yes/No, if given); Allotment, Annuity and Identification Numbers (if given).

4630; Moeller (Marshall), Jennie; F; 1891-41; plus 1/4; Wd; Head; 4557; Yes; Yes; Al. 4529 An. 4543

4631; Moeller, Sallie; F; 5/29/12-19; 1/4; S; Daughter; 4558; Yes; Yes; Id. U-10026 An. 4544

4632; Moeller, Mary E; F; 11/4/16-15; plus 1/4; S; Daughter; 4559; Yes; Yes; Id. U-10027 An. 4545

4633; Moeller, Emery D; M; 8/15/19-12; 1/4; S; Son; 4560; Yes; Yes; Id. U-10028 An. 4546

4634; Moeller, Tilly; F; 5/7/23-8; 1/4; S; Daughter; 4561; Yes; Yes; Id. U-13069 An. 4547

4635; Moeller, Moroni J; M; 7/30/26-5; 1/4; S; Son; 4562; Yes; Yes; Id. U-13171 An. none

4636; Monroe, Aloysius; M; 1893-39; 1/4; S; Head; 4563; Yes; Yes; Al. 2320 An. 4548

4637; Monroe, John; M; 1870-62; Plus 1/4; M; Head; 4564; Yes; Yes; Al. 2318 An. 4549

4638; Monroe (no data), Sophia; F; 1865-67; 1/4; M; Wife; 4565; Yes; Yes; Al. 2319 An. 4550

4639; Monroe, William; M; 1901-31; 1/4; M; Head; 4566; Yes; Yes; Al. 2323 An. 4553

N.E.: Monroe (Howard), Minnie; F; ------; Rosebud Sioux; 1/4; M; Wife;

4640; Monroe, Mark W; M; 10/5/30-1; 1/4; S; Son; 4567; Yes; Yes; Id. U-13654 An. none

4641; Montileaux (no data), Julia; F; 1881-51; 1/4; Wd; Head; 4568; Yes; No; Al. 3571 An. 4557

4642; Montileaux, Wesley; M; 9/5/11-20; 1/4; S; Son; 4569; Yes; Yes; Al. 7223 An. 4560

4643; Montileaux, Bert; M; 5/20/16-15; 1/4; S; Son; 4570; Yes; Yes; Al. 8075 An. 4561

4644; Montileaux, Emma; F; 1/14/18-14; 1/4; S; Daughter; 4571; Yes; Yes; Id. U-10031 An. 4562

4645; Montileaux, Floyd; M; 1/1/21-11; 1/4; S; Son; 4572; Yes; Yes; Id. U-10032 An. 4563

4646; Montileaux, Della; F; 4/6/24-7; 1/4; S; Daughter; 4573; Yes; Yes; Id. U-11320 An. 4564

4647; Montileaux, Joseph; M; 11/10/08-23; 1/4; S; Head; 4574; Yes; Yes; Al. 3576 An. 4559

Census of the **Pine Ridge** reservation of the **Pine Ridge, South Dakota** jurisdiction, as of **April 1**, 1932, taken by **James H. McGregor**, Superintendent.

Key: Number; Surname, Given; Sex; Date of Birth-Age at Last Birthday; Tribe (Oglala Sioux, unless stated otherwise); Degree of Blood; Marital Status; Relationship to Head of Family [Last Census Roll Number]; At Jurisdiction Where Enrolled (Yes/No); (If no – Where); Ward (Yes/No, if given); Allotment, Annuity and Identification Numbers (if given).

4648; Monto, Enoch; M; 1876-56; 1/4; M; Head; 4575; Yes; Yes; Al. 4191 An. 4565

~~N.E.: Monto (Bonser), Clara; F; ------; Rosebud Sioux; 1/4; M; Wife;~~

4649; Moore, Della; F; 1907-25; 1/4; S; Head; 4577; No; Phoenix, city, Maricopa, Ariz.; Yes; Al. 2501 An. 4569

4650; Moore, Norval; M; 1901-31; 1/4; M; Head; 4578; Yes; Yes; Al. 2501 An. 4573

4651; Moore (Provost), Mary; F; 1905-27; 1/4; M; Wife; 4579; Yes; Yes; Al. 2342 An. 4571

4652; Moore, Norma; F; 5/21/22-9; 1/4; S; Daughter; 4580; Yes; Yes; Id. U-11012 An. 4572

4653; Moore, Norval L; M; 5/27/26-5; 1/4; S; Son; 4581; Yes; Yes; Id. U-12633 An. none

4654; Moore, Henry; M; 4/23/28-3; 1/4; S; Son; 4582; Yes; Yes; Id. U-12634 An. none

4655; Moore, Oliver F; M; 4/25/18-13; 1/4; S; Ward; 4583; Yes; Yes; Id. U-10033 An. 4570

4656; Moore, Mary A; F; 4/11/31-11/12; 1/4; S; Daughter; ---; Yes; Yes; U-13811

4657; Moore, William; M; 1902-30; 1/4; M; Head; 4584; Yes; Yes; Al. 2502 An. 4574

4658; Moore (Condelario), Lucinda; F; 3/6/08-24; 1/4; M; Wife; 4585; Yes; Yes; Al. 4952 An. 1583

4659; Moore, Willard; M; 3/17/29-3; 1/4; S; Son; 4586; Yes; Yes; Id. U-13343 An. none

4660; Moore, Oliver D; M; 7/25/30-1; 1/4; S; Son; 4587; Yes; Yes; Id. U-13702 An. none

4661; Moose, Paul; M; 1873-59; F; M; Head; 4588; Yes; Yes; Al. 354 An. 4575

4662; Moose (no data), Grace; F; 1876-56; plus 1/4; M; Wife; 4589; Yes; Yes; Al. 5548 An. 4576

4663; Moose, Abraham; M; 2/26/10-22; 1/4; S; Son; 4590; Yes; Yes; Al. 6950 An. 4578

4664; Moose, Cecelia; F; 1/27/20-12; 1/4; S; Daughter; 4592; Yes; Yes; Id. U-10034 An. 4580

4665; Moose, Charles; M; 11/4/12-19; 1/4; S; Son; 4591; Yes; Yes; Al. 6950 An. 4579

4666; Morejon (Corn), Emma; F; 1886-46; 1/4; M; Head; 4593; No; New York, city, City, N.Y.; Yes; Al. 405 An. 1636

Census of the __Pine Ridge__ reservation of the __Pine Ridge, South Dakota__ jurisdiction, as of __April 1__, 1932, taken by __James H. McGregor__, Superintendent.

Key: Number; Surname, Given; Sex; Date of Birth-Age at Last Birthday; Tribe (Oglala Sioux, unless stated otherwise); Degree of Blood; Marital Status; Relationship to Head of Family [Last Census Roll Number]; At Jurisdiction Where Enrolled (Yes/No); (If no – Where); Ward (Yes/No, if given); Allotment, Annuity and Identification Numbers (if given).

4667; Morgan (Green), Viola; F; 1899-33; -1/4; M; Head; 4594; No; Seminole, town, Okla.; Yes; Al. 7751 An. 4581

4668; Morgan, Norma; F; 6/3/18-13; -1/4; S; Daughter; 4595; No; Same; Yes; Id. U-10035 An. 4582

4669; Morgan, Mary I; F; 7/24/20-11; -1/4; S; Daughter; 4596; No; Seminole, town, Okla.; Yes; Id. U-10036 An. 4583

4670; Morgan (Merrival), Keva; F; 1893-39; plus 1/4; M; Head; 4597; No; Hay Springs, town, Sheridan, Nebr.; Yes; Al. 314 An. 4249

4671; Beuch, Madeline; F; 1/3/17-15; -1/4; S; Daughter; 4598; No; Same; Yes; Id. U-9138 An. 4250

4672; Looking Elk, Lester; M; 10/22/19-12; -1/4; S; Son; 4599; No; Same; Yes; Id. U-9955 An. 4251

4673; Looking Elk, Norwood; M; 12/29/22-9; -1/4; S; Son; 4600; No; Same; Yes; Id. U-11483 An. 4252

4674; Morgan, Duane; M; 2/27/28-4; -1/4; S; Son; 4601; No; Same; Yes; Id. U-12522 An. none

4675; Morgan, Delmer; M; 9/17/29-2; -1/4; S; Son; 4602; No; Same; Yes; Id. U-13344 An. none

4676; Morgan, Kenneth; M; 1/9/32-2/12; -1/4; S; Son; ---; No; Same; Yes; U-14066

4677; Morrisette, Dawson; M; 1901-31; plus1/4; M; Head; 4603; Yes; Yes; Al. 4864 An. 1384

4678; Morrisette (Knife)(Red Owl), Bessie; F; 1902-30; F; M; Wife; 4604; Yes; Yes; Al. 1370 An. 5517

4679; Knife, Maxine; F; 7/31/28-3; F; S; S. Daughter; 4605; Yes; Yes; Id. U-12759 An. none

4680; Morrisette (no data), Lucy; F; 1869-63; F; M; Head; 4607; Yes; Yes; Al. 6102 An. 4585

4681; Morrisette, James; M; 12/25/12-19; plus 1/4; S; Son; 4608; Yes; Yes; Id. U-10037 An. none

4682; Morrison, Albert; M; 1890-42; 1/4; M; Head; 4609; Yes; Yes; Al. 3844 An. 4587

N.E.: Morrison (Two Horse) or Quigley, Anna; F; -------; Rosebud Sioux; 1/4; M; Wife;

4683; Morrrison[sic], William; M; 6/5/18-13; 1/4; S; Son; 4610; Yes; Yes; Id. U-10038 An. 4588

4684; Morrison, Charles; M; 1892-40; 1/4; M; Head; 4611; Yes; Yes; Al. 243 An. 4589

Census of the **Pine Ridge** reservation of the **Pine Ridge, South Dakota** jurisdiction, as of **April 1**, 19**32**, taken by **James H. McGregor**, Superintendent.

Key: Number; Surname, Given; Sex; Date of Birth-Age at Last Birthday; Tribe (Oglala Sioux, unless stated otherwise); Degree of Blood; Marital Status; Relationship to Head of Family [Last Census Roll Number]; At Jurisdiction Where Enrolled (Yes/No); (If no – Where); Ward (Yes/No, if given); Allotment, Annuity and Identification Numbers (if given).

4685; Morrison (Short Bear), Nettie; F; 1892-40; 1/4; M; Wife; 4612; Yes; Yes; Al. 5231 An. 4590

4686; Morrison, Carl; M; 4/24/14-17; plus 1/4; S; Son; 4613; Yes; Yes; Al. 8154 An. 4591

4687; Morrison, Aloysius; M; 11/1/16-15; 1/4; S; Son; 4614; Yes; Yes; Id. U-10040 An. 4593

4688; Morrison, Elmer; M; 11/23/19-12; 1/4; S; Son; 4615; Yes; Yes; Id. U-10042 An. 4595

4689; Morrison, Rebecca; F; 2/22/22-10; 1/4; S; Daughter; 4616; Yes; Yes; Id. U-10842 An. 4596

4690; Morrison, Ethel; F; 4/11/23-8; 1/4; S; Daughter; 4617; Yes; Yes; Id. U-13092 An. 4597

4691; Morrison, Roy G; M; 1/6/25-7; 1/4; S; Son; 4618; Yes; Yes; Id. U-11538 An. 4598

4692; Morrison, Mary A; F; 2/4/28-4; 1/4; S; Daughter; 4619; Yes; Yes; Id. U-12584 An. none

4693; Morrison, Rhoda; F; 8/2/29-2; 1/4; S; Daughter; 4620; Yes; Yes; Id. U-13249 An. none

4694; Morrison, Russell; M; 7/1/31-9/12; 1/4; S; Son; ---; Yes; Yes; U-13871

4695; Morrison, George G; M; 3/3/07-25; 1/4; S; Head; 4621; Yes; Yes; Al. 4929 An. 4600

4696; Morrison (no data), Lucy; F; 1870-62; F; M; Wife; 4623; Yes; Yes; Al. 4251 An. 4607

4697; Morrison, Bennie; M; 4/6/12-19; plus 1/4; S; Son; 4624; Yes; Yes; Al. 7047 An. 4608

4698; Morrison, James; M; 1899-33; 1/4; M; Head; 4625; Yes; Yes; Al. 5501 An. 4609

4699; Morrison (Salway), Alice; F; 1901-31; 1/4; M; Wife; 4626; Yes; Yes; Al. 5518 An. 4610

4700; Morrison, Roland; M; 1/26/23-9; 1/4; S; Son; 4627; Yes; Yes; Id. U-13081 An. 4611

4701; Morrison, Vincent M; M; 7/10/26-5; 1/4; S; Son; 4628; Yes; Yes; Id. U-12116 An. none

4702; Morrison, James Jr.; M; 4/17/29-2; 1/4; S; Son; 4629; Yes; Yes; Id. U-12145 An. none

4703; Morrison, Martina; F; 12/14/31-3/12; 1/4; S; Daughter; ---; Yes; Yes; U-14101

4704; Morrison, John; M; 1890-42; plus 1/4; Wd; Head; 4630; Yes; Yes; Al. 242 An. 4612

Census of the **Pine Ridge** reservation of the **Pine Ridge, South Dakota** jurisdiction, as of **April 1**, 19**32**, taken by **James H. McGregor**, Superintendent.

Key: Number; Surname, Given; Sex; Date of Birth-Age at Last Birthday; Tribe (Oglala Sioux, unless stated otherwise); Degree of Blood; Marital Status; Relationship to Head of Family [Last Census Roll Number]; At Jurisdiction Where Enrolled (Yes/No); (If no – Where); Ward (Yes/No, if given); Allotment, Annuity and Identification Numbers (if given).

4705; Morrison, Joseph; M; 1885-47; 1/4; M; Head; 4631; Yes; Yes; Al. 1690 An. 4614

4706; Morrison (Yankton), Helena; F; 1887-45; F; M; Wife; 4632; Yes; Yes; Al. 1744 An. 4615

4707; Morrison, Charley; M; 1/28/18-14; plus 1/4; S; Son; 4633; Yes; Yes; Id. U-10044 An. 4618

4708; Morrison, Clifford; M; 7/5/28-3; 1/4; S; Son; 4634; Yes; Yes; Id. U-12743 An. none

4709; Morrison, Peter; M; 1858-74; 1/4; M; Head; 4635; Yes; Yes; Al. 5497 An. 4623

4710; Morrison (no data), Wing; F; 1855-77; F; M; Wife; 4636; Yes; Yes; Al. 5498 An. 4624

4711; Mortensen (no data), Ida; F; 1/8/70-62; 1/4; M; Head; 4637[sic]; Yes; Yes; Id. U-13849

N.E.: ~~Mountain, Moses; M; -------; Cheyenne Sioux; plus 1/4; M; Head;~~

4712; Mountain (Morisette), Edith; F; 12/7/09-22; plus 1/4; M; Wife; 4637; Yes; Yes; Al. 4865 An. 1383

4713; Mountain, Jennet; F; 2/20/28-4; 1/4; S; Daughter; 4638; Yes; Yes; Id. U-12523 An. none

4714; Mountain, Joseph R; M; 9/18/30-1; 1/4; S; Son; 4639; Yes; Yes; Id. U-13703 An. none

4715; Mountain Sheep, ---; M; 1867-65; F; M; Head; 4640; Yes; Yes; Al. 3501 An. 4626

4716; Mountain Sheep (no data), Millie; F; 1871-61; F; M; Wife; 4641; Yes; Yes; Al. 3502 An. 4627

4717; Mousseau, Alex; M; 1856-76; plus 1/4; M; Head; 4642; Yes; Yes; Al. 695 An. 4631

4718; Medicine Woman, ---; F; 1860-72; F; M; Wife; 4643; Yes; Yes; Al. 5790 An. 4632

4719; Mousseau, Robert; M; 9/9/15-16; plus 1/4; S; Ward; 4644; Yes; Yes; Al. 8072 An. 5977

4720; Mousseau, David; M; 9/13/11-20; 1/4; S; Head; 4645; Yes; Yes; Al. 5959 An. 4635

4721; Mousseau, Gilbert; M; 1903-29; 1/4; S; Head; 4646; Yes; Yes; Al. 2213 An. 4636

Census of the **Pine Ridge** reservation of the **Pine Ridge, South Dakota** jurisdiction, as of **April 1**, 19**32**, taken by **James H. McGregor**, Superintendent.

Key: Number; Surname, Given; Sex; Date of Birth-Age at Last Birthday; Tribe (Oglala Sioux, unless stated otherwise); Degree of Blood; Marital Status; Relationship to Head of Family [Last Census Roll Number]; At Jurisdiction Where Enrolled (Yes/No); (If no – Where); Ward (Yes/No, if given); Allotment, Annuity and Identification Numbers (if given).

4722; Mousseau, James Sr.; M; 1872-60; 1/4; M; Head; 4647; Yes; No; Al. 2206 An. 4637

4723; Mousseau (Lone Wolf), Rosa; F; 1872-60; F; M; Wife; 4648; Yes; Yes; Al. 2207 An. 4638

4724; Mousseau, James Jr.; M; 4/8/07-24; plus 1/4; S*M*; Head; 4649; Yes; Yes; Al. 2211 An. 4369

4725; Mousseau, James; M; 1/7/10-22; plus 1/4; S; Head; 4650; Yes; Yes; Al. 4539 An. 4634

4726; Mousseau, Jennie; F; 1902-30; 1/4; S; Head; 4651; Yes; Yes; Al. 703 An. 4640

4727; Mousseau, Joseph Sr.; M; 1865-67; 1/4; M; Head; 4652; Yes; No; Al. 2326 An. 4641

4728; Mousseau, Richard Jr.; M; 12/4/13-18; 1/4; S; Gr. Son; 4653; Yes; Yes; Id. U-10047 An. 4643

4729; Mousseau, Joseph; M; 1893-39; plus 1/4; S; Head; 4654; Yes; Yes; Al. 1858 An. 4644

4730; Mousseau, Louis C; M; 4/24/08-23; 1/4; M; Head; 4655; Yes; Yes; Al. 5957 An. 4633

4731; Mousseau (Rouillard), Isabell; F; 9/25/10-21; 1/4; M; Wife; 4656; Yes; Yes; Al. 6176 An. 5848

4732; Mousseau, Louis Jr.; M; 5/30/28-3; 1/4; S; Son; 4657; Yes; Yes; Id. U-12660 An. none

4733; Mousseau, Rebecca; F; 3/18/30-2; 1/4; S; Daughter; 4658; Yes; Yes; Id. U-13420 An. none

4734; Mousseau, Louis P Sr.; M; 1870-62; 1/4; M; Head; 4659; Yes; No; Al. 1856 An. 4645

4735; Mousseau (Broken Leg), Lucy; F; 1872-60; 1/4; M; Wife; 4660; Yes; Yes; Al. 1862 An. 4646

4736; Mousseau, Louis Jr.; M; 1894-38; 1/4; M; Head; 4661; Yes; No; Al. 1859 An. 4647

4737; Mousseau (Bad Iron), Winnie; F; 1900-32; 1/4; M; Wife; 4662; Yes; Yes; Al. 5254 An. 4648

4738; Mousseau, Daniel; M; 8/15/17-14; plus 1/4; S; Son; 4663; Yes; Yes; Id. U-10048 An. 4649

Census of the   **Pine Ridge**   reservation of the **Pine Ridge, South Dakota** jurisdiction, as of   **April 1**   , 19**32**, taken by   **James H. McGregor**   , Superintendent.

Key: Number; Surname, Given; Sex; Date of Birth-Age at Last Birthday; Tribe (Oglala Sioux, unless stated otherwise); Degree of Blood; Marital Status; Relationship to Head of Family [Last Census Roll Number]; At Jurisdiction Where Enrolled (Yes/No); (If no – Where); Ward (Yes/No, if given); Allotment, Annuity and Identification Numbers (if given).

4739; Mousseau, Zouie; F; 5/2/19-12; 1/4; S; Daughter; 4664; Yes; Yes; Id. U-10049 An. 4650

4740; Mousseau, Alexander; M; 5/17/22-9; 1/4; S; Son; 4665; Yes; Yes; Id. U-10990 An. 4651

4741; Mousseau, Raymond; M; 6/20/25-6; 1/4; S; Son; 4666; Yes; Yes; Id. U-12448 An. none

4742; Mousseau, Maglorie; M; 1892-40; plus 1/4; M; Head; 4667; Yes; Yes; Al. 2329 An. 4652

N.E.: Mousseau (Wooden Ring), Esther; F; -------; Rosebud Sioux; M; Wife; Yes;

4743; Mousseau, Mathiss; M; 2/24/30-2; plus 1/4; S; Son; 4668/; Yes; Yes; Id. U-13517 An. none

4744; Mousseaum[sic], Paul; M; 1903-29; 1/4; M; Head; 4669; Yes; Yes; Al. 2212 An. 4653

4745; Mousseaum[sic] (Iron Crow), Anna; F; 1904-28; F; M; Wife; 4670; Yes; Yes; Al. 5875 An. 3168

4746; Iron Crow, Garfield; M; 4/9/22-9; F; S; S Son; 4671; Yes; Yes; Id. U-12008 An. 3169

4747; Moves Camp, ---; M; 1870-62; F; M; Head; 4672; Yes; Yes; Al. 1818 An. 4654

4748; Moves Camp (Running Horse), Lizzie; F; 1862-70; F; M; Wife; 4673; Yes; Yes; Al. 3683 An. 4655

4749; Moves Camp, Nora; F; 5/24/14-17; F; S; Daughter; 4674; Yes; Yes; Id. U-9543 An. 4656

4750; Moves Camp, Samuel; M; 1894-38; F; M; Head; 4675; Yes; Yes; Al. 1887 An. 4657

4751; Moves Camp (Iron Rope), Winnie; F; 1892-40; F; M; Wife; 4676; Yes; Yes; Al. 1999 An. 4658

4752; Moves Camp, Bernard; M; 6/22/11-20; F; S; Son; 4677; Yes; Yes; Al. 5810 An. 4659

4753; Moves Camp, Annie; F; 5/4/14-17; F; S; Daughter; 4678; Yes; Yes; Al. 7722 An. 4660

4754; Moves Camp, Mary; F; 12/24/16-15; F; S; Daughter; 4679; Yes; Yes; Id. U-10053 An. 4661

4755; Moves Camp, Dick; M; 5/18/19-12; F; S; Son; 4680; Yes; Yes; Id. U-10054 An. 4662

4756; Moves Camp, James; M; 7/1/25-6; F; S; Son; 4681; Yes; Yes; Id. U-11648 An. none

4757; Moves Camp, Marian; F; 4/14/31-11/12; F; S; Daughter; ---; Yes; Yes; U-13812

Census of the **Pine Ridge** reservation of the **Pine Ridge, South Dakota** jurisdiction, as of **April 1**, 19**32**, taken by **James H. McGregor**, Superintendent.

Key: Number; Surname, Given; Sex; Date of Birth-Age at Last Birthday; Tribe (Oglala Sioux, unless stated otherwise); Degree of Blood; Marital Status; Relationship to Head of Family [Last Census Roll Number]; At Jurisdiction Where Enrolled (Yes/No); (If no – Where); Ward (Yes/No, if given); Allotment, Annuity and Identification Numbers (if given).

4758; McCabe (Kelly), Clara; F; 1880-52; 1/4; M; Head; 4684; No; Cheyenne, city, Laramie, Wyo.; No; Al. 4141 An. 4665

4759; McConnell (O'Rourke), Pansy; F; 2/21/08-24; 1/4; M; Head; 4685; No; Rapid City, city, Pennington, S.D.; Yes; Al. 7267 An. 4835

4760; McConnell, Clifford; M; 1/20/30-2; 1/4; S; Son; 4686; No; Same; Yes; Id. U-13366 An. none

4761; McConnell, Beverly; F; 9/26/31-6/12; 1/4; S; Daughter; ---; No; Same; Yes; U-13996

4762; McGaa, Albert; M; 1888-44; 1/4; Wd; Head; 4687; No; Kennebec, town, Lyman, S.D.; No; Al. 2996 An. 4666

4763; McGaa (Davidson), Anna; F; 1889-43; 1/4; Wd; Head; 4688; Yes; No; Al. 1620 An. 4667

4764; McGaa, Roy; M; 12/22/09-22; 1/4; S; Son; 4689; Yes; Yes; Al. 7530 An. 4668

4765; McGaa, Louis; M; 9/26/15-15; 1/4; S; Son; 4690; Yes; Yes; Id. U-10056 An. 4669

4766; McGaa, Denver; M; 1902-30; 1/4; S; Head; 4691; Yes; Yes; Al. 2999 An. 4671

4767; McGaa, George L; M; 1893-39; plus 1/4; M; Head; 4692; Yes; Yes; Al. 2998 An. 4672

4768; McGaa, Harold; M; 5/14/22-9; plus 1/4; S; Son; 4693; Yes; Yes; Id. U-12871 An. none

4769; McGaa (Pouier), Mary P; F; 1884-48; 1/4; Wd; Head; 4694; Yes; Yes; Al. 2995 An. 4675

4770; McGaa, Isadore; F; 4/11/12-19; 1/4; S; Daughter; 4695; Yes; Yes; Al. 7407 An. 4678

4771; McGaa, Leona; F; 12/11/15-16; 1/4; S; Daughter; 4696; Yes; Yes; Id. U-10055 An. 4679

4772; McGaa, Hazel; F; 1/11/10-22; 1/4; S; Head; 4697; Yes; Yes; Al. 7528 An. 4677

4773; McGaa, Raymond; M; 9/25/11-20; 1/4; S; Head; 4698; Yes; Yes; Al. 7529 An. 3088

4774; McGaa, William Jr.; M; 1882-50; 1/4; M; Head; 4699; Yes; No; Al. 2674 An. 4680

4775; McGaa (Russell), Julia; F; 1893-39; 1/4; M; Wife; 4700; Yes; No; Al. 2745 An. 4681

Census of the ___**Pine Ridge**___ reservation of the ___**Pine Ridge, South Dakota**___ jurisdiction, as of ___**April 1**___, 19**32**, taken by ___**James H. McGregor**___, Superintendent.

Key: Number; Surname, Given; Sex; Date of Birth-Age at Last Birthday; Tribe (Oglala Sioux, unless stated otherwise); Degree of Blood; Marital Status; Relationship to Head of Family [Last Census Roll Number]; At Jurisdiction Where Enrolled (Yes/No); (If no – Where); Ward (Yes/No, if given); Allotment, Annuity and Identification Numbers (if given).

4776; McGaa, Albert; M; 2/1/11-21; 1/4; S; Son; 4701; Yes; Yes; Al. 7358 An. 4682

4777; McGaa, Mildred; F; 4/14/12-19; 1/4; S; Daughter; 4702; Yes; Yes; Al. 7359 An. 4683

4778; McGaa, Corbin; M; 11/6/13-18; 1/4; S; Son; 4703; Yes; Yes; Al. 7360 An. 4684

4779; McGaa, Russell; M; 3/25/17-15; 1/4; S; Son; 4704; Yes; Yes; Id. U-10057 An. 4686

4780; McGaa, Bernice; F; 3/25/19-13; plus 1/4; S; Daughter; 4705; Yes; Yes; Id. U-10058 An. 4687

4781; McGaa, Lavina; F; 5/5/24-7; plus 1/4; S; Daughter; 4706; Yes; Yes; Id. U-11347 An. 4688

4782; McGaa, Orion; F; 8/25/21-10; 1/4; S; Daughter; 4707; Yes; Yes; Id. U-11348 An. 4689

4783; McGaa, Aldine; F; 11/28/28-3; 1/4; S; Daughter; 4708; Yes; Yes; Id. U-13456 An. none

4784; McGaa, DeWayne; M; 10/2/26-5; 1/4; S; Son; 4709; Yes; Yes; Id. U-13457 An. 4686

4785; McGaa, William; M; 7/1/31-8/12; 1/4; S; Son; ---; Yes; Yes; U-13897

4786; McGrew (Dixon), Ruth; F; 1903-29; 1/4; M; Head; 4710; No; Gordon, town, Sheridan, Nebr.; Yes; Al. 413 An. 4690

4787; McGrew, Glen; M; 4/3/23-9; 1/4; S; Son; 4711; No; Same; Yes; Id. U-11631 An. 4691

4788; McGrew, Virginia; F; 10/15/24-7; 1/4; S; Daughter; 4712; No; Same; Yes; Id. U-11801 An. none

N.E.: Mc Lane, David; M; -------; Rosebud Sioux; 1/4; M; Head;

4789; Mc Lane (Provost), Gertrude (Maude); F; 4/7/12-19; plus1/4; M; Wife; 5214; No; Rapid City, city, Pennington, S.D.; Yes; Al. 6811 An. 5179

4790; Mc Lane, Gladys; F; 4/16/31-11/12; plus1/4; S; Daughter; ---; No; Same; Yes; U-14102

4791; McNeil (Ingersol), Sarah; F; 1865-67; 1/4; S; Head; 4716; No; Somewhere in Canada; ; Yes; Al. 7188 An. 4694

4792; McWilliams, Benj.; M; 1887-45; -1/4; M; Head; 4717; Yes; Yes; Al. 1347 An. 4696

4793; Nelson, Charles; M; 1901-31; plus 1/4; M; Head; 4718; Yes; No; Al. 5211 An. 4698

4794; Nelson (Yellow Hawk), Susie; F; 1904-28; F; M; Wife; 4719; Yes; Yes; Al. 4811 An. 4699

Census of the **Pine Ridge** reservation of the **Pine Ridge, South Dakota** jurisdiction, as of **April 1**, 19**32**, taken by **James H. McGregor**, Superintendent.

Key: Number; Surname, Given; Sex; Date of Birth-Age at Last Birthday; Tribe (Oglala Sioux, unless stated otherwise); Degree of Blood; Marital Status; Relationship to Head of Family [Last Census Roll Number]; At Jurisdiction Where Enrolled (Yes/No); (If no – Where); Ward (Yes/No, if given); Allotment, Annuity and Identification Numbers (if given).

4795; Nelson, Peter; M; 4/22/22-9; plus 1/4; S; Son; 4720; Yes; Yes; Id. U-10975 An. 4700

4796; Nelson, Narcisse; M; 2/11/27-5; 1/4; S; Son; 4721; Yes; Yes; Id. U-12324 An. none

4797; Nelson, Florine; F; 1/16/31-1; 1/4; S; Daughter; 4722; Yes; Yes; Id. U-13704 An. none

4798; Nelson, Francis; M; 1895-37; plus 1/4; M; Head; 4723; Yes; No; Al. 5220 An. 4701

N.E.: Nelson (Bird), Bessie; F; ------; Flandreau Sioux; M; Wife;

4799; Nelson, Frances; F; 1873-59; F; M; Head; 4724; Yes; No; Al. 6058 An. 4704

4800; Nelson, Emily; F; 12/3/13-18; plus 1/4; S; Daughter; 4725; Yes; Yes; Al. 7604 An. 4706

4801; Make Shine, Oliver; M; 9/5/22-9; 1/4; S; Ward; 4726; Yes; Yes; Id. U-11068 An. 4294

4802; Nelson, John; M; 1866-66; plus 1/4; M; Head; 4727; Yes; No; Al. 262 An. 4707

4803; Nelson (Janis), Lizzie; F; 1865-67; 1/4; M; Wife; 4728; Yes; Yes; Al. 2216 An. 4708

4804; Nelson (Milk), Lillian; F; 1904-28; F; Wd; Head; 4729; Yes; Yes; Al. 4556 An. 4505

4805; Nelson, Ruben; M; 3/24/24-8; F; S; Son; 4730; Yes; Yes; Id. U-11527 An. 4506

4806; Nelson, Daniel Jr; M; 6/10/30-1; F; S; Son; 4731; Yes; Yes; Id. U-13570 An. none

4807; Nelson, Patrick; M; 1898-34; plus 1/4; M; Head; 4732; Yes; No; Al. 5210 An. 4711

4808; Nelson (Little Hoop), Sallie; F; 1900-32; F; M; Wife; 4733; Yes; Yes; Al. 4545 An. 3964

4809; Nelson, Cecelia; F; 8/31/26-5; plus 1/4; S; Daughter; 4734; Yes; Yes; Id. U-12142 An. none

4810; Nelson, Delbert; M; 5/22/28-3; 1/4; S; Son; 4735; Yes; Yes; Id. U-12585 An. none

4811; Nelson, Sophia; F; 1/30/30-2; 1/4; S; Daughter; 4736; Yes; Yes; Id. U-13385 An. none

4812; Nelson, Samuel; M; 1890-42; 1/4; M; Head; 4737; Yes; No; Al. 2218 An. 4712

N.E.: Nelson (La Force), Mary; F; ------; Iroquois; F; M; Wife;

Census of the____**Pine Ridge**____reservation of the__**Pine Ridge, South Dakota**
jurisdiction, as of____**April 1**____, 19**32**, taken by____**James H. McGregor**____,
Superintendent.

Key: Number; Surname, Given; Sex; Date of Birth-Age at Last Birthday; Tribe (Oglala Sioux, unless stated otherwise); Degree of Blood; Marital Status; Relationship to Head of Family [Last Census Roll Number]; At Jurisdiction Where Enrolled (Yes/No); (If no – Where); Ward (Yes/No, if given); Allotment, Annuity and Identification Numbers (if given).

4813; Nelson, Annie; F; 6/8/15-16; 1/4; S; Daughter; 4738; Yes; Yes; Id. U-10064 An. 4713

4814; Nelson, Agnis; M; 5/9/17-14; 1/4; S; Son; 4739; Yes; Yes; Id. U-10065 An. 4714

4815; Nelson, Thomas; M; 1864-68; 1/4; M; Head; 4740; Yes; No; Al. 5188 An. 4715

4816; Nelson (Salway), Susie; F; 1877-55; 1/4; M; Wife; 4741; Yes; Yes; Al. 4189 An. 4716

4817; Nelson, William; M; 1888-44; 1/4; Wd; Head; 4742; Yes; No; Al. 2217 An. 4719

4818; Nelson, Henrietta; F; 4/5/15-16; 1/4; S; Daughter; 4743; Yes; Yes; Al. 8107 An. 4721

4819; Nelson, Marie; F; 11/26/16-15; 1/4; S; Daughter; 4744; Yes; Yes; Id. U-10061 An. 4722

4820; Nelson, Neville; M; 4/20/18-13; 1/4; S; Son; 4745; Yes; Yes; Id. U-10062 An. 4723

4821; Nelson, Cleveland; M; 6/22/20-11; 1/4; S; Son; 4746; Yes; Yes; Id. U-10063 An. 4724

4822; Nelson, Ida B; F; 12/19/22-9; 1/4; S; Daughter; 4747; Yes; Yes; Id. U-12076 An. 4725

N.E.: Never Miss A Shot, Abel; M; 1910-22; ------; Rosebud Sioux; F; M; Head;
4823; Never Miss A Shot (Two Lance), Elaine; F; 11/10/13-18; plus 1/4; M; Wife; 4760; No; Rosebud, S.D.; Yes; Id. U-10641 An. 7145

N.E.: Never Miss A Shot, Roger; M; ------; Rosebud Sioux; F; M; Head;
4824; Never Miss A Shot (Kills On Horse Back), Sallie; F; 1903-29; plus 1/4; M; Wife; 3163; Yes; Yes; Al. 2833 An. 3182

4825; Iron Elk, Mary; F; 11/17/25-6; 1/4; S; S. Daughter; 3164; Yes; Yes; Id. U-11767 An. none

N.E.: New, Thomas Jr.; M; ------; Rosebud Sioux; M; Head;
4826; New (Merrival), Pauline; F; 9/13/16-15; plus 1/4; M; Wife; ---; No; Rosebud, S.D.; Yes; Id. U-9999 An. 2366

4827; New Holy, Sadie; F; 1863-69; F; Wd; Head; 4749; Yes; Yes; Al. 7037 An. 4727

4828; New Holy, Frank; M; 1897-35; F; M; Head; 4750; Yes; Yes; Al. 6448 An. 4731

Census of the **Pine Ridge** reservation of the **Pine Ridge, South Dakota** jurisdiction, as of **April 1**, 19**32**, taken by **James H. McGregor**, Superintendent.

Key: Number; Surname, Given; Sex; Date of Birth-Age at Last Birthday; Tribe (Oglala Sioux, unless stated otherwise); Degree of Blood; Marital Status; Relationship to Head of Family [Last Census Roll Number]; At Jurisdiction Where Enrolled (Yes/No); (If no – Where); Ward (Yes/No, if given); Allotment, Annuity and Identification Numbers (if given).

4829; New Holy (Little Cloud), Blanche; F; 1899-33; F; M; Wife; 4751; Yes; Yes; Al. 4126 An. 4729

4830; New Holy, Milbea; F; 2/1/23-9; F; S; Daughter; 4752; Yes; Yes; Id. U-13044 An. 4730

4831; New Holy, Myrle; F; 4/23/27-4; F; S; Daughter; 4753; Yes; Yes; Id. U-12963 An. none

4832; New Holy, Joseph; M; 1893-39; F; m; Head; 4754; Yes; Yes; Al. 6447 An. 4731

4833; New Holy (Kills At Lodge), Julia; F; 1898-34; F; M; Wife; 4755; Yes; Yes; Al. 3422 An. 4732

4834; New Holy, Aloysius; M; 6/13/19-12; F; S; Son; 4756; Yes; Yes; Id. U-10070 An. 4733

4835; New Holy, Ambrose; M; 3/1/21-11; F; S; Son; 4757; Yes; Yes; Id. U-10071 An. 4734

4836; New Holy, Alice; F; 7/26/25-6; F; S; Daughter; 4758; Yes; Yes; Id. U-11722 An. none

4837; New Holy, Daniel; M; 10/26/29-2; F; S; Son; 4759; Yes; Yes; Id. U-13345 An. 4734

N.E.: Night Chase, Ernest; M; ———; Rosebud Sioux; F; M; Head;

4838; Night Chase (Yellow Wolf), Nancy (Sallie); F; 1899-33; F; M; Wife; 4761; Yes; Yes; Al. 1339 An. 4736

4839; No Belt, George; M; 1902-30; F; M; Head; 4762; Yes; Yes; Al. 628 An. 4738

4840; No Belt (One Feather), Julia; F; 1904-28; F; M; Wife; 4763; Yes; Yes; Al. 1328 An. 4800

4841; No Belt, Sarah; F; 3/24/27-5; F; S; Daughter; 4764; Yes; Yes; Id. U-12292 An. none

4842; No Belt, Paul; M; 1862-70; F; Wd; Head; 4765; Yes; Yes; Al. 627 An. 4739

4843; No Braid (no data), Julia; F; 1871-61; F; Wd; Head; 4766; Yes; Yes; Al. 2944 An. 4742

4844; No Braid, Charles; M; 1905-27; F; S; Head; 4767; Yes; Yes; Al. 6814 An. 4744

4845; No Braid, Oliver; M; 9/9/16-15; F; S; Alone; 5800; Yes; Yes; Al. 10072 An. 4746

Census of the **Pine Ridge** reservation of the **Pine Ridge, South Dakota** jurisdiction, as of **April 1**, 1932, taken by **James H. McGregor**, Superintendent.

Key: Number; Surname, Given; Sex; Date of Birth-Age at Last Birthday; Tribe (Oglala Sioux, unless stated otherwise); Degree of Blood; Marital Status; Relationship to Head of Family [Last Census Roll Number]; At Jurisdiction Where Enrolled (Yes/No); (If no – Where); Ward (Yes/No, if given); Allotment, Annuity and Identification Numbers (if given).

4846; No Fat (no data), Edna; F; 1857-75; F; Wd; Head; 4768; Yes; Yes; Al. 3112 An. 4750

4847; No Fat, Adam; M; 1879-53; F; M; Head; 4769; Yes; Yes; Al. 4026 An. 4751
4848; No Fat (Dreamer), Rosa; F; 1868-64; F; M; Wife; 4770; Yes; Yes; Al. 4027 An. 4752
4849; No Fat, Emma; F; 2/4/08-24; F; S; Daughter; 4771; Yes; Yes; Al. 6164 An. 4753
4850; Dreamer, Verbena; F; 10/3/29-2; F; S; Ward; 4772; Yes; Yes; Id. U-13287 An. none

4851; No Name, ---; F; 1858-74; F; Wd; Head; 4774; Yes; Yes; Al. 5127 An. 171

4852; No Neck, Peter; M; 1906-26; F; M; Head; 4775; Yes; Yes; Al. 2259 An. 177
4853; No Neck (Little Bull), Jessie; F; 9/12/12-19; F; M; Wife; 4776; Yes; Yes; Al. 7832 An. 3895
4854; No Neck, John; M; 6/12/30-1; F; S; Son; 4777; Yes; Yes; Id. U-13609 An. none
4855; No Neck, Lottie; F; 1/21/32-2/12; F; S; Daughter; ---; Yes; Yes; U-14132

4856; No Neck (Little Killer), Bessie; F; 1904-28; plus 1/4; M; Head; 4779; Yes; Yes; Al. 6613 An. 4757
4857; No Neck, Leroy; M; 7/2/25-6; 1/4; S; Son; 4780; Yes; Yes; Id. U-11696 An. none
4858; No Neck, Robert; M; 1/10/28-4; 1/4; S; Son; 4781; Yes; Yes; Id. U-12473 An. none

4859; Nose, ---; M; 1873-59; F; M; Head; 4783; Yes; Yes; Al. 6556 An. 4760
4860; Nose (no data), Ada; F; 1856-76; F; M; Wife; 4784; Yes; Yes; Al. 3804 An. 4761

4861; Not Help Him (no data), Jennie; F; 1874-58; F; Wd; Head; 4785; Yes; Yes; Al. 2845 An. 4764

4862; No Two Horns, Paul; M; 1884-48; Plus 1/4; M; Head; 4786; Yes; Yes; Al. 5524 An. 4766
N.E.: No Two Horns (Six Shooter), Maggie; F; ------; Rosebud Sioux; M; Wife;
4863; No Two Horns, Lawrence; M; 12/12/22-9; 1/4; S; Son; 4787; Yes; Yes; Id. U-11565 An. 4767
4864; No Two Horns, Luella; F; 3/14/27-5; 1/4; S; Daughter; 4788; Yes; Yes; Id. U-13191 An. none
4865; No Two Horns, Chris; M; 10/11/29-2; 1/4; S; Son; 4789; Yes; Yes; Id. U-13421 An. none

Census of the __Pine Ridge__ reservation of the __Pine Ridge, South Dakota__ jurisdiction, as of __April 1__, 19**32**, taken by __James H. McGregor__, Superintendent.

Key: Number; Surname, Given; Sex; Date of Birth-Age at Last Birthday; Tribe (Oglala Sioux, unless stated otherwise); Degree of Blood; Marital Status; Relationship to Head of Family [Last Census Roll Number]; At Jurisdiction Where Enrolled (Yes/No); (If no – Where); Ward (Yes/No, if given); Allotment, Annuity and Identification Numbers (if given).

4866; No Water, George; M; 1900-32; F; Wd; Head; 4790; Yes; Yes; Al. 6400 An. 4768

4867; No Water, Thomas; M; 1880-52; F; M; Head; 4791; Yes; Yes; Al. 6214 An. 4770

4868; No Water (Sword), Louisa; F; 1877-55; F; M; Wife; 4792; Yes; Yes; Al. 4161 An. 4771

4869; No Water, Eugene; M; 3/12/17-15; F; S; Son; 4793; Yes; Yes; Id. U-10076 An. 4774

4870; Old Eagle, James; M; 1899-33; F; M; Head; 4794; No; Cincinnati, city, Hamilton, Ohio; Yes; Al. 4093 An. 4775

4871; Old Hair (Brings) (Parts His Hair), Bessie; F; 1904-28; F; Wd; Head; 4795; Yes; Yes; Al. 1187 An. 4779

4872; Brings, Ernestine; F; 11/12/29-2; F; S; Daughter; 4796; Yes; Yes; Id. U-13373 An. none

4873; Old Horse, George; M; 1892-40; F; M; Head; 4797; Yes; Yes; Al. 2435 An. 4780

4874; Old Horse (Bull Bear), Julia; F; 1892-40; plus 1/4; M; Wife; 4798; Yes; Yes; Al. 4533 An. 1192

4875; Bull Bear, Moses; M; 2/28/15-17; 1/4; S; S. Son; 4799; Yes; Yes; Al. 8184 An. 1193

4876; Bull Bear, Helena; F; 1/27/17-15; 1/4; S; S. Daughter; 4800; Yes; Yes; Id. U-9287 An. 1194

4877; Bull Bear, Morris; M; 4/19-12; 1/4; S; S. Son; 4801; Yes; Yes; Id. U-9288 An. 1195

4878; Bull Bear, Lawrence; M; 4/24/21-10; 1/4; S; S. Son; 4802; Yes; Yes; Id. U-9289 An. 1196

4879; Bull Bear, Ethel M; F; 1/12/28-14; 1/4; S; S. Daughter; 4803; Yes; Yes; Id. U-10166 An. none

4880; Old Horse, Theodore; M; 8/28/30-1; 1/4; S; Son; 4804; Yes; Yes; Id. U-13572 An. none

4881; Old Horse, Ralph Sr.; M; 1862-70; F; M; Head; 4805; Yes; Yes; Al. 1756 An. 4781

4882; Old Horse (Little Wound), Belle; F; 1868-64; F; M; Wife; 4806; Yes; Yes; Al. 7799 An. 4782

4883; Old Horse, Ralph Jr.; M; 1897-35; F; M; Head; 4807; Yes; Yes; Al. 3778 An. 4783

Census of the __Pine Ridge__ reservation of the __Pine Ridge, South Dakota__ jurisdiction, as of __April 1__, 19**32**, taken by __James H. McGregor__, Superintendent.

Key: Number; Surname, Given; Sex; Date of Birth-Age at Last Birthday; Tribe (Oglala Sioux, unless stated otherwise); Degree of Blood; Marital Status; Relationship to Head of Family [Last Census Roll Number]; At Jurisdiction Where Enrolled (Yes/No); (If no – Where); Ward (Yes/No, if given); Allotment, Annuity and Identification Numbers (if given).

4884; Old Horse (Gets There First), Mabel; F; 1901-31; F; M; Wife; 4808; Yes; Yes; Al. 1492 An. 4784

4885; Old Horse, David; M; 9/4/20-11; F; S; Son; 4809; Yes; Yes; Id. U-10077 An. 4785

4886; Old Horse, Bertha; F; 1/26/22-10; F; S; Daughter; 4810; Yes; Yes; Id. U-10945 An. 4786

4887; Old Horse, Oliver; M; 11/11/27-4; F; S; Son; 4811; Yes; Yes; Id. U-12449 An. none

4888; Old Shield, Alfred; M; 1868-64; F; M; Head; 4812; Yes; Yes; Al. 483 An. 4789

4889; Old Shield (Two Bulls), Nellie; F; 1879-53; F; M; Wife; 4813; Yes; Yes; Al. 350 An. 4790

4890; Old Shield, John; M; 1895-37; F; M; Head; 4814; Yes; Yes; Al. 483 An. 4789

4891; Old Shield (Brave Heart), Mary; F; 1886-46; F; M; Wife; 4815; Yes; Yes; Al. 7391 An. 4792

4892; Old Shield, Ethel; F; 5/3/24-7; F; S; Daughter; 4816; Yes; Yes; Id. U-11258 An. 4794

N.E.: Old Shield (Abrams), ---; F; ------; Seneca; plus 1/4; Wd; Head;

4893; Old Shield, Wilson; M; 12/8/26-5; 1/4; S; Son; 4817; No; Olean, city, Chattaraugua, N.Y.; Yes; Id. U-12196 An. none

4894; One Bear, Samuel; M; 1877-55; F; Wd; Head; 4818; Yes; Yes; Al. 1428 An. 4797

4895; One Crow, James; M; 1893-39; F; S; Head; 4819; Yes; Yes; Al. 5421 An. 4798

4896; One Feather, Jackson; M; 1902-30; F; S; Head; 4820; Yes; Yes; Al. 1327 An. 4799

4897; One Feather, Moses; M; 1855-77; F; Wd; Head; 4821; Yes; Yes; Al. 4357 An. 4801

4898; One Feather, Moses; M; 1854-78; F; M; Head; 4822; Yes; Yes; Al. 1331 An. 4803

4899; Old Feather (Red Plume), Girl; F; 1852-80; F; M; Wife; 4823; Yes; Yes; Al. 1465 An. 4804

Census of the **Pine Ridge** reservation of the **Pine Ridge, South Dakota** jurisdiction, as of **April 1**, 1932, taken by **James H. McGregor**, Superintendent.

Key: Number; Surname, Given; Sex; Date of Birth-Age at Last Birthday; Tribe (Oglala Sioux, unless stated otherwise); Degree of Blood; Marital Status; Relationship to Head of Family [Last Census Roll Number]; At Jurisdiction Where Enrolled (Yes/No); (If no – Where); Ward (Yes/No, if given); Allotment, Annuity and Identification Numbers (if given).

4900; One Feather, William; M; 1881-51; F; M; Head; 4824; Yes; Yes; Al. 1326 An. 4805

4901; Old Feather, Isaac; M; 10/14/19-13; F; S; Son; 4826; Yes; Yes; Id. U-10081 An. 4809

4902; Old Feather, Enoch; M; 3/17/16-16; F; S; Son; 4827; Yes; Yes; Id. U-10080 An. 4810

4903; Oney (Craven), Minnie; F; 1903-29; Plus 1/4; M; Head; 4828; Yes; Yes; Al. 3797 An. 4811

4904; Oney, Maxine, F; 12/6/24-7; 1/4; S; Daughter; 4829; Yes; Yes; Id. U-11569 An. 4812

4905; Oney, Wilmar, M; 3/21/27-5; 1/4; S; Son; 4830; Yes; Yes; Id. U-12325 An. none

4906; O'Rourke, Charles; M; 1883-49; plus 1/4; M; Head; 4831; Yes; No; Al. 2916 An. 4813

4907; O'Rourke (no data), Lizzie; F; 1883-49; 1/4; M; Wife; 4832; Yes; No; Al. 2917 An. 4814

4908; O'Rourke, McCoy; M; 11/19/13-18; 1/4; S; Son; 4833; Yes; Yes; Al. 7712 An. 4816

4909; O'Rourke , Violet; F; 8/15/18-13; 1/4; S; Daughter; 4834; Yes; Yes; Id. U-10084 An. 4817

4910; O'Rourke; Louise; F; 11/1/08-23; 1/4; S; Head; 4835; Yes; Yes; Al. 7711 An. 4815

4911; O'Rourke, Jack; M; 1905-27; 1/4; S; Head; 4836; Yes; Yes; Al. 2918 An. 4819

4912; O'Rourke, John; M; 1894-38; 1/4; Wd; Head; 4837; Yes; No; Al. 1613 An. 4820

4913; O'Rourke , Barbara; F; 5/2/18-13; 1/4; S; ~~Son~~Daughter; 4838; Yes; Yes; Id. U-10087 An. 4822

4914; O'Rourke , Glesner; F; 11/4/19-12; 1/4; S; Daughter; 4839; Yes; Yes; Id. U-10088 An. 4823

4915; O'Rourke , Kenneth; M; 3/24/21-11; 1/4; S; Son; 4840; Yes; Yes; Id. U-10089 An. 4824

4916; O'Rourke , Kermit; M; 1/2/12/24[sic]-7; 1/4; S; Son; 4841; Yes; Yes; Id. U-11494 An. 4825

4917; O'Rourke , Laverne; M~~F~~; 12/29/22-9; 1/4; S; ~~Daughter~~Son; 4842; Yes; Yes; Id. U-12554 An. none

4918; O'Rourke , William; M; 5/20/27-4; 1/4; S; Son; 4843; Yes; Yes; Id. U-12555 An. none

Census of the **Pine Ridge** reservation of the **Pine Ridge, South Dakota** jurisdiction, as of **April 1**, 19**32**, taken by **James H. McGregor**, Superintendent.

Key: Number; Surname, Given; Sex; Date of Birth-Age at Last Birthday; Tribe (Oglala Sioux, unless stated otherwise); Degree of Blood; Marital Status; Relationship to Head of Family [Last Census Roll Number]; At Jurisdiction Where Enrolled (Yes/No); (If no – Where); Ward (Yes/No, if given); Allotment, Annuity and Identification Numbers (if given).

4919; O'Rourke, Samuel; M; 1888-44; plus 1/4; M; Head; 4844; Yes; No; Al. 1612 An. 4826

4920; O'Rourke (Shangreau), Pearl; F; 1894-38; 1/4; M; Wife; 4845; Yes; No; Al. 7226 An. 4827

4921; O'Rourke, Henry; M; 6/12/12-19; 1/4; S; Son; 4846; Yes; Yes; Al. 7228 An. 4829

4922; O'Rourke, Patrick; M; 8/5/17-14; 1/4; S; Son; 4847; Yes; Yes; Id. U-10085 An. 4830

4923; O'Rourke, Alvera; F; 8/6/20-11; 1/4; S; Daughter; 4848; Yes; Yes; Id. U-10086 An. 4831

4924; O'Rourke, Eleanora; F; 7/15/26-5; 1/4; S; Daughter; 4849; Yes; Yes; Id. U-12293 An. none

4925; O'Rourke, Delbert; M; 12/9/27-4; 1/4; S; Son; 4850; Yes; Yes; Id. U-12524 An. none

4926; O'Rourke, Robert L.; M; 12/29/30-1; 1/4; S; Son; 4851; Yes; Yes; Id. U-13705 An. none

4927; O'Rourke, Thomas; M; 1877-55; 1/4; M; Head; 4852; Yes; No; Al. 1607 An. 4833

4928; O'Rourke (no data), Rosa; F; 1875-57; 1/4; M; Wife; 4853; Yes; No; Al. 7265 An. 4834

4929; O'Rourke, Lloyd; M; 9/25/10-21; 1/4; S; Son; 4854; Yes; Yes; Al. 7268 An. 4836

4930; O'Rourke, Annie; F; 3/11/12-20; 1/4; S; Daughter; 4855; Yes; Yes; Al. 7269 An. 4837

4931; O'Rourke, Thomas L. (Lawrence); M; 2/15/14-18; 1/4; S; Son; 4856; Yes; Yes; Al. 7441 An. 4838

4932; Owen (Condelario), Marguerite; F; 1906-26; 1/4; M; Head; 4857; Yes; Yes; Al. 2104 An. 1579

4933; Drury, Keith; M; 12/5/27-4; 1/4; S; Son; 4858; Yes; Yes; Id. U-12819 An. none

4934; Drury, Harry; M; 9/26/29-2; 1/4; S; Son; 4859; Yes; Yes; Id. U-13778 An. none

4935; Owns Many Horses, William; M; 1870-62; F; M; Head; 4860; Yes; Yes; Al. 4892 An. 4840

4936; Owns Many Horses (Black Road), Maggie; F; 1880-52; F; M; Wife; 4861; Yes; Yes; Al. 3343 An. 4841

4937; Owns Many Horses, Edith, F; 2/3/16-16; F; S; Daughter; 4862; Yes; Yes; Id. U-10090 An. 4843

Census of the __**Pine Ridge**__ reservation of the __**Pine Ridge, South Dakota**__ jurisdiction, as of __**April 1**__, 19**32,** taken by __**James H. McGregor**__, Superintendent.

Key: Number; Surname, Given; Sex; Date of Birth-Age at Last Birthday; Tribe (Oglala Sioux, unless stated otherwise); Degree of Blood; Marital Status; Relationship to Head of Family [Last Census Roll Number]; At Jurisdiction Where Enrolled (Yes/No); (If no – Where); Ward (Yes/No, if given); Allotment, Annuity and Identification Numbers (if given).

4938; Pablo, Alex; M; 1885-47; plus 1/4; M; Head; 4864; Yes; Yes; Al. 353 An. 4844

4939; Pablo (Little Bald Eagle), Nancy; F; 1884-48; F; M; Wife; 4865; Yes; Yes; Al. 2316 An. 4845

4940; Pablo, Louis, M; 1906-26; 1/4; M; Head; 4868; Yes; Yes; Al. 2317 An. 4854

4941; Pablo (Pourier), Grace; F; 10/7/09-22; 1/4; M; Wife; 4869; Yes; Yes; Al. 6660 An. 5072

4942; Pacer, Joseph; M; 1898-34; F; M; Head; 4871; Yes; Yes; Al. 1137 An. 4852

4943; Pacer (Fast Thunder), Mary; F; 1893-39; F; M; Wife; 4872; Yes; Yes; Al. 4081 An. 4853

4944; Pacer, Vida; F; 3/25/30-2; F; S; Daughter; 4873; Yes; Yes; Id. U-13422 An. none

4945; Packed, Frank; M; 1889-43; F; M; Head; 4874; Yes; Yes; Al. 5991 An. 4856

4946; Packed (Charging Crow), Minnie; F; 1898-34; F; M; Wife; 4878; Yes; Yes; Al. 5284 An. 1399

4947; Packed, Rosa; F; 7/13/13-18; F; S; Daughter; 4875; Yes; Yes; Al. 7830 An. 4858

4948; Packed, Grace; F; 2/19/16-16; F; S; Daughter; 4876; Yes; Yes; Id. U-10094 An. 4859

4949; Packed, Riley; M; 8/8/19-12; F; S; Son; 4877; Yes; Yes; Id. U-10095 An. 4860

4950; Chief Bear, Joseph Jr.; M; 9/2/19-12; F; S; S. Son; 4879; Yes; Yes; Id. U-9333 An. 1400

4951; Chief Bear, Arena; F; 10/29/22-9; F; S; S. Daughter; 4880; Yes; Yes; Id. U-13070 An. 1401

4952; Chief Bear, Vera; F; 4/19/29-2; F; S; Daughter; 4882; Yes; Yes; Id. U-13172 An. none

4953; Chief Bear, Jennie; F; 4/5/25-6; F; S; Daughter; 4881; Yes; Yes; Id. U-11586 An. none

4954; Packed, Jacob; M; 1885-47; F; Wd; Head; 4883; Yes; Yes; Al. 3746 An. 4863

4955; Pain On Hip, Charles; M; 1889-43; F; ~~MD~~.; Head; 4884; Yes; Yes; Al. 1727 An. 4867

4956; Pain On Hip, Millie; F; 12/25/18-13; F; S; Daughter; 4885; Yes; Yes; Id. U-10096 An. 4869

4957; Pain On Hip, Charles Jr.; M; 1/3/28-4; F; S; Son; 4886; Yes; Yes; Id. U-12463 An. none

4958; Palmer (Dixon), Josephine; F; 1901-31; Plus 1/4; S; Head; 4887; No; Gordon, town, Sheridan, Nebr.; No; Al. 412 An. 1922

Census of the **Pine Ridge** reservation of the **Pine Ridge, South Dakota** jurisdiction, as of **April 1**, 1932, taken by **James H. McGregor**, Superintendent.

Key: Number; Surname, Given; Sex; Date of Birth-Age at Last Birthday; Tribe (Oglala Sioux, unless stated otherwise); Degree of Blood; Marital Status; Relationship to Head of Family [Last Census Roll Number]; At Jurisdiction Where Enrolled (Yes/No); (If no – Where); Ward (Yes/No, if given); Allotment, Annuity and Identification Numbers (if given).

4959; Palmer, James H.; M; 11/10/23-8; -1/4; S; Son; 4888; No; Same; Yes; Id. U-11670 An. none

4960; Palmer, Helen; F; 1/17/25-7; -1/4; S; Daughter; 4889; No; Same; Yes; Id. U-11671 An. none

4961; Palmer, Teddy; M; 12/22/21-10; -1/4; S; Son; 4890; No; Same; Yes; Id. U-11919 An. none

4962; Palmer, Hope; F; 1/10/31-1; -1/4; S; Daughter; 4891; No; Same; Yes; Id. U-13706 An. none

4963; Palmier, Albert; M; 1883-49; Plus 1/4; M; Head; 4892; Yes; Yes; Al. 2707 An. 4871

4964; Palmier (Twiss), Minnie; F; 1895-37; 1/4; M; Wife; 4893; Yes; Yes; Al. 2690 An. 4872

4965; Palmier, Wonder; F; 11/3/24-7; 1/4; S; Daughter; 4895; No; Same; Yes; Id. U-11493 An. 4874

4966; Palmier, Taylor; M; 1907-25; 1/4; S; Head; 4894; Yes; Yes; Al. 2710 An. 4873

4967; Palmier, William; M; 1908-24; 1/4; M; Head; 4896; Yes; Yes; Al. 2717 An. 4877

4968; Palmier (Shangreau), Pacific; F; 1902-30; 1/4; M; Wife; 4897; Yes; Yes; Al. 5963 An. 6124

4969; Shangreau, Donroy; M; 5/8/21-10; 1/4; S. Son; 4898; Yes; Yes; Id. U-10379 An. 6125

4970; Palmier, Maynard; M; 5/17/25-6; 1/4; S; Son; 4899; Yes; Yes; Id. U-12837 An. none

4971; Palmier, Theodore; M; 8/27/26-5; 1/4; S; Son; 4900; Yes; Yes; Id. U-12838 An. none

4972; Palmier, Nicholas; M; 3/5/10-22; 1/4; S; Head; 4901; Yes; Yes; Al. 7252 An. 4878

4973; Palmier, William; M; 1874-58; 1/4; M; Head; 4902; Yes; Yes; Al. 2711 An. 4884

4974; Palmier (no data), Emily; F; 1874-58; 1/4; M; Wife; 4903; Yes; Yes; Al. 2712 An. 4885

4975; Parker (Williams), Susie; F; 1880-52; 1/4; M; Head; 4904; No; Hyattville, town, Big Horn, Wyo.; Yes; Al. 1109 An. 4886

4976; Parker, Lawrence C; M; 5/30/13-18; 1/4; S; Son; 4905; No; Same; Yes; Id. U-10100 An. 4888

Census of the **Pine Ridge** reservation of the **Pine Ridge, South Dakota** jurisdiction, as of **April 1**, 19**32**, taken by **James H. McGregor**, Superintendent.

Key: Number; Surname, Given; Sex; Date of Birth-Age at Last Birthday; Tribe (Oglala Sioux, unless stated otherwise); Degree of Blood; Marital Status; Relationship to Head of Family [Last Census Roll Number]; At Jurisdiction Where Enrolled (Yes/No); (If no – Where); Ward (Yes/No, if given); Allotment, Annuity and Identification Numbers (if given).

4977; Parker, Curtis; M; 5/5/16-15; 1/4; S; Son; 4906; No; Same; Yes; Id. U-10101 An. 4889

4978; Parker, Dora; F; 5/12/18-13; 1/4; S; Daughter; 4907; No; Same; Yes; Id. U-10102 An. 4890

4979; Parker, John H.; M; 12/23/21-10; Plus 1/4; S; Son; 4908; No; Hyattville, town, Big Horn, Wyo.; Yes; Id. U-10858 An. 4891

4980; Parker, Rhoda; F; 8/24/24-7; 1/4; S; Daughter; 4909; No; Same; Yes; Id. U-11920 An. none

N.E.: Parkhurst, Charles D; M; ~~-- -- --~~; Oneida Indian; 1/4; M; Head;

4981; Parkhurst (Martinez), Nora; F; 1894-38; 1/4; M; Wife; 4910; No; Redby, town, Beltrami, Minn; No; Al. 834 An. 4892

4982; Parkhurst, Lawrence; M; 5/13/15-16; 1/4; S; Son; 4911; No; Same; Yes; Al. 7996 An. 4893

4983; Parkhurst, Collins; M; 10/15/17-14; 1/4; S; Son; 4912; No; Same; Yes; Id. U-10103 An. 4894

4984; Parkhurst, Lillie; F; 6/25/20-11; 1/4; S; Daughter; 4913; No; Same; Yes; Id. U-10105 An. 4895

4985; Parkhurst, Murphy; M; 11/26/22-9; 1/4; S; Son; 4914; No; Same; Yes; Id. U-12058 An. 4896

4986; Parkhurst, Elizabeth; F; 6/12/25-6; 1/4; S; Daughter; 4915; No; Same; Yes; Id. U-11736 An. none

4987; Parkhurst, Patrick; M; 9/4/27-4; 1/4; S; Son; 4916; No; Same; Yes; Id. U-12489 An. none

4988; Parkhurst, Manuel; M; 6/6/30-1; 1/4; S; Son; 4917; No; Same; Yes; Id. U-13611 An. none

4989; Parts His Hair, Moses; M; 1899-33; F; S; Head; 4918; Yes; Yes; Al. 779 An. 4900

4990; Parts His Hair, Ephraim; M; 1878-54; F; M; Head; 4919; Yes; Yes; Al. 1387 An. 4901

4991; Parts His Hair (Kills Bad), Augusta; F; 1896-36; F; M; Wife; 4922; Yes; Yes; Al. 4291 An. 4904

4992; Parts His Hair, Abraham; M; 12/21/10-21; F; S; Son; 4920; Yes; Yes; Al. 4291 An. 4904

4993; Parts His Hair, Ethel; F; 1/5/14-18; F; S; Daughter; 4921; Yes; Yes; Id. U-10106 An. 4903

4994; Patton (Gillespie), Sarah; F; 1907-25; plus 1/4; Wd; Head; 4923; Yes; Yes; Al. 3792 An. 4900

4995; Patton, Grace; F; 4/9/26-5; 1/4; S; Daughter; 4924; Yes; Yes; Id. U-11921 An. none

Census of the____Pine Ridge____reservation of the__Pine Ridge, South Dakota__ jurisdiction, as of____April 1____, 19**32**, taken by____James H. McGregor____, Superintendent.

Key: Number; Surname, Given; Sex; Date of Birth-Age at Last Birthday; Tribe (Oglala Sioux, unless stated otherwise); Degree of Blood; Marital Status; Relationship to Head of Family [Last Census Roll Number]; At Jurisdiction Where Enrolled (Yes/No); (If no – Where); Ward (Yes/No, if given); Allotment, Annuity and Identification Numbers (if given).

4996; Patton, Lottie; F; 1875-57; 1/4; Wd; Head; 4925; Yes; Yes; Al. 2930 An. 4909

4997; Patton, George; M; 11/30/10-21; 1/4; S; Head; 4926; Yes; Yes; Al. 6803 An. 534

4998; Patton, Thomas; M; 1903-29; 1/4; M; Head; 4927; Yes; Yes; Al. 2931 An. 4911

4999; Patton (Bear Robe), Alice; F; 1902-30; F; M; Wife; 4928; Yes; Yes; Al. 6275 An. 383

5000; Patton, Vincent; M; 4/16/29-2; plus 1/4; S; Son; 4929; Yes; Yes; Id. U-13173 An. none

5001; Patton, Chauncey; M; 8/13/30-1; 1/4; S; Son; 4930; Yes; Yes; Id. U-13580 An. none

5002; Patton, William; M; 1895-37; plus 1/4; M; Head; 4931; Yes; NoYes; Al. 6801 An. 4912

5003; Patton (Merrivall), Laura; F; 1895-37; 1/4; M; Wife; 4932; Yes; No; Al. 51 An. 4913

5004; Patton, Clara; F; 10/22/16-15; 1/4; S; Daughter; 4933; Yes; Yes; Id. U-10107 An. 4914

5005; Patton, Henry; M; 7/17/18-13; 1/4; S; Son; 4934; Yds[sic]; Yes; Id. U-10108 An. 4815

5006; Patton, Wm. Vincent; M; 3/27/20-12; 1/4; S; Son; 4935; Yes; Yes; Id. U-10109 An. 4816

5007; Patton, Thymer; M; 11/25/21-10; 1/4; S; Son; 4936; Yes; Yes; Id. U-10963 An. 4817

5008; Patton, Pearl; F; 6/29/23-8; 1/4; S; Daughter; 4937; Yes; Yes; Id. U-12491 An. none

5009; Patton, Norbert; M; 3/24/26-6; 1/4; S; Son; 4938; Yes; Yes; Id. U-11927 An. none

5010; Patton, Irene; F; 12/25/27-4; 1/4; S; Daughter; 4939; Yes; Yes; Id. U-12490 An. none

5011; Patton, Elizabeth; F; 11/12/31-4/12; 1/4; S; Daughter; ---; Yes; Yes; U-13969

5012; Pawnee Leggins, George; M; 1883-49; F; M; Head; 4940; Yes; Yes; Al. 1403 An. 4920

5013; Pawnee Leggins (Last Horse), Kate; F; 1893-39; F; M; Wife; 4941; Yes; Yes; Al. 6963 An. 4921

5014; Pawnee Leggins, Josephine; F; 10/16/16-15; F; S; Daughter; 4942; Yes; Yes; Id. U-10110 An. 4923

5015; Pawnee Leggins, David; M; 3/18/19-13; F; S; Son; 4943; Yes; Yes; Id. U-10111 An. 4924

5016; Pawnee Leggins, Lalie; F; 8/7/21-10; F; S; Daughter; 4944; Yes; Yes; Id. U-10112 An. 4925

Census of the____**Pine Ridge**____reservation of the____**Pine Ridge, South Dakota**
jurisdiction, as of____**April 1**____, 19**32**, taken by____**James H. McGregor**____,
Superintendent.

Key: Number; Surname, Given; Sex; Date of Birth-Age at Last Birthday; Tribe (Oglala Sioux, unless stated otherwise); Degree of Blood; Marital Status; Relationship to Head of Family [Last Census Roll Number]; At Jurisdiction Where Enrolled (Yes/No); (If no – Where); Ward (Yes/No, if given); Allotment, Annuity and Identification Numbers (if given).

5017; Pawnee Leggins, Delphine; F; 3/9/28-4; F; S; Daughter; 4945; Yes; Yes; Id. U-12525 An. none

5018; Pawnee Leggins, Philip; M; 10/9/30-1; F; S; Son; 4946; Yes; Yes; Id. U-13610 An. none

5019; Peano, Delilah; F; 9/3/01-31; plus 1/4; S; Head; 4947; Yes; Yes; Al. 1627 An. 4926

5020; Peck (Cuny), Louise; F; 1907-25; plus 1/4; M; Head; 4948; Yes; Yes; Al. 2992 An. 1809

5021; Peck, Marvin; M; 5/12/31-10/12; -1/4; S; Son; ---; Yes; Yes; U-13839

5022; Peck, Louis; M; 1880-52; 1/4; M; Head; 4949; Yes; Yes; Al. 2464 An. 4927

5023; Peck (no data), Nancy; F; 1882-50; 1/4; M; Wife; 4950; Yes; Yes; Al. 2465 An. 4928

5024; Peck, Ernest; M; 11/30/09-22; 1/4; S; Son; 4951; Yes; Yes; Al. 6892 An. 4930

5025; Peck, Gilbert; M; 2/8/12-20; 1/4; S; Son; 4952; Yes; Yes; Al. 6891 An. 4931

5026; Peck, Lucille; F; 11/21/20-11; 1/4; S; Daughter; 4953; Yes; Yes; Id. U-10915 An. 4933

5027; Peck, Joseph J; M; 1907-25; 1/4; M; Head; 4954; Yes; Yes; Al. 2468 An. 4829[sic]

5028; Peck (Young), Mary; F; 1908-24; -1/4; M; Wife; 8062; Yes; Yes; Al. 4866 An. 7964

5029; Bowman, Loran; M; 11/4/27-4; 1/4; S; S. Son; ---; Yes; Yes; U-13793

5030; Peck, Mary; F; 3/28/30-2; 1/4; S; S. Daughter; ---; Yes; Yes; U-13791

5031; Peck, Louis R; M; 1904-28; 1/4; M; Head; 4955; Yes; Yes; Al. 2467 An. 4934

5032; Peck (Hawkins), Agnes; F; 1906-26; 1/4; M; Wife; 4956; Yes; Yes; Al. 4616 An. 2760

5033; Peck, Lois; F; 3/20/28-4; 1/4; S; Daughter; 4957; Yes; Yes; Id. U-12689 An. none

5034; Peck, William; M; 7/26/29-2; 1/4; S; Son; 4958; Yes; Yes; Id. U-13346 An. none

5035; Peck, Wanda; F; 7/27/31-8/12; 1/4; S; Daughter; ---; Yes; Yes; U-13874

5036; Peck, Owen; M; 1897-35; 1/4; Wd; Head; 4959; Yes; No~~Yes~~; Al. 5446 An. 4935

5037; Peck, Walter Jr.; M; 10/24/26-5; -1/4; S; Son; 4960; Yes; Yes; Id. U-13707 An. none

5038; Pemican, ---; M; 1867-65; F; S; Head; 4961; Yes; Yes; Al. 2986 An. 4936

Census of the **Pine Ridge** reservation of the **Pine Ridge, South Dakota** jurisdiction, as of **April 1**, 19**32**, taken by **James H. McGregor**, Superintendent.

Key: Number; Surname, Given; Sex; Date of Birth-Age at Last Birthday; Tribe (Oglala Sioux, unless stated otherwise); Degree of Blood; Marital Status; Relationship to Head of Family [Last Census Roll Number]; At Jurisdiction Where Enrolled (Yes/No); (If no – Where); Ward (Yes/No, if given); Allotment, Annuity and Identification Numbers (if given).

5039; Perea? (Griffith), Eleanor; F; 1907-25; -1/4; Wd; Head; 4963; No; San Diego, city, San Diego, Cal.; Yes; Al. 3911 An. 2691

5040; Perea, Patsy; F; 5/2/27-4; -1/4; S; Daughter; 4964; No; Same; Yes; Id. U-12993 An. none

N.E.: Pereau, Joseph; M; -------; Ft. Peck Indian; M; Head;

5041; Pereau (American Horse), Alice; F; 1881-51; F; M; Wife; 4962; No; Poplar, town, Sheridan, Wyo.; Yes; Al. 618 An. 4937

5042; Pflug (Clifford), Mary; F; 1904-28; plus 1/4; M; Head; 4965; Yes; Yes; Al. 4476 An. 1478

5043; Pflug, Elaine; F; 1/18/27-5; -1/4; S; Daughter; 4966; Yes; Yes; Id. U-12495 An. none

5044; Peterson (Bettelyoun), Rene; F; 1899-33; plus 1/4; M; Head; 4967; Yes; NoYes; Al. 4075 An. 4939

5045; Peterson, Vera; F; 7/12/18-13; -1/4; S; Daughter; 4968; Yes; Yes; Id. U-10113 An. 4940

5046; Peterson, Irene; F; 9/23/19-12; -1/4; S; Daughter; 4969; Yes; Yes; Id. U-10114 An. 4941

5047; Peterson, James A; M; 1/3/21-11; -1/4; S; Son; 4970; Yes; Yes; Id. U-10115 An. 4942

5048; Peterson, Maxum; M; 3/19/22-10; -1/4; S; Son; 4971; Yes; Yes; Id. U-10916 An. 4943

5049; Peterson, Roger W; M; 7/19/23-8; -1/4; S; Son; 4972; Yes; Yes; Id. U-11193 An. 4944

5050; Peterson, Virginia; F; 11/19/24-7; -1/4; S; Daughter; 4973; Yes; Yes; Id. U-11651 An. none

5051; Peterson, Ramon; M; 2/28/26-6; -1/4; S; Son; 4974; Yes; Yes; Id. U-12493 An. none

5052; Peterson, Maxine; F; 6/3/27-4; -1/4; S; Daughter; 4975; Yes; Yes; Id. U-12492 An. none

5053; Peterson, Eileen; F; 6/24/29-2; -1/4; S; Daughter; 4976; Yes; Yes; Id. U-13404 An. none

5054; Peterson, Berdine; F; 3/5/31-1; -1/4; S; Daughter; ---; Yes; Yes; U-13813

5055; Picotte, Victoria; F; 12/20/10-21; Plus 1/4; S; Head; 4977; Yes; Yes; Al. 5480 An. 4947

5056; Pipe On Head, James; M; 1882-50; F; M; Head; 4978; Yes; Yes; Al. 3279 An. 4960

5057; Pipe On Head (Red Elk), Mary; F; 1883-49; F; M; Wife; 4979; Yes; Yes; Al. 3287 An. 4961

Census of the **Pine Ridge** reservation of the **Pine Ridge, South Dakota** jurisdiction, as of **April 1**, 19**32**, taken by **James H. McGregor**, Superintendent.

Key: Number; Surname, Given; Sex; Date of Birth-Age at Last Birthday; Tribe (Oglala Sioux, unless stated otherwise); Degree of Blood; Marital Status; Relationship to Head of Family [Last Census Roll Number]; At Jurisdiction Where Enrolled (Yes/No); (If no – Where); Ward (Yes/No, if given); Allotment, Annuity and Identification Numbers (if given).

5058; Pipe On Head, Arleane; F; 1/18/17-15; F; S; Daughter; 4980; Yes; Yes; Id. U-10120 An. 4963

5059; Pipe On Head, Mercy; F; 3/2/13-15; F; S; Daughter; 4981; Yes; Yes; Id. U-10121 An. 4964

5060; Pipe On Head, Flossie; F; 1/4/22-10; F; S; Daughter; 4982; Yes; Yes; Id. U-10878 An. 4965

5061; Pipe On Head, Norman; M; 7/6/08-23; F; M; Head; 4983; Yes; Yes; Al. 6171 An. 4962

5062; Pipe On Head (Black Tail Deer), Jennie; F; 1910-22; F~~Plus 1/4~~; M; Wife; 4985; Yes; Yes; Al. 7415 An. 806

5063; Pipe On Head, Mathew; M; 2/23/26-6; Plus 1/4; S; Son; 4984; Yes; Yes; Id. U-11950 An. none

5064; Pipe On Head, Darrell; M; 6/19/31-9/12; F; S; Son; ---; Yes; Yes; U-13900

5065; Plenty Arrows, William; M; 1896-36; F; M; Head; 4986; Yes; Yes; Al. 5423 An. 4969

5066; Plenty Arrows (White Eagle), Mary; F; 1897-35; F; M; Wife; 4987; Yes; Yes; Al. 5345 An. 4970

5067; Plenty Arrows, Leo; M; 9/15/21-10; F; S; Son; 4988; Yes; Yes; Id. U-10126 An. 4973

5068; Plenty Arrows, Patty; F; 9/17/26-5; F; S; Daughter; 4989; Yes; Yes; Id. U-12254 An. none

5069; Plenty Arrows, Sarah; F; 11/26/29-2; F; S; Daughter; 4990; Yes; Yes; Id. U-13298 An. none

5070; Plenty Arrows, Leroyal; M; 2/10/32-1/12; F; S; Son; ---; Yes; Yes; U-14103

5071; Plenty Brothers, ---; F; 1853-79; F; Wd; Head; 4991; Yes; Yes; Al. 2385 An. 4982

5072; Plenty Haranger, ---; M; 1850-82; F; Wd; Head; 4992; Yes; Yes; Al. 1279 An. 4983

5073; Plenty Holes, Eunice; F; 6/29/09-22; F; S; Head; 4993; Yes; Yes; Al. 6767 An. 4464

5074; Plenty Holes, George; M; 1897-35; F; M; Head; 4994; Yes; Yes; Al. 5725 An. 4986

5075; Plenty Holes (White), Louisa; F; 1901-31; plus 1/4; M; Wife; 4995; Yes; Yes; Al. 2742 An. 4987

5076; Plenty Holes, Annie; F; 4/22/24-7; 1/4; S; Daughter; 4996; Yes; Yes; Id. U-11349 An. 4988

5077; Plenty Holes, Rosa; F; 12/28/27-4; 1/4; S; Daughter; 4997; Yes; Yes; Id. U-12553 An. none

Census of the _____Pine Ridge_____ reservation of the _Pine Ridge, South Dakota_ jurisdiction, as of_____April 1_____, 1932, taken by_____James H. McGregor_____, Superintendent.

Key: Number; Surname, Given; Sex; Date of Birth-Age at Last Birthday; Tribe (Oglala Sioux, unless stated otherwise); Degree of Blood; Marital Status; Relationship to Head of Family [Last Census Roll Number]; At Jurisdiction Where Enrolled (Yes/No); (If no – Where); Ward (Yes/No, if given); Allotment, Annuity and Identification Numbers (if given).

5078; Plenty Holes, Christine; F; 4/11/30-1; 1/4; S; Daughter; 4998; Yes; Yes; Id. U-13488 An. none

5079; Plenty Horses, ---; F; 1862-70; F; Wd; Head; 4999; Yes; Yes; Al. 1828 An. 6256

5080; Plenty Wolf, George; M; 1901-31; F; Wd; Head; 5001; Yes; Yes; Al. 889 An. 4993

5081; Plenty Wolf, John; M; 1885-47; F; M; Head; 5002; Yes; Yes; Al. 856 An. 4994

5082; Plenty Wolf (no data), Louisa; F; 1884-48; F; M; Wife; 5003; Yes; Yes; Al. 4383 An. 4995

5083; Plenty Wolf, Victoria; F; 9/28/14-17; F; S; Daughter; 5004; Yes; Yes; Al. 7941 An. 4997

5084; Plenty Wolf, Kiva; F; 12/8/16-15; F; S; Daughter; 5005; Yes; Yes; Id. U-10128 An. 4998

5085; Plenty Wolf, Alvina; F; 7/22/20-11; F; S; Daughter; 5006; Yes; Yes; Id. U-10129 An. 4999

5086; Plenty Wolf, Mattie; F; 4/14/23-8; F; S; Daughter; 5007; Yes; Yes; Id. U-13085 An. 5000

5087; Plenty Wolf, Selvin; M; 1/21/26-6; F; S; Son; 5008; Yes; Yes; Id. U-11817 An. none

5088; Plenty Wolf, Bernard; M; 7/17/29-2; F; S; Son; 5009; Yes; Yes; Id. U-13228 An. none

5089; Plenty Wounds, ---; M; 1871-61; F; M; Head; 5010; Yes; Yes; Al. 421 An. 5001

5090; Plenty Wounds (no data), Ida; F; 1878-54; F; M; Wife; 5011; Yes; Yes; Al. 8059 An. 5002

5091; Plenty Wounds, Paul W.; M; 8/6/16-15; F; S; Son; 5012; Yes; Yes; Id. U-10130 An. 5003

5092; Plenty Wounds, Emma; F; 9/1/20-11; F; S; Daughter; 5013; Yes; Yes; Id. U-10131 An. 5004

5093; Plenty Wounds, George; M; 1898-34; F; M; Head; 5014; Yes; Yes; Al. 422 An. 5006

5094; Plenty Wounds (Crooked Eyes), Rosa; F; 1907-25; F; M; Wife; 5015; Yes; Yes; Al. 5924 An. 7761

5095; Plenty Wounds, Raymond; M; 6/3/30-1; F; S; Son; 5016; Yes; Yes; Id. U-13553 An. none

Census of the **Pine Ridge** reservation of the **Pine Ridge, South Dakota** jurisdiction, as of **April 1**, 19**32**, taken by **James H. McGregor**, Superintendent.

Key: Number; Surname, Given; Sex; Date of Birth-Age at Last Birthday; Tribe (Oglala Sioux, unless stated otherwise); Degree of Blood; Marital Status; Relationship to Head of Family [Last Census Roll Number]; At Jurisdiction Where Enrolled (Yes/No); (If no – Where); Ward (Yes/No, if given); Allotment, Annuity and Identification Numbers (if given).

5096; Plenty Wounds, Joseph; M; 1900-32; F; S; Head; 5017; Yes; Yes; Al. 423 An. 5007

5097; Plenty Wounds, John; M; 1890-42; F; M; Head; 5018; Yes; Yes; Al. 298 An. 5008

5098; Plenty Wounds (Two Eagles), Katie; F; 1891-41; F; M; Wife; 5019; Yes; Yes; Id. U-10132 An. 5009

5099; Plenty Wounds, Charles; M; 2/12/11-21; F; S; Son; 5020; Yes; Yes; Id. U-10134 An. 5010

5100; Plenty Wounds, Claude; M; 2/28/23-9; F; S; Son; 5021; Yes; Yes; Id. U-12097 An. 5013

5101; Plenty Wounds, William; M; 4/28/25-6; F; S; Son; 5023; Yes; Yes; Id. U-11626 An. none

5102; Plenty Wounds, Katie; F; 7/9/28-3; F; S; Daughter; 5024; Yes; Yes; Id. U-12744 An. none

5103; Plenty Wounds, Moses; M; 8/3/30-1; F; S; Son; 5025; Yes; Yes; Id. U-13671 An. none

5104; Plenty Wounds, Thomas; M; 1900-32; F; S; Head; 5026; Yes; Yes; Al. 425 An. 5014

5105; Plucks Porcupine, Philip; M; 1865-67; F; M; Head; 5027; Yes; Yes; Al. 582 An. 5015

5106; Plucks Porcupine (Red Star), Sallie; F; 1861-71; F; M; Wife; 5028; Yes; Yes; Al. 1849 An. 5584

5107; Plucks Porcupine, William; M; 1899-33; F; M; Head; 5029; Yes; Yes; Al. 585 An. 5016

5108; Plucks Porcupine (Milk), Elizabeth; F; 2/25/12-20; F; M; Wife; 4508; Yes; Yes; Al. 7078 An. 5017[sic]

5109; Two Elk, Collins; M; 5/14/30-1; F; S; S. Son; 4509; Yes; Yes; Id. U-13766 An. none

5110; Plume, Amos; M; 1905-27; plus 1/4; S; Head; 5030; Yes; Yes; Al. 6770 An. 5017

5111; Plume, Hobart; M; 1875-57; F; M; Head; 5032; Yes; Yes; Al. 5716 An. 5018

5112; Plume, Paul; M; 6/4/13-18; plus 1/4; S; Son; 5034; Yes; Yes; Al. 8252 An. 5022

5113; Poor Bear, Albert; M; 1882-50; 1/4; S; Head; 5035; Yes; Yes; Al. 2115 An. 5023

Census of the __Pine Ridge__ reservation of the __Pine Ridge, South Dakota__ jurisdiction, as of __April 1__, 1932, taken by __James H. McGregor__, Superintendent.

Key: Number; Surname, Given; Sex; Date of Birth-Age at Last Birthday; Tribe (Oglala Sioux, unless stated otherwise); Degree of Blood; Marital Status; Relationship to Head of Family [Last Census Roll Number]; At Jurisdiction Where Enrolled (Yes/No); (If no – Where); Ward (Yes/No, if given); Allotment, Annuity and Identification Numbers (if given).

5114; Poor Bear (Two Elk), Bessie; F; 1889-43; F; M; Wife; 5036; Yes; Yes; Al. 4321 An. 5024
5115; Poor Bear, Theodore; M; 8/7/11-20; plus 1/4; S; Son; 5037; Yes; Yes; Al. 6967 An. 5026
5116; Poor Bear, Gordon; M; 9/5/14-17; 1/4; S; Son; 5038; Yes; Yes; Al. 8263 An. 5027
5117; Poor Bear, Ellice; F; 7/17/16-15; 1/4; S; Daughter; 5039; Yes; Yes; Al. 8264 An. 5028
5118; Poor Bear, Peter; M; 6/1/21-10; 1/4; S; Son; 5040; Yes; Yes; Id. U-10140 An. 5029
5119; Poor Bear, Eliza; F; 1/19/27-5; 1/4; S; Daughter; 5041; Yes; Yes; Id. U-12255 An. none

5120; Poor Bear, William E.; M; 12/8/10-21; F; S; Head; 5042; Yes; Yes; Al. 5993 An. 5041

5121; Poor Bear, George; M; 1891-41; F; M; Head; 5043; Yes; Yes; Al. 2141 An. 5031
5122; Poor Bear (Star), Susie; F; 1896-36; F; M; Wife; 5044; Yes; Yes; Al. 7429 An. 5032
5123; Star, Joseph; M; 9/18/13-18; plus 1/4; S; Son; 5045; Yes; Yes; Id. U-10141 An. 5033
5124; Poor Bear, Ruth; F; 7/16/22-9; F; S; Daughter; 5046; Yes; Yes; Id. U-9182 An. 5034
5125; Poor Bear, Anderson; M; 12/30/25-6; F; S; Son; 5047; Yes; Yes; Id. U-12690 An. none
5126; Poor Bear, Robert; M; 8/10/26-5; F; S; Son; 5048; Yes; Yes; Id. U-12691 An. none
5127; Poor Bear, Raymond; M; 5/4/28-3; F; S; Son; 5049; Yes; Yes; Id. U-12692 An. none
5128; Poor Bear, Leona; F; 11/14/31-4/12; F; S; Daughter; ---; Yes; Yes; U-13970

5129; Poor Bear nee (Quiver), Fannie; F; 1885-47; F; Wd; Head; 5050; Yes; Yes; Al. 4207 An. 5036
5130; Poor Bear, Enos; M; 4/10/12-19; F; S; Son; 5051; Yes; Yes; Al. 7033 An. 5037
5131; Poor Bear, Harry Jr.; M; 4/27/17-15; F; S; Son; 5052; Yes; Yes; Id. U-10138 An. 5038

5132; Poor Bear, Philip; M; 1886-46; plus 1/4; M; Head; 5053; Yes; Yes; Al. 5115 An. 5039
5133; Poor Bear (Moves Camp) (Yellow Eyes), Belle; F; 1905-27; F; M; Wife; 5054; Yes; Yes; Al. 1889 An. 7875

Census of the **Pine Ridge** reservation of the **Pine Ridge, South Dakota** jurisdiction, as of **April 1**, 19**32**, taken by **James H. McGregor**, Superintendent.

Key: Number; Surname, Given; Sex; Date of Birth-Age at Last Birthday; Tribe (Oglala Sioux, unless stated otherwise); Degree of Blood; Marital Status; Relationship to Head of Family [Last Census Roll Number]; At Jurisdiction Where Enrolled (Yes/No); (If no – Where); Ward (Yes/No, if given); Allotment, Annuity and Identification Numbers (if given).

5134; Poor Bear, Weldon; M; 6/13/27-14; plus 1/4; S; Son; 5055; Yes; Yes; Id. U-12369 An. none

5135; Poor Bear, Edith; F; 12/13/23-8; 1/4; S; Daughter; 5056; Yes; Yes; Id. U-11185 An. none

5136; Poor Bear, Raymond; M; 5/22/29-2; 1/4; S; Son; 5057; Yes; Yes; Id. U-13212 An. none

5137; Yellow Eyes, Edna; F; 10/12/20-11; F; S; S. Daughter; 5058; Yes; Yes; Id. U-10803 An. 7876

5138; Poor Bear, Irene; F; 8/1/31-7/12; plus 1/4; S; Daughter; ---; Yes; Yes; U-13901

5139; Poor Bear, Pierre; M; 1907-25; F; S; Head; 5059; Yes; Yes; Al. 2140 An. 5042

5140; Poor Buffalo (Sound Sleeper), Lily; F; 1849-83; F; Wd; Head; 5060; Yes; Yes; Al. 6490 An. 5043

5141; Poor Elk, Jacob; M; 6/1/07-24; F; M; Head; 5061; Yes; Yes; Al. 6599 An. 50

5142; Poor Elk (Good Voice Flute), Louisa; F; 12/10/11-20; F; M; Wife; 2633; Yes; Yes; Al. 6225 An. 2621

5143; Poor Elk, Virginia; F; 12/10/11-20; F; S; Head; 5062; Yes; Yes; Id. U-10147 An. 7265

N.E.: ~~Poor Thunder, George; M; ------; Rosebud Sioux; M; Head;~~

5144; Poor Thunder (Morrison), Emma; F; 1890-42; F; M; Wife; 5063; Yes; Yes; Al. 5499 An. 7431

5145; Poor Thunder (Weasel), Mary; F; 1859-73; F; Wd; Head; 5064; Yes; Yes; Al. 3466 An. 5047

5146; Poor Thunder, Philip; M; 11/29/20-11; F; S; Gr Son; 5065; Yes; Yes; Id. U-10148 An. 5147

5147; Poor Thunder, John; M; 1896-36; F; M; Head; 5066; Yes; Yes; Al. 7210 An. 5049

5148; Poor Thunder (Sound Sleeper), Bessie; F; 7/3/07-24; F; M; Wife; 5067; Yes; Yes; Al. 4145 An. 6044

5149; Poor Thunder, Isadore; M; 10/23/19-12; F; S; Son; 5068; Yes; Yes; Id. U-10149 An. 5051

5150; Poor Thunder, Evylain; F; 5/10/25-6; F; S; Daughter; 5069; Yes; Yes; Id. U-11638 An. none

5151; Poor Thunder, Ollie; F; 10/9/30-1; F; S; Daughter; 5070; Yes; Yes; Id. U-13708 An. none

Census of the_____**Pine Ridge**_____reservation of the **Pine Ridge, South Dakota** jurisdiction, as of_____**April 1**_____, 1932, taken by_____**James H. McGregor**_____, Superintendent.

Key: Number; Surname, Given; Sex; Date of Birth-Age at Last Birthday; Tribe (Oglala Sioux, unless stated otherwise); Degree of Blood; Marital Status; Relationship to Head of Family [Last Census Roll Number]; At Jurisdiction Where Enrolled (Yes/No); (If no – Where); Ward (Yes/No, if given); Allotment, Annuity and Identification Numbers (if given).

5152; Poor Thunder, Luke; M; 1892-40; F; M; Head; 5071; Yes; Yes; Al. 7209 An. 5053

5153; Poor Thunder, Lillian; F; 2/11/25-7; plus 1/4; S; Daughter; 5072; Yes; Yes; Id. U-11566 An. none

5154; Poor Thunder, Ruth; F; 4/3/28-4; 1/4; S; Daughter; 5073; Yes; Yes; Id. U-12693 An. none

5155; Poor Thunder, Wilson; M; 12/30/29-2; 1/4; S; Son; 5074; Yes; Yes; Id. U-13347 An. none

5156; Porcupine (Good Cloud), Augusta; F; 1870-62; F; Wd; Head; 5075; Yes; Yes; Al. 7492 An. 5055

5157; Porcupine, Joseph; M; 10/24/12-19; F; S; Son; 5976[sic]; Yes; Yes; Al. 7661 An. 5056

5158; Porcupine, Edward; M; 1874-58; F; M; Head; 5077; Yes; Yes; Al. 5789 An. 5057

5159; Porcupine (Chasing Jumper), Bertha; F; 1871-61; F; M; Wife; 5078; Yes; Yes; Al. 4356 An. 5058

5160; Horse Stands In Sight, Esther; F; 7/28/25-6; F; S; Ward; 5079; Yes; Yes; Id. U-11703 An. none

5161; Porcupine, Eugene; M; 1885-47; F; S; Head; 5080; Yes; Yes; Al. 553 An. 5059

5162; Pourier (no data), Josephine; F; 1852-80; plus 1/4; Wd; Head; 5081; Yes; No; Al. 2609 An. 5062

5163; Pourier, Baptiste; M; 1899-33; -1/4; M; Head; 5082; Yes; Yes; Al. 721 An. 5063

5164; Pourier (O'Rourke), Pearl; F; 1901-31; plus 1/4; M; Wife; 5083; Yes; Yes; Al. 1609 An. 5064

5165; Pourier, Learn; M; 8/25/21-10; 1/4; S; Son; 5084; Yes; Yes; Id. U-10867 An. 5065

5166; Pourier, Verna; F; 9/10/25-6; 1/4; S; Daughter; 5085; Yes; Yes; Id. U-11884 An. none

5167; Pourier, Melven; M; 3/2/27-5; 1/4; S; Son; 5086; Yes; Yes; Id. U-12527 An. 5065

5168; Pourier, Lucille; F; 7/17/31-8/12; 1/4; S; Daughter; ---; Yes; Yes; U-13875

5169; Pourier, Charles; M; 1893-39; -1/4; M; Head; 5087; Yes; Yes; Al. 2613 An. 5066

5170; Pourier (Provost), Bessie; F; 1899-33; plus 1/4; M; Wife; 5088; Yes; Yes; Al. 46 An. 5067

Census of the __Pine Ridge__ reservation of the __Pine Ridge, South Dakota__ jurisdiction, as of __April 1__, 19**32**, taken by __James H. McGregor__, Superintendent.

Key: Number; Surname, Given; Sex; Date of Birth-Age at Last Birthday; Tribe (Oglala Sioux, unless stated otherwise); Degree of Blood; Marital Status; Relationship to Head of Family [Last Census Roll Number]; At Jurisdiction Where Enrolled (Yes/No); (If no – Where); Ward (Yes/No, if given); Allotment, Annuity and Identification Numbers (if given).

5171; Pourier, Rosa; F; 6/7/23-8; 1/4; S; Daughter; 5089; Yes; Yes; Id. U-14001 An. 5968

5172; Pourier, Edward; M; 11/19/25-6; 1/4; S; Son; 5090; Yes; Yes; Id. U-11788 An. none

5173; Pourier, Emil; M; 1882-50; -1/4; M; Head; 5091; Yes; No; Al. 2610 An. 5070

5174; Pourier (Lee), Emma; F; 1887-45; plus 1/4; M; Wife; 5092; Yes; Yes; Al. 54 An. 5071

5175; Pourier, Ethel; F; 6/8/15-16; 1/4; S; Daughter; 5093; Yes; Yes; Id. Al. 7930 An. 5073

5176; Pourier, Lorene; F; 7/25/17-14; 1/4; S; Daughter; 5094; Yes; Yes; Id. U-10150 An. 5074

5177; Pourier, Bernice; F; 7/30/22-9; 1/4; S; Daughter; 5095; Yes; Yes; Id. U-11066 An. 5075

5178; Pourier, Emil A; M; 1903-29; -1/4; M; Head; 5096; Yes; Yes; Al. 722 An. 5076

5179; Pourier, Calvin; M; 2/8/25-7; 1/4; S; Son; 5098; Yes; Yes; Id. U-11444 An. 5078

5180; Pourier, Christine; F; 11/29/26-5; 1/4; S; Daughter; 5099; Yes; Yes; Id. U-12145 An. none

5181; Pourier, Ramona; F; 2/17/29-3; 1/4; S; Daughter; 5100; Yes; Yes; Id. U-13279 An. none

5182; Pourier, Lawton; M; 9/2/31-6/12; 1/4; S; Son; ---; Yes; Yes; U-13923

5183; Pourier, Hobart; M; 1904-28; -1/4; M; Head; 5101; Yes; Yes; Al. 723 An. 5079

5184; Pourier (O'Rourke), Isabelle; F; 1907-25; plus 1/4; M; Wife; 5102; Yes; Yes; Al. 2919 An. 5080

5185; Pourier, Edna; F; 4/6/24-7; 1/4; S; Daughter; 5103; Yes; Yes; Id. U-11291 An. 5081

5186; Pourier, Cecile; M; 2/8/26-6; 1/4; S; Son; 5104; Yes; Yes; Id. U-11883 An. none

5187; Pourier, Clarence; M; 5/11/28-3; 1/4; S; Son; 5105; Yes; Yes; Id. U-12590 An. none

5188; Pourier, Lavon; F; 3/4/30-2; 1/4; S; Daughter; 5106; Yes; Yes; Id. U-13423 An. none

5189; Pourier, Lester; M; 11/19/31-4/12; 1/4; S; Son; ---; Yes; Yes; U-13971

5190; Pourier, John; M; 1872-60; -1/4; M; Head; 5107; Yes; No; Al. 717 An. 5082

5191; Pourier (no data), Josie; F; 1875-57; plus 1/4; M; Wife; 5108; Yes; No; Al. 7692 An. 5083

5192; Pourier, Wilber; M; 10/5/09-22; 1/4; S; Son; 5109; Yes; Yes; Al. 4685 An. 5085

Census of the **Pine Ridge** reservation of the **Pine Ridge, South Dakota** jurisdiction, as of **April 1**, 19**32,** taken by **James H. McGregor**, Superintendent.

Key: Number; Surname, Given; Sex; Date of Birth-Age at Last Birthday; Tribe (Oglala Sioux, unless stated otherwise); Degree of Blood; Marital Status; Relationship to Head of Family [Last Census Roll Number]; At Jurisdiction Where Enrolled (Yes/No); (If no – Where); Ward (Yes/No, if given); Allotment, Annuity and Identification Numbers (if given).

5193; Pourier, Raymond; M; 1/5/12-20; 1/4; S; Son; 5110; Yes; Yes; Al. 7680 An. 5086

5194; Pourier, Benjamin; M; 5/11/14-17; 1/4; S; Son; 5111; Yes; Yes; Al. 7536 An. 5087

5195; Pourier, Francis; M; 5/11/14-17; 1/4; S; Son; 5112; Yes; Yes; Al. 7537 An. 5088

5196; Pourier, Elizabeth; F; 4/20/16-15; 1/4; S; Daughter; 5113; Yes; Yes; Id. U-10154 An. 5089

5197; Pourier, Joseph; M; 11/17/06-25; 1/4; S; Head; 5114; Yes; Yes; Al. 2616 An. 5090

5198; Pourier, Levi; M; 1906-26; plus 1/4; M; Head; 5115; Yes; Yes; Al. 4684 An. 5091

5199; Pourier (Shangreau), Agatha; F; 1906-26; 1/4; M; Wife; 5116; Yes; Yes; Al. 3598 An. 6099

5200; Pourier, Marlene; F; 8/16/31-7/12; 1/4; S; Daughter; ---; Yes; Yes; U-13902

5201; Pourier, William; M; 1909-24; plus 1/4; S; Head; 5117; Yes; Yes; Al. 7679 An. 5084

5202; Pourier, Louis; M; 1880-52; -1/4; M; Head; 5118; Yes; No; Al. 4471 An. 5092

5203; Pourier (Dubray), Minnie; F; 1892-40; plus 1/4; M; Wife; 5119; Yes; No; Al. 4580 An. 5094

5204; White, Millicent; F; 1/13/14-18; 1/4; S; S. Daughter; 5120; Yes; Yes; Al. 8073 An. 5095

5205; White, Mary; F; 8/6/15-16; 1/4; S; S. Daughter; 5121; Yes; Yes; Al. 8074 An. 5096

5206; White, Irene; F; 11/22/17-14; 1/4; S; S. Daughter; 5122; Yes; Yes; Id. U-10714 An. 5097

5207; White, Evelyn; F; 8/14/20-11; 1/4; S; S. Daughter; 5123; Yes; Yes; Id. U-10715 An. 5098

5208; Pourier, Baptiste; M; 9/15/22-9; 1/4; S; Son; 5124; Yes; Yes; Id. U-12018 An. 5099

5209; Pourier, Stanley; M; 12/28/24-7; 1/4; S; Son; 5125; Yes; Yes; Id. U-11480 An. 5100

5210; Pourier, Doris; F; 8/21/30-1; 1/4; S; Daughter; 5126; Yes; Yes; Id. U-13573 An. none

5211; Pourier, Peter; M; 1888-44; -1/4; M; Head; 5127; Yes; No; Al. 2611 An. 5101

Census of the **Pine Ridge** reservation of the **Pine Ridge, South Dakota** jurisdiction, as of **April 1**, 19**32**, taken by **James H. McGregor**, Superintendent.

Key: Number; Surname, Given; Sex; Date of Birth-Age at Last Birthday; Tribe (Oglala Sioux, unless stated otherwise); Degree of Blood; Marital Status; Relationship to Head of Family [Last Census Roll Number]; At Jurisdiction Where Enrolled (Yes/No); (If no – Where); Ward (Yes/No, if given); Allotment, Annuity and Identification Numbers (if given).

5212; Pourier (Standing Bear), Hattie; F; 1890-41; plus 1/4; M; Wife; 5128; Yes; No; Al. 937 An. 5102

5213; Pourier, Edith; F; 3/23/19-19; 1/4; S; Daughter; 5129; Yes; Yes; Al. 6793 An. 5104

5214; Pourier, Louis; M; 12/3/14-17; 1/4; S; Son; 5130; Yes; Yes; Al. 7889 An. 5105

5215; Pourier, Margaret; ~~M~~F; 10/16-15; 1/4; S; Daughter; 5131; Yes; Yes; Id. U-10151 An. 5106

5216; Pourier, Percie; M; 8/29/20-11; 1/4; S; Son; 5132; Yes; Yes; Id. U-10152 An. 5107

5217; Pourier, Floyd; M; 9/10/18-13; 1/4; S; Son; 5133; Yes; Yes; Id. U-10153 An. 5108

5218; Pourier, Gertreude[sic]; F; 2/38[sic]/23-9; 1/4; S; Daughter; 5134; Yes; Yes; Id. U-13052 An. 5109

5219; Pourier, Crispean; F; 12/10/24-7; 1/4; S; Daughter; 5135; Yes; Yes; Id. U-11418 An. 5110

5220; Pourier, Alvina; F; 12/5/09-22; 1/4; S; Head; 5136; Yes; Yes; Al. 6791 An. 5103

5221; Pourier, William; M; 3/31/07-25; 1/4; M; Head; 5137; Yes; Yes; Al. 4473 An. 5093

5222; Pourier (Irving), Ella; F; 7/27/06-25; 1/4; M; Wife; 5138; Yes; Yes; Al. 4659 An. 3048

5223; Powder Woman, John; M; 1902-30; F; M; Head; 5139; Yes; Yes; Al. 4296 An. 5111

N.E.: ~~Powder Woman (Good Shield), Sophia; F; ------; Rosebud Sioux; F; M; Wife; yes~~

5224; Powder Woman, Abraham; M; 5/20/22-9; F; S; Son; 5140; Yes; Yes; Id. U-11039 An. 5112

5225; Powder Woman, Nathan; M; 6/29/23-8; F; S; Son; 5141; Yes; Yes; Id. U-14028 An. 5113

5226; Powers (O'Rourke), Josephine; F; 1899-33; plus 1/4; M; Wife; 5143; Yes; Yes; Al. 1608 An. 5115

5227; Powers, Darrel; M; 5/17/24-7; -1/4; S; Son; 5144; Yes; Yes; Id. U-11570 An. 5116

5228; Prairie Chicken, Archie; M; 1862-70; F; M; Head; 5145; Yes; Yes; Al. 1972 An. 5117

5229; Prairie Chicken (no data), Eliza; F; 1873-59; F; M; Wife; 5146; Yes; Yes; Al. 1973 An. 5118

Census of the __Pine Ridge__ reservation of the __Pine Ridge, South Dakota__ jurisdiction, as of __April 1__, 19**32**, taken by __James H. McGregor__, Superintendent.

Key: Number; Surname, Given; Sex; Date of Birth-Age at Last Birthday; Tribe (Oglala Sioux, unless stated otherwise); Degree of Blood; Marital Status; Relationship to Head of Family [Last Census Roll Number]; At Jurisdiction Where Enrolled (Yes/No); (If no – Where); Ward (Yes/No, if given); Allotment, Annuity and Identification Numbers (if given).

5230; Walking Bull, Lydia; F; 6/10/17-14; F; S; Adopted Daughter; 5147; Yes; Yes; Id. U-12046 An. 5120

5231; Prairie Chicken, Solomon; M; 1907-25; F; S; Head; 5148; Yes; Yes; Al. 5266 An. 5119

5232; Prairie Hen, Benjamin; M; 1887-45; F; M; Head; 5149; ~~Yes~~No; Rapid City, city, Pennington, S.D.; No; Al. 7658 An. 5122

5233; Prairie Hen, Ramona; F; 7/12/17-14; F; S; Daughter; 5150; No; Same; Yes; Id. U-10155 An. 5123

5234; Prairie Hen, Benjamin F; M; 11/2/21-10; F; S; Son; 5151; No; Same; Yes; Id. U-11164 An. 5124

N.E.: ~~Pratt, Oscar; M; ------; Arapahoe; M; Head;~~

5235; Pratt (Guerrier), Annie; F; 6/6/11-20; 1/4; M; Wife; 5152; No; Geary, town, Blaine, Okla; Yes; Al. 5770 An. 2707

5236; Pratt, Dorothy; F; 9/18/30-1; 1/4; S; Daughter; 5153; No; Same; Yes; Id. U-13630 An. none

5237; Prays to Her, ---; F; 1863-69; F; Wd; Head; 5154; Yes; Yes; Al. 5330 An. 5126

5238; Prescott (no data), Millie; F; 1870-62; plus 1/4; M; Wife; 5155; Yes; Yes; Al. 5268 An. 5127

N.E.: ~~Presho, Wallace; M; ------; Rosebud Sioux; 1/4; M; Head;~~

5239; Presho (Young), Carrie; F; 1905-27; 1/4; M; Wife; 5156; No; Rosebud, S.D.; Yes; Al. 2516 An. 5128

5240; Pretty Back, George; M; 9/30/03-28; F; M; Head; 5157; Yes; Yes; Al. 782 An. 3129

5241; Pretty Back (Yellow Thunder), Jessie; F; 9/14/06-25; F; M; Wife; 5158; Yes; Yes; Al. 6859 An. 7923

5242; Pretty Back, Edward; M; 9/28/28-3; F; S; Son; 5159; Yes; Yes; Id. U-12851 An. none

5243; Pretty Back, Lorene; F; 5/11/31-10/12; F; S; Daughter; ---; Yes; Yes; U-13840

5244; Pretty Back, Thomas; ~~F~~M; 1879-53; F; M; Head; 5160; Yes; Yes; Al. 751 An. 5130

5245; Pretty Back (no data), Augusta; F; 1882-50; F; M; Wife; 5161; Yes; Yes; Al. 5662 An. 5131

5246; Pretty Back, Romeo; M; 9/20/10-21; F; S; Son; 5162; Yes; Yes; Al. 5664 An. 5132

Census of the __Pine Ridge__ reservation of the __Pine Ridge, South Dakota__ jurisdiction, as of __April 1__, 19**32**, taken by __James H. McGregor__, Superintendent.

Key: Number; Surname, Given; Sex; Date of Birth-Age at Last Birthday; Tribe (Oglala Sioux, unless stated otherwise); Degree of Blood; Marital Status; Relationship to Head of Family [Last Census Roll Number]; At Jurisdiction Where Enrolled (Yes/No); (If no – Where); Ward (Yes/No, if given); Allotment, Annuity and Identification Numbers (if given).

5247; Pretty Back, Eva; F; 8/2/14-17; F; S; Daughter; 5163; Yes; Yes; Al. 7710 An. 5134

5248; Pretty Back, Jacob; M; 5/18/18-14; F; S; Son; 5164; Yes; Yes; Id. U-10156 An. 5135

5249; Pretty Back, Asa; M; 6/24/20-11; F; S; Son; 5165; Yes; Yes; Id. U-10157 An. 5136

5250; Pretty Back, Noah; M; 11/1/20[sic]-9; F; S; Son; 5166; Yes; Yes; Id. U-13055 An. 5137

5251; Pretty Back, Annie; F; 1/13/28-4; F; S; Daughter; 5167; Yes; Yes; Id. U-12730 An. none

5252; Pretty Bird, Henry; M; 1879-53; F; M; Head; 5168; Yes; Yes; Al. 880 An. 5138

5253; Pretty Bird, Harrison; M; 9/22/10-21; F; S; Son; 5170; Yes; Yes; Al. 6757 An. 5141

5254; Pretty Bird, John; M; 1886-46; F; M; Head; 5171; Yes; Yes; Al. 2890 An. 5142

5255; Pretty Bird (Poor Thunder), Anna; F; 1899-33; F; M; Wife; 5172; Yes; Yes; Al. 7211 An. 5140

5256; Pretty Bird, Phoebe; F; 10/29/15-16; F; S; Daughter; 5173; Yes; Yes; Id. U-10158 An. 5144

5257; Pretty Bird, Samuel; M; 3/14/18-14; F; S; Son; 5174; Yes; Yes; Id. U-10159 An. 5145

5258; Pretty Bird, Viola; F; 7/27/26-5; F; S; Daughter; 5175; Yes; Yes; Id. U-12146 An. none

5259; Pretty Bird, Ethel; F; 8/8/28-3; F; S; Daughter; 5176; Yes; Yes; Id. U-12762 An. none

5260; Pretty Bird, Grace; F; 3/26/12-20; F; S; Head; 5177; Yes; Yes; Al. 7490 An. 5143

5261; Pretty Bird, Joseph; M; 1858-74; F; Wd; Head; 5178; Yes; Yes; Al. 2888 An. 5148

5262; Pretty Boy, Benjamin; M; 1896-36; F; M; Head; 5179; Yes; Yes; Al. 2413 An. 5149

5263; Pretty Boy (White Belly), Mattie; F; 1878-54; F; M; Wife; 5180; Yes; Yes; Al. 3684 An. 5150

5264; Pretty Boy, Levi; M; 9/16/13-18; F; S; Ward; 5181; Yes; Yes; Id. U-10161 An. 5153

5265; Pretty Boy, Edith; F; 1/14/16-16; F; S; Ward; 5182; Yes; Yes; Id. U-10162 An. 5154

Census of the **Pine Ridge** reservation of the **Pine Ridge, South Dakota** jurisdiction, as of **April 1**, 19**32**, taken by **James H. McGregor**, Superintendent.

Key: Number; Surname, Given; Sex; Date of Birth-Age at Last Birthday; Tribe (Oglala Sioux, unless stated otherwise); Degree of Blood; Marital Status; Relationship to Head of Family [Last Census Roll Number]; At Jurisdiction Where Enrolled (Yes/No); (If no – Where); Ward (Yes/No, if given); Allotment, Annuity and Identification Numbers (if given).

5266; Pretty Boy, Lydia; F; 1911-20; F; S; Head; 5183; No; Omaha, city, Douglas, Nebr.; Yes; Id. U-10160 An. 5152

5267; Pretty Boy, Louis; M; 3/17/28-4; F; S; Son; 5184; No; Unknown; Yes; Id. U-12159 An. none

5268; Pretty Bull, Marshall; M; 1858-74; F; M; Head; 5185; Yes; Yes; Al. 493 An. 5156

5269; Pretty Bull (Pine Bird), Alice; F; 1857-75; F; M; Wife; 5186; Yes; Yes; Al. 7094 An. 4951

5270; Pine Bird, Hazel; F; 4/8/15-16; F; S; Ward; 5187; Yes; Yes; Id. U-10118 An. 4956

N.E.: Pratty Cloud, William; M; ---- ---; Rosebud Sioux; F; M; Head;

5271; Pratty Cloud (Bad Heart Bull), Dollie; F; 1872-60; F; M; Wife; 5188; Yes; Yes; Al. 3232 An. 265

N.E.: Pretty Voice, Walter C; M; ---- ---; Cheyenne Sioux; F; M; Head;

5272; Pretty Voice (no data), Emma; F; 1899-33; plus 1/4; M; Wife; 5189; Yes; Yes; Al. 3050 An. 5158

5273; Pretty Voice, Bernice; F; 2/11/23-9; 1/4; S; Daughter; 5190; Yes; Yes; Id. U-13742 An. none

5274; Pretty Voice, John; M; 4/21/29-2; F; S; Son; 5191; Yes; Yes; Id. U-13741 An. none

5275; Pretty Voice, Mercy; F; 12/18/30-1; 1/4; S; Daughter; 5192; Yes; Yes; Id. U-13709 An. none

N.E.: Pretty Voice Crane, Abraham; M; ---- ---; Cheyenne Sioux; F; M; Head;

5276; Pretty Voice Crane (Morrison), Josie; F; 1894-38; plus 1/4; M; Wife; 554; No; Cheyenne River, S.D.; Yes; Al. 5500 An. 560

5277; Bingham, Leon; M; 6/25/18-13; 1/4; S; S. Son; 555; No; Same; Yes; Id. U-9147 An. 561

5278; Pretty Weasel, Owen; M; 1892-40; F; M; Head; 5193; Yes; Yes; Al. 6160 An. 5160

N.E.: Pretty Weasel (Shane), Bessie; F; ---- ---; Crow; plus 1/4; M; Wife;

N.E.: Primeau, Joseph; M; ---- ---; Standing Rock Sioux; plus 1/4; M; Head;

5279; Primeau (Janis), Mary; F; 1895-37; plus 1/4; M; Wife; 5194; No; Rapid City, city, Pennington, S.D.; Yes; Al. 1632 An. 5161

5280; Protector, ---; M; 1861-71; F; M; Head; 5195; Yes; Yes; Al. 862 An. 5162

Census of the **Pine Ridge** reservation of the **Pine Ridge, South Dakota** jurisdiction, as of **April 1**, 19**32**, taken by **James H. McGregor**, Superintendent.

Key: Number; Surname, Given; Sex; Date of Birth-Age at Last Birthday; Tribe (Oglala Sioux, unless stated otherwise); Degree of Blood; Marital Status; Relationship to Head of Family [Last Census Roll Number]; At Jurisdiction Where Enrolled (Yes/No); (If no – Where); Ward (Yes/No, if given); Allotment, Annuity and Identification Numbers (if given).

5281; Protector (no data), Lizzie; F; 1875-57; F; M; Wife; 5196; Yes; Yes; Al. 6452 An. 5163

5282; Protector, Adam; M; 4/7/15-16; F; M[sic]; Son; 5197; Yes; Yes; Al. 7851 An. 5165

5283; Protector, Alexander; M; 2/29/20-12; F; M[sic]; Son; 5198; Yes; Yes; Id. U-10165 An. 5166

5284; Provost, Albert; M; 1902-30; plus 1/4; M; Head; 5199; Yes; Yes; Al. 45 An. 5189

5285; Provost (Russel), Lena; F; 3/5/09-23; 1/4; M; Wife; 5200; Yes; Yes; Al. 7697 An. 5990

5286; Provost, Medar; M; 12/20/25-6; 1/4; S; Son; 5201; Yes; Yes; Id. U-11790 An. none

5287; Provost, Howard; M; 9/14/28-3; 1/4; S; Son; 5202; Yes; Yes; Id. U-12808 An. none

5288; Provost, Jewell; F; 3/5/31-1; 1/4; S; Daughter; 5203; Yes; Yes; Id. U-13767 An. none

5289; Provost, Alfred; M; 1898-34; 1/4; M; Head; 5204; Yes; No; Al. 6712 An. 5168

5290; Provost, Anthony; M; 10/14/20-11; -1/4; S; Son; 5205; Yes; Yes; Id. U-10168 An. 5169

5291; Provost, John; M; 8/19/22-9; -1/4; S; Son; 5206; Yes; Yes; Id. U-12032 An. 5170

5292; Provost, Alfred J.; M; 11/11/24-7; -1/4; S; Son; 5207; Yes; Yes; Id. U-11443 An. 5171

5293; Provost, Antoine; M; 1863-69; 1/4; M; Head; 5208; Yes; Yes; Al. 6325 An. 5173

5294; Provost, Julia; F; 11/23/09-22; 1/4; S; Daughter; 5209; Yes; Yes; Id. U-10167 An. 5174

5295; Provost (Baker) (Pedigo), Beth; F; 1868-64; 1/4; M; Head; 5210; Yes; Yes; Al. 2194 An. 5175

5296; Provost, Charles; M; 7/28/65-66; 1/4; M; Head; 5211; Yes; Yes; Al. 2189 An. 5176

5297; Provost (no data), Josephine; F; 1875-57; 1/4; M; Wife; 5212; Yes; Yes; Al. 2190 An. 5177

5298; Provost, Charles Jr.; M; 1/28/10-22; 1/4; S; Son; 5213; Yes; Yes; Al. 5431 An. 5178

5299; Provost, Grace; F; 4/11/15-16; 1/4; S; Daughter; 5215; Yes; Yes; Id. U-10169 An. 5180

Census of the ____Pine Ridge____ reservation of the __Pine Ridge, South Dakota__ jurisdiction, as of ____April 1____, 19**32**, taken by ____James H. McGregor____, Superintendent.

Key: Number; Surname; Given; Sex; Date of Birth-Age at Last Birthday; Tribe (Oglala Sioux, unless stated otherwise); Degree of Blood; Marital Status; Relationship to Head of Family [Last Census Roll Number]; At Jurisdiction Where Enrolled (Yes/No); (If no – Where); Ward (Yes/No, if given); Allotment, Annuity and Identification Numbers (if given).

5299; Provost, Grace; F; 4/11/15-16; 1/4; S; Daughter; 5215; Yes; Yes; Id. U-10169 An. 5180

5300; Provost, Harold; M; 12/12/17-14; 1/4; S; Son; 5216; Yes; Yes; Id. U-10170 An. 5181

5301; Provost, Clinton; M; 1900-32; plus 1/4; M; Head; 5217; Yes; Yes; Al. 47 An. 5182

5302; Provost (Cottier), Maggie; F; 1898-34; 1/4; M; Wife; 5218; Yes; Yes; Al. 4661 An. 1674

5303; Provost, Pelhomine; F; 6/5/25-6; 1/4; S; Daughter; 5219; Yes; Yes; Id. U-11681 An. none

5304; Provost, Dorothy; F; 1904-28; 1/4; S; Head; 5220; Yes; Yes; Al. 5769 An. 5183

5305; Provost, George D; M; 1900-32; 1/4; M; Head; 5221; No; Omaha, city, Douglas, Nebr.; Yes; Al. 4483 An. 5184

5306; Provost, Alma; F; 8/24/29-2; -1/4; S; Daughter; 5222; No; Same; Yes; Id. U-13348 An. none

5307; Provost, Jack; M; 6/3/98-33; plus 1/4; M; Head; 5223; No; Omaha, city, Douglas, Nebr.; No; Al. 4482 An. 5185

N.E.: Provost (Brandon), Ethel; F; ------; Rosebud Sioux; -1/4; M; Wife;

5308; Provost, John W; M; 8/29/28-3; -1/4; S; Son; 5224; No; ; Omaha, city, Douglas, Nebr.; Yes; Id. U-13114 An. none

5309; Provost, John B; M; 1903-29; plus 1/4; Wd; Head; 5225; Yes; Yes; Al. 2241 An. 3186

5310; Provost, Dorothy; F; 9/15/25-6; 1/4; S; Daughter; 5226; Yes; Yes; Id. U-12148 An. none

5311; Provost, Alonzo; M; 7/27/26-5; 1/4; S; Son; 5227; Yes; Yes; Id. U-12147 An. none

N.E.: Provost, William; M; ------; Omaha Indian; plus 1/4; M; Head;

5312; Provost (no data), Lucy; F; 1882-50; 1/4; M; Wife; 5228; Yes; Yes; Al. 45 An. 5189

5313; Provost, William; M; 1856-76; plus 1/4; Wd; Head; 5229; Yes; Yes; Al. 8273 An. 5191

5314; Provost, William; M; 1884-48; 1/4; Wd; Head; 5230; Yes; No; Al. 3817 An. 5192

Census of the __**Pine Ridge**__ reservation of the __**Pine Ridge, South Dakota**__ jurisdiction, as of __**April 1**__, 19**32**, taken by __**James H. McGregor**__, Superintendent.

Key: Number; Surname, Given; Sex; Date of Birth-Age at Last Birthday; Tribe (Oglala Sioux, unless stated otherwise); Degree of Blood; Marital Status; Relationship to Head of Family [Last Census Roll Number]; At Jurisdiction Where Enrolled (Yes/No); (If no – Where); Ward (Yes/No, if given); Allotment, Annuity and Identification Numbers (if given).

5315; Pugh, Jennie; F; 1871-61; 1/4; Wd; Head; 5231; Yes; No; Al. 1077 An. 5193

5316; Pugh, Stanley; M; 1889-43; 1/4; M; Head; 5232; No; Cheyenne River, S.D.; No; Al. 1078 An. 5194

N.E.: Pugh (Robertson), Emily; F; ———; Sisseton Sioux; 1/4; M; Wife;

5317; Pugh, Norman; M; 8/11/20-11; 1/4; S; Son; 5233; No; Cheyenne River, S.D.; Yes; Id. U-10172 An. 5195

5318; Pugh, Klaura; F; 1/4/26-6; 1/4; S; Daughter; 5234; No; Same; Yes; Id. U-11793 An. none

5319; Pugh, Mary; F; 3/19/28-4; 1/4; S; Daughter; 5235; No; Same; Yes; Id. U-12526 An. none

5320; Pugh, William; M; 1891-41; 1/4; M; Head; 5236; Yes; Yes; Al. 1079 An. 5196

5321; Pugh (Babby), Irene; F; 4/1/06-26; -1/4; M; Wife; 5237; Yes; Yes; Al. 4610 An. 232

5322; Pugh, Robert; M; 1/6/22-10; -1/4; S; Son; 5238; Yes; Yes; Id. U-11002 An. 5197

5323; Pugh, George; M; 10/7/29-2; -1/4; S; Son; 5239; Yes; Yes; Id. U-13312 An. none

5324; Pulliam, Amos; M; 1896-36; plus 1/4; S; Head; 5240; Yes; Yes; Al. 5964 An. 5199

5325; Pulliam, James; M; 1892-40; plus 1/4; M; Head; 5241; Yes; No; Al. 1567 An. 5201

5326; Pulliam (Nelson), Rosa; F; 1896-36; 1/4; M; Wife; 5242; Yes; Yes; Al. 2219 An. 5202

5327; Pulliam, Charlotte; F; 10/4/17-14; 1/4; S; Daughter; 5243; Yes; Yes; Id. U-10174 An. 5203

5328; Pulliam, Evelyn; F; 10/24/21-10; 1/4; S; Daughter; 5244; Yes; Yes; Id. U-11006 An. 5204

5329; Pulliam, James Jr.; M; 11/26/24-10; 1/4; S; Son; 5245; Yes; Yes; Id. U-11474 An. 5205

5330; Pulliam, Ruth; F; 1912-19; 1/4; S; Head; 5246; No; Omaha, city, Douglas, Nebr; Yes; Al. 7833 An. 5210

5331; Pulliam, Mary; F; 5/19/28-3; 1/4; S; Daughter; 5247; No; Unknown; Yes; Id. U-13158 An. none

5332; Pulliam (no data), Lucinda; F; 1873-59; 1/4; Wd; Head; 5248; Yes; No; Al. 3632 An. 5207

5333; Pulliam, Wilma; F; 10/26/15-16; 1/4; S; Daughter; 5249; Yes; Yes; Al. 8198 An. 5211

Census of the _____**Pine Ridge**_____ reservation of the _**Pine Ridge, South Dakota**_ jurisdiction, as of _____**April 1**_____, 19**32**, taken by _____**James H. McGregor**_____, Superintendent.

Key: Number; Surname, Given; Sex; Date of Birth-Age at Last Birthday; Tribe (Oglala Sioux, unless stated otherwise); Degree of Blood; Marital Status; Relationship to Head of Family [Last Census Roll Number]; At Jurisdiction Where Enrolled (Yes/No); (If no – Where); Ward (Yes/No, if given); Allotment, Annuity and Identification Numbers (if given).

5334; Pulliam, Maggie; F; 1908-24; 1/4; S; Head; 5250; Yes; Yes; Al. 5962 An. 5208

5334[sic];Pulliam, Martin; M; 1899-33; 1/4; M; Head; 5251; Yes; Yes; Al. 5965 An. 5213

5336; Pulliam, Stella; F; 1905-27; 1/4; S; Head; 5252; Yes; Yes; Al. 5960 An. 5214

5337; Pumpkin Seed, Asa; M; 1864-68; F; M; Head; 5253; Yes; Yes; Al. 678 An. 5215

5338; Pumpkin Seed, Hobert; M; 12/25/11-20; F; S; Son; 5254; Yes; Yes; Al. 7677 An. 5218

5339; Pumpkin Seed, John; M; 1889-43; F; M; Head; 5256; Yes; Yes; Al. 682 An. 5219

5340; Pumpkin Seed (Eagle Shield), Helen; F; 1895-37; F; M; Wife; 5257; Yes; Yes; Al. 7208 An. 5220

5341; Pumpkin Seed, Charles; M; 5/8/16-15; F; S; Son; 5258; Yes; Yes; Id. U-10179 An. 5221

5342; Pumpkin Seed, Clarence; M; 5/8/20-11; F; S; Son; 5260; Yes; Yes; Id. U-10180 An. 5223

5343; Pumpkin Seed, Edgar; M; 9/14/22-9; F; S; Son; 5261; Yes; Yes; Id. U-10181 An. 5224

5344; Pumpkin Seed, Dallas; M; 4/17/24-7; F; S; Son; 5262; Yes; Yes; Id. U-11305 An. 5225

5345; Pumpkin Seed, Winnie; F; 7/2/26-5; F; S; Daughter; 5263; Yes; Yes; Id. U-11984 An. none

5346; Pumpkin Seed, Ida; F; 5/24/18-13; F; S; Head; 5259; Yes; Yes; Id. U-10181 An. 5222

5347; Pumpkin Seed, Jacob; M; 12/12/31-3/12; F; S; Son; ---; Yes; Yes; U-14074

5348; Pumpkin Seed, Joseph; M; 1900-32; F; Wd; Head; 5264; Yes; Yes; Al. 684 An. 5226

5349; Pumpkin Seed, Lucy; F; 3/12/20-12; F; S; Daughter; 5265; Yes; Yes; Id. U-10182 An. 5228

5350; Pumpkin Seed, Noah; M; 12/9/23-8; F; S; Son; 5267; Yes; Yes; Id. U-11293 An. 5230

5351; Pumpkin Seed, Sophia; F; 4/18/27-4; F; S; Daughter; 5268; Yes; Yes; Id. U-12327 An. none

Census of the __**Pine Ridge**__ reservation of the __**Pine Ridge, South Dakota**__ jurisdiction, as of __**April 1**__, 1932, taken by __**James H. McGregor**__, Superintendent.

Key: Number; Surname, Given; Sex; Date of Birth-Age at Last Birthday; Tribe (Oglala Sioux, unless stated otherwise); Degree of Blood; Marital Status; Relationship to Head of Family [Last Census Roll Number]; At Jurisdiction Where Enrolled (Yes/No); (If no – Where); Ward (Yes/No, if given); Allotment, Annuity and Identification Numbers (if given).

5352; Pumpkin Seed, Robert; M; 1886-46; F; M; Head; 5269; Yes; Yes; Al. 681 An. 5231

5353; Pumpkin Seed (Eagle Bear), Mabel; F; 1892-40; F; M; Wife; 5270; Yes; Yes; Al. 748 An. 5232

5354; Pumpkin Seed, Rosa; F; 6/25/14-17; F; S; Daughter; 5271; Yes; Yes; Al. 7678 An. 5234

5355; Pumpkin Seed, Stanley; M; 8/24/16-15; F; S; Son; 5272; Yes; Yes; Id. U-10176 An. 5235

5356; Pumpkin Seed, Noah; M; 8/29/18-13; F; S; Son; 5273; Yes; Yes; Id. U-10177 An. 5236

5357; Pumpkin Seed, Louie; M; 2/7/28-4; F; S; Son; 5274; Yes; Yes; Id. U-12591 An. none

5358; Pumpkin Seed, James; M; 9/22/29-2; F; S; Son; 5275; Yes; Yes; Id. U-13270 An. none

5359; Pumpkin Seed, Cora; F; 7/31/31-8/12; F; S; Daughter; ---; Yes; Yes; U-13876

5360; Pumpkin Seed, Rose; F; 10/30/08-23; F; S; Head; 5276; Yes; Yes; Id. U-10187 An. 5234

5361; Pumpkin Seed, William; M; 1882-50; F; M; Head; 5277; Yes; Yes; Al. 5076 An. 5240

5362; Pumpkin Seed (Jarvis), Lizzie; F; 1882-50; F; M; Wife; 5278; Yes; Yes; Al. 3862 An. 5241

5363; Pumpkin Seed, William Jr.; M; 3/16/15-17; F; M[sic]; Son; 5279; Yes; Yes; Id. U-10186 An. 5242

5364; Pumpkin Seed, Evelyn; F; 11/12/17-14; F; S; Daughter; 5280; Yes; Yes; Id. U-10183 An. 5243

5365; Pumpkin Seed, Joyce; F; 9/25/20-11; F; S; Daughter; 5281; Yes; Yes; Id. U-10184 An. 5244

5366; Pumpkin Seed, Baptiste; M; 3/2/23-9; F; S; Son; 5282; Yes; Yes; Id. U-12088 An. 5245

5367; Pumpkin Seed, Madeline; F; 1/25/25-7; F; S; Daughter; 5283; Yes; Yes; Id. U-10333 An. 5246

N.E.: ~~Quick Bear, Philip; M; ------; Rosebud Sioux; F; Wd; Head;~~
5368; Quick Bear, Eunice; F; 3/17/23-9; plus 1/4; S; Daughter; 5284; No; Rosebud, S.D.; Yes; Id. U-11573 An. 5248

5369; Quick Bear, Virginia J; F; 8/25/24-7; 1/4; S; Daughter; 5285; No; Rosebud, S.D.; Yes; Id. U-11621 An. 5249

N.E.: ~~Quick Bear, Philip; M; ------; Rosebud Sioux; F; M; Head;~~
5370; Quick Bear (LaBuff), Jeannette; F; 1902-30; 1/4; M; Wife; 5286; Yes; Yes; Al. 2264 An. 3610

286

Census of the **Pine Ridge** reservation of the **Pine Ridge, South Dakota** jurisdiction, as of **April 1**, 19**32**, taken by **James H. McGregor**, Superintendent.

Key: Number; Surname, Given; Sex; Date of Birth-Age at Last Birthday; Tribe (Oglala Sioux, unless stated otherwise); Degree of Blood; Marital Status; Relationship to Head of Family [Last Census Roll Number]; At Jurisdiction Where Enrolled (Yes/No); (If no – Where); Ward (Yes/No, if given); Allotment, Annuity and Identification Numbers (if given).

5371; Quick Hawk (Little Bear), Zuzella; F; 1860-72; 1/4; Wd; Head; 5287; Yes; Yes; Al. 1181 An. 5250

5372; Quiver, ---; M; 1853-79; F; M; Head; 5291; Yes; Yes; Al. 4206 An. 5252
5373; Rattling Hawk, ---; F; 1857-75; F; M; Wife; 5292; Yes; Yes; Al. 4310 An. 5253

5374; Quiver, Dennis; M; 1895-37; F; M; Head; 5293; Yes; Yes; Al. 4228 An. 5254
5375; Quiver (Bad Wound), Agnes; F; 1891-41; F; M; Wife; 5294; Yes; Yes; Al. 2074 An. 5255
5376; Quiver, Harry; M; 11/5/14-17; F; S; Son; 5295; Yes; Yes; Al. 7957 An. 5256
5377; Quiver, Nancy; F; 1/16/18-14; F; S; Daughter; 5296; Yes; Yes; Id. U-10189 An. 5257
5378; Quiver, Eva; F; 4/4/25-6; F; S; Daughter; 5297; Yes; Yes; Id. U-12712 An. none
5379; Quiver, James N; M; 4/16/27-4; F; S; Son; 5298; Yes; Yes; Id. U-12328 An. none
5380; Quiver, David; M; 5/10/30-1; F; S; Son; 5299; Yes; Yes; Id. U-13491 An. none

5381; Quiver, Joseph; M; 1903-29; F; S; Head; 5300; Yes; Yes; Al. 4231 An. 5259

5382; Quiver, Harry; M; 1870-62; F; M; Head; 5301; Yes; Yes; Al. 4227 An. 5260
5383; Wild Horse, ---; F; 1875-57; F; M; Wife; 5302; Yes; Yes; Al. 5373 An. 5261
5384; Quiver, Albert; M; 3/3/12-20; F; S; Son; 5303; Yes; Yes; Al. 7035 An. 5262
5385; Quiver, Daniel; M; 11/22/14-17; F; S; Son; 5304; Yes; Yes; Al. 7903 An. 5264
5386; Little Killer, Owen; M; 3/25/15-17; F; S; Son; 5305; Yes; Yes; Al. 8164 An. 5265

5387; Quiver, James Jonas; M; 1907-25; F; M; Head; 5308; Yes; Yes; Al. 4232 An. 5266
5388; Quiver (Richard), Lucinda; F; 11/2/10-21; F; M; Wife; 5309; Yes; Yes; Al. 5707 An. 5657
5389; Quiver, Millie; F; 7/13/29-2; F; S; Daughter; 5310; Yes; Yes; Id. U-13229 An. none
5390; Quiver, Phoebe; F; 8/28/30-1; F; S; Daughter; 5311; Yes; Yes; Id. U-13581 An. none
5391; Quiver, Bernard; M; 3/7/32-1/12; F; S; Son; ---; Yes; Yes; U-14133

5392; Quiver, Thomas; M; 1890-42; F; M; Head; 5312; Yes; Yes; Al. 4309 An. 5267
5393; Quiver (Standing Bear), Esther; F; 1889-43; F; M; Wife; 5313; Yes; Yes; Al. 4010 An. 5268

Census of the **Pine Ridge** reservation of the **Pine Ridge, South Dakota** jurisdiction, as of **April 1**, 19**32**, taken by **James H. McGregor**, Superintendent.

Key: Number; Surname, Given; Sex; Date of Birth-Age at Last Birthday; Tribe (Oglala Sioux, unless stated otherwise); Degree of Blood; Marital Status; Relationship to Head of Family [Last Census Roll Number]; At Jurisdiction Where Enrolled (Yes/No); (If no – Where); Ward (Yes/No, if given); Allotment, Annuity and Identification Numbers (if given).

5394; Quiver, Bert; M; 11/5/15-16; F; S; Son; 5314; Yes; Yes; Al. 8237 An. 5270

5395; Randall, Andrew; M; 5/29/11-20; plus 1/4; M; Head; 5315; Yes; Yes; Al. 5675 An. 5314

5396; Randall (Hawkins, Sophia), Sophia; F; 9/7/08-23; plus 1/4; M; Wife; 5316; Yes; Yes; Al. 4617 An.2764

5397; Randall, Antoine; M; 1863-69; plus 1/4; Wd.; Head; 5317; Yes; Yes; Al. 1807 An. 5271

5398; Randall, Benjamin; M; 1902-30; plus 1/4; M; Head; 5318; Yes; Yes; Al. 1845 An. 5273

N.E.: Randall (Hollow Horn Bear, Leah), Leah; F; -------; Rosebud Sioux; M; Wife;

5399; Randall, Charles Sr.; M; 1871-61; plus 1/4; Wd.; Head; 5319; Yes; No; Al. 4669 An. 5275

5400; Randall, Charles Jr.; M; 1903-29; plus 1/4; M; Head; 5320; Yes; Yes; Al. 4672 An. 5276

5401; Randall (Hornbeck, Elizabeth), Elizabeth; F; 6/2/03-28; plus 1/4; M; Wife; 5321; Yes; Yes; Al. 836 An.3024

5402; Hornbeck, Archie Joseph; M; 1/15/24-8; plus 1/4; S; Stepson; 5322; Yes; Yes; Id. U-12892 An. none

5403; Randall, Edward; M; 1904-27; plus 1/4; M; Head; 5323; Yes; Yes; Al. 1846 An. 5277

5404; Randall (Little Killer, Mabel), Mabel; F; 1902-29; F; M; Wife; 5324; Yes; Yes; Al. 5576 An.5278

5405; Randall, Frank; M; 1900-32; plus 1/4; M; Head; 5329; Yes; Yes; Al. 1964 An. 5285

5406; Randall (Hornbeck, Maggie), Maggie; F; 1906-26; plus 1/4; M; Wife; 5331; Yes; Yes; Al. 7690 An.2039

5407; Randall, Anna; F; 10/9/21-10; plus 1/4; S; Daughter; 5330; Yes; Yes; Id. U-10872 An. 5286

5408; Randall, Mary M.; F; 9/4/28-3; plus 1/4; S; Daughter; 5332; Yes; Yes; Id. U-12779 An. none

5409; Randall, Victoria; F; 12/5/30-1; plus 1/4; S; Daughter; 5333; Yes; Yes; Id. U-13672 An. none

5410; Randall, George; M; 1876-56; F; M; Head; 5334; Yes; Yes; Al. 5557 An. 5288

Census of the＿＿**Pine Ridge**＿＿reservation of the＿**Pine Ridge, South Dakota**
jurisdiction, as of＿＿**April 1**＿＿, 19**32**, taken by＿**James H. McGregor**＿,
Superintendent.

Key: Number; Surname, Given; Sex; Date of Birth-Age at Last Birthday; Tribe (Oglala Sioux, unless stated otherwise); Degree of Blood; Marital Status; Relationship to Head of Family [Last Census Roll Number]; At Jurisdiction Where Enrolled (Yes/No); (If no – Where); Ward (Yes/No, if given); Allotment, Annuity and Identification Numbers (if given).

5411; Randall (Fox Belly, Lucy), Lucy; F; 1899-33; F; M; Wife; 5335; Yes; Yes; Al. 7199 An.5289

5412; Randall, Lizzie; F; 5/21/24-7; F; S; Daughter; 5336; Yes; Yes; Id. U-11280 An. 5293

5413; Randall, Patrick; M; 2/26/31-1; F; S; Son; 5338; Yes; Yes; Id. U-13768 An. none

5414; Randall, John; M; 1891-41; plus 1/4; M; Head; 5341; Yes; Yes; Al. 5765 An. 5298

N.E.: ~~Randall (Hunter or Garreau, Alice), Alice; F; ------; Cheyenne River Sioux; M; Wife;~~

5415; Randall, Ramona; F; 10/21/27-4; plus 1/4; S; Daughter; 5342; Yes; Yes; Id. U-12694 An. none

5416; Randall, Jeanette; F; 5/14/29-2; plus 1/4; S; Daughter; 5343; Yes; Yes; Id. U-13192 An. none

5417; Randall, Owen James; M; 1904-28; plus 1/4; M; Head; 5344; Yes; Yes; Al. 4871 An. 5302

N.E.: ~~Randall (Little Chief, Emma), Emma; F; ------; Rosebud Sioux; plus 1/4 M; Wife;~~

5418; Randall, Robert; M; 4/27/27-4; Sioux; plus 1/4; S; Son; 5345; Yes; Yes; Id. U-12357 An. none

5419; Randall, Julia May; F; 4/27/29-2; Sioux; plus 1/4; S; Daughter; ---; Yes; Yes; Id. U-14048 An. none

5420; Randall, Florence L.; F; 4/22/31-11/12; plus 1/4; S; Daughter; ---; Yes; Yes; Id. U-13972 An. none

5421; Randall, Robert; M; 1854-78; plus 1/4; Wd.; Head; 5346; Yes; Yes; Al. 4531 An. 5303

5422; Randall, Sarah; F; 1880-52; plus 1/4; Wd.; Head; 5347; Yes; Yes; Al. 1844 An. 5304

5423; Randall, Joseph Jr.; M; 7/4/11-20; plus 1/4; S; Son; 5348; Yes; Yes; Al. 5764 An. 5306

5424; Randall, Rose; F; 3/28/14-18; plus 1/4; S; Daughter; 5349; Yes; Yes; Al. 8124 An. 5307

5425; Randall, Mark; M; 8/9/17-14; plus 1/4; S; Son; 5350; Yes; Yes; Id. U-10196 An. 5308

5426; Randall, Stephen; M; 8/30/23-8; plus 1/4; S; Son; 5351; Yes; Yes; Id. U-11613 An. 5309

5427; Randall, Todd; M; 1899-33; plus 1/4; M; Head; 5352; Yes; Yes; Al. 2008 An. 5310

Census of the __Pine Ridge__ reservation of the __Pine Ridge, South Dakota__ jurisdiction, as of __April 1__, 1932, taken by __James H. McGregor__, Superintendent.

Key: Number; Surname, Given; Sex; Date of Birth-Age at Last Birthday; Tribe (Oglala Sioux, unless stated otherwise); Degree of Blood; Marital Status; Relationship to Head of Family [Last Census Roll Number]; At Jurisdiction Where Enrolled (Yes/No); (If no – Where); Ward (Yes/No, if given); Allotment, Annuity and Identification Numbers (if given).

N.E.: Randall (Left Hand Bull, Mary), Minnie Mary; F; ------; Rosebud Sioux; M; Wife;

5428; Randall, William; M; 1867-65; plus 1/4; M; Head; 5353; Yes; Yes; Al. 2037 An. 5311

5429; Randall (no data), Susie; F; 1870-62; F; M; Wife; 5354; Yes; Yes; Al. 2038 An.5312

5430; Randall, Martin; M; 11/10/13-18; plus 1/4; S; Son; 5355; Yes; Yes; Al. 7725 An.5315

5431; Rattling Chase, John; M; 1879-53; F; Wd.; Head; 5357; Yes; Yes; Al. 2861 An. 5317

5432; Rattling Chase, Isaac; M; 9/16/09-22; F; M; Head; 5359; Yes; Yes; Al. 7670 An. 5319

5433; Rattling Chase (Black Bear, Agnes), Agnes; F; 10/13/09-22; F; M; Wife; 5360; Yes; Yes; Al. 5942 An.677

5434; Red Nest, Edison; M; 9/9/27-4; F; S; Ward; 5527; Yes; Yes; Id. U-12389 An. none

5435; Red Bear, Dick; M; 1885-47; F; M; Head; 5361; Yes; Yes; Al. 205 An. 5324

5436; Red Bear (Romero, Maggie), Maggie; plus 1/4; 1878-54; plus 1/4; M; Wife; 5362; Yes; Yes; Al. 871 An.5325

5437; Romero, Emma; F; 4/25/13-18; plus 1/4; S; Stepdaughter; 5363; Yes; Yes; Al. 7296 An. 5327

5438; Mesteth, Louis; M; 2/23/16-16; plus 1/4; S; Ward; 5364; Yes; Yes; Id. U-10010 An. none

5439; Red Bear, George; M; 1879-53; F; M; Head; 5365; Yes; Yes; Al. 6360 An. 5328

5440; Red Bear (Eagle Louse, Lizzie), Lizzie; plus ; 1857-75; F; M; Wife; 5366; Yes; Yes; Al. 3410 An.5329

5441; Red Bear, Howard; M; 1874-58; plus 1/4; M; Head; 5367; Yes; Yes; Al. 1515 An. 5330

5442; Red Bear (No data, Jessie), Jessie; F; 1877-55; F; M; Wife; 5368; Yes; Yes; Al. 4651 An.5331

5443; Red Bear, Isaac; M; 2/11/17-15; plus 1/4; S; Grandson; 5369; Yes; Yes; Id. U-10202 An. 5332

5444; Red Bear, Joseph; M; 1886-46; F; M; Head; 5370; Yes; Yes; Al. 6609 An. 5333

Census of the **Pine Ridge** reservation of the **Pine Ridge, South Dakota** jurisdiction, as of **April 1**, 19**32**, taken by **James H. McGregor**, Superintendent.

Key: Number; Surname, Given; Sex; Date of Birth-Age at Last Birthday; Tribe (Oglala Sioux, unless stated otherwise); Degree of Blood; Marital Status; Relationship to Head of Family [Last Census Roll Number]; At Jurisdiction Where Enrolled (Yes/No); (If no – Where); Ward (Yes/No, if given); Allotment, Annuity and Identification Numbers (if given).

5445; Red Bear (Whirlwind Bear, Susie), Susie; F; 1874-58; F; M; Wife; 5371; Yes; Yes; Al. 6610 An.5334

5446; Red Bear, Julia; F; 1878-54; plus 1/4; Wd.; Head; 5372; Yes; Yes; Al. 4091 An. 7276

5447; Red Bear, Ben Jr.; M; 9/23/21-10; plus 1/4; S; Alone; 5373; No; Verdel, town, Neb.; Yes; Id. U-11485 An. 5323

5448; Red Bear, Martin; M; 1874-58; F; M; Head; 5374; Yes; Yes; Al. 88 An. 5335
5449; Red Bear (No data), Julia; F; 1878-54; plus 1/4; M; Wife; 5375; Yes; Yes; Al. 6753 An. 5336
5450; Red Bear, John; M; 10/2/22-9; plus 1/4; S; Son; 5376; Yes; Yes; Id. U-11084 An. 5338
5451; Red Bear, Roote; M; 1907-25; F; S; Head; 5377; Yes; Yes; Id. U-10205 An. 3340

5452; Red Bear, Philip; M; 1848-84; F; M; Head; 5378; Yes; Yes; Al. 5163 An. 5341
5453; Shell Woman, ---; F; 1849-83; F; M; Wife; 5379; Yes; Yes; Al. 5164 An. 5342

5454; Red Bear, Ralph; M; 1901-31; F; M; Head; 5381; Yes; Yes; Id. U-10206 An. 5344
5455; Red Bear (Takes The Shield, Josie), Josie; F; 1895-37; F; M; Wife; 5382; Yes; Yes; Al. 1223 An. 5345
5456; Takes The Shield, Clara M.; F; 4/ /18-13; F; S; Stepdaughter; 5383; Yes; Yes; Id. U-10207 An. 5346

5457; Red Blanket, Charles; M; 1899-33; F; M; Head; 5385; Yes; Yes Al. 655 An. 5349
5458; Red Blanket (Wounded Head, Sarah), Sarah; F; 1907-25; F; M; Wife; 5386; Yes; Yes; Al. 3807 An. 7774
5459; Red Blanket, Walter; M; 10/24/26-5; F; S; Son; 5387; Yes; Yes; Id. U-12118 An. none
5460; Red Blanket, Thomas; M; 8/22/28-3; F; S; Son; 5388; Yes; Yes; Id. U-12780 An. none
5461; Red Blanket, Leslie; M; 12/13/30-1; F; S; Son; 5389; Yes; Yes; Id. U-13655 An. none

5462; Red Bow, Joseph; M; 1899-33; F; M; Head; 5390; Yes; Yes Al. 3354 An. 5350
5463; Red Bow (Living Outside, Susie), Susie; F; 1896-36; F; M; Wife; 5391; Yes; Yes; Al. 2898 An. 5351

Census of the **Pine Ridge** reservation of the **Pine Ridge, South Dakota** jurisdiction, as of **April 1**, 19**32**, taken by **James H. McGregor**, Superintendent.

Key: Number; Surname, Given; Sex; Date of Birth-Age at Last Birthday; Tribe (Oglala Sioux, unless stated otherwise); Degree of Blood; Marital Status; Relationship to Head of Family [Last Census Roll Number]; At Jurisdiction Where Enrolled (Yes/No); (If no – Where); Ward (Yes/No, if given); Allotment, Annuity and Identification Numbers (if given).

5464; Red Bow, John; M; 1/14/21-11; F; S; Son; 5392; Yes; Yes; Id. U-10209 An. 5352

5465; Red Bow, Wallace; M; 7/16/31-9/12; F; S; Son; ---; Yes; Yes; Id. U-13877 An. none

5466; Red Bow, Richard; M; 1875-57; F; M; Head; 5393; Yes; Yes Al. 3170 An. 3354

5467; Red Bow (No data), Annie; F; 1876-56; F; M; Wife; 5394; Yes; Yes; Al. 6231 An. 5355

5468; Red Bow, Steven; M; 4/17/21-10; F; S; Ward; 5395; Yes; Yes; Id. U-10854 An. 6055

5469; Red Boy, George; M; 1895-37; F; M; Head; 5396; No; Chadron, town, Dawes, Nebr.; Yes Al. 6361 An. 5357

5470; Red Breath Bear, Charles; M; 1890-42; F; M; Head; 5397; Yes; Yes Al. 7551 An. 5360

N.E.: ~~Red Breath Bear (Crier, Mary), Mary; F; ---- ---; Rosebud Sioux; M; Wife;~~

5471; Red Breath Bear, Leslie; F; 10/27/25-6; F; S; Daughter; 5398; Yes; Yes; Id. U-11740 An. none

5472; Red Breath Bear, Pearl; F; 3/29/28-4; F; S; Daughter; 5399; Yes; Yes; Id. U-12556 An. none

5473; Red Breath Bear, Percy; M; 10/27/31-5/12; F; S; Son; ---; Yes; Yes; Id. U-13951 An. none

5474; Red Breath Bear, Taylor; M; 1896-36; F; Wd.; Head; 5400; Yes; Yes Al. 6431 An. 5362

5475; Red Cloud, Alfred; M; 1897-35; F; M; Head; 5401; Yes; Yes Al. 1269 An. 5363

5476; Red Cloud (Kills Enemy, Nellie), Nellie; F; 1901-31; F; M; Wife; 5402; Yes; Yes; Al. 7321 An. 5364

5477; Red Cloud, Bernard; M; 2/18/29-3; F; S; Son; 5403; Yes; Yes; Id. U-13115 An. none

5478; Red Cloud, Charles; M; 1885-47; F; M; Head; 5404; Yes; Yes Al. 6462 An. 5365

5479; Red Cloud (Black Bear, Laura), Laura; F; 1886-46; F; M; Wife; 5405; Yes; Yes; Al. 1241 An. 5366

5480; Red Cloud, Susie; F; 8/11/14-17; F; S; Daughter; 5406; Yes; Yes; Id. U-10216 An. 5368

5481; Red Cloud, Oliver; M; 12/14/20-11; F; S; Son; 5407; Yes; Yes; Id. U-10217 An. 5369

Census of the   **Pine Ridge**   reservation of the **Pine Ridge, South Dakota** jurisdiction, as of   **April 1**   , 19**32**, taken by   **James H. McGregor**   , Superintendent.

Key: Number; Surname, Given; Sex; Date of Birth-Age at Last Birthday; Tribe (Oglala Sioux, unless stated otherwise); Degree of Blood; Marital Status; Relationship to Head of Family [Last Census Roll Number]; At Jurisdiction Where Enrolled (Yes/No); (If no – Where); Ward (Yes/No, if given); Allotment, Annuity and Identification Numbers (if given).

5482; Red Cloud, Nancy; F; 1859-73; F; Wd.; Head; 5408; Yes; Yes; Al. 7820 An. 5387

5483; Red Cloud, Edgar; M; 1897-35; plus 1/4; M; Head; 5409; Yes; Yes Al. 3736 An. 5371
5484; Red Cloud (Bissonette, Lottie), Lottie; F; 1903-29; plus 1/4; M; Wife; 5410; Yes; Yes; Al. 1241 An. 5366
5485; Red Cloud, Benjamin; M; 7/27/25-5; plus 1/4; S; Son; 5411; Yes; Yes; Id. U-12194 An. none
5486; Red Cloud, Vance; M; 6/24/28-3; plus 1/4; S; Son; 5412; Yes; Yes; Id. U-12897 An. none
5487; Red Cloud, Marie; F; 2/2/31-1; plus 1/4; S; Daughter; 5413; Yes; Yes; Id. U-13743 An. none

5488; Red Cloud, James; M; 1877-53; F; M; Head; 5414; Yes; Yes Al. 2875 An. 5374
5489; Red Cloud (No data), Delia; F; 1886-46; F; M; Wife; 5415; Yes; Yes; Al. 5130 An. 5375
5490; Red Cloud, Louis; M; 12/4/11-20; F; S; Son; 5416; Yes; Yes; Al. 6488 An. 5376
5491; Red Cloud, Agnes; F; 11/15/18-13; F; S; Daughter; 5417; Yes; Yes; Id. U-10215 An. 5377

5492; Red Cloud, James; M; 1892-40; F; M; Head; 5418; Yes; Yes Al. 1267 An. 5372
5493; Red Cloud (White Bear, Alice), Alice; F; 1895-37; F; M; Wife; 5419; Yes; Yes; Al. 1794 An. 5373
5494; Red Cloud, Lydia Naomi; F; 8/5/15-16; F; S; Daughter; 5420; Yes; Yes; Id. U-10212 An. 5374
5495; Red Cloud, Melvin; M; 11/21/17-14; F; S; Son; 5421; Yes; Yes; Id. U-10213 An. 5375
5496; Red Cloud, William; M; 1/20/20-12; F; S; Son; 5422; Yes; Yes; Id. U-10214 An. 5376
5497; Red Cloud, Walter Jay; M; 6/10/22-9; F; S; Son; 5423; Yes; Yes; Id. U-11020 An. 5377
5498; Red Cloud, Gladys Ruby; F; 12/30/24-7; F; S; Daughter; 5424; Yes; Yes; Id. U-11431 An. 5378
5499; Red Cloud, Louisa; F; 5/6/27-4; F; S; Daughter; 5425; Yes; Yes; Id. U-12558 An. none

5500; Red Cloud, Joseph; M; 1899-33; F; M; Head; 5426; Yes; Yes Al. 1270 An. 5385

Census of the __**Pine Ridge**__ reservation of the __**Pine Ridge, South Dakota**__ jurisdiction, as of __**April 1**__, 19**32**, taken by __**James H. McGregor**__, Superintendent.

Key: Number; Surname, Given; Sex; Date of Birth-Age at Last Birthday; Tribe (Oglala Sioux, unless stated otherwise); Degree of Blood; Marital Status; Relationship to Head of Family [Last Census Roll Number]; At Jurisdiction Where Enrolled (Yes/No); (If no – Where); Ward (Yes/No, if given); Allotment, Annuity and Identification Numbers (if given).

5501; Red Cloud (Wounded, Bessie), Bessie; F; 1897-35; F; M; Wife; 5427; Yes; Yes; Al. 3201 An. 5386

5502; Red Cloud, Dorene; F; 2/18/27-5; F; S; Daughter; 5428; Yes; Yes; Id. U-12559 An. none

5503; Red Cloud, Nancy; F; 6/14/09-22; F; S; Head; 5408; Yes; Yes; Al. 7307 An. 5387

5504; Red Cow, ---; F; 1848-84; F; Wd.; Head; 5430; Yes; Yes; Al. 5051 An. 4102

5505; Red Dog, Samuel; M; 1890-42; F; Wd.; Head; 5431; Yes; Yes; Al. 6366 An. 5393

5506; Red Dog, Irene; F; 4/27/15-16; plus 1/4; S; Daughter; 5432; Yes; Yes; Al. 8016 An. 5397

5507; Red Dog, Virginia; F; 12/4/19-12; plus 1/4; S; Daughter; 5433; Yes; Yes; Id. U-10219 An. 5398

5508; Red Dog, Peter; M; 9/30/22-9; plus 1/4; S; Son; 5434; Yes; Yes; Id. U-11089 An. 5399

5509; Red Dog, Norah; F; 7/28/26-5; plus 1/4; S; Daughter; 5435; Yes; Yes; Id. U-12119 An. none

5510; Red Dog, Huron; M; 6/3/09-22; plus 1/4; S; Head; 5436; Yes; Yes; Al. 7639 An. 5395

5511; Red Dog, Esther; F; 1/6/12-20; plus 1/4; S; Head; 5437; Yes; Yes; Al. 7640 An. 5396

N.E.: Red Dog, Baptiste; M; ------; Cheyenne River Sioux; F; M; Head;
5512; Red Dog (Runs Above, Lizzie), Lizzie; F; 1898-34; plus 1/4; M; Wife; 5438; Yes; Yes; Al. 7585 An. 5406

5513; Red Dog, ---; F; 1860-72; F; Wd.; Wife; 5439; Yes; Yes; Al. 4050 An. 5409
N.E.: Reddy, William; M; ------; WHITE; Head;
5514; Reddy (Garnette, Emma), Emma; F; 1889-43; plus 1/4; M; Wife; 5440; Yes; No; Al. 3663 An. 5400

5515; Garnette, Theodore; M; 11/17/11-20; plus 1/4; S; Son (Step); 5441; Yes; Yes; Al. 7213 An. 5401

5516; Garnette, Frances E.; F; 1/ /17-15; plus 1/4; S; Stepdaughter; 5442; Yes; Yes; Id. U-9555 An. 5402

5517; Garnette, Cynthia B.; F; 1/15/19-12; plus 1/4; S; Stepdaughter; 5443; Yes; Yes; Id. U-9556 An. 5403

5518; Reddy, Florence; F; 7/1/22-9; -1/4; S; Daughter; 5444; Yes; Yes; Id. U-12081 An. 5404

Census of the **Pine Ridge** reservation of the **Pine Ridge, South Dakota** jurisdiction, as of **April 1**, 1932, taken by **James H. McGregor**, Superintendent.

Key: Number; Surname, Given; Sex; Date of Birth-Age at Last Birthday; Tribe (Oglala Sioux, unless stated otherwise); Degree of Blood; Marital Status; Relationship to Head of Family [Last Census Roll Number]; At Jurisdiction Where Enrolled (Yes/No); (If no – Where); Ward (Yes/No, if given); Allotment, Annuity and Identification Numbers (if given).

5519; Reddy, William Jr.; M; 10/27/24-7; -1/4; S; Son; 5445; Yes; Yes; Id. U-11557 An. 5405

5520; Reddy, Magdaline; F; 3/1/27-5; -1/4; S; Daughter; 5446; Yes; Yes; Id. U-12695 An. none

5521; Reddy, Rose Mary; F; 12/24/29-2; -1/4; S; Daughter; 5447; Yes; Yes; Id. U-13349 An. none

5522; Red Eagle, Amos; M; 1889-43; F; M; Head; 5448; Yes; Yes; Al. 625 An. 5411

5523; Red Eagle (Runs Against, Irene), Irene; F; 1898-34; F; M; Wife; 5449; Yes; Yes; Al. 2976 An. 5412

5524; Red Eagle, Anna; F; 1859-73; F; Wd.; Head; 5450; Yes; Yes; Al. 3719 An. 5416

5525; Red Ear Horse, Dora; F; 8/14/06-26; F; S; Head; 5451; Yes; Yes; Al. 3272 An. 5417

5526; Red Ear Horse, Harry; M; 1878-54; F; M; Head; 5452; Yes; Yes; Al. 3262 An. 5418

5527; Red Ear Horse (Little Bird,), Opal; F; 1886-46; F; M; Wife; 5453; Yes; Yes; Al. 3263 An. 5419

5528; Red Ear Horse, Margery; F; 10/23/15-16; F; S; Daughter; 5454; Yes; Yes; Id. U-10222 An. 5422

5529; Red Ear Horse, Jacob; M; 11/27/26-5; F; S; Son; 5455; Yes; Yes; Id. U-12226 An. none

5530; Red Ear Horse, Stephen; M; 10/22/06-26; F; M; Head; 5456; Yes; Yes; Al. 2891 An. 5423

5531; Red Ear Horse (Wounded Horse, Hazel), Hazel; F; 2/8/11-21; F; M; Wife; 5457; Yes; Yes; Al. 3329a An. 7780

5532; Red Ear Horse, Melvina B.; F; 10/24/31-5/12; F; S; Daughter; ---; Yes; Yes; Id. U-14104 An. none

5533; Red Elk, ---; M; 1860-76; F; Wd.; Head; 5458; Yes; Yes; Al. 5648 An. 5427

5534; Red Elk, Emil; M; 1894-38; F; Wd.; Head; 5459; No; Leavenworth, Kans,; Yes; Al. 6995 An. 5429

5535; Red Elk, Peter; M; 1892-40; F; M; Head; 5460; Yes; Yes; Al. 7567 An. 5436

5536; Red Elk (Black Tail Deer, Fannie), Fannie; F; 1898-34; F; M; Wife; 5461; Yes; Yes; Al. 5072 An. 5437

5537; Red Elk, Steven; M; 3/13/17-15; F; S; Son; 5462; Yes; Yes; Id. U-10227 An. 5438

Census of the __Pine Ridge__ reservation of the __Pine Ridge, South Dakota__ jurisdiction, as of __April 1__, 1932, taken by __James H. McGregor__, Superintendent.

Key: Number; Surname, Given; Sex; Date of Birth-Age at Last Birthday; Tribe (Oglala Sioux, unless stated otherwise); Degree of Blood; Marital Status; Relationship to Head of Family [Last Census Roll Number]; At Jurisdiction Where Enrolled (Yes/No); (If no – Where); Ward (Yes/No, if given); Allotment, Annuity and Identification Numbers (if given).

5538; Red Elk, Wilbert; M; 1/21/20-12; F; S; Son; 5463; Yes; Yes; Id. U-10228 An. 5439

5539; Red Elk, Rosie; F; 8/25/21-10; F; S; Daughter; 5464; Yes; Yes; Id. U-10229 An. 5440

5540; Red Elk, Violet; F; 4/3/23-8; F; S; Daughter; 5465; Yes; Yes; Id. U-13023 An. 5441

5541; Red Elk, James; M; 2/24/27-5; F; S; Son; 5466; Yes; Yes; Id. U-12260 An. none

5542; Red Elk, Aloysius; M; 9/10/30-1; F; S; Son; 5467; Yes; Yes; Id. U-13582 An. none

5543; Red Elk, William; M; 1889-43; F; M; Head; 5468; Yes; Yes; Al. 5649 An. 5443

5544; Red Elk (Thompson, Lizzie), Lizzie; F; 1889-43; F; M; Wife; 5469; Yes; Yes; Al. 1908 An. 6852

5545; Red Elk, Virginia; F; 2/6/13-19; F; S; Daughter; 5470; Yes; Yes; Al. 7050 An. 5445

5546; Red Elk, Elmore; M; 4/15/15-16; F; S; Son; 5471; Yes; Yes; Al.8165 An. 5446

5547; Red Elk, Stephen; M; 1/22/19-13; F; S; Son; 5472; Yes; Yes; Id. U-10226 An. 5448

5548; Red Elk, Mollie; F; 5/13/21-10; F; S; Daughter; 5473; Yes; Yes; Id. U-11032 An. 5449

5549; Red Eyes, Daniel; M; 1880-52; F; Wd.; Head; 5474; Yes; No; Al. 658 An. 5452

5550; Red Eyes, Reuben; M; 1/4/15-17; F; S; Son; 5475; Yes; Yes; Id. U-10233 An. 5456

5551; Red Eyes, Earnest; M; 2/28/18-14; F; S; Son; 5476; Yes; Yes; Id. U-10234 An. 5457

5552; Red Eyes, Lucy; F; 6/12/10-21; F; S; Head; 5478; Yes; Yes; Al. 6880 An. 5455

5553; Red Eyes, Ella; F; 1901-25; F; S; Head; 5479; Yes; Yes; Al. 7929 An. 5458

5554; Red Eyes, Elmore; M; 1877-55; F; M; Head; 5480; Yes; No; Al. 3698 An. 5459

5555; Red Eyes (No data), Mollie; F; 1880-52; F; M; Wife; 5481; Yes; Yes; Al. 7818 An. 5460

5556; Red Eyes, Homer; M; 9/16/17-14; F; S; Son; 5482; Yes; Yes; Id. U-10231 An. 5462

Census of the **Pine Ridge** reservation of the **Pine Ridge, South Dakota** jurisdiction, as of **April 1**, 19**32**, taken by **James H. McGregor**, Superintendent.

Key: Number; Surname, Given; Sex; Date of Birth-Age at Last Birthday; Tribe (Oglala Sioux, unless stated otherwise); Degree of Blood; Marital Status; Relationship to Head of Family [Last Census Roll Number]; At Jurisdiction Where Enrolled (Yes/No); (If no – Where); Ward (Yes/No, if given); Allotment, Annuity and Identification Numbers (if given).

5557; Red Eyes, Walter; M; 2/15/09-23; F; S; Head; 5483; Yes; Yes; Al. 6858 An. 5461

5558; Red Feather, Dinah; F; 1893-39; F; Wd.; Head; 5485; Yes; Yes; Al. 3413 An. 5466

5559; Red Feather, Mary Lona; F; 11/23/23-8; F; S; Daughter; 5486; Yes; Yes; Id. U-11169 An. 5467

5560; Red Feather, Elva M.; F; 1/2/28-4; F; S; Daughter; 5487; Yes; Yes; Id. U-12464 An. none

5561; Red Feather, Christopher; M; 1879-35; F; M; Head; 5488; Yes; Yes; Al. 6494 An. 5468

5562; Red Feather (Lone Dog, Mollie), Mollie; F; 1903-29; F; M; Wife; 5489; Yes; Yes; Al. 322 An. 5469

5563; Red Feather, Paul; M; 1901-31; F; M; Head; 5494; Yes; Yes; Al. 2290 An. 5478

5564; Red Feather (Holy Elk, Julia), Julia; F; 1901-31; plus 1/4; M; Wife; 5495; Yes; Yes; Al. 5492 An. none

5565; Red Feather, Elizabeth; F; 4/22/30-1; plus 1/4; S; Daughter; 5498; Yes; Yes; Id. U-13656 An. none

5566; Holy Elk, Roy; M; 9/10/19-12; plus 1/4; S; Stepson; 5496; Yes; Yes; Id. U-9697 An. none

5567; Young, Wallace; M; 7/28/27-4; plus 1/4; S; Stepson; 5497; Yes; Yes; Id. U-12396 An. none

5568; Red Feather, Stanley; M; 1859-73; F; M; Head; 5499; Yes; Yes; Al. 6491 An. 5479

5569; Red Feather (No data), Barbara; F; 1859-73; F; M; Wife; 5500; Yes; Yes; Al. 6492 An. 5480

5570; Red Hair, William; M; 1887-45; F; M; Head; 5501; Yes; Yes; Al. 336 An. 5485

5571; Red Hair (Brave Heart, Mary), Mary; F; 1876-56; plus 1/4; M; Wife; 5502; Yes; Yes; Al. 4178 An. 5486

5572; Red Hair, Leo; M; 2/10/14-18; plus 1/4; S; Son; 5503; Yes; Yes; Id. U-10243 An. 5488

5573; Red Hair, Rosa; F; 1/9/11-21; plus 1/4; S; Head; 5404; Yes; Yes; Id. U-10242 An. 5487

5574; Red Hawk, Alice; F; 1857-75; F; Wd.; Head; 5505; Yes; Yes; Al. 2812 An. 5491

Census of the __Pine Ridge__ reservation of the __Pine Ridge, South Dakota__ jurisdiction, as of __April 1__, 19**32**, taken by __James H. McGregor__, Superintendent.

Key: Number; Surname, Given; Sex; Date of Birth-Age at Last Birthday; Tribe (Oglala Sioux, unless stated otherwise); Degree of Blood; Marital Status; Relationship to Head of Family [Last Census Roll Number]; At Jurisdiction Where Enrolled (Yes/No); (If no – Where); Ward (Yes/No, if given); Allotment, Annuity and Identification Numbers (if given).

5575; Red Hawk, John; M; 12/16/96-35; F; M; Head; 5506; Yes; Yes; Id. U-10244 An. 5492

5576; Red Hawk (Make Shine, Julia), Julia; F; 9/15/02-29; F; M; Wife; 5507; Yes; Yes; Al. 4992 An. 4301

5577; Red Hawk, Ward Nelson; M; 11/20/25-6; F; S; Son; 5508; Yes; Yes; Id. U-11858 An. none

5578; Red Hawk, Suey San; F; 10/14/29-2; F; S; Daughter; 5509; Yes; Yes; Id. U-13299 An. none

5579; Red Hawk, Martha; F; 1903-29; F; S; Head; 5510; Yes; Yes; Al. 7717a An. 5493

5580; Red Hawk, Thomas; M; 1896-36; F; M; Head; 5511; Yes; Yes; Id. U-10246 An. 5494

5581; Red Hawk (Plenty Wounds, Louisa), Louisa; F; 1908-24; F; M; Wife; 5512; Yes; Yes; Id. U-10133 An. 5495

N.E.: ~~Red Horse, Charles; M; ------; Cheyenne River Sioux; M; Head;~~
5582; Red Horse (Two Tails, Sarah), Sarah; F; 1905-27; F; M; Wife; 5513; Yes; Yes; Al. 3836 An. 674

N.E.: ~~Red Horse, Henry; M; ------; Cheyenne River Sioux; M; Head;~~
5583; Red Horse (Bald Eagle, Sarah), Sarah Susan; F; 1902-30; F; M; Wife; 5514; Yes; Yes; Al. 3546 An. 5498

5584; Red Kettle, Alice; F; 1865-67; F; S; Head; 5515; Yes; Yes; Al. 5388 An. 5499

5585; Red Kettle, Chester; M; 1892-40; plus 1/4; M; Head; 5516; Yes; Yes; Al. 1675 An. 5500

5586; Red Kettle (Little Wound, Jessie), Jessie; F; 1877-55; F; M; Wife; 5517; Yes; Yes; Al. 5842 An. 5501

5587; Red Kettle, Minnie; F; 6/30/16-15; plus 1/4; S; Daughter; 5518; Yes; Yes; Id. U-10250 An. 5502

5588; Red Kettle, Jennie; F; 1858-74; plus 1/4; Wd.; Head; 5519; Yes; Yes; Al. 1803 An. 5503

5589; Red Kettle, Joseph; M; 1889-43; plus 1/4; Wd.; Head; 5520; No; Denver, city, Denver, Colo.; Yes; Al. 1674 An. 5504

5590; Red Kettle, Burgis; M; 11/1/13-18; plus 1/4; S; Son; 5521; Yes; Yes; Al. 7728 An. 5505

5591; Red Neckless, ---; F; 1857-75; F; Wd.; Head; 5522; Yes; Yes; Al. 5147 An. 5507

Census of the **Pine Ridge** reservation of the **Pine Ridge, South Dakota** jurisdiction, as of **April 1**, 19**32**, taken by **James H. McGregor**, Superintendent.

Key: Number; Surname, Given; Sex; Date of Birth-Age at Last Birthday; Tribe (Oglala Sioux, unless stated otherwise); Degree of Blood; Marital Status; Relationship to Head of Family [Last Census Roll Number]; At Jurisdiction Where Enrolled (Yes/No); (If no – Where); Ward (Yes/No, if given); Allotment, Annuity and Identification Numbers (if given).

5592; Red Nest, ---; M; 1863-69; F; Wd.; Head; 5523; Yes; Yes; Al. 5148 An. 5508

5593; Red Nest, Adam; M; 9/30/10-21; F; M; Head; 5524; Yes; Yes; Al. 5337 An. 5511
5594; Red Nest, Irene; F; 3/17/22-10; F; S; Sister; 5525; Yes; Yes; Id. U-10913 An. 5512
5595; Loafer, Eugene; M; 6/9/17-14; F; S; Brother; 5527; Yes; Yes; Id. U-9492 An. 5513

5596; Red Owl, Amos; M; 1861-71; F; M; Head; 5528; Yes; Yes; Al. 1324 An. 5514
5597; Red Owl (No data), Jessie; F; 1865-67; F; M; Wife; 5529; Yes; Yes; Al. 3941 An. 5515

5598; Red Owl, Henry; M; 1889-43; F; M; Head; 5537; Yes; Yes; Al. 1366 An. 5518
N.E.: Red Owl (Smith, Della), Della; F; ------; Rosebud Sioux; plus 1/4; M; Wife;
5599; Red Owl, Theodore; M; 2/17/15-17; plus 1/4; S; Son; 5538; Yes; Yes; Id. U-10251 An. 5519
5600; Red Owl, Henry C.; M; 3/4/17-15; plus 1/4; S; Son; 5539; Yes; Yes; Id. U-10252 An. 5520
5601; Red Owl, Archie L.; M; 7/31/29-2; plus 1/4; S; Son; 5540; Yes; Yes; Id. U-13230 An. none

5602; Red Owl, Levi; M; 1892-40; F; M; Head; 5530; Yes; Yes; Al. 1367 An. 5521
5603; Red Owl (Whirlwind Horse, Zetta), Zetta; F; 1891-41; F; M; Wife; 5531; Yes; Yes; Al. 4960 An. 5522
5604; Red Owl, Veronica; F; 2/5/17-15; F; S; Daughter; 5532; Yes; Yes; Id. U-10253 An. 5523
5605; Red Owl, Millie; F; 11/30/18-13; F; S; Daughter; 5533; Yes; Yes; Id. U-10254 An. 5524
5606; Red Owl, Hazel; F; 9/3/23-8; F; S; Daughter; 5534; Yes; Yes; Id. U-11127 An. 5525
5607; Red Owl, Pearl; F; 12/6/25-6; F; S; Daughter; 5535; Yes; Yes; Id. U-11789 An. none
5608; Red Owl, Rachel; F; 10/10/28-3; F; S; Daughter; 5536; Yes; Yes; Id. U-12848 An. none

5609; Red Owl, Lizzie; F; 1898-34; F; S; Head; 5541; Yes; Yes; Al. 1369 An. 5527

5610; Red Owl, Paul; M; 1906-26; F; M; Head; 5542; Yes; Yes; Al. 3957 An. 5528
5611; Red Owl (One Feather, Nellie), Nellie; F; 1907-25; F; M; Wife; 5543; Yes; Yes; Id. U-10079 An. 4808

Census of the **Pine Ridge** reservation of the **Pine Ridge, South Dakota** jurisdiction, as of **April 1**, 19**32**, taken by **James H. McGregor**, Superintendent.

Key: Number; Surname, Given; Sex; Date of Birth-Age at Last Birthday; Tribe (Oglala Sioux, unless stated otherwise); Degree of Blood; Marital Status; Relationship to Head of Family [Last Census Roll Number]; At Jurisdiction Where Enrolled (Yes/No); (If no – Where); Ward (Yes/No, if given); Allotment, Annuity and Identification Numbers (if given).

5612; Red Owl, Vastana E.; F; 11/16/29-2; F; S; Daughter; 5544; Yes; Yes; Id. U-13300 An. none

5613; Red Owl, Elizabeth; F; 11/1/31-5/12; F; S; Daughter; ---; Yes; Yes; Id. U-13973 An. none

5614; Red Paint, Alfred; M; 1886-46; F; M; Head; 5545; Yes; Yes; Al. 3357 An. 5529

5615; Red Paint (Weasel Bear, Edna), Edna; F; 1892-40; F; M; Wife; 5546; Yes; Yes; Al. 6076 An. 5530

5616; Red Paint, Amos; M; 7/6/24-7; F; S; Son; 5547; Yes; Yes; Id. U-11300 An. 5532

5617; Red Paint, Noah; M; 10/20/27-4; F; S; Son; 5548; Yes; Yes; Id. U-12430 An. none

5618; Red Paint, Louis; M; 1891-41; F; M; Head; 5549; Yes; Yes; Al. 3355 An. 5533

5619; Red Paint (High Horse, Eva), Eva; F; 1893-39; F; M; Wife; 5550; Yes; Yes; Al. 7107 An. 5534

5620; Red Paint, Zona E.; F; 5/13/15-16; F; S; Daughter; 5551; Yes; Yes; Al. 7885 An. 5537

5621; Red Paint, Ross; M; 11/22/17-14; F; S; Son; 5552; Yes; Yes; Id. U-10257 An. 5538

5622; Red Paint, Moses; M; 11/16/19-12; F; S; Son; 5553; Yes; Yes; Id. U-10258 An. 5539

5623; Red Paint, Lucy; F; 10/5/27-4; F; S; Daughter; 5554; Yes; Yes; Id. U-12429 An. none

5624; Red Paint, Flora; F; 6/19/29-2; F; S; Daughter; 5555; Yes; Yes; Id. U-13213 An. none

5625; Red Paint, Theresa; F; 1/2/12-20; F; S; Head; 5556; Yes; Yes; Al. 7109 An. 5536

5626; Red Paint, Roger; M; 1867-65; F; WD.; Head; 5558; Yes; Yes; Al. 3162 An. 5540

5627; Red Shirt, Abraham; M; 1905-27; F; M; Head; 5559; Yes; Yes; Al. 6512 An. 5549

5628; Red Shirt (Nelson, Pearl), Pearl; F; 6/1/07-24; plus 1/4; M; Wife; 5560; Yes; Yes; Al. 6124 An. 4705

5629; Red Shirt, Guy; M; 6/3/28-3; plus 1/4; S; Son; 5561; Yes; Yes; Id. U-12636 An. none

Census of the **Pine Ridge** reservation of the **Pine Ridge, South Dakota** jurisdiction, as of **April 1**, 1932, taken by **James H. McGregor**, Superintendent.

Key: Number; Surname, Given; Sex; Date of Birth-Age at Last Birthday; Tribe (Oglala Sioux, unless stated otherwise); Degree of Blood; Marital Status; Relationship to Head of Family [Last Census Roll Number]; At Jurisdiction Where Enrolled (Yes/No); (If no – Where); Ward (Yes/No, if given); Allotment, Annuity and Identification Numbers (if given).

5630; Red Shirt, Alfred; M; 1895-37; plus 1/4; S; Head; 5562; Yes; Yes; Al. 3451 An. 5550

5631; Red Shirt, Charles; M; 1890-42; plus 1/4; M; Head; 5563; Yes; Yes; Al. 3450 An. 5551

5632; Red Shirt (Girten, May), May; F; 1894-38; plus 1/4; M; Wife; 5564; Yes; Yes; Al. 1035 An. 5552

5633; Red Shirt, Clara; F; 4/15/19-12; plus 1/4; S; ---; 5565; Yes; Yes; Id. U-10259 An. 5553

5634; Red Shirt, Mabel; F; 6/15/23-8; plus 1/4; S; Dau.; 5566; Yes; Yes; Id. U-11689 An. none

5635; Red Shirt, Ollie; F; 11/15/25-6; plus 1/4; S; Daughter; 5567; Yes; Yes; Id. U-11772 An. none

5636; Red Shirt, Edith; F; 11/17/29-2; plus 1/4; S; Daughter; 5568; Yes; Yes; Id. U-13459 An. none

5637; Red Shirt, Marian; F; 2/3/18-14; F; S; Alone; 5572; Yes; Yes; Id. U-10261 An. 5559

5638; Red Shirt, Henry; M; 1859-73; F; Wd.; Head; 5574; Yes; Yes; Al. 3447 An. 5560

5639; Yellow Bird, Charles; M; 4/2/12-19; plus 1/4; S; Grandson; 5575; Yes; Yes; Al. 7545 An. 5562

5640; Red Shirt, John; M; 1882-50; plus 1/4; M; Head; 5576; Yes; Yes; Al. 3449 An. 5563

5641; Red Shirt (Pumpkinseed, Mary), Mary; F; 1892-40; F; M; Wife; 5577; Yes; Yes; Al. 683 An. 5564

5642; Red Shirt, Raymond; M; 8/2/15-16; plus 1/4; S; Son; 5578; Yes; Yes; Al. 8022 An. 5565

5643; Red Shirt, Lillie; F; 11/12/18-13; plus 1/4; S; Daughter; 5579; Yes; Yes; Id. U-10260 An. 5566

5644; Red Shirt, Irene; F; 10/1/21-10; plus 1/4; S; Daughter; 5580; Yes; Yes; Id. U-11037 An. 5567

5645; Red Shirt, Simon; M; 2/8/24-7; plus 1/4; S; Son; 5581; Yes; Yes; Id. U-12592 An. none

5646; Red Shirt, Esther; F; 1/4/30-2; plus 1/4; S; Daughter; 5582; Yes; Yes; Id. U-13351 An. none

5647; Red Shirt, Matthew; M; 1/30/32-2/12; plus 1/4; S; Son; ---; Yes; Yes; Id. U-14105 An. none

5648; Red Shirt, Kacy; M; 1883-49; plus 1/4; M; Head; 5583; No; Rosebud, S.D.; Yes; Al. 5459 An. 5570

Census of the **Pine Ridge** reservation of the **Pine Ridge, South Dakota** jurisdiction, as of **April 1**, 19**32**, taken by **James H. McGregor**, Superintendent.

Key: Number; Surname, Given; Sex; Date of Birth-Age at Last Birthday; Tribe (Oglala Sioux, unless stated otherwise); Degree of Blood; Marital Status; Relationship to Head of Family [Last Census Roll Number]; At Jurisdiction Where Enrolled (Yes/No); (If no – Where); Ward (Yes/No, if given); Allotment, Annuity and Identification Numbers (if given).

5649; Red Shirt, Wallace; M; 1903-29; F; M; Head; 5584; Yes; Yes; Al. 6511 An. 5572

5650; Red Shirt (Martin, Frances), Frances; F; 1906-26; plus 1/4; M; Wife; 5585; Yes; Yes; Al. 7587 An. 4352

5651; Red Shirt, Margaret; F; 10/15/26-5; plus 1/4; S; Daughter; 5586; Yes; Yes; Id. U-12149 An. none

5652; Red Shirt, Grace; F; 3/12/29-3; plus 1/4; S; Daughter; 5587; Yes; Yes; Id. U-13116 An. none

5653; Red Shirt, Ignitius; M; 9/26/31-6/12; plus 1/4; S; Son; ---; Yes; Yes; Id. U-13945 An. none

5654; Red Shirt, Owen; M; 9/30/12-19; plus 1/4; S; Head; 3112; Yes; Yes; Id. U-10262 An. 5576

5655; Red Shirt, Delphine; F; 2/24/17-15; plus 1/4; S; Sister; 5588; Yes; Yes; Id. U-10263 An. 5577

5656; Red Shirt, Alice; F; 1/14/20-12; plus 1/4; S; Sister; 3113; Yes; Yes; Id. U-10264 An. 5578

5657; Red Star, Calvin; M; 1893-39; F; S; Head; 5589; Yes; Yes; Al. 5585 An. 5580

5658; Red Star, David; M; 1891-41; F; Wd.; Head; 5590; Yes; Yes; Al. 441 An. 5581

5659; Red Star, Paul; M; 1895-37; F; M; Head; 5591; Yes; Yes; Al. 2663 An. 5585

5660; Red Star (Blunt Horn, Vina), Vina; F; 1905-27; F; M; Wife; 5592; Yes; Yes; Al. 2497 An. 884

5661; Red Star, Merdol N.; M; 5/5/28-3; F; S; Son; 5593; Yes; Yes; Id. U-12638 An. none

5662; Red Star, Neville C.; M; 3/13/31-1; F; S; Son; 5594; Yes; Yes; Id. U-13769 An. none

5663; Red Star, Raymond; M; 1888-44; F; M; Head; 5595; Yes; Yes; Al. 5584 An. 5586

5664; Red Star (Spider, Nellie), Nellie; F; 1893-39; F; M; Wife; 5596; Yes; Yes; Al. 807 An. 5587

5665; Red Star, David; M; 6/21/15-16; F; S; Son; 5597; Yes; Yes; Id. U-10265 An. 5588

5666; Red Star, Lavina L.; F; 5/29/28-3; F; S; Daughter; 5598; Yes; Yes; Id. U-12637 An. none

5667; Red Star, Austin P; M; 2/26/31-1; F; S; Son; 5599; Yes; Yes; Id. U-13744 An. none

5668; Red Top, ---; F; 1850-82; F; Wd.; Head; 5601; Yes; Yes; Al. 5281 An. 5591

Census of the **Pine Ridge** reservation of the **Pine Ridge, South Dakota** jurisdiction, as of **April 1**, 19**32**, taken by **James H. McGregor**, Superintendent.

Key: Number; Surname, Given; Sex; Date of Birth-Age at Last Birthday; Tribe (Oglala Sioux, unless stated otherwise); Degree of Blood; Marital Status; Relationship to Head of Family [Last Census Roll Number]; At Jurisdiction Where Enrolled (Yes/No); (If no – Where); Ward (Yes/No, if given); Allotment, Annuity and Identification Numbers (if given).

5669; Red Track, ---; F; 1858-74; F; Wd.; Head; 5602; Yes; Yes; Al. 3806 An. 5592

5670; Red Willow, ---; M; 1859-73; F; M; Head; 5603; Yes; Yes; Al. 1854 An. 5594
5671; Red Willow (No Data), Anna; F; 1866-66; F; M; Wife; 5604; Yes; Yes; Al. 1855 An. 5595

5672; Red Willow, Peter; M; 1891-41; F; Wd.; Head; 5605; Yes; Yes; Al. 5795 An. 5596
5673; Red Willow, Amandaline; F; 12/20/16-15; F; S; Daughter; 5606; Yes; Yes; Id. U-10272 An. 5598
5674; Red Willow, Foster; M; 1/27/21-11; F; S; Son; 5607; Yes; Yes; Id. U-10273 An. 5599
5675; Red Willow, Edith; F; 4/9/23-8; F; S; Daughter; 5608; Yes; Yes; Id. U-13024 An. 5600
5676; Red Willow, Bertha; F; 7/25/25-6; F; S; Daughter; 5609; Yes; Yes; Id. U-11981 An. none
5677; Red Willow, Lucille; F; 9/10/28-3; F; S; Daughter; 5610; Yes; Yes; Id. U-12782 An. none

5678; Red Water, ---; F; 1848-84; F; Wd.; Head; 5611; Yes; Yes; Al. 5377 An. 5601

N.E.: Red Wing, John; M; ------; Santee Sioux; F; M; Head;
5679; Red Wing (Valandry, Jennie), Jennie; F; 1885-47; plus 1/4; M; Wife; 5612; Yes; Yes; Al. 1082 An. 5602
5680; Red Wing, Lawrence; M; 4/20/12-19; plus 1/4; S; Son; 5613; Yes; Yes; Al. 7493 An. 5603
5681; Red Wing, Robert B.; M; 11/30/15-16; plus 1/4; S; Son; 5614; Yes; Yes; Id. U-10275 An. 5605
5682; Red Wing, Stanley O.; M; 10/22/18-13; plus 1/4; S; Son; 5615; Yes; Yes; Id. U-10276 An. 5606
5683; Red Wing, Alice D.; F; 8/11/20-11; plus 1/4; S; Daughter; 5616; Yes; Yes; Id. U-10277 An. 5607
5684; Red Wing, Sarah E.; F; 8/29/24-7; plus 1/4; S; Daughter; 5617; Yes; Yes; Id. U-11408 An. 5608
5685; Red Wing, Ruby E.; F; 10/27/22-9; plus 1/4; S; Daughter; 5618; Yes; Yes; Id. U-11415 An. 5609

5686; Red With Blood, ---; M; 1867-65; F; S; Head; 5619; Yes; Yes; Al. 4424 An. 5611

5687; Red Wolf, John; M; 1901-31; F; M; Head; 5620; Yes; Yes; Al. 1312 An. 5612
5688; Red Wolf (Chief Eagle, Josephine), Josephine; F; 1886-46; F; M; Wife; 5621; Yes; Yes; Al. 1768 An. 1415

Census of the **Pine Ridge** reservation of the **Pine Ridge, South Dakota** jurisdiction, as of **April 1**, 19**32**, taken by **James H. McGregor**, Superintendent.

Key: Number; Surname, Given; Sex; Date of Birth-Age at Last Birthday; Tribe (Oglala Sioux, unless stated otherwise); Degree of Blood; Marital Status; Relationship to Head of Family [Last Census Roll Number]; At Jurisdiction Where Enrolled (Yes/No); (If no – Where); Ward (Yes/No, if given); Allotment, Annuity and Identification Numbers (if given).

5689; Red Wolf, Sophia; F; 5/8/30-1; F; S; Daughter; 5624; Yes; Yes; Id. U-13492 An. none

5690; Chief Eagle, Anna; F; 11/15/19-12; F; S; Stepdaughter; 5623; Yes; Yes; Id. U-9337 An. 1417

5691; Red Wolf, Paul; M; 1906-26; F; M; Head; 5625; Yes; Yes; Al. 5010 An. 5613

5692; Red Wolf (Kills Right, Emma), Emma; F; 1907-25; F; M; Wife; 5626; Yes; Yes; Al. 4975 An. 1954

5693; Red Wolf, Timothy; M; 7/8/28-3; F; S; Son; 5627; Yes; Yes; Id. U-12745 An. none

5694; Red Wolf, Chris; M; 12/25/30-1; F; S; Son; 5628; Yes; Yes; Id. U-13658 An. none

5695; Resist, ---; F; 1849-83; F; Wd.; Head; 5629; Yes; Yes; Al. 3085 An. 5615

5696; Respects Nothing, Alex; M; 1900-32; F; M; Head; 5630; Yes; Yes; Al. 6444 An. 5618

5697; Respects Nothing (No Braid, Mary), Mary; F; 1900-32; F; M; Wife; 5631; Yes; Yes; Al. 5697 An. 3062

5698; Respects Nothing, Sylvan; F; 5/11/27-4; F; S; Daughter; 5632; Yes; Yes; Id. U-12408 An. none

5699; Respects Nothing, Raymond; M; 2/21/31-1; F; S; Son; 5633; Yes; Yes; Id. U-13745 An. none

5700; Respects Nothing, George; M; 1890-42; F; M; Head; 5634; Yes; Yes; Al. 6443 An. 5619

5701; Respects Nothing (Red Bear, Rosa), Rosa; F; 1899-33; plus 1/4; M; Wife; 5635; Yes; Yes; Al. 6423 An. 5620

5702; Respects Nothing, Woodrow G.; M; 12/15/23-8; plus 1/4; S; Son; 5636; Yes; Yes; Id. U-11150 An. 5622

5703; Respects Nothing, Florine; F; 2/25/26-6; plus 1/4; S; Daughter; 5637; Yes; Yes; Id. U-11835 An. none

5704; Respects Nothing, Hildegarde B.; F; 2/4/32-2/12; plus 1/4; S; Daughter; ---; Yes; Yes; Id. U-14106 An. none

5705; Returns From Scout, John; M; 1884-48; F; M; Head; 5638; Yes; Yes; Al. 6332 An. 5624

5706; Returns From Scout (White Whirlwind, Alice), Alice; F; 1890-42; F; M; Wife; 5639; Yes; Yes; Al. 254 An. 5625

5707; Returns From Scout, Elizabeth; F; 8/31/18-13; F; S; Daughter; 5640; Yes; Yes; Id. U-10281 An. 5628

5708; Returns From Scout, Vincent; M; 2/2/20-12; F; S; Son; 5641; Yes; Yes; Id. U-10282 An. 5629

Census of the __Pine Ridge__ reservation of the __Pine Ridge, South Dakota__ jurisdiction, as of __April 1__, 19**32**, taken by __James H. McGregor__, Superintendent.

Key: Number; Surname, Given; Sex; Date of Birth-Age at Last Birthday; Tribe (Oglala Sioux, unless stated otherwise); Degree of Blood; Marital Status; Relationship to Head of Family [Last Census Roll Number]; At Jurisdiction Where Enrolled (Yes/No); (If no – Where); Ward (Yes/No, if given); Allotment, Annuity and Identification Numbers (if given).

5709; Returns From Scout, Albert; M; 10/10/21-10; F; S; Son; 5642; Yes; Yes; Id. U-10284 An. 5630

5710; Returns From Scout, Edith; F; 10/9/26-5; F; S; Daughter; 5643; Yes; Yes; Id. U-12184 An. none

5711; Returns From Scout, Katherine; F; 7/9/28-3; F; S; Daughter; 5644; Yes; Yes; Id. U-12746 An. none

5712; Returns From Scout, Joseph; M; 12/13/07-24; F; M; Head; 5645; Yes; Yes; Al. 7624 An. 5626

5713; Returns From Scout (Catches, Mary), Mary; F; 1904-28; F; M; Wife; 3292; Yes; Yes; Al. 7007 An. 3297

5714; Returns From Scout, Melvin; M; 9/25/31-6/12; F; S; Son; ---; Yes; Yes; Id. U-13974 An. none

5715; Janis, Mary Marian; F; 7/23/24-7; plus 1/4; S; Stepdaughter; 3293; tes[sic]; Yes; Id. U-11396 An. 3298

5716; Returns From Scout, Seth; M; 1878-54; F; M; Head; 5646; Yes; Yes; Al. 5721 An. 5635

5717; Returns From Scout (Chief, Julia), Julia; F; 1864-68; F; M; Wife; 5647; Yes; Yes; Al. 4193 An. 5636

5718; Revenger, ---; F; 1858-74; F; Wd.; Head; 5648; Yes; Yes; Al. 4931 An. 5637

5719; Rexroat, Clara; F; 1893-39; plus 1/4; Wd.: Head; 5649; Yes; Yes; Al. 2256 An. 5638

5720; Rexroat, Verona J.; F; 12/30/15-16; -1/4; S; Daughter; 5650; Yes; Yes; Id. U-10285 An. 5639

5721; Rexroat, Ola Mildred; F; 8/29/17-14; -1/4; S; Daughter; 5651; Yes; Yes; Id. U-10286 An. 5640

5722; Rexroat, Wynona; F; 12/15/19-12; -1/4; S; Daughter; 5652; Yes; Yes; Id. U-12072 An. 5641

5723; Reynolds, Estella L.; F; 6/20/1886-66; plus 1/4; Wd.; Head; 5653; Yes; Yes; Al. 6661 1/2 An. 5642

N.E.: Reynolds, Louis; M; ------; Oglala Sioux; plus 1/4; M; Head; not enrolled;

5724; Reynolds (Valandry, Mary Ione), Mary Ione; F; 1895-37; -1/4; M; Wife; 5654; No; Quemado, town, Socorro, N.M.; Yes; Al. 2461 An. 5643

5725; Ribman, Alfred; M; 1881-51; F; M; Head; 5655; Yes; Yes; Al. 3055 An. 5644

5726; Ribman (Red Feather, Claudia), Claudia; F; 1891-41; F; M; Wife; 5656; Yes; Yes; Al. 7361 An. 5645

5727; Ribman, Emily; F; 8/6/15-16; F; S; Daughter; 5657; Yes; Yes; Id. U-10287 An. 5647

Census of the __Pine Ridge__ reservation of the __Pine Ridge, South Dakota__ jurisdiction, as of __April 1__, 19**32**, taken by __James H. McGregor__, Superintendent.

Key: Number; Surname, Given; Sex; Date of Birth-Age at Last Birthday; Tribe (Oglala Sioux, unless stated otherwise); Degree of Blood; Marital Status; Relationship to Head of Family [Last Census Roll Number]; At Jurisdiction Where Enrolled (Yes/No); (If no – Where); Ward (Yes/No, if given); Allotment, Annuity and Identification Numbers (if given).

5728; Ribman, Nellie; F; 5/17/26-5; F; S; Daughter; 5658; Yes; Yes; Id. U-12872 An. none

5729; Ribman, Mary; F; 12/19/28-3; F; S; Daughter; 5659; Yes; Yes; Id. U-12977 An. none

5730; Ribman, Thomas; M; 1874-58; F; S; Head; 5660; Yes; Yes; Al. 2617 An. 5650

5731; Ribs, (Mrs.), White Mountain; F; 1850-62; F; Wd.; Head; 5661; Yes; Yes; Al. 3463 An. 5652

5732; Richard, Alex; M; 1901-31; plus 1/4; S; Head; 5662; Yes; Yes; Al. 2112 An. 5653

5733; Richard, Alfred; M; 1902-30; plus 1/4; S; Head; 5663; Yes; Yes; Al. 4695 An. 5654

5734; Richard, Alfred; M; 1896-36; plus 1/4; M; Head; 5672; Yes; Yes; Al. 2342 An. 5664

5735; Richard (Black Bear, Ella), Ella; F; 1894-38; F; M; Wife; 5675; Yes; Yes; Al. 2068 An. 667

5736; Richard, Jeanette; F; 8/20/20-11; plus 1/4; S; Daughter; 5673; Yes; Yes; Id. U-10296 An. 5666

5737; Richard, Thomas; M; 5/12/22-9; plus 1/4; S; Son; 5674; Yes; Yes; Id. U-10988 An. 5667

5738; Black Bear, Rebecca; F; 12/31/26-5; F; S; Stepdaughter; 5676; Yes; Yes; Id. U-12676 An. none

5739; Richard, Alfred; M; 1882-50; plus 1/4; M; Head; 5664; Yes; Yes; Al. 4673 An. 5655

5740; Richard (Randall, Nellie), Nellie; F; 1892-40; plus 1/4; M; Wife; 5665; Yes; Yes; Al. 4674 An. 5656

5741; Richard, Bernard; M; 2/28/13-19; plus 1/4; S; Son; 5666; Yes; Yes; Al. 8191 An. 5658

5742; Richard, Jennie C.; F; 11/5/17-14; plus 1/4; S; Daughter; 5667; Yes; Yes; Id. U-10294 An. 5660

5743; Richard, Oliver; M; 7/11/20-11; plus 1/4; S; Son; 5668; Yes; Yes; Id. U-10295 An. 5661

5744; Richard, Angelina; F; 5/19/22-9; plus 1/4; S; Daughter; 5669; Yes; Yes; Id. U-11013 An. 5662

5745; Richard, Rudolph; M; 7/29/27-4; plus 1/4; S; Son; 5670; Yes; Yes; Id. U-12391 An. none

5746; Richard, Rachel; F; 11/7/30-1; plus 1/4; S; Daughter; 5671; Yes; Yes; Id. U-13659 An. none

Census of the **Pine Ridge** reservation of the **Pine Ridge, South Dakota** jurisdiction, as of **April 1**, 19**32**, taken by **James H. McGregor**, Superintendent.

Key: Number; Surname, Given; Sex; Date of Birth-Age at Last Birthday; Tribe (Oglala Sioux, unless stated otherwise); Degree of Blood; Marital Status; Relationship to Head of Family [Last Census Roll Number]; At Jurisdiction Where Enrolled (Yes/No); (If no – Where); Ward (Yes/No, if given); Allotment, Annuity and Identification Numbers (if given).

5747; Richard, Antoine; M; 1900-32; plus 1/4; M; Head; 5677; Yes; Yes; Al. 2336 An. 5668

5748; Richard (Ruff, Vina A.), Vina A.; F; 1904-28; plus 1/4; M; Wife; 5678; Yes; Yes; Al. 6898 An. 5669

5749; Richard, Caroline M.; F; 4/15/25-6; plus 1/4; S; Daughter; 5679; Yes; Yes; Id. U-11617 An. none

5750; Richard, Spencer; M; 5/21/26-5; plus 1/4; S; Son; 5680; Yes; Yes; Id. U-11976 An. none

5751; Richard, Isabelle; F; 9/20/27-4; plus 1/4; S; Daughter; 5681; Yes; Yes; Id. U-12639 An. none

5752; Richard, Benjamin; M; 1880-52; plus 1/4; M; Head; 5682; Yes; Yes; Al. 2333 An. 5670

5753; Richard (Eldridge, Nettie), Nettie; F; 1878-54; plus 1/4; M; Wife; 5683; Yes; Yes; Al. 2334 An. 5671

5754; Richard, Virginia; F; 11/6/14-17; plus 1/4; S; Daughter; 5684; Yes; Yes; Id. U-10302 An. 5675

5755; Richard, Edison; M; 1/28/17-14; plus 1/4; S; Son; 5685; Yes; Yes; Id. U-10303 An. 5676

5756; Richard, Benjamin Jr.; M; 5/17/19-12; plus 1/4; S; Son; 5686; Yes; Yes; Id. U-10304 An. 5677

5757; Richard, Ida; F; 3/6/12-20; plus 1/4; S; Head; 5687; Yes; Yes; Id. U-10301 An. 5674

5758; Richard, Marcline M.; F; 5/5/28-3; plus 1/4; S; Daughter; 5688; Yes; Yes; Id. U-12719 An. none

5759; Richard, Charles P.; M; 1905-27; plus 1/4; M; Head; 5689; Yes; Yes; Al. 2338 An. 5678

5760; Richard, Sylvan C.; M; 1/21/29-3; plus 1/4; S; Son; 5690; Yes; Yes; Id. U-13214 An. none

5761; Richard, Virginia J.; F; 1/25/30-2; plus 1/4; S; Daughter; 5691; Yes; Yes; Id. U-13460 An. none

5762; Richard, Charles; M; 1873-59; plus 1/4; M; Head; 5692; Yes; Yes; Al. 2602 An. 5679

5763; Richard (Gerry, Louisa), Louisa; F; 1875-57; plus 1/4; M; Wife; 5693; Yes; Yes; Al. 2603 An. 5680

5764; Richard, Irene; F; 3/20/10-22; plus 1/4; S; Head; 5694; Yes; Yes; Al. 4747 An. 5681

Census of the __Pine Ridge__ reservation of the __Pine Ridge, South Dakota__ jurisdiction, as of __April 1__, 19**32**, taken by __James H. McGregor__, Superintendent.

Key: Number; Surname, Given; Sex; Date of Birth-Age at Last Birthday; Tribe (Oglala Sioux, unless stated otherwise); Degree of Blood; Marital Status; Relationship to Head of Family [Last Census Roll Number]; At Jurisdiction Where Enrolled (Yes/No); (If no – Where); Ward (Yes/No, if given); Allotment, Annuity and Identification Numbers (if given).

5765; Richard, Edward; M; 1890-42; plus 1/4; Wd.; Head; 5695; Yes; Yes; Al. 814 An. 5683

5766; Richard, Edward, Jr.; M; 3/18/17-15; plus 1/4; S; Son; 5697; Yes; Yes; Id. U-10290 An. 5686

5767; Richard, Francis; M; 2/16/19-12; plus 1/4; S; Son; 5698; Yes; Yes; Id. U-10291 An. 5687

5768; Richard, Mercy; F; 5/8/22-9; plus 1/4; S; Daughter; 5699; Yes; Yes; Id. U-10979 An. 5688

5769; Richard, Sam Percy; M; 5/21/24-7; plus 1/4; S; Son; 5700; Yes; Yes; Id. U-11284 An. 5689

5770; Richard, Gladys; F; 4/9/28-3; plus 1/4; S; Daughter; 5701; Yes; Yes; Id. U-12593 An. none

5771; Richard, Kenneth D.; M; 9/5/29-7; plus 1/4; S; Son; 5702; Yes; Yes; Id. U-13256 An. none

5772; Richard, Emil; M; 5/16/26-5; plus 1/4; S; Son; 5703; Yes; Yes; Id. U-13493 An. none

5773; Richard, James; M; 1857-75; plus 1/4; M; Head; 5704; Yes; Yes; Al. 2109 An. 5690

5774; Richard (Salway, Sophia), Sophia; F; 1860-72; plus 1/4; M; Wife; 5705; Yes; Yes; Al. 2110 An. 5691

5775; Richard, Theresa M.; F; 11/2/24-7; plus 1/4; S; granddaughter; 5706; Yes; Yes; Id. U-11594 An. none

5776; Morrison, Andrew; M; 7/5/16-15; plus 1/4; S; Grandson; 5707; Yes; Yes; Id. U-10039 An. 4613

5777; Richard, James; M; 1875-57; plus 1/4; M; Head; 5708; Yes; Yes; Al. 1226 An. 5692

5778; Richard (No data), Julia; F; 1873-59; F; M; Wife; 5709; Yes; Yes; Al. 6063 An. 5693

5779; Richard, Walter; M; 5/11/11-20; plus 1/4; S; Son; 5710; Yes; Yes; Al. 7460 An. 5694

5780; Richard, George; M; 6/4/14-17; plus 1/4; S; Son; 5711; ues[sic]; Yes; Al. 7591 An. 5695

5781; Richard, James; M; 1877-55; plus 1/4; M; Head; 5712; Yes; Yes; Al. 4693 An. 5697

5782; Richard (Fast Wolf, Eva), Eva; F; 1881-51; plus 1/4; M; Wife; 5713; Yes; Yes; Al. 4694 An. 5698

5783; Richard, Agatha; F; 7/4/13-18; plus 1/4; S; Daughter; 5714; Yes; Yes; Al. 7191 An. 5699

5784; Richard, Ason; M; 9/8/18-13; plus 1/4; S; Son; 5715; Yes; Yes; Id. U-10300 An. 5700

Census of the _____ **Pine Ridge** _____ reservation of the **Pine Ridge, South Dakota** jurisdiction, as of _____ **April 1** _____, 19**32**, taken by _____ **James H. McGregor** _____, Superintendent.

Key: Number; Surname, Given; Sex; Date of Birth-Age at Last Birthday; Tribe (Oglala Sioux, unless stated otherwise); Degree of Blood; Marital Status; Relationship to Head of Family [Last Census Roll Number]; At Jurisdiction Where Enrolled (Yes/No); (If no – Where); Ward (Yes/No, if given); Allotment, Annuity and Identification Numbers (if given).

5785; Richard, John; M; 1/ /04-28; plus 1/4; M; Head; 5716; Yes; Yes; Al. 4745 An. 5701
5786; Richard (Babby, Wilma), Wilma; F; 4/15/04-27; -1/4; M; Wife; 5717; Yes; Yes; Al. 4609 An. 5702
5787; Richard, Darlene M.; F; 12/4/25-6; plus 1/4; S; Daughter; 5718; Yes; Yes; Id. U-11757 An. none
5788; Richard, Wildene I.; F; 9/15/28-3; plus 1/4; S; Daughter; 5719; Yes; Yes; Id. U-13147 An. none

5789; Richard, Joseph; M; 1881-51; plus 1/4; M; Head; 5720; Yes; Yes; Al. 4463 An. 5703
5790; Richard (Brewer, Ellen), Ellen; F; 1886-46; plus 1/4; M; Wife; 5721; Yes; Yes; Al. 5588 An. 5704
5791; Richard, Francis; M; 11/7/12-19; plus 1/4; S; Son; 5722; Yes; Yes; Al. 6938 An. 5709
5792; Richard, Alfreda; F; 10/7/19-12; plus 1/4; S; Daughter; 5723; Yes; Yes; Id. U-10305 An. 5710
5793; Richard, John B.; M; 2/9/21-11; plus 1/4; S; Son; 5724; Yes; Yes; Id. U-10306 An. 5711
5794; Richard, Elma; F; 11/8/23-8; plus 1/4; S; Daughter; 5725; Yes; Yes; Id. U-11524 An. 5712
5795; Richard, Esther M.; F; 10/19/26-5; plus 1/4; S; Daughter; 5726; Yes; Yes; Id. U-12926 An. none

5796; Richard, Henry; M; 4/19/08-23; plus 1/4; S; Head; 5727; Yes; Yes; Al. 4247 An. 5705

5797; Richard, Louis; M; 1875-57; plus 1/4; Wd.; Head; 5728; Yes; Yes; Al. 4696 An. 5714
5798; Richard, Garfield; M; 11/24/09-22; plus 1/4; S; Son; 5729; Yes; Yes; Al. 5448 An. 5715
5799; Richard, Elvina M.; F; 5/6/15-16; plus 1/4; S; Daughter; 5730; Yes; Yes; Id. U-10298 An. 5716

5800; Richard, Louis; M; 1896-36; plus 1/4; M; Head; 5731; Yes; Yes; Al. 4743 An. 5717
5801; Richard, Denzel; M; 3/12/22-10; -1/4; S; Son; 5732; Yes; Yes; Id. U-10989 An. 5718
5802; Richard, Laverne; F; 4/16/25-6; -1/4; S; Daughter; 5733; Yes; Yes; Id. U-11620 An. none
5803; Richard, Rosella M.; F; 5/15/29-2; -1/4; S; Daughter; 5734; Yes; Yes; Id. U-13388 An. none

Census of the __**Pine Ridge**__ reservation of the __**Pine Ridge, South Dakota**__ jurisdiction, as of __**April 1**__, 19**32**, taken by __**James H. McGregor**__, Superintendent.

Key: Number; Surname, Given; Sex; Date of Birth-Age at Last Birthday; Tribe (Oglala Sioux, unless stated otherwise); Degree of Blood; Marital Status; Relationship to Head of Family [Last Census Roll Number]; At Jurisdiction Where Enrolled (Yes/No); (If no – Where); Ward (Yes/No, if given); Allotment, Annuity and Identification Numbers (if given).

5804; Richard, Luella M; F; 5/15/29-2; -1/4; S; Daughter; 5735; Yes; Yes; Id. U-13387 An. none

5805; Richard, Oliver Warfield; M; 11/5/22-9; plus 1/4; S; Alone; 5736; Yes; Yes; Id. U-11328 An. 5720

5806; Richard, Peter; M; 1888-34; plus 1/4; M; Head; 5737; Yes; Yes; Al. 2335 An. 5724

5807; Richard (Nelson, Lillian), Lillian; F; 1906-26; plus 1/4; M; Wife; 5738; Yes; Yes; Al. 5259 An. 5710

5808; Richard, Pearl; F; 12/4/24-7; plus 1/4; S; Daughter; 5739; Yes; Yes; Id. U-11669 An. none

5809; Richard, Alexander; M; 6/6/26-5; plus 1/4; S; Son; 5740; Yes; Yes; Id. U-12261 An. none

5810; Richard, David; M; 3/20/28-4; plus 1/4; S; Son; 5741; Yes; Yes; Id. U-12697 An. none

5811; Richard, Florence; F; 5/5/30-1; plus 1/4; S; Daughter; 5742; Yes; Yes; Id. U-13519 An. none

5812; Richard, Julia; F; 3/6/32-1/12; plus 1/4; S; Daughter; ---; Yes; Yes; Id. U-14134 An. none

5813; Richard, Susanna; F; 8/2/11-20; plus 1/4; S; Head; 5743; Yes; Yes; Al. 6931 An. 5726

5814; Richard, Samuel; M; 1891-41; plus 1/4; M; Head; 5744; Yes; Yes; Al. 2489 An. 5727

N.E.: ~~Richard, (Giroux, Martha) Martha; F; -------; Rosebud Sioux; plus 1/4; M; Wife;~~

5815; Richard, Delmar P.; M; 3/17/22-10; plus 1/4; S; Son; 5745; Yes; Yes; Id. U-9602 An. 5729

5816; Richard, Mervin; M; 3/15/27-5; plus 1/4; S; Son; 5746; Yes; Yes; Id. U-12494 An. none

5817; Richard, Theodore; M; 1907-25; plus 1/4; M; Head; 5747; Yes; Yes; Al. 4746 An. 5730

5818; Richard (Rooks, Zona), Zona; F; 1906-26; plus 1/4; M; Wife; 5748; Yes; Yes; Al. 2600 An. 5822

5819; Richard, Leverne C.; M; 7/30/28-3; plus 1/4; S; Son; 5749; Yes; Yes; Id. U-12764 An. none

5820; Richard, Leroy; M; 3/25/30-2; plus 1/4; S; Son; 5750; Yes; Yes; Id. U-13447 An. none

Census of the **Pine Ridge** reservation of the **Pine Ridge, South Dakota** jurisdiction, as of **April 1**, 19**32**, taken by **James H. McGregor**, Superintendent.

Key: Number; Surname, Given; Sex; Date of Birth-Age at Last Birthday; Tribe (Oglala Sioux, unless stated otherwise); Degree of Blood; Marital Status; Relationship to Head of Family [Last Census Roll Number]; At Jurisdiction Where Enrolled (Yes/No); (If no – Where); Ward (Yes/No, if given); Allotment, Annuity and Identification Numbers (if given).

5821; Richard, Thomas E.; M; 1903-29; plus 1/4; M; Head; 5751; Yes; Yes; Al. 4726 An. 5732

N.E.: Richard, (Little, Sarah) Sarah; F; ------; Rosebud Sioux; plus 1/4; M; Wife;

5822; Richardson, Jessie; F; 1907-25; plus 1/4; M; Head; 5752; Yes; Yes; Al. 7731 An. 11
5823; Richardson, Ace D.; M; 4/24/30-1; plus 1/4; S; Son; 5753; Yes; Yes; Id. U-13494 An. none
5824; Richardson, Caroline L.; F; 5/2/31-10/12; plus 1/4; S; Daughter; ---; Yes; Yes; Id. U-13842 An. none

N.E.: Riley, James; M; ------; Cheyenne; plus 1/4; Head;
5825; Riley (Stover, Grace), Grace; F; 1895-37; plus 1/4; M; Wife; 5754; No; Belle Fourche, town, Butte, S.D.; Yes; Al. 1117 An. 5733
5826; Riley Lawrence; M; 8/14/15-16; Oglala Sioux & Chey.; plus 1/4; S; Son; 5755; No; Belle Fourche, town, Butte, S.D.; Yes; Id. U-10308 An. 5734
5827; Riley James G.; M; 12/24/17-14; Oglala Sioux & Chey.; plus 1/4; S; Son; 5756; No; Ditto; ---; Id. U-10309 An. 5735
5828; Riley Harriet C.; F; 5/26/19-12; Oglala Sioux & Chey.; plus 1/4; S; Daughter; 5757; No; Ditto; Yes; Id. U-10310 An. 5736
5829; Riley Nina M.; F; 1/26/21-11; Oglala Sioux & Chey.; plus 1/4; S; Daughter; 5758; No; Ditto; Yes; Id. U-10311 An. 5737
5830; Riley Patrick; M; 5/12/24-7; Oglala Sioux & Chey.; plus 1/4; S; Son; 5759; No; Ditto; Yes; Id. U-11306 An. 5738

5831; Ringing Shield, Moses; M; 1899-33; F; M; Head; 5760; Yes; Yes; Al. 2421 An. 5740

N.E.: Ringing Shield, (Henry, Martha) Martha; F; ------; Yankton Sioux; F; M; Wife;

5832; Ringing Shield, Kenneth; M; 3/30/28-4; Sioux; F; S; Son; 5761; Yes; Yes; Id. U-12594 An. none
5833; Ringing Shield, Zelma Una; F; 2/12/30-2; Sioux; F; S; Daughter; 5762; Yes; Yes; Id. U-13386 An. none

5834; Ringing Shield, William; M; 1906-26; F; M; Head; 5763; Yes; Yes; Al. 2424 An. 5741
5835; Ringing Shield (Iron Teeth, Nancy), Nancy; F; 1906-26; plus 1/4; M; Wife; 5764; Yes; Yes; Al. 2732 An. 3223
5836; Ringing Shield, Ella; F; 12/2/28-3; F; S; Daughter; 5765; Yes; Yes; Id. U-12956 An. none

5837; Risse, Lucille M.; F; 8/28/08-24; -1/4; M; Head; 5766; Yes; Yes; Al. 4797 An. 4098

Census of the **Pine Ridge** reservation of the **Pine Ridge, South Dakota** jurisdiction, as of **April 1**, 19**32**, taken by **James H. McGregor**, Superintendent.

Key: Number; Surname, Given; Sex; Date of Birth-Age at Last Birthday; Tribe (Oglala Sioux, unless stated otherwise); Degree of Blood; Marital Status; Relationship to Head of Family [Last Census Roll Number]; At Jurisdiction Where Enrolled (Yes/No); (If no – Where); Ward (Yes/No, if given); Allotment, Annuity and Identification Numbers (if given).

5838; Roan Eagle, William; M; 9/29/10-21; F; S; Head; 5767; Yes; Yes; Al. 6101 An. 5744

5839; Roan Eagle, George; M; 1902-30; F; M; Head; 5768; Yes; Yes; Al. 3091 An. 5746

5840; Roan Eagle (Shangreau, Angelina), Angelina; F; 1895-37; plus 1/4; M; Wife; 5769; Yes; Yes; Al. 1209 An. 4440

5841; Roan Eagle, Joseph; M; 10/1/28-3; plus 1/4; S; Son; 5774; Yes; Yes; Id. U-21927 An. none

5842; Roan Eagle, Verna May; F; 7/4/30-1; plus 1/4; S; Daughter; 5775; Yes; Yes; Id. U-13554 An. none

5843; Mesteth, George L.; M; 1/18/18-14; plus 1/4; S; Stepson; 5770; Yes; Yes; Id. U-10002 An. 4441

5844; Mesteth, Gladys R.; F; 5/27/19-12; plus 1/4; S; Stepdaughter; 5771; Yes; Yes; Id. U-10003 An. 4442

5845; Mesteth, Ferne Doris; F; 7/23/22-9; plus 1/4; S; Stepdaughter; 5772; Yes; Yes; Id. U-11589 An. 4443

5846; Shangreau, Lillie; F; 2/18/27-5; plus 1/4; S; Stepdaughter; 5773; Yes; Yes; Id. U-12265 An. none

5847; Roan Eagle, James; M; 1894-38; F; M; Head; 5776; Yes; Yes; Al. 3089 An. 5747

5848; Roan Eagle (Martin, Bessie), Bessie; F; 1881-51; plus 1/4; M; Wife; 4347; Yes; Yes; Al.7584 An. 4346

5849; Robinson, James M.; M; 1898-34; -1/4; S; Head; 5777; Yes; Yes; Al. 7356 An. 5750

N.E.: Robinson, Philip; M; -------; Flandreau Sioux; F; M; Head;

5850; Robinson (Luhan, Millie), Millie; F; 1870-62; plus 1/4; M; Wife; 5778; Yes; Yes; Al. 694 An. 5751

5851; Robinson, Patsy; F; 1891-41; -1/4; M; Head; 5779; Yes; Yes; Al.1348 An. 5752

5852; Robinson, Myrtle I.; F; 3/6/15-17; -1/4; S; Daughter; 5780; Yes; Yes; Al.7897 An. 5753

5853; Robinson, Irma I.; F; 6/16/18-13; -1/4; S; Daughter; 5781; Yes; Yes; Id. U-10313 An. 5754

5854; Robinson, Joan A.; F; 10/24/24-7; -1/4; S; Daughter; 5782; Yes; Yes; Id. U-11403 An. 5753

5855; Robinson, Ruth; F; 1881-51; plus 1/4; M; Head; 5783; Yes; No; Al.416 An. 5756

Census of the __Pine Ridge__ reservation of the __Pine Ridge, South Dakota__ jurisdiction, as of __April 1__, 1932, taken by __James H. McGregor__, Superintendent.

Key: Number; Surname, Given; Sex; Date of Birth-Age at Last Birthday; Tribe (Oglala Sioux, unless stated otherwise); Degree of Blood; Marital Status; Relationship to Head of Family [Last Census Roll Number]; At Jurisdiction Where Enrolled (Yes/No); (If no – Where); Ward (Yes/No, if given); Allotment, Annuity and Identification Numbers (if given).

5856; Robinson, Clark J.; M; 4/25/14-17; -1/4; S; Son; 5784; Yes; Yes; Al.7488 An. 5757

5857; Rock, Charles; M; 1884-48; F; M; Head; 5785; Yes; Yes; Al. 693 An. 5758
5858; Rock (Lone Hill, Helen), Helen; F; 1887-45; plus 1/4; M; Wife; 5786; Yes; Yes; Al. 6840 An. 5759
5859; Rock, Hannah; F; 9/13/25-6; plus 1/4; S; Daughter; 5787; Yes; Yes; Id. U-11712 An. none

5860; Rock, John; M; 1886-46; F; M; Head; 5788; Yes; Yes; Al. 831 An. 5760
5861; Rock (Lone Hill, Florence), Florence; F; 1889-43; plus 1/4; M; Wife; 5789; Yes; Yes; Al. 6841 An. 5761
5862; Rock, Edgar; M; 2/4/12-20; plus 1/4; M; Son; 5790; Yes; Yes; Al. 7141 An. 5762
5863; Rock, Zackary; M; 9/6/15-16; plus 1/4; M; Son; 5791; Yes; Yes; Al. 8123 An. 5763
5864; Rock, Edith; F; 9/6/17-14; plus 1/4; S; Daughter; 5792; Yes; Yes; Id. U-10314 An. 5764
5865; Rock, Grace M; F; 8/26/19-12; plus 1/4; S; Daughter; 5793; Yes; Yes; Id. U-10315 An. 5765
5866; Rock, Beulah; F; 9/6/21-10; plus 1/4; S; Daughter; 5794; Yes; Yes; Id. U-10316 An. 5766
5867; Rock, Rachel; F; 2/17/26-6; plus 1/4; S; Daughter; 5795; Yes; Yes; Id. U-11831 An. none
5868; Rock, Bessie; F; 7/15/29-2; plus 1/4; S; Daughter; 5796; Yes; Yes; Id. U-13231 An. none

5869; Rock, Samuel; M; 1861-71; F; M; Head; 5797; Yes; Yes; Al. 843 An. 5768
5870; Rock (Red Bird, Mary), Mary; F; 1859-73; F; M; Wife; 5798; Yes; Yes; Al. 4176 An. 5769

5871; Rock Mountain, Fannie; F; 1879-53; F; Wd.; Head; 5801; Yes; Yes; Al. 5019 An. 5773
5872; Rock Mountain, Moses; M; 5/27/17-14; F; S; Son; 5802; Yes; Yes; Id. U-10317 An. 5774
5873; Rock Mountain, Thomas; M; 11/4/19-12; F; S; Son; 5803; Yes; Yes; Id. U-10318 An. 5775

5874; Rogers, Josephine; F; 6/29/86-55; -1/4; M; Head; 5804; Yes; Yes; Al. 4621 An. 5776
5875; Rogers, Elmer James; M; 10/17/12-19; -1/4; S; Son; 5805; Yes; Yes; Id. U-10319 An. 5778

Census of the **Pine Ridge** reservation of the **Pine Ridge, South Dakota** jurisdiction, as of **April 1**, 19**32**, taken by **James H. McGregor**, Superintendent.

Key: Number; Surname, Given; Sex; Date of Birth-Age at Last Birthday; Tribe (Oglala Sioux, unless stated otherwise); Degree of Blood; Marital Status; Relationship to Head of Family [Last Census Roll Number]; At Jurisdiction Where Enrolled (Yes/No); (If no – Where); Ward (Yes/No, if given); Allotment, Annuity and Identification Numbers (if given).

5876; Rogers, William G.; M; 1/20/09-22; -1/4; S; Head; 5806; Yes; Yes; Al. 4649 An. 5777

5877; Romero, John; M; 8/7/08-24; plus 1/4; M; Head; 5807; Yes; Yes; Al. 7295 An. 3526

5878; Romero (Means, Jessie), Jessie; F; 1906-26; plus 1/4; M; Wife; 5808; Yes; Yes; Al. 4080 An. 4395

5879; Romero, Aloysius; M; 9/25/30-1; plus 1/4; S; Son; 5809; Yes; Yes; Id. U-13612 An. none

5880; Romero, Sophia; F; 10/31/10-21; plus 1/4; S; Head; 5810; Yes; Yes; Al. 5734 An. 5780

5881; Romero, Thomas; M; 11/25/12-19; plus 1/4; S; Brother; 5811; Yes; Yes; Al. 7006 An. 5781

5882; Romero, Vetal; M; 3/28/15-16; plus 1/4; S; Brother; 5812; Yes; Yes; Al. 8095 An. 5782

5883; Romero, Susie; F; 12/17/17-14; plus 1/4; S; Sister; 5813; Yes; Yes; Id. U-10320 An. 5783

5884; Romero, Philip; M; 1872-60; plus 1/4; M; Head; 5814; Yes; Yes; Al. 3891 An. 5788

5885; Romero (No data), Katie; F; 1871-61; F; M; Wife; 5815; Yes; Yes; Al. 8029 An. 5789

5886; Romero, Albert; M; 3/19/14-18; plus 1/4; S; Son; 5816; Yes; Yes; Al. 8030 An. 5792

5887; Rooks, Charles; M; 1876-56; plus 1/4; M; Head; 5820; Yes; No; Al. 2599 An. 5794

5888; Rooks, Anna; F; 1878-54; plus 1/4; M; Wife; 5821; Yes; No; Al. 4065 An. 5795

5889; Rooks, Evaline M.; F; 6/19/14-17; plus 1/4; S; Daughter; 5822; Yes; Yes; Al. 7952 An. 5798

5890; Rooks, William L.; M; 12/9/16-15; plus 1/4; S; Son; 5823; Yes; Yes; Id. U-10323 An. 5799

5891; Rooks, Audre; F; 1/4/20-11; plus 1/4; S; Daughter; 5824; Yes; Yes; Id. U-10324 An. 5800

5892; Rooks, Eugene; M; 7/28/22-9; plus 1/4; S; Son; 5825; Yes; Yes; Id. U-12882 An. none

5893; Rooks, Charles Jr.; M; 1898-34; plus 1/4; M; Head; 5826; Yes; Yes; Al. 6886 An. 5802

~~N.E.: Rooks, (Beva, Emma) Emma; F; ------; Rosebud Sioux; M; Wife;~~

Census of the **Pine Ridge** reservation of the **Pine Ridge, South Dakota** jurisdiction, as of **April 1**, 19**32**, taken by **James H. McGregor**, Superintendent.

Key: Number; Surname, Given; Sex; Date of Birth-Age at Last Birthday; Tribe (Oglala Sioux, unless stated otherwise); Degree of Blood; Marital Status; Relationship to Head of Family [Last Census Roll Number]; At Jurisdiction Where Enrolled (Yes/No); (If no – Where); Ward (Yes/No, if given); Allotment, Annuity and Identification Numbers (if given).

5894; Rooks, Edward; M; 1902-30; plus 1/4; Wd.; Head; 5827; Yes; Yes; Al. 1737 An. 5801

5895; Rooks, Eric; M; 1903-29; plus 1/4; M; Head; 5832; Yes; Yes; Al. 4062 An. 5806

5896; Rooks, Frank; M; 1873-59; plus 1/4; M; Head; 5833; Yes; Yes; Al. 4097 An. 5807

N.E.:   Rooks, (Larabee, Alice) Alice; F; ------; Rosebud Sioux; plus 1/4; M; Wife;

5897; Rooks, Dennis; M; 3/5/14-18; Sioux; plus 1/4; S; Son; 5834; Yes; Yes; Al. 8114 An. 5808

5898; Rooks, Jacob; M; 1900-32; plus 1/4; S; Head; 5835; Yes; Yes; Al. 6919 An. 5809

5899; Rooks, James; M; 1892-40; plus 1/4; Wd.; Head; 5836; Yes; Yes; Al. 4055 An. 5810

5900; Rooks, John Eric; M; 1/5/20-12; plus 1/4; S; Son; 5838; Yes; Yes; Id. U-9829 An. 3612

5901; Rooks, Patricia I.; F; 3/17/23-9; plus 1/4; S; Daughter; 5839; Yes; Yes; Id. U-13042 An. 3613

5902; Rooks, Lucille L.; F; 6/5/26-5; plus 1/4; S; Daughter; 5840; Yes; Yes; Id. U-12150 An. none

5903; Rooks, Elaine R.; F; 3/16/25-7; plus 1/4; S; Daughter; 5841; Yes; Yes; Id. U-12262 An. none

5904; Rooks, Joseph; M; 6/6/13-18; plus 1/4; M; Head; 5843; Yes; Yes; Al. 5735 An. 5815

5905; Rooks (Little Warrior, Dorothy), Dorothy; F; 5/12/13-18; F; M; Wife; 113; Yes; Yes; Al. 7827 An. 4037

5906; Rooks, George B.; M; 12/27/08-24; plus 1/4; M; Head; 5844; Yes; Yes; Al. 3693 An. 5813

5907; Rooks (Blue Legs, Edna), Edna; F; 2/10/12-19; F; M; Wife; 5845; Yes; Yes; Al. 7705 An. 5814

5908; Rooks, William; M; 1888-44; plus 1/4; Wd.; Head; 5846; Yes; Yes; Al. 4054 An. 5817

5909; Rooks, Zouie; M; 1888-44; plus 1/4; Wd.; Head; 5847; Yes; Yes; Al. 2262 An. 5818

5910; Rooks, George Jr.; M; 8/20/12-19; plus 1/4; S; Son; 5848; Yes; Yes; Al. 6986 An. 5819

Census of the __Pine Ridge__ reservation of the __Pine Ridge, South Dakota__ jurisdiction, as of __April 1__, 19**32**, taken by __James H. McGregor__, Superintendent.

Key: Number; Surname, Given; Sex; Date of Birth-Age at Last Birthday; Tribe (Oglala Sioux, unless stated otherwise); Degree of Blood; Marital Status; Relationship to Head of Family [Last Census Roll Number]; At Jurisdiction Where Enrolled (Yes/No); (If no – Where); Ward (Yes/No, if given); Allotment, Annuity and Identification Numbers (if given).

5911; Rooks, Alex J.; M; 12/8/13-18; plus 1/4; S; Son; 5849; Yes; Yes; Al. 8111 An. 5820

5912; Rooks, Sarah N.; F; 8/27/15-16; plus 1/4; S; Daughter; 5850; Yes; Yes; Al. 8112 An. 5821

5913; Rooks, Hazel Amy; F; 8/18/27-4; plus 1/4; S; Daughter; 5851; Yes; Yes; Id. U-12377 An. none

5914; Rope Neckless, Sadie; F; 4/4/17-14; F; S; Alone; 5852; Yes; Yes; Al. 7705 An. 5814

5915; Rose, Joseph; M; 8/6/10-21; -1/4; S; Head; 5853; Yes; Yes; Al. 7158 An. 5825

5916; Rose, Louisa; F; 1895-37; -1/4; M; Head; 5854; Yes; Yes; Al. 5043 An. 5826

5917; Rose, Melda C.; F; 5/13/24-7; -1/4; S; Daughter; 5855; Yes; Yes; Id. U-11290 An. 5827

5918; Rose, Richard; M; 5/19/25-6; -1/4; S; Son; 5856; Yes; Yes; Id. U-13174 An. none

5919; Ross, Amos Jr.; M; 1895-37; plus 1/4; M; Head; 5857; Yes; Yes; Al. 5279 An. 5828

5920; Ross, Jean Alva; F; 1/24/23-9; plus 1/4; S; Daughter; 5858; Yes; Yes; Id. U-11277 An. none

5921; Ross, Glen Lyle; M; 6/18/27-4; plus 1/4; S; Son; 5859; Yes; Yes; Id. U-12530 An. none

N.E.: Ross, Owen D.; M; ------; Santee Sioux; plus 1/4; Head; No; Ft. Berthold, N.D.

5922; Ross (Armstrong, Cecelia), Cecelia; F; 1888-50; plus 1/4; M; Wife; 5860; No; Ditto; Yes; Al. 2107 An. 5830

5923; Ross, Henry; M; 2/28/10-22; plus 1/4; S; Son; 5861; No; Ft. Berthold, N.D.; Yes; Al. 4983 An. 5832

5924; Ross, Elsie M.; F; 6/30/13-18; plus 1/4; S; Daughter; 5862; No; Ditto; Yes; Al. 7045 An. 5833

5925; Ross, Russell; M; 10/27/15-16; plus 1/4; S; Son; 5863; No; Ditto; Yes; Id. U-10326 An. 5838

5926; Ross, H. James; M; 3/10/98-34; plus 1/4; M; Head; 5864; Yes; Yes; Al. 4984 An. 5835

5927; Ross (Valandry, Maude), Maude; F; 1899-33; plus 1/4; M; Wife; 5865; Yes; Yes; Al. 1087 An. 5836

5928; Ross, Rachel; F; 2/17/21-11; plus 1/4; S; Daughter; 5866; Yes; Yes; Id. U-10327 An. 5837

Census of the __Pine Ridge__ reservation of the __Pine Ridge, South Dakota__ jurisdiction, as of __April 1__, 19**32**, taken by __James H. McGregor__, Superintendent.

Key: Number; Surname, Given; Sex; Date of Birth-Age at Last Birthday; Tribe (Oglala Sioux, unless stated otherwise); Degree of Blood; Marital Status; Relationship to Head of Family [Last Census Roll Number]; At Jurisdiction Where Enrolled (Yes/No); (If no – Where); Ward (Yes/No, if given); Allotment, Annuity and Identification Numbers (if given).

5929; Ross, William; M; 3/22/03-29; plus 1/4; S; Head; 5867; Yes; Yes; Al. 4981 An. 5838

N.E.: Roubideaux, Antoine; M; ------; Rosebud Sioux; plus ---; Head;
5930; Roubideaux (LaPointe, Anna), Anna; F; 1899-33; plus 1/4; M; Wife; 5868; Yes; Yes; Al. 4677 An. 3686

5931; Roubideaux, Maggie; F; 1882-50; plus 1/4; Wd.; Head; 5869; Yes; Yes; Al. 356 An. 5840
5932; Roubideaux, Vernie; M; 3/ /10-22; plus 1/4; S; Son; 5870; Yes; Yes; Al. 4773 An. 5842
5933; Roubideaux, Annie; F; 1/23/12-20; plus 1/4; S; Daughter; 5871; Yes; Yes; Id. U-10312 An. 5843
5934; Rough Feather, ---; M; 1863-69; F; M; Head; 5872; Yes; Yes; Al. 5861 An. 5844
5935; Rough Feather (Eagle Dress, Mary), Mary; F; 1864-68; F; M; Wife; 5873; Yes; Yes; Al. 5862 An. 5845

N.E.: Rouillard, Samuel; MF; 1880; Flandreau Sioux; plus 1/4; M; Head;
5936; Rouillard (Gillispie, Jennie), Jennie; F; 1880-52; plus 1/4; M; Wife; 5874; Yes; Yes; Al. 6175 An. 5846
5937; Rouillard, Edith; F; 8/24/16-15; plus 1/4; S; Daughter; 5875; Yes; Yes; Id. U-10328 An. 5849

5938; Rouillard, Samuel, Jr.; M; 10/10/13-18; plus 1/4; Wd.; Head; 5876; Yes; Yes; Al. 7630 An. 5849
5939; Rouillard, Edith (Ruth) Marie; F; 1/31/31-1; plus 1/4; S; Daughter; 5878; Yes; Yes; Id. U-13710 An. none

N.E.: Rouillard, Peter A.; F[sic]; Santee Sioux; M; Head;
5940; Rouillard (Dismounts Thrice, Sophia), Sophia; F; 1903-29; F; M; Wife; 5879; Yes; Yes; Al. 1441 An. 1901
5941; Rouillard, Peter Seymour; M; 9/12/29-2; Sioux; plus 1/4; S; Son; 5880; Yes; Yes; Id. U-13711 An. none
5942; Rouillard, Mary Evelyn; F; 8/24/31-7/12; Sioux; plus 1/4; S; Daughter; ---; Yes; Yes; Id. U-14049 An. none

N.E.: Rowland, Benton; M; Nor. Cheyenne; plus 1/4; M; Head;
5943; Rowland (Breaks In, Anna), Anna; F; 1905-27; F; M; Wife; 5881; Yes; Yes; Al. 6471 An. 969
5944; Rowland, Rose May; F; 10/7/30-1; Sioux & Chey.; plus 1/4; S; Daughter; 5882; Yes; Yes; Id. U-13660 An. none

Census of the **Pine Ridge** reservation of the **Pine Ridge, South Dakota** jurisdiction, as of **April 1**, 19**32**, taken by **James H. McGregor**, Superintendent.

Key: Number; Surname, Given; Sex; Date of Birth-Age at Last Birthday; Tribe (Oglala Sioux, unless stated otherwise); Degree of Blood; Marital Status; Relationship to Head of Family [Last Census Roll Number]; At Jurisdiction Where Enrolled (Yes/No); (If no – Where); Ward (Yes/No, if given); Allotment, Annuity and Identification Numbers (if given).

5945; Bartlett, Lena; F; 9/22/19-12; plus 1/4; S; Ward; 5883; Yes; Yes; Id. U-10411 An. 435

N.E.: Rowland, Clay; M; 1880-52; Cheyenne (Tongue Riv); plus 1/4; M; Head;
5946; Rowland (Brown, Jennie), Jennie; F; 1876-56; plus 1/4; M; Wife; 5884; No; Tongue River, Mont.; Yes; Al. 7355 An. 5853

5947; Rowland, Nellie; F; 1869-63; F; Wd.; Head; 5885; Yes; Yes; Al. 1643 An. 5856

5948; Ruff, Arthur; M; 1883-49; plus 1/4; M; Head; 5887; Yes; Yes; Al. 4498 An. 5858

5949; Ruff (Peano, Hilda), Hilda; F; 1900-32; plus 1/4; M; Wife; 5888; Yes; Yes; Al. 1626 An. 5859

5950; Ruff, Eloise E.; F; 8/15/20-11; plus 1/4; S; Daughter; 5889; Yes; Yes; Id. U-10329 An. 5860

5951; Ruff, William H.; M; 4/8/26-5; plus 1/4; S; Son; 5890; Yes; Yes; Id. U-11885 An. none

5952; Ruff, Phyllisarna; F; 9/4/27-4; plus 1/4; S; Daughter; 5891; Yes; Yes; Id. U-12392 An. none

5953; Ruff, Geoffrey; M; 1898-34; -1/4; M; Head; 5892; Yes; Yes; Al. 4702 An. 5863

5954; Ruff (Ruleau, Isabel), Isabel; F; 1901-31; plus 1/4; M; Wife; 5893; Yes; Yes; Al. 2148 An. 5864

5955; Ruff, Inez; F; 8/20/20-11; -1/4; S; Daughter; 5894[sic]; Yes; Yes; Id. U-10336 An. 5865

5956; Ruff, Paul N.; M; 1/23/23-9; -1/4; S; Son; 5894; Yes; Yes; Id. U-11242 An. 5866

5957; Ruff, Marguerite; F; 1/29/24-8; -1/4; S; Daughter; 5895; Yes; Yes; Id. U-11241 An. 5867

5958; Ruff, George; M; 1869-63; plus 1/4; M; Head; 5897; Yes; Yes; Al. 4478 An. 5868

5959; Ruff (No data), Rosa; F; 1872-60; plus 1/4; M; Wife; 5898; Yes; No; Al. 7302 An. 5869

5960; Ruff, George W.; M; 10/30/16-15; plus 1/4; S; Son; 5899; Yes; Yes; Id. U-10335 An. 5871

5961; Ruff, Emma V.; F; 10/5/10-21; plus 1/4; S; Head; 5900; Yes; Yes; Al. 5471 An. 5870

Census of the __Pine Ridge__ reservation of the __Pine Ridge, South Dakota__ jurisdiction, as of __April 1__, 1932, taken by __James H. McGregor__, Superintendent.

Key: Number; Surname, Given; Sex; Date of Birth-Age at Last Birthday; Tribe (Oglala Sioux, unless stated otherwise); Degree of Blood; Marital Status; Relationship to Head of Family [Last Census Roll Number]; At Jurisdiction Where Enrolled (Yes/No); (If no – Where); Ward (Yes/No, if given); Allotment, Annuity and Identification Numbers (if given).

5962; Ruff, John; M; 1881-63; plus 1/4; M; Head; 5901; Yes; Yes; Al. 4504 An. 5872
5963; Ruff (Smith, Alice), Alice; F; 1885-47; plus 1/4; M; Wife; 5902; Yes; Yes; Al. 2379 An. 5873
5964; Ruff, Jennie E.; F; 5/14/14-17; plus 1/4; S; Daughter; 5903; Yes; Yes; Al. 7866 An. 5875
5965; Ruff, Seth G.; M; 4/2/17-15; plus 1/4; S; Son; 5904; Yes; Yes; Id. U-10330 An. 5876
5966; Ruff, Viola T.; F; 4/8/19-12; plus 1/4; S; Daughter; 5905; Yes; Yes; Id. U-10331 An. 5877
5967; Ruff, Emma G.; F; 11/5/24-7; plus 1/4; S; Daughter; 5906; Yes; Yes; Id. U-10447 An. 5878

5968; Ruff, William; M; 1887-45; plus 1/4; M; Head; 5907; Yes; No; Al. 4506 An. 5880
5969; Ruff (Williams, Lizzie), Lizzie; F; 1890-42; plus 1/4; M; Wife; 5908; Yes; Yes; Al. 4571 An. 5881
5970; Ruff, Elva M.; F; 10/25/14-17; plus 1/4; S; Daughter; 5909; Yes; Yes; Id. U-10332 An. 5882
5971; Ruff, Weldon A.; M; 8/16/17-14; plus 1/4; S; Son; 5910; Yes; Yes; Id. U-10333 An. 5883
5972; Ruff, Delbert; M; 11/3/23-8; plus 1/4; S; Son; 5911; Yes; Yes; Id. U-11327 An. 5885
5973; Ruff, Eileen G.; F; 5/9/29-2; plus 1/4; S; Daughter; 5912; Yes; Yes; Id. U-13257 An. none
5974; Ruff, Irene A.; F; 5/9/29-2; plus 1/4; S; Daughter; 5913; Yes; Yes; Id. U-13258 An. none

5975; Ruggles, Isabelle; F; 1878-54; plus 1/4; Wd.; Head; 5914; Yes; No; Al. 2592 An. 5886

5976; Ruleau, Hobart; M; 1897-35; plus 1/4; M; Head; 5915; Yes; Yes; Al. 2146 An. 5887
5977; Ruleau, Betty L.; F; 3/7/25-7; -1/4; S; Daughter; 5916; Yes; Yes; Id. U-11664 An. none
5978; Ruleau, Cecelia L.; F; 11/16/26-5; -1/4; S; Daughter; 5917; Yes; Yes; Id. U-12185 An. none
5979; Ruleau, Geraldine; F; 7/10/28-3; -1/4; S; Daughter; 5918; Yes; Yes; Id. U-12766 An. none
5980; Ruleau, Phyllis E.; F; 10/16/29-2; -1/4; S; Daughter; 5919; Yes; Yes; Id. U-13390 An. none
5981; Ruleau, Donald D.; M; 6/19/31-9/12; -1/4; S; Son; ---; Yes; Yes; Id. U-13903 An. none

Census of the____Pine Ridge____reservation of the **Pine Ridge, South Dakota** jurisdiction, as of____**April 1**____, 19**32**, taken by____**James H. McGregor**____, Superintendent.

Key: Number; Surname, Given; Sex; Date of Birth-Age at Last Birthday; Tribe (Oglala Sioux, unless stated otherwise); Degree of Blood; Marital Status; Relationship to Head of Family [Last Census Roll Number]; At Jurisdiction Where Enrolled (Yes/No); (If no – Where); Ward (Yes/No, if given); Allotment, Annuity and Identification Numbers (if given).

5982; Ruleau, Paul; M; 5/31/16-15; plus 1/4; S; Alone; 5920; Yes; Yes; Id. U-10338 An. 5889

5983; Ruleau, Hazel; F; 12/17/13-18; plus 1/4; S; Head; 5921; Yes; Yes; Id. U-10337 An. 5892

5984; Ruleau, William; M; 10/4/09-23; plus 1/4; S; Head; 5922; Yes; Yes; Al. 7841 An. 5890

5985; Ruleau, Frank; M; 7/9/07-25; plus 1/4; S; Head; 5923; Yes; Yes; Al. 2149 An. 5888

5986; Ruleau, Edward; M; 11/17/11-20; plus 1/4; S; Head; 5924; Yes; Yes; Al. 6906 An. 5891

5987; Rump Bone, ---; F; 1858-74; F; Wd.; Head; 775; Yes; Yes; Al. 6450 An. 804

5988; Runnels, Maude; F; 1884-48; plus 1/4; Wd.; Head; 5925; Yes; Yes; Al. 2962 An. 5896

5989; Runnels, Raymond; M; 1906-26; plus 1/4; M; Head; 5926; Yes; Yes; Al. 2965 An. 5897

5990; Runnels (Conroy, Cecelia), Cecelia; F; 11/13/06-25; plus 1/4; M; Wife; 5927; Yes; hes[sic]; Al. 4583 An. 1611

5991; Runnels, Betty G.; F; 5/23/28-3; plus 1/4; S; Daughter; 5928; Yes; Yes; Id. U-12783 An. none

5992; Runnels, Jack Ray; M; 9/23/29-2; plus 1/4; S; Son; 5929; Yes; Yes; Id. U-13391 An. none

N.E.: Running, Frank Isadore; M; Rosebud Sioux; F; M; Head;

5993; Running (Janis, Alice), Alice; F; 1899-33; plus 1/4; M; Wife; 5930; Yes; Yes; Al. 1635 An. 5898

5994; Running Bear, Albert; M; 1871-61; F; Wd.; Head; 5931; Yes; Yes; Al. 148 An. 5901

5995; Running Bear, Dick; M; 1892-40; F; M; Head; 5932; Yes; Yes; Al. 4854 An. 5902

5996; Running Bear (Good Soldier, Hazel), Hazel; F; 1892-40; F; M; Wife; 5933; Yes; Yes; Al. 3391 An. 5903

5997; Running Bear, Jonas; M; 3/20/22-9; F; S; Son; 5934; Yes; Yes; Id. U-11047 An. 5905

Census of the **Pine Ridge** reservation of the **Pine Ridge, South Dakota** jurisdiction, as of **April 1**, 19**32,** taken by **James H. McGregor**, Superintendent.

Key: Number; Surname, Given; Sex; Date of Birth-Age at Last Birthday; Tribe (Oglala Sioux, unless stated otherwise); Degree of Blood; Marital Status; Relationship to Head of Family [Last Census Roll Number]; At Jurisdiction Where Enrolled (Yes/No); (If no – Where); Ward (Yes/No, if given); Allotment, Annuity and Identification Numbers (if given).

5998; Running Bear, Emerson; M; 2/11/25-6; F; S; Son; 5935; Yes; Yes; Id. U-12853 An. none
5999; Running Bear, Richard; M; 7/4/27-4; F; S; Son; 5936; Yes; Yes; Id. U-12854 An. none
6000; Running Bear, Loranda; F; 3/25/28-4; F; S; Daughter; 5938[sic]; Yes; Yes; Id. U-12855 An. none

6001; Running Eagle, Mark; M; 1890-42; F; M; Head; 5938; Yes; Yes; Al. 3174 An. 5906
6002; Running Eagle (Chief Eagle, Nellie), Nellie; F; 1900-32; F; M; Wife; 5939; Yes; Yes; Al. 3041 An. 5907
6003; Running Eagle, Florine; F; 3/4/25-7; F; S; Daughter; 5940; Yes; Yes; Id. U-11489 An. none
6004; Running Eagle, Hoover; M; 8/29/29-2; F; S; Son; 5941; Yes; Yes; Id. U-13271 An. none
6005; Running Eagle, Thomas; M; 5/9/31-10/12; F; S; Son; ---; Yes; Yes; Id. U-13911 An. none

6006; Running Eagle, Wallace; M; 1875-57; F; M; Head; 5942; Yes; Yes; Al. 3058 An. 5910
6007; Running Eagle (No data), Jennie; F; 1879-53; F; M; Wife; 5943; Yes; Yes; Al. 3059 An. 5911
6008; Running Eagle, Charles; M; 1/9/10-22; F; S; Son; 5944; Yes; Yes; Al. 6165 An. 5912
6009; Running Eagle, Oliver; M; 7/4/15-16; F; S; Son; 5945; Yes; Yes; Id. U-10341 An. 5913
6010; Running Eagle, Silas; M; 11/16/19-12; F; S; Son; 5946; Yes; Yes; Id. U-10342 An. 5914

6011; Running Elk, ---; M; 1849-83; F; M; Head; 5947; Yes; Yes; Al. 6787 An. 5915
6012; Pouting, ---; F; 1858-74; F; M; Wife #1; 5948; Yes; Yes; Al. 7565 An. 5916
6013; Ask Them Something, ---; F; 1861-71; F; M; Wife #2; 5949; Yes; Yes; Al. 7136 An. 5917

6014; Running Hawk, Ellen; F; 1884-48; plus 1/4; Wd.; Head; 5951; Yes; Yes; Al. 6502 An. 5919

6015; Running Hawk, Claude; M; 1879-53; F; M; Head; 5952; Yes; Yes; Al. 4153 An. 5920
6016; Running Hawk (Marrow Bone, Emma), Emma; plus 1/4; 1880-52; plus 1/4; M; Wife; 5953; Yes; Yes; Al. 6473 An. 5921
6017; Running Hawk, Charles; M; 10/16/14-17; plus 1/4; S; Son; 5954; Yes; Yes; Id. U-10343 An. 5926

Census of the **Pine Ridge** reservation of the **Pine Ridge, South Dakota** jurisdiction, as of **April 1**, 19**32**, taken by **James H. McGregor**, Superintendent.

Key: Number; Surname, Given; Sex; Date of Birth-Age at Last Birthday; Tribe (Oglala Sioux, unless stated otherwise); Degree of Blood; Marital Status; Relationship to Head of Family [Last Census Roll Number]; At Jurisdiction Where Enrolled (Yes/No); (If no – Where); Ward (Yes/No, if given); Allotment, Annuity and Identification Numbers (if given).

6018; Marrow Bone, Victoria; F; 10/28/13-18; plus 1/4; S; Stepdaughter; 5955; Yes; Yes; Id. U-9981 An. 5922

6019; Running Hawk, Lucy; F; 12/3/11-20; plus 1/4; S; Head; 5956; Yes; Yes; Al. 7921 An. 5920

6020; Running Hawk, Eugene; M; 10/3/07-24; plus 1/4; S; Head; 5957; Yes; Yes; Al. 4156 An. 5923

6021; Running Hawk, Harry; M; 1875-57; F; M; Head; 5958; Yes; Yes; Al. 4910 An. 5927

6022; Running Hawk (No data), Victoria; F; 1880-52; plus 1/4; M; Wife; 5959; Yes; Yes; Al. 6497 An. 5928

6023; Running Hawk, Joseph; M; 10/29/09-22; F; S; Son; 5960; Yes; Yes; Al. 6500 An. 5929

6024; Running Hawk, Lawrence; M; 2/1/07-25; F; M; Head; 5961; No; Checotah, town, Mackintosh, Okla.; Yes; Al. 6499 An. 5930

N.E.: Running Hawk, (Swadley, Ethel) Ethel; F; ------; Creek; 1/16; Wife;

6025; Running Hawk, William; M; 1902-30; F; S; Head; 5962; Yes; Yes; Al. 6498 An. 5931

N.E.: Running Horse, Jesse; M; Rosebud Sioux; Head;

6026; Running Horse (Little Bear, Alice), Alice; F; 3/30/11-21; F; M; Wife; 5964; Yes; Yes; Al. 6765 An. 3869

6027; Running Horse, Hobart; M; 11/27/31-4/12; F; S; Son; ---; Yes; Yes; Id. U-14067 An. none

6028; Running Horse, Alice; F; 1863-69; F; Wd.; Head; 5963; Yes; Yes; Al. 6026 An. 5933

6029; Running Horse, Peter; M; 1887-45; F; M; Head; 5965; Yes; No; Al. 6015 An. 5934

6030; Running Horse (Sword, Jessie), Jessie; F; 1888-44; F; M; Wife; 5966; Yes; No; Al. 1164 An. 5935

6031; Running Horse, George; M; 1/13/12-20; F; S; Son; 5967; Yes; Yes; Al. 6062 An. 5936

6032; Running Horse, Peter Jr.; M; 6/29/15-16; F; S; Son; 5968; Yes; Yes; Al. 8099 An. 5937

6033; Running Horse, George; M; 1875-57; F; M; Head; 5969; Yes; Yes; Al. 1836 An. 5938

Census of the **Pine Ridge** reservation of the **Pine Ridge, South Dakota** jurisdiction, as of **April 1**, 1932, taken by **James H. McGregor**, Superintendent.

Key: Number; Surname, Given; Sex; Date of Birth-Age at Last Birthday; Tribe (Oglala Sioux, unless stated otherwise); Degree of Blood; Marital Status; Relationship to Head of Family [Last Census Roll Number]; At Jurisdiction Where Enrolled (Yes/No); (If no – Where); Ward (Yes/No, if given); Allotment, Annuity and Identification Numbers (if given).

6034; Running Horse (Romero, Lillie), Lillie; F; 1877-55; plus 1/4; M; Wife; 5970; Yes; Yes; Al. 1837 An. 5939

6035; Running Horse, Judson; M; 3/6/14-18; plus 1/4; S; Son; 5971; Yes; Yes; Al. 7772 An. 5941

6036; Running Shield, Dawson; M; 1903-29; plus 1/4; M; Head; 5972; Yes; Yes; Al. 2511 An. 5942

6037; Running Shield (White Bear, Jessie), Jessie; F; 1902-30; F; M; Wife; 5974; Yes; Yes; Al. 1796 An. 1233

6038; Running Shield, Lucille; F; 1/16/27-5; plus 1/4; M; Wife; 5973; Yes; Yes; Id. U-12595 An. none

6039; Running Shield, Louis; M; 2/18/31-1; plus 1/4; S; Son; 5975; Yes; Yes; Id. U-13746 An. none

6040; Running Shield, Leon; M; 1873-59; Wd.; M; Head; 5976; Yes; Yes; Al. 58 An. 5943

6041; Running Shield, Isaac; M; 2/25/11-21; F; S; Son; 5977; Yes; Yes; Al. 6740 An. 5945

6042; Running Shield, Sarah; F; 6/5/13-18; F; S; Daughter; 5978; Yes; Yes; Al. 7908 An. 5946

6043; Running Shield, Abraham; M; 5/3/20-11; F; S; Son; 5980; Yes; Yes; Id. U-10347 An. 5948

6044; Running Shield, Marie; F; 5/20/24-7; F; S; Daughter; 5981; Yes; Yes; Id. U-11318 An. 5950

6045; Running Shield, Wilson; M; 7/8/10-21; plus 1/4; S; Head; 5982; Yes; Yes; Al. 6674 An. 2194

6046; Running Shield, Louisa; F; 11/1/14-17; plus 1/4; S; Sister; 5983; Yes; Yes; Al. 7992 An. 2195

6047; Runs Above, Peter; M; 1881-51; F; S; Head; 5984; Yes; Yes; Al. 7610 An. 5953

6048; Runs Above, Lloyd L.; M; 10/18/25-6; plus 1/4; S; Son; 5985; Yes; Yes; Id. U-11823 An. none

6049; Runs Above, George; M; 3/16/28-4; plus 1/4; S; Son; 5986; Yes; Yes; Id. U-12560 An. none

6050; Runs For Hill, Peter; M; 1862-70; F; M; Head; 7706; Yes; Yes; Al. 1145 An. 5976

6051; Runs Against, Moses; M; 1898-34; F; M; Head; 5987; Yes; Yes; Al. 6782 An. 5960

Census of the __**Pine Ridge**__ reservation of the __**Pine Ridge, South Dakota**__ jurisdiction, as of __**April 1**__, 19**32**, taken by __**James H. McGregor**__, Superintendent.

Key: Number; Surname, Given; Sex; Date of Birth-Age at Last Birthday; Tribe (Oglala Sioux, unless stated otherwise); Degree of Blood; Marital Status; Relationship to Head of Family [Last Census Roll Number]; At Jurisdiction Where Enrolled (Yes/No); (If no – Where); Ward (Yes/No, if given); Allotment, Annuity and Identification Numbers (if given).

6052; Runs Against (Picket Pin, Delia), Delia; F; 1896-36; F; M; Wife; 5988; Yes; Yes; Al. 7515 An. 5961

6053; Runs Against, Katherine; F; 1/30/22-10; F; S; Daughter; 5989; Yes; Yes; Id. U-10855 An. 5962

6054; Runs Against, Calvert; M; 3/3/25-7; F; S; Son; 5990; Yes; Yes; Id. U-11450 An. 5963

6055; Runs Against, Cornelia; F; 11/27/26-5; F; S; Daughter; 5991; Yes; Yes; Id. U-12151 An. none

6056; Runs Against, Claudia; F; 1/2/29-3; F; S; Daughter; 5992; Yes; Yes; Id. U-12995 An. none

6057; Runs Along The Edge, ---; M; 1869-63; F; M; Head; 5993; Yes; Yes; Al. 1097 An. 5964

6058; Runs Along The Edge (No data), Delia; F; 1873-59; F; M; Wife; 5994; Yes; Yes; Al. 5296 An. 5965

6059; Runs Along The Edge, Moses; M; 8/24/10-21; F; S; Son; 5995; Yes; Yes; Id. U-10350 An. 5966

6060; Runs Along The Edge, Solomon; M; 1907-25; plus 1/4; M; Head; 5996; Yes; Yes; Al. 5350 An. 5968

6061; Runs Along The Edge (Slow Dog, Jessie), Jessie; F; 1907-25; F; M; Wife; 5997; Yes; Yes; Al. 5369 An. 6391

6062; Runs Close To Lodge, Lottie; F; 1894-38; F; Wd.; Head; 5999; Yes; Yes; Al. 2475 An. 4702

6063; Runs On, Mary; F; 1865-67; F; Wd.; Head; 6000; Yes; Yes; Al. 3645 An. 5872

6064; Runs On The Edge, Peter; M; 1866-66; F; M; Head; 6001; Yes; Yes; Al. 590 An. 5978

6065; Runs On The Edge (No data), Mary; F; 1868-64; F; M; Wife; 6002; Yes; Yes; Al. 4143 An. 5979

6066; Weston, Grace; F; 5/19/26-5; F; S; Granddaughter; 6003; Yes; Yes; Id. U-12651 An. none

6067; Russell, Albert; M; 1898-34; plus 1/4; M; Head; 6004; No; Rapid City, town, Pennington, S.D.; Yes; Al. 2747 An. 5980

6068; Russell, Shirley A.; F; 1/10/28-4; -1/4; S; Daughter; 6005; No; Ditto; Yes; Id. U-12891 An. none

6069; Russell, Andrew; M; 1869-63; plus 1/4; M; Head; 6006; Yes; Yes; Al. 4628 An. 5981

Census of the __Pine Ridge__ reservation of the __Pine Ridge, South Dakota__ jurisdiction, as of __April 1__, 1932, taken by __James H. McGregor__, Superintendent.

Key: Number; Surname, Given; Sex; Date of Birth-Age at Last Birthday; Tribe (Oglala Sioux, unless stated otherwise); Degree of Blood; Marital Status; Relationship to Head of Family [Last Census Roll Number]; At Jurisdiction Where Enrolled (Yes/No); (If no – Where); Ward (Yes/No, if given); Allotment, Annuity and Identification Numbers (if given).

6070; Russell (No data), Sophia; F; 1879-59; -1/4; M; Wife; 6007; Yes; Yes; Al. 4629 An. 5982

6071; Russell, Alma L.; F; 4/1/16-16; plus 1/4; S; Daughter; 6008; Yes; Yes; Al. 8171 An. 5982

6072; Russell, Robert J.; M; 12/23/19-12; plus 1/4; S; Son; 6009; Yes; Yes; Id. U-10353 An. 5984

6073; Russell, Dorothy N.; F; 4/5/22-9; plus 1/4; S; Daughter; 6010; Yes; Yes; Id. U-10955 An. 5985

6074; Russell, Floyd; M; 1904-28; plus 1/4; M; Head; 6011; Yes; Yes; Al. 4631 An. 5986

6075; Russell, Mary; F; 1865-67; plus 1/4; Wd.; Wife; 6013; Yes; Yes; Al. 2738 An. 5988

6076; White, Florine; F; 1/23/20-12; plus 1/4; S; Granddaughter; ---; Yes; Yes; Id. U-13794 An. none

6077; Ryan, Evaline; F; 5/24/11-20; -1/4; S; Head; 6016; Yes; Yes; Id. U-10355 An. 5994

6078; Ryan, Gerald J.; M; 10/17/09-22; -1/4; S; Head; 6015; Yes; Yes; Id. U-10354 An. 5993

6079; Ryan, Louis; M; 1888-44; plus 1/4; Wd.; Head; 6014; Yes; No; Al. 5487 An. 5992

6080; Salvis, Enoch; M; 1898-34; plus 1/4; M; Head; 6017; Yes; Yes; Al. 2372 An. 5996

N.E.: Salvis, (Bordeaux, Mary) Mary; F; -------; Rosebud Sioux; 1/2; Wife;

6081; Salvis, Eileen; F; 11/20/26-5; plus 1/4; S; Daughter; 6018; Yes; Yes; Id. U-12186 An. none

6082; Salvis, Lemoyne R.; M; 1/7/29-3; plus 1/4; S; Son; 6019; Yes; Yes; Id. U-13232 An. none

6083; Salvis, George; M; 1898-39; plus 1/4; Wd.; Head; 6020; Yes; Yes; Al. 2370 An. 5997

6084; Salvis, Levi; M; 1888-44; plus 1/4; M; Head; 6021; Yes; Yes; Al. 2368 An. 5999

N.E.: Salvis, (Left Hand Bull, Nancy) Nancy; F; -------; Rosebud Sioux; Wife;

6085; Salvis, Leon; M; 1905-27; plus 1/4; M; Head; 6022; Yes; Yes; Al. 5519 An. 6000

Census of the **Pine Ridge** reservation of the **Pine Ridge, South Dakota** jurisdiction, as of **April 1**, 19**32**, taken by **James H. McGregor**, Superintendent.

Key: Number; Surname, Given; Sex; Date of Birth-Age at Last Birthday; Tribe (Oglala Sioux, unless stated otherwise); Degree of Blood; Marital Status; Relationship to Head of Family [Last Census Roll Number]; At Jurisdiction Where Enrolled (Yes/No); (If no – Where); Ward (Yes/No, if given); Allotment, Annuity and Identification Numbers (if given).

6086; Salvis (Ruff, Mary), Mary; F; 7/22/12-19; plus 1/4; M; Wife; 6023; Yes; Yes; Al. 6899 An. 5874

6087; Salvis, Iris Pauline; F; 8/5/29-2; plus 1/4; S; Daughter; 6024; Yes; Yes; Id. U-13241 An. none

6088; Salvis, Myrtle Grace; F; 3/29/31-1; plus 1/4; S; Daughter; 6025; Yew[sic]; Yes; Id. U-13784 An. none

6089; Salvis, Oliver; M; 1876-56; plus 1/4; M; Head; 6026; Yes; No; Al. 2366 An. 6001

6090; Salvis (No data), Mary; F; 1876-56; plus 1/4; M; Wife; 6027; Yes; Yes; Al. 5263 An. 6002

6091; Salvis, Oliver, Jr.; M; 5/7/13-18; plus 1/4; S*M*; Son; 6028; Yes; Yes; Id. U-10356 An. 6004

6092; Salvis, John; M; 10/16/15-16; plus 1/4; S; Son; 6029; Yes; Yes; Id. U-10357 An. 6005

6093; Salvis, George True; M; 12/28/18-13; plus 1/4; S; Alone; 6030; Yes; Yes; Id. U-10831 An. 5998

6094; Salvis, William; M; 1895-37; plus 1/4; M; Head; 6032; Yes; Yes; Al. 2371 An. 6006

6095; Salvis, Freida Marie; F; 9/9/24-7; plus 1/4; S; Daughter; 6033; Yes; Yes; Id. U-11668 An. none

6096; Salway, Alex Sr.; M; 1856-76; plus 1/4; M; Head; 6034; Yes; Yes; Al. 5233 An. 6007

6097; Salway (Sanders, Millie), Millie; F; 1858-74; plus 1/4; M; Wife; 6035; Yes; Yes; Al. 5234 An. 6008

6098; Salway, Alex Jr.; M; 1887-45; plus 1/4; S; Head; 6036; Yes; Yes; Al. 5235 An. 6009

6099; Salway, Matilda; F; 7/20/14-17; plus 1/4; S; Head; 6037; Yes; Yes; Id. U-10358 An. 6013

6100; Salway, Clementine; F; 4/24/18-13; plus 1/4; S; Sister; 6038; Yes; Yes; Id. U-10359 An. 6014

6101; Salway, Nancy; F; 3/30/21-11; plus 1/4; S; Sister; 6039; Yes; Yes; Id. U-10360 An. 6015

6102; Salway, James; M; 1898-34; plus 1/4; M; Head; 6040; Yes; Yes; Al. 5237 An. 6016

6103; Salway (Ladeaux, Maggie), Maggie; F; 1894-38; plus 1/4; M; Wife; 6041; Yes; Yes; Al. 3586 An. 6017

Census of the **Pine Ridge** reservation of the **Pine Ridge, South Dakota** jurisdiction, as of **April 1**, 1932, taken by **James H. McGregor**, Superintendent.

Key: Number; Surname, Given; Sex; Date of Birth-Age at Last Birthday; Tribe (Oglala Sioux, unless stated otherwise); Degree of Blood; Marital Status; Relationship to Head of Family [Last Census Roll Number]; At Jurisdiction Where Enrolled (Yes/No); (If no – Where); Ward (Yes/No, if given); Allotment, Annuity and Identification Numbers (if given).

6104; Salway, Eleanor; F; 7/13/18-18; plus 1/4; S; Daughter; 6042; Yes; Yes; Id. U-10364 An. 6018

6105; Salway, Genevieve; F; 1/20/21-11; plus 1/4; S; Daughter; 6043; Yes; Yes; Id. U-10365 An. 6019

6106; Salway, Sylvia M.; F; 11/4/23-8; plus 1/4; S; Daughter; 6044; Yes; Yes; Id. U-11459 An. 6020

6107; Salway, James A.; M; 10/31/25-6; plus 1/4; S; Son; 6045; Yes; Yes; Id. U-11824 An. none

6108; Salway, Harley Warren; M; 10/1/31-6/12; plus 1/4; S; Son; 6046; Yes; Yes; Id. U-13946 An. none

6109; Salway, Stacy; M; 1890-42; plus 1/4; M; Head; 6046; Yes; Yes; Al. 5236 An. 6021

6110; Salway (Richard, Emma), Emma; F; 1904-28; plus 1/4; M; Wife; 6047; Yes; Yes; Al. 2337 An. 6022

6111; Salway, Marvin; M; 7/6/23-8; plus 1/4; S; Son; 6048; Yes; Yes; Id. U-11702 An. 6023

6112; Salway, William; M; 1883-49; plus 1/4; M; Head; 6049; Yes; No; Al. 4648 An. 6024

6113; Salway (Janis, Winnie), Winnie; F; 1887-45; plus 1/4; M; Wife; 6050; Yes; Yes; Al. 8071 An. 6025

6114; Salway, Marceal; M; 3/29/16-16; plus 1/4; S; Son; 6051; Yes; Yes; Id. U-10361 An. 6028

6115; Salway, Stacy Wm.; M; 7/1/18-13; plus 1/4; S; Son; 6052; Yes; Yes; Id. U-10362 An. 6029

6116; Salway, Mandala C.; F; 12/11/20-11; plus 1/4; S; Daughter; 6053; Yes; Yes; Id. U-10363 An. 6030

6117; Salway, Orville; M; 10/23/23-8; plus 1/4; S; Son; 6054; Yes; Yes; Id. U-11228 An. 6031

6118; Salway, Clement; M; 6/1/26-5; plus 1/4; S; Son; 6055; Yes; Yes; Id. U-11954 An. none

6119; Salway, Vincent W.; M; 10/5/28-3; plus 1/4; S; Son; 6056; Yes; Yes; Id. U-12812 An. none

6120; Salway, Theodore; M; 11/21/10-21; plus 1/4; S; Head; 6057; Yes; Yes; Al. 5794 An. 6026

6121; Salway, Magdaline; F; 12/24/12-19; plus 1/4; S; Head; 6058; Yes; Yes; Al. 6990 An. 6027

6122; Donohue, Adeline L.; F; 1/6/32-3/12; plus 1/4; S; Daughter; ---; ues[sic]; Yes; Id. U-14068 An. none

Census of the **Pine Ridge** reservation of the **Pine Ridge, South Dakota** jurisdiction, as of **April 1**, 19**32**, taken by **James H. McGregor**, Superintendent.

Key: Number; Surname, Given; Sex; Date of Birth-Age at Last Birthday; Tribe (Oglala Sioux, unless stated otherwise); Degree of Blood; Marital Status; Relationship to Head of Family [Last Census Roll Number]; At Jurisdiction Where Enrolled (Yes/No); (If no – Where); Ward (Yes/No, if given); Allotment, Annuity and Identification Numbers (if given).

6123; Sanders, Norah; F; 1894-38; -1/4; M; Head; 6059; Yes; Yes; Al. 4839 An. 6032

6124; Sanders, Pauline; F; 4/17/16-15; -1/4; S; Daughter; 6060; Yes; Yes; Id. U-10366 An. 6033

6125; Sanders, Thomas A.; M; 1/10/18-14; -1/4; S; Son; 6061; Yes; Yes; Id. U-10367 An. 6034

6126; Sanders, Ellen M.; F; 3/28/20-12; -1/4; S; Daughter; 6062; Yes; Yes; Id. U-11109 An. 6035

6127; Sanders, Betty Jean; F; 8/14/24-7; -1/4; S; Daughter; 6063; Yes; Yes; Id. U-12561 An. none

6128; Sanovia, James; M; 1884-48; plus 1/4; M; Head; 6064; Yes; Yes; Al. 4362 An. 6036

6129; Sanovia (Fire Thunder, Louisa), Louisa; F; 1871-61; plus 1/4; M; Wife; 6065; Yes; Yes; Al. 1950 An. 6037

6130; Sanovia, Lloyd; M; 9/28/12-19; plus 1/4; S; Son; 6066; Yes; Yes; Id. U-11110 An. 6039

6131; Sasse, Alice D.; F; 1894-38; plus 1/4; M; Head; 6067; Yes; Yes; Al. 409 An. 6040

6132; Sasse, Charles D.; M; 12/5/17-14; -1/4; S; Son; 6068; Yes; Yes; Id. U-11111 An. 6041

6133; Sasse, Martha H.; F; 12/29/21-10; -1/4; S; Daughter; 6069; Yes; Yes; Id. U-11056 An. 6042

6134; Sasse, Earnest L.; M; 3/16/19-12; -1/4; S; Son; 6070; Yes; Yes; Id. U-11057 An. 6043

6135; Sasse, Mary A.; F; 2/22/23-8; -1/4; S; Daughter; 6071; Yes; Yes; Id. U-11632 An. 6044

6136; Sasse, Elane H.; F; 4/14/24-7; -1/4; S; Daughter; 6072; Yes; Yes; Id. U-11633 An. 6045

6137; Sasse, Carl Jr.; M; 1/8/30-2; -1/4; S; Son; 6073; Yes; Yes; Id. U-13461 An. none

6138; Sauser, Alma A.; F; 1888-44; -1/4; M; Head; 6074; Yes; Yes; Al. 3911 An. 6046

6139; Sauser, Arthur P.; M; 8/29/09-23; -1/4; S; Son; 6075; Yes; Yes; Al. 4102 An. 6047

6140; Sauser, Raymond P.; M; 2/14/11-21; -1/4; S; Son; 6076; Yes; Yes; Al. 5761 An. 6048

6141; Sauser, Maurice W.; M; 4/14/13-18; -1/4; S; Son; 6077; Yes; Yes; Al. 7177 An. 6049

6142; Sauser, Harold E.; M; 7/30/15-16; -1/4; S; Son; 6078; Yes; Yes; Al. 8109 An. 6050

Census of the **Pine Ridge** reservation of the **Pine Ridge, South Dakota** jurisdiction, as of **April 1**, **1932**, taken by **James H. McGregor**, Superintendent.

Key: Number; Surname, Given; Sex; Date of Birth-Age at Last Birthday; Tribe (Oglala Sioux, unless stated otherwise); Degree of Blood; Marital Status; Relationship to Head of Family [Last Census Roll Number]; At Jurisdiction Where Enrolled (Yes/No); (If no – Where); Ward (Yes/No, if given); Allotment, Annuity and Identification Numbers (if given).

6143; Sauser, Philip M.; M; 9/25/18-13; -1/4; S; Son; 6079; Yes; Yes; Id. U-11112 An. 6051

6144; Sauser, Margaret; F; 3/21/21-11; -1/4; S; Daughter; 6080; Yes; Yes; Id. U-11113 An. 6052

N.E.: Saves Life, George; M; Standing Rock Sioux; M; Head;

6145; Saves Life (Randall, Mabel), Mabel; F; 3/2/10-22; plus 1/4; M; Wife; 6081; Yes; Yes; Al. 5791 An. 5281

6146; Saves Life, Earl Wayne; M; 7/5/31-9/12; plus 1/4; S; Son; ---; Yes; Yes; Id. U-13878 An. none

6147; Scabby Face, Johnson; M; 1873-59; F; M; Head; 6085; Yes; Yes; Al. 2873 An. 6057

6148; Scabby Face (Red Ear Horse, Sallie), Sallie; F; 1877-54; F; M; Wife; 6086; Yes; Yes; Al. 3360 An. 6058

6149; Scabby Face, Jessie; F; 5/10/12-19; F; S; Daughter; 6087; Yes; Yes; Al. 7625 An. 6060

6150; Scabby Face, Bennie; M; 1903-29; F; Wd.; Head; 6082; Yes; Yes; Al. 3128 An. 6053

6151; Scabby Face, Victoria; F; 3/12/30-2; F; S; Daughter; 6084; Yes; Yes; Id. U-13448 An. none

6152; Scabby Face, Alexander; M; 1904-28; F; S; Head; 6088; Yes; Yes; Al. 3129 An. 6061

6153; Schnitger, Ida; F; 1873-59; plus 1/4; M; Head; 6089; No; Long Beach, city, Los Angeles, Cal.; No; Al. 5372 An. 6063

6154; Schroeder, Emma; F; 1885-47; plus 1/4; Wd.; Head; 6090; Yes; Yes; Al. 979 An. 6064

6155; Schwartz, Estelle; F; 1895-37; plus 1/4; M; Head; 6091; Yes; Yes; Al. 1350 An. 6065

6156; Schwartz, Thomas A.; M; 11/27/20-11; -1/4; S; Son; 6092; Yes; Yes; Id. U-10369 An. 6066

6157; Schwartz, Harold B.; M; 9/7/22-9; -1/4; S; Son; 6093; Yes; Yes; Id. U-12035 An. 6067

6158; Schwartz, Wilma E.; F; 4/23/25-6; -1/4; S; Daughter; 6094; Yes; Yes; Id. U-11729 An. none

6159; Scott, Ida; F; 1899-33; -1/4; M; Head; 6095; Yes; Yes; Al. 1356 An. 6069

Census of the __Pine Ridge__ reservation of the __Pine Ridge, South Dakota__ jurisdiction, as of __April 1__, 19**32**, taken by __James H. McGregor__, Superintendent.

Key: Number; Surname, Given; Sex; Date of Birth-Age at Last Birthday; Tribe (Oglala Sioux, unless stated otherwise); Degree of Blood; Marital Status; Relationship to Head of Family [Last Census Roll Number]; At Jurisdiction Where Enrolled (Yes/No); (If no – Where); Ward (Yes/No, if given); Allotment, Annuity and Identification Numbers (if given).

6160; Scott, Ashley Lee; M; 4/8/20-11; -1/4; S; Son; 6096; Yes; Yes; Id. U-10370 An. 6070

6161; Scott, Robert £D.; M; 3/13/23-9; -1/4; S; Son; 6097; Yes; Yes; Id. U-13026 An. 6071

6162; Scott, Lavon M.; F; 11/4/24-7; -1/4; S; Daughter; 6098; Yes; Yes; Id. U-11732 An. none

6163; Scott, Laverne L.; F; 4/12/27-4; -1/4; S; Daughter; 6099; Yes; Yes; Id. U-12393 An. none

6164; Scout, Jasper; M; 1871-61; F; M; Head; 6100; Yes; Yes; Al. 1122 & 6933 An. 6072

6165; Scout (Red Bear, Mary), Mary; F; 1872-60; plus 1/4; M; Wife; 6101; Yes; Yes; Al. 6759 An. 6073

6166; Crow, Catherine; F; 4/6/20-11; plus 1/4; S; Ward; 6102; Yes; Yes; Id. U-9409 An. 6075

6167; Sears, Jesse; M; 1901-31; plus 1/4; S; Head; 6104; Yes; Yes; Al. 381 An. 6077

6168; Sears, John; M; 1897-35; plus 1/4; S; Head; 6105; Yes; Yes; Al. 2178 An. 6078

6169; Sears, Clarence; M; 1878-54; plus 1/4; M; Head; 6106; No; Pawhuska, town Osage, Oklahoma; No; Al. 4755 An. 6079

6170; Sears (No data), Ida; F; 1883-49; plus 1/4; M; Wife; 6107; No; Ditto; No; Al. 4756 An. 6080

6171; Sears, Maxine; F; 7/15/12-19; plus 1/4; S; Daughter; 6108; No; Ditto; Yes; Al. 7911 An. 6083

6172; Sears, Christiana; F; 9/28/18-13; plus 1/4; S; Daughter; 6109; No; Ditto; Yes; Id. U-10376 An. 6084

6173; Sears, Ruth; F; 1907-25; plus 1/4; S; Head; 6110; No; Ditto; Yes; Al. 4759 An. 6081

6174; Sears, Agnes E.; F; 7/16/10-21; plus 1/4; S; Head; 6111; No; Ditto; Yes; Al. 7910 An. 6082

6175; Sears, Joseph; M; 1904-28; plus 1/4; S; Head; 6112; No; Arkansas City, city, Desha, Ark; Yes; Al. 4758 An. 6088

6176; Sears, Leander; M; 1890-32[sic]; plus 1/4; S; Head; 6113; No; Lincoln city, Lancaster, Nebr.; Yes; Al. 2176 An. 6086

Census of the __Pine Ridge__ reservation of the __Pine Ridge, South Dakota__ jurisdiction, as of __April 1__, 1932, taken by __James H. McGregor__, Superintendent.

Key: Number; Surname, Given; Sex; Date of Birth-Age at Last Birthday; Tribe (Oglala Sioux, unless stated otherwise); Degree of Blood; Marital Status; Relationship to Head of Family [Last Census Roll Number]; At Jurisdiction Where Enrolled (Yes/No); (If no – Where); Ward (Yes/No, if given); Allotment, Annuity and Identification Numbers (if given).

6177; Sears, Vincent; M; 1875-57; plus 1/4; M; Head; 6114; No; Arkansas City, city, Desha, Ark; Yes; Al. 376 An. 6087

6178; Sears (No data), Pacific; F; 1880-52; plus 1/4; M; Wife; 6115; No; Ditto; No; Al. 4950 An. 6088

6179; Sears, Glenn; M; 2/17/11-21; plus 1/4; S; Son; 6116; No; Ditto; Yes; Al. 7867 An. 6090

6180; Sears, Vesta L.; F; 3/28/18-14; plus 1/4; S; Daughter; 6117; No; Ditto; Yes; Id. U-10375 An. 6091

6181; Sears, William; M; 1892-40; plus 1/4; M; Head; 6118; Yes; No; Al. 2177 An. 6093

6182; Sears, Florence; F; 3/7/15-17; -1/4; S; Daughter; 6119; Yes; Yes; Al. 7909 An. 6094

6183; Sears, Elmer; M; 2/8/17-15; -1/4; S; Son; 6120; Yes; Yes; Id. U-10372 An. 6094

6184; Sears, Christina; F; 7/23/18-13; -1/4; S; Daughter; 6121; Yes; Yes; Id. U-10373 An. 6095

6185; Sears, William; M; 3/31/21-11; -1/4; S; Son; 6122; Yes; Yes; Id. U-10374 An. 6096

6186; Sears, Jesse R.; M; 11/5/23-9; -1/4; S; Son; 6123; Yes; Yes; Id. U-12264 An. none

6187; Sedacek, Mary J.; F; 1903-29; plus 1/4; M; Head; 6124; Yes; Yes; Al. 4496 An. 6097

6188; Sedacek, Harriet; F; 7/1/28-3; -1/4; S; Daughter; 6125; Yes; Yes; Id. U-13504 An. none

6189; Sedacek, Jerald Dean; M; 1/27/30-2; -1/4; S; Son; 6126; Yes; Yes; Id. U-13504 An. none

6190; Shald (Trueblood, Gladys), Gladys; F; 4/4/09-23; -1/4; M; Head; 6127; Yes; Yes; Al. 5327 An. 6075

6191; Shald, Margaret; F; 8/18/29-2; -1/4; S; Daughter; 6128; Yes; Yes; Id. U-13301 An. none

6192; Shangreau, Annie; F; 1907-25; plus 1/4; S; Head; 6130; Yes; Yes; Al. 3599 An. 6100

6193; Shangreau, Antoine; M; 1884-48; plus 1/4; M; Head; 6131; Yes; Yes; Al. 1206 An. 6101

6194; Shangreau (Fuller, Nora), Nora; F; 1886-46; plus 1/4; M; Wife; 6132; Yes; Yes; Al. 209 An. 6102

6195; Shangreau, Jessie; F; 3/28/17-15; plus 1/4; S; Daughter; 6133; Yes; Yes; Al. 6116 An. 6104

Census of the ___Pine Ridge___ reservation of the **Pine Ridge, South Dakota** jurisdiction, as of ___April 1___, 19**32**, taken by ___**James H. McGregor**___, Superintendent.

Key: Number; Surname, Given; Sex; Date of Birth-Age at Last Birthday; Tribe (Oglala Sioux, unless stated otherwise); Degree of Blood; Marital Status; Relationship to Head of Family [Last Census Roll Number]; At Jurisdiction Where Enrolled (Yes/No); (If no – Where); Ward (Yes/No, if given); Allotment, Annuity and Identification Numbers (if given).

6196; Shangreau, Frances; F; 9/9/19-12; plus 1/4; S; Daughter; 6134; Yes; Yes; Id. U-10383 An. 6105

6197; Shangreau, Isidora; F; 4/4/23-8; plus 1/4; S; Daughter; 6135; Yes; Yes; Id. U-13053 An. 6107

6198; Fuller, Margaret; F; 12/14/13-18; -1/4; S; Stepdaughter; 6136; Yes; Yes; Id. U-9023 An. 98

6199; Shangreau, Bat Richard; M; 1902-30; plus 1/4; M; Head; 6137; Yes; Yes; Al. 6117 An. 6108

6200; Shangreau (Richard, Jessie), Jessie; F; 1903-29; plus 1/4; M; Wife; 6138; Yes; Yes; Al. 1227 An. 6109

6201; Shangreau, Peter; M; 8/23/25-6; plus 1/4; S; Son; 6139; Yes; Yes; Id. U-11822 An. none

6202; Shangreau, Richard Wm.; M; 10/11/31-5/12; plus 1/4; S; Son; ---; Yes; Yes; Id. U-13947 An. none

6203; Shangreau, Claude; M; 10/17/12-19; plus 1/4; S; Alone; 6144; No; Cody, town, Cherry, Neb.; Yes; Al. 6971 An. 6116

6204; Shangreau, Darrell; M; 3/25/10-22; plus 1/4; M; Head; 6141; No; Cody, town, Cherry, Neb.; Yes; Al. 4784 An. 6114

6205; Shangreau, Delores; F; 12/27/30-1; -1/4; S; Daughter; 6142; No; Ditto; Yes; Id. U-13785 An. none

6206; Shangreau, Desmond; M; 3/25/10-22; plus 1/4; S; Head; 6143; No; Ditto; Yes; Al. 4785 An. 6115

6207; Shangreau, Florence; F; 1901-31; plus 1/4; S; Head; 6140; No; Ditto; Yes; Al. 2563 An. 6110

6208; Shangreau, Leon; M; 1887-45; plus 1/4; M; Head; 6145; Yes; Yes; Al. 2561 An. 6117

6209; Shangreau (Black Eyes, Anna), Anna; F; 1874-58; F; M; Wife; 6146; Yes; Yes; Al. 2105 An. 6118

6210; Shangreau, Lizzie; F; 1875-57; plus 1/4; Wd.; Head; 6147; Yes; Yes; Al. 3596 An. 6119

6211; Shangreau, Martin; M; 2/7/09-23; plus 1/4; S; Son; 6148; Yes; Yes; Al. 3601 An. 6120

6212; Shangreau, Philomena; F; 12/18/12-19; plus 1/4; S; Daughter; 6149; Yes; Yes; Al. 7229 An. 6121

6213; Shangreau, Margaret; F; 11/30/17-14; plus 1/4; S; Daughter; 6150; Yes; Yes; Id. U-10380 An. 6122

Census of the ___**Pine Ridge**___ reservation of the ___**Pine Ridge, South Dakota**___ jurisdiction, as of ___**April 1**___, 1932, taken by ___**James H. McGregor**___, Superintendent.

Key: Number; Surname, Given; Sex; Date of Birth-Age at Last Birthday; Tribe (Oglala Sioux, unless stated otherwise); Degree of Blood; Marital Status; Relationship to Head of Family [Last Census Roll Number]; At Jurisdiction Where Enrolled (Yes/No); (If no – Where); Ward (Yes/No, if given); Allotment, Annuity and Identification Numbers (if given).

6214; Shangreau, Louis; M; 1900-32; plus 1/4; Wd.; Head; 6151; Yes; Yes; Al. 1211 An. 6123

6215; Shangreau, Mary; F; 1887-45; plus 1/4; S; Head; 6152; Yes; Yes; Al. 2554 An. 6127

6216; Shangreau, Martin; M; 1887-45; plus 1/4; M; Head; 6153; Yes; Yes; Al. 3602 An. 6128

6217; Shangreau (Jones, Louisa), Louisa; F; 6/28/97-35; plus 1/4; M; Wife; 6154; Yes; Yes; Al. 2699 An. 6129

6218; Shangreau, Flora; F; 9/27/14-17; plus 1/4; S; Daughter; 6155; Yes; Yes; Al. 8067 An. 6130

6219; Shangreau, Mildred; F; 9/5/19-12; plus 1/4; S; Daughter; 6156; Yes; Yes; Id. U-10377 An. 6131

6220; Shangreau, Bernice; F; 1/10/21-11; plus 1/4; S; Daughter; 6157; Yes; Yes; Id. U-10378 An. 6132

6221; Shangreau, Charles; M; 5/21/23-9; plus 1/4; S; Son; 6158; Yes; Yes; Id. U-13099 An. 6133

6222; Shangreau, Wesley; M; 10/30/26-5; plus 1/4; S; Son; 6159; Yes; Yes; Id. U-12266 An. none

6223; Shangreau, Calvin; M; 3/10/25-6; plus 1/4; S; Son; 6160; Yes; Yes; Id. U-11492 An. 4832

6224; Shangreau, Peter; M; 1860-72; plus 1/4; M; Head; 6161; Yes; Yes; Al. 1205 An. 6134

6225; Shangreau (Janis, Lucy), Lucy; F; 1863-69; plus 1/4; M; Wife; 6162; Yes; Yes; Al. 6094 An. 6135

6226; Shangreau, William; M; 7/1/08-23; plus 1/4; M; Head; 6163; No; Pawhuska, town, Osage, Okla.; Yes; Al. 6096 An. 6136

N.E.: Shangreau, (Big Heart, Dorothy) Dorothy; F; ------; Osage; M; Wife;

6227; Shangreau, Willie Ann; F; 2/18/30-2; Sioux & Osage; plus 1/4; S; Daughter; 6164; No; Ditto; Yes; Id. U-13613 An. none

6228; Shangreau, William; M; 1861-71; plus 1/4; M; Head; 6165; Yes; Yes; Al. 2552 An. 6139

6229; Shangreau (Lee, Erma), Erma; F; 1866-66; plus 1/4; M; Wife; 6166; Yes; Yes; Al. 2553 An. 6140

6230; Shangreau, William; M; 1907-25; plus 1/4; S; Head; 6167; Yes; Yes; Al. 2558 An. 6141

Census of the **Pine Ridge** reservation of the **Pine Ridge, South Dakota** jurisdiction, as of **April 1**, 19**3**2, taken by **James H. McGregor**, Superintendent.

Key: Number; Surname, Given; Sex; Date of Birth-Age at Last Birthday; Tribe (Oglala Sioux, unless stated otherwise); Degree of Blood; Marital Status; Relationship to Head of Family [Last Census Roll Number]; At Jurisdiction Where Enrolled (Yes/No); (If no – Where); Ward (Yes/No, if given); Allotment, Annuity and Identification Numbers (if given).

6231; Sharp, Frances E.; F; 1898-34; -1/4; Wd.; Head; 6168; No; San Jose, city, Santa Clara, Cal.; Yes; Id. U-10387 An. 6142
6232; Sharp, Frances Edna; F; 5/30/18-13; -1/4; S; Daughter; 6169; No; Ditto; Yes; Id. U-10388 An. 6143
6233; Sharp, Louis Roy; M; 12/6/19-12; -1/4; S; Son; 6170; No; Ditto; Yes; Id. U-10389 An. 6144

6234; Sharp (Jacobs, Wilma), Wilma; F; 1899-33; plus 1/4; M; Head; 6171; Yes; Yes; Al. 3618 An. 6145
6235; Sharp, Julia; F; 6/5/14-17; -1/4; S; Daughter; 6172; Yes; Yes; Al. 7880 An. 6146
6236; Sharp, Clyde V.; M; 5/20/15-16; -1/4; S; Son; 6173; Yes; Yes; Id. U-10384 An. 6147
6237; Sharp, Wilson; M; 11/7/18-13; -1/4; S; Son; 6174; Yes; Yes; Id. U-10385 An. 6148
6238; Sharp, Goldie; F; 7/17/20-11; -1/4; S; Daughter; 6175; Yes; Yes; Id. U-10386 An. 6149
6239; Sharp, William; M; 1/26/22-10; -1/4; S; Son; 6176; Yes; Yes; Id. U-11500 An. 6150
6240; Sharp, Celesta; F; 7/22/23-8; -1/4; S; Daughter; 6177; Yes; Yes; Id. U-11547 An. 6151
6241; Sharp, Albert L.; M; 2/13/25-7; -1/4; S; Son; 6178; Yes; Yes; Id. U-11546 An. 6152
6242; Sharp, Wallard; M; 6/10/26-5; -1/4; S; Son; 6179; Yes; Yes; Id. U-11977 An. none
6243; Sharp, Bud Russell; M; 11/12/27-4; -1/4; S; Son; 6180; Yes; Yes; Id. U-13393 An. none
6244; Sharp, Calvin; M; 5/31/29-2; -1/4; S; Son; 6181; Yes; Yes; Id. U-13392 An. none
6245; Sharp, Ben Franklyn; M; 7/16/31-9/12; -1/4; S; Son; ---; Yes; Yes; Id. U-13904 An. none

6246; Sharp Pointed, Mary; F; 1853-79; F; Wd.; Head; 6182; Yes; Yes; Al. 6311 An. 6164

6247; Shell Woman, #2; F; 1842-90; F; Wd.; Head; 6183; Yes; Yes; Al. 7395 An. 6164

6248; Shell Woman, Leo; M; 1889-43; F; M; Head; 6184; Yes; Yes; Al. 6679 An. 6165
6249; Shell Woman (Iron Heart, Julia), Julia; F; 1906-26; plus 1/4; M; Wife; 6185; Yes; Yes; Al. 4105 An. 3196

Census of the **Pine Ridge** reservation of the **Pine Ridge, South Dakota** jurisdiction, as of **April 1**, 19**32,** taken by **James H. McGregor**, Superintendent.

Key: Number; Surname, Given; Sex; Date of Birth-Age at Last Birthday; Tribe (Oglala Sioux, unless stated otherwise); Degree of Blood; Marital Status; Relationship to Head of Family [Last Census Roll Number]; At Jurisdiction Where Enrolled (Yes/No); (If no – Where); Ward (Yes/No, if given); Allotment, Annuity and Identification Numbers (if given).

6250; Shell Woman, Charles; M; 4/7/13-18; F; S; Son; 6186; Yes; Yes; Al. 7365 An. 6167
6251; Shell Woman, Sadie; F; 5/14/16-15; F; S; Daughter; 6187; Yes; Yes; Id. U-10390 An. 6168
6252; Iron Heart, Clara; F; 4/2/25-6; plus 1/4; S; Stepdaughter; 6188; Yes; Yes; Id. U-11515 An. none
6253; Shell Woman, Vivian; F; 10/21/29-2; plus 1/4; S; Daughter; 6189; Yes; Yes; Id. U-13302 An. none
6254; Shell Woman, Lydia; F; 2/4/32-2/12; plus 1/4; S; Daughter; ---; Yes; Yes; Id. U-14108 An. none

6255; Shelton, Emma; F; 3/14/11-21; -1/4; M; Head; 6190; Yes; Yes; Al. 7494 An. 221
6256; Shelton, Fredell J.; F; 10/21/27-4; -1/4; S; Daughter; 6191; Yes; Yes; Id. U-12820 An. none
6257; Shelton, James V.; M; 10/22/31-5/12; -1/4; S; Son; ---; Yes; Yes; Id. U-12975 An. none

6258; Sherman, George; M; 1894-38; plus 1/4; M; Head; 6192; Yes; Yes; Al. 3664 An. 6171
6259; Sherman (Montileaux, Louisa), Louisa; F; 1900-32; plus 1/4; M; Wife; 6193; Yes; Yes; Al. 3572 An. 6172
6260; Sherman, Verine J.; F; 6/24/18-13; plus 1/4; S; Daughter; 6194; Yes; Yes; Id. U-10394 An. 6173
6261; Sherman, Elvira K.; F; 1/10/21-11; plus 1/4; S; Daughter; 6195; Yes; Yes; Id. U-10395 An. 6174
6262; Sherman, Adeline F.; F; 8/20/22-9; plus 1/4; S; Daughter; 6196; Yes; Yes; Id. U-11077 An. 6175
6263; Sherman, Rosalie E.; F; 9/22/25-6; plus 1/4; S; Daughter; 6197; Yes; Yes; Id. U-11784 An. none

6264; Sherman, Lizzie; F; 1864-68; plus 1/4; Wd.; Head; 6198; Yes; Yes; Al. 3661 An. 6176

N.E.: ~~Sherman, William; M; Ponca Indian; -1/4; M; Head;~~
6265; Sherman (Hunter, Victoria), Victoria; F; 1894-38; plus 1/4; M; Wife; 6199; Yes; Yes; Al. 3656 An. 6179
6266; Sherman, Angeline; F; 4/15/14-17; Sioux & Ponca; plus 1/4; S; Daughter; 6200; Yes; Yes; Al. 7872 An. 6180
6267; Sherman, Emma E.; F; 5/13/16-15; Sioux & Ponca; plus 1/4; S; Daughter; 6201; Yes; Yes; Id. U-10392 An. 6181
6268; Sherman, Mark R.; M; 11/1/17-14; plus 1/4; S; Son; 6202; Yes; Yes; Id. U-10393 An. 6182

Census of the **Pine Ridge** reservation of the **Pine Ridge, South Dakota** jurisdiction, as of **April 1**, 1932, taken by **James H. McGregor**, Superintendent.

Key: Number; Surname, Given; Sex; Date of Birth-Age at Last Birthday; Tribe (Oglala Sioux, unless stated otherwise); Degree of Blood; Marital Status; Relationship to Head of Family [Last Census Roll Number]; At Jurisdiction Where Enrolled (Yes/No); (If no – Where); Ward (Yes/No, if given); Allotment, Annuity and Identification Numbers (if given).

6269; Sherman, Geraldine; F; 9/8/22-9; plus 1/4; S; Daughter; 6203; Yes; Yes; Id. U-12067 An. 6183

6270; Sherman, Cornelia; F; 6/5/28-3; plus 1/4; S; Daughter; 6204; Yes; Yes; Id. U-12641 An. none

6271; Sherman, Bertha Mae; F; 12/25/31-3/12; plus 1/4; S; Daughter; ---; Yes; Yes; Id. U-14069 An. none

6272; Shield, Henry; M; 12/28/08-24; F; S; Head; 6205; Yes; Yes; Al. 3979 An. 6186

6273; Shield, Louis; M; 1868-64; F; M; Head; 6209; Yes; Yes; Al. 957 An. 6184

6274; Shield (Horse Woman, Lizzie), Lizzie; F; 1874-58; F; M; Wife; 6210; Yes; Yes; Al. 3976 An. 6185

6275; Shields, Edward J.; M; 1906-26; -1/4; S; Head; 6211; Yes; Yes; Al. 5546 An. 6199

6276; Shields, Lottie; F; 1887-45; plus 1/4; Wd.; Head; 6212; Yes; Yes; Al. 86 An. 6200

6277; Shields, Raymond L.; M; 3/4/16-16; -1/4; S; Son; 6213; Yes; Yes; Id. U-10400 An. 6201

6278; Shiver (Stahl, Esther), Esther; F; 7/23/11-20; -1/4; M; Head; 6214; Yes; Yes; Al. 6992 An. 6524

~~N.E.: Shoots Off, Douglas; Chey. River Sioux; F; M; Head;~~

6279; Shoots Off, Lucy; F; 1879-53; F; M; Wife; 6215; No; Chey. River, S.D.;Yes; Al. 3461 An. 6203

6280; Short Bear, Jennie; F; 1906-26; plus 1/4; S; Head; 6216; Yes; Yes; Al. 5849 An. 6207

6281; White Whirl Wind, Jennie V.; F; 5/25/31-10/12; plus 1/4; S; Daughter; ---; Yes; Yes; Id. U-13847 An. none

6282; Short Bear, Joseph; M; 1901-31; plus 1/4; M; Head; 6217; Yes; Yes; Al. 5604 An. 6208

6283; Short Bear (Swallow, Helen), Helen; F; 1908-24; F; M; Wife; 6218; Yes; Yes; Id. U-10519 An. 6736

6284; Short Bear, Floyd; M; 7/22/28-3; plus 1/4; S; Son; 6219; Yes; Yes; Id. U-12784 An. none

6285; Short Bear, Moses; M; 4/24/31-11/12; plus 1/4; S; Son; ---; Yes; Yes; Id. U-13815 An. none

Census of the __Pine Ridge__ reservation of the __Pine Ridge, South Dakota__ jurisdiction, as of __April 1__, 19**32**, taken by __James H. McGregor__, Superintendent.

Key: Number; Surname, Given; Sex; Date of Birth-Age at Last Birthday; Tribe (Oglala Sioux, unless stated otherwise); Degree of Blood; Marital Status; Relationship to Head of Family [Last Census Roll Number]; At Jurisdiction Where Enrolled (Yes/No); (If no – Where); Ward (Yes/No, if given); Allotment, Annuity and Identification Numbers (if given).

6286; Short Bear, Silas; M; 1880-52; F; M; Head; 6220; Yes; Yes; Al. 5363 An. 6210

6287; Short Bear (No data), Millie; F; 1886-46; plus 1/4; M; Wife; 6221; Yes; Yes; Al. 5370 An. 6211

6288; Short Bear, William; M; 2/10/15-17; plus 1/4; S; Son; 6222; Yes; Yes; Id. U-10403 An. 6213

6289; Short Bear, Peter A.; M; 5/28/20-11; plus 1/4; S; Son; 6223; Yes; Yes; Id. U-10404 An. 6214

6290; Short Bear, Mildred A.; F; 10/1/23-8; plus 1/4; S; Daughter; 6224; Yes; Yes; Id. U-11118 An. 6215

6291; Short Bear, Sylvia; F; 4/15/27-4; plus 1/4; S; Daughter; 6225; Yes; Yes; Id. U-12330 An. none

6292; Short Bull, Abraham; M; 6/3/16-15; plus 1/4; S; Alone; 6228; Yes; Yes; Al. 8146 An. 6224

6293; Short Bull, Norman E.; M; 3/11/18-14; plus 1/4; S; Brother; 6227; Yes; Id. U-10406 An. 6225

6294; Short Bull, Charles; M; 1886-46; F; M; Head; 6229; Yes; Yes; Al. 3172 An. 6219

6295; Short Bull (White Horse, Susie), Susie; F; 1889-43; F; M; Wife; 6232; Yes; Yes; Al. 6224 An. 7589

6296; Short Bull, Eugene; M; 1/24/15-17; F; S; Son; 6230; Yes; Yes; Id. U-10408 An. 6220

6297; Short Bull, Kerman; M; 5/21/26-5; F; S; Son; 6231; Yes; Yes; Id. U-11972 An. none

6298; Short Bull, Eastman; M; 4/20/30-1; F; S; Son; 6233; Yes; Yes; Id. U-13495 An. none

6299; White Horse, Nellie; F; 1/22/26-6; F; S; Stepdaughter; 6234; Yes; Yes; Id. U-11833 An. none

6300; Short Bull, Grant; M; 1872-80; F; Wd.; Head; 6235; Yes; Yes; Al. 3130 An. 6221

6301; Short Bull, Chauncey; M; 6/3/15-16; F; S; Alone; 6236; Yes; Yes; Al. 8110 An. 6218

6302; Short Bull, Thomas; M; 1874-58; F; Wd.; Head; 6237; Yes; Yes; Al. 5580 An. 6227

6303; Short Horn, Frank; M; 1897-35; F; M; Head; 6238; Yes; Yes; Al. 579 An. 6228

Census of the __Pine Ridge__ reservation of the __Pine Ridge, South Dakota__ jurisdiction, as of __April 1__, 19**32**, taken by __James H. McGregor__, Superintendent.

Key: Number; Surname, Given; Sex; Date of Birth-Age at Last Birthday; Tribe (Oglala Sioux, unless stated otherwise); Degree of Blood; Marital Status; Relationship to Head of Family [Last Census Roll Number]; At Jurisdiction Where Enrolled (Yes/No); (If no – Where); Ward (Yes/No, if given); Allotment, Annuity and Identification Numbers (if given).

6304; Short Horn (Janis, Sadie), Sadie; F; 1901-31; plus 1/4; M; Wife; 6239; Yes; Yes; Al. 3863 An. 3337
6305; Short Horn, Gladys May; F; 2/10/27-5; plus 1/4; S; Daughter; 6240; Yes; Yes; Id. U-12267 An. none
6306; Short Horn, Frances A.; F; 12/9/28-3; plus 1/4; S; Daughter; 6241; Yes; Yes; Id. U-12117 An. none
6307; Short Horn, Edna Lucille; F; 6/5/30-1; plus 1/4; S; Daughter; 6242; Yes; Yes; Id. U-13532 An. none

6308; Short Man, Josephine; F; 1848-84; F; Wd.; Head; 6243; Yes; Yes; Al. 6013 An. 6230

6309; Short Step, Charles; M; 1881-51; F; M; Head; 6244; Yes; Yes; Al. 4275 An. 6231
6310; Short Step (Red Feather, Eva), Eva; F; 1879-53; F; M; Wife; 5490; Yes; Yes; Al. 2288 An. 5471
6311; Short Step, Oscar; M; 8/10/18-13; F; S; Son; 6246; Yes; Yes; Id. U-9484 An. 2095
6312; Short Step, Isaac; M; 7/19/24-7; F; S; Son; 6247; Yes; Yes; Id. U-11310 An. 6234
6313; Short Step, Alma; F; 12/25/27-4; F; S; Daughter; 6248; Yes; Yes; Id. U-12465 An. none
6314; Red Feather, Flent; M; 5/18/12-19; F; S; Stepson; 5491; Yes; Yes; Id. U-10238 An. 5473
6315; Red Feather, Winnie; F; 2/19/17-15; F; S; Stepdaughter; 5492; Yes; Yes; Id. U-10240 An. 5475
6316; Red Feather, Joseph; M; 9/22/19-12; F; S; Stepson; 5493; Yes; Yes; Id. U-10241 An. 5476

6317; Shot, Charles; M; 1891-41; F; M; Head; 6249; Yes; Yes; Al. 196 An. 6236
6318; Shot (Medicine Boy, Susie), Susie; F; 1895-37; F; M; Wife; 6250; Yes; Yes; Al. 1894 An. 6237
6319; Shot, Gilbert; M; 2/18/17-15; F; S; Son; 6251; Yes; Yes; Id. U-10413 An. 6238
6320; Shot, Winona; F; 1/3/20-12; F; S; Daughter; 6252; Yes; Yes; Id. U-10414 An. 6239
6321; Shot, Clement; M; 4/6/26-5; F; S; Son; 6253; Yes; Yes; Id. U-11886 An. none
6322; Shot, Leo C.; M; 9/28/28-3; F; S; Son; 6254; Yes; Yes; Id. U-12929 An. none
6323; Shot, Rose; F; 2/16/30-2; F; S; Daughter; 6255; Yes; Yes; Id. U-13425 An. none
6324; Shot, Anna Theresa; F; 3/21/32-1/12; F; S; Daughter; 6256[sic]; Yes; Yes; Id. U-14135 An. none

Census of the **Pine Ridge** reservation of the **Pine Ridge, South Dakota** jurisdiction, as of **April 1**, 19**32**, taken by **James H. McGregor**, Superintendent.

Key: Number; Surname, Given; Sex; Date of Birth-Age at Last Birthday; Tribe (Oglala Sioux, unless stated otherwise); Degree of Blood; Marital Status; Relationship to Head of Family [Last Census Roll Number]; At Jurisdiction Where Enrolled (Yes/No); (If no – Where); Ward (Yes/No, if given); Allotment, Annuity and Identification Numbers (if given).

6325; Shot, David; M; 1863-69; F; M; Head; 6256; Yes; Yes; Al. 168 An. 6242
6326; Shot (Pretty Eagle, Mary), Mary; F; 1871-61; F; M; Wife; 6257; Yes; Yes; Al. 5037 An. 6243

6327; Shot To Pieces, Charles; M; 1876-56; F; M; Head; 6258; Yes; Yes; Al. 16 An. 6248
6328; Shot To Pieces, (Stabber, Julia), Julia; F; 1871-61; F; M; Wife; 6257; Yes; Yes; Al. 5037 An. 6243
6329; Shot To Pieces, Ross; M; 9/19/14-17; F; S; Son; 6261; Yes; Yes; Id. U-10415 An. 6250
6330; Shot To Pieces, Hobert; M; 5/20/16-15; F; S; Son; 6260; Yes; Yes; Id. U-10416 An. 6251

6331; Shot To Pieces, Helen; F; 12/23/10-21; F; S; Head; 6262; Yes; Yes; Al. 5587 An. 6250

6332; Shot With Arrows, Reuben; M; 1902-30; F; M; Head; 6263; Yes; Yes; Id. U-10417 An. 6257
N.E.: Shot With Arrows, (Knuth, Geneva) Geneva; F; ------; Omaha Indian; M; Wife;
6333; Shot With Arrows, Catalina; F; 9/24/22-9; F; S; Daughter; 6264; Yes; Yes; Id. U-12003 An. 6259
6334; Shot With Arrows, Louisa; F; 4/16/26-5; F; S; Daughter; 6265; Yes; Yes; Id. U-11887 An. none
6335; Shot With Arrows, Delila; F; 7/10/29-2; Omaha & Sioux; F; S; Daughter; 6266; Yes; Yes; Id. U-13233 An. none
6336; Shot With Arrows, Cleveland B.; M; 11/13/31-4/12; Omaha & Sioux; F; S; Son; ---; Yes; Yes; Id. U-13976 An. none

6337; Shot In, Silas; M; 1869-63; F; M; Head; 6267; Yes; Yes; Al. 1789 An. 6261
6338; Shot In, (No data), Carrie; F; 1870-62; F; M; Wife; 6268; Yes; Yes; Al. 1790 An. 6262
6339; Star, Kermit; M; 8/29/20-11; F; S; Ward; 6269; Yes; Yes; Id. U-10492 An. 6615

6340; Shoulder, Andrew; M; 1900-32; F; M; Head; 6270; Yes; Yes; Al. 5657 An. 6263
6341; Shoulder, (Kills Red, Julia), Julia; F; 12/31/09-23; F; M; Wife; 6271; Yes; Yes; Al. 6642 An. 3529

6342; Shoulder, James; M; 1874-58; F; M; Head; 6272; Yes; Yes; Al. 3898 An. 6264
6343; Shoulder, (No data), Mary; F; 1877-55; F; M; Wife; 6273; Yes; Yes; Al. 5623 An. 6265

Census of the __Pine Ridge__ reservation of the __Pine Ridge, South Dakota__ jurisdiction, as of __April 1__, 19**32**, taken by __James H. McGregor__, Superintendent.

Key: Number; Surname, Given; Sex; Date of Birth-Age at Last Birthday; Tribe (Oglala Sioux, unless stated otherwise); Degree of Blood; Marital Status; Relationship to Head of Family [Last Census Roll Number]; At Jurisdiction Where Enrolled (Yes/No); (If no – Where); Ward (Yes/No, if given); Allotment, Annuity and Identification Numbers (if given).

6344; Shoulder, Napoleon; M; 8/15/19-12; F; S; Son; 6274; Yes; Yes; Id. U-10419 An. 6267

6345; Shoulder, Reuben; M; 1877-55; F; M; Head; 6275; Yes; Yes; Al. 4812 An. 6268

6346; Shoulder, (Kills Enemy In Morning, Etta), Etta; F; 1877-55; F; M; Wife; 6276; Yes; Yes; Al. 1293 An. 6269

6347; Shoulder, Johnson; M; 8/5/09-23; F; S; Son; 6277; Yes; Yes; Al. 4813 An. 6270

6348; Shout At, Reuben; M; 1871-61; F; M; Head; 6278; Yes; Yes; Al. 4815 An. 6272

6349; Shout At, (Living Bear, Annie), Annie; F; 1874-58; F; M; Wife; 6279; Yes; Yes; Al. 4853 An. 6273

6350; Sickler, Earl; M; 1898-34; plus 1/4; S; Head; 6281; Yes; Yes; Al. 3842 An. 6280

6351; Sickler, John; M; 1868-64; plus 1/4; S; Head; 6282; Yes; Yes; Al. 7745 An. 6281

6352; Sierro, Bennett; M; 1889-43; plus 1/4; M; Head; 6283; Yes; Yes; Al. 1194 An. 6282

6353; Sierro, (Yellow Boy, Mary), Mary; F; 1896-36; F; M; Wife; 6284; Yes; Yes; Al. 228 An. 6283

6354; Sierro, Christopher; M; 6/12/24-7; plus 1/4; S; Son; 6286; Yes; Yes; Id. U-11297 An. 6287

6355; Sierro, Virginia May; F; 5/10/28-3; plus 1/4; S; Daughter; 6287; Yes; Yes; Id. U-12596 An. none

6356; Yellow Boy, Harold; M; 6/18/16-15; F; S; Stepson; 6285; Yes; Yes; Id. U-10422 An. 6284

6357; Sierro, Joseph; M; 1896-36; plus 1/4; M; Head; 6288; Yes; Yes; Al. 1196 An. 6288

6358; Sierro, (Red Hawk, Susie), Susie; F; 1899-33; F; M; Wife; 6289; Yes; Yes; Id. U-10248 An. 6289

6359; Sierro, Joseph Ben; M; 4/6/24-7; plus 1/4; S; Son; 6290; Yes; Yes; Id. U-11462 An. 6291

6360; Sierro, Howard E.; M; 1/24/27-5; plus 1/4; S; Son; 6291; Yes; Yes; Id. U-12211 An. none

6361; Sierro, Phylliseta; F; 3/26/30-2; plus 1/4; S; Daughter; 6292; Yes; Yes; Id. U-13462 An. none

Census of the __Pine Ridge__ reservation of the __Pine Ridge, South Dakota__ jurisdiction, as of __April 1__, 19**32**, taken by __James H. McGregor__, Superintendent.

Key: Number; Surname, Given; Sex; Date of Birth-Age at Last Birthday; Tribe (Oglala Sioux, unless stated otherwise); Degree of Blood; Marital Status; Relationship to Head of Family [Last Census Roll Number]; At Jurisdiction Where Enrolled (Yes/No); (If no – Where); Ward (Yes/No, if given); Allotment, Annuity and Identification Numbers (if given).

6362; Siers, James; M; 1894-38; plus 1/4; M; Head; 6293; Yes; Yes; Al. 4844 An. 6292

6363; Siers, (Bettelyoun, Lucinda), Lucinda; F; 1897-35; F; M; Wife; 6294; Yes; Yes; Al. 2184 An. 6293

6364; Siers, Zenola; F; 8/25/20-11; plus 1/4; S; Daughter; 6295; Yes; Yes; Id. U-10426 An. 6294

6365; Siers, Irene; F; 3/31/23-8; plus 1/4; S; Daughter; 6296; Yes; Yes; Id. U-11591 An. 6295

6366; Siers, Emily; F; 12/3/24-7; plus 1/4; S; Daughter; 6297; Yes; Yes; Id. U-11592 An. 6296

6367; Siers, Iola May; F; 7/27/26-5; plus 1/4; S; Daughter; 6298; Yes; Yes; Id. U-12120 An. none

6368; Siers, Robert C.; M; 9/17/28-3; plus 1/4; S; Son; 6299; Yes; Yes; Id. U-12813 An. none

6369; Siers, Albert Henry; M; 4/4/30-1; plus 1/4; S; Son; 6300; Yes; Yes; Id. U-13506 An. none

6370; Siers, Jennie; F; 1964[sic]-68; F; Wd.; Head; 6301; Yes; Yes; Al. 4842 An. 6297

6371; Siers, Frank; M; 9/8/09-23; plus 1/4; M; Head; 6302; Yes; Yes; Al. 4852 An. 6298

6372; Siers, (Allman, Lillie), Lillie; F; 2/25/12-20; plus 1/4; M; Wife; 6303; Yes; Yes; Al. 6895 An. 93

6373; Siers, Victoria Mae; F; 12/22/31-3/12; plus 1/4; S; Daughter; ---; Yes; Yes; Id. U-14050 An. none

6374; Siers, John; M; 6/16/92-40; plus 1/4; M; Head; 6304; Yes; Yes; Al. 4843 An. 6300

6375; Siers, (Fast Horse, Rosa), Rosa; F; 1907-25; plus 1/4; M; Wife; 6305; Yes; Yes; Al. 6738 An. 2133

6376; Siers, John Jr.; M; 6/6/28-3; plus 1/4; S; Son; 6306; Yes; Yes; Id. U-12964 An. none

6377; Siers, Fannie; F; 5/31/30-1; plus 1/4; S; Daughter; 6307; Yes; Yes; Id. U-13747 An. none

6378; Siers, Louis; M; 1898-34; plus 1/4; S; Head; 6308; Yes; Yes; Al. 4846 An. 6298

6379; Siers, Treffle; M; 9/10/03-29; plus 1/4; S; Head; 6309; Yes; Yes; Al. 4849 An. 6303

Census of the **Pine Ridge** reservation of the **Pine Ridge, South Dakota** jurisdiction, as of **April 1**, 19**32**, taken by **James H. McGregor**, Superintendent.

Key: Number; Surname, Given; Sex; Date of Birth-Age at Last Birthday; Tribe (Oglala Sioux, unless stated otherwise); Degree of Blood; Marital Status; Relationship to Head of Family [Last Census Roll Number]; At Jurisdiction Where Enrolled (Yes/No); (If no – Where); Ward (Yes/No, if given); Allotment, Annuity and Identification Numbers (if given).

6380; Siers, Victoria; F; 5/10/12-19; plus 1/4; S; Head; 6310; Yes; Yes; Al. 6666 An. 6299

6381; Sioux Bob, Henry; M; 1877-55; F; M; Head; 6311; Yes; Yes; Al. 1891 An. 6304

6382; Sioux Bob, (High Bull, Victoria), Victoria; F; 1883-49; F; M; Wife; 6312; Yes; Yes; Al. 4988 An. 6305

6383; Sioux Bob, Frank; M; 4/4/14-17; F; S; Son; 6313; Yes; Yes; Al. 7892 An. 6306

6384; Sioux Bob, Christin; M; 9/27/20-11; F; S; Son; 6314; Yes; Yes; Id. U-10428 An. 6307

6385; Sioux Bob, Mabel; F; 9/24/26-5; F; S; Daughter; 6315; Yes; Yes; Id. U-12121 An. none

6386; Sitting Bear, Thomas; M; 1887-45; F; M; Head; 6322; Yes; Yes; Al. 630 An. 6317

6387; Sitting Bear, (Bear Robe, Alice), Alice; F; 1904-28; F; M; Wife; 6323; Yes; Yes; Al. 2437 An. 6318

6388; Sitting Bear, Eugene; M; 6/18/25-6; F; S; Son; 6324; Yes; Yes; Id. U-11647 An. none

6389; Sitting Bear, Mary; F; 5/6/26-5; F; S; Daughter; 6325; Yes; Yes; Id. U-12331 An. none

6390; Sitting Bear, Aloysius; M; 6/21/29-2; F; S; Son; 6326; Yes; Yes; Id. U-13215 An. none

6391; Sitting Bear, Cecelia; F; 9/15/31-6/12; F; S; Daughter; ---; Yes; Yes; Id. U-13925 An. none

6392; Bear Robe, Lena; F; 6/9/19-12; F; S; Stepdaughter; 6327; Yes; Yes; Id. U-11140 An. 6319

6393; Sitting Eagle, ---; M; 1849-83; F; M; Head; 6328; Yes; Yes; Al. 1730 An. 6321

6394; Sitting Eagle, (No data), Mary; F; 1863-69; F; M; Wife; 6329; Yes; Yes; Al. 3676 An. 6322

6395; Sitting Eagle, Albert; M; 1873-59; F; M; Head; 6330; Yes; Yes; Al. 1425 An. 6323

6396; Sitting Eagle, (No data), Lizzie; F; 1883-49; F; M; Wife; 6331; Yes; Yes; Al. 7771 An. 6324

6397; Sitting Eagle, Ellis; M; 12/18/10-21; F; S; Son; 6332; Yes; Yes; Al. 7948 An. 6326

6398; Sitting Eagle, Grace; F; 1/16/20-12; F; S; Daughter; 6333; Yes; Yes; Id. U-10429 An. 6327

Census of the **Pine Ridge** reservation of the **Pine Ridge, South Dakota** jurisdiction, as of **April 1**, 19**32**, taken by **James H. McGregor**, Superintendent.

Key: Number; Surname, Given; Sex; Date of Birth-Age at Last Birthday; Tribe (Oglala Sioux, unless stated otherwise); Degree of Blood; Marital Status; Relationship to Head of Family [Last Census Roll Number]; At Jurisdiction Where Enrolled (Yes/No); (If no – Where); Ward (Yes/No, if given); Allotment, Annuity and Identification Numbers (if given).

6399; Sitting Eagle, Joseph; M; 1898-34; F; M; Head; 6334; Yes; Yes; Al. 1731 An. 6328

6400; Sitting Eagle, (Spotted Eagle, Jessie), Jessie; F; 1898-34; F; M; Wife; 6335; Yes; Yes; Al. 1681 An. 6329

6401; Sitting Hawk, Rosa; F; 1862-70; F; Wd.; Head; 6337; Yes; Yes; Al. 2490 An. 6333

6402; Sitting Hawk, Levi; M; 1886-46; F; Wd.; Head; 6338; Yes; Yes; Al. 82 An. 6334

6403; Sitting Hawk, Jessie; F; 10/27/16-15; F; S; Daughter; 6339; Yes; Yes; Id. U-10430 An. 6336

6404; Sitting Hawk, Albert; M; 8/10/18-13; F; S; Son; 6340; Yes; Yes; Id. U-10431 An. 6337

6405; Sitting Hawk, Thomas; M; 10/4/20-11; F; S; Son; 6341; Yes; Yes; Id. U-10432 An. 6338

6406; Sitting Hawk, Marie; F; 2/26/24-8; F; S; Daughter; 6342; Yes; Yes; Id. U-12251 An. 6339

6407; Sitting Up, Alex; M; 1901-31; F; M; Head; 6343; Yes; Yes; Al. 1912 An. 6344

6408; Sitting Up, (Richard, Leona), Leona; F; 1907-25; plus 1/4; M; Wife; 6344; Yes; Yes; Al. 5374 An. 5706

6409; Sitting Up, Herman J.; M; 4/14/27-4; plus 1/4; S; Son; 6345; Yes; Yes; Id. U-12724 An. none

6410; Sitting Up, Leo C.; M; 2/6/29-3; plus 1/4; S; Son; 6346; Yes; Yes; Id. U-13234 An. none

6411; Sitting Up, Ellen Louise; F; 9/25/30-1; plus 1/4; S; Daughter; 6347; Yes; Yes; Id. U-13673 An. none

6412; Sitting Up, Benjamin; M; 1904-28; F; M; Head; 6348; Yes; Yes; Al. 1913 An. 6345

6413; Sitting Up, (Breast, Gertie), Gertie; F; 1903-29; F; M; Wife; 6349; Yes; Yes; Al. 4249 An. 6345

6414; Sitting Up, Francis; M; 1/11/24-8; F; S; Son; 6350; Yes; Yes; Id. U-11192 An. 6347

6415; Sitting Up, Josephine; F; 4/26/28-3; F; S; Daughter; 6351; Yes; Yes; Id. U-12597 An. none

6416; Sitting Up, Benjamin Jr.; M; 1/15/30-2; F; S; Son; 6352; Yes; Yes; Id. U-13370 An. none

6417; Sits Poor, Frank; M; 1880-52; F; M; Head; 6318; Yes; Yes; Al. 2807 An. 6311

Census of the **Pine Ridge** reservation of the **Pine Ridge, South Dakota** jurisdiction, as of **April 1**, 19**32**, taken by **James H. McGregor**, Superintendent.

Key: Number; Surname, Given; Sex; Date of Birth-Age at Last Birthday; Tribe (Oglala Sioux, unless stated otherwise); Degree of Blood; Marital Status; Relationship to Head of Family [Last Census Roll Number]; At Jurisdiction Where Enrolled (Yes/No); (If no – Where); Ward (Yes/No, if given); Allotment, Annuity and Identification Numbers (if given).

N.E.: Sits Poor, (Drop Two, Sarah) Sarah; F; ----; Cheyenne River; F; M; Wife;
6418; Sits Poor, Jessie; F; 4/8/16-15; F; S; Daughter; 6319; Yes; Id. U-10435 An. 6314
6419; Sits Poor, Sophia; F; 1/9/21-11; F; S; Daughter; 6320; Yes; Yes; Id. U-10436 An. 6315
6420; Sits Poor, Henrietta; F; 9/24/27-4; F; S; Daughter; 6321; Yes; Yes; Yes; Id. U-12431 An. none

6421; Six Feathers, Albert; M; 1906-26; plus 1/4; M; Head; 6353; Yes; Yes; Al. 5177 An. 6343
6422; Six Feathers, (Young, Nora), Nora; F; 1906-26; plus 1/4; M; Wife; 6354; Yes; Yes; Al. 2525 An. 7989
6423; Young, Chery; M; 8/19/24-7; plus 1/4; S; Stepson; 6355; Yes; Yes; Id. U-11583 An. 7090

6424; Six Feathers, John; M; 1880-52; F; M; Head; 6356; Yes; Yes; Al. 4622 An. 6351
6425; Six Feathers, (No data), Josephine; F; 1880-52; plus 1/4; M; Wife; 6357; Yes; Yes; Al. 5174 An. 6352
6426; Six Feathers, Russell; M; 1/30/16-16; plus 1/4; S; Son; 6359; Yes; Yes; Id. U-10438 An. 6354
6427; Six Feathers, Lizzie; F; 8/15/11-20; plus 1/4; S; Head; 6358; Yes; Id. U-10437 An. 6353
6428; Six Feathers, Emma; F; 3/17/31-1; plus 1/4; S; Daughter; ---; Yes; Id. U-13816 An. none

6429; Skalander, Arthur; M; 1888-44; -1/4; M; Head; 6361; Yes; Yes; Al. 4500 An. 6356
6430; Skalander, (Ruleau, Zouie), Zouie; F; 1899-33; plus 1/4; M; Wife; 6362; Yes; Yes; Al. 2147 An. 6357
6431; Skalander, Herbert; M; 12/1/21-10; F-1/4; S; Son; 6363; Yes; Yes; Id. U-10853 An. 6358
6432; Skalander, Essie A.; F; 12/19/25-6; -1/4; S; Daughter; 6364; Yes; Yes; Id. U-11956 An. none
6433; Skalander, Mary Ann; F; 5/4/28-3; -1/4; S; Daughter; 6365; Yes; Yes; Id. U-12699 An. none
6434; Skalander, Margaret C.; F; 8/1/30-1; -1/4; S; Daughter; 6366; Yes; Yes; Id. U-13631 An. none

6435; Skalander, Louis; M; 1903-29; -1/4; M; Head; 6367; Yes; Yes; Al. 4503 An. 6359

Census of the **Pine Ridge** reservation of the **Pine Ridge, South Dakota** jurisdiction, as of **April 1**, 19**32**, taken by **James H. McGregor**, Superintendent.

Key: Number; Surname, Given; Sex; Date of Birth-Age at Last Birthday; Tribe (Oglala Sioux, unless stated otherwise); Degree of Blood; Marital Status; Relationship to Head of Family [Last Census Roll Number]; At Jurisdiction Where Enrolled (Yes/No); (If no – Where); Ward (Yes/No, if given); Allotment, Annuity and Identification Numbers (if given).

6436; Skalander, (Brown, Pansy), J Pansy; F; 1900-32; -1/4; M; Wife; 6368; Yes; Yes; Al. 4453 An. 6360

6437; Skalander, Eldene M.; F; 7/31/24-7; -1/4; S; Daughter; 6369; Yes; Yes; Id. U-11369 An. 6361

6438; Skalander, Lois I.; F; 12/17/25-6; -1/4; S; Daughter; 6370; Yes; Yes; Id. U-11813 An. none

6439; Skalander, Lyle F.; M; 6/15/29-2; -1/4; S; Son; 6371; Yes; Yes; Id. U-13426 An. none

6440; Skalander, Velma June; F; 11/13/31-4/12; -1/4; S; Daughter; 6372; Yes; Yes; Id. U-14109 An. none

6441; Skalander, William; M; 4/21/12-19; -1/4; S; Alone; 6372; Yes; Yes; Al. 6928 An. 6363

N.E.: Skenandore, Eli; Oneida; 3/4; M; Head;

6442; Skenandore, (Williams, Anna), Anna; F; 1888-44; plus 1/4; M; Wife; 6373; Yes; Yes; Al. 4570 An. 6364

6443; Skenandore, Vivian; F; 7/16/16-15; Sioux & Oneida; plus1/4; S; Daughter; 6374; Yes; Yes; Al. 8125 An. 6365

6444; Skenandore, Marvin E.; M; 11/17/19-12; Sioux & Oneida; plus1/4; S; Son; 6375; Yes; Yes; Id. U-10442 An. 6366

6445; Skenandore, Albert E.; M; 6/25/21-10; plus1/4; S; Son; 6376; Yes; Yes; Id. U-10882 An. 6367

6446; Skenandore, Darold W.; M; 5/22/23-8; plus1/4; S; Son; 6377; Yes; Yes; Id. U-13090 An. 6368

6447; Skenandore, Pearl L.; F; 3/25/25-7; plus1/4; S; Daughter; 6378; Yes; Yes; Id. U-11529 An. 6269

6448; Sleeps, Asay; M; 8/10/08-24; F; M; Head; 6379; Yes; Yes; Id. U-10443 An. 6372

N.E.: Sleeps, (Sharp Fish, Ora) Ora; F; ------; Rosebud Sioux; F; M; Wife;

6449; Sleeps, Eli; M; 1862-70; F; M; Head; 6381; Yes; Yes; Al. 3074 An. 6370

6450; Sleeps, (No Data), Betsy; F; 1866-66; F; M; Wife; 6382; Yes; Yes; Al. 6085 An. 6371

6451; Sleeps, Hartley; M; 1889-43; F; S; Head; 6383; Yes; Yes; Al. 6086 An. 6373

6452; Sleeps, Joseph; M; 1906-26; F; S; Head; 6384; Yes; Yes; Id. U-9516 An. 6374

6453; Sleeps, Saul; M; 1898-34; F; M; Head; 6385; Yes; Yes; Al. 6088 An. 6375

Census of the **Pine Ridge** reservation of the **Pine Ridge, South Dakota** jurisdiction, as of **April 1**, 19**32**, taken by **James H. McGregor**, Superintendent.

Key: Number; Surname, Given; Sex; Date of Birth-Age at Last Birthday; Tribe (Oglala Sioux, unless stated otherwise); Degree of Blood; Marital Status; Relationship to Head of Family [Last Census Roll Number]; At Jurisdiction Where Enrolled (Yes/No); (If no – Where); Ward (Yes/No, if given); Allotment, Annuity and Identification Numbers (if given).

6454; Sleeps, (Runs Close To Lodge, Lillie), Lillie; F; 6/28/11-20; F; M; Wife; 6386; Yes; Yes; Al. 5824 An. 5971

6455; Sleeps, William; M; 5/1/27-4; F; S; Son; 6387; Yes; Yes; Id. U-12340 An. none

6456; Sleeps, Hobert; M; 2/5/31-1; F; S; Son; ---; Yes; Yes; Id. U-13817 An. none

6457; Slow, ---; F; 1850-82; F; Wd.; Head; 6388; Yes; Yes; Al. 7278 An. 6683

6458; Slow Bear, Baptiste; M; 7/6/11-20; plus 1/4; M; Head; 6394; Yes; Yes; Al. 6288 An. 6379

6459; Slow Bear, (Bear Robe, Rose), Rose; F; 1/3/09-23; F; M; Wife; 6395; Yes; Yes; Al. 6230 An. 390

6460; Slow Bear, Katherine; F; 10/17/29-2; plus 1/4; S; Daughter; 6396; Yes; Yes; Id. U-13303 An. none

6461; Slow Bear, Kate; F; 7/6/31-9/12; plus 1/4; S; Daughter; ---; Yes; Yes; Id. U-13905 An. none

6462; Slow Bear, Donald; M; 2/8/09-23; F; S; Head; 6397; Yes; Yes; Al. 7150 An. 6384

6463; Slow Bear, Martin; M; 2/24/18-14; F; S; Brother; 6398; Yes; Yes; Id. U-10445 An. 6385

6464; Slow Bear, Andrew; M; 1/21/21-11; F; S; Brother; 6399; Yes; Yes; Id. U-10446 An. 6386

6465; Slow Bear, Felix; M; 1879-53; F; M; Head; 6389; Yes; Yes; Al. 5158 An. 6377

6466; Slow Bear, (Door, Mary), Mary; F; 1891-41; F; M; Wife; 6390; Yes; Yes; Al. 7394 An. 6378

6467; Slow Bear, Angeline; F; 1/13/20-12; F; S; Daughter; 6391; Yes; Yes; Id. U-10444 An. 6380

6468; Slow Bear, Elfreda; F; 6/20/27-4; F; S; Daughter; 6392; Yes; Yes; Id. U-12394 An. none

6469; Slow Bear, Roland; M; 5/29/30-1; F; S; Son; 6393; Yes; Yes; Id. U-13520 An. none

6470; Slow Bear, Libbie; F; 1847-85; F; Wd.; Head; 6400; Yes; Yes; Al. 3125 An. 6387

6471; Slow Bear, McKinley; M; 1900-32; F; M; Head; 6401; Yes; Yes; Al. 3124 An. 6388

6472; Slow Bear, (Little Bald Eagle, Rosa), Rosa; F; 1907-25; F; M; Wife; 6402; Yes; Yes; Al. 7853 An. 3858

6473; Slow Bear, Irene; F; 9/12/27-4; F; S; Daughter; 6403; Yes; Yes; Id. U-12410 An. none

Census of the __Pine Ridge__ reservation of the __Pine Ridge, South Dakota__ jurisdiction, as of __April 1__, 19**32**, taken by __James H. McGregor__, Superintendent.

Key: Number; Surname, Given; Sex; Date of Birth-Age at Last Birthday; Tribe (Oglala Sioux, unless stated otherwise); Degree of Blood; Marital Status; Relationship to Head of Family [Last Census Roll Number]; At Jurisdiction Where Enrolled (Yes/No); (If no – Where); Ward (Yes/No, if given); Allotment, Annuity and Identification Numbers (if given).

6474; Slow Bear, Mary Rose; F; 1/6/29-3; F; S; Daughter; 6404; Yes; Yes; Id. U-13355 An. none

6475; Slow Dog, Philip; M; 1861-71; F; M; Head; 6405; Yes; Yes; Al. 5258 An. 6389

6476; Wears White, ---; F; 1864-68; F; M; Wife; 6406; Yes; Yes; Id. U-10447 An. 6390

6477; Slow Heart, Solomon; M; 5/26/09-23; F; S; Head; 6407; Yes; Yes; Al. 3934 An. 4313

6478; Smith, Clara; F; 4/15/06-36; plus 1/4; M; Head; 6408; Yes; Yes; Al. 4059 An. 6394

6479; Smith, Thelma R.; F; 1/23/17-15; -1/4; S; Daughter; 6409; Yes; Yes; Id. U-10448 An. 6395

6480; Smith, Lola May; F; 1/24/19-13; -1/4; S; Daughter; 6410; Yes; Yes; Id. U-10449 An. 6396

6481; Smith, Charles G.; M; 6/24/23-8; -1/4; S; Son; 6411; Yes; Yes; Id. U-14025 An. 6397

6482; Smith, (Gresh, Mary), Mary; F; 1864-68; plus 1/4; M; Head; 6412; Yes; Yes; Al. 4443 An. 6398

6483; Smith, (Monroe, Mary), Mary; F; 1896-36; plus 1/4; M; Head; 6413; Yes; Yes; Al. 2321 An. 6399

6484; Smith, Samuel; M; 1860-72; plus 1/4; M; Head; 6414; Yes; Yes; Al. 1873 An. 6400

6485; Smith, (No data), Julia; F; 1862-70; F; M; Wife; 6415; Yes; Yes; Al. 1874 An. 6401

6486; Smith (Youman, Susie M.), Susie Mildred; F; 11/26/11-20; -1/4; M; Head; 6416; Yes; Yes; Al. 7170 An. 7950

6487; Smith, Sophia; F; 1874-58; plus 1/4; Wd.; Head; 6417; Yes; No; Al. 2128 An. 6402

6488; Smith (Allen, Viola), Viola; F; 1907-25; -1/4; M; Head; 6418; Yes; Yes; Al. 4635 An. 63

6489; Smith, Joseph O.; M; 3/22/25-7; -1/4; S; Son; 6419; Yes; Yes; Id. U-11634 An. none

6490; Smith, Rose Marie; F; 7/10/26-5; -1/4; S; Daughter; 6420; Yes; Yes; Id. U-12294 An. none

Census of the **Pine Ridge** reservation of the **Pine Ridge, South Dakota** jurisdiction, as of **April 1**, 19**32**, taken by **James H. McGregor**, Superintendent.

Key: Number; Surname, Given; Sex; Date of Birth-Age at Last Birthday; Tribe (Oglala Sioux, unless stated otherwise); Degree of Blood; Marital Status; Relationship to Head of Family [Last Census Roll Number]; At Jurisdiction Where Enrolled (Yes/No); (If no – Where); Ward (Yes/No, if given); Allotment, Annuity and Identification Numbers (if given).

6491; Smith, Sylvia F; F; 12/7/27-4; -1/4; S; Daughter; 6421; Yes; Yes; Id. U-12643 An. none

6492; Smith, Dean DeCleo; M; 8/19/29-2; -1/4; S; Son; 6422; Yes; Yes; Id. U-13273 An. none

6493; Smith (Youmans, Mabel A.), Mabel A.; F; 2/18/13-19; -1/4; M; Head; 6423; Yes; Yes; Al. 7171 An. 7951

6494; Smith, Sidney D.; M; 8/22/29-2; -1/4; S; Son; 6424; Yes; Yes; Id. U-13394 An. none

6495; Smoke, Elizabeth; F; 2/5/09-23; F; S; Head; 6425; Yes; Yes; Al. 4096 An. 6404

6496; Smoke, Sophia; F; 1906-26; F; S; Head; 6426; Yes; Yes; Al. 4095 An. 6407

6497; Smoke Woman, ---; F; 1861-71; F; Wd.; Head; 6427; Yes; Yes; Al. 3337 An. 6408

6498; Snyder, Rachel; F; 1877-55; plus 1/4; Wd.; Head; 6428; Yes; Yes; Al. 3965 An. 6412

6499; Snyder, Francene M.; F; 4/10/18-13; -1/4; S; Daughter; 6429; Yes; Yes; Id. U-10917 An. 6415

6500; Snyder, Iola; F; 6/24/13-18; -1/4; S; Head; 6430; No; Milwaukee, city, Wis.; Yes; Al. 7721 An. 6414

6501; Snyder, Tressa; F; 1/15/11-21; -1/4; S; Head; 6431; No; Milwaukee, city, Wis.; Yes; Al. 7720 An. 6412

6502; Soldier Hawk, Henry; M; 1877-55; F; M; Head; 6432; Yes; Yes; Al. 3099 An. 6416

6503; Soldier Hawk (No data), Alice; F; 1877-55; F; M; Wife; 6433; Yes; Yes; Al. 3100 An. 6417

6504; Sounding Side, Logan; M; 1893-39; F; M; Head; 6434; Yes; Yes; Al. 3362 An. 6420

6505; Sounding Side (Stands, Susie), Susie; F; 1900-32; F; M; Wife; 6435; Yes; Yes; Al. 3315 An. 6421

6506; Sounding Side, Theresa; F; 5/10/20-11; F; S; Daughter; 6436; Yes; Yes; Id. U-11000 An. 6423

6507; Sounding Side, Stella; F; 4/17/21-10; F; S; Daughter; 6437; Yes; Yes; Id. U-10999 An. 6424

Census of the **Pine Ridge** reservation of the **Pine Ridge, South Dakota** jurisdiction, as of **April 1**, 1932, taken by **James H. McGregor**, Superintendent.

Key: Number; Surname, Given; Sex; Date of Birth-Age at Last Birthday; Tribe (Oglala Sioux, unless stated otherwise); Degree of Blood; Marital Status; Relationship to Head of Family [Last Census Roll Number]; At Jurisdiction Where Enrolled (Yes/No); (If no – Where); Ward (Yes/No, if given); Allotment, Annuity and Identification Numbers (if given).

6508; Sounding Side, Mollie; F; 6/17/24-7; F; S; Daughter; 6438; Yes; Yes; Id. U-11488 An. 6435

6509; Sounding Side, Philip; M; 8/8/26-5; F; S; Son; 6439; Yes; Yes; Id. U-12122 An. none

6510; Sounding Side, Jerry; M; 10/25/29-2; F; S; Son; 6440; Yes; Yes; Id. U-13304 An. none

6511; Stands, Hobart; M; 7/3/15-16; F; S; Stepson; 6441; Ues[sic]; Yes; Al. 7984 An. 6422

6512; Sound Sleeper, Joseph; M; 1883-49; F; M; Head; 6442; Yes; Yes; Al. 4144 An. 6426

6513; Sound Sleeper (Plenty Wolf, Susie), Susie A.; F; 1903-29; F; M; Wife; 6443; Yes; Yes; Al. 4384 An. 6427

6514; Sound Sleeper, Alice; F; 5/13/21-10; F; S; Daughter; 6444; Yes; Yes; Id. U-10454 An. 6428

6515; Sound Sleeper, Paul; M; 5/24/24-7; F; S; Son; 6445; Yes; Yes; Id. U-11338 An. 6429

6516; Sound Sleeper, Patrick; M; 10/20/26-5; F; S; Son; 6446; Yes; Yes; Id. U-12152 An. none

6517; Sound Sleeper, Emma; F; 8/15/29-2; F; S; Daughter; 6447; Yes; Yes; Id. U-13305 An. none

6518; Southerland, George C.; M; 8/23/96-36; -1/4; S; Head; 6448; No; Cheyenne, city, Laramie, Wyo.; No; Al. 4689 An. 6431

6519; Southerland, Maude M.; F; 8/23/03-29; -1/4; S; Head; 6449; No; Laramie, town, Albany, Wyo.; Yes; Al. 4692 An. 6432

6520; Southerland, Robert E.; M; 12/21/1900-32; -1/4; S; Head; 6450; No; Cheyenne, city, Laramie, Wyo.; Yes; Al. 4691 An. 6433

6521; Southerland, William; M; 12/21/98-32[sic]; -1/4; S; Head; 6451; No; Wheatland, city, Platt, Wyo.; Yes; Al. 4690 An. 6434

6522; Spaulding (Skalander, Elsie), Elsie; F; 1892-40; -1/4; M; Head; 6452; No; Flandreau, town, Moody, S.D.; Yes; Al. 4502 An. 6435

6523; Spaulding, Thelma; F; 10/4/20-11; -1/4; S; Daughter; 6453; No; Ditto; Yes; Id. U-10455 An. 6436

6524; Spaulding, Evon Jean; F; 10/11/26-5; -1/4; S; Daughter; 6454; No; Ditto; Yes; Id. U-14070 An. none

6525; Speck (Larabee, Mary), Mary; F; 8/14/10-21; plus 1/4; M; Head; 6455; Yes; Yes; Al. 5364 An. 3719

Census of the __Pine Ridge__ reservation of the __Pine Ridge, South Dakota__ jurisdiction, as of __April 1__, 19**32**, taken by __James H. McGregor__, Superintendent.

Key: Number; Surname, Given; Sex; Date of Birth-Age at Last Birthday; Tribe (Oglala Sioux, unless stated otherwise); Degree of Blood; Marital Status; Relationship to Head of Family [Last Census Roll Number]; At Jurisdiction Where Enrolled (Yes/No); (If no – Where); Ward (Yes/No, if given); Allotment, Annuity and Identification Numbers (if given).

6526; Speck, Eva Mary; F; 4/14/30-1; -1/4; S; Daughter; 6456; Yes; Yes; Id. U-13712 An. none

6527; Speck, Lola Iris; F; 1/23/32-2/12; -1/4; S; Daughter; ---; Yes; Yes; Id. U-14070 An. none

6528; Spider, Albert; M; 1895-37; F; M; Head; 6457; Yes; Yes; Al. 808 An. 6437

6529; Spider (Grass, Julia), Julia; F; 1902-30; F; M; Wife; 6458; Yes; Yes; Al. 689 An. 6438

6530; Spider, Caroline; F; 8/13/22-9; F; S; Daughter; 6459; Yes; Yes; Id. U-11098 An. 6439

6531; Spider, Avaha; F; 7/1/25-6; F; S; Daughter; 6460; Yes; Yes; Id. U-11752 An. none

6532; Spider, Adam; M; 9/26/27-4; F; S; Son; 6461; Yes; Yes; Id. U-12411 An. none

6533; Spider, Florence R.; F; 4/3/31-11/12; F; S; Daughter; ---; Yes; Yes; Id. U-13818 An. none

6534; Spider, Mack; M; 1864-68; F; Wd.; Head; 6462; Yes; Yes; Al. 544 An. 6430

6535; Spider, Oliver; M; 1897-35; F; M; Head; 6463; Yes; Yes; Al. 809 An. 6442

6536; Spider (Black Bear, Jessie), Jessie; F; 1901-31; F; M; Wife; 6464; Yes; Yes; Al. 5312 An. 6443

6537; Spider, Emerson; M; 6/17/21-10; F; S; Son; 6465; Yes; Yes; Id. U-11584 An. 6444

6538; Spider, Pauline; F; 10/15/26-5; F; S; Daughter; 6466; Yes; Yes; Id. U-12153 An. none

6539; Spider, Raymond; M; 10/8/28-3; F; S; Son; 6467; Yes; Yes; Id. U-12839 An. none

6540; Spider, Melvin; M; 5/31/30-1; F; S; Son; 6468; Yes; Yes; Id. U-13521 An. none

6541; Spider Back Bone, ---; M; 1876-56; F; M; Head; 6469; Yes; Yes; Al. 6259 An. 6446

6542; Spider Back Bone, Julia; F; 1880-52; F; M; Wife; 6470; Yes; Yes; Al. 6260 An. 6447

6543; Spider Back Bone, Matthew; M; 3/16/13-19; F; S; Son; 6471; Yes; Yes; Id. U-10457 An. 6449

6544; Spider Back Bone, Victoria; F; 9/7/18-13; F; S; Daughter; 6472; Yes; Yes; Id. U-10458 An. 6450

6545; Spotted Bear, Charles; M; 1906-26; plus 1/4; S; Head; 6473; Yes; Yes; Al. 2286 An. 6451

Census of the____Pine Ridge____reservation of the__Pine Ridge, South Dakota__ jurisdiction, as of____April 1____, 19**32,** taken by__James H. McGregor__, Superintendent.

Key: Number; Surname, Given; Sex; Date of Birth-Age at Last Birthday; Tribe (Oglala Sioux, unless stated otherwise); Degree of Blood; Marital Status; Relationship to Head of Family [Last Census Roll Number]; At Jurisdiction Where Enrolled (Yes/No); (If no – Where); Ward (Yes/No, if given); Allotment, Annuity and Identification Numbers (if given).

6546; Spotted Bear, Edward; M; 12/13/08-23; plus 1/4; S; Head; 6474; Yes; Yes; Al. 5152 An. 6454

6547; Spotted Bear, Thomas, Sr.; M; 1873-59; F; M; Head; 6475; Yes; Yes; Al. 41 An. 6452

6548; Spotted Bear (Broken Rope, Sallie), Sallie; F; 1895-37; plus 1/4; M; Wife; 6476; Yes; Yes; Al. 7090 An. none

6549; Spotted Bear, Agatha; F; 11/23/14-17; plus 1/4; S; Daughter; 6477; Yes; Yes; Al. 8036 An. 6456

6550; Spotted Bear, Gladys; F; 7/6/18-13; plus 1/4; S; Daughter; 6478; Yes; Yes; Id. U-10459 An. 6457

6551; Spotted Bear, Emerson; M; 4/19/28-3; plus 1/4; S; Son; 6479; Yes; Yes; Id. U-12598 An. none

6552; Spotted Bear, Joseph; M; 3/8/30-2; plus 1/4; S; Son; 6480; Yes; Yes; Id. U-13427 An. none

6553; Broken Rope, Vance; M; 3/28/20-12; plus 1/4; S; Stepson; 6481; Yes; Yes; Id. U-9255 An. 1042

6554; Broken Rope, Loranzo; M; 3/7/22-10; plus 1/4; S; Stepson; 6482; Yes; Yes; Id. U-10911 An. 1043

6555; Broken Rope, Everett; M; 5/10/23-8; plus 1/4; S; Stepson; 6483; Yes; Yes; Id. U-13088 An. 1044

6556; Spotted Bear, Thomas L.; M; 1902-30; plus 1/4; S; Head; 6484; Yes; Yes; Al. 2284 An. none

6557; Spotted Bear, Thomas Jr.; M; 1897-35; plus 1/4; M; Head; 6485; Yes; Yes; Al. 280 An. 6459

6558; Spotted Bear (Yellow Rope, Sallie R.), Sallie Rosie; F; 1907-25; F; M; Wife; 7953; Yes; Yes; Al. 5700 An. 7870

6559; Spotted Bear, Homer F.; M; 10/13/30-1; plus 1/4; S; Son; 7954; Yes; Yes; Id. U-13661 An. none

6560; Spotted Bear, Pearl Mary; F; 3/25/32-1/12; plus 1/4; S; Daughter; ---; Yes; Yes; Id. U-14136 An. none

6561; Spotted Crow, Edward; M; 1878-54; F; Wd.; Head; 6486; Yes; Yes; Al. 3722 An. 6460

6562; Spotted Crow, William; M; 1873-59; F; M; Head; 6487; Yes; Yes; Al. 4720 An. 6462

6563; Spotted Crow, Ellen; F; 1879-53; F; M; Wife; 6488; Yes; Yes; Al. 4771 An. 6463

Census of the **Pine Ridge** reservation of the **Pine Ridge, South Dakota** jurisdiction, as of **April 1**, 19**32**, taken by **James H. McGregor**, Superintendent.

Key: Number; Surname, Given; Sex; Date of Birth-Age at Last Birthday; Tribe (Oglala Sioux, unless stated otherwise); Degree of Blood; Marital Status; Relationship to Head of Family [Last Census Roll Number]; At Jurisdiction Where Enrolled (Yes/No); (If no – Where); Ward (Yes/No, if given); Allotment, Annuity and Identification Numbers (if given).

6564; Spotted Eagle, ---; M; 1867-65; F; M; Head; 6489; Yes; Yes; Al. 4260 An. 6465

6565; Spotted Eagle (No data), Kate; F; 1867-65; F; M; Wife; 6490; Yes; Yes; Al. 4261 An. 6466

6566; Spotted Eagle, Emma; F; 1902-30; F; S; Daughter; 6491; Yes; Yes; Al. 7747 An. 6467

6567; Spotted Eagle, Charles; M; 1894-38; F; M; Head; 6492; Yes; Yes; Al. 1053 An. 6468

6568; Spotted Eagle (Lone Wolf, Agnes), Agnes; F; 1897-35; F; M; Wife; 6493; Yes; Yes; Al. 2209 An. 6469

6569; Spotted Eagle, Grace; F; 7/3/21-10; F; S; Daughter; 6494; Yes; Yes; Id. U-11028 An. 6471

6570; Spotted Eagle, Lorene; F; 12/22/30-1; F; S; Daughter; 6495; Yes; Yes; Id. U-13713 An. none

6571; Spotted Eagle, Harry; M; 1860-72; F; M; Head; 6496; Yes; Yes; Al. 1678 An. 6474

6572; Spotted Eagle (No data), Nellie; F; 1869-63; F; M; Wife; 6497; Yes; Yes; Al. 5956 An. 6475

6573; Spotted Eagle, John; M; 1892-40; F; M; Head; 6498; Yes; Yes; Al. 1679 An. 6476

6574; Spotted Eagle (American Bear, Mary), Mary; F; 1892-40; F; M; Wife; 108; Yes; Yes; Al. 1235 An. 113

6575; Spotted Eagle, Joseph; M; 7/ /16-15; F; S; Son; 6499; Yes; Yes; Id. U-10461 An. 6479

6576; Spotted Eagle, Pauline; F; 3/10/12-15; F; S; Daughter; 6500; Yes; Yes; Id. U-10462 An. 6480

6577; Spotted Eagle, Louis; M; 9/8/22-9; F; S; Son; 6501; Yes; Yes; Id. U-11078 An. 6481

6578; Shield, Hazel; F; 2/12/15-17; F; S; Ward; 6206; Yes; Yes; Id. U-10396 An. 6191

6579; Shield, Stephen; M; 10/12/16-15; F; S; Ward; 6207; Yes; Yes; Id. U-10397 An. 6192

6580; Shield, Joseph; M; 12/30/19-12; F; S; Ward; 6208; Yes; Yes; Id. U-10398 An. 6193

6581; Spotted Eagle, Oscar; M; 1899-33; F; M; Head; 6502; Yes; Yes; Al. 1054 An. 6482

6582; Spotted Eagle (Bush, Elizabeth), Elizabeth; F; 1906-26; plus 1/4; M; Wife; 1192; Yes; Yes; Al. 3690 An. 1239

Census of the **Pine Ridge** reservation of the **Pine Ridge, South Dakota** jurisdiction, as of **April 1**, 19**32,** taken by **James H. McGregor**, Superintendent.

Key: Number; Surname, Given; Sex; Date of Birth-Age at Last Birthday; Tribe (Oglala Sioux, unless stated otherwise); Degree of Blood; Marital Status; Relationship to Head of Family [Last Census Roll Number]; At Jurisdiction Where Enrolled (Yes/No); (If no – Where); Ward (Yes/No, if given); Allotment, Annuity and Identification Numbers (if given).

6583; Spotted Eagle, Joseph; M; 5/24/31-10/12; plus 1/4; S; Son; ---; Yes; Yes; Id. U-13843 An. none

6584; Spotted Eagle, William B.; M; 3/2/11-21; F; M; Head; 6503; Yes; Yes; Al. 5923 An. 6478

6585; Spotted Eagle (No Neck, Ellen), Ellen; F; 2/25/13-19; plus 1/4; M; Wife; 6504; Yes; Yes; Id. U-9043 An. none

6586; Spotted Eagle, Agnes Ellen; F; 6/20/30-1; plus 1/4; S; Daughter; 6505; Yes; Yes; Id. U-13615 An. none

6587; Spotted Elk, Earnest; M; 1888-44; F; M; Head; 6506; Yes; Yes; Al. 7049 An. 6483

6588; Spotted Elk (Brave Heart, Frankie), Frankie; F; 1892-40; F; M; Wife; 6507; Yes; Yes; Al. 3180 An. 6484

6589; Spotted Elk, Ellen; F; 11/3/13-18; F; S; Daughter; 6508; Yes; Yes; Al. 7979 An. 6485

6590; Spotted Elk, Victoria; F; 7/4/31-9/12; F; S; Daughter; ---; Yes; Yes; Id. U-13906 An. none

6591; Spotted Elk, Esther; F; 5/24/15-16; F; S; Alone; 6509; Yes; Yes; Id. U-10466 An. 6487

6592; Spotted Elk, Louisa; F; 1/16/19-13; F; S; Sister; 6510; Yes; Yes; Id. U-10467 An. 6490

6593; Spotted Elk, Jasper; M; 1891-41; F; M; Head; 6512; Yes; Yes; Al. 3079 An. 6492

6594; Spotted Elk (Fast, Annie), Annie; F; 1891-41; F; M; Wife; 6513; Yes; Yes; Al. 7012 An. 6493

-----; ~~Spotted Elk, Richard; M; 6/21/13-18; F; S; Son; 6514; Yes; Died 2/18/32; Yes; Al. 7013 An. 6494~~

6595; Spotted Elk, Alice; F; 7/2/23-8; F; S; Daughter; 6515; Yes; Yes; Id. U-14010[sic] An. 6495

6596; Spotted Elk, Jasper Jr.; M; 3/1/27-5; F; S; Son; 6516; Yes; Yes; Id. U-12268 An. none

6597; Spotted Horse, Eli; M; 12/26/09-23; F; S; Head; 6511; Yes; Yes; Al. 6330 An. 3849

6598; Spotted Horse, Carrie; F; 1882-50; F; Wd.; Head; 6518; Yes; Yes; Al. 3812 An. 6505

6599; White Face, Psific; F; 2/13/20-12; F; S; Niece; 6519; Yes; Yes; Id. U-10655 An. 6501

Census of the **Pine Ridge** reservation of the **Pine Ridge, South Dakota** jurisdiction, as of **April 1**, 19**32**, taken by **James H. McGregor**, Superintendent.

Key: Number; Surname, Given; Sex; Date of Birth-Age at Last Birthday; Tribe (Oglala Sioux, unless stated otherwise); Degree of Blood; Marital Status; Relationship to Head of Family [Last Census Roll Number]; At Jurisdiction Where Enrolled (Yes/No); (If no – Where); Ward (Yes/No, if given); Allotment, Annuity and Identification Numbers (if given).

6600; Spotted Horse, Mack; M; 1993-39; F; M; Head; 6520; Yes; Yes; Al. 1656 An. 6502

6601; Spotted Horse (Stabber, Emma), Emma; F; 1864-58; F; M; Wife; 6521; Yes; Yes; Al. 3687 An. 6516

6602; Spotted Owl, Joshua; M; 1868-68; F; Wd.; Head; 6524; Yes; Yes; Al. 7523 An. 6508

6603; Spotted Owl, Nancy; F; 9/1/15-16; F; S; Daughter; 6525; Yes; Yes; Id. U-10471 An. 6512

6604; Spotted Snake, ---; M; 1862-70; F; Wd.; Head; 6526; Yes; Yes; Al. 3697 An. 2120

6605; Fast Eagle, Martha; F; 12/13/21-10; F; S; Granddaughter; 6527; Yes; Yes; Id. U-10075 An. none

6606; Fast Eagle, Orlando; M; 6/4/24-7; F; S; Grandson; 6528; Yes; Yes; Id. U-11279 An. none

6607; Fast Eagle, Comer Paul; M; 12/1/26-5; F; S; Grandson; 6529; Yes; Yes; Id. U-12204 An. none

6608; Spotted Weasel, Cedar; M; 1851-81; F; Wd.; Head; 6530; Yes; Yes; Al. 4564 An. 6514

6609; Stabber, Louis; M; 1907-25; F; S; Head; 6531; Yes; Yes; Al. 5901 An. 2182

6610; Stabber, Madger; F; 8/20/26-5; F; S; Alone; 6532; Yes; Yes; Id. U-12195 An. none

6611; Stabber, Sylvia; F; 4/24/27-4; F; S; Alone (Sister); 6533; Yes; Yes; Id. U-12466 An. none

6612; Stabber, Thomas; M; 1874-58; F; M; Head; 6534; Yes; Yes; Al. 526 An. 6519

6613; Stabber (Three Stars, Sallie), Sallie; F; 1872-60; F; M; Wife; 6535; Yes; Yes; Al. 6691 An. 6520

6614; Stahl, Christina; M; 1890-42; plus 1/4; M; Head; 6536; Yes; Yes; Al. 4057 An. 6522

6615; Stahl, Belle; F; 4/12/14-17; -1/4; S; Daughter; 6537; Yes; Yes; Al. 7954 An. 6525

6616; Stair, Isabel; F; 1893-39; -1/4; M; Head; 6538; Yes; Yes; Al. 3822 An. 6521

6617; Stair, Neoma I; F; 12/13/21-10; -1/4; S; Daughter; 6539; Yes; Yes; Id. U-12700 An. none

6618; Stair, Patsy Jean; F; 1/9/25-7; -1/4; S; Daughter; 6540; Yes; Yes; Id. U-12701 An. none

Census of the ___Pine Ridge___ reservation of the ___Pine Ridge, South Dakota___ jurisdiction, as of ___April 1___, 1932, taken by ___James H. McGregor___, Superintendent.

Key: Number; Surname, Given; Sex; Date of Birth-Age at Last Birthday; Tribe (Oglala Sioux, unless stated otherwise); Degree of Blood; Marital Status; Relationship to Head of Family [Last Census Roll Number]; At Jurisdiction Where Enrolled (Yes/No); (If no – Where); Ward (Yes/No, if given); Allotment, Annuity and Identification Numbers (if given).

6619; Standing Bear, ---; M; 1859-73; F; M; Head; 6541; Yes; Yes; Al. 936 An. 6526

6620; Two Bonnets, Violet R.; F; 2/3/16-16; plus 1/4; S; Granddaughter; 6542; Yes; Yes; Id. U-10613 An. 4446

6621; Two Bonnets, Lulu M.; F; 1/9/18-14; plus 1/4; S; Granddaughter; 6543; Yes; Yes; Id. U-10614 An. 4447

6622; Two Bonnets, Helena; F; 5/8/20-11; plus 1/4; S; Granddaughter; 6544; Yes; Yes; Id. U-10615 An. 4448

6623; Standing Bear, David; M; 1881-51; F; M; Head; 6545; Yes; Yes; Al. 2415 An. 6527

6624; Standing Bear, Bessie; F; 1906-26; plus 1/4; S; Head; 6546; No; Ambler, town, Montgomery, Pa; Yes; Al. 5060 An. 6528

6625; Standing Bear, Henry; M; 1869-63; plus 1/4; M; Head; 6548; Yes; Yes; Al. 2604 An. 6531

6626; Standing Bear (Irving, Martha), Martha; F; 1884-48; plus 1/4; M; Wife; 6549; Yes; Yes; Al. 63 An. 3239

6627; Irving, Wilbert; M; 5/3/12-19; plus 1/4; S; Stepson; 3220; Yes; Yes; Al. 6708 An. 3241

6628; Irving, Clara; F; 6/12/14-17; plus 1/4; S; Stepsondaughter; 3221; Yes; Yes; Id. U-9746 An. 3242

6629; Irving, Eugene; M; 2/29/16-16; plus 1/4; S; Stepson; 3222; Yes; Yes; Id. U-9747 An. 3243

6630; Irving, Monica; F; 1/16/18-14; plus 1/4; S; Stepdaughter; 3223; Yes; Yes; Id. U-9748 An. 3244

6631; Irving, Mary; F; 3/12/20-12; plus 1/4; S; Stepdaughter; 3224; Yes; Yes; Id. U-9749 An. 3245

6632; Irving, Seth Chas.; M; 5/3/22-9; plus 1/4; S; Stepson; 3225; Yes; Yes; Id. U-10996 An. 3246

6633; Irving, Catherine; F; 10/11/23-8; plus 1/4; S; Stepdaughter; 3226; Yes; Yes; Id. U-11126 An. none

6634; Irving, Cecelia; F; 12/28/25-6; plus 1/4; S; Stepdaughter; 3227; Yes; Yes; Id. U-11797 An. none

6635; Standing Bear, Margaret; F; 2/23/11-21; plus 1/4; S; Head; 6549; No; New York, city, New York, N.Y.; Yes; Al. 7848 An. 6532

6636; Standing Bear, Henry; M; 1894-38; plus 1/4; M; Head; 6551; No; Flandreau, town, Moody, S.D.; No; Al. 2055 An. 6534

6637; Standing Bear (Lessert, Olive), Olive; F; 1903-29; plus 1/4; M; Wife; 6552; No; Ditto; No; Al. 968 An. 6535

Census of the __Pine Ridge__ reservation of the __Pine Ridge, South Dakota__ jurisdiction, as of __April 1__, 19**32**, taken by __James H. McGregor__, Superintendent.

Key: Number; Surname, Given; Sex; Date of Birth-Age at Last Birthday; Tribe (Oglala Sioux, unless stated otherwise); Degree of Blood; Marital Status; Relationship to Head of Family [Last Census Roll Number]; At Jurisdiction Where Enrolled (Yes/No); (If no – Where); Ward (Yes/No, if given); Allotment, Annuity and Identification Numbers (if given).

6638; Standing Bear, Roy Thomas; M; 9/3/22-9; plus 1/4; S; Son; 6553; No; Ditto; Yes; Id. U-12011 An. 6536

6639; Standing Bear, Carmel G.; F; 8/29/24-7; plus 1/4; S; Daughter; 6554; No; Ditto; Yes; Id. U-11341 An. 6537

6640; Standing Bear, George; M; 1906-26; plus 1/4; M; Head; 6555; No; Osage, Okla.; Yes; Al. 4647 An. 5538

N.E.: Standing Bear, (Lookout, Nora) Nora; F; -------; Osage; M; Wife;

6641; Standing Bear, Geo. Eugene; M; 10/31/29-1; Osage & Sioux; plus 1/4; S; Son; 6556; No; Ditto; Yes; Id. U-13352 An. none

6642; Standing Bear, Howard; M; 1885-47; F; S; Head; 6557; Yes; Yes; Id. U-10473 An. 6539

6643; Standing Bear, Edgar; M; 2/14/03-29; plus 1/4; M; Head; 6558; Yes; Yes; Al. 5168 An. 6540

6644; Standing Bear (Dubray, Vivian), Vivian; F; 2/8/09-23; plus 1/4; M; Wife; 6559; Yes; Yes; Al. 4492 An. 1964

6645; Standing Bear, Edsel; M; 4/10/27-4; plus 1/4; S; Son; 6560; Yes; Yes; Id. U-12295 An. none

6646; Standing Bear, Victoria; F; 1/27/29-3; plus 1/4; S; Daughter; 6561; Yes; Yes; Id. U-12996 An. none

6647; Standing Bear, Luther; M; 1863-69; plus 1/4; Wd.; Head; 6562; Yes; 3/4 Indian. See 3902-35 and 3904/35; Yes; Al. 4644 An. 6544

6648; Standing Bear, Richard; M; 1898-34; plus 1/4; M; Head; 6563; Yes; Yes; Al. 4013 An. 6545

N.E.: Standing Bear, (Neck Shield, Martha) Martha; F; -------; Rosebud Sioux; plus 1/4 M; Wife;

6649; Standing Bear, Deloris; F; 10/9/28-3; Sioux; plus 1/4; S; Daughter; 6564; Yes; Yes; Id. U-12930 An. none

6650; Standing Bear, Stephen; M; 1892-40; plus 1/4;Wd.; Head; 6565; Yes; Yes; Al. 4011 An. 6546

6651; Standing Bear, Gladys A.; F; 1/21/2-5; plus 1/4; S; Daughter; 6566; Yes; Yes; Id. U-13119 An. none

6652; Standing Bear, Willard; M; 1868-64; plus 1/4; Wd.; Head; 6567; Yes; Yes; Al. 4008 An. 6549

N.E.: Standing Buffalo, Jesse; M; -------; Rosebud Sioux; M; Head;

Census of the **Pine Ridge** reservation of the **Pine Ridge, South Dakota** jurisdiction, as of **April 1**, 1932, taken by **James H. McGregor**, Superintendent.

Key: Number; Surname, Given; Sex; Date of Birth-Age at Last Birthday; Tribe (Oglala Sioux, unless stated otherwise); Degree of Blood; Marital Status; Relationship to Head of Family [Last Census Roll Number]; At Jurisdiction Where Enrolled (Yes/No); (If no – Where); Ward (Yes/No, if given); Allotment, Annuity and Identification Numbers (if given).

6653; Standing Buffalo (Black Crow, Ethel), Ethel; F; 1904-28; F; M; Wife; 6568; Yes; Yes; Al. 4492 An. 1964

6654; Standing Buffalo, Purcell; M; 1/125/31-1; F; S; Son; 6569; Yes; Yes; Id. U-13748 An. none

6655; Standing Cloud, Charles; M; 1876-56; F; M; Head; 6570; Yes; Yes; Al. 1517 An. 6553

6656; Standing Cloud (Has No Horses, Julia), Julia; F; 1872-60; F; M; Wife; 6571; Yes; Yes; Al. 5326 An. 6554

6657; Standing Elk, Julia; F; 1850-82; F; Wd.; Head; 6572; Yes; Yes; Al. 4423 An. 6558

6658; Standing Elk, Thomas; M; 1892-40; F; M; Head; 6573; Yes; Yes; Al. 959 An. 6560

6659; Standing Elk (Good Crow, Frances), Frances; F; 1894-38; F; M; Wife; 6577; Yes; Yes; Al. 1544 An. 2573

6660; Standing Elk, Mary M.; F; 5/29/16-15; plus 1/4; S; Daughter; 6574; Yes; Yes; Id. U-10476 An. 6562

6661; Standing Elk, Barnard; M; 2/24/18-14; plus 1/4; S; Son; 6575; Yes; Yes; Id. U-10477 An. 6553

6662; Standing Elk, Joseph; M; 2/28/22-10; plus 1/4; S; Son; 6576; Yes; Yes; Id. U-11564 An. 6554

6663; Standing Elk, Theodore; M; 12/9/28-3; plus 1/4; S; Son; 6582; Yes; Yes; Id. U-13353 An. none

6664; Good Crow, Eva; F; 4/21/15-16; F; S; Stepdaughter; 6578; Yes; Yes; Al. 8077 An. 2574

6665; Good Crow, Raymond; M; 9/9/17-14; F; S; Stepson; 6579; Yes; Yes; Id. U-9600 An. 2575

6666; Good Crow, Charles S.; M; 2/24/20-12; F; S; Stepson; 6580; Yes; Yes; Id. U-9601 An. 2576

6667; Good Crow, Elizabeth; F; 10/24/22-9; F; S; Stepdaughter; 6581; Yes; Yes; Al. 9601 An. 2577

6668; Standing Soldier, Edwardd[sic]; M; 1882-50; F; M; Head; 6583; Yes; No; Al. 5872 An. 6555

6669; Standing Soldier (No data), Louisa; F; 1880-52; F; M; Wife; 6584; Yes; Yes; Al. 3324 An. 6556

6670; Standing Soldier, Lavina; F; 2/14/18-14; F; S; Daughter; 6586; Yes; Yes; Id. U-10479 An. 6558

6671; Standing Soldier, Elk; M; 1872-60; F; M; Head; 6587; Yes; Yes; Al. 1929 An. 6559

Census of the __Pine Ridge__ reservation of the __Pine Ridge, South Dakota__ jurisdiction, as of __April 1__, 1932, taken by __James H. McGregor__, Superintendent.

Key: Number; Surname, Given; Sex; Date of Birth-Age at Last Birthday; Tribe (Oglala Sioux, unless stated otherwise); Degree of Blood; Marital Status; Relationship to Head of Family [Last Census Roll Number]; At Jurisdiction Where Enrolled (Yes/No); (If no – Where); Ward (Yes/No, if given); Allotment, Annuity and Identification Numbers (if given).

6672; Standing Soldier (No data), Julia; F; 1864-68; plus 1/4; M; Wife; 6588; Yes; Yes; Al. 1930 An. 6560

6673; Standing Soldier, Andrew; M; 2/1/17-15; plus 1/4; S; Son; 6589; Yes; Yes; Id. U-10478 An. 6562

6674; Standing Soldier, Felix; M; 1897-35; plus 1/4; Wd.; Head; 6590; Yes; Yes; Al. 1932 An. 6563

6675; Standing Soldier, Joseph; M; 1899-33; plus 1/4; M; Head; 6591; Yes; Yes; Al. 1933 An. 6564

6676; Standing Soldier (Moves Camp, Clara), Clara; F; 1898-34; plus 1/4; M; Wife; 6592; Yes; Yes; Al. 2096 An. 6565

6677; Standing Soldier, Stanley; M; 1/16/23-9; plus 1/4; S; Son; 6593; Yes; Yes; Id. U-12063 An. 6568

6678; Standing Soldier, Maude L.; F; 3/18/25-7; plus 1/4; S; Daughter; 6594; Yes; Yes; Id. U-11514 An. 6569

6679; Standing Soldier, Viola; F; 3/29/27-5; plus 1/4; S; Daughter; 6595; Yes; Yes; Id. U-12702 An. none

6680; Standing Soldier, Elizabeth; F; 11/14/28-3; plus 1/4; S; Daughter; 6596; Yes; Yes; Id. U-12931 An. none

6681; Standing Soldier, Robert; M; 10/6/30-1; plus 1/4; S; Son; 6597; Yes; Yes; Id. U-13714 An. none

6682; Standing Soldier, Paul; M; 1893-39; plus 1/4; M; Head; 6598; Yes; Yes; Al. 1931 An. 6571

N.E.: Standing Soldier, (Witt, May) May; F; ------; Cherokee; plus 1/4 M; Wife;

6683; Standing Soldier, Helen; F; 10/12/24-7; Sioux & Cherokee; plus 1/4; S; Daughter; 6599; Yes; Yes; Id. U-11516 An. 6572

6684; Standing Soldier, Rita; F; 3/30/26-6; Sioux & Cherokee; plus 1/4; S; Daughter; 6600; Yes; Yes; Id. U-12703 An. none

6685; Standing Soldier, Julianna; F; 12/2/27-4; Sioux & Cherokee; plus 1/4; S; Daughter; 6601; Yes; Yes; Id. U-12450 An. none

6686; Standing Soldier, Andrew; M; 6/4/29-2; Sioux & Cherokee; plus 1/4; S; Son; 6602; Yes; Yes; Id. U-13194 An. none

6687; Standing Soldier, Mildred L.; F; 9/4/31-7/12; Sioux & Cherokee; plus 1/4; S; Daughter; ---; Yes; Yes; Id. U-14071 An. none

6688; Standing Soldier, Philip; M; 1877-55; F; Wd.; Head; 6603; Yes; Yes; Al. 3554 An. 6573

6689; Standing Soldier, Johnson; M; 8/12/08-23; F; M; Head; 6604; Yes; Yes; Al. 3556 An. 6574

Census of the **Pine Ridge** reservation of the **Pine Ridge, South Dakota** jurisdiction, as of **April 1**, 1932, taken by **James H. McGregor**, Superintendent.

Key: Number; Surname, Given; Sex; Date of Birth-Age at Last Birthday; Tribe (Oglala Sioux, unless stated otherwise); Degree of Blood; Marital Status; Relationship to Head of Family [Last Census Roll Number]; At Jurisdiction Where Enrolled (Yes/No); (If no – Where); Ward (Yes/No, if given); Allotment, Annuity and Identification Numbers (if given).

6690; Standing Soldier (Yellow Boy, Mabel), Mabel; F; 12/1/10-21; F; M; Wife; 6605; Yes; Yes; Al. 5701 An. 7854

6691; Standing Soldier, William; M; 1874-58; F; M; Head; 6606; Yes; Yes; Al. 282 An. 6577

6692; Standing Soldier (Whalen, Mary), Mary; F; 1886-46; plus 1/4; M; Wife; 6607; Yes; Yes; Al. 317 An. 6578

6693; Standing Soldier, George; M; 6/28/20-11; plus 1/4; S; Son; 6608; Yes; Yes; Id. U-10480 An. 6580

6694; Standing Soldier, Thomas; M; 6/20/23-8; plus 1/4; S; Son; 6609; Yes; Yes; Id. U-13097 An. 6581

6695; Stands Soldier, Andrew; M; 1899-33; F; S; Head; 6610; Yes; Yes; Al. 3305 An. 6582

6696; Stands, Peter; M; 1872-60; F; M; Head; 6611; Yes; Yes; Al. 3303 An. 6583
6697; Stands (No data), Nellie; F; 1878-54; F; M; Wife; 6612; Yes; Yes; Al. 7613 An. 6584
6698; Stands, Stella; F; 4/5/19-12; F; ~~M~~S; Daughter; 6613; Yes; Yes; Id. U-10481 An. 6585

6699; Stands, Samuel; M; 1895-37; F; M; Head; 6614; Yes; Yes; Al. 6252 An. 6586
6700; Stands (Dreaming Bear, Lucy), Lucy; F; 1896-36; F; M; Wife; 6615; Yes; Yes; Al. 6146 An. 6586
6701; Stands, Vincent; M; 6/10/17-14; F; S; Son; 6616; Yes; Yes; Id. U-10487 An. 6588
6702; Stands, Evalyne; F; 11/17/21-10; F; S; Daughter; 6617; Yes; Yes; Id. U-10490 An. 6589
6703; Stands, Paul V.; M; 2/28/24-8; F; S; Son; 6618; Yes; Yes; Id. U-11218 An. none
6704; Stands, Juanita; F; 9/10/26-5; F; S; Daughter; 6619; Yes; Yes; Id. U-12123 An. none
6705; Stands, Cornia; F; 5/3/28-3; F; S; Daughter; 6620; Yes; Yes; Id. U-12644 An. none
6706; Stands, Vivian; F; 11/1/30-1; F; S; Daughter; 6621; Yes; Yes; Id. U-13715 An. none

6707; Stands, Silas; M; 1894-38; F; M; Head; 6622; Yes; Yes; Al. 3304 An. 6591
6708; Stands (LaPointe, Annie), Annie; F; 1899-33; plus 1/4; M; Wife; 6623; Yes; Yes; Al. 6510 An. 6592
6709; Stands, Daniel; M; 8/30/17-14; plus 1/4; S; Son; 6624; Yes; Yes; Id. U-10482 An. 6593

Census of the **Pine Ridge** reservation of the **Pine Ridge, South Dakota** jurisdiction, as of **April 1**, 19**32**, taken by **James H. McGregor**, Superintendent.

Key: Number; Surname, Given; Sex; Date of Birth-Age at Last Birthday; Tribe (Oglala Sioux, unless stated otherwise); Degree of Blood; Marital Status; Relationship to Head of Family [Last Census Roll Number]; At Jurisdiction Where Enrolled (Yes/No); (If no – Where); Ward (Yes/No, if given); Allotment, Annuity and Identification Numbers (if given).

6710; Stands, Jobe; M; 1/1/19-13; plus 1/4; S; Son; 6625; Yes; Yes; Id. U-10483 An. 6594
6711; Stands, Jacob; M; 6/10/21-10; plus 1/4; S; Son; 6626; Yes; Yes; Id. U-10485 An. 6595
6712; Stands, Titus; M; 1/27/23-9; plus 1/4; S; Son; 6627; Yes; Yes; Id. U-13066 An. 6596
6713; Stands, Isaac; M; 12/13/24-7; plus 1/4; S; Son; 6628; Yes; Yes; Id. U-11422 An. 6597
6714; Stands, Jonas; M; 5/15/26-5; plus 1/4; S; Son; 6629; Yes; Yes; Id. U-11958 An. none
6715; Stands, Levi Moses; M; 11/13/27-4; plus 1/4; S; Son; 6630; Yes; Yes; Id. U-12497 An. none
6716; Stands, Mary; F; 7/11/29-2; plus 1/4; S; Daughter; 6631; Yes; Yes; Id. U-13235 An. none
6717; Stands, Hannah; F; 3/21/31-1; plus 1/4; S; Daughter; ---; Yes; Yes; Id. U-13844 An. none

6718; Stands Up, Peter; M; 1894-38; F; M; Head; 6632; Yes; Yes; Al. 908 An. 6603
6719; Red Horse or Iron Tail, ---; F; 1856-76; F; M; Wife; 6633; Yes; Yes; Al. 4112 An. 6604

6720; Star Yellow Wood, Louisa; F; 1899-33; plus 1/4; M; Head; 6634; Yes; Yes; Al. 5426 An. 6607
6721; Star Yellow Wood, Samuel; M; 4/8/22-9; plus 1/4; S; Son; 6635; Yes; Yes; Id. U-10985 An. 6608
6722; Star Yellow Wood, Theda; F; 8/25/24-7; plus 1/4; S; Daughter; 6636; Yes; Yes; Id. U-11519 An. 6609
6723; Star Yellow Wood, Willard; M; 2/12/25-7; plus 1/4; S; Son; 6637; Yes; Yes; Id. U-11520 An. 6610
6724; Star Yellow Wood, Loma; F; 10/28/27-4; plus 1/4; S; Daughter; 6638; Yes; Yes; Id. U-12498 An. none
6725; Star Yellow Wood, Ramona; F; 8/19/28-3; plus 1/4; S; Daughter; 6639; Yes; Yes; Id. U-12814 An. none
6726; Star Yellow Wood, Thelma Sue; F; 6/15/30-1; plus 1/4; S; Daughter; 6640; Yes; Yes; Id. U-13662 An. none
6727; Star, Paddy; M; 1859-73; plus 1/4; Wd.; Head; 6641; Yes; Yes; Al. 1776 An. 6613
6728; Star, Paddy Jr.; M; 1896-36; plus 1/4; Wd.; Head; 6642; Yes; Yes; Al. 1780 An. 6614
6729; Star, Noah; M; 1/22/27-5; plus 1/4; S; Son; 6643; Yes; Yes; Id. U-12212 An. none

Census of the **Pine Ridge** reservation of the **Pine Ridge, South Dakota** jurisdiction, as of **April 1**, 1932, taken by **James H. McGregor**, Superintendent.

Key: Number; Surname, Given; Sex; Date of Birth-Age at Last Birthday; Tribe (Oglala Sioux, unless stated otherwise); Degree of Blood; Marital Status; Relationship to Head of Family [Last Census Roll Number]; At Jurisdiction Where Enrolled (Yes/No); (If no – Where); Ward (Yes/No, if given); Allotment, Annuity and Identification Numbers (if given).

6730; Star, Reuben; M; 1870-62; F; M; Head; 6644; Yes; Yes; Al. 5170 An. 6616
6731; Star (Pine Bird, Jennie), Jennie; F; 1871-61; F; M; Wife; 6645; Yes; Yes; Al. 4858 An. 4958

6732; Star Comes Out, Ivan; M; 1875-57; F; M; Head; 6646; Yes; Yes; Al. 3347 An. 6618
6733; Star Comes Out (No data), Lizzie; F; 1877-55; F; M; Wife; 6647; Yes; Yes; Al. 3348 An. 6619
6734; Star, Comes Out; Stephen; M; 2/21/11-21; F; S; Son; 6648; Yes; Yes; Al. 6359 An. 6621

6735; Star Comes Out, Nancy; F; 7/3/04-27; F; S; Head; 6649; Yes; Yes; Al. 3361 An. 6625

6736; Steals Horses, Thomas; M; 1877-55; F; M; Head; 6650; Yes; Yes; Al. 1683 An. 6625
6737; Steals Horses (Long Visitor, Ellen), Ellen; F; 1873-59; F; M; Wife; 6651; Yes; Yes; Al. 6045 An. 6626

6738; Steffensmeir, Caroline; F; 5/30/09-23; plus 1/4; M; Head; 6652; Yes; Yes; Al. 3974 An. 6810
6739; Steffensmeir, Merlin G.; M; 9/29/28-3; -1/4; S; Son; 6653; Yes; Yes; Id. U-13120 An. none

6740; Stiff Tail, Emma; F; 1878-53; F; Wd.; Head; 6657; Yes; Yes; Al. 4921 An. 6403
6741; Smoke, Lena; F; 1912-20; F; S; Daughter; 6658; Yes; Yes; Id. U-10450 An. 6405
6742; Smoke, Melvin; M; 11/21/15-16; F; S; Son; 6659; Yes; Yes; Id. U-10451 An. 6406

6743; Stinking Bear, Charles; M; 1881-51; F; M; Head; 6660; Yes; Yes; Al. 3338 An. 6628
6744; Stinking Bear (Little Killer, Ida), Ida; F; 1873-59; F; M; Wife; 6661; Yes; Yes; Al. 6611 An. 6629
6745; Stinking Bear, Elva; F; 9/15/15-16; F; S; Daughter; 6662; Yes; Yes; Id. U-10496 An. 6631

6746; Stirk, Anthony; M; 1879-53; plus 1/4; M; Head; 6663; Yes; Yes; Al. 2605 An. 6633
6747; Stirk (No Data), Emma; F; 1882-50; plus 1/4; M; Wife; 6664; Yes; Yes; Al. 2606 An. 6634

Census of the____Pine Ridge____reservation of the__Pine Ridge, South Dakota__ jurisdiction, as of____April 1____, 1932, taken by____James H. McGregor____, Superintendent.

Key: Number; Surname, Given; Sex; Date of Birth-Age at Last Birthday; Tribe (Oglala Sioux, unless stated otherwise); Degree of Blood; Marital Status; Relationship to Head of Family [Last Census Roll Number]; At Jurisdiction Where Enrolled (Yes/No); (If no – Where); Ward (Yes/No, if given); Allotment, Annuity and Identification Numbers (if given).

6748; McGaa, Jessie; F; 4/6/14-17; plus 1/4; S; Niece; 6665; Yes; Yes; Al. 7527 An. 6635

6749; Stirk (No Data), Emma; F; 1859-73; plus 1/4; Wd.; Head; 6666; Yes; Yes; Al. 2665 An. 6636

6750; Stirk, George; M; 1891-41; plus 1/4; M; Head; 6667; Yes; Yes; Al. 2669 An. 6637

6751; Stirk (Cottier, Elizabeth), Elizabeth; F; 1892-40; plus 1/4; M; Wife; 6668; Yes; Yes; Al. 982 An. 6638

6752; Stirk, Mavis; F; 8/13/18-13; plus 1/4; S; Daughter; 6669; Yes; Yes; Id. U-10500 An. 6640

6753; Stirk, Louisa; F; 9/24/23-8; plus 1/4; S; Daughter; 6670; Yes; Yes; Id. U-11575 An. 6641

6754; Stirk, Maxine; F; 8/10/11-20; plus 1/4; S; Head; 6671; Yes; Yes; Al. 5977 An. 6639

6755; Stirk, Richard; M; 1886-46; plus 1/4; M; Head; 6672; Yes; Yes; Al. 2667 An. 6642

N.E.:   Stirk, (Keith, Alice) Alice; F; ; Yankton Sioux; 1/4 M; Wife;

6756; Stirk, James L.; M; 6/6/11-20; Sioux; -1/4; S; Son; 6673; Yes; Yes; Al. 5983 An. 6643

6757; Stirk, Richard M.; M; 10/15/13-18; Sioux; -1/4; S; Son; 6675; Yes; Yes; Al. 7453 An. 6645

6758; Stirk, Violet; F; 7/4/15-16; Sioux; -1/4; S; Daughter; 6676; Yes; Yes; Al. 7959 An. 6646

6759; Stirk, Fern Eleanor; F; 7/5/19-12; Sioux; -1/4; S; Daughter; 6677; Yes; Yes; Id. U-10499 An. 6647

6760; Stoldt, Herman; M; 3/9/08-24; plus 1/4; S; Head; 6678; Yes; Yes; Al. 5473 An. 6648

6761; Stoldt, Frank; M; 8/19/10-21; plus 1/4; S; Head; 6679; Yes; Yes; Al. 5474 An. 6649

6762; Stone (Yellow Bird, Jo.), Josephine; F; 1884-48; plus 1/4; M; Head; 6680; Yes; Yes; Al. 2777 An. 6650

6763; Stone, Walter; M; 11/30/13-18; plus1/4; S; Son; 6681; Yes; Yes; Id. U-10501 An. 6651

6764; Stone, Melvin; M; 10/24/17-14; plus1/4; S; Son; 6682; Yes; Yes; Id. U-10502 An. 6652

Census of the   **Pine Ridge**   reservation of the **Pine Ridge, South Dakota** jurisdiction, as of   **April 1** , **1932**, taken by   **James H. McGregor** , Superintendent.

Key: Number; Surname, Given; Sex; Date of Birth-Age at Last Birthday; Tribe (Oglala Sioux, unless stated otherwise); Degree of Blood; Marital Status; Relationship to Head of Family [Last Census Roll Number]; At Jurisdiction Where Enrolled (Yes/No); (If no – Where); Ward (Yes/No, if given); Allotment, Annuity and Identification Numbers (if given).

6765; Stone, Robert; M; 10/9/19-12; plus1/4; S; Son; 6683; Yes; Yes; Id. U-10503 An. 6653

6766; Stone, Emerson F.; M; 3/30/27-4; plus1/4; S; Son; 6684; Yes; Yes; Id. U-12336 An. 6654

6767; Stover, Edward; M; 1877-55; plus 1/4; M; Head; 6685; Yes; Yes; Al. 4636 An. 6654

6768; Stover (Swallow, Susan), Susan; F; 1883-49; plus 1/4; M; Wife; 6686; Yes; Yes; Al. 3227 An. 6655

6769; Stover, Edward; M; 10/20/13-18; plus 1/4; S; Son; 6687; Yes; Yes; Al. 7965 An. 6656

6770; Stover, Ralph W.; M; 3/22/15-17; plus 1/4; S; Son; 6688; Yes; Yes; Al. 7966 An. 6657

6771; Stover, Dorothy P.; F; 3/17/16-16; plus 1/4; S; Daughter; 6693; Yes; Yes; Id. U-10504 An. 6658

6772; Stover, Oliver; M; 2/11/18-14; plus1/4; S; Son; 6689; Yes; Yes; Id. U-10505 An. 6659

6773; Stover, George W.; M; 3/3/19-13; plus1/4; S; Son; 6690; Yes; Yes; Id. U-10506 An. 6660

6774; Stover, Eli; M; 3/10/21-11; plus1/4; S; Son; 6691; Yes; Yes; Id. U-10507 An. 6661

6775; Stover, Loyal E.; M; 1/27/24-8; plus1/4; S; Son; 6692; Yes; Yes; Id. U-11233 An. 6662

6776; Stover, John; M; 1899-33; plus 1/4; M; Head; 6694; Yes; Yes; Al. 4638 An. 6665

6777 Stover, Eugene L.; M; 10/22/27-4; plus1/4; S; Son; 6695; Yes; Yes; Id. U-12467 An. none

6778; Straight Forhead[sic], ---; M; 1858-74; F; M; Head; 6696; Yes; Yes; Al. 4633 An. 6666

6779; Straight Forhead[sic], Alice; F; 1864-68; F; M; Wife; 6697; Yes; Yes; Al. 6902 An. 6667

6780; Strikes Enemy, George; M; 1897-35; F; M; Head; 6698; Yes; Yes; Al. 2446 An. 6668

6781; Strikes Enemy (Running Horse, Alice), Alice; F; 1908-24; plus 1/4; M; Wife; 6699; Yes; Yes; Al. 3590 An. 6669

6782; Strikes Enemy, Leo; M; 6/30/25-6; plus1/4; S; Son; 6700; Yes; Yes; Id. U-11653 An. none

6783; Strikes Enemy, Lucy; F; 10/2/27-4; plus1/4; S; Daughter; 6701; Yes; Yes; Id. U-12432 An. none

Census of the __**Pine Ridge**__ reservation of the __**Pine Ridge, South Dakota**__ jurisdiction, as of __**April 1**__, 19**32**, taken by __**James H. McGregor**__, Superintendent.

Key: Number; Surname, Given; Sex; Date of Birth-Age at Last Birthday; Tribe (Oglala Sioux, unless stated otherwise); Degree of Blood; Marital Status; Relationship to Head of Family [Last Census Roll Number]; At Jurisdiction Where Enrolled (Yes/No); (If no – Where); Ward (Yes/No, if given); Allotment, Annuity and Identification Numbers (if given).

6784; Strikes Enemy, Bernard; M; 3/3/30-2; plus1/4; S; Son; 6702; Yes; Yes; Id. U-13428 An. none

6785; Strikes Plenty, Jefferson; M; 1879-53; F; M; Head; 6703; Yes; Yes; Al. 1377 An. 6671

6786; Strikes Plenty (Holy Bear, Julia), Julia; F; 1889-43; F; M; Wife; 6704; Yes; Yes; Al. 7072 An. 6672

6787; Strikes Plenty, Lillie; F; 8/9/13-18; F; S; Daughter; 6705; Yes; Yes; Al. 6857 An. 6675

6788; Strikes Plenty, Mary; M; 11/2/21-10; F; S; Son; 6706; Yes; Yes; Id. U-10508 An. 6676

6789; Strikes Plenty, Ollie; F; 2/9/10-21; F; S; Head; 6707; Yes; Yes; Al. 7069 An. 6673

6790; Strikes Plenty, Theresa; F; 11/7/30-1; F; S; Daughter; ---; Yes; Yes; Id. U-14072 An. none

6791; Strikes Three Times, ---; M; 1875-57; F; M; Head; 6708; Yes; Yes; Al. 1042 An. 6677

6792; Pleases Herself, ---; F; 1875-57; F; M; Wife; 6709; Yes; Yes; Al. 6940 An. 6678

6793; Strong Talk, ---; M; 1863-69; F; M; Head; 6710; Yes; Yes; Al. 1148 An. 6679
6794; Her Door, ---; F; 1873-79; F; M; Wife; 6711; Yes; Yes; Al. 6111 An. 6680

6795; Sullivan (Cummings, Mary), Mary; F; 1906-26; -1/4; M; Head; 6712; Yes; Yes; Al. 2157 An. 6687

6796; Sullivan, Raymond; M; 5/10/25-6; -1/4; S; Son; 6713; Yes; Yes; Id. U-11654 An. none

6797; Sullivan, Frank J.; M; 8/29/26-5; -1/4; S; Son; 6714; Yes; Yes; Id. U-11747 An. none

6798; Sullivan, William F.; M; 4/3/28-3; -1/4; S; Son; 6715; Yes; Yes; Id. U-12932 An. none

6799; Sun Bear Jesse; M; 1902-30; F; Wd.; Head; 6716; Yes; Yes; Al. 195 An. 6688
6800; Sun Bear, Vincent; M; 1/2/23-9; F; S; Son; 6718; Yes; Yes; Id. U-13068 An. 6690

6801; Sun Bear, Randolph; M; 7/19/27-4; F; S; Son; 6719; Yes; Yes; Id. U-12645 An. none

6802; Sun Bear, Julia; F; 1902-30; F; Wd.; Head; 6717; Yes; Yes; Al. 132 An. 6689
6803; Running Bear, Vernice; F; 3/15/31-1; F; S; Daughter; ---; Yes; Yes; Id. U-14107 An. none

Census of the __Pine Ridge__ reservation of the __Pine Ridge, South Dakota__ jurisdiction, as of __April 1__, 19**32**, taken by __James H. McGregor__, Superintendent.

Key: Number; Surname, Given; Sex; Date of Birth-Age at Last Birthday; Tribe (Oglala Sioux, unless stated otherwise); Degree of Blood; Marital Status; Relationship to Head of Family [Last Census Roll Number]; At Jurisdiction Where Enrolled (Yes/No); (If no – Where); Ward (Yes/No, if given); Allotment, Annuity and Identification Numbers (if given).

6804; Sun Bear, Amelia; F; 7/5/09-22; F; S; Head; 6726; Yes; Yes; Al. 5679 An. 6693

6805; Wounded Horse, Mary Jane; F; 11/29/31-4/12; F; S; Daughter; ---; Yes; Yes; Id. U-14076 An. none

6806; Sun Bear, Oliver; M; 1887-45; F; M; Head; 6720; Yes; Yes; Al. 560 An. 6691

6807; Sun Bear (Black Bird, Rosa), Rosa; F; 1883-49; F; M; Wife; 6723; Yes; Yes; Al. 928 An. 691

6808; Sun Bear, Clarence C.; M; 1/8/11-21; F; S; Son; 6721; Yes; Yes; Id. U-10511 An. 6694

6809; Sun Bear, Clifford; M; 12/6/13-18; F; S; Son; 6722; Yes; Yes; Id. U-10512 An. 6695

6810; Black Bird, Moses; M; 3/10/11-21; F; S; Stepson; 6724; Yes; Yes; Al. 6434 An. 692

6811; Black Bird, Rebecca; F; 6/22/20-11; F; S; Stepdaughter; 6725; Yes; Yes; Id. U-9173 An. 693

6812; Surrounded In Woods, ---; M; 1867-65; F; Wd.; Head; 6727; Yes; Yes; Al. 2029 An. 6698

6813; Surrounded In Woods, Matthew; M; 1908-24; F; M; Head; 6728; Yes; Yes; Al. 4306 An. 6700

6814; Surrounded In Woods (Her Horses, Alice), Alice; F; 11/9/10-21; F; M; Wife; 2858; Yes; Yes; Al. 5819 An. 2835

6815; Surrounded In Woods, Peter; M; 10/26/31-4/12; F; S; Son; ---; Yes; Yes; Id. U-14051 An. none

6816; Swain, Bernice; F; 1907-25; plus 1/4; S; Head; 6729; Yes; Yes; Al. 4069 An. 6702

6817; Swain, Inez; F; 1908-24; plus 1/4; S; Head; 6730; Yes; Yes; Al. 4070 An. 2106

6818; Swallow, Antoine; M; 1888-44; plus 1/4; M; Head; 6731; Yes; Yes; Al. 6177 An. 6703

6819; Swallow (Pourier, Etta), Etta; F; 1884-48; plus 1/4; M; Wife; 6732; Yes; Yes; Al. 3002 An. 6704

6820; Swallow, Leslie; M; 9/21/14-17; plus 1/4; S; Son; 6733; Yes; Yes; Al. 7950 An. 6705

6821; Swallow, Inez E.; F; 4/11/17-14; plus 1/4; S; Daughter; 6734; Yes; Yes; Id. U-10522 An. 6707

6822; Swallow, Helen A.; F; 1/25/25-7; plus 1/4; S; Daughter; 6735; Yes; Yes; Id. U-11553 An. 6708

Census of the **Pine Ridge** reservation of the **Pine Ridge, South Dakota** jurisdiction, as of **April 1**, 19**32**, taken by **James H. McGregor**, Superintendent.

Key: Number; Surname, Given; Sex; Date of Birth-Age at Last Birthday; Tribe (Oglala Sioux, unless stated otherwise); Degree of Blood; Marital Status; Relationship to Head of Family [Last Census Roll Number]; At Jurisdiction Where Enrolled (Yes/No); (If no – Where); Ward (Yes/No, if given); Allotment, Annuity and Identification Numbers (if given).

6823; Swallow, Lois Regina; F; 5/26/21-10; plus 1/4; S; Daughter; 6736; Yes; Yes; Id. U-10524 An. 6707

6824; Swallow, Benjamin; M; 1894-38; plus 1/4; M; Head; 6737; Yes; Yes; Al. 3216 An. 6709

6825; Swallow (Brown, Josephine), Josephine; F; 1898-34; -1/4; M; Wife; 6738; Yes; Yes; Al. 4452 An. 6710

6826; Swallow, Wilma A.; F; 6/9/21-10; -1/4; S; Daughter; 6739; Yes; Yes; Id. U-10521 An. 6711

6827; Swallow, Wildene; F; 11/17/23-8; -1/4; S; Daughter; 6740; Yes; Yes; Id. U-11156 An. 6712

6828; Swallow, Roylene; F; 11/17/23-8; -1/4; S; Daughter; 6741; Yes; Yes; Id. U-11157 An. 6713

6829; Swallow, Melba; F; 12/21/27-4; -1/4; S; Daughter; 6742; Yes; Yes; Id. U-12599 An. none

6830; Swallow, Charles; M; 1905-27; plus 1/4; M; Head; 6743; Yes; Yes; Al. 3245 An. 6714

6831; Swallow (Monroe, Zouie), Zouie; F; 1898-34; plus 1/4; M; Wife; 6744; Yes; Yes; Al. 2322 An. 4554

6832; Swallow, Bernice; F; 10/1/26-5; plus 1/4; S; Daughter; 6745; Yes; Yes; Id. U-12154 An. none

6833; Swallow, Marie; F; 9/26/28-3; plus 1/4; S; Daughter; 6746; Yes; Yes; Id. U-12840 An. none

6834; Swallow, Charles W.; M; 6/30/30-1; plus 1/4; S; Son; 6747; Yes; Yes; Id. U-13616 An. none

6835; Swallow, Daniel; M; 1900-32; plus 1/4; M; Head; 6748; Yes; Yes; Al. 3244 An. 6715

6836; Swallow (Cuny, Eva), Eva; F; 1900-32; plus 1/4; M; Wife; 6749; Yes; Yes; Al. 2913 An. 6716

6837; Swallow, Louis; M; 6/10/19-12; plus 1/4; S; Son; 6750; Yes; Yes; Id. U-10517 An. 6717

6838; Swallow, Marcella; F; 12/5/20-11; plus 1/4; S; Daughter; 6751; Yes; Yes; Id. U-13046 An. 6718

6839; Swallow, Lucille; F; 1/4/24-8; plus 1/4; S; Daughter; 6752; Yes; Yes; Id. U-11690 An. none

6840; Swallow, Lawrence; M; 12/24/27-4; plus 1/4; S; Son; 6753; Yes; Yes; Id. U-12867 An. none

6841; Swallow, Oliver W.; M; 12/22/29-2; plus 1/4; S; Son; 6754; Yes; Yes; Id. U-13437 An. none

6842; Swallow, Armine; F; 12/3/25-6; plus 1/4; S; Daughter; 6755; Yes; Yes; Id. U-12866 An. none

Census of the **Pine Ridge** reservation of the **Pine Ridge, South Dakota** jurisdiction, as of **April 1**, 1932, taken by **James H. McGregor**, Superintendent.

Key: Number; Surname, Given; Sex; Date of Birth-Age at Last Birthday; Tribe (Oglala Sioux, unless stated otherwise); Degree of Blood; Marital Status; Relationship to Head of Family [Last Census Roll Number]; At Jurisdiction Where Enrolled (Yes/No); (If no – Where); Ward (Yes/No, if given); Allotment, Annuity and Identification Numbers (if given).

6843; Swallow, Eli; M; 5/5/98-34; plus 1/4; S; Head; 6756; Yes; Yes; Al. 3217 An. 6719

6844; Swallow, Hattie; F; 1878-54; plus 1/4; Wd.; Head; 6757; Yes; Yes; Al. 2161 An. 6720

6845; Stover, Sarah Grace; F; 3/29/18-14; plus 1/4; S; Daughter; 6758; Yes; Yes; Id. U-10518 An. 6721

6846; Swallow, Mary; F; 1891-41; plus 1/4; S; Head; 6759; Yes; Yes; Al. 3215 An. 6724

6847; Swallow, Oliver; M; 1870-62; plus 1/4; M; Head; 6760; Yes; Yes; Al. 3241 An. 6784

6848; Swallow (Gillispie, Bettie), Bettie; F; 1880-52; plus 1/4; M; Wife; 6761; Yes; Yes; Al. 3242 An. 6785

6849; Swallow, John; M; 6/5/11-20; plus 1/4; S; Son; 6762; Yes; Yes; Al. 6193 An. 6727

6850; Swallow, Edna; F; 9/18/14-17; plus 1/4; S; Daughter; 6763; Yes; Yes; Id. U-10514 An. 6728

6851; Swallow, Josephine; F; 6/26/16-15; plus 1/4; S; Daughter; 6764; Yes; Yes; Id. U-10515 An. 6729

6852; Swallow, Lizzie; F; 3/1/19-13; plus 1/4; S; Daughter; 6765; Yes; Yes; Id. U-10516 An. 6730

6853; Swallow, Woodrow W.; M; 1/5/24-8; plus 1/4; S; Son; 6766; Yes; Yes; Id. U-11607 An. 6731

6854; Swallow, Richard; M; 1900-32; F; M; Head; 6767; Yes; Yes; Al. 398 An. 6732

N.E.: ~~Swallow, (White Feather, Mary) Mary; F; ------; Rosebud Sioux; F; M; Wife;~~

6855; Swallow, Joseph; M; 8/6/30-1; Sioux; F; S; Son; ---; Yes; Yes; Id. U-13819 An. none

6856; Swallow, Rosa; F; 1904-28; -1/4; S; Head; 6768; Yes; Yes; Al. 3239 An. 6733
6857; Sitting Up, Theresa; F; 1/20/30-2; plus 1/4; S; Daughter; 6769; Yes; Yes; Id. U-13429 An. none

6858; Swallow, Stephen; M; 1879-53; F; M; Head; 6770; Yes; Yes; Al. 397 An. 6734

6859; Swallow (No data), Susie; F; 1879-53; F; M; Wife; 6771; Yes; Yes; Al. 2416 An. 6735

6860; Swallow, John; M; 12/14/18-13; F; S; Son; 6772; Yes; Yes; Id. U-10520 An. 6737

Census of the __Pine Ridge__ reservation of the __Pine Ridge, South Dakota__ jurisdiction, as of __April 1__, 19**32**, taken by __James H. McGregor__, Superintendent.

Key: Number; Surname, Given; Sex; Date of Birth-Age at Last Birthday; Tribe (Oglala Sioux, unless stated otherwise); Degree of Blood; Marital Status; Relationship to Head of Family [Last Census Roll Number]; At Jurisdiction Where Enrolled (Yes/No); (If no – Where); Ward (Yes/No, if given); Allotment, Annuity and Identification Numbers (if given).

6861; Swallow, Davis; M; 3/29/28-4; F; S; Son; 6773; Yes; Yes; Id. U-12933 An. none

6862; Swallow, Willie; M; 1886-46; plus 1/4; M; Head; 6774; Yes; Yes; Al. 3237 An. 6738

6863; Swallow (Pourier, Helena), Helena; F; 1886-46; -1/4; M; Wife; 6775; Yes; Yes; Al. 3238 An. 6739

6864; Swallow, Wilbur J.; M; 9/4/11-20; -1/4; S; Son; 6776; Yes; Yes; Al. 7629 An. 6742

6865; Swallow, Marie; F; 2/10/16-16; -1/4; S; Daughter; 6777; Yes; Yes; Id. U-10525 An. 6743

6866; Swallow, Carl L.; M; 3/17/20-12; -1/4; S; Son; 6778; Yes; Yes; Id. U-10526 An. 6744

6867; Swallow, Lloyd W.; M; 7/10/25-6; -1/4; S; Son; 6779; Yes; Yes; Id. U-11694 An. none

6868; Swallow, Walter; M; 5/25/08-23; -1/4; M; Head; 6780; Yes; Yes; Al. 3240 An. 6740

6869; Swallow (Swallow, Louisa), Louisa; F; 1/30/15-17; plus 1/4; M; Wife; 4867; Yes; Yes; Id. U-10091 An. 4848

6870; Swallow, Thelma D.; F; 3/17/32-1/12; plus 1/4; S; Daughter; ---; Yes; Yes; Id. U-14137 An. none

6871; Swanson (Lang, Helen), Helen; F; 4/17/04-27; -1/4; M; Head; 6781; No; Rapid City, city, Pennington, S.D.; Yes; Al. 3706 An. 6745

6872; Swanson, Evelyn; F; 6/20/23-8; -1/4; S; Daughter; 6782; No; Ditto; ; Yes; Id. U-12750 An. none

6873; Swanson, Oliver H.; M; 10/25/24-7; -1/4; S; Son; 6783; No; Ditto; ; Yes; Id. U-12751 An. none

6874; Swanson (Glick, Ione), Ione; F; 1901-31; -1/4; M; Head; 6784; No; San Bernardino, Cal.; Yes; Al. 3967 An. 6746

6875; Swanson, Keith E.; M; 1/13/21-11; -1/4; S; Son; 6785; No; Ditto; ; Yes; Id. U-9583 An. 6747

6876; Swanson (Lang, Mabel), Mabel; F; 3/30/08-24; -1/4; M; Head; 6786; No; Rapid City, city, Pennington, S.D.; Yes; Al. 3708 An. 3679

6877; Swanson, Ruth L.; F; 9/9/26-5; -1/4; S; Daughter; 6787; No; Ditto; ; Yes; Id. U-12749 An. none

6878; Swanson, Mary A.; F; 5/18/29-2; -1/4; S; Daughter; 6788; No; Ditto; ; Yes; Id. U-13430 An. none

Census of the ___Pine Ridge___ reservation of the ___Pine Ridge, South Dakota___ jurisdiction, as of ___April 1___, 19**32**, taken by ___James H. McGregor___, Superintendent.

Key: Number; Surname, Given; Sex; Date of Birth-Age at Last Birthday; Tribe (Oglala Sioux, unless stated otherwise); Degree of Blood; Marital Status; Relationship to Head of Family [Last Census Roll Number]; At Jurisdiction Where Enrolled (Yes/No); (If no – Where); Ward (Yes/No, if given); Allotment, Annuity and Identification Numbers (if given).

6879; Sweat, Thelma; F; 1/26/20-12; plus 1/4; S; Alone; 6789; No; Edgemont, town, Fall River, S.D.; Yes; Id. U-10527 An. 6749

6880; Swick (Dripping, Susie), Susie; F; 1883-49; plus 1/4; M; Head; 6790; Yes; Yes; Al. 6095 An. 6750

6881; Swick, Robert; M; 12/29/18-13; plus 1/4; S; Son; 6791; Yes; Yes; Id. U-9455 An. 6753

6882; Swick, Ethel; F; 12/2/20-11; plus 1/4; S; Daughter; 6792; Yes; Yes; Id. U-9456 An. 6754

6883; Swick, Henry; M; 12/10/22-9; plus 1/4; S; Son; 6793; Yes; Yes; Id. U-12048 An. 6755

6884; Swick, Joseph; M; 11/24/31-4/12; plus 1/4; S; Son; ---; Yes; Yes; Id. U-13977 An. none

6885; Dripping, Maude; F; 1/31/16-16; plus 1/4; S; Daughter; 6794; Yes; Yes; Id. U-9454 An. 6752

6886; Swift Bird, Charles; M; 1899-33; plus 1/4; S; Head; 6795; Yes; Yes; Al. 273 An. 6757

6887; Swift Bird, George; M; 1896-36; plus 1/4; M; Head; 6796; Yes; Yes; Al. 144 An. 6758

6888; Swift Bird (Red Star, Stella), Stella; F; 1897-35; F; M; Wife; 6797; Yes; Yes; Al. 2664 An. 6759

6889; Swift Bird, Francis; M; 7/7/17-14; plus 1/4; S; Son; 6798; Yes; Yes; Id. U-10528 An. 6760

6890; Swift Bird, Cornelius; M; 2/13/19-13; plus 1/4; S; Son; 6799; Yes; Yes; Id. U-10529 An. 6761

6891; Swift Bird, Joseph; M; 1/16/21-11; plus 1/4; S; Son; 6800; Yes; Yes; Id. U-10530 An. 6762

6892; Swift Bird, Peter; M; 2/19/23-9; plus 1/4; S; Son; 6801; Yes; Yes; Id. U-13075 An. 6763

6893; Swift Bird, Julia; F; 5/27/25-6; plus 1/4; S; Daughter; 6802; Yes; Yes; Id. U-12269 An. none

6894; Swift Bird, George Jr.; M; 7/4/27-4; plus 1/4; S; Son; 6803; Yes; Yes; Id. U-12371 An. none

6895; Swift Bird, Leo; M; 9/17/29-2; plus 1/4; S; Son; 6804; Yes; Yes; Id. U-13274 An. none

6896; Swimmer, John; M; 1875-57; F; M; Head; 6803[sic]; Yes; Yes; Al. 2655 An. 6765

6897; Swimmer (No data), Nellie; F; 1883-49; plus 1/4; M; Wife; 6804[sic]; Yes; Yes; Al. 4368 An. 6766

Census of the __Pine Ridge__ reservation of the __Pine Ridge, South Dakota__ jurisdiction, as of __April 1__, 19**32**, taken by __James H. McGregor__, Superintendent.

Key: Number; Surname, Given; Sex; Date of Birth-Age at Last Birthday; Tribe (Oglala Sioux, unless stated otherwise); Degree of Blood; Marital Status; Relationship to Head of Family [Last Census Roll Number]; At Jurisdiction Where Enrolled (Yes/No); (If no – Where); Ward (Yes/No, if given); Allotment, Annuity and Identification Numbers (if given).

6898; Swimmer, Gustavus; M; 12/1/18-13; plus 1/4; S; Son; 6807; Yes; Yes; Id. U-10531 An. 6767
6899; Swimmer, Keva; F; 5/9/22-9; plus 1/4; S; Daughter; 6808; Yes; Yes; Id. U-10983 An. 6768

6900; Swimmer, Joseph; M; 1904-28; plus 1/4; S; Head; 6809; Yes; Yes; Al. 6785 An. 6769

N.E.: Swimmer, Thomas; M; --------; Rosebud Sioux; F; M; Head;
6901; Swimmer (Star, Lucy), Lucy; F; 1894-38; plus 1/4; M; Wife; 6810; Yes; Yes; Al. 1779 An. 6611
6902; Swimmer, Wallace; M; 3/25/31-1; Sioux; plus 1/4; S; Son; 0000; Yes; Yes; Id. U-138201 An. none
6903; Red Kettle, Lydia; F; 7/9/15-16; plus 1/4; S; Stepdaughter; 6811; Yes; Yes; Id. U-10494 An. 6612

6904; Tail, Charles; M; 1901-31; F; M; Head; 6812; Yes; Yes; Al. 389 An. 6771
6905; Tail (Ghost Bear), Rosa; F; 11/4/10-21; F; M; Wife; 6813; Yes; Yes; Al. 5739 An. 2441
6906; Tail, Cleveland; M; 8/21/31-7/12; F; S; Son; ---; Yes; Yes; U-13907

6907; Tail, Daniel; M; 1895-37; F; M; Head; 6814; Yes; Yes; Al. 387 An. 6772
6908; Tail (Grass), Jennie; F; 1894-38; F; M; Wife; 6815; Yes; Yes; Al. 7674 An. 6774
6909; Tail, Irving; M; 4/10/23-8; F; S; Son; 6816; Yes; Yes; Id. U-13040 An. 6775

6910; Tail, Jackson; M; 1897-35; F; M; Head; 6817; Yes; Yes; Al. 388 An. 6778
6911; Tail (Young Bear), Helen; F; 10/14/07-24; F; M; Wife; 6818; Yes; Yes; Al. 7392 An. 4793
6912; Tail, Edalbert; M; 4/10/27-4; F; S; Son; 6819; Yes; Yes; Id. U-12296 An. none
6913; Tail, Lula; F; 1/12/31-1; F; S; Daughter; 6820; Yes; Yes; Id. U-13674 An. none

6914; Tail, Richard; M; 1872-60; F; M; Head; 6821; Yes; Yes; Al. 386 An. 6783
6915; Tail (Big Owl), Lucy; F; 1868-64; F; M; Wife; 6822; Yes; Yes; Al. 6851 An. 6784

6916; Takes Enemy (no data), Laura; F; 1867-65; F; Wd.; Head; 6823; Yes; Yes; Al. 4359 An. 6789

N.E.: Takes The Horse, Joseph; M; --------; Cheyenne Sioux; M; Head;
6917; Takes The Horse (Black Crow), Ellen; F; 1905-27; F; M; Wife; 6824; Yes; Yes; Al. 2378 An. 6790

Census of the __Pine Ridge__ reservation of the __Pine Ridge, South Dakota__ jurisdiction, as of __April 1__, 19**32**, taken by __James H. McGregor__, Superintendent.

Key: Number; Surname, Given; Sex; Date of Birth-Age at Last Birthday; Tribe (Oglala Sioux, unless stated otherwise); Degree of Blood; Marital Status; Relationship to Head of Family [Last Census Roll Number]; At Jurisdiction Where Enrolled (Yes/No); (If no – Where); Ward (Yes/No, if given); Allotment, Annuity and Identification Numbers (if given).

6918; Takes The Horse, Nelson; M; 1/27/25-7; F; S; Son; 6825; Yes; Yes; Id. U-11452 An. 6791

6919; Takes The Horse, Max; M; 1/13/30-2; F; S; Son; 6826; Yes; Yes; Id. U-13522 An. none

6920; Takes Too Much, ---; F; 1850-82; F; Wd; Head; 6827; Yes; Yes; Al. 4422 An. 2027

6921; Takes War Bonnet, Oscar; M; 1891-41; F; M; Head; 6828; Yes; Yes; Al. 1694 An. 6792

6922; Takes War Bonnet (Gets There First), Jennie; F; 1895-37; F; M; Wife; 6829; Yes; Yes; Al. 1592 An. 6793

6923; Takes War Bonnet, Rebecca; F; 5/15/14-17; F; S; Daughter; 6830; Yes; Yes; Id. U-10537 An. 6794

6924; Takes War Bonnet, Leo; M; 3/4/30-2; F; S; Son; 6831; Yes; Yes; Id. U-13431 An. none

6925; Takes War Bonnet, Lottie; F; 6/21/31-9/12; F; S; Daughter; ---; Yes; Yes; U-13908

6926; Tall, Noah; M; 1891-41; F; M; Head; 6832; Yes; Yes; Al. 4414 An. 6800
6927; Tall (Shield), Mary; F; 1903-29; F; M; Wife; 6836; Yes; Yes; Al. 3977 An. 6188
6928; Tall, Verne; M; 9/14/16-15; F; S; Son; 6833; Yes; Yes; Id. U-10541 An. 6801
6929; Tall, Richard; M; 4/19/19-12; F; S; Son; 6834; Yes; Yes; Id. U-10542 An. 6802
6930; Tall, Margaret; F; 8/18/21-10; F; S; Daughter; 6835; Yes; Yes; Id. U-11181 An. 6803
6931; Janis, Hermos; M; 2/5/28-4; F; S. Son; 6837; Yes; Yes; Id. U-12478 An. none

6932; Tanner, Josephine; F; 5/4/17-14; Plus 1/4; S; Alone; 6838; No; Sturgis, town, Meade, S.D.; Yes; Id. U-10543 An. 6804

N.E.: Tapia, Richard; M; ------; Oglala Sioux; 1/4; Wd; Head;
6933; Tapia, Rita; F; 1/27/21-11; 1/4; S; Dauthter[sic]; 6839; Yes; Yes; Id. U-10548 An. 6806
6934; Tapia, Delvina; F; 5/21/22-9; 1/4; S; Daughter; 6840; Yes; Yes; Id. U-10943 An. 6807
6935; Tapia, Joseph; M; 3/18/24-8; 1/4; S; Son; 6841; Yes; Yes; Id. U-11240 An. 6808
6936; Tapia, Louis; M; 3/8/26-6; 1/4; S; Son; 6842; Yes; Yes; Id. U-11923 An. none

Census of the __Pine Ridge__ reservation of the __Pine Ridge, South Dakota__ jurisdiction, as of __April 1__, 19**32**, taken by __James H. McGregor__, Superintendent.

Key: Number; Surname, Given; Sex; Date of Birth-Age at Last Birthday; Tribe (Oglala Sioux, unless stated otherwise); Degree of Blood; Marital Status; Relationship to Head of Family [Last Census Roll Number]; At Jurisdiction Where Enrolled (Yes/No); (If no – Where); Ward (Yes/No, if given); Allotment, Annuity and Identification Numbers (if given).

6937; Tapia, Mercy; F; 3/9/27-5; 1/4; S; Daughter; 6843; Yes; Yes; Id. U-12271 An. none

6938; Tapia, Richard; M; 8/7/29-2; 1/4; S; Son; 6844; Yes; Yes; Id. U-13275 An. none

6939; Tapia (Allman), Julia; F; 10/13/07-24; plus 1/4; M; Wife; 93; Yes; Yes; Al. 5713 An. 91

6940; Tapia, Joseph; M; 1872-60; 1/4; M; Head; 6845; Yes; No; Al. 3973 An. 6809

6941; Tapia, Mannelita; F; 10/30/11-20; 1/4; S; Daughter; 6846; Yes; Yes; Id. U-10544 An. 6811

6942; Tapia, Talis; M; 1879-53; 1/4; M; Head; 6847; Yes; No; Al. 3971 An. 6812

6943; Tapia, Mary; F; 12/25/14-18; 1/4; S; Daughter; 6848; Yes; Yes; Id. U-10546 An. 6813

6944; Tapia, Agnes; F; 1/31/19-13; 1/4; S; Daughter; 6849; Yes; Yes; Id. U-10547 An. 6814

6945; Tapia, Cecelia; F; 7/20/21-10; 1/4; S; Daughter; 6850; Yes; Yes; Id. U-10875 An. 6815

6946; Tapia, Nelson; M; 5/25/23-8; 1/4; S; Son; 6851; Yes; Yes; Id. U-14012 An. 6816

6947; Tapia, Romania; F; 1/1/26-6; 1/4; S; Daughter; 6852; Yes; Yes; Id. U-11958 An. none

6948; Tapia, Martha; F; 1/14/31-1; 1/4; S; Daughter; 6853; Yes; Yes; Id. U-13675 An. none

6949; Tapia, Beatrice; F; 2/14/28-4; 1/4; S; Daughter; ---; Yes; Yes; U-13857

6950; Taylor (Thompson), Julia; F; 1904-28; -1/4; M; Head; 6854; Yes; Yes; Al. 457 An. 6851

6951; Taylor, Sarah; F; 2/5/28-4; -1/4; S; Daughter; 6855; Yes; Yes; Id. U-12934 An. none

6952; Taylor, Alta J; F; 4/8/29-2; -1/4; S; Daughter; 6856; Yes; Yes; Id. U-13250 An. none

6953; Tells His Name, George; M; 1901-31; F; M; Head; 6858; Yes; Yes; Al. 661 An. 6817

6954; Tells His Name (Black Bear), Rosa; F; 1908-24; F; M; Wife; 6859; Yes; Yes; Al. 4964 An. 634

6955; Tender, ---; M; 1850-82; F; Wd; Head; 6860; Yes; Yes; Al. 4187 An. 6819

6956; Ten Fingers, ---; M; 1861-71; F; M; Head; 6861; Yes; Yes; Al. 2834 An. 6820

6957; Ten Fingers (no data), Ella; F; 1868-64; F; M; Wife; 6862; Yes; Yes; Al. 2935 An. 6821

Census of the **Pine Ridge** reservation of the **Pine Ridge, South Dakota** jurisdiction, as of **April 1**, **1932**, taken by **James H. McGregor**, Superintendent.

Key: Number; Surname, Given; Sex; Date of Birth-Age at Last Birthday; Tribe (Oglala Sioux, unless stated otherwise); Degree of Blood; Marital Status; Relationship to Head of Family [Last Census Roll Number]; At Jurisdiction Where Enrolled (Yes/No); (If no – Where); Ward (Yes/No, if given); Allotment, Annuity and Identification Numbers (if given).

6958; Ten Fingers, Charles; M; 1897-35; F; S; Head; 6863; Yes; Yes; Al. 6267 An. 6823

6959; Ten Fingers, Asa; M; 1891-41; F; M; Head; 6864; Yes; Yes; Al. 6266 An. 6824

6960; Ten Fingers (Broken Nose), Lucy; F; 1900-32; F; M; Wife; 6865; Yes; Yes; Al. 6530 An. 1037

6961; Ten Fingers, Evelyn; F; 6/1/30-1; F; S; Daughter; 6866; Yes; Yes; Id. U-13534 An. none

6962; Ten Fingers, Helen; F; 11/19/31-4/12; F; S; Daughter; ---; Yes; Yes; Id. U-14110

6963; Ten Fingers, Henry; M; 1881-51; F; M; Head; 6867; Yes; Yes; Al. 6265 An. 6826

6964; Ten Fingers (Big Boy), Annie; F; 1881-51; F; M; Wife; 6868; Yes; Yes; Al. 6279 An. 6827

6965; Ten Fingers, Leroy; M; 5/17/09-22; F; S; Son; 6869; Yes; Yes; Al. 6280 An. 6828

6966; Ten Fingers, Alfred; M; 7/20/13-18; F; S; Son; 6870; Yes; Yes; Al. 7534 An. 6830

6967; Ten Fingers, Lena; F; 3/22/17-15; F; S; Daughter; 6871; Yes; Yes; Id. U-10550 An. 6832

6968; Ten Fingers, Eliza; F; 7/12/22-9; F; S; Daughter; 6872; Yes; Yes; Id. U-11051 An. 6833

6969; Ten Fingers, Nancy; F; 8/20/26-5; F; S; Daughter; 6873; Yes; Yes; Id. U-12124 An. none

6970; Ten Fingers, Frances; F; 9/8/11-20; F; S; Head; 6874; Yes; Yes; Al. 6281 An. 6829

6971; Ten Fingers, Isabelle; F; 1906-26; F; S; Head; 6875; Yes; Yes; Al. 2836 An. 6834

6972; Ten Fingers, Walter; M; 1888-44; F; M; Head; 6876; Yes; Yes; Al. 7868 An. 6835

6973; Ten Fingers (Gillispie), Emma; F; 1894-38; plus 1/4; M; Wife; 6881; Yes; Yes; Al. 3249 An. 795

6974; Ten Fingers, Ida; F; 7/20/13-19; plus 1/4; S; Daughter; 6877; Yes; Yes; Al. 7473 An. 6838

6975; Ten Fingers, Ruth; F; 10/19/19-12; F; S; Daughter; 6878; Yes; Yes; Id. U-10552 An. 6839

6976; Ten Fingers, Walter Jr.; M; 5/9/21-10; F; S; Son; 6879; Yes; Yes; Id. U-10553 An. 6840

Census of the __Pine Ridge__ reservation of the __Pine Ridge, South Dakota__ jurisdiction, as of __April 1__, 19**32**, taken by __James H. McGregor__, Superintendent.

Key: Number; Surname, Given; Sex; Date of Birth-Age at Last Birthday; Tribe (Oglala Sioux, unless stated otherwise); Degree of Blood; Marital Status; Relationship to Head of Family [Last Census Roll Number]; At Jurisdiction Where Enrolled (Yes/No); (If no – Where); Ward (Yes/No, if given); Allotment, Annuity and Identification Numbers (if given).

6977; Ten Fingers, Nevill; M; 9/16/23-8; F; S; Son; 6880; Yes; Yes; Id. U-11101 An. 6841

6978; Flood, Elizabeth; F; 9/15/14-17; F; S; S. Daughter; 6882; Yes; Yes; Id. U-9533 An. 796

6979; Flood, Etta; F; 3/27/22-10; F; S; S. Daughter; 6883; Yes; Yes; Id. U-11059 An. 797

6980; Ten Fingers, Rosa; F; 7/20/11-20; 1/4; S; Head; 6884; Yes; Yes; Al. 7472 An. 6837

6981; Terkeldsen? (Brown), Anita; F; 1901-31; 1/4; M; Head; 6885; Yes; Yes; Al. 4022 An. 6842

6982; Terkeldsen, Geraldine; F; 1/27/23-9; -1/4; S; Daughter; 6886; Yes; Yes; Id. U-13025 An. 6843

6983; Terkeldsen, Calvin; M; 6/9/21-10; -1/4; S; Son; 6887; Yes; Yes; Id. U-12272 An. none

6984; Terkeldsen, Dorothy; F; 5/31/24-7; -1/4; S; Daughter; 6888; Yes; Yes; Id. U-12274 An. none

6985; Terkeldsen, Dahlman W; M; 12/10/25-6; -1/4; S; Son; 6889; Yes; Yes; Id. U-12273 An. none

6986; Terkeldsen, Thos. G.; M; 6/24/28-3; -1/4; S; Son; 6890; Yes; Yes; Id. U-13786 An. none

6987; Terkeldsen, Raymond; M; 12/27/30-1; -1/4; S; Son; 6891; Yes; Yes; Id. U-13787 An. none

N.E.: Thompson, George; M; ------; Lower Brule Sioux; 1/4; M; Head;

6988; Thompson (Ladeaux), Alice; F; 1878-54; 1/4; M; Wife; 5325; Yes; Yes; Al. 1991 An. 5280

6989; Randall, Stella; F; 5/29/17-14; 1/4; S; S. Daughter; 5327; Yes; Yes; Id. U-10192 An. 5283

6990; Randall, Jessie; F; 12/20/20-11; 1/4; S; S. Daughter; 5328; Yes; Yes; Id. U-10193 An. 5284

N.E.: Thompson, Thomas; M; ------; Rosebud Sioux; F; Wd; Head;

6991; Thompson, Angelic; F; 10/5/23-8; plus 1/4; S; Daughter; 6893; Yes; Yes; Id. U-11100 An. 6849

6992; Thunder Hawk, Andrew; M; 2/18/23-9; 1/4; S; Ward; 6894; Yes; Yes; Id. U-9334 An. 7943

6993; Thompson, Francis; M; 1907-25; -1/4; S; Head; 6895; Yes; Yes; Al. 6677 An. 6850

6994; Thompson (no data), Sarah; F; 1883-49; plus1/4; M; Head; 6896; Yes; Yes; Al. 312 An. 6853

Census of the _____**Pine Ridge**_____ reservation of the_**Pine Ridge, South Dakota**_ jurisdiction, as of_____**April 1**_____, 19**32,** taken by_____**James H. McGregor**_____, Superintendent.

Key: Number; Surname, Given; Sex; Date of Birth-Age at Last Birthday; Tribe (Oglala Sioux, unless stated otherwise); Degree of Blood; Marital Status; Relationship to Head of Family [Last Census Roll Number]; At Jurisdiction Where Enrolled (Yes/No); (If no – Where); Ward (Yes/No, if given); Allotment, Annuity and Identification Numbers (if given).

6995; Thompson, Joseph; M; 1/3/14-18; -1/4; S; Son; 6897; Yes; Yes; Id. U-10554 An. 6857

6996; Thompson, Ollie; F; 1/3/14-18; -1/4; S; Daughter; 6898; Yes; Yes; Id. U-10555 An. 6858

6997; Thompson, Clarence; M; 3/3/18-14; -1/4; S; Son; 6899; Yes; Yes; Id. U-10556 An. 6859

6998; Thompson, Sarah J; F; 4/26/20-11; -1/4; S; Daughter; 6900; Yes; Yes; Id. U-10557 An. 6860

6999; Thompson, Evaline; F; 4/11/22-9; -1/4; S; Daughter; 6901; Yes; Yes; Id. U-11094 An. 6861

7000; Thompson, Oliver; M; 1/24/24-8; -1/4; S; Son; 6902; Yes; Yes; Id. U-12893 An. none

7001; Thompson, William; M; 3/23/11-21; -1/4; S; Head; 6903; Yes; Yes; Al. 6680 An. 6856

7002; Three Stars, Mary; F; 4/13/11-20; plus1/4; S; Head; 6905; Yes; Yes; Id. U-10559 An. 6863

7003; Three Stars, Clarence Jr.; M; 1899-33; 1/4; M; Head; 6906; Yes; Yes; Al. 2063 An. 6864

7004; Three Stars, Bessie; F; 9/5/28-3; 1/4; S; Daughter; 6907; Yes; Yes; Id. U-12815 An. none

7005; Three Stars, Jennie; F; 8/26/29-2; 1/4; S; Daughter; 6908; Yes; Yes; Id. U-13356 An. none

7006; Three Stars, Paul; M; 1895-37; 1/4; M; Head; 6909; Yes; Yes; Al. 2061 An. 6866

7007; Three Stars (Red Horse), Sarah; F; 1893-39; F; M; Wife; 6910; Yes; Yes; Al. 2025 An. 6867

7008; Three Stars, Ruth; F; 11/25/17-14; plus 1/4; S; Daughter; 6911; Yes; Yes; Id. U-10560 An. 6868

7009; Three Stars, Louisa; F; 8/9/23-8; 1/4; S; Daughter; 6912; Yes; Yes; Id. U-11171 An. 6870

7010; Three Stars, Peter; M; 2/11/27-5; 1/4; S; Son; 6913; Yes; Yes; Id. U-12230 An. none

7011; Three Stars, Sophia; F; 6/20/92-39; 1/4; S; Head; 6914; No; Canton Hospital, S.D.; Yes; Al. 2060 An. 6871

7012; Three Stars, Thomas; M; 1905-27; 1/4; M; Head; 6915; Yes; Yes; Al. 6872 An. 4976

Census of the   **Pine Ridge**   reservation of the **Pine Ridge, South Dakota**
jurisdiction, as of   **April 1**   , 19**32**, taken by   **James H. McGregor**   ,
Superintendent.

Key: Number; Surname, Given; Sex; Date of Birth-Age at Last Birthday; Tribe (Oglala Sioux, unless stated otherwise); Degree of Blood; Marital Status; Relationship to Head of Family [Last Census Roll Number]; At Jurisdiction Where Enrolled (Yes/No); (If no – Where); Ward (Yes/No, if given); Allotment, Annuity and Identification Numbers (if given).

7013; Thunder Beard (No data), Alice; F; 1853-79; F; Wd; Head; 6916; Yes; Yes; Al. 3292 An. 6874

7014; Thunder Bull, Charles Jr.; M; 1890-42; F; M; Head; 6917; Yes; Yes; Al. 3987 An. 6877

7015; Thunder Bull (Plenty Bird), Nancy; F; 1888-44; F; M; Wife; 6918; Yes; Yes; Al. 7250 An. 6878

7016; Thunder Bull, Thomas (Inez); M; 5/22/16-15; F; M[sic]; Son; 6919; Yes; Yes; Id. U-10562 An. 6879

7017; Thunder Bull, Shield; M; 1879-53; F; M; Head; 6920; Yes; Yes; Al. 5980 An. 6882

7018; Thunder Bull (no data), Josephine; F; 1882-50; plus 1/4; M; Wife; 6921; Yes; Yes; Al. 2133 An. 6883

7019; Thunder Bull, Veronica; F; 10/5/12-19; 1/4; S; Daughter; 6922; Yes; Yes; Id. U-10565 An. 6886

7020; Thunder Bull, Vincent; M; 6/29/16-15; 1/4; S; Son; 6923; Yes; Yes; Id. U-10566 An. 6887

7021; Thunder Bull, Grace; F; 5/5/19-12; 1/4; S; Daughter; 6924; Yes; Yes; Id. U-10567 An. 6888

7022; Thunder Bull, Alma; F; 3/23/23-9; 1/4; S; Daughter; 6925; Yes; Yes; Id. U-13022 An. 6889

7023; Thunder Bull, Mildred; F; 9/26/27-4; 1/4; S; Daughter; 6926; Yes; Yes; Id. U-12533 An. none

7024; Thunder Club, Paul; M; 1869-63; F; M; Head; 6927; Yes; Yes; Al. 6591 An. 6890

7025; Holy Lodge, ---; F; 1874-58; F; M; Wife; 6928; Yes; Yes; Al. 7636 An. 6891

7026; Thunder Club, Tobin; M; 1874-58; F; Wd; Head; 6929; Yes; Yes; Al. 6590 An. 6892

7027; Thunder Hawk, (Thomas); M; 1869-63; F; M; Head; 6930; Yes; Yes; Al. 1890 An. 6894

7028; Thunder Hawk (Sitting Up), Emma; F; 1893-39; F; M; Wife; 6931; Yes; Yes; Al. 3785 An. 6895

7029; Thunder Hawk, Romero; M; 4/10/24-7; F; S; Son; 6932; Yes; Yes; Id. U-11405 An. 6896

7030; Thunder Hawk, Rebecca; F; 7/12/27-4; F; S; Daughter; 6933; Yes; Yes; Id. U-12378 An. none

7031; Thunder Hawk, Francis; M; 2/10/30-2; F; S; Son; 6934; Yes; Yes; Id. U-13395 An. none

Census of the ___Pine Ridge___ reservation of the ___Pine Ridge, South Dakota___ jurisdiction, as of ___April 1___, 19**32**, taken by ___James H. McGregor___, Superintendent.

Key: Number; Surname, Given; Sex; Date of Birth-Age at Last Birthday; Tribe (Oglala Sioux, unless stated otherwise); Degree of Blood; Marital Status; Relationship to Head of Family [Last Census Roll Number]; At Jurisdiction Where Enrolled (Yes/No); (If no – Where); Ward (Yes/No, if given); Allotment, Annuity and Identification Numbers (if given).

7032; Thunder Hawk, Charles; M; 1894-38; plus 1/4; M; Head; 6935; Yes; Yes; Al. 2684 An. 6897

7033; Thunder Hawk (Jealous Of Him), Susie; F; 1904-28; F; M; Wife; 6936; Yes; Yes; Al. 608 An. 6899

7034; Thunder Hawk, Fannie; F; 3/18/25-7; plus 1/4; S; Daughter; 6937; Yes; Yes; Id. U-11579 An. 6901

7035; Thunder Hawk, Martin; M; 6/4/27-4; 1/4; S; Son; 6938; Yes; Yes; Id. U-13121 An. none

7036; Thunder Hawk, Gladys; F; 12/9/29-2; 1/4; S; Daughter; 6939; Yes; Yes; Id. U-13313 An. none

7037; Thunder Hawk, George; M; 1900-32; 1/4; M; Head; 6940; Yes; Yes; Al. 2686 An. 6902

7038; Thunder Hawk (Bone), Helen; F; 10/20/07-24; F; M; Wife; 6941; Yes; Yes; Al. 4292 An. 887

7039; Thunder Hawk, Martin; M; 1867-65; plus 1/4; M; Head; 6942; Yes; Yes; Al. 2682 An. 6906

7040; Thunder Hawk (Kills In Lodge), Rosa; F; 1862-70; F; M; Wife; 6943; Yes; Yes; Al. 3838 An. 6907

7041; Thunder Horse, Alex; M; 1898-34; F; M; Head; 6944; Yes; Yes; Al. 167 An. 6908

7042; Thunder Horse (Bad Bear), Mary; F; 1904-28; F; M; Wife; 6945; Yes; Yes; Al. 3560 An. 6909

7043; Thunder Horse, Lydia; F; 5/25/23-8; F; S; Daughter; 6946; Yes; Yes; Id. U-11151 An. 6910

7044; Thunder Horse, Walter; M; 6/15/30-1; F; S; Son; 6947; Yes; Yes; Id. U-13535 An. none

7045; Thunder Tail, Blaine; M; 1895-37; F; Wd; Head; 6948; Yes; Yes; Al. 6202 An. 6914

7046; Thunder Tail, Rachel; F; 8/2/21-10; F; S; Daughter; 6949; Yes; Yes; Id. U-10571 An. 6916

7047; Thunder Tail, Hilda; F; 3/11/23-9; F; S; Daughter; 6950; Yes; Yes; Id. U-13001 An. 6917

7048; Thunder Tail (Black Feather), Nellie; F; 1900-32; F; M; Wife; 6951; Yes; Yes; Al. 2822 An. 770

7049; Tibbits, Thomas; M; 1897-35; plus 1/4; M; Head; 6952; Yes; Yes; Al. 3628 An. 6919

7050; Tibbits (Pourier), Florence; F; 9/4/97-34; 1/4; M; Wife; 6953; Yes; Yes; Al. 720 An. 6920

Census of the __Pine Ridge__ reservation of the __Pine Ridge, South Dakota__ jurisdiction, as of __April 1__, 1932, taken by __James H. McGregor__, Superintendent.

Key: Number; Surname, Given; Sex; Date of Birth-Age at Last Birthday; Tribe (Oglala Sioux, unless stated otherwise); Degree of Blood; Marital Status; Relationship to Head of Family [Last Census Roll Number]; At Jurisdiction Where Enrolled (Yes/No); (If no – Where); Ward (Yes/No, if given); Allotment, Annuity and Identification Numbers (if given).

7051; Tibbits, Thelma; F; 5/25/16-15; 1/4; S; Daughter; 6954; Yes; Yes; Id. U-10576 An. 6921

7052; Tibbits, Deloris; F; 8/19/17-14; 1/4; S; Daughter; 6955; Yes; Yes; Id. U-10577 An. 6922

7053; Tibbits, Vesta; F; 12/19/21-10; 1/4; S; Daughter; 6956; Yes; Yes; Id. U-11614 An. 6923

7054; Tibbits, Derona; F; 7/19/25-6; 1/4; S; Daughter; 6957; Yes; Yes; Id. U-11688 An. none

7055; Tibbits, Thomas B; M; 8/10/28-3; 1/4; S; Son; 6958; Yes; Yes; Id. U-12821 An. none

7056; Tibbits, Phyliss; F; 6/2/31-9/12; 1/4; S; Daughter; ---; Yes; Yes; U-13858

7057; Tibbits, Mary; F; 3/24/11-20; 1/4; S; Head; 6959; Yes; Yes; Al. 5744 An. 6926

7058; Tibbits, William; M; 1882-50; 1/4; M; Head; 6960; Yes; Yes; Al. 2572 An. 6924

7059; Tibbits (Pourier), Rose; F; 1889-43; -1/4; M; Wife; 6961; Yes; Yes; Al. 2612 An. 6925

7060; Tibbits, Emil; M; 4/22/13-18; -1/4; S; Son; 6962; Yes; Yes; Al. 6794 An. 6927

7061; Tibbits, Theodore; M; 2/19/16-16; -1/4; S; Son; 6963; Yes; Yes; Id. U-10572 An. 6928

7062; Tibbits, Beatrice; F; 6/11/17-14; -1/4; S; Daughter; 6964; Yes; Yes; Id. U-10573 An. 6929

7063; Tibbits, Charles; M; 11/9/18-13; -1/4; S; Son; 6965; Yes; Yes; Id. U-10574 An. 6930

7064; Tibbits, Cecelia; F; 7/23/20-11; -1/4; S; Daughter; 6966; Yes; Yes; Id. U-10575 An. 6931

7065; Tibbits, Benjamin; M; 5/21/22-9; -1/4; S; Son; 6967; Yes; Yes; Id. U-11017 An. 6932

7066; Tibbits, Arline; F; 6/18/25-7; -1/4; S; Daughter; 6968; Yes; Yes; Id. U-11659 An. none

7067; Tibbits, Theresa; F; 5/29/27-4; -1/4; S; Daughter; 6969; Yes; Yes; Id. U-12349 An. none

7068; Tibbits, Sylvester; M; 3/25/31-1; -1/4; S; Son; 6970; Yes; Yes; Id. U-13770 An. none

7069; Tobacco (Irving), Ellen; F; 1866-66; plus 1/4; Wd; Head; 6971; Yes; Yes; Al. 17 An. 6934

7070; Tobacco, Archie; M; 1895-37; 1/4; M; Head; 6972; Yes; Yes; Al. 6519 An. 6935

7071; Tobacco (Standing Bear), Lillie; F; 1892-40; 1/4; M; Wife; 6973; Yes; Yes; Al. 938 An. 6936

Census of the __Pine Ridge__ reservation of the __Pine Ridge, South Dakota__ jurisdiction, as of __April 1__, 19**32**, taken by __James H. McGregor__, Superintendent.

Key: Number; Surname, Given; Sex; Date of Birth-Age at Last Birthday; Tribe (Oglala Sioux, unless stated otherwise); Degree of Blood; Marital Status; Relationship to Head of Family [Last Census Roll Number]; At Jurisdiction Where Enrolled (Yes/No); (If no – Where); Ward (Yes/No, if given); Allotment, Annuity and Identification Numbers (if given).

7072; Tobacco, Evelyne; F; 11/29/14-17; 1/4; S; Daughter; 6974; Yes; Yes; Al. 7000 An. 6937
7073; Tobacco, Roy; M; 2/4/17-15; 1/4; S; Son; 6975; Yes; Yes; Id. U-10579 An. 6938
7074; Tobacco, Rudolph; M; 5/5/19-12; 1/4; S; Son; 6976; Yes; Yes; Id. U-10580 An. 6939
7075; Tobacco, Vincent; M; 8/20/21-10; 1/4; S; Son; 6977; Yes; Yes; Id. U-10966 An. 6940
7076; Tobacco, Elmer; M; 4/11/24-7; 1/4; S; Son; 6978; Yes; Yes; Id. U-11257 An. 6941
7077; Tobacco, Ethel; F; 8/3/26-5; 1/4; S; Daughter; 6979; Yes; Yes; Id. U-12125 An. none
7078; Tobacco, Leroy; M; 6/6/31-9/12; 1/4; S; Son; ---; Yes; Yes; U-13859

~~N.E.: Tools, James; M; ------; Rosebud Sioux; F; M; Head;~~
7079; Tools (Strikes Plenty), Sallie; F; 1899-33; F; M; Wife; 6980; No; Rosebud, S.D.; Yes; Al. 1378 An. 6942
7080; Walking Bull, Cornelia; F; 8/25/20-11; F; S; Daughter; 6981; No; Rosebud, S.D.; Yes; Id. U-10509 An. 6943

7081; Todd (Lamb), Mary; F; 1897-35; -1/4; M; Head; 6984; No; Cheyenne, city, Laramie, Wyo; Yes; Al. 2580 An. 2228
7082; Finney, Virginia; F; 4/10/18-13; -1/4; S; Daughter; 6985; No; same; Yes; Id. U-9519 An. 2229
7083; Todd, Billie; F; 6/17/24-7; -1/4; S; Daughter; 6986; No; same; Yes; Id. U-12914 An. none
7084; Todd, Robert; M; 2/1/29-3; -1/4; S; Son; 6987; No; same; Yes; Id. U-13150 An. none

7085; Top Bear, Hugh; M; 1876-56; F; M; Head; 6988; Yes; Yes; Al. 657 An. 6946
7086; Top Bear (Last Horse), Georgiana; F; 1882-50; F; M; Wife; 6989; Yes; Yes; Al. 2309 An. 6947
7087; Top Bear, William; M; 1907-25; F; S; Head; 6990; Yes; Yes; Al. 5867 An. 6948

7088; Traveler, ---; M; 1856-76; F; M; Head; 6991; Yes; Yes; Al. 4390 An. 6952

7089; Tree Leg, Charles; M; 1858-74; F; M; Head; 6992; Yes; Yes; Al. 4948 An. 6953
7090; Tree Leg (no data), Lucy; F; 1858-74; F; M; Wife; 6993; Yes; Yes; Al. 6480 An. 6954

Census of the __Pine Ridge__ reservation of the __Pine Ridge, South Dakota__ jurisdiction, as of __April 1__, 19**32**, taken by __James H. McGregor__, Superintendent.

Key: Number; Surname, Given; Sex; Date of Birth-Age at Last Birthday; Tribe (Oglala Sioux, unless stated otherwise); Degree of Blood; Marital Status; Relationship to Head of Family [Last Census Roll Number]; At Jurisdiction Where Enrolled (Yes/No); (If no – Where); Ward (Yes/No, if given); Allotment, Annuity and Identification Numbers (if given).

7091; Trimble (Randall), Lucy; F; 1899-43; plus 1/4; M; Head; 6994; Yes; Yes; Al. 4873 An. 6957

7092; Trimble, Gertrude; F; 7/25/13-18; 1/4; S; Daughter; 6995; Yes; Yes; Al. 7735 An. 6958

7093; Trimble, Grace; F; 7/25/13-18; 1/4; S; Daughter; 6996; Yes; Yes; Al. 7756 An. 6959

7094; Trimble, Cora; F; 2/25/15-17; 1/4; S; Daughter; 6997; Yes; Yes; Al. 8090 An. 6960

7095; Trimble, Emma; F; 9/22/16-15; 1/4; S; Daughter; 6998; Yes; Yes; Al. 8201 An. 6961

7096; Trimble, Leola; F; 5/23/18-13; 1/4; S; Daughter; 6999; Yes; Yes; Id. U-10585 An. 6962

7097; Trimble, Shirley; F; 11/18/20-11; 1/4; S; Daughter; 7000; Yes; Yes; Id. U-10586 An. 6963

7098; Trimble, James; M; 3/12/24-8; 1/4; S; Son; 7001; Yes; Yes; Id. U-11231 An. 6964

7099; Trimble, William A; M; 8/21/28-3; 1/4; S; Son; 7002; Yes; Yes; Id. U-12767 An. none

7100; Trimble, Nelson; M; 5/18/30-1; 1/4; S; Son; 7003; Yes; Yes; Id. U-13507 An. none

7101; Trimble, John H; M; 1903-29; 1/4; M; Head; 7004; Yes; Yes; Al. 3796 An. 6955

7102; Trimble (Jacobs), Celesta; F; 1902-30; 1/4; M; Wife; 7005; Yes; Yes; Al. 3621 An. 6956

7103; Trimble, John H Jr.; M; 8/2/26-5; 1/4; S; Son; 7006; Yes; Yes; Id. U-11990 An. none

7104; Trimble, Lyle L; M; 3/8/31-1; 1/4; S; Son; 7007; Yes; Yes; Id. U-13771 An. none

7105; Trott, Theodore; M; 1907-25; -1/4; M; Head; 7008; No; Lame Deer, Mont.; Yes; Al. 4667 An. 4319

7106; Trouble In Front, ---; M; 1858-74; F; Wd; Head; 7009; Yes; Yes; Al. 1007 An. 6965

7107; Trouble In Front, Albert; M; 1890-42; F; M; Head; 7010; Yes; Yes; Al. 1008 An. 6967

7108; Trouble In Front (Chips), Emma; F; 1905-27; F; M; Wife; 7011; Yes; Yes; Al. 5116 An. 2231

7109; Fire Place, Pansy; F; 5/3/20-11; F; S; S. Daughter; 7012; Yes; Yes; Id. U-9520 An. none

Census of the **Pine Ridge** reservation of the **Pine Ridge, South Dakota** jurisdiction, as of **April 1**, 1932, taken by **James H. McGregor**, Superintendent.

Key: Number; Surname, Given; Sex; Date of Birth-Age at Last Birthday; Tribe (Oglala Sioux, unless stated otherwise); Degree of Blood; Marital Status; Relationship to Head of Family [Last Census Roll Number]; At Jurisdiction Where Enrolled (Yes/No); (If no – Where); Ward (Yes/No, if given); Allotment, Annuity and Identification Numbers (if given).

7110; Fire Place, Thomas; M; 10/1/25-6; F; S; S. Son; 7013; Yes; Yes; Id. U-11773 An. none

7111; Trouble In Front, Rose; F; 1/7/30-2; F; S; Daughter; 7014; Yes; Yes; Id. U-13357 An. none

7112; Trueblood, Glenn; M; 10/25/11-20; -1/4; S; Head; 7015; No; Gordon, town, Sheridan, Nebr; Yes; Al. 7789 An. 6975

7113; Trueblood (Sears), Lulu; F; 1886-46; 1/4; S; Head; 7016; No; Gordon, town, Sheridan, Nebr; No; Al. 377 An. 6973

7114; Trueblood, Jesse; M; 7/12/13-18; -1/4; S; Son; 7017; No; Same; Yes; Al. 7790 An. 6976

7115; Trueblood, Maxine; F; 8/25/15-16; -1/4; S; Daughter; 7018; No; same; Yes; Id. U-10590 An. 6977

7116; Trueblood, Frances; F; 12/17-14; -1/4; S; Daughter; 7019; No; same; Yes; Id. U-10591 An. 6978

7117; Trueblood, Jack; M; 4/7/21-10; -1/4; S; Son; 7020; No; same; Yes; Id. U-10592 An. 6979

7118; Trueblood, Richard; M; 10/8/25-6; -1/4; S; Son; 7021; No; same; Yes; Id. U-12648 An. none

7119; Trueblood, Edward; M; 7/31/27-4; -1/4; S; Son; 7022; No; same; Yes; Id. U-12647 An. none

7120; Trueblood, Thomas; M; 12/4/29-2; -1/4; S; Son; 7023; No; same; Yes; Id. U-13463 An. none

N.E.: ~~Turning Bear, Joseph; M; ------ ; Rosebud Sioux; F; M; Head;~~

7121; Turning Bear (yellow boy), Elizabeth; F; 1904-28; F; M; Wife; 7024; No; Rosebud, S.D.; Yes; Id. U-10795 An. 6980

7122; Turning Bear, Lydia; F; 1867-65; F; S; Head; 7025; Yes; Yes; Al. 6188 An. 6981

7123; Turning Bear, Theodore; M; 1901-31; F; S; Head; 7026; Yes; Yes; Al. 3359 An. 6984

7124; Turning Hawk, Charles; M; 1858-74; F; S; Head; 7027; Yes; Yes; Al. 1670 An. 6985

7125; Turning Hawk (no data), Philomena; F; 1856-76; F; M; Wife; 7028; Yes; Yes; Al. 5887 An. 6986

7126; Turning Hawk, Hobart; M; 1886-46; F; M; Head; 7029; Yes; Yes; Al. 1671 An. 6987

Census of the **Pine Ridge** reservation of the **Pine Ridge, South Dakota** jurisdiction, as of **April 1**, 19**32**, taken by **James H. McGregor**, Superintendent.

Key: Number; Surname, Given; Sex; Date of Birth-Age at Last Birthday; Tribe (Oglala Sioux, unless stated otherwise); Degree of Blood; Marital Status; Relationship to Head of Family [Last Census Roll Number]; At Jurisdiction Where Enrolled (Yes/No); (If no – Where); Ward (Yes/No, if given); Allotment, Annuity and Identification Numbers (if given).

7127; Turning Hawk (Holy Elk), Gertrude; F; 1899-33; F; M; Wife; 7030; Yes; Yes; Al. 1669 An. 6988
7128; Turning Hawk, Dora; F; 3/26/18-14; F; S; Daughter; 7031; Yes; Yes; Id. U-10593 An. 6989
7129; Turning Hawk, Philomene; F; 8/22/21-10; F; S; Daughter; 7032; Yes; Yes; Id. U-10594 An. 6991
7130; Turning Hawk, Jona; M; 12/10/23-8; F; S; Son; 7033; Yes; Yes; Id. U-11182 An. 6992
7131; Turning Hawk, Vera; F; 7/30/26-5; F; S; Daughter; 7034; Yes; Yes; Id. U-12127 An. none
7132; Turning Hawk, Zoey; F; 8/24/30-1; F; S; Daughter; 7035; Yes; Yes; Id. U-13574 An. none

7133; Turning Holy, Frank; M; 1888-44; F; M; Head; 7036; Yes; Yes; Al. 2126 An. 6995
7134; Turning Holy (Hand Soldier), Louisa; F; 1886-46; F; M; Wife; 7037; Yes; Yes; Al. 2125 An. 6996
7135; Turning Holy, Moses; M; 2/10/25-7; F; S; Son; 7038; Yes; Yes; Id. U-11430 An. 6999
7136; Turning Holy, Joshua; M; 1/5/12-20; F; M; Head; 7039; Yes; Yes; Id. U-10596 An. 6997
7137; Turning Holy (Strikes Plenty), Susie; F; 9/28/11-20; F; M; Wife; 7040; Yes; Yes; Id. U-7070 An. 6674
7138; Turning Holy, Altine; F; 5/15/31-10/12; F; S; Daughter; ---; Yes; Yes; U-13845

7139; Turning Holy, Henry; M; 1852-80; F; M; Head; 7041; Yes; Yes; Al. 4668 An. 7000
7140; Yellow Bug, ---; F; 1862-70; F; M; Wife; 7042; Yes; Yes; Al. 5276 An. 7001

N.E.: ~~Tuttle, Henry J; M; ------; Santee Sioux; F; M; Head;~~
7141; Tuttle (Bush), Julia; F; 1898-34; plus 1/4; M; Wife; 7043; Yes; Yes; Al. 735 An. 7002
7142; Tuttle, David; M; 8/30/16-15; 1/4; S; Son; 7044; Yes; Yes; Id. U-10598 An. 7003
7143; Tuttle, John A Jr.; M; 1/6/18-14; 1/4; S; Son; 7045; Yes; Yes; Id. U-10599 An. 7004
7144; Tuttle, Isaac; M; 12/31/19-12; 1/4; S; Son; 7046; Yes; Yes; Id. U-10600 An. 7005
7145; Tuttle, Margaret; F; 9/30/21-10; 1/4; S; Daughter; 7047; Yes; Yes; Id. U-10931 An. 7006

Census of the **Pine Ridge** reservation of the **Pine Ridge, South Dakota** jurisdiction, as of **April 1**, 19**32**, taken by **James H. McGregor**, Superintendent.

Key: Number; Surname, Given; Sex; Date of Birth-Age at Last Birthday; Tribe (Oglala Sioux, unless stated otherwise); Degree of Blood; Marital Status; Relationship to Head of Family [Last Census Roll Number]; At Jurisdiction Where Enrolled (Yes/No); (If no – Where); Ward (Yes/No, if given); Allotment, Annuity and Identification Numbers (if given).

7146; Tuttle, Lillian; F; 5/24/23-8; 1/4; S; Daughter; 7048; Yes; Yes; Id. U-11686 An. none
7147; Tuttle, Celesta; F; 5/26/25-6; 1/4; S; Daughter; 7049; Yes; Yes; Id. U-11675 An. none
7148; Tuttle, Edward; M; 5/23/27-4; 1/4; S; Son; 7050; Yes; Yes; Id. U-12349 An. none
7149; Tuttle, Marvin; M; 7/18/28-3; 1/4; S; Son; 7051; Yes; Yes; Id. U-12768 An. none
7150; Tuttle, Florence; F; 7/5/30-1; plus 1/4; S; Daughter; 7052; Yes; Yes; Id. U-13617 An. none

7151; Tway (no data), Mary; F; 1867-65; 1/4; Wd; Head; 7053; Yes; Yes; Al. 4837 An. 7007

7152; Tway, Thomas; M; 1896-36; -1/4; M; Head; 7054; No; Gordon, town, Sheridan, Nebr; No; Al. 5493 An. 7008
7153; Tway, Chester; M; 2/24/15-17; -1/4; S; Son; 7055; No; same; Yes; Id. U-10601 An. 7009
7154; Tway, Maurice; M; 10/29/16-15; -1/4; S; Son; 7056; No; same; Yes; Id. U-10602 An. 7010
7155; Tway, Helen; F; 6/14/18-13; -1/4; S; Daughter; 7057; No; same; Yes; Id. U-10603 An. 7011

7156; Twin, Fred; M; 1869-63; F; M; Head; 7058; Yes; Yes; Al. 4115 An. 7012
7157; Scratcher, ---; F; 1868-64; F; M; Wife; 7059; Yes; Yes; Al. 4116 An. 7013
7158; Twin, Lily; F; 7/4/13-18; F; S; Daughter; 7060; Yes; Yes; Al. 4118 An. 7015
7159; Chips, Isabelle; F; 5/12/15-16; F; S; Daughter; 7061; Yes; Yes; Id. U-9338 An. 1420

7160; Twin, Victoria; F; 1/21/10-22; F; S; Head; 7062; Yes; Yes; Al. 5602 An. 7014

7161; Twin, Reuben; M; 1876-56; F; M; Head; 7063; Yes; Yes; Al. 4113 An. 7016
N.E.: Twin (Black Bull), Alice; F; ------; Rosebud Sioux; F; M; Wife;
7162; Twin, John; M; 5/26/14-17; F; S; Son; 7064; Yes; Yes; Al. 7744 An. 7017

7163; Twiss, Charles; M; 1899-33; plus 1/4; M; Head; 7065; Yes; Yes; Al. 2925 An. 7018

7164; Twiss, Frank; M; 1893-39; 1/4; M; Head; 7066; Yes; Yes; Al. 828 An. 7019
7165; Twiss (Bissonette), Jessie; F; 1894-38; 1/4; M; Wife; 7067; Yes; Yes; Al. 2928 An. 7020
7166; Twiss, Seymore; M; 5/19/19-12; 1/4; S; Son; 7068; Yes; Yes; Id. U-10609 An. 7021

Census of the **Pine Ridge** reservation of the **Pine Ridge, South Dakota** jurisdiction, as of **April 1**, 19**32**, taken by **James H. McGregor**, Superintendent.

Key: Number; Surname, Given; Sex; Date of Birth-Age at Last Birthday; Tribe (Oglala Sioux, unless stated otherwise); Degree of Blood; Marital Status; Relationship to Head of Family [Last Census Roll Number]; At Jurisdiction Where Enrolled (Yes/No); (If no – Where); Ward (Yes/No, if given); Allotment, Annuity and Identification Numbers (if given).

7167; Twiss, Theodore; M; 12/19/20-11; 1/4; S; Son; 7069; Yes; Yes; Id. U-11644 An. 7022

7168; Twiss, William; M; 10/13/23-8; 1/4; S; Son; 7070; Yes; Yes; Id. U-11139 An. 7023

7169; Twiss, Peter; M; 5/7/27-4; 1/4; S; Son; 7071; Yes; Yes; Id. U-12706 An. none

7170; Twiss, Casper; M; 1/6/30-2; 1/4; S; Son; 7072; Yes; Yes; Id. U-13358 An. none

7171; Twiss, Frank; M; 1871-61; 1/4; M; Head; 7073; Yes; Yes; Al. 724 An. 7024

7172; Twiss (no data), Adelia; F; 1870-62; 1/4; M; Wife; 7074; Yes; Yes; Al. 2142 An. 7025

7173; Twiss, Hattie; F; 1904-28; 1/4; S; Head; 7075; Yes; Al. 823 An. 7027

7174; Twiss, Jesse; M; 1892-40; plus 1/4; Wd; Head; 7076; Yes; No; Al. 817 An. 7028

7175; Twiss, Joseph; M; 1866-66; 1/4; Wd; Head; 7077; Yes; Yes; Al. 824 An. 7031

7176; Twiss, Leon; M; 1898-34; 1/4; M; Head; 7078; Yes; Yes; Al. 830 An. 7032

7177; Twiss (Red Owl), Hattie; F; 1896-36; F; M; Wife; 7079; Yes; Yes; Al. 1386 An. 7033

7178; Twiss, Evalyn; F; 11/30/19-12; plus 1/4; S; Daughter; 7080; Yes; Yes; Id. U-10608 An. 7034

7179; Twiss, Bessie; F; 12/13/23-8; 1/4; S; Daughter; 7081; Yes; Yes; Id. U-11252 An. 7036

7180; Twiss, Amos; M; 12/24/25-6; 1/4; S; Son; 7082; Yes; Yes; Id. U-13175 An. none

7181; Twiss, Lula; F; 7/5/29-2; 1/4; S; Daughter; 7083; Yes; Yes; Id. U-13236 An. none

7182; Twiss (no data), Louise; F; 1871-61; 1/4; Wd; Wife; 7084; Yes; No; Al. 3961 An. 7040

7183; Twiss, Robert; M; 10/24/11-20; 1/4; S; Head; 7085; Yes; Yes; Id. U-10610 An. 7042

7184; Twiss, Lizzie; F; 1907-25; 1/4; S; Head; 7086; Yes; Yes; Al. 3963 An. 7041

7185; Twiss, Mary; F; 1906-26; plus 1/4; S; Head; 7087; Yes; Yes; Al. 3962 An. 7043

7186; Twiss, Paul; M; 1904-28; 1/4; M; Head; 7088; Yes; Yes; Al. 7535 An. 7044

Census of the **Pine Ridge** reservation of the **Pine Ridge, South Dakota** jurisdiction, as of **April 1**, 19**32**, taken by **James H. McGregor**, Superintendent.

Key: Number; Surname, Given; Sex; Date of Birth-Age at Last Birthday; Tribe (Oglala Sioux, unless stated otherwise); Degree of Blood; Marital Status; Relationship to Head of Family [Last Census Roll Number]; At Jurisdiction Where Enrolled (Yes/No); (If no – Where); Ward (Yes/No, if given); Allotment, Annuity and Identification Numbers (if given).

7187; Twiss (Russell), Marguerite; F; 1907-25; 1/4; M; Wife; 7089; Yes; Yes; Al. 2744 An. 5989

7188; Twiss, Thomas; M; 1886-46; 1/4; M; Head; 7090; Yes; No; Al. 827 An. 7046
7189; Twiss (Galligo (Angel), Frances; F; 1897-35; plus 1/4; M; Wife; 164; Yes; Yes; Al. 2790 An. 166
7190; Twiss, Mary; F; 11/18/13-18; 1/4; S; Daughter; 7091; Yes; Yes; Id. U-10605 An. 7048
7191; Twiss, Joseph L; M; 9/4/15-16; 1/4; S; Son; 7092; Yes; Yes; Id. U-10606 An. 7049
7192; Twiss, David; M; 9/8/18-13; 1/4; S; Son; 7093; Yes; Yes; Id. U-10607 An. 7050
7193; Twiss, Floredah; F; 2/16/22-10; 1/4; S; Daughter; 7094; Yes; Yes; Id. U-10907 An. 7051
7194; Twiss, Cecelia; F; 12/23/23-8; 1/4; S; Daughter; 7095; Yes; Yes; Id. U-11200 An. 7052
7195; Galligo, Joseph; M; 5/5/22-9; plus 1/4; S; S. Son; 165; Yes; Yes; Id. U-11454 An. 167
7196; Twiss, Lawrence; M; 1/20/31-1; 1/4; S; Son; ---; Yes; Yes; U-13821

7197; Twiss, Wallace; M; 1906-26; 1/4; M; Head; 7096; Yes; Yes; Al. 7521 An. 7053
7198; Twiss (Clifford), Hattie; F; 1907-25; plus 1/4; M; Wife; 1402; Yes; Yes; Al. 2755 An. 1446
7199; Twiss, George; M; 11/8/31-4/12; 1/4; S; Son; ---; Yes; Yes; U-14111

7200; Twiss, William; M; 1862-70; 1/4; M; Head; 7097; Yes; Yes; Al. 2922 An. 7054
7201; Twiss (no data), Lizzie; F; 1865-67; 1/4; M; Wife; 7098; Yes; Yes; Al. 2925 An. 7055

7202; Twiss, Gilbert; M; 4/23/10-21; plus 1/4; S; Head; 7099; Yes; Yes; Al. 7506 An. 7057

7203; Twiss, Joseph; M; 11/14/07-24; 1/4; S; Head; 7100; Yes; Yes; Al. 2926 An. 7056

7204; Twiss, William; M; 1897-35; 1/4; M; Head; 7101; Yes; Yes; Al. 335 An. 7058
7205; Twiss (Tobacco), Susan; F; 1900-32; 1/4; M; Wife; 7102; Yes; Yes; Al. 5871 An. 7059
7206; Twiss, Ellen; F; 1/15/21-11; 1/4; S; Daughter; 7103; Yes; Yes; Id. U-10612 An. 7060

Census of the __Pine Ridge__ reservation of the __Pine Ridge, South Dakota__ jurisdiction, as of __April 1__, 19__32__, taken by __James H. McGregor__, Superintendent.

Key: Number; Surname, Given; Sex; Date of Birth-Age at Last Birthday; Tribe (Oglala Sioux, unless stated otherwise); Degree of Blood; Marital Status; Relationship to Head of Family [Last Census Roll Number]; At Jurisdiction Where Enrolled (Yes/No); (If no – Where); Ward (Yes/No, if given); Allotment, Annuity and Identification Numbers (if given).

7207; Twiss, Edith; F; 6/4/28-3; 1/4; S; Daughter; 7104; Yes; Yes; Id. U-12649 An. none

7208; Twist, Joseph; M; 1906-26; 1/4; S; Head; 7105; Yes; Yes; Al. 5621 An. 7064

7209; Twist, Levi; M; 1904-28; 1/4; S; Head; 7106; Yes; Yes; Al. 3673 An. 7065

7210; Two Bonnets, John; M; 1874-58; F; M; Head; 7107; Yes; Yes; Al. 4378 An. 7068

7211; Two Bonnets (no data), Susie; F; 1874-58; F; M; Wife; 7108; Yes; Yes; Al. 4379 An. 7067

7212; Two Bulls, Amos; M; 1875-57; plus 1/4; M; Head; 7109; Yes; Yes; Al. 2652 An. 7068

7213; Two Bulls, Gale; M; 2/12/15-17; 1/4; S; Son; 7110; Yes; Yes; Id. U-10619 An. 7069

7214; Two Bulls, Edward; M; 1894-38; plus 1/4; Wd; Head; 7111; Yes; Yes; Al. 3475 An. 7071

7215; Two Bulls, Mathew; M; 11/1/21-10; 1/4; S; Son; 7112; Yes; Yes; Id. U-11943 An. 7073

7216; Two Bulls, Mary; F; 1873-59; F; Wd; Head; 7113; Yes; Yes; Al. 3471 An. 7075

7217; Two Bulls, Maggie; F; 12/2/13-18; plus 1/4; S; Daughter; 7114; Yes; Yes; Al. 7478 An. 7077

7218; Two Bulls, Delphine; F; 10/22/16-15; 1/4; S; Daughter; 7115; Yes; Yes; Id. U-10616 An. 7078

7219; Two Bull[sic], George; M; 1898-34; 1/4; S; Head; 7116; Yes; Yes; Al. 6790 An. 7080

7220; Two Bulls, John; M; 1897-35; 1/4; M; Head; 7117; Yes; Yes; Al. 3475 An. 7081

7221; Two Bulls, Lizzie; F; 1907-25; 1/4; S; Head; 7120; Yes; Yes; Al. 3479 An. 7082

7222; Two Bulls, Jacob; M; 1909-23; 1/4; S; Head; 7121; Yes; Yes; Al. 7477 An. 7076

7223; Two Bulls, Moses; M; 1903-29; plus 1/4; M; Head; 7122; Yes; Yes; Al. 3477 An. 7083

Census of the __Pine Ridge__ reservation of the __Pine Ridge, South Dakota__ jurisdiction, as of __April 1__, 19**32**, taken by __James H. McGregor__, Superintendent.

Key: Number; Surname, Given; Sex; Date of Birth-Age at Last Birthday; Tribe (Oglala Sioux, unless stated otherwise); Degree of Blood; Marital Status; Relationship to Head of Family [Last Census Roll Number]; At Jurisdiction Where Enrolled (Yes/No); (If no – Where); Ward (Yes/No, if given); Allotment, Annuity and Identification Numbers (if given).

7224; Two Bulls (Rouillard), Effie; F; 2/16/09-23; 1/4; M; Wife; 7123; Yes; Yes; Al. 6174 An. 5847

7225; Two Bulls, Fred; M; 10/5/29-2; 1/4; S; Son; 7124; Yes; Yes; Id. U-13276 An. none

7226; Two Bulls, Peter; M; 1901-31; 1/4; M; Head; 7125; Yes; Yes; Al. 3476 An. 7084

7227; Two Bulls (Helper), Melissa; F; 1904-28; F; M; Wife; 7126; Yes; Yes; Al. 3332 An. 7085

7228; Two Bulls, Maizie; F; 11/27/24-7; plus 1/4; S; Daughter; 7127; Yes; Yes; Id. U-10475 An. 7086

7229; Two Bulls, Elizabeth; F; 10/20/26-5; 1/4; S; Daughter; 7128; Yes; Yes; Id. U-12156 An. none

7230; Two Bulls, Lucille; F; 12/6/28-3; 1/4; S; Daughter; 7129; Yes; Yes; Id. U-12957 An. none

7231; Two Bulls, Norene; F; 7/17/30-1; 1/4; S; Daughter; 7130; Yes; Yes; Id. U-13618 An. none

7232; Two Bulls, Stearn; M; 1890-42; 1/4; M; Head; 7131; Yes; Yes; Al. 3472 An. 7087

7233; Two Bulls, Isabell; F; 12/31/14-17; plus 1/4; S; Daughter; 7133; Yes; Yes; Al. 8239 An. 7089

7234; Two Bulls, Abraham; M; 10/20/17-14; 1/4; S; Son; 7134; Yes; Yes; Id. U-10617 An. 7090

7235; Two Bulls, Earl; M; 6/16/20-11; 1/4; S; Son; 7135; Yes; Yes; Id. U-10618 An. 7091

7236; Two Bulls, Floyd; M; 3/2/26-6; 1/4; S; Son; 7136; Yes; Yes; Id. U-11850 An. none

7237; Two Crow, Henry; M; 1900-32; plus 1/4; M; Head; 7137; Yes; Yes; Al. 1480 An. 7093

7238; Two Crow (Marshall), Annie; F; 1889-43; 1/4; M; Wife; 7138; Yes; Yes; Al. 7288 An. 7094

7239; Mesteth, Amanda; F; 7/7/12-19; 1/4; S; S. Daughter; 7139; Yes; Yes; Al. 7289 An. 7096

7240; Two Crow, Judson; M; 3/8/15-17; 1/4; S; Son; 7140; Yes; Yes; Al. 8265 An. 7097

7241; Two Crow, Edith; F; 5/30/17-14; 1/4; S; Daughter; 7141; Yes; Yes; Id. U-10620 An. 7098

7242; Two Crow, Ruth; F; 2/19/19-13; 1/4; S; Daughter; 7142; Yes; Yes; Id. U-10621 An. 7091

7243; Two Crow, Emma; F; 2/3/21-11; 1/4; S; Daughter; 7143; Yes; Yes; Id. U-10622 An. 7100

Census of the **Pine Ridge** reservation of the **Pine Ridge, South Dakota** jurisdiction, as of **April 1**, 19**32**, taken by **James H. McGregor**, Superintendent.

Key: Number; Surname, Given; Sex; Date of Birth-Age at Last Birthday; Tribe (Oglala Sioux, unless stated otherwise); Degree of Blood; Marital Status; Relationship to Head of Family [Last Census Roll Number]; At Jurisdiction Where Enrolled (Yes/No); (If no – Where); Ward (Yes/No, if given); Allotment, Annuity and Identification Numbers (if given).

7244; Two Crow, Russell; M; 3/26/24-8; 1/4; S; Son; 7144; Yes; Yes; Id. U-11469 An. 7101

7245; Two Crow, Myrtle; F; 1/19/26-6; 1/4; S; Daughter; 7145; Yes; Yes; Id. U-11815 An. none

7246; Two Crow, Hazel; F; 3/26/27-5; 1/4; S; Daughter; 7146; Yes; Yes; Id. U-12935 An. none

7247; Two Crow, Chester; M; 7/10/31-8/12; 1/4; S; Son; ---; Yes; Yes; U-13926

7248; Two Crow, Hobert; M; 1891-41; 1/4; M; Head; 7147; Yes; Yes; Al. 1478 An. 7102

7249; Two Crow (Spotted Horse), Frances; F; 1881-51; F; M; Wife; 7149; Yes; Yes; Al. 155 An. 6500

7250; Two Crow, Irene; F; 11/20/19-12; 1/4; M[sic]; Daughter; 7148; Yes; Yes; Id. U-14043 An. 7104

7251; Two Crow, John; M; 1880-52; plus 1/4; Wd; Head; 7150; Yes; Yes; Al. 1482 An. 7105

7252; Two Crow, Dallas; M; 6/29/15-16; 1/4; S; Son; 7152; Yes; Yes; Id. U-10626 An. 7109

7253; Two Crow, Frank; M; 8/16/17-14; 1/4; S; Son; 7153; Yes; Yes; Id. U-10627 An. 7110

7254; Two Crow, Rufus; M; 1/5/20-12; 1/4; S; Son; 7154; Yes; Yes; Id. U-10628 An. 7111

7255; Two Crow, Earl; M; 12/27/21-10; 1/4; S; Son; 7155; Yes; Yes; Id. U-10857 An. 7112

7256; Two Crow, Raural; F; 3/20/24-8; 1/4; S; Daughter; 7156; Yes; Yes; Id. U-11468 An. 7113

7257; Two Crow, Grace; F; 12/14/09-22; plus 1/4; S; Head; 7157; Yes; Yes; Al. 5919 An. 7108

7258; Two Crow, Joseph; M; 1888-44; 1/4; M; Head; 7158; Yes; Yes; Al. 1476 An. 7114

7259; Two Crow (Heart Man), Anna; F; 1890-42; F; M; Wife; 7159; Yes; Yes; Al. 8175 An. 7115

7260; Two Crow, Joseph F; M; 7/11/16-15; plus 1/4; S; Son; 7160; Yes; Yes; Id. U-10623 An. 7116

7261; Two Crow, Arnold; M; 8/30/23-8; 1/4; S; Son; 7161; Yes; Yes; Id. U-14046 An. 7118

7262; Two Crow, Peter; M; 6/26/26-5; plus 1/4; S; Son; 7162; Yes; Yes; Id. U-12126 An. none

7263; Two Crow, Phoebe; F; 8/24/28-3; 1/4; S; Daughter; 7163; Yes; Yes; Id. U-12794 An. none

Census of the **Pine Ridge** reservation of the **Pine Ridge, South Dakota** jurisdiction, as of **April 1**, 19**32**, taken by **James H. McGregor**, Superintendent.

Key: Number; Surname, Given; Sex; Date of Birth-Age at Last Birthday; Tribe (Oglala Sioux, unless stated otherwise); Degree of Blood; Marital Status; Relationship to Head of Family [Last Census Roll Number]; At Jurisdiction Where Enrolled (Yes/No); (If no – Where); Ward (Yes/No, if given); Allotment, Annuity and Identification Numbers (if given).

7264; Two Crow, Romeo; M; 1905-27; plus 1/4; M; Head; 7165; Yes; Yes; Al. 5894 An. 7120

7265; Two Crow (Brown Ears), Belle M; F; 3/28/10-22; F; M; Wife; 7166; Yes; Yes; Al. 7218 An. 2069

7266; Two Dogs, Edward; M; 1907-25; F; S; Head; 7167; Yes; Yes; Al. 3716 An. 3052

7267; Two Dogs, Oscar; M; 1886-46; F; M; Head; 7168; Yes; Yes; Al. 1342 An. 7121

7268; Two Dogs (Running Hawk), Maggie; F; 1890-42; plus 1/4; M; Wife; 7169; Yes; Yes; Al. 6536 An. 7122

7269; Running Hawk, Joseph; M; 4/23/13-18; 1/4; S; S. Son; 7170; Yes; Yes; Al. 8031 An. 7123

7270; Two Eagles, George; M; 1873-59; F; M; Head; 7171; Yes; Yes; Al. 7100 An. 7125

7271; Two Eagles (Black Kettle), Jessie; F; 1855-77; F; M; Wife; 7172; Yes; Yes; Al. 7627 An. 7126

7272; Two Eagles, John; M; 1897-35; F; M; Head; 7173; Yes; Yes; Al. 231 An. 7127

7273; Two Eagles, Joseph; M; 1894-38; F; M; Head; 7174; Yes; Yes; Al. 232 An. 7128

7274; Two Eagles, Lucille; F; 7/8/28-3; plus 1/4; S; Daughter; 7175; Yes; Yes; Id. U-12748 An. none

7275; Two Eagles, Oscar; M; 1895-37; F; M; Head; 7176; Yes; Yes; Al. 6066 An. 7129

7276; Two Eagles (Chief), Nancy; F; 1906-26; plus 1/4; M; Wife; 7177; Yes; Yes; Al. 5256 An. 7130

7277; Two Eagles, Hank; M; 9/13/22-9; 1/4; S; Son; 7178; Yes; Yes; Id. U-11426 An. 7131

7278; Two Eagles, Stella; F; 7/22/09-22; F; S; Head; 7179; Yes; Yes; Id. U-10635 An. 7170

7279; Two Elk, Philip; M; 1905-27; F; M; Head; 7180; Yes; Yes; Al. 4318 An. 7132

N.E.: Two Elk (Fire), Nellie; F; ------; Rosebud Sioux; F; M; Wife;

7280; Two Elk, Twellie; F; 7/17/30-1; F; S; Daughter; 7181; Yes; Yes; Id. U-13556 An. none

7281; Two Elk, Robert; M; 1875-57; F; M; Head; 7182; Yes; Yes; Al. 4314 An.7133

Census of the **Pine Ridge** reservation of the **Pine Ridge, South Dakota** jurisdiction, as of **April 1**, 19**32**, taken by **James H. McGregor**, Superintendent.

Key: Number; Surname, Given; Sex; Date of Birth-Age at Last Birthday; Tribe (Oglala Sioux, unless stated otherwise); Degree of Blood; Marital Status; Relationship to Head of Family [Last Census Roll Number]; At Jurisdiction Where Enrolled (Yes/No); (If no – Where); Ward (Yes/No, if given); Allotment, Annuity and Identification Numbers (if given).

N.E.:   Two Elk (Day Boy), Josephine; F; ‒‒‒‒‒‒; Lower Brule Sioux; F; M; Wife;
7282;   Two Elk, Royal; M; 5/28/20-11; F; S; Son; 7183; Yes; Yes; Id. U-10637 An. 7136

7283;   Two Elk, Thomas; M; 1895-37; F; S; Head; 7184; Yes; Yes; Al. 4316 An.7138

7284;   Two Elk, William; M; 1901-31; F; S; Head; 7185; Yes; Yes; Al. 1232 An. 7139

7285;   Two Gray Cows, ---; F; 1845-87; F; Wd; Head; 7186; Yes; Yes; Al. 5180 An. 7140

7286;   Two Lance (no data), Hattie; F; 1862-70; F; Wd.; Head; 7188; Yes; Yes; Al. 4742 An.7144

7287;   Two Lance, Isadore; M; 1907-25; F; M; Head; 7189; Yes; Yes; Al. 6692 An.7147

7288;   Two Lance (Tail), Ida; F; 7/26/10-21; F; M; Wife; 7190; Yes; Yes; Al. 7115 An. 5785

7289;   Two Lance, Christina; F; 10/27/31-5/12; F; S; Daughter; ---; Yes; Yes; U-13978

7290;   Two Lance, Thomas; M; 1883-49; F; M; Head; 7191; Yes; Yes; Al. 22 An. 7148

7291;   Two Lance (Yellow Hawk), Julia; F; 1882-50; F; M; Wife; 7192; Yes; Yes; Al. 414 An. 7149

7292;   Two Lance, Louisa; F; 1/4/13-19; F; S; Daughter; 7193; Yes; Yes; Al. 6690 An. 7152

7293;   Two Lance, Mabel; F; 1/26/15-17; F; S; Daughter; 7194; Yes; Yes; Id. U-10638 An. 7153

7294;   Two Lance, Thomas Jr.; M; 4/28/17-15; F; S; Son; 7195; Yes; Yes; Id. U-10639 An. 7154

7295;   Two Lance, Naomi; F; 7/28/19-12; F; S; Daughter; 7196; Yes; Yes; Id. U-10640 An. 7155

7296;   Two Lance, Rebecca; F; 10/4/21-10; F; S; Daughter; 7197; Yes; Yes; Id. U-10896 An. 7156

7297;   Two Lance, Ellis; M; 1/7/24-8; F; S; Son; 7198; Yes; Yes; Id. U-11542 An. 7157

7298;   Two Lance, Almaria; F; 12/1/26-5; F; S; Daughter; 7199; Yes; Yes; Id. U-12873 An. none

7299;   Two Lance, David F; M; 1/21/09-23; F; M; Head; 7200; Yes; Yes; Al. 5530 An. 7150

Census of the **Pine Ridge** reservation of the **Pine Ridge, South Dakota** jurisdiction, as of **April 1**, 1932, taken by **James H. McGregor**, Superintendent.

Key: Number; Surname, Given; Sex; Date of Birth-Age at Last Birthday; Tribe (Oglala Sioux, unless stated otherwise); Degree of Blood; Marital Status; Relationship to Head of Family [Last Census Roll Number]; At Jurisdiction Where Enrolled (Yes/No); (If no – Where); Ward (Yes/No, if given); Allotment, Annuity and Identification Numbers (if given).

7300; Two Lance (Running Shield), Bessie; F; 4/22/08-23; F; M; Wife; 7201; Yes; Yes; Al. 6673 An. 2293

7301; Two Lance, Vincent; M; 1/31/31-11; F; S; Son; 7202; Yes; Yes; Id. U-13716 An. none

7302; Two Sticks, David ; M; 1893-39; F; S; Head; 7203; Yes; Yes; Al. 7096 An. 7158

7303; Two Sticks, Fred ; M; 1884-48; F; M; Head; 7204; Yes; Yes; Al. 533 An. 7159

7304; Two Sticks (Understanding Crow), Hattie; F; 1877-55; F; M; Wife; 7205; Yes; Yes; Al. 5329 An. 7160

7305; Two Sticks, Isabel; F; 5/15/21-10; F; S; Daughter; 7206; Yes; Yes; Id. U-10643 An. 7162

7306; Two Sticks, Daisy; F; 4/29/26-5; F; S; Daughter; 7207; Yes; Yes; Id. U-11960 An. none

7307; Two Sticks, John; M; 1896-36; F; M; Head; 7208; Yes; Yes; Al. 3040 An. 7163

7308; Two Sticks (Hawkins), Theresa; F; 1899-33; plus 1/4; M; Wife; 7209; Yes; Yes; Al. 4614 An. 7164

7309; Two Sticks, Gladys; F; 6/17/20-11; 1/4; S; Daughter; 7210; Yes; Yes; Id. U-10644 An. 7165

7310; Two Sticks, Clarence; M; 4/6/23-8; 1/4; S; Son; 7211; Yes; Yes; Id. U-13080 An. 7166

7311; Two Sticks, Vivian; F; 2/14/29-3; 1/4; S; Daughter; 7212; Yes; Yes; Id. U-13152 An. none

7312; Two Sticks, Eleanor; F; 6/7/31-9/12; 1/4; S; Daughter; ---; Yes; Yes; U-13860

7313; Two Sticks, Thomas; M; 1880-52; F; M; Head; 7213; Yes; Yes; Al. 2360 An. 7167

7314; Two Sticks (Eagle Shawl), Hattie; F; 1877-55; F; M; Wife; 7214; Yes; Yes; Al. 2361 An. 7168

7315; Two Two, Alexander; M; 1877-55; plus 1/4; M; Head; 7215; Yes; Yes; Al. 198 An. 7174

7316; Two Two (One Feather), Rosa; F; 1893-39; F; M; Wife; 7216; Yes; Yes; Al. 6752 An. 7175

7317; Two Two, Andrew; M; 2/1/14-18; plus 1/4; S; Son; 7217; Yes; Yes; Id. U-10651 An. 7176

7318; Two Two, Mary; F; 4/9/28-3; 1/4; S; Daughter; 7218; Yes; Yes; Id. U-12601 An. none

Census of the __Pine Ridge__ reservation of the __Pine Ridge, South Dakota__ jurisdiction, as of __April 1__, 19**32**, taken by __James H. McGregor__, Superintendent.

Key: Number; Surname, Given; Sex; Date of Birth-Age at Last Birthday; Tribe (Oglala Sioux, unless stated otherwise); Degree of Blood; Marital Status; Relationship to Head of Family [Last Census Roll Number]; At Jurisdiction Where Enrolled (Yes/No); (If no – Where); Ward (Yes/No, if given); Allotment, Annuity and Identification Numbers (if given).

7319; Two Two, Agnes; F; 6/6/15-16; 1/4; M; Head; 7219; Yes; Yes; Id. U-10652 An. 7177
7320; Yellow Horse, Elmer; M; 11/20/31-4/12; plus 1/4; S; Son; ---; Yes; Yes; U-14056

7321; Two Two, James; M; 1889-43; F; M; Head; 7220; Yes; Yes; Al. 263 An. 7180
7322; Two Two (Little Dog), Julia; F; 1889-43; F; M; Wife; 7221; Yes; Yes; Al. 1714 An. 7181
7323; Two Two, Marie; F; 12/20/28-3; F; S; Daughter; 7222; Yes; Yes; Id. U-13123 An. none

7324; Two Two, Joseph; M; 1879-53; plus 1/4; M; Head; 7223; Yes; Yes; Al. 156 An. 7185
7325; Two Two, Adam; M; 2/20/14-18; 1/4; M[sic]; Son; 7224; Yes; Yes; Al. 8003 An. 7188
7326; Two Two, Raymond; M; 9/1/20-11; 1/4; M[sic]; Son; 7225; Yes; Yes; Id. U-10633 An. 7189

7327; Two Two, Richard; M; 1896-36; plus 1/4; M; Head; 7226; Yes; Yes; Al. 265 An. 7192
N.E.: Two Two (Head), Evangeline; F; ------; Crow Creek Sioux; F; M; Wife;
7328; Two Two, Lorene; F; 11/30/22-9; plus 1/4; S; Daughter; 7227; Yes; Yes; Id. U-12534 An. none
7329; Two Two, Earl; M; 5/3/24-7; 1/4; S; Son; 7228; Yes; Yes; Id. U-12533 An. none
7330; Two Two, Leonard; M; 3/21/27-5; 1/4; S; Son; 7229; Yes; Yes; Id. U-12536 An. none

7331; Two Two, Stephen; M; 1906-26; 1/4; M; Head; 7230; Yes; Yes; Al. 4722 An. 7183
N.E.: Two Two (Foote), Thelma; F; ------; North Cheyenne Sioux; M; Wife;

7332; Tyndall, Alex J; M; 1900-32; 1/4; M; Head; 7231; Yes; Yes; Al. 4806 An. 7194
7333; Tyndall, Vurene; F; 7/6/30-1; -1/4; S; Daughter; 7232; Yes; Yes; Id. U-13557 An. none

7334; Tyndall, Elizabeth; F; 1906-26; plus 1/4; S; Head; 7233; Yes; Yes; Al. 4803 An. 7195
N.E.: Tyndall, Joel; M; ------; Omaha Indian; F; M; Head;
7335; Tyndall (Hill), Lizzie; F; 1874-58; 1/4; M; Wife; 7234; Yes; Yes; Al. 4802 An. 7196

Census of the __Pine Ridge__ reservation of the __Pine Ridge, South Dakota__ jurisdiction, as of __April 1__, 19**32**, taken by __James H. McGregor__, Superintendent.

Key: Number; Surname, Given; Sex; Date of Birth-Age at Last Birthday; Tribe (Oglala Sioux, unless stated otherwise); Degree of Blood; Marital Status; Relationship to Head of Family [Last Census Roll Number]; At Jurisdiction Where Enrolled (Yes/No); (If no – Where); Ward (Yes/No, if given); Allotment, Annuity and Identification Numbers (if given).

7336; Tyndall, Joel W; M; 7/0[sic]/09-22; 1/4; S; Head; 7235; Yes; Yes; Al. 4807 An. 7198

7337; Tyndall, Robert; M; 10/29/10-21; 1/4; S; Head; 7236; Yes; Yes; Al. 5430 An. 7199

7338; Tyndall, Jacob E; M; 1907-25; plus 1/4; S; Head; 7237; Yes; Yes; Al. 4804 An. 7197

7339; Tyndall, Richard; M; 1903-29; 1/4; S; Head; 7238; Yes; Yes; Al. 4805 An. 7194

7340; Tyon (no data), Isabelle; F; 1864-68; F; Wd; Head; 7239; Yes; Yes; Al. 3397 An. 7202

7341; Tyon, Oliver Jr.; M; 1883-49; plus 1/4; M; Head; 7240; Yes; Yes; Al. 3423 An. 7203
7342; Tyon (no data), Lucy; F; 1884-48; 1/4; M; Wife; 7241; Yes; Yes; Al. 3424 An. 7204
7343; Tyon, Elizabeth; F; 12/3/13-18; 1/4; S; Daughter; 7242; Yes; Yes; Al. 7582 An. 7207
7344; Tyon, Ellen; F; 5/10/16-15; 1/4; S; Daughter; 7243; Yes; Yes; Id. U-10658 An. 7208
7345; Galligo, Carl D; M; 1/13/21-11; 1/4; S; Ward; 7244; Yes; Yes; Id. U-9552 An. 2374

7346; Tyon, Denver; M; 10/14/07-24; 1/4; M; Head; 7245; Yes; Yes; Al. 3426 An. 7205
7347; Tyon (Jarvis), Julia; F; 6/15/11-20; 1/4; M; Wife; 3368; Yes; Yes; Al. 5613 An. 3357

7348; Tyon, George; M; 12/7/10-21; 1/4; M; Head; 7246; Yes; Yes; Al. 7581 An. 7206
7349; Tyon (Little Bear), Sarah; F; 1/21/14-18; 1/4; M; Wife; 7247; Yes; Yes; Al. 7400 An. 3864
7350; Tyon, Eugene; M; 6/9/31-9/12; 1/4; S; Son; ---; Yes; Yes; Id. U-13861

7351; Tyon, Thomas Jr.; M; 1898-34; plus 1/4; M; Head; 7248; Yes; Yes; Al. 3418 An. 7209
7352; Tyon (Little Moon), Sarah; F; 1896-36; F; M; Wife; 7249; Yes; Yes; Al. 6725 An. 7210
7353; Tyon, Leo; M; 12/28/17-14; plus 1/4; S; Son; 7250; Yes; Yes; Id. U-10656 An. 7211

Census of the **Pine Ridge** reservation of the **Pine Ridge, South Dakota** jurisdiction, as of **April 1**, 1932, taken by **James H. McGregor**, Superintendent.

Key: Number; Surname, Given; Sex; Date of Birth-Age at Last Birthday; Tribe (Oglala Sioux, unless stated otherwise); Degree of Blood; Marital Status; Relationship to Head of Family [Last Census Roll Number]; At Jurisdiction Where Enrolled (Yes/No); (If no – Where); Ward (Yes/No, if given); Allotment, Annuity and Identification Numbers (if given).

7354; Tyon, Harry; M; 2/4/20-12; 1/4; S; Son; 7251; Yes; Yes; Id. U-10657 An. 7212

7355; Tyon, Jonas; M; 1/14/24-8; 1/4; S; Son; 7252; Yes; Yes; Id. U-11245 An. 7213

7356; Tyon, Louisa; F; 9/18/26-5; 1/4; S; Daughter; 7253; Yes; Yes; Id. U-12841 An. none

7357; Tyon, Mary; F; 9/29/28-3; 1/4; S; Daughter; 7254; Yes; Yes; Id. U-12842 An. none

7358; Tyon, William; M; 1904-28; 1/4; S; Head; 7255; Yes; Yes; Al. 3425 An. 7214

7359; Understanding Crow, Joshua; M; 1905-27; F; M; Head; 7256; Yes; Yes; Al. 5757 An. 7218

7360; Understanding Crow (no data), Melisse; F; 1/5/12-20; F; M; Wife; 7257; Yes; Yes; Al. 5321 An. 723

7361; Understanding Crow, Dorthia; F; 1/30/31-1; F; S; Daughter; 7258; Yes; Yes; Id. U-13717 An. none

7362; Under The Baggage, Charles; M; 1903-29; F; M; Head; 7259; Yes; Yes; Al. 1511 An. 7219

7363; Under The Baggage (Takes Enemy), Nancy; F; 1901-31; F; M; Wife; 7260; Yes; Yes; Al. 4324 An. 7220

7364; Under The Baggage, Charles; M; 4/16/23-8; F; S; Son; 7261; Yes; Yes; Id. U-11799 An. none

7365; Under The Baggage, Russell; M; 6/6/26-5; F; S; Son; 7262; Yes; Yes; Id. U-11961 An. none

7366; Under The Baggage, Alfred; M; 4/16/28-3; F; S; Son; 7263; Yes; Yes; Id. U-12602 An. none

7367; Under The Baggage, Norman; M; 2/9/32-1/12; F; S; Son; ---; Yes; Yes; U-14138

7368; Under The Baggage, Josephine; F; 7/12-19; F; S; Head; 7264; Yes; Yes; Al. 7702 An. 4309

7369; Usher nee (Stover), Hattei[sic]; F; 1904-28; plus 1/4; M; Head; 7265; Yes; Yes; Al. 4640 An. 6663

7370; Usher, Dean E; M; 5/29/29-3; 1/4; S; Son; 7266; Yes; Yes; Id. U-12732 An. none

7371; Usher, Dorothy; F; 7/25/30-1; 1/4; S; Daughter; 7267; Yes; Yes; Id. U-13619 An. none

Census of the **Pine Ridge** reservation of the **Pine Ridge, South Dakota** jurisdiction, as of **April 1**, 19**32**, taken by **James H. McGregor**, Superintendent.

Key: Number; Surname, Given; Sex; Date of Birth-Age at Last Birthday; Tribe (Oglala Sioux, unless stated otherwise); Degree of Blood; Marital Status; Relationship to Head of Family [Last Census Roll Number]; At Jurisdiction Where Enrolled (Yes/No); (If no – Where); Ward (Yes/No, if given); Allotment, Annuity and Identification Numbers (if given).

7372; Usher (Frazier), Ethel; F; 1/15/13-19; -1/4; M; Head; 2330; Yes; Yes; Al. 6717 An. 2332

7373; Valandry, Owen H.; M; 1896-36; plus 1/4; M; Head; 7268; Yes; No; Al. 1086 An. 7221

7374; Valandry (Condelario), Sophia; F; 1902-30; 1/4; M; Wife; 7269; Yes; Yes; Al. 2031 An. 7222

7375; Valandry, Isabel; F; 7/2/23-8; 1/4; S; Daughter; 7270; Yes; Yes; Id. U-11608 An. 7223

7376; Valandry, Paul; M; 1899-33; -1/4; M; Head; 7271; Yes; No; Al. 2462 An. 7224

7377; Valandry (Clifford), Eleanor; F; 1899-33; plus 1/4; M; Wife; 7272; Yes; Yes; Al. 4474 An. 7225

7378; Valandry, Philomene; F; 8/22/22-9; -1/4; S; Daughter; 7273; Yes; Yes; Id. U-12017 An. 7227

7379; Valandry, Alice; F; 7/7/24-7; -1/4; S; Daughter; 7274; Yes; Yes; Id. U-11416 An. 7228

7380; Valandry, Paul H.; M; 6/23/26-5; -1/4; S; Son; 7275; Yes; Yes; Id. U-11980 An. none

7381; Valandry, Lawrence; M; 9/1/28-3; -1/4; S; Son; 7276; Yes; Yes; Id. U-12804 An. none

7382; Valandry, Robert; M; 1889-43; plus 1/4; S; Head; 7277; Yes; Yes; Al. 1084 An. 7229

7383; Valandry, Vetal; M; 1871-61; 1/4; Wd; Head; 7278; Yes; No; Al. 2460 An. 7231

7384; Valandry, Gilbert; M; 8/20/10-21; -1/4; S; Son; 7279; Yes; Yes; Al. 5507 An. 7232

7385; Valandry, William; M; 3/8/53-79; plus 1/4; M; Head; 7280; Yes; No; Al. 5396 An. 7233

7386; Valandry (no data), Emma; F; 1866-66; 1/4; M; Wife; 7281; Yes; No; Al. 1081 An. 7234

7387; Valandry, William Jr.; M; 1887-45; 1/4; M; Head; 7282; Yes; No; Al. 1083 An. 7235

7388; Valandry, Willard; M; 8/17/15-16; -1/4; S; Son; 7283; Yes; Yes; Id. U-10660 An. 7236

7389; Valandry, Mildred; F; 12/19/18-13; -1/4; S; Daughter; 7284; Yes; Yes; Id. U-10661 An. 7237

Census of the **Pine Ridge** reservation of the **Pine Ridge, South Dakota** jurisdiction, as of **April 1**, 19**32**, taken by **James H. McGregor**, Superintendent.

Key: Number; Surname, Given; Sex; Date of Birth-Age at Last Birthday; Tribe (Oglala Sioux, unless stated otherwise); Degree of Blood; Marital Status; Relationship to Head of Family [Last Census Roll Number]; At Jurisdiction Where Enrolled (Yes/No); (If no – Where); Ward (Yes/No, if given); Allotment, Annuity and Identification Numbers (if given).

7390; Valandry, Lois; F; 2/20/22-10; -1/4; S; Daughter; 7285; Yes; Yes; Id. U-10924 An. 7238

7391; Vegar (Little Bull), Julia; F; 1889-43; F; M; Head; 7286; No; Temecula, town, Riverside Cal.; Yes; Al. 3289 An. 7241
7392; Vegar, Dionisio; M; 7/16/15-16; 1/4; S; Son; 7288; No; Same; Yes; Id. U-10664 An. 7244
7393; Vegar, Carlos; M; 2/6/18-14; 1/4; S; Son; 7289; No; Same; Yes; Id. U-10665 An. 7245
7394; Vegar, Marcus; M; 10/7/11-20; 1/4; S; Son; 7290; No; Same; Yes; Id. U-10663 An. 7243

7395; Vert (Allen), Julia; F; 1890-42; -1/4; M; Head; 7291; No; Unknown; No; Al. 1107 An. 7246
7396; Vert, James E.; M; 8/1/13-18; -1/4; S; Son; 7292; No; Unknown; Yes; Id. U-10666 An. 7247
7397; Vert, Helen; F; 8/23/14-17; -1/4; S; Daughter; 7293; No; Unknown; Yes; Id. U-10667 An. 7248
7398; Vert, Naomi; F; 1/3/16-16; -1/4; S; Daughter; 7294; No; Unknown; Yes; Id. U-10668 An. 7249
7399; Vert, Ethel A; F; 10/2/20-11; -1/4; S; Daughter; 7296; No; Unknown; Yes; Id. U-10670 An. 7251
7400; Vert, Murle; F; 8/31/17-14; -1/4; S; Daughter; 7295; No; Unknown; Yes; Id. U-10669 An. 7250
7401; Vert, Wesley; M; 6/24/24-7; -1/4; S; Son; 7297; No; Unknown; Yes; Id. U-11735 An. none
7402; Vert, Stanley; M; 4/13/27-4; -1/4; S; Son; 7298; No; Unknown; Yes; Id. U-12775 An. none

7403; Victor (Shangreau), Vesta; F; 1904-28; plus 1/4; M; Head; 7299; Yes; Yes; Al. 2564 An. 6138

7404; Vierling, Gwendoline; F; 8/9/11-20; -1/4; S; Head; 7300; Yes; Yes; Al. 7254 An. 6988

7405; Vierling (Allen), Jessie; F; 1884-48; -1/4; M; Head; 7301; Yes; Yes; Al. 1104 An. 7252
7406; Vierling, Anna; F; 3/24/15-17; -1/4; S; Daughter; 7302; Yes; Yes; Al. 7933 An. 7255
7407; Vierling, Earnest; M; 11/18/16-15; -1/4; S; Son; 7303; Yes; Yes; Id. U-10671 An. 7256

Census of the **Pine Ridge** reservation of the **Pine Ridge, South Dakota** jurisdiction, as of **April 1**, 1932, taken by **James H. McGregor**, Superintendent.

Key: Number; Surname, Given; Sex; Date of Birth-Age at Last Birthday; Tribe (Oglala Sioux, unless stated otherwise); Degree of Blood; Marital Status; Relationship to Head of Family [Last Census Roll Number]; At Jurisdiction Where Enrolled (Yes/No); (If no – Where); Ward (Yes/No, if given); Allotment, Annuity and Identification Numbers (if given).

7408; Vocu (Giago), Lucy; F; 10/17/02-29; plus 1/4; M; Head; 7305; Yes; Yes; Al. 1424 An. 2462
7409; Vocu, Leo; M; 10/12/27-4; -1/4; S; Son; 7306; Yes; Yes; Id. U-12538 An. none
7410; Vocu, Robert; M; 12/19/28-3; -1/4; S; Son; 7307; Yes; Yes; Id. U-13152 An. none
7411; Vocu, Melvin; M; 3/31/31-1; -1/4; S; Son; 7308; Yes; Yes; Id. U-13789 An. none
7412; Fergusion, Earl; M; 1/18/30-2; -1/4; S; Nephew; 7309; Yes; Yes; Id. U-13325 An. none

N.E.: Wafford, Jesse; M; ------; Cherokee; plus 1/4; M; Head;
7413; Wafford (Merrival), Lema; F; 1900-32; plus 1/4; M; Head; 7310; No; Detroit, city, Wayne, Mich; Yes; Al. 3593 An. 7258
7414; Wafford, Josephine; F; 6/20/23-8; 1/4; S; Daughter; 7311; No; Same; Yes; Id. U-14038 An. 7259
7415; Wafford, Fay; F; 10/28/28-3; 1/4; S; Daughter; 7312; No; Same; Yes; Id. U-12958 An. none

7416; Walking, Cyrus; M; 1904-28; F; S; Head; 7313; No; Akron, city, Summit, Ohio; Yes; Id. U-9438 An. 7260
7417; Walking, Felix; M; 6/4/06-26; F; S; Head; 7314; Yes; Yes; Id. U-9439 An. 7261

N.E.: Walking Bull, Charles; M; ------; Rosebud Sioux; M; Head;
7418; Walking Bull (Weasel), Edna; F; 1908-24; F; M; Wife; 7315; Yes; Yes; Al. 7548 An. 7338
7419; Walking Bull, Florence; F; 12/28/27-4; F; S; Daughter; 7316; Yes; Yes; Id. U-12894 An. none
7420; Walking Bull, Allen; M; 12/12/28-3; F; S; Son; 7317; Yes; Yes; Id. U-12997 An. none
7421; Walking Bull, Junior G; M; 6/19/30-1; F; S; Son; 7318; Yes; Yes; Id. U-13558 An. none

7422; Walking Elk, ---; M; 1857-75; F; M; Head; 7319; Yes; Yes; Al. 3098 An. 7269
7423; Walking Elk (No data), Edna; F; 1864-68; F; M; Wife; 7320; Yes; Yes; Id. U-10674 An. 7270

7424; Walking Elk, Ben; M; 1888-44; F; M; Head; 7321; Yes; Yes; Id. U-10765 An. 7271
7425; Walking Elk (Heart Heart), Rosa; F; 1885-47; F; M; Wife; 7323; Yes; Yes; Al. 5122 An. 7274

Census of the __Pine Ridge__ reservation of the __Pine Ridge, South Dakota__ jurisdiction, as of __April 1__, 19**32**, taken by __James H. McGregor__, Superintendent.

Key: Number; Surname, Given; Sex; Date of Birth-Age at Last Birthday; Tribe (Oglala Sioux, unless stated otherwise); Degree of Blood; Marital Status; Relationship to Head of Family [Last Census Roll Number]; At Jurisdiction Where Enrolled (Yes/No); (If no – Where); Ward (Yes/No, if given); Allotment, Annuity and Identification Numbers (if given).

7426; Walking Elk, James; M; 8/5/17-14; F; S; Son; 7322; Yes; Yes; Id. U-10676 An. 7272
7427; Walking Elk, Sarah; F; 1/16/26-6; F; S; Daughter; 7324; Yes; Yes; Id. U-11795 An. none

7428; Walking Hail, ---; F; 1834-98; F; Wd; Head; 7325; Yes; Yes; Al. 3152 An. 7278

7429; Walks Fast, Adam; M; 1883-49; F; M; Head; 7326; Yes; Yes; Al. 652 An. 7279
7430; Walks Fast (Kills In Winter), Lizzie; F; 1888-44; F; M; Wife; 7327; Yes; Yes; Al. 3776 An. 7280

7431; Walks Out, ---; M; 1861-71; F; M; Head; 7328; Yes; Yes; Al. 3295 An. 7282
7432; Walks Out (no data), Eureka; F; 1864-68; F; M; Wife; 7329; Yes; Yes; Al. 6237 An. 7283

7433; Walks Out, Asa; M; 1905-27; F; M; Head; 7330; Yes; Yes; Al. 6238 An. 7284
7434; Walks Out, Blondy; M; 4/28/27-4; F; S; Son; 7331; Yes; Yes; Id. U-12334 An. none
N.E.: Walks Out, Elizabeth; F; ------; Cheyenne R. Sioux; M; Wife;
7435; Walks Out, Aurelia; F; 11/2/28-3; F; S; Daughter; 7332; Yes; Yes; Id. U-12959 An. none
7436; Walks Out, Hermus; M; 11/4/30-1; F; S; Son; 7333; Yes; Yes; Id. U-13750 An. none

7437; Walks Under Ground, Enos; M; 1876-56; F; M; Head; 7334; Yes; Yes; Al. 738 An. 7285
7438; Walks Under Ground (Charging), Louisa; F; 1870-62; F; M; Wife; 7335; Yes; Yes; Al. 6584 An. 7286
7439; Walks Under Ground, Jonas; M; 4/2/12-20; F; S; Son; 7336; Yes; Yes; Al. 7484 An. 7288

7440; Walks Under Ground, Jacob; M; 1874-58; F; M; Head; 7337; Yes; Yes; Al. 1677 An. 7291
7441; Walks Under Ground, Philip; M; 4/17/11-20; F; S; Son; 7338; Yes; Yes; Al. 7804 An. 7294

7442; Walks Under Ground, Reuben; M; 3/5/09-23; F; M; Head; 7339; Yes; Yes; Al. 7803 An. 7293
7443; Walks Under Ground (Little Warrior), Sadie; F; 9/19/08-23; F; M; Wife; 7340; Yes; Yes; Al. 4052 An. 4036

Census of the **Pine Ridge** reservation of the **Pine Ridge, South Dakota** jurisdiction, as of **April 1**, 1932, taken by **James H. McGregor**, Superintendent.

Key: Number; Surname, Given; Sex; Date of Birth-Age at Last Birthday; Tribe (Oglala Sioux, unless stated otherwise); Degree of Blood; Marital Status; Relationship to Head of Family [Last Census Roll Number]; At Jurisdiction Where Enrolled (Yes/No); (If no – Where); Ward (Yes/No, if given); Allotment, Annuity and Identification Numbers (if given).

7444; Walks Under Ground, Douglas; M; 1/4/31-1; M[sic]; S; Son; ---; Yes; Yes; U-13676

7445; Walks Under Ground, Joshua J; M; 1897-35; F; M; Head; 7341; Yes; tes[sic]; Al. 740 An. 7298

7446; Walks Under Ground, Francis; M; 7/16/28-3; F; S; Son; 7342; Yes; Yes; Id. U-12769 An. none

7447; Walks Under Ground, Burdick; M; 4/16/31-11/12; F; S; Son; ---; Yes; Yes; U-13846

7448; Walters, Ulysses; M; 11/11/08-23; 1/4; S; Head; 7348; Yes; Yes; Al. 5006 An. 2361

N.E.: ~~War Bonnet, Charles; M; ------; Rosebud Sioux; F; M; Head;~~

7449; War Bonnet (Eagle Shawl), Agnes; F; 3/15/11-21; F; M; Wife; 7349; Yes; Yes; Al. 7343 An. 6157

7450; War Bonnet, Conrad; M; 1871-61; F; M; Head; 7350; Yes; Yes; Al. 446 An. 7301

7451; War Bonnet (no data), Rosa; F; 1871-61; F; M; Wife; 7351; Yes; Yes; Al. 6952 An. 7302

7452; War Bonnet, Caroline; F; 3/28/26-6; F; S; Ward; 7352; Yes; Yes; Id. U-11925 An. none

7453; War Bonnet, Joseph; M; 1900-32; F; M; Head; 7353; Yes; Yes; Al. 446 An. 7301

7454; War Bonnet (White Thunder), Mary; F; 1900-32; F; M; Wife; 7354; Yes; Yes; Al. 4938 An. 7647

7455; War Bonnet, Thelma; F; 10/10/27-4; F; S; Daughter; 7355; Yes; Yes; Id. U-12451 An. none

7456; War Bonnet, Philip; M; 1/27/31-1; F; S; Son; 7356; Yes; Yes; Id. U-13718 An. none

7457; War Bonnet, Joseph; M; 1875-57; F; M; Head; 7357; Yes; No; Al. 5748 An. 7307

7458; Ward, Eldridge; M; 1869-63; plus 1/4; M; Head; 7358; Yes; No; Al. 2065 An. 7308

7459; Ward, Genevieve; F; 9/20/13-18; -1/4; S; Daughter; 7359; Yes; Yes; Id. U-10681 An. 7311

7460; Ward, Florence; F; 4/8/17-14; -1/4; S; Daughter; 7360; Yes; Yes; Id. U-10682 An. 7312

Census of the __Pine Ridge__ reservation of the __Pine Ridge, South Dakota__ jurisdiction, as of __April 1__, 19**32**, taken by __James H. McGregor__, Superintendent.

Key: Number; Surname, Given; Sex; Date of Birth-Age at Last Birthday; Tribe (Oglala Sioux, unless stated otherwise); Degree of Blood; Marital Status; Relationship to Head of Family [Last Census Roll Number]; At Jurisdiction Where Enrolled (Yes/No); (If no – Where); Ward (Yes/No, if given); Allotment, Annuity and Identification Numbers (if given).

7461; Ward, Woodrow; M; 10/12/18-13; -1/4; S; Son; 7361; Yes; Yes; Id. U-10683 An. 7313
7462; Ward, Gerald; M; 1/10/22-10; -1/4; S; Son; 7362; Yes; Yes; Id. U-10840 An. 7314

7463; Ward, Edison; M; 1907-25; -1/4; S; Head; 7363; Yes; Yes; Al. 4445 An. 7309

7464; Ward, Mary; F; 9/5/11-20; -1/4; S; Head; 7364; Yes; Yes; Al. 7004 An. 7310

7465; Ward (Williams), Irene; F; 8/21/09-22; plus 1/4; M; Head; 7365; No; Hyattville, town, Bighorn, Wyo; Yes; Al. 5362 An. 4887
7466; Ward, Robert; M; 12/19/28-3; -1/4; S; Son; 7366; No; Same; Yes; Id. U-13153 An. none
7467; Ward, William M; M; 7/12/30-1; -1/4; S; Son; 7367; No; Same; Yes; Id. U-13620 An. none

7468; Warrior, Fargo; M; 1900-32; F; M; Head; 7368; Yes; Yes; Al. 6273 An. 7315
7469; Warrior (Spider Back Bone), Stella; F; 1905-27; F; M; Wife; 7369; Yes; Yes; Al. 6262 An. 7616
7470; Warrior, Irene; F; 1/5/26-6; F; S; Daughter; 7370; Yes; Yes; Id. U-11791 An. none
7471; Warrior, Harvey; M; 3/29/28-4; F; S; Son; 7371; Yes; Yes; Id. U-12563 An. none
7472; Warrior, Wilber; M; 4/15/30-1; F; S; Son; 7372; Yes; Yes; Id. U-13498 An. none

7473; Water, Alex; M; 1866-66; plus 1/4; M; Head; 7373; Yes; No; Al. 4925 An. 7317
7474; Water (no data), Maggie; F; 1867-65; F; M; Wife; 7374; Yes; Yes; Al. 4926 An. 7318
7475; Water, Jessie; F; 12/19/10-21; plus 1/4; S; Head; 7375; Yes; Yes; Al. 8225 An. 7320
7476; Water, Aloysius; M; 1/8/32-2/12; 1/4; S; Son; ---; Yes; Yes; U-14073
7477; Water, Fred; M; 1895-37; plus 1/4; M; Head; 7376; Yes; Yes; Al. 8222 An. 7321
7478; Water (White Wolf), Susie; F; 1901-31; F; M; Wife; 7377; Yes; Yes; Id. U-10685 An. 7322
7479; Water, Ruth; F; 1/21/20-12; plus 1/4; S; Daughter; 7378; Yes; Yes; Id. U-10686 An. 7323
7480; Water, Thomas; M; 12/31/24-7; 1/4; S; Son; 7379; Yes; Yes; Id. U-10474 An. 7325

Census of the __Pine Ridge__ reservation of the __Pine Ridge, South Dakota__ jurisdiction, as of __April 1__, 19**32,** taken by __James H. McGregor__, Superintendent.

Key: Number; Surname, Given; Sex; Date of Birth-Age at Last Birthday; Tribe (Oglala Sioux, unless stated otherwise); Degree of Blood; Marital Status; Relationship to Head of Family [Last Census Roll Number]; At Jurisdiction Where Enrolled (Yes/No); (If no – Where); Ward (Yes/No, if given); Allotment, Annuity and Identification Numbers (if given).

7481; Water, Kathrine; F; 9/4/26-5; 1/4; S; Daughter; 7380; Yes; Yes; Id. U-12190 An. none

7482; Water, Athalia; F; 2/24/28-4; 1/4; S; Daughter; 7381; Yes; Yes; Id. U-12603 An. none

7483; Water, Leroy; M; 5/1/30-1; 1/4; S; Son; 7382; Yes; Yes; Id. U-13497 An. none

7484; Water, George; M; 1900-32; 1/4; Wd; Head; 7383; Yes; Yes; Al. 8223 An. 7326

7485; Water nee (Nelson), Katie; F; 1902-30; 1/4; Wd; Head; 7384; Yes; Yes; Al. 5024 An. 7327

7486; Water, Herman; M; 1890-42; plus 1/4; M; Head; 7385; Yes; Yes; Al. 6523 An. 7329

7487; Water (Brings White), Ella; F; 1890-42; 1/4; M; Wife; 7386; Yes; Yes; Al. 898 An. 7330

7488; Water, Emily; F; 8/12/15-16; 1/4; S; Daughter; 7387; Yes; Yes; Id. U-10684 An. 7331

7489; Water, Ida; F; 1/24/24-8; 1/4; S; Daughter; 7388; Yes; Yes; Id. U-11461 An. 7332

7490; Water, Norman; M; 3/1/08-24; 1/4; M; Head; 7389; Yes; Yes; Al. 5227 An. 7319

7491; Water (White Butterfly), Louisa; F; 10/5/07-24; F; M; Wife; 7390; Yes; Yes; Al. 6470 An. 3639

7492; Water, Rebecca; F; 5/17/30-1; plus 1/4; S; Daughter; 7391; Yes; Yes; Id. U-13536 An. none

7493; Water, Harry; M; 1903-29; 1/4; M; Head; 7392; Yes; Yes; Al. 8224 An. 7328

7494; Water (Red Feather), Fosa; F; 9/2/09-22; F; M; Wife; 7393; Yes; Yes; Al. 5328 An. 5472

7495; Water, William; M; 5/14/29-2; plus 1/4; S; Son; 7394; Yes; Yes; Id. U-13196 An. none

7496; Water, Martha; F; 5/14/31-10/12; 1/4; S; Daughter; ---; Yes; Yes; U-13880

7497; Wears Leaf, ---; F; 1862-70; F; Wd; Head; 7395; Yes; Yes; Al. 5376 An. 4968

7498; Wears The Eagle, ---; F; 1855-77; F; Wd; Head; 7396; Yes; Yes; Al. 7603 An. 7335

7499; Weasel, Henry; M; 1881-51; F; M; Head; 7397; Yes; Yes; Al. 3519 An. 7336
7500; Weasel (Iron Crow), Lucy; F; 1891-41; F; M; Wife; 7398; Yes; Yes; Al. 6910 An. 5957

Census of the **Pine Ridge** reservation of the **Pine Ridge, South Dakota** jurisdiction, as of **April 1**, 19**32**, taken by **James H. McGregor**, Superintendent.

Key: Number; Surname, Given; Sex; Date of Birth-Age at Last Birthday; Tribe (Oglala Sioux, unless stated otherwise); Degree of Blood; Marital Status; Relationship to Head of Family [Last Census Roll Number]; At Jurisdiction Where Enrolled (Yes/No); (If no – Where); Ward (Yes/No, if given); Allotment, Annuity and Identification Numbers (if given).

7501; Weasel, Alexander; M; 8/22/15-16; F; S; Son; 7399; Yes; Yes; Al. 8180 An. 7340

7502; Weasel, Villance; F; 10/14/24-7; F; S; Daughter; 7400; Yes; Yes; Id. U-11355 An. 7341

7503; Weasel, Van; M; 5/23/30-1; F; S; Son; 7401; Yes; Yes; Id. U-13499 An. none

7504; Weasel, Alta; F; 5/24/12-19; F; S; Head; 7402; Yes; Yes; Al. 7549 An. 7339

7505; Weasel Bear, Charles; M; 1880-52; F; M; Head; 7404; Yes; Yes; Al. 3065 An. 7342

7506; Weasel Bear (Bear Louse), Amy; F; 1889-43; F; M; Wife; 7405; Yes; Yes; Al. 3805 An. 7343

7507; Weasel Bear, Jefferson; M; 8/25/14-17; F; S; Son; 7406; Yes; Yes; Id. U-10688 An. 7345

7508; Weasel Bear, Samuel; M; 10/27/17-14; F; S; Son; 7407; Yes; Yes; Id. U-10689 An. 7346

7509; Weasel Bear, Philip; M; 10/27/22-9; F; S; Son; 7408; Yes; Yes; Id. U-12022 An. 7347

7510; Weasel Bear, Alice; F; 2/10/26-6; F; S; Daughter; 7409; Yes; Yes; Id. U-11846 An. none

7511; Weasel Bear, Luke; M; 5/6/08-23; F; S; Head; 7410; Yes; Yes; Al. 6077 An. 1290

7512; Weasel Bear (no data), Louisa; F; 1852-80; F; Wd; Wife; 7412; Yes; Yes; Al. 6074 An. 7348

7513; Weasel Bear, Willie; M; 1900-32; F; M; Head; 7413; Yes; Yes; Al. 3066 An. 7349

7514; Weasel Bear (Little Soldier), Jennie; F; 1901-31; F; M; Wife; 7414; Yes; Yes; Al. 6348 An. 7350

7515; Weasel Bear, Cleveland; M; 2/11/23-9; F; S; Son; 7415; Yes; Yes; Id. U-12082 An. 7351

7516; Weasel Bear, Benjamin; M; 4/3/25-6; F; S; Son; 7416; Yes; Yes; Id. U-11533 An. none

7517; Weasel Bear, Grace; F; 7/4/27-4; F; S; Daughter; 7417; Yes; Yes; Id. U-12433 An. none

7518; Weasel Bear, Tex; M; 11/23/29-2; F; S; Son; 7418; Yes; Yes; Id. U-13360 An. none

7519; Weber (no data), Emma; F; 1869-63; plus 1/4; M; Head; 7419; No; Merriman, town, Cherry, Nebr; No; Al. 1352 An. 7352

Census of the **Pine Ridge** reservation of the **Pine Ridge, South Dakota** jurisdiction, as of **April 1**, 1932, taken by **James H. McGregor**, Superintendent.

Key: Number; Surname, Given; Sex; Date of Birth-Age at Last Birthday; Tribe (Oglala Sioux, unless stated otherwise); Degree of Blood; Marital Status; Relationship to Head of Family [Last Census Roll Number]; At Jurisdiction Where Enrolled (Yes/No); (If no – Where); Ward (Yes/No, if given); Allotment, Annuity and Identification Numbers (if given).

7520; Weber, Dorothy; F; 5/23/15-16; -1/4; S; Daughter; 7420; No; Same; Yes; Id. U-10693 An. 7356

7521; Weber, Winnie; F; 5/11/09-22; -1/4; S; Head; 7421; No; Merriman, town, Cherry, Nebr; Yes; Al. 5438 An. 7354

7522; Weber, Kenneth; M; 12/7/11-20; -1/4; S; Head; 7422; No; Merriman, town, Cherry, Nebr; Yes; Id. U-10692 An. 7355

7523; Weber, Frank; M; 1892-40; -1/4; M; Head; 7423; No; Merriman, town, Cherry, Nebr; No; Al. 1353 An. 7357

7524; Weber, Glenn; M; 8/17/15-16; -1/4; S; Son; 7424; No; Same; Yes; Id. U-10694 An. 7358

7525; Weber, Noel; M; 10/17/17-14; -1/4; S; Son; 7425; No; Same; Yes; Id. U-10695 An. 7359

7526; Weber, George; M; 6/14/24-7; -1/4; S; Son; 7426; No; Same; Yes; Id. U-11315 An. 7360

7527; Weber, Fred; M; 1907-25; -1/4; M; Head; 7427; No; Merriman, town, Cherry, Nebr; Yes; Al. 5437 An. 7353

7528; Weber, Bonnie L; F; 11/20/28-3; -1/4; S; Daughter; 7428; No; Same; Yes; Id. U-12936 An. none

7529; Weber, John; M; 1905-27; -1/4; M; Head; 7429; No; Merriman, town, Cherry, Nebr; Yes; Al. 5436 An. 7361

7530; Weber, Jackie B; M; 6/29/29-2; -1/4; S; Son; 7430; No; Same; Yes; Id. U-13238 An. none

7531; Weber, Joseph; M; 10/14/97-34; -1/4; S; Head; 7431; No; Merriman, town, Cherry, Nebr; Yes; Al. 1355 An. 7362

7532; Weber, Julia; F; 1895-37; -1/4; S; Head; 7432; No; Merriman, town, Cherry, Nebr; No; Al. 1354 An. 7363

7533; Weber, William; M; 1902-30; -1/4; M; Head; 7433; No; Merriman, town, Cherry, Nebr; Yes; Al. 1357 An. 7364

7534; Weber, Wilda; F; 12/1/30-1; -1/4; S; Daughter; 7434; No; Same; Yes; Id. U-13719 An. none

7535; Wellborn (Midkiff), Lorraine; F; 10/27/97-34; -1/4; S; Head; 7435; No; Bono, town, Craighead, Ark.; No; Al. 3921 An. 7365

7536; Wellborn, William; M; 9/23/17-14; -1/4; S; Son; 7436; No; Same; Yes; Id. U-10696 An. 7366

Census of the __Pine Ridge__ reservation of the __Pine Ridge, South Dakota__ jurisdiction, as of __April 1__, 19__32__, taken by __James H. McGregor__, Superintendent.

Key: Number; Surname, Given; Sex; Date of Birth-Age at Last Birthday; Tribe (Oglala Sioux, unless stated otherwise); Degree of Blood; Marital Status; Relationship to Head of Family [Last Census Roll Number]; At Jurisdiction Where Enrolled (Yes/No); (If no – Where); Ward (Yes/No, if given); Allotment, Annuity and Identification Numbers (if given).

7537; Wellborn, Virginia; F; 11/15/18-13; -1/4; S; Daughter; 7437; No; Same; Yes; Id. U-10697 An. 7367

7538; Wellborn, Frances; F; 7/7/23-8; -1/4; S; Daughter; ---; No; Same; Yes; U-13862

7539; Wells, Mark; M; 1894-38; -1/4; S; Head; 7438; Yes; No; Al. 3913 An. 7368

7540; Wells, Patrick; M; 1/23/97-35; -1/4; S; Head; 7439; Yes; No; Al. 3914 An. 7369

7541; Wells, Maurice; M; 1907-25; -1/4; S; Head; 7440; Yes; Yes; Al. 3916 An. 7371

7542; Wells, Philip Jr.; M; 1892-40; -1/4; M; Head; 7442; Yes; Yes; Al. 2912 An. 7372

7543; Wells, Frederick; M; 7/30/15-16; -1/4; S; Son; 7443; Yes; Yes; Al. 8088 An. 7373

7544; Wells, Helen M; F; 5/4/17-14; -1/4; S; Daughter; 7444; Yes; Yes; Id. U-10698 An. 7374

7545; Wells, Elroy P; M; 3/7/21-11; -1/4; S; Son; 7445; Yes; Yes; Id. U-10699 An. 7375

7546; Wells, Philip Sr.; M; 1851-81; -1/4; M; Head; 7440; Yes; No; Al. 3909 An. 7370

7547; Wells, Thomas H.; M; 1886-46; -1/4; S; Head; 7446; Yes; No; Al. 3910 An. 7376

7548; Wells, William W.; M; 7/19/00-31; -1/4; S; Head; 7447; Yes; Yes; Al. 3915 An. 7377

7549; Wentzel (Peck), Nellie; F; 1890-42; plus 1/4; M; Head; 7448; Yes; No; Al. 2255 An. 7378

7550; Wentzel, Betty; F; 7/20/17-14; -1/4; S; Daughter; 7449; Yes; Yes; Id. U-11367 An. 7379

7551; Wentzel, Helean A; F; 8/30/19-12; -1/4; S; Daughter; 7450; Yes; Yes; Id. U-11368 An. 7380

7552; Wentzel, Roberta; F; 2/16/23-9; -1/4; S; Daughter; 7451; Yes; Yes; Id. U-11625 An. 7381

N.E.: ~~Weston, Gilbert; M; ------; Santee Sioux; F; M; Head;~~

7553; Weston (Brown Eyes), Mary; F; 6/30/03-28; plus 1/4; M; Wife; 7452; Yes; Yes; Al. 576 An. 7382

Census of the   **Pine Ridge**   reservation of the **Pine Ridge, South Dakota** jurisdiction, as of   **April 1**   , 19**32**, taken by   **James H. McGregor**   , Superintendent.

Key: Number; Surname, Given; Sex; Date of Birth-Age at Last Birthday; Tribe (Oglala Sioux, unless stated otherwise); Degree of Blood; Marital Status; Relationship to Head of Family [Last Census Roll Number]; At Jurisdiction Where Enrolled (Yes/No); (If no – Where); Ward (Yes/No, if given); Allotment, Annuity and Identification Numbers (if given).

7554; Weston, Harry L; M; 10/6/26-5; 1/4; S; Son; 7453; Yes; Yes; Id. U-12128 An. none

7555; Weston, Lourina; F; 8/12/28-3; 1/4; S; Daughter; 7454; Yes; Yes; Id. U-12770 An. none

7556; Weston, Belle L; F; 6/25/30-1; 1/4; S; Daughter; 7455; Yes; Yes; Id. U-13559 An. none

N.E.:   Weston, Reuben; M; ------; Flandreau Sioux; F; M; Head;

7557; Weston (White Bull), Susan; F; 11/8/20-11; F; M; Wife; 7456; Yes; Yes; Al. 427 An. 7385

7558; Weston, Roy R; M; 7/15/26-5; F; S; Son; 7457; Yes; Yes; Id. U-12129 An. none

7559; Weston, Elinora; F; 8/6/28-3; F; S; Daughter; 7458; Yes; Yes; Id. U-12785 An. none

7560; Weston, Ruby; F; 2/20/31-1; F; S; Daughter; 7459; Yes; Yes; Id. U-13752 An. none

7561; Weston, Samuel C; M; 1/6/32-2/12; F; S; Son; ---; Yes; Yes; U-14139

7562; Whalen, James; M; 1881-51; plus 1/4; S; Head; 7460; No; Chadron, town, Dawes, Nebr.; Yes; Al. 318 An. 7388

7563; Whalen, Richard; M; 1891-41; 1/4; S; Head; 7461; Yes; No; Al. 320 An. 7389

N.E.:   Whalen (Henry), Emma R; F; ------; Winnegago[sic]; M; Wife;

7564; Whalen, Thelma; F; 8/17/12-19; Oglala Sioux-Winnebago; 1/4; S; Daughter; 7462; No; Sac & Fox, San., Iowa; Yes; Al. 7315 An. 7391

7565; Weston, Richard Jr.; M; 5/29/14-17; Oglala Sioux-Winnebago; 1/4; S; Son; 7463; Yes; Yes; Id. U-10702 An. 7392

7566; Weston, Myron; M; 6/5/28-3; Oglala Sioux-Winnebago; 1/4; S; Son; 7464; Yes; Yes; Id. U-12708 An. none

7567; Weston, Merle; M; 6/20/31-9/12; Oglala Sioux-Winnebago; 1/4; S; Son; ---; Yes; Yes; U-13862

7568; Whetstone, Joseph; M; 1882-50; F; Wd; Head; 7465; Yes; Yes; Al. 587 An. 7394

7569; Whirlwind, ---; F; 1854-78; F; Wd; Head; 7467; Yes; Yes; Al. 2307 An. 595

7570; Whirlwind, ---; M; 1871-61; F; M; Head; 7468; Yes; Yes; Al. 1024 An. 7401

7571; Whirlwind (Red Eyes), Lucy; F; 1888-44; F; M; Wife; 7469; Yes; Yes; Al. 1394 An. 7402

7572; Whirlwind, Theodore; M; 11/18/26-5; F; S; Son; 7470; Yes; Yes; Id. U-12168 An. none

Census of the **Pine Ridge** reservation of the **Pine Ridge, South Dakota** jurisdiction, as of **April 1**, 19**32**, taken by **James H. McGregor**, Superintendent.

Key: Number; Surname, Given; Sex; Date of Birth-Age at Last Birthday; Tribe (Oglala Sioux, unless stated otherwise); Degree of Blood; Marital Status; Relationship to Head of Family [Last Census Roll Number]; At Jurisdiction Where Enrolled (Yes/No); (If no – Where); Ward (Yes/No, if given); Allotment, Annuity and Identification Numbers (if given).

7573; Whirlwind, Stacy; M; 5/24/12-19; F; S; Head; 7471; Yes; Yes; Al. 7243 An. 7403

7574; Whirlwind, Bartholemew; M; 8/3/13-18; F; S; Head; 7472; Yes; Yes; Al. 7244 An. 7404

7575; Whirlwind, Pugh; M; 1904-28; F; M; Head; 7473; Yes; Yes; Al. 5232 An. 7408

7576; Whirlwind (Bad Wound), Grace; F; 7/3/09-22; F; M; Wife; 285; Yes; Yes; Al. 5081 An. 290

7577; Bad Wound, Stella; F; 5/29/27-4; plus 1/4; S; S. Daughter; 286; Yes; Yes; U-12677

7578; Whirlwind Bear (She Stops), ---; F; 1865-67; F; Wd; Head; 7474; Yes; Yes; Al. 5340 An. 7410

7579; Whirlwind Horse, William; M; 7/10/08-23; F; S; Head; 7475; Yes; Yes; Al. 4985 An. 7415

7580; Whirlwind Horse, James; M; 1900-32; F; S; Head; 7476; Yes; Yes; Al. 4958 An. 7416

7581; Whirlwind Horse, John; M; 1892-40; F; M; Head; 7477; Yes; Yes; Al. 4957 An. 7417

7582; Whirlwind Horse (Six Feathers), Mollie; F; 1901-31; plus 1/4; M; Wife; 7478; Yes; Yes; Al. 5175 An. 7418

7583; Whirlwind Horse, Raymond; M; 3/15/26-6; 1/4; S; Son; 7479; Yes; Yes; Id. U-11856 An. none

7584; Whirlwind Horse, Verda; F; 4/29/30-1; 1/4; S; Daughter; 7480; Yes; Yes; Id. U-13500 An. none

7585; Whirlwind Horse, Joseph; M; 1897-35; F; M; Head; 7481; Yes; Yes; Al. 4961 An. 7421

7586; Whirlwind Horse (Bissonette), Bertha; F; 1899-33; plus 1/4; M; Wife; 7310; Yes; Yes; Al. 5175 An. 7422

7587; Whirlwind Horse, Cecelia; F; 8/18/17-14; 1/4; S; Daughter; 7483; Yes; Yes; Id. U-10710 An. 7423

7588; Whirlwind Horse, Adolph; M; 12/3/18-13; 1/4; S; Son; 7484; Yes; Yes; Id. U-10711 An. 7424

7589; Whirlwind Horse, Robert; M; 9/8/20-11; 1/4; S; Son; 7485; Yes; Yes; Id. U-10712 An. 7425

7590; Whirlwind Horse, Maurice; M; 8/1/23-8; 1/4; S; Son; 7486; Yes; Yes; Id. U-11168 An. 7426

Census of the ___Pine Ridge___ reservation of the ___Pine Ridge, South Dakota___ jurisdiction, as of ___April 1___, 19**32**, taken by ___James H. McGregor___, Superintendent.

Key: Number; Surname, Given; Sex; Date of Birth-Age at Last Birthday; Tribe (Oglala Sioux, unless stated otherwise); Degree of Blood; Marital Status; Relationship to Head of Family [Last Census Roll Number]; At Jurisdiction Where Enrolled (Yes/No); (If no – Where); Ward (Yes/No, if given); Allotment, Annuity and Identification Numbers (if given).

7591; Whirlwind Horse, Louis; M; 1902-30; F; M; Head; 7487; Yes; Yes; Al. 4962 An. 7427

N.E.: Whirlwind Horse (Zwimiega), Sadie; F; ------; Cherokee; 1/4; M; Wife;

7592; Whirlwind Horse, Anthony; M; 11/20/27-4; plus 1/4; S; Son; 7488; Yes; Yes; Id. U-12883 An. none

7593; Whirlwind Horse, Thelma; F; 3/13/31-1; 1/4; S; Daughter; 7490; Yes; Yes; Id. U-13772 An. none

7594; Whirlwind Man, ---; M; 1857-75; F; M; Head; 7491; Yes; Yes; Al. 6614 An. 7428

7595; Whirlwind Man (no data), Florence; F; 1853-79; F; M; Wife; 7492; Yes; Yes; Al. 6615 An. 7428

N.E.: Whirlwind Soldier, Clement; M; ------; Rosebud Sioux; F; M; Head;

7596; Whirlwind Soldier (Levering), Sallie; F; 1873-59; plus 1/4; M; Wife; 7493; No; Winnebago, Nebr.; No; Al. 4645 An. 3835

7597; Whistler, Charles; M; 1896-36; F; M; Head; 7494; Yes; No; Al. 4302 An. 7430

N.E.: Whistler (Little Chief), Mary; F; ------; Rosebud Sioux; F; M; Wife;

7598; Whistler, Julian; M; 1861-71; F; M; Head; 7495; Yes; Yes; Al. 4301 An. 7432
7599; Her Door, ---; F; 1869-63; F; M; Wife; 7496; Yes; Yes; Al. 7193 An. 7433

N.E.: White, Francis; M; ------; Rosebud Sioux; F; M; Head;

7600; White (Bull Tail), Ada; F; 1894-38; F; M; Wife; 7497; Yes; Yes; Al. 602 An. 7434

7601; White, Frank; M; 1890-42; plus 1/4; Wd; Head; 7499; No; Yankton, town, Yankton, S.D.; Yes; Al. 2739 An. 7435

7602; White, Jefferson; M; 1905-27; F; S; Head; 7500; Yes; Yes; Al. 5680 An. 7436

7603; White (Henderson), Lucy; F; 1897-35; plus 1/4; M; Head; 7501; No; Hay Springs, town, Sheridan, Nebr.; No; Al. 1351 An. 7437
7604; White, Helen; F; 8/3/15-16; -1/4; S; Daughter; 7502; No; Same; Yes; Id. U-10717 An. 7438
7605; White, Elaine; F; 3/4/17-15; -1/4; S; Daughter; 7503; No; Same; Yes; Id. U-10718 An. 7439
7606; White, Robert; M; 3/13/24-8; -1/4; S; Son; 7504; No; Same; Yes; Id. U-11232 An. 7440
7607; White, Neil; M; 9/28/27-5; -1/4; S; Son; 7505; No; Same; Yes; Id. U-12452 An. none

Census of the **Pine Ridge** reservation of the **Pine Ridge, South Dakota** jurisdiction, as of **April 1**, 1932, taken by **James H. McGregor**, Superintendent.

Key: Number; Surname, Given; Sex; Date of Birth-Age at Last Birthday; Tribe (Oglala Sioux, unless stated otherwise); Degree of Blood; Marital Status; Relationship to Head of Family [Last Census Roll Number]; At Jurisdiction Where Enrolled (Yes/No); (If no – Where); Ward (Yes/No, if given); Allotment, Annuity and Identification Numbers (if given).

7608; White, Martin; M; 1903-29; plus 1/4; M; Head; 7506; Yes; Yes; Al. 2743 An. 7441

7609; White (Jones), Josephine; F; 1907-25; 1/4; M; Wife; 7507; Yes; Yes; Al. 2704 An. 3317

7610; White, Doris; F; 4/8/29-2; 1/4; S; Daughter; 7508; Yes; Yes; Id. U-13280 An. none

7611; White, Marie; F; 10/24/30-1; 1/4; S; Daughter; 7509; Yes; Yes; Id. U-13632 An. none

7612; White (Montileaux), Emily; F; 1907-25; 1/4; Wd; Head; 7510; Yes; Yes; Al. 3575 An. 4558

7613; White, Verine; F; 6/30/25-6; 1/4; S; Daughter; 7511; Yes; Yes; Id. U-11828 An. none

7614; White, Irene; F; 2/27/28-4; 1/4; S; Daughter; 7512; Yes; Yes; Id. U-12816 An. none

7615; White, Mathew; M; 4/9/10-21; F; S; Head; 7513; Yes; Yes; Al. 5681 An. 7444

7616; White, Katie; F; 9/28/14-17; F; S; Head; 7514; Yes; Yes; Id. U-10713 An. 7445

7617; White, Robert; M; 1872-60; F; M; Head; 7515; Yes; Yes; Al. 3798 An. 7446
7618; White (no data), Jessie; F; 1872-60; F; M; Wife; 7516; Yes; Yes; Al. 3799 An. 7447

7619; White Bear (no data), Day; F; 1860-72; F; Wd; Head; 7517; Yes; Yes; Al. 3564 An. 7450

7620; White Bear, John; M; 1906-26; F; M; Head; 7518; Yes; Yes; Id. U-9901 An. 7451

7621; White Bear (Broken Nose), Winnie; F; 5/18/11-20; F; M; Wife; 7519; Yes; Yes; Al. 6531 An. 1033

7622; White Bear, Katie; F; 11/6/31-4/12; F; S; Daughter; ---; Yes; Yes; U-14113

7623; White Bear, Jacob; M; 12/22/06-25; F; M; Head; 7520; Yes; Yes; Al. 5773 An. 7452

7624; White Bear (Lone Hill), Edna; F; 4/3/14-17; plus 1/4; M; Wife; 7521; Yes; Yes; Al. 8116 An. 4153

7625; White Bear, William; M; 11/25/31-4/12; 1/4; S; Son; ---; Yes; Yes; U-14052

7626; White Bear, William; M; 1867-65; F; M; Head; 7522; Yes; Yes; Al. 1792 An. 7453

Census of the **Pine Ridge** reservation of the **Pine Ridge, South Dakota** jurisdiction, as of **April 1**, 1932, taken by **James H. McGregor**, Superintendent.

Key: Number; Surname, Given; Sex; Date of Birth-Age at Last Birthday; Tribe (Oglala Sioux, unless stated otherwise); Degree of Blood; Marital Status; Relationship to Head of Family [Last Census Roll Number]; At Jurisdiction Where Enrolled (Yes/No); (If no – Where); Ward (Yes/No, if given); Allotment, Annuity and Identification Numbers (if given).

7627; White Bear (no data), Jennie; F; 1872-60; F; M; Wife; 7523; Yes; Yes; Al. 1793 An. 7454

7628; White Bear, Benjamin; M; 12/2/19-12; F; S; Adopted Son; 7524; Yes; Yes; Id. U-10247 An. 7455

7629; White Bear Claws, James; M; 1885-47; F; M; Head; 7525; Yes; Yes; Al. 3443 An. 7456

7630; White Bear Claws (Flesh), Mary; F; 1886-46; F; M; Wife; 7526; Yes; Yes; Al. 4665 An. 7457

7631; White Belly, Frank; M; 1876-56; F; M; Head; 7528; Yes; Yes; Al. 4914 An. 7460

7632; White Belly (Grass), Victoria; F; 1895-37; plus 1/4; M; Wife; 7529; Yes; Yes; Al. 7673 An. 7461

7633; White Belly, Augustine; F; 6/18/15-16; 1/4; S; Daughter; 7530; Yes; Yes; Id. U-9623 An. none

7634; White Belly, Willard; M; 1878-54; F; M; Head; 7531; Yes; Yes; Al. 752 An. 7462

7635; White Belly (no data), Mary; F; 1882-50; F; M; Wife; 7532; Yes; Yes; Al. 3869 An. 7463

7636; White Belly, Albert; M; 8/4/12-19; F; S; Son; 7533; Yes; Yes; Al. 7701 An. 7464

7637; White Bird, James; M; 1893-39; F; M; Head; 7534; Yes; Yes; Al. 6570 An. 7465

7638; White Bird (Chase In Sight), Winnie; F; 1900-32; F; Wd; Head; 7535; Yes; Yes; Al. 4881 An. 7466

7639; Chase In Sight, Garcia; M; 6/9/27-4; F; S; Son; 7536; Yes; Yes; Id. U-12733 An. none

7640; Yellow Thunder, Winfred; M; 11/10/31-4/12; F; S; Son; ---; Yes; Yes; U-14114

7641; White Bull, #1; M; 1857-75; F; M; Head; 7537; Yes; Yes; Al. 434 An. 7470

7642; White Bull (no data), Fannie; F; 1853-79; F; M; Wife; 7538; Yes; Yes; Al. 5943 An. 1350

7643; White Bull, #2; M; 1859-73; F; Wd; Head; 7539; Yes; Yes; Al. 462 An. 7472

7644; White Bull, Martin; M; 9/13/11-20; F; M; Head; 7540; Yes; Yes; Id. U-10721 An. 7474

Census of the __Pine Ridge__ reservation of the __Pine Ridge, South Dakota__ jurisdiction, as of __April 1__, 19**32**, taken by __James H. McGregor__, Superintendent.

Key: Number; Surname, Given; Sex; Date of Birth-Age at Last Birthday; Tribe (Oglala Sioux, unless stated otherwise); Degree of Blood; Marital Status; Relationship to Head of Family [Last Census Roll Number]; At Jurisdiction Where Enrolled (Yes/No); (If no – Where); Ward (Yes/No, if given); Allotment, Annuity and Identification Numbers (if given).

7645; White Bull, George; M; 1896-36; F; M; Head; 7541; Yes; Yes; Al. 438 An. 7476

7646; White Bull (White Bull), Ella; F; 1877-55; F; M; Wife; 7542; Yes; Yes; Al. 6958 An. 7477

7647; White Bull, Isaac; M; 12/23/09-22; F; M; Head; 7543; Yes; Yes; Al. 6959 An. 7478

N.E.: White Bull (Little Thunder), Winnie; F; ------; Rosebud Sioux; F; M; Wife;

7648; White Bull, James; M; 1895-37; F; M; Head; 7544; Yes; No; Al. 437 An. 7480

N.E.: White Bull (Skenandare), Ida; F; ------; Oneida; plus 1/4; M; Wife;

7649; White Bull, Lucille; F; 7/10/19-12; plus 1/4; S; Daughter; 7545; Yes; Yes; Id. U-10938 An. 7481

7650; White Bull, Theodore; M; 8/28/20-11; 1/4; S; Son; 7546; Yes; Yes; Id. U-10940 An. 7482

7651; White Bull, Phyllis; F; 11/21/21-10; 1/4; S; Daughter; 7547; Yes; Yes; Id. U-10959 An. 7483

7652; White Bull, James; M; 6/10/25-6; 1/4; S; Son; 7548; Yes; Yes; Id. U-12916 An. none

7653; White Bull, Levi; M; 1907-25; F; M; Head; 7549; Yes; Yes; Al. 4601 An. 7484

7654; White Bull (Brown Ear Horse), Katie; F; 12/2/12-19; F; M; Wife; 1079; Yes; Yes; Al. 7649 An. 1122

7655; White Bull, Kiva; F; 11/9/28-3; F; S; Daughter; 7550; Yes; Yes; Id. U-13124 An. none

7656; White Bull, Seth; M; 1892-40; F; M; Head; 7551; Yes; Yes; Al. 436 An. 7485

7657; White Bull (Howling Horse), Mary; F; 1892-40; F; M; Wife; 7552; Yes; Yes; Al. 2856 An. 7486

7658; White Bull, Leonard; M; 8/4/18-13; F; S; Son; 7553; Yes; Yes; Id. U-10720 An. 7487

7659; White Bull, Vernie; F; 1/18/29-3; F; S; Daughter; 7554; Yes; Yes; Id. U-13154 An. none

7660; White Butterfly (Lame Dog), Rosa; F; 1892-40; F; WD; Head; 7555; Yes; Yes; Al. 3724 An. 7490

7661; White Butterfly, Louisa; F; 8/9/16-15; F; S; Daughter; 7556; Yes; Yes; Id. U-10724 An. 7493

7662; White Butterfly, Roy; M; 7/12/20-11; F; S; Son; 7557; Yes; Yes; Id. U-10725 An. 7494

Census of the   **Pine Ridge**   reservation of the **Pine Ridge, South Dakota** jurisdiction, as of   **April 1** , 19**32,** taken by   **James H. McGregor** , Superintendent.

Key: Number; Surname, Given; Sex; Date of Birth-Age at Last Birthday; Tribe (Oglala Sioux, unless stated otherwise); Degree of Blood; Marital Status; Relationship to Head of Family [Last Census Roll Number]; At Jurisdiction Where Enrolled (Yes/No); (If no – Where); Ward (Yes/No, if given); Allotment, Annuity and Identification Numbers (if given).

7663; White Butterfly, Victoria; F; 12/19/22-9; F; S; Daughter; 7558; Yes; Yes; Id. U-12041 An. 7495

7664; White Butterfly, Benjamin; M; 1/1/25-7; F; S; Son; 7559; Yes; Yes; Id. U-11445 An. 7496

7665; White Butterfly, Paul; M; 11/17/31-4/12; F; S; Son; ---; Yes; Yes; U-14053

7666; White Butterfly, Ollie; F; 5/25/11-20; F; S; Head; 7560; Yes; Yes; Al. 5786 An. 7491

7667; White Butterfly, Lucy; F; 1899-33; F; Wd; Head; 7561; Yes; Yes; Al. 6469 An. 7497

7668; White Calf, Clarence; M; 1906-26; F; M; Head; 7563; Yes; Yes; Al. 7683 An. 7499

7669; White Calf (High Pine), Berdena; F; 1907-25; plus 1/4; M; Wife; 7564; Yes; Yes; Id. U-10116 An. 2727

7670; White Calf, Melbeta; F; 4/13/28-3; 1/4; S; Daughter; 7565; Yes; Yes; Id. U-12605 An. none

7671; White Calf, Lindy; M; 1/30/31-1; 1/4; S; Son; 7566; Yes; Yes; Id. U-13720 An. none

7672; White Calf, Philip; M; 1901-31; F; M; Head; 7567; Yes; Yes; Al. 7666 An. 7500

7673; White Calf (Lays Bear), Sarah; F; 1904-28; F; M; Wife; 7568; Yes; Yes; Al. 3341 An. 7502

7674; White Calf, Evelyn; F; 12/15/24-7; F; S; Daughter; 7569; Yes; Yes; Id. U-11427 An. 7503

7675; White Calf, Lema; F; 12/18/28-3; F; S; Daughter; 7570; Yes; Yes; Id. U-12961 An. none

7676; White Calf (no data), Maggie; F; 1872-60; F; Wd; Head; 7571; Yes; Yes; Al. 7462 An. 7505

7677; White Cow Bull, ---; M; 1852-80; F; M; Head; 7573; Yes; Yes; Al. 6406 An. 7507

7678; White Cow Bull (no data), Agnes; F; 1857-75; F; M; Wife; 7574; Yes; Yes; Al. 7663 An. 7508

7679; White Cow Killer, Jacob; M; 1877-55; F; M; Head; 7575; Yes; Yes; Al. 892 An. 7509

7680; White Cow Killer (no data), Emma; F; 1878-54; F; M; Wife; 7576; Yes; Yes; Al. 4184 An. 7510

Census of the **Pine Ridge** reservation of the **Pine Ridge, South Dakota** jurisdiction, as of **April 1**, 1932, taken by **James H. McGregor**, Superintendent.

Key: Number; Surname, Given; Sex; Date of Birth-Age at Last Birthday; Tribe (Oglala Sioux, unless stated otherwise); Degree of Blood; Marital Status; Relationship to Head of Family [Last Census Roll Number]; At Jurisdiction Where Enrolled (Yes/No); (If no – Where); Ward (Yes/No, if given); Allotment, Annuity and Identification Numbers (if given).

7681; White Cow Killer, Marian; F; 8/12/21-10; F; S; Daughter; 7577; Yes; Yes; Id. U-10726 An. 7511

7682; White Cow Killer, Thomas; M; 1899-33; F; M; Head; 7578; Yes; Yes; Al. 4185 An. 7512

7683; White Cow Killer (Tyon), Ida; F; 1901-31; plus 1/4; M; Wife; 7579; Yes; Yes; Al. 3419 An. 7513

7684; White Cow Killer, Lynn; M; 10/26/23-8; 1/4; S; Son; 7580; Yes; Yes; Id. U-11152 An. 7514

7685; White Cow Killer, Thomas Jr.; M; 2/17/25-7; plus 1/4; S; Son; 7581; Yes; Yes; Id. U-11490 An. 7515

7686; White Cow Killer, Verene; F; 1/4/30-2; 1/4; S; Daughter; 7582; Yes; Yes; Id. U-13361 An. none

7687; White Cow Killer, Celeste; F; 3/23/32-1/12; 1/4; S; Daughter; ---; Yes; Yes; U-14140

7688; White Coyote, Joseph; M; 1871-61; F; M; Head; 7583; Yes; Yes; Al. 3653 An. 7517

7689; White Coyote (Parts His Hair), Maggie; F; 1872-60; F; M; Wife; 7584; Yes; Yes; Al. 778 An. 7518

7690; White Coyote, Bessie; F; 12/13/12-19; F; S; Daughter; 7585; Yes; Yes; Al. 6809 An. 7519

N.E.: White Crane Walking, Isaac; M; ------; Rosebud Sioux; M; Head;

7691; White Crane Walking (Shout At), Jessie; F; 1899-33; F; M; Wife; 7572; Yes; Yes; Al. 4818 An. 6277

7692; White Crow, ---; F; 1836-96; F; Wd; Head; 7586; Yes; Yes; Al. 3680 An. 1141

7693; White Crow, Alfred; M; 1891-41; F; S; Head; 7587; Yes; Yes; Al. 1850 An. 7529

7694; White Crow, Edward; M; 1866-66; F; M; Head; 7588; Yes; Yes; Al. 2443 An. 7521

7695; White Crow (Bush), Ellen; F; 1874-58; F; M; Wife; 7589; Yes; Yes; Al. 4412 An. 7522

7696; White Crow, Peter; M; 1912-19; plus 1/4; S; Son; 7590; Yes; Yes; Al. 7368 An. 7524

7697; White Crow, Paul; M; 10/30/14-17; 1/4; S; Son; 7591; Yes; Yes; Al. 8167 An. 7525

7698; Bush, Eugene; M; 9/16/14-17; 1/4; S; S. Son; 7593; Yes; Yes; Id. U-9301 An. 7527

Census of the **Pine Ridge** reservation of the **Pine Ridge, South Dakota** jurisdiction, as of **April 1**, 19**32**, taken by **James H. McGregor**, Superintendent.

Key: Number; Surname, Given; Sex; Date of Birth-Age at Last Birthday; Tribe (Oglala Sioux, unless stated otherwise); Degree of Blood; Marital Status; Relationship to Head of Family [Last Census Roll Number]; At Jurisdiction Where Enrolled (Yes/No); (If no – Where); Ward (Yes/No, if given); Allotment, Annuity and Identification Numbers (if given).

7699; White Deer (no data), Margaret; F; 1855-77; 1/4; Wd; Head; 7594; Yes; Yes; Al. 1868 An. 7530

7700; White Dress, James; M; 1901-31; F; M; Head; 7595; Yes; Yes; Al. 3695 An. 7531
7701; White Dress (Bald Head), Amelia; F; 1903-29; F; M; Wife; 7596; Yes; Yes; Al. 91 An. 7532
7702; White Dress, Pearl; F; 4/6/27-4; F; S; Daughter; 7597; Yes; Yes; Id. U-12468 An. none
7703; White Dress, Francis; M; 9/16/29-2; F; S; Son; 7598; Yes; Yes; Id. U-13721 An. none
7704; White Dress, Edward; M; 3/25/31-1; F; S; Son; 7599; Yes; Yes; Id. U-13773 An. none

7705; White Dress, John; M; 12/24/08-23; F; S; Head; 7600; Yes; Yes; Al. 4051 An. 2279

7706; White Dress, Silas; M; 1906-26; F; M; Head; 7601; Yes; Yes; Al. 3696 An. 7534
7707; White Dress (Bad Yellow Hair), Marie; F; 8/3/12-19; F; M; Wife; 7602; Yes; Yes; Al. 7409 An. 309
7708; White Dress, William; M; 12/27/31-3/12; F; S; Son; ---; Yes; Yes; U-14054

7709; White Eagle, Robert; M; 1862-70; F; M; Head; 7603; Yes; Yes; Al. 1026 An. 7535
7710; White Eagle (Stand Up), Julia; F; 1865-67; F; M; Wife; 7604; Yes; Yes; Al. 6600 An. 7536

7711; White Elk (no data), Alice; F; 1862-70; F; Wd; Head; 7605; Yes; Yes; Al. 6208 An. 7539

7712; White Eyes, ---; M; 1858-74; F; M; Head; 7606; Yes; Yes; Al. 218 An. 7540
7713; White Eyes (no data), Jennie; F; 1862-70; F; M; Wife; 7607; Yes; Yes; Al. 7971 An. 7541

7714; White Eyes, Ida; F; 1875-57; F; Wd; Head; 7608; Yes; Yes; Al. 5425 An. 7542

7715; White Eyes, James Clarence; M; 1900-32; F; M; Head; 7609; Yes; Yes; Al. 7607 An. 7543
7716; White Eyes (Romero), Stella; F; 1900-32; plus 1/4; M; Wife; 7610; Yes; Yes; Al. 3893 An. 7544

Census of the __Pine Ridge__ reservation of the __Pine Ridge, South Dakota__ jurisdiction, as of __April 1__, 19**3**2, taken by __James H. McGregor__, Superintendent.

Key: Number; Surname, Given; Sex; Date of Birth-Age at Last Birthday; Tribe (Oglala Sioux, unless stated otherwise); Degree of Blood; Marital Status; Relationship to Head of Family [Last Census Roll Number]; At Jurisdiction Where Enrolled (Yes/No); (If no – Where); Ward (Yes/No, if given); Allotment, Annuity and Identification Numbers (if given).

7717; White Eyes, Francis; M; 12/19/21-10; 1/4; S; Son; 7611; Yes; Yes; Id. U-10972 An. 7545

7718; White Eyes, Albert; M; 1/6/26-6; 1/4; S; Son; 7612; Yes; Yes; Id. U-11794 An. none

7719; White Eyes, Mildred; F; 2/6/28-4; 1/4; S; Daughter; 7613; Yes; Yes; Id. U-12885 An. none

7720; White Eyes, Robert; M; 11/22/29-2; 1/4; S; Son; 7614; Yes; Yes; Id. U-13314 An. none

7721; White Eyes, Daniel; M; 1881-51; F; M; Head; 7615; Yes; Yes; Al. 220 An. 7546

7722; White Eyes (no data), Ida; F; 1871-61; F; M; Wife; 7616; Yes; Yes; Id. U-10730 An. 7547

7723; White Eyes, George; M; 1903-29; F; M; Head; 7617; Yes; Yes; Id. U-10732 An. 7549

N.E.: White Eyes (White Hollow Horn), Florence; F; ——–; Rosebud Sioux; F; M; Wife;

7724; White Eyes, Claudia; F; 5/16/30-1; F; S; Daughter; 7618; Yes; Yes; Id. U-13501 An. none

7725; White Eyes, Jeanette; F; 3/13/31-1; F; S; Daughter; ---; Yes; Yes; U-14115

7726; White Eyes, Jacob; M; 1870-62; F; M; Head; 7619; Yes; Yes; Al. 3616 An. 7553

7727; White Eyes (Brown Eyes), Susie; F; 1889-43; F; M; Wife; 7620; Yes; Yes; Al. 1659 An. 7554

7728; White Eyes, Mildred; F; 3/30/14-18; F; S; Daughter; 7621; Yes; Yes; Al. 7326 An. 7555

7729; White Eyes, Lillie; F; 5/4/21-10; F; S; Daughter; 7622; Yes; Yes; Id. U-10729 An. 7557

7730; White Eyes, Christine; F; 1/29/28-14; F; S; Daughter; 7623; Yes; Yes; Id. U-12500 An. none

7731; White Eyes, John; M; 1898-34; F; M; Head; 7624; Yes; Yes; Al. 6979 An. 7550

7732; White Eyes (Brown), Helen; F; 1903-29; -1/4; M; Wife; 7625; Yes; Yes; Al. 4454 An. 7551

7733; White Eyes, Joseph; M; 7/8/24-7; -1/4; S; Son; 7626; Yes; Yes; Id. U-11354 An. 7552

7734; White Eyes, Juanita; F; 1/14/26-6; plus 1/4; S; Daughter; 7627; Yes; Yes; Id. U-11830 An. none

7735; White Eyes, John M; M; 8/5/27-4; 1/4; S; Son; 7628; Yes; Yes; Id. U-12652 An. none

Census of the __Pine Ridge__ reservation of the __Pine Ridge, South Dakota__ jurisdiction, as of __April 1__, 1932, taken by __James H. McGregor__, Superintendent.

Key: Number; Surname, Given; Sex; Date of Birth-Age at Last Birthday; Tribe (Oglala Sioux, unless stated otherwise); Degree of Blood; Marital Status; Relationship to Head of Family [Last Census Roll Number]; At Jurisdiction Where Enrolled (Yes/No); (If no – Where); Ward (Yes/No, if given); Allotment, Annuity and Identification Numbers (if given).

7736; White Eyes, Lawrence; M; 8/8/29-2; 1/4; S; Son; 7629; Yes; Yes; Id. U-13251 An. none

7737; White Eyes, Dorothy; F; 1/7/32-2/12; 1/4; S; Daughter; ---; Yes; Yes; U-14075

7738; White Face, Charles; M; 1894-38; F; M; Head; 7630; Yes; Yes; Al. 1599 An. 7561

7739; White Face (Fast Eagle), Mary; F; 1902-30; F; M; Wife; 7631; Yes; Yes; Al. 5898 An. 2122

7740; White Face, Joseph; M; 1904-28; F; M; Head; 7632; Yes; Yes; Al. 6847 An. 7562

7741; White Face (Ghost Bear), Jessie; F; 1904-28; F; M; Wife; 7633; Yes; Yes; Al. 307 An. 7563

7742; White Face, Isaac; M; 11/5/25-6; F; S; Son; 7634; Yes; Yes; Id. U-11743 An. none

7743; White Face, Susan; F; 7/7/30-1; F; S; Daughter; 7635; Yes; Yes; Id. U-13560 An. none

7744; White Face, Vine; M; 2/23/32-1/12; F; S; Son; ---; Yes; Yes; U-14116

7745; White Face, Lucy; F; 1852-80; F; Wd; Head; 7636; Yes; Yes; Al. 2032 An. 7564

7746; White Face (nee Clifford), Maggie; F; 1894-38; plus 1/4; WD; Wife; 7637; Yes; Yes; Al. 1639 An. 7565

7747; White Face, Winnie; F; 3/25/20-12; 1/4; S; Daughter; ---; Yes; Yes; U-13953

7748; White Face, Frederick; M; 5/9/22-9; 1/4; S; Son; ---; Yes; Yes; U-13954

7749; White Face, Clifford; M; 3/21/26-6; 1/4; S; Son; ---; Yes; Yes; U-13955

7750; White Face, Thomas; M; 1877-55; F; M; Head; 7638; Yes; Yes; Al. 383 An. 7566

7751; White Face (Crooked Eyes), Susie; F; 1880-52; F; M; Wife; 7639; Yes; Yes; Al. 6732 An. 7567

7752; White Face, Mathew; M; 1/17/11-21; F; S; Son; 7641; Yes; Yes; Al. 6734 An. 7569

7753; White Face, Rex; M; 4/17/16-15; F; S; Son; 7642; Yes; Yes; Id. U-10733 An. 7570

7754; White Face, Chauncey; M; 3/17/18-14; F; S; Son; 7643; Yes; Yes; Id. U-10734 An. 7571

7755; White Face, Winnie; F; 8/25/20-11; F; S; Daughter; 7644; Yes; Yes; Id. U-10735 An. 7572

7756; White Face, Bennie; M; 7/13/09-22; F; M; Head; 7640; Yes; Yes; Al. 6733 An. 7568

Census of the __Pine Ridge__ reservation of the __Pine Ridge, South Dakota__ jurisdiction, as of __April 1__, 19**32**, taken by __James H. McGregor__, Superintendent.

Key: Number; Surname, Given; Sex; Date of Birth-Age at Last Birthday; Tribe (Oglala Sioux, unless stated otherwise); Degree of Blood; Marital Status; Relationship to Head of Family [Last Census Roll Number]; At Jurisdiction Where Enrolled (Yes/No); (If no – Where); Ward (Yes/No, if given); Allotment, Annuity and Identification Numbers (if given).

7757; White Face (Her Horses), Lucy; F; 10/24/15-16; F; M; Wife; 2857; Yes; Yes; Al. 8168 An. 2836

7758; White Face, William; M; 1884-48; F; M; Head; 7645; Yes; Yes; Al. 393 An. 7573

7759; White Face (Two Eagles), Eunice; F; 2/00-32; F; M; Wife; 7646; Yes; Yes; Al. 4905 An. 7574

7760; White Face, Aggie; F; 3/15/20-12; F; S; Daughter; 7647; Yes; Yes; Id. U-10737 An. 7577

7761; White Face, Hattie; F; 2/1/25-7; F; S; Daughter; 7648; Yes; Yes; Id. U-11432 An. 7578

7762; White Face, Hannah; F; 11/2/30-1; F; S; Daughter; 7649; Yes; Yes; Id. U-13722 An. none

7763; White Face, Hobert; M; 5/21/11-20; F; S; Head; 7650; Yes; Yes; Id. U-10736 An. 7576

7764; White Hawk (no data), Mattie; F; 1868-64; plus 1/4; Wd; Head; 7652; Yes; Yes; Al. 3048 An. 7580

7765; White Hawk, Clarence; M; 1891-41; 1/4; M; Head; 7653; Yes; Yes; Al. 7393 An. 7581

7766; White Hawk (Kills Enemy), Jessie; F; 1895-37; F; M; Wife; 7654; Yes; Yes; Al. 7852 An. 7582

7767; White Hawk, Ernest; M; 12/20/14-17; plus 1/4; S; Son; 7655; Yes; Yes; Id. U-10738 An. 7583

7768; White Hawk, Vervina; F; 9/16/18-13; 1/4; S; Daughter; 7656; Yes; Yes; Id. U-10739 An. 7584

7769; White Hawk, Leo; M; 1/1/14-18; 1/4; S; Son; 7657; Yes; Yes; Id. U-11481 An. 7585

7770; White Hawk, Joseph; M; 2/21/27-5; 1/4; S; Son; 7658; Yes; Yes; Id. U-12606 An. none

7771; White Hawk, Roselyn; F; 4/18/30-1; 1/4; S; Daughter; 7659; Yes; Yes; Id. U-13502 An. none

7772; White Horse, Grover; M; 1886-46; F; Wd; Head; 7660; Yes; Yes; Al. 8039 An. 7590

7773; White Horse, Esther; F; 4/14/18-13; F; S; Daughter; 7661; Yes; Yes; Id. U-10740 An. 7592

7774; White Horse, Kate; F; 1/17/21-11; F; S; Daughter; 7662; Yes; Yes; Id. U-10741 An. 7593

7775; White Horse, Henry; M; 1884-48; F; S; Head; 7663; Yes; Yes; Al. 2431 An. 7594

Census of the **Pine Ridge** reservation of the **Pine Ridge, South Dakota** jurisdiction, as of **April 1**, 19**32**, taken by **James H. McGregor**, Superintendent.

Key: Number; Surname, Given; Sex; Date of Birth-Age at Last Birthday; Tribe (Oglala Sioux, unless stated otherwise); Degree of Blood; Marital Status; Relationship to Head of Family [Last Census Roll Number]; At Jurisdiction Where Enrolled (Yes/No); (If no – Where); Ward (Yes/No, if given); Allotment, Annuity and Identification Numbers (if given).

7776; White Horse (Yellow Wood), Mary; F; 1857-75; F; Wd; Head; 7665; Yes; Yes; Al. 222 An. 7596

7777; White Lance, Daniel; M; 1869-63; F; M; Head; 7666; Yes; Yes; Al. 1543 An. 7599

7778; White Lance (no data), Julia; F; 1873-59; F; M; Wife; 7667; Yes; Yes; Al. 3681 An. 7600

7779; White Lance, John; M; 1907-25; F; S; Head; 7668; Yes; Yes; Al. 3682 An. 7601

7780; White Magpie, Paul; M; 1879-53; F; M; Head; 7669; Yes; Yes; Al. 6182 An. 7603

7781; White Magpie, Mabel; F; 9/7/13-18; F; S; Daughter; 7671; Yes; Yes; Al. 7646 An. 7606

7782; White Magpie, George; M; 7/26/15-16; F; S; Son; 7672; Yes; Yes; Al. 7923 An. 7607

7783; White Magpie, Josie; F; 1/15/17-15; F; S; Daughter; 7673; Yes; Yes; Id. U-10745 An. 7608

7784; White Magpie, Dortha; F; 9/24/18-13; F; S; Daughter; 7674; Yes; Yes; Id. U-10746 An. 7609

7785; White Magpie, Jacob; M; 4/21/22-9; F; S; Son; 7675; Yes; Yes; Id. U-11629 An. 7611

7786; White Magpie, Samuel; M; 8/1/24-7; F; S; Son; 7676; Yes; Yes; Id. U-11324 An. 7612

7787; White Magpie, Elijah; M; 3/30/11-21; F; M; Head; 7670; Yes; Yes; Al. 6233 An. 7605

7788; White Magpie (Red Paint), Mary; F; 8/2/10-21; F; M; Wife; 5557; Yes; Yes; Id. U-10256 An. 5535

7789; White Magpie, Wallace; M; 1886-46; F; M; Head; 7677; Yes; Yes; Al. 3209 An. 7613

7790; White Magpie (Warrior), Alice; F; 1874-58; F; M; Wife; 7678; Yes; Yes; Al. 3178 An. 7614

7791; White Magpie, George; M; 6/8/15-16; F; S; Son; 7679; Yes; Yes; Id. U-10744 An. 7615

7792; White Magpie, Ida; F; 4/14/17-14; F; S; Daughter; 7680; Yes; Yes; Id. U-10743 An. 7616

7793; White Magpie, Lucy; F; 11/8/19-12; F; S; Daughter; 7681; Yes; Yes; Id. U-10742 An. 7617

7794; Lakota, Amelia; F; 9/22/23-8; F; S; Ward; 7682; Yes; Yes; Id. U-11136 An. 7275

Census of the __Pine Ridge__ reservation of the __Pine Ridge, South Dakota__ jurisdiction, as of __April 1__, 1932, taken by __James H. McGregor__, Superintendent.

Key: Number; Surname, Given; Sex; Date of Birth-Age at Last Birthday; Tribe (Oglala Sioux, unless stated otherwise); Degree of Blood; Marital Status; Relationship to Head of Family [Last Census Roll Number]; At Jurisdiction Where Enrolled (Yes/No); (If no – Where); Ward (Yes/No, if given); Allotment, Annuity and Identification Numbers (if given).

7795; White Man Bear, Amos; M; 1863-69; F; M; Head; 7683; Yes; Yes; Al. 3306 An. 7618

7796; White Man Bear (no date), Alice; F; 1875-57; F; M; Wife; 7684; Yes; Yes; Al. 3307 An. 7619

7797; White Mouse, ---; M; 1858-74; F; M; Head; 7685; Yes; Yes; Al. 366 An. 7620

7798; White Mouse (Lays Bad-Smith), Jeanette; F; 1868-64; F; M; Wife; 7686; Yes; Yes; Al. 2736 An. 3747

7799; White Plume, ---; M; 1850-82; F; M; Head; 7687; Yes; Yes; Al. 2884 An. 7623

7800; White Plume (no date), Fannie; F; 1850-82; F; M; Wife; 7688; Yes; Yes; Al. 2885 An. 7624

7801; White Plume, Carl; M; 1881-51; F; M; Head; 7689; Yes; Yes; Al. 2886 An. 7626

7802; White Plume (Little Finger), Jessie; F; 1903-29; F; M; Wife; 7692; Yes; Yes; Al. 6593 An. 3946

7803; White Plume, Raymond; M; 6/5/14-17; F; S; Son; 7690; Yes; Yes; Al. 7994 An. 7627

7804; White Plume, Roy; M; 11/23/17-14; F; S; Son; 7691; Yes; Yes; Id. U-10748 An. 7628

7805; White Plume, Robert; M; 1885-47; F; M; Head; 7693; Yes; Yes; Al. 2887 An. 7629

7806; White Plume (Mexican), Millie; F; 1884-48; F; M; Wife; 7694; Yes; Yes; Al. 2803 An. 7630

7807; White Plume, Esther; F; 12/5/14-17; F; S; Daughter; 7695; Yes; Yes; Al. 7938 An. 7632

7808; White Plume, Percy; M; 7/11/19-12; F; S; Son; 7696; Yes; Yes; Id. U-10749 An. 7633

7809; White Plume, Robert Jr.; M; 5/13/11-20; F; S; Son; 7697; Yes; Yes; Al. 6820 An. 7631

7810; White Rabbit, (Robert); M; 1854-78; F; M; Head; 7698; Yes; Yes; Al. 4444 An. 7634

7811; White Rabbit (no data), Millie; F; 1864-68; F; M; Wife; 7699; Yes; Yes; Al. 4521 An. 7635

7812; White Rabbit, Elmer; M; 3/18/12-20; F; S; Son; 7700; Yes; Yes; Al. 6896 An. 7636

7813; White Rabbit, Philip; M; 1883-49; F; M; Head; 7701; Yes; Yes; Al. 5104 An. 7637

Census of the ____Pine Ridge____ reservation of the __Pine Ridge, South Dakota__ jurisdiction, as of ____April 1____, 1932, taken by ____James H. McGregor____, Superintendent.

Key: Number; Surname, Given; Sex; Date of Birth-Age at Last Birthday; Tribe (Oglala Sioux, unless stated otherwise); Degree of Blood; Marital Status; Relationship to Head of Family [Last Census Roll Number]; At Jurisdiction Where Enrolled (Yes/No); (If no – Where); Ward (Yes/No, if given); Allotment, Annuity and Identification Numbers (if given).

7814; White Rabbit (Adams), Lizzie; F; 1887-45; F; M; Wife; 7702; Yes; Yes; Al. 512 An. 7638

7815; White Rabbit, Philip Jr.; M; 12/25/24-7; F; S; Son; 7703; Yes; Yes; Id. U-10407 An. 7640

7816; White Rabbit, Andrew; M; 4/3/29-3; F; S; Son; 7704; Yes; Yes; Id. U-13155 An. none

N.E.: White Thunder, Charles; M; ---- ---; Rosebud Sioux; F; M; Head;

7817; White Thunder (Bear Killer), Bene; F; 1879-53; plus 1/4; M; Wife; 7707; Yes; Yes; Al. 5200 An. 7643

7818; White Thunder, Harrison; M; 1876-56; F; M; Head; 7708; Yes; Yes; Al. 503 An. 7645

7819; White Thunder (no data), Vina; F; 1879-53; F; M; Wife; 7709; Yes; Yes; Al. 4918 An. 7646

7820; White Thunder, William; M; 9/12/12-19; F; S; Son; 7710; Yes; Yes; Id. U-10751 An. 7648

N.E.: White Thunder, Albert; M; ---- ---; Rosebud Sioux; F; M; Head;

7821; White Thunder (Long Bull), Susie; F; 1898-34; F; M; Wife; 7711; Yes; Yes; Al. 5927 An. 7650

7822; White Thunder, Emma; F; 11/17/21-10; F; S; Daughter; 7712; Yes; Yes; Id. U-10995 An. 7651

7823; White Thunder, Lucille; F; 1/18/24-8; F; S; Daughter; 7713; Yes; Yes; Id. U-11665 An. none

7824; White Thunder, Pearl; F; 3/16/28-4; F; S; Daughter; 7714; Yes; Yes; Id. U-12653 An. none

7825; White Thunder, Pierre; M; 3/16/28-4; F; S; Son; 7715; Yes; Yes; Id. U-12654 An. none

7826; White Thunder, Dorothy; F; 12/28/29-2; F; S; Daughter; 7716; Yes; Yes; Id. U-13396 An. none

N.E.: White Wash, Lyman; M; ---- ---; Rosebud Sioux; F; M; Head;

7827; White Wash (Little Warrior), Dallas; F; 1905-27; F; M; Wife; 7717; Yes; Yes; Al. 4038 An. 7655

7828; White Whirlwind, Gilbert; M; 1886-46; F; M; Head; 7719; Yes; Yes; Al. 1237 An. 7656

7829; White Whirlwind (Dripping), Julia; F; 1886-46; F; M; Wife; 1951; Yes; Yes; Al. 4409 An. 1952

7830; White Whirlwind, Frank; M; 8/17/10-21; F; M; Head; 7720; Yes; Yes; Al. 6582 An. 7658

Census of the __Pine Ridge__ reservation of the __Pine Ridge, South Dakota__ jurisdiction, as of __April 1__, 19**32**, taken by __James H. McGregor__, Superintendent.

Key: Number; Surname, Given; Sex; Date of Birth-Age at Last Birthday; Tribe (Oglala Sioux, unless stated otherwise); Degree of Blood; Marital Status; Relationship to Head of Family [Last Census Roll Number]; At Jurisdiction Where Enrolled (Yes/No); (If no – Where); Ward (Yes/No, if given); Allotment, Annuity and Identification Numbers (if given).

7831; White Whirlwind (Wounded), Cecelia; F; 10/1/11-20; F; M; Wife; 7834; Yes; Yes; Al. 7543 An. 7749

7832; White Whirlwind, Louis; M; 4/23/10-21; F; S; Head; 7721; Yes; Yes; Id. U-10283 An. 5627

7833; White Whirlwind (Spotted Crow), Susie; F; 1875-57; F; Wd; Wife; 7722; Yes; Yes; Al. 7611 An. 7661

7834; White Wolf, Luke; M; 1854-78; F; Wd; Head; 7723; Yes; Yes; Al. 1799 An. 7662

7835; White Wolf, Charles; M; 1896-36; F; M; Head; 7724; Yes; Yes; Id. U-10753 An. 7665

7836; White Wolf (Eagle Bird), Winnie; F; 1900-32; F; M; Wife; 7725; Yes; Yes; Al. 1170 An. 7666

7837; White Wolf, Robert; M; 3/26/25-7; F; S; Son; 7726; Yes; Yes; Id. U-11549 An. 7667

7838; White Wolf, Vincent; M; 7/16/27-4; F; S; Son; 7727; Yes; Yes; Id. U-12710 An. none

7839; White Wolf, Louis; M; 11/13/30-1; F; S; Son; 7728; Yes; Yes; Id. U-13677 An. none

7840; White Woman, John; M; 1891-41; F; M; Head; 7729; Yes; Yes; Al. 1941 An. 7671

7841; White Woman (Strong Talk), Jessie; F; 1893-39; F; M; Wife; 7730; Yes; Yes; Al. 1149 An. 7672

7842; White Woman, Bessie; F; 12/15/23-8; F; S; Daughter; 7731; Yes; Yes; Id. U-11167 An. 7676

7843; White Woman, Rufus; M; 9/1/28-3; F; S; Son; 7732; Yes; Yes; Id. U-12789 An. none

7844; White Wolf, John; M; 1871-61; F; M; Head; 7733; Yes; Yes; Al. 891 An. 7668

7845; White Wolf (no data), Alice; F; 1873-59; F; M; Wife; 7734; Yes; Yes; Al. 5873 An. 7669

7846; White Woman, ---; F; 1870-62; F; S; Head; 7735; Yes; Yes; Al. 1940 An. 7670

7847; Wilcox (Quiver), Anna; F; 1900-32; F; M; Head; 7736; Yes; Yes; Al. 4229 An. 7677

7848; Quiver, Mike; M; 6/23/21-10; F; S; Son; 7737; Yes; Yes; Id. U-10188 An. 7678

Census of the **Pine Ridge** reservation of the **Pine Ridge, South Dakota** jurisdiction, as of **April 1**, 1932, taken by **James H. McGregor**, Superintendent.

Key: Number; Surname, Given; Sex; Date of Birth-Age at Last Birthday; Tribe (Oglala Sioux, unless stated otherwise); Degree of Blood; Marital Status; Relationship to Head of Family [Last Census Roll Number]; At Jurisdiction Where Enrolled (Yes/No); (If no – Where); Ward (Yes/No, if given); Allotment, Annuity and Identification Numbers (if given).

7849; Wilcox, Geneva; F; 2/20/24-8; Plus 1/4; S; Daughter; 7738; Yes; Yes; Id. U-11226 An. 7679
7850; Wilcox, Billie; M; 8/13/25-6; 1/4; S; Son; 7739; Yes; Yes; Id. U-11766 An. none
7851; Wilcox, Zona; F; 9/14/27-4; 1/4; S; Daughter; 7740; Yes; Yes; Id. U-12414 An. none
7852; Wilcox, Ollie; F; 7/5/29-2; 1/4; S; Daughter; 7741; Yes; Yes; Id. U-13237 An. none
7853; Wilcox (LaBuff), Angelique; F; 1906-26; 1/4; M; Head; 7742; Yes; Yes; Al. 2266 An. 3608

7854; Wilcox (nee Rooks), Evelyn; F; 2/24/11-21; 1/4; M; Head; 7743; Yes; Yes; Al. 5920 An. 5798
7855; Wilcox, Howard J; M; 7/17/28-3; 1/4; S; Son; 7744; Yes; Yes; Id. U-12771 An. none
7856; Wilcox, Curtis J; M; 7/21/30-1; 1/4; S; Son; 7745; Yes; Yes; Id. U-13562 An. none

7857; Wilde, Charley J; M; 12/21/19-12; 1/4; S; Alone; 7746; Yes; Yes; Id. U-10757 An. 7680
7858; Wilde, Norman; M; 6/3/21-10; 1/4; S; Alone; 7747; Yes; Yes; Id. U-10758 An. 7681

7859; Wilde, James; M; 1877-55; 1/4; M; Head; 7748; Yes; No; Al. 3759 An. 7682
7860; Wilde (Babby), Grace; F; 5/5/79-52; -1/4; M; Wife; 7749; Yes; No; Al. 3820 An. 7683

7861; Williams, Louis; M; 1899-33; plus 1/4; M; Head; 7750; Yes; Yes; Al. 4575 An. 7685
7862; Williams (Wilson), Ramona; F; 6/15/10-21; 1/4; M; Wife; 7772; Yes; No; Al. 6969 An. 7698

7863; Williams, Maggie; F; 1872-60; 1/4; Wd; Head; 7751; Yes; No; Al. 4086 An. 7686

7864; Williams (no data), Mary; F; 1858-74; 1/4; Wd; Head; 7752; Yes; Yes; Al. 4541 An. 7687

7865; Williams, Maurice; M; 1895-37; 1/4; S; Head; 7753; Yes; Yes; Al. 4573 An. 7688

7866; Williams, Ray; M; 5/2/02-29; 1/4; M; Head; 7754; No; Carey, town, Blaine, Idaho; Yes; Al. [5359] An. 7689

Census of the **Pine Ridge** reservation of the **Pine Ridge, South Dakota** jurisdiction, as of **April 1**, 1932, taken by **James H. McGregor**, Superintendent.

Key: Number; Surname, Given; Sex; Date of Birth-Age at Last Birthday; Tribe (Oglala Sioux, unless stated otherwise); Degree of Blood; Marital Status; Relationship to Head of Family [Last Census Roll Number]; At Jurisdiction Where Enrolled (Yes/No); (If no – Where); Ward (Yes/No, if given); Allotment, Annuity and Identification Numbers (if given).

7867; Williams, Alberta; F; 12/2/28-3; 1/4; S; Daughter; 7755; Noe(sic); Same; Yes; Id. U-13156 An. none

7868; Williams, Helen; F; 4/22/30-1; 1/4; S; Daughter; 7756; No; Carey, town, Blaine, Idaho; Yes; Id. U-13585 An. none

7869; Williams, Richard; M; 4/25/04-27; 1/4; S; Head; 7757; No; Hyattville, town, Bighorn, Wyo; Yes; Al. 5360 An. 7690

7870; Williams (Griffith), Murle; F; 4/24/09-22; -1/4; M; Head; 7758; No; El Paso, city, El Paso, Tex.; Yes; Al. 3902 An. 2692

7871; Williams (Valandry), Stella; F; 3/8/06-26; -1/4; M; Head; 7759; No; Hot Springs, Town, River, S.D.; Yes; Al. 2463 An. 7230

7872; Williams, Joseph; M; 8/21/28-3; -1/4; S; Son; 7760; No; Same; Yes; Id. U-13464 An. none

7873; Williams, Rosemary; F; 1/17/30-2; -1/4; S; Daughter; 7761; No; Same; Yes; Id. U-13465 An. none

7874; Williams, John; M; 6/13/31-9/12; -1/4; S; Son; ---; No; Same; Yes; U-13864

7875; Williams, Wendell; M; 1903-29; plus 1/4; S; Head; 7762; No; Split Rock, town, Natrona, Wyo.; Yes; Al. 4576 An. 7691

7876; Wilson, Dorothy; F; 1899-33; -1/4; M; Head; 7763; Yes; Yes; Al. 7916 An. 7692

7877; Twiss, Anna W; F; 10/10/24-7; -1/4; S; Daughter; 7764; Yes; Yes; Id. U-10164 An. 7694

N.E.: Wilson, Louis; M; -------; Cheyenne Sioux; plus 1/4; M; Head;
7878; Wilson (Tobacco), Clara; F; 9/1/03-28; F; M; Wife; 5982; No; Chey, & Arapahoe, Okla.; tes(sic); Al. 5539 An. 6944

7879; Wilson, Henrietta; F; 4/30/29-2; plus 1/4; S; Daughter; 5983; No; Chey, & Arapahoe, Okla.; Yes; Id. U-13218 An. none

7880; Wilson, Morgan; M; 2/23/31-1; 1/4; S; Son; ---; No; Chey, & Arapahoe, Okla.; Yes; U-14118

7881; Wilson, Francis; M; 1902-30; -1/4; M; Head; 7765; Yes; Yes; Al. 3434 An. 7695

7882; Wilson, Lois M; F; 6/7/24-7; -1/4; S; Daughter; 7766; Yes; Yes; Id. U-12373 An. none

7883; Wilson, Frank G; M; 1883-49; plus 1/4; M; Head; 7767; Yes; No; Al. 3772 An. 7696

Census of the __Pine Ridge__ reservation of the __Pine Ridge, South Dakota__ jurisdiction, as of __April 1__, 1932, taken by __James H. McGregor__, Superintendent.

Key: Number; Surname, Given; Sex; Date of Birth-Age at Last Birthday; Tribe (Oglala Sioux, unless stated otherwise); Degree of Blood; Marital Status; Relationship to Head of Family [Last Census Roll Number]; At Jurisdiction Where Enrolled (Yes/No); (If no – Where); Ward (Yes/No, if given); Allotment, Annuity and Identification Numbers (if given).

7884; Wilson (Salvois Adams), Alice; F; 1879-53; 1/4; M; Wife; 7768; Yes; Yes; Al. 2159 An. 7697

7885; Wilson, Ogden; M; 5/24/12-19; 1/4; S; Son; 7769; Yes; Yes; Al. 6968 An. 7699

7886; Wilson, Millie; F; 10/24/14-17; 1/4; S; Daughter; 7770; Yes; Yes; Id. U-10759 An. 7700

7887; Wilson, Corrine; F; 12/12/18-13; 1/4; S; Daughter; 7771; Yes; Yes; Id. U-10760 An. 7701

7888; Wilson, James J; M; 1897-35; -1/4; M; Head; 7773; Yes; Yes; Al. 7915 An. 7702

7889; Wilson (Janis), Julia; F; 1896-36; plus 1/4; M; Wife; 7774; Yes; No; Al. 1784 An. 7703

7890; Wilson, George F; M; 2/10/18-14; 1/4; S; Son; 7775; Yes; Yes; Id. U-10762 An. 7704

7891; Wilson, Woodrow; M; 1/4/20-12; 1/4; S; Son; 7776; Yes; Yes; Id. U-10763 An. 7705

7892; Wilson, Lester; M; 4/18/22-9; 1/4; S; Son; 7777; Yes; Yes; Id. U-10195 An. 7707

7893; Wilson, Edna; F; 12/17/24-7; 1/4; S; Daughter; 7778; Yes; Yes; Id. U-11083 An. 7706

7894; Wilson, Lyle; M; 8/17/28-3; 1/4; S; Son; 7779; Yes; Yes; Id. U-12790 An. none

7895; Wilson, James J; M; 10/23/31-5/12; 1/4; S; Son; ---; Yes; Yes; U-13949

7896; Wilson, John; M; 1898-34; -1/4; M; Head; 7780; Yes; Yes; Al. 3433 An. 7708

7897; Wilson, Enid; F; 9/30/18-13; -1/4; S; Daughter; 7781; Yes; Yes; Id. U-11598 An. 7709

7898; Wilson, Thomas; M; 10/22/19-12; -1/4; S; Son; 7782; Yes; Yes; Id. U-11599 An. 7710

7899; Wilson, Owen; M; 7/8/12-19; -1/4; S; Head; 7783; Yes; Yes; Id. Al. [8248] An. 7713

7900; Wilson, Charles; M; 1900-32; -1/4; M; Head; 7784; Yes; Yes; Al. 8246 An. 7714

7901; Wilson, Arlene; F; 8/22/23-8; -1/4; S; Daughter; 7785; Yes; Yes; Id. U-11420 An. 7715

7902; Wilson, Alice; F; 4/20/26-5; -1/4; S; Daughter; 7786; Yes; Yes; Id. U-12130 An. none

7903; Wilson, Nadine; F; 5/28/30-1; -1/4; S; Daughter; 7787; Yes; Yes; Id. U-13776 An. none

Census of the **Pine Ridge** reservation of the **Pine Ridge, South Dakota** jurisdiction, as of **April 1**, **1932,** taken by **James H. McGregor**, Superintendent.

Key: Number; Surname, Given; Sex; Date of Birth-Age at Last Birthday; Tribe (Oglala Sioux, unless stated otherwise); Degree of Blood; Marital Status; Relationship to Head of Family [Last Census Roll Number]; At Jurisdiction Where Enrolled (Yes/No); (If no – Where); Ward (Yes/No, if given); Allotment, Annuity and Identification Numbers (if given).

7904; Wilson, Zona C; F; 9/23/31-6/12; -1/4; S; Daughter; ---; Yes; Yes; U-13927

N.E.: Winfred, Ray; M; ------; Walapai; F; M; Head;
7905; Winfred (Amiotte), Maude; F; 1889-43; plus 1/4; M; Wife; 7788; No; Prescott, town, Yavapai, Ariz.; No; Al. 2583 An. 7716
7906; Winfred, Rosalind; F; 11/12/13-18; Oglala Sioux- Walapai; 1/4; S; Daughter; 7789; No; Same; Yes; Al. 8145 An. 7717
7907; Winfred, Winona; F; 11/15/15-16; Oglala Sioux- Walapai; 1/4; S; Daughter; 7790; No; Same; Yes; Id. U-10764 An. 7718
7908; Winfred, Leslie; M; 4/28/20-11; Oglala Sioux- Walapai; 1/4; S; Son; 7791; No; Same; Yes; Id. U-10765 An. 7719
7909; Winfred, Jean; F; 8/30/22-9; Oglala Sioux- Walapai; 1/4; S; Daughter; 7792; No; Same; Yes; Id. U-12053 An. 7720
7910; Not Used;
7911; Winfred, Charlotte; F; 1/1/25-7; Oglala Sioux- Walapai; 1/4; S; Daughter; 7793; No; Same; Yes; Id. U-11706 An. none

N.E.: Witt, Nathaniel; M; ------; Cherokee; 1/4; M; Head;
7912; Witt (Distribution), Minnie; F; 1892-40; F; M; Wife; 7794; Yes; Yes; Al. 4408 An. 1907
7913; Witt, Geralda; F; 1/13/21-11; Oglala Sioux- Cherokee; plus 1/4; S; Daughter; 7795; Yes; Yes; Id. U-9440 An. 1908
7914; Witt, Lawrence; M; 1/16/28-4; Oglala Sioux- Cherokee; 1/4; S; Son; 7796; Yes; Yes; Id. U-12474 An. none
7915; Witt, Nathaniel Jr.; M; 3/16/25-7; Oglala Sioux- Cherokee; 1/4; S; Son; 7797; Yes; Yes; Id. U-12504 An. none
7916; Witt, Eugenia; F; 10/4/29-2; Oglala Sioux- Cherokee; 1/4; S; Daughter; 7798; Yes; Yes; Id. U-13282 An. none

N.E.: Witt, Charles; M; ------; Cherokee; 1/4; M; Head;
7917; Witt (Quiver), Julia; F; 1901-31; F; M; Wife; 7799; Yes; Yes; Al. 4230 An. 7721
7917(sic);Witt, John; M; 6/24/22-9; Oglala Sioux- Cherokee; plus 1/4; S; Son; 7800; Yes; Yes; Id. U-14026 An. 7722
7918; Witt, Mary; F; 2/4/25-7; Oglala Sioux- Cherokee; 1/4; S; Daughter; 7801; Yes; Yes; Id. U-11484 An. 7723
7919; Witt, Lillian; F; 11/11/26-5; Oglala Sioux- Cherokee; 1/4; S; Daughter; 7802; Yes; Yes; Id. U-12297 An. none
7920; Witt, Mildred; F; 6/13/30-1; Oglala Sioux- Cherokee; 1/4; S; Daughter; 7803; Yes; Yes; Id. U-13537 An. none

N.E.: Witt, Floyd; M; ------; Cherokee; 1/4; M; Head;

Census of the **Pine Ridge** reservation of the **Pine Ridge, South Dakota** jurisdiction, as of **April 1**, 19**32**, taken by **James H. McGregor**, Superintendent.

Key: Number; Surname, Given; Sex; Date of Birth-Age at Last Birthday; Tribe (Oglala Sioux, unless stated otherwise); Degree of Blood; Marital Status; Relationship to Head of Family [Last Census Roll Number]; At Jurisdiction Where Enrolled (Yes/No); (If no – Where); Ward (Yes/No, if given); Allotment, Annuity and Identification Numbers (if given).

7921; Witt (Quiver), Stella; F; 11/12/12-19; F; M; Wife; 7804; Yes; Yes; Al. 7065 An. 5269

7922; Witt, Delane; M; 1/14/31-1; Oglala Sioux- Cherokee; 1/4; S; Son; 7805; Yes; Yes; Id. U-13723 An. none

7923; Wolf (Harvey), Mary; F; 1899-33; 1/4; M; Head; 7806; Yes; Yes; Al. 2725 An. 7724

7924; Wolf, Bernard; M; 11/30/24-7; 1/4; S; Son; 7807; Yes; Yes; Id. U-11478 An. 7725

7925; Wolf, Verna J; F; 7/17/27-4; 1/4; S; Son[sic]; 7808; Yes; Yes; Id. U-12753 An. none

7926; Wolf, Ruth; F; 10/13/29-2; 1/4; S; Daughter; 7809; Yes; Yes; Id. U-13362 An. none

7927; Wolf, Myrtle; F; 3/14/32-1/12; 1/4; S; Daughter; ---; Yes; Yes; U-14141

7928; Wolf Ears, Jerome; M; 1884-48; F; M; Head; 7810; Yes; Yes; Al. 1245 An. 7726

7929; Wolf Ears (Brings), Alice; F; 1880-52; F; M; Wife; 7812; Yes; Yes; Al. 6024 An. 7728

7930; Wolf Ears, Lavina; F; 1/14/17-15; F; S; Daughter; 7811; Yes; Yes; Id. U-10766 An. 7727

7931; Brings, Owen; M; 1917-15; F; S; Ward; 7813; Yes; Yes; Id. U-9250 An. none

N.E.: Wolf Guts, Silas; M; ------; Rosebud Sioux; F; M; Head;

7932; Wolf Guts (Logan), Amelia; F; 1905-27; F; M; Wife; 7814; Yes; Yes; Al. 5635 An. 7739

7933; Woman Dress, Bennie; M; 1882-50; F; M; Head; 7815; Yes; Yes; Al. 875 An. 7731

7934; Woman Dress (Long Cat), Lizzie; F; 1885-47; F; M; Wife; 7816; Yes; Yes; Al. 136 An. 7732

7935; Woman Dress, Jessie; F; 7/3/17-14; F; S; Daughter; 7817; Yes; Yes; Id. U-10767 An. 7735

7936; Woman Dress, John; M; 7/31/26-5; F; S; Son; 7818; Yes; Yes; Id. U-11982 An. none

7937; Woman Dress, Jennie; F; 12/8/09-22; F; S; Head; 7819; Yes; Yes; Al. 5723 An. 7733

7938; Woman Dress, Joseph; M; 3/3/12-20; F; S; Head; 7820; Yes; Yes; Al. 6722 An. 7734

Census of the __Pine Ridge__ reservation of the __Pine Ridge, South Dakota__ jurisdiction, as of __April 1__, 1932, taken by __James H. McGregor__, Superintendent.

Key: Number; Surname, Given; Sex; Date of Birth-Age at Last Birthday; Tribe (Oglala Sioux, unless stated otherwise); Degree of Blood; Marital Status; Relationship to Head of Family [Last Census Roll Number]; At Jurisdiction Where Enrolled (Yes/No); (If no – Where); Ward (Yes/No, if given); Allotment, Annuity and Identification Numbers (if given).

7939; Woman Dress, Edward; M; 1879-53; F; M; Head; 7821; Yes; Yes; Al. 2233 An. 7736
7940; Woman Dress (Loafer Joe), Lizzie; F; 1900-32; F; M; Wife; 7822; Yes; Yes; Al. 6627 An. 7737
7941; Woman Dress, Arthur; M; 7/25/20-11; F; S; Son; 7823; Yes; Yes; Id. U-10768 An. 7738
7942; Woman Dress, Lema; F; 5/15/25-6; F; S; Daughter; 7824; Yes; Yes; Id. U-11642 An. none
7943; Woman Dress, Raymond; M; 11/3/28-3; F; S; Son; 7825; Yes; Yes; Id. U-12938 An. none
7944; Woman Dress, Joseph; M; 3/13/31-1; F; S; Son; 7826; Yes; Yes; Id. U-13775 An. none

7945; Wood (Terrapin Lights), ---; F; 1850-82; F; Wd; Head; 7827; Yes; Yes; Al. 392 An. 6844

7946; Wooden Gun, Albert; M; 1869-63; F; M; Head; 7828; Yes; Yes; Al. 4219 An. 7744

N.E.: ~~Wooden Ring, Eli; M; ------; Rosebud Sioux; F; M; Head;~~
7947; Wooden Ring (Looking Cloud), Nancy; F; 1862-70; F; M; Wife; 7839; Yes; Yes; Al. 5780 An. 4247

7948; Woodley (Many Horses), Elizabeth; F; 1903-29; plus 1/4; M; Head; 4315; Yes; Yes; Al. 3366 An. 4316
7949; Woodley, Beverly; F; 6/4/30-1; 1/4; S; Daughter; ---; Yes; Yes; U-13865

7950; Wounded, Denver; M; 12/13/04-27; F; M; Head; 7831; Yes; Yes; Al. 3203 An. 7746
7951; Wounded (Little Soldier), Lizzie; F; 5/13/10-21; F; M; Wife; 4014; Yes; Yes; Al. 6543 An. 3999
7952; Wounded, Ruby; F; 10/17/31-5/12; F; S; Daughter; ---; Yes; Yes; U-13979

7953; Wounded, Samuel; M; 1895-37; F; M; Head; 7835; Yes; Yes; Al. 6546 An. 7750
7954; Wounded (Brown Cloud), Julia; F; 1890-42; F; M; Wife; 7836; Yes; Yes; Al. 631 An. 7751
7955; Wounded, Noah; M; 6/18/21-10; F; S; Son; 7837; Yes; Yes; Id. U-11460 An. 7752
7956; Wounded, Frances C; M[sic]; 6/28/28-3; F; S; Daughter; 7838; Yes; Yes; Id. U-12709 An. none

Census of the____Pine Ridge____reservation of the__Pine Ridge, South Dakota__ jurisdiction, as of____April 1____, 19**32**, taken by____James H. McGregor____, Superintendent.

Key: Number; Surname, Given; Sex; Date of Birth-Age at Last Birthday; Tribe (Oglala Sioux, unless stated otherwise); Degree of Blood; Marital Status; Relationship to Head of Family [Last Census Roll Number]; At Jurisdiction Where Enrolled (Yes/No); (If no – Where); Ward (Yes/No, if given); Allotment, Annuity and Identification Numbers (if given).

7957; Wounded, Saul; M; 1899-33; F; M; Head; 7839; Yes; Yes; Al. 6547 An. 7754

7958; Wounded (Lays Bear), Mary; F; 1882-50; F; M; Wife; 7840; Yes; Yes; Al. 3340 An. 7755

7959; Lays Bear, Lucy; F; 1882-50; F; S; S. Daughter; 7841; Yes; Yes; Al. 7495 An. 7757

7960; Wounded, Willie; M; 1901-31; F; M; Head; 7842; Yes; Yes; Al. 6548 An. 7758

~~N.E.: Wounded (Owns The Fire), Cora; F; — — — —; Rosebud Sioux; F; M; Wife;~~

7961; Wounded, Irene; F; 7/11/21-20; F; S; Daughter; 7843; Yes; Yes; Id. U-10770 An. 7759

7962; Wounded, Zona; F; 10/28/25-6; F; S; Daughter; 7844; Yes; Yes; Id. U-13397 An. none

7963; Wounded, Maurice; M; 8/10/27-4; F; S; Son; 7845; Yes; Yes; Id. U-12395 An. none

7964; Wounded Arrows, Harry; M; 1899-33; F; M; Head; 7847; Yes; Yes; Al. 566 An. 7760

7965; Wounded Arrows (Bush), Lucy; F; 8/10/10-21; plus 1/4; M; Wife; 7848; Yes; Yes; Al. 5857 An. 1243

7966; Wounded Arrows, Cecelia; F; 6/17/30-1; 1/4; S; Daughter; 7849; Yes; Yes; Id. U-13538 An. none

7967; Wounded Arrows, Harry J; M; 8/2/31-7/12; 1/4; S; Son; ---; Yes; Yes; U-13910

7968; Wounded Head, Brooks; M; 1887-45; F; M; Head; 7850; Yes; Yes; Al. 1667 An. 7763

7969; Wounded Head (Rooks), Jessie; F; 1897-35; plus 1/4; M; Wife; 7851; Yes; Yes; Al. 1735 An. 7764

7970; Wounded Head, Mollie; F; 1/6/19-13; 1/4; S; Daughter; 7852; Yes; Yes; Id. U-10773 An. 7766

7971; Wounded Head, Herbert; M; 7/15/22-9; 1/4; S; Son; 7853; Yes; Yes; Id. U-11501 An. 7767

7972; Wounded Head, Robert; M; 12/17/26-5; 1/4; S; Son; 7854; Yes; Yes; Id. U-12191 An. none

7973; Wounded Head, Peter; M; 1901-31; F; M; Head; 7855; Yes; Yes; Al. 1739 An. 7770

7974; Wounded Head (Bush), Eva; F; 1901-31; plus 1/4; M; Wife; 7856; Yes; Yes; Al. 1707 An. 7771

7975; Wounded Head, Felix; M; 2/28/28-4; 1/4; S; Son; 7857; Yes; Yes; Id. U-12540 An. none

Census of the __Pine Ridge__ reservation of the __Pine Ridge, South Dakota__ jurisdiction, as of __April 1__, 19**32,** taken by __James H. McGregor__, Superintendent.

Key: Number; Surname, Given; Sex; Date of Birth-Age at Last Birthday; Tribe (Oglala Sioux, unless stated otherwise); Degree of Blood; Marital Status; Relationship to Head of Family [Last Census Roll Number]; At Jurisdiction Where Enrolled (Yes/No); (If no – Where); Ward (Yes/No, if given); Allotment, Annuity and Identification Numbers (if given).

7976; Iron Crow, Pearl; F; 8/30/20-11; 1/4; S; S. Daughter; 7858; Yes; Yes; Id. U-9206 An. 7773

7977; Wounded Horse, ---; F; 1848-84; F; Wd; Head; 7859; Yes; Yes; Al. 6761 An. 7775

7978; Wounded Horse, Howard; M; 7/15/05-26; F; M; Head; 7860; Yes; Yes; Al. 4375 An. 7777
7979; Wounded Horse (Twiss), Agatha; F; 1907-25; plus 1/4; M; Wife; 7861; Yes; Yes; Al. 7682 An. 7026
7980; Wounded Horse, Olson; M; 6/4/27-4; 1/4; S; Son; 7862; Yes; Yes; Id. U-12415 An. none
7981; Wounded Horse, Ollie; F; 1/30/30-2; 1/4; S; Daughter; 7863; Yes; Yes; Id. U-13367 An. none

7982; Wounded Horse, Joseph; M; 1874-58; F; Wd; Head; 7864; Yes; Yes; Al. 3310 An. 7778

7983; Wounded Horse, Pugh; M; 1904-28; F; M; Head; 7865; Yes; Yes; Al. 3311 An. 7782
7984; Wounded Horse (Young Dog), Emma; F; 11/28/09-22; F; M; Wife; 8094; Yes; Yes; Al. 5833 An. 8027
7985; Wounded Horse, Delores; F; 10/18/31-4/12; F; S; Daughter; ---; Yes; Yes; U-14120

7986; Yaeger (Hudspeth, Thelma), Thelma; F; 1897-35; plus 1/4; M; Wife; 7866; Yes; Yes; Al. 3371 An. 7783
7987; Yaeger, Sylvia E.; F; 8/31/21-10; -1/4; S; Daughter; 7867; Yes; Yes; Id. U-10887 An. 7784
7988; Yaeger, Nellie; F; 7/13/23-8; -1/4; S; Daughter; 7868; Yes; Yes; Id. U-11361 An. 7785
7989; Yaeger, Freda; F; 9/16/25-6; -1/4; S; Daughter; 7869; Yes; Yes; Id. U-11893 An. none
7990; Yaeger, Ruth L.; F; 7/17/27-4; -1/4; S; Daughter; 7870; Yes; Yes; Id. U-12434 An. none
7991; Yaeger, Mary Ann; F; 3/14/30-2; -1/4; S; Daughter; 7871; Yes; Yes; Id. U-13449 An. none

7992; Yankton, Albert; M; 1902-30; plus 1/4; M; Head; 7872; Yes; Yes; Al. 128 An. 7786
7993; Yankton (Ladeaux, Josephine), Josephine; F; 6/1/06-26; plus 1/4; M; Wife; 7873; Yes; Yes; Id. U-9830 An. 3629

Census of the __Pine Ridge__ reservation of the __Pine Ridge, South Dakota__ jurisdiction, as of __April 1__, 19**32**, taken by __James H. McGregor__, Superintendent.

Key: Number; Surname, Given; Sex; Date of Birth-Age at Last Birthday; Tribe (Oglala Sioux, unless stated otherwise); Degree of Blood; Marital Status; Relationship to Head of Family [Last Census Roll Number]; At Jurisdiction Where Enrolled (Yes/No); (If no – Where); Ward (Yes/No, if given); Allotment, Annuity and Identification Numbers (if given).

7994; Yankton, Vina G.; F; 3/5/30-2; plus 1/4; S; Daughter; 7874; Yes; Yes; Id. U-13433 An. none

7995; Yankton, Julia; F; 1860-72; F; Wd; Head; 7875; Yes; Yes; Al. 5870 An. 7788

7996; Yankton, James; M; 1891-41; F; M; Head; 7876; Yes; Yes; Al. 1745 An. 7789
7997; Yankton (Cloud Horse, Winnie), Winnie; F; 1894-38; F; M; Wife; 7877; Yes; Yes; Al. 1323 An. 7790
7998; Yankton, Royal; M; 11/13/12-19; F; S; Son; 7878; Yes; Yes; Al. 7788 An. 7791
7999; Yankton, Nellie; F; 11/3/15-16; F; S; Daughter; 7879; Yes; Yes; Al. 8190 An. 7792
8000; Yankton, Harvey; M; 4/16/18-13; F; S; Son; 7880; Yes; Yes; Id. U-10775 An. 7793
8001; Yankton, Dorothy; F; 12/21/27-4; F; S; Daughter; 7881; Yes; Yes; Id. U-12470 An. none

8002; Yankton, Jennie; F; 1877-55; plus 1/4; Wd; Head; 7882; Yes; Yes; Al. 4707 An. 7796
8003; Yankton, Raymond; M; 7/16/12-19; plus 1/4; S; Son; 7883; Yes; Yes; Al. 8043 An. 7797
8004; Yankton, Hannah; F; 7/5/16-15; plus 1/4; S; Daughter; 7884; Yes; Yes; Id. U-10777 An. none

8005; Yankton, John; M; 1895-37; F; S; Head; 7885; Yes; Yes; Al. 1746 An. 7799

8006; Yankton, Noah; M; 1895-37; plus 1/4; M; Head; 7886; Yes; Yes; Al. 126 An. 7800
8007; Yankton (Boyer, Maggie), Maggie; F; 1892-40; plus 1/4; M; Wife; 7887; Yes; Yes; Al. 550 An. 7801
8008; Yankton, Edward; M; 1/13/21-11; plus 1/4; S; Son; 7888; Yes; Yes; Id. U-10779 An. 7803
8009; Yankton, Cecelia; F; 8/4/24-7; plus 1/4; S; Daughter; 7889; Yes; Yes; Id. U-11346 An. 7804
8010; Yankton, Stephen; M; 12/27/29-2; plus 1/4; S; Son; 7890; Yes; Yes; Id. U-13363 An. none

8011; Yankton Woman, ---; F; 1845-87; F; Wd; Wife; 7891; Yes; Yes; Al. 7287 An. 7806

8012; Yellow Bear, Charles; M; 1886-46; F; M; Head; 7892; Yes; Yes; Al. 810 An. 7809

Census of the **Pine Ridge** reservation of the **Pine Ridge, South Dakota** jurisdiction, as of **April 1**, 1932, taken by **James H. McGregor**, Superintendent.

Key: Number; Surname, Given; Sex; Date of Birth-Age at Last Birthday; Tribe (Oglala Sioux, unless stated otherwise); Degree of Blood; Marital Status; Relationship to Head of Family [Last Census Roll Number]; At Jurisdiction Where Enrolled (Yes/No); (If no – Where); Ward (Yes/No, if given); Allotment, Annuity and Identification Numbers (if given).

8013; Yellow Bear (Bear Robe, Bessie), Bessie; F; 1906-26; F; M; Wife; 7894; Yes; Yes; Al. 4841 An. 387

8014; Yellow Bear, William; M; 11/2/14-17; 1/4; S; Son; 7893; Yes; Yes; Al. 7944 An. 7812

8015; Bear Robe, Alouius(sic) Denver; M; 4/8/30-1; F; S; Stepson; 7895; Yes; Yes; Id. U-13419 An. none

8016; Yellow Bear, Edgar; M; 1896-36; F; M; Head; 7896; Yes; Yes; Al. 4410 An. 7815

8017; Yellow Bear (Young Dog, Nancy), Nancy; F; 1908-24; F; M; Wife; 7897; Yes; Yes; Al. 4407 An. 8026

8018; Yellow Bear, Ryan; M; 7/11/29-2; F; S; Son; 7898; Yes; Yes; Id. U-13306 An. none

8019; Yellow Bear, James; M; 1874-58; F; M; Head; 7899; Yes; Yes; Al. 7327 An. 7816

8020; Yellow Bear (Garter, Bessie), Bessie; F; 1885-47; F; M; Wife; 7900; Yes; Yes; Al. 5801 An. 7817

8021; Yellow Bear, Charles; M; 4/1/26-5; F; S; Son; 7901; Yes; Yes; Id. U-11894 An. none

8022; Yellow Bear, Peter; M; 4/2/28-3; F; S; Son; 7902; Yes; Yes; Id. U-12607 An. none

8023; Yellow Bird, Alexander; M; 1895-37; plus 1/4; S; Head; 7903; Yes; Yes; Al. 2780 An. 7821

8024; Yellow Bird, David; M; 1878-54; plus 1/4; M; Head; 7904; Yes; No; Al. 2762 An. 7822

8025; Yellow Bird (Pourier, Ellen), Ellen; F; 1895-36; plus 1/4; M; Wife; 7905; Yes; Yes; Al. 719 An. 7823

8026; Yellow Bird, Ruth; F; 10/1/16-15; plus 1/4; S; Daughter; 7906; Yes; Yes; Id. U-10790 An. 7824

8027; Yellow Bird, Henry; M; 9/1/14-17; plus 1/4; S; Son; 7907; Yes; Yes; Id. U-10791 An. 7825

8028; Yellow Bird, Hope; F; 6/11/19-12; plus 1/4; S; Daughter; 7908; Yes; Yes; Id. U-10792 An. 7826

8029; Yellow Bird, Clara J.; F; 12/1/21-10; plus 1/4; S; Daughter; 7909; Yes; Yes; Id. U-10861 An. 7827

8030; Yellow Bird, David L.; M; 4/14/24-7; plus 1/4; S; Son; 7910; Yes; Yes; Id. U-11262 An. 7828

8031; Yellow Bird, Clayton; M; 10/24/26-5; plus 1/4; S; Son; 7911; Yes; Yes; Id. U-12167 An. none

Census of the **Pine Ridge** reservation of the **Pine Ridge, South Dakota** jurisdiction, as of **April 1**, 19**32**, taken by **James H. McGregor**, Superintendent.

Key: Number; Surname, Given; Sex; Date of Birth-Age at Last Birthday; Tribe (Oglala Sioux, unless stated otherwise); Degree of Blood; Marital Status; Relationship to Head of Family [Last Census Roll Number]; At Jurisdiction Where Enrolled (Yes/No); (If no – Where); Ward (Yes/No, if given); Allotment, Annuity and Identification Numbers (if given).

8032; Yellow Bird, Alex D.; M; 9/12/29-2; plus 1/4; S; Son; 7912; Yes; Yes; Id. U-13398 An. none

8033; Yellow Bird, Eddie; M; 1890-42; plus 1/4; M; Head; 7913; Yes; Yes; Al. 2779 An. 7829

8034; Yellow Bird (Shangreau, Winnie), Winnie; F; 1889-43; plus 1/4; M; Wife; 7914; Yes; Yes; Al. 2555 An. 7830

8035; Yellow Bird, Earnest; M; 1/11/23-9; plus 1/4; S; Son; 7914(sic); Yes; Yes; Id. U-13002 An. 7831

8036; Yellow Bird, Evaline; F; 6/12/24-7; plus 1/4; S; Daughter; 7915(sic); Yes; Yes; Id. U-11286 An. 7832

8037; Yellow Bird, Frank; M; 1897-35; plus 1/4; M; Head; 7917; Yes; Yes; Al. 4216 An. 7833

8038; Yellow Bird (Palmier, Mamie), Mamie; F; 1899-33; plus 1/4; M; Wife; 7918; Yes; Yes; Al. 2713 An. 7834

8039; Yellow Bird, William; M; 2/28/21-11; plus 1/4; S; Son; 7919; Yes; Yes; Id. U-12055 An. 7835

8040; Yellow Bird, Hermoine; F; 6/2/24-7; plus 1/4; S; Daughter; 7920; Yes; Yes; Id. U-11428 An. 7836

8041; Yellow Bird, Fern; F; 2/2/26-6; plus 1/4; S; Daughter; 7921; Yes; Yes; Id. U-12275 An. none

8042; Yellow Bird, Frank E.; M; 9/3/28-3; plus 1/4; S; Son; 7923; Yes; Yes; Id. U-13126 An. none

8043; Yellow Bird, Beulah; F; 6/3/30-1; plus 1/4; S; Daughter; 7924; Yes; Yes; Id. U-13725 An. none

8044; Yellow Bird, Chester; M; 6/25/31-10/12; plus 1/4; S; Son; ---; Yes; Yes; Id. U-14055 An. none

8045; Yellow Bird, Harry; M; 1887-45; plus 1/4; M; Head; 7925; Yes; Yes; Al. 2778 An. 7837

8046; Yellow Bird (Carlow, Jennie), Jennie; F; 1886-46; plus 1/4; M; Wife; 7926; Yes; Yes; Al. 1070 An. 7838

8047; Yellow Bird, Thelma; F; 3/18/14-18; plus 1/4; S; Daughter; 7927; Yes; Yes; Al. 7694 An. 7839

8048; Yellow Bird, Gladys; F; 3/14/16-16; plus 1/4; S; Daughter; 7928; Yes; Yes; Id. U-10783 An. 7840

8049; Yellow Bird, Harry, Jr.; M; 6/11/18-13; plus 1/4; S; Son; 7929; Yes; Yes; Id. U-10784 An. 7841

8050; Yellow Bird, Jeanette; F; 12/22/20-11; plus 1/4; S; Daughter; 7930; Yes; Yes; Id. U-10785 An. 7842

8051; Yellow Bird, Jack; M; 5/26/23-8; plus 1/4; S; Son; 7931; Yes; Yes; Id. U-14000 An. 7843

Census of the __Pine Ridge__ reservation of the __Pine Ridge, South Dakota__ jurisdiction, as of __April 1__, 19**32**, taken by __James H. McGregor__, Superintendent.

Key: Number; Surname, Given; Sex; Date of Birth-Age at Last Birthday; Tribe (Oglala Sioux, unless stated otherwise); Degree of Blood; Marital Status; Relationship to Head of Family [Last Census Roll Number]; At Jurisdiction Where Enrolled (Yes/No); (If no – Where); Ward (Yes/No, if given); Allotment, Annuity and Identification Numbers (if given).

8052; Yellow Bird, Raymond J.; M; 5/6/27-4; plus 1/4; S; Son; 7932; Yes; Yes; Id. U-12884 An. none

8053; Yellow Bird, Harry; M; 1858-74; plus 1/4; Wd.; Head; 7933; Yes; Yes; Al. 4202 An. 7844

8054; Yellow Boy, Adolph; M; 1902-30; plus 1/4; M; Head; 7934; Yes; Yes; Al. 4284 An. 7846

8055; Yellow Boy (Protector, Lucy), Lucy; F; 1/14/09-23; F; M; Wife; 7939; Yes; Yes; Al. 7425 An. 5764

8056; Yellow Boy, Sophia; F; 6/28/19-12; plus 1/4; S; Daughter; 7935; Yes; Yes; Id. U-10797 An. 7848

8057; Yellow Boy, Levi; M; 4/19/22-9; plus 1/4; S; Son; 7936; Yes; Yes; Id. U-10949 An. 7849

8058; Yellow Boy, Eugene; M; 3/9/24-8; plus 1/4; S; Son; 7937; Yes; Yes; Id. U-11237 An. 7850

8059; Yellow Boy, Carrie J.; F; 9/4/27-4; plus 1/4; S; Daughter; 7938; Yes; Yes; Id. U-12435 An. none

8060; Yellow Boy, Dorothy; F; 10/25/31-5/12; plus 1/4; S; Daughter; ---; Yes; Yes; Id. U-13952 An. none

8061; Yellow Boy, Charles; M; 1882-50; F; M; Head; 7940; Yes; No; Al. 217 An. 7852

8062; Yellow Boy (Fly, Josephine), Josephine; F; 1881-51; F; M; Wife; 7941; Yes; Yes; Al. 5699 An. 7853

8063; Yellow Boy, Grover; M; 12/5/12-19; F; S; Son; 7942; Yes; Yes; Id. U-10798 An. 7855

8064; Yellow Boy, George; M; 1894-38; plus 1/4; M; Head; 7943; Yes; Yes; Al. 248 An. 7857

N.E.: ~~Yellow Boy (Industrious, Jessie Annie), Annie; F; ------; Cheyenne River Sioux; F; M; Wife;~~

8065; Yellow Boy, Joseph; M; 2/8/24-8; Sioux; plus 1/4; S; Son; 7944; Yes; Yes; Id. U-11197 An. 7859

8066; Yellow Boy, Winona; F; 3/28/29-3; Sioux; plus 1/4; S; Daughter; 7945; Yes; Yes; Id. U-13157 An. none

8067; Yellow Boy, Theodore; M; 10/5/31-3/12; Sioux; plus 1/4; S; Son; ---; Yes; Yes; Id. U-14077 An. none

8068; Yellow Boy, Grover; M; 1870-62; plus 1/4; M; Head; 7946; Yes; Yes; Al. 246 An. 7860

8069; Yellow Boy (No data), Lizzie; F; 1880-52; F; M; Wife; 7947; Yes; No; Al. 4281 An. 7861

Census of the **Pine Ridge** reservation of the **Pine Ridge, South Dakota** jurisdiction, as of **April 1**, 19**32**, taken by **James H. McGregor**, Superintendent.

Key: Number; Surname, Given; Sex; Date of Birth-Age at Last Birthday; Tribe (Oglala Sioux, unless stated otherwise); Degree of Blood; Marital Status; Relationship to Head of Family [Last Census Roll Number]; At Jurisdiction Where Enrolled (Yes/No); (If no – Where); Ward (Yes/No, if given); Allotment, Annuity and Identification Numbers (if given).

8070; Yellow Boy, Lucy; F; 10/11/13-18; plus 1/4; S; Head; 7948; Yes; Yes; Al. 7857 An. 7863

8071; Yellow Boy, Philip; M; 1883-49; F; M; Head; 7949; Yes; Yes; Al. 4376 An. 7865

8072; Yellow Boy (Walking Elk, Agnes), Agnes; F; 1884-48; F; M; Wife; 7950; Yes; Yes; Al. 4377 An. 7866

8073; Yellow Boy, Thomas; M; 3/15/18-14; F; S; Son; 7951; Yes; Yes; Id. U-10800 An. 7867

8074; Yellow Boy, Julia; F; 9/10/20-11; F; S; Daughter; 7952; Yes; Yes; Id. U-10801 An. 7868

8075; Yellow Boy, Silas; M; 1889-43; F; M; Head; 7955; Yes; Yes; Al. 884 An. 7871

8076; Yellow Boy (Big Crow, Susie), Susie; F; 1873-59; F; M; Wife; 7956; Yes; Yes; Al. 261 An. 2986

8077; Yellow Boy, Bessie; F; 6/15/17-14; F; S; Daughter; 7957; Yes; Yes; Id. U-10371 An. 6074

8078; Yellow Bull, Albert; M; 1891-41; F; M; Head; 7958; Yes; Yes; Al. 7834 An. 7873

8079; Yellow Bull (Spotted Horse, Jo), Josephine; F; 1897-35; F; M; Wife; 7959; Yes; Yes; Al. 6832 An. 7874

8080; Yellow Bull, Alberta; F; 5/16/25-6; F; S; Daughter; 7960; Yes; Yes; Id. U-11639 An. none

8081; Yellow Bull, Isaac; M; 1/26/31-1; F; S; Son; 7961; Yes; Yes; Id. U-13726 An. none

N.E.: Yellow Bull, Thomas; M; ------; Rosebud Sioux; F; M; Head;

8082; Yellow Bull (Fast Horse, Annie), Annie; F; 1875-57; plus 1/4; M; Wife; 7962; Yes; Yes; Al. 2237 An. 2133

8083; Yellow Hair, Daniel; M; 1882-50; F; Wd.; Head; 7963; Yes; Yes; Al. 4591 An. 7878

8084; Yellow Hair, Stephen; M; 6/10/18-13; F; S; Alone; 7964; Yes; Yes; Id. U-10804 An. 7881

8085; Yellow Hair, Leo; M; 7/3/21-10; F; S; Brother; 7965; Yes; Ues(sic); Id. U-11035 An. 7882

8086; Yellow Hawk, #2; M; 1872-60; F; M; Head; 7966; Yes; Yes; Al. 3982 An. 7884

Census of the _____Pine Ridge_____ reservation of the _Pine Ridge, South Dakota_ jurisdiction, as of_____April 1_____, 19**32**, taken by_____**James H. McGregor**_____, Superintendent.

Key: Number; Surname, Given; Sex; Date of Birth-Age at Last Birthday; Tribe (Oglala Sioux, unless stated otherwise); Degree of Blood; Marital Status; Relationship to Head of Family [Last Census Roll Number]; At Jurisdiction Where Enrolled (Yes/No); (If no – Where); Ward (Yes/No, if given); Allotment, Annuity and Identification Numbers (if given).

8087; Yellow Hawk (Sitting Up, Ellen), Ellen; F; 1879-53; F; M; Wife; 7967; Yes; Yes; Al. 3927 An. 7885

8088; Yellow Hawk, Jacob; M; 3/25/12-19; F; S; Son; 7968; Yes; Yes; Al. 7842 An. 7886

8089; Yellow Hawk, John; M; 1876-56; F; M; Head; 7969; Yes; Yes; Al. 5354 An. 7888

8090; Yellow Hawk (Imitates Dog, Belle), Belle; F; 1877-55; F; M; Wife; 7971; Yes; Yes; Al. 7086 An. 3116

8091; Yellow Hawk, Katie; F; 1/21/19-13; F; S; Daughter; 7970; Yes; Yes; Id. U-10806 An. 7893

8092; Imitates Dog, Victoria; F; 9/28/16-15; F; S; Stepdaughter; 7973; Yes; Yes; Id. U-9718 An. 3119

8093; Imitates Dog, Andrew; M; 10/3/18-13; F; S; Stepson; 7974; Yes; Yes; Id. U-9719 An. 3120

8094; Imitates Dog, Ella; F; 12/8/20-11; F; S; Stepdaughter; 7975; Yes; Yes; Id. U-9720 An. 3121

8095; Imitates Dog, Jonas; M; 5/13/24-7; F; S; Stepson; 7976; Yes; Yes; Id. U-11264 An. 3122

8096; Yellow Hawk, Samuel; M; 1904-28; F; M; Head; 7977; Yes; Yes; Al. 5357 An. 7894

8097; Yellow Hawk (Cut Grass), Lucy; F; 10/12/09-22; F; M; Wife; 7978; Yes; Yes; Id. U-9336 An. 1411

8098; Yellow Hawk, Harlin; M; 1/30/28-4; F; S; Son; 7979; Yes; Yes; Id. U-12656 An. none

8099; Yellow Horse, Alfred; M; 1904-28; F; M; Head; 7980; Yes; Yes; Al. 3740 An. 7895

8100; Yellow Horse (Bird Eagle), Agnes; F; 1905-27; F; M; Wife; 7981; Yes; Yes; Al. 7595 An. 7896

8101; Yellow Horse, Bertha; F; 12/20/25-6; F; S; Daughter; 7982; Yes; Yes; Id. U-11803 An. none

8102; Yellow Horse, Mary; F; 12/21/27-4; F; S; Daughter; 7983; Yes; Yes; Id. U-12471 An. none

8103; Yellow Horse, Annie I; F; 3/25/31-1; F; S; Daughter; ---; Yes; Yes; U-13823

8104; Yellow Horse, James; M; 1861-71; F; Wd; Head; 7985; Yes; Yes; Al. 1191 An. 7897

8105; Yellow Horse, Joseph; M; 1878-54; F; M; Head; 7986; Yes; Yes; Al. 2607 An. 7898

Census of the __Pine Ridge__ reservation of the __Pine Ridge, South Dakota__ jurisdiction, as of __April 1__, 1932, taken by __James H. McGregor__, Superintendent.

Key: Number; Surname, Given; Sex; Date of Birth-Age at Last Birthday; Tribe (Oglala Sioux, unless stated otherwise); Degree of Blood; Marital Status; Relationship to Head of Family [Last Census Roll Number]; At Jurisdiction Where Enrolled (Yes/No); (If no – Where); Ward (Yes/No, if given); Allotment, Annuity and Identification Numbers (if given).

8106; Yellow Horse (Patton), Susie; F; 1877-55; plus 1/4; M; Wife; 7987; Yes; Yes; Al. 2618 An. 7899

8107; Yellow Horse, Thomas; M; 8/3/13-18; 1/4; S; Son; 7988; Yes; Yes; Al. 8105 An. 7901

8108; Yellow Horse, Ruth; F; 2/27/16-16; 1/4; S; Daughter; 7989; Yes; Yes; Id. U-10807 An. none

8109; Yellow Horse, Wilbert; M; 9/28/18-13; 1/4; S; Son; 7990; Yes; Yes; Al. 8106 An. 7902

8110; Yellow Horse, Leonard; M; 1903-29; 1/4; M; Head; 7991; Yes; Yes; Al. 6798 An. 7904

8111; Yellow Horse (Running Shield), Fannie; F; 1902-30; F; M; Wife; 7992; Yes; Yes; Al. 83 An. 7905

8112; Yellow Horse, Morris; M; 1/5/27-5; plus 1/4; S; Son; 7993; Yes; Yes; Id. U-12885 An. none

8113; Yellow Horse, Velma; F; 11/23/29-2; 1/4; S; Daughter; 7994; Yes; Yes; Id. U-13435 An. none

8114; Yellow Horse, Wilson; M; 5/6/31-10/12; 1/4; S; Son; ---; Yes; Yes; U-14119

8115; Yellow Shield, David; M; 1907-25; F; S; Head; 7995; Yes; Yes; Al. 4716 An. 7907

8116; Yellow Shirt, Jefferson; M; 1875-57; F; M; Head; 7996; Yes; Yes; Al. 925 An. 7908

8117; Yellow Shirt (no Data), Stella; F; 1874-58; F; M; Wife; 7997; Yes; Yes; Al. 6438 An. 7909

8118; Yellow Shirt, Levi; M; 12/12/13-18; F; S; Son; 7998; Yes; Yes; Al. 8153 An. 7912

8119; Yellow Shirt, Stella; F; 7/23/18-13; F; S; Daughter; 7999; Yes; Yes; Id. U-10808 An. 7913

8120; Yellow Shirt, Mathew; M; 2/17/03-29; F; M; Head; 8000; Yes; Yes; Al. 6439 An. 7914

8121; Yellow Shirt (Thunder Bull), Cora; F; 1908-24; plus 1/4; M; Wife; 8001; Yes; Yes; Al. 5988 An. 6885

8122; Yellow Shirt, Vien; M; 7/10/31-8/12; 1/4; S; Son; ---; Yes; Yes; U-13950

8123; Yellow Thunder, Andrew; M; 1878-54; F; M; Head; 8002; Yes; Yes; Al. 1364 An. 7915

8124; Yellow Thunder (no data), Jennie; F; 1880-52; F; M; Wife; 8003; Yes; Yes; Al. 6875 An. 7916

8125; Yellow Thunder, Winnie; F; 2/14/14-18; F; S; Daughter; 8004; Yes; Yes; Al. 7815 An. 7918

Census of the **Pine Ridge** reservation of the **Pine Ridge, South Dakota** jurisdiction, as of **April 1**, 19**32**, taken by **James H. McGregor**, Superintendent.

Key: Number; Surname, Given; Sex; Date of Birth-Age at Last Birthday; Tribe (Oglala Sioux, unless stated otherwise); Degree of Blood; Marital Status; Relationship to Head of Family [Last Census Roll Number]; At Jurisdiction Where Enrolled (Yes/No); (If no – Where); Ward (Yes/No, if given); Allotment, Annuity and Identification Numbers (if given).

8126; Yellow Thunder, Norman; M; 10/26/16-15; F; S; Son; 8005; Yes; Yes; Id. U-10812 An. 7919

8127; Yellow Thunder, Clarence; M; 5/28/19-12; F; S; Son; 8006; Yes; Yes; Id. U-10813 An. 7920

8128; Yellow Thunder, Raymond; M; 1/9/21-11; F; S; Son; 8007; Yes; Yes; Id. U-10814 An. 7921

8129; Yellow Thunder, Russell; M; 8/21/24-7; F; S; Son; 8008; Yes; Yes; Id. U-11355 An. 7922

8130; Yellow Thunder, Joseph; M; 1895-37; F; M; Head; 8009; Yes; Yes; Al. 3960 An. 7924

8131; Yellow Thunder (Two Two), Theresa; F; 1903-29; plus 1/4; M; Wife; 8010; Yes; Yes; Al. 160 An. 7926

8132; Yellow Thunder, Marguerite; F; 6/25/24-7; 1/4; S; Daughter; 8011; Yes; Yes; Id. U-12874 An. none

8133; Yellow Thunder, Thomas; M; 1868-64; F; Wd; Head; 8012; Yes; Yes; Al. 1382 An. 7928

8134; Yellow Thunder, Julia; F; 7/11/12-19; F; S; Daughter; 8013; Yes; Yes; Al. 7829 An. 7930

8135; Yellow Thunder, Wallace; M; 10/1/15-16; F; S; Son; 8014; Yes; Yes; Id. U-10809 An. 7931

8136; Yellow Thunder, Nellie; F; 3/13/19-13; F; S; Daughter; 8015; Yes; Yes; Id. U-10811 An. 7932

8137; Yellow Thunder, Nancy; F; 3/21/22-10; F; S; Daughter; 8016; Yes; Yes; Id. U-10932 An. 7933

8138; Yellow Thunder, William; M; 1888-44; F; S; Head; 8017; Yes; Yes; Al. 1383 An. 7935

8139; Yellow Wolf, Alex; M; 1863-69; F; Wd; Head; 8018; Yes; Yes; Al. 1338 An. 7936

8140; Chips, Lawrence; M; 4/10/25-6; plus 1/4; S; Ward; 8020; Yes; Yes; Id. U-11643 An. none

8141; Yellow Wolf, Charles; M; 1882-50; F; M; Head; 8021; Yes; Yes; Al. 5113 An. 7939

8142; Yellow Wolf, Joseph; M; 7/10/10-21; F; S; Head; 8023; Yes; Yes; Al. 5415 An. 7945

8143; Youman (Bettelyoun), Alice; F; 1874-58; plus 1/4; M; Head; 8025; Yes; Yes; Al. 4072 An. 7947

Census of the __Pine Ridge__ reservation of the __Pine Ridge, South Dakota__ jurisdiction, as of __April 1__, 1932, taken by __James H. McGregor__, Superintendent.

Key: Number; Surname, Given; Sex; Date of Birth-Age at Last Birthday; Tribe (Oglala Sioux, unless stated otherwise); Degree of Blood; Marital Status; Relationship to Head of Family [Last Census Roll Number]; At Jurisdiction Where Enrolled (Yes/No); (If no – Where); Ward (Yes/No, if given); Allotment, Annuity and Identification Numbers (if given).

8144; Youman, Katherine; F; 3/4/15-17; -1/4; S; Daughter; 8026; Yes; Yes; Al. 8108 An. 7952

8145; Youman, David; M; 7/8/18-13; -1/4; S; Son; 8027; Yes; Yes; Id. U-10817 An. 7953

8146; Youmans (no data), Amelia; F; 1873-59; plus 1/4; M; Head; 8028; Yes; No; Al. 4697 An. 7954

8147; Youman, Charles; M; 9/28/08-23; -1/4; S; Head; 8029; Yes; Yes; Al. 4074 An. 7948

8148; Youman, Elnora; F; 10/7/10-21; -1/4; S; Head; 8030; Yes; Yes; Al. 7169 An. 7949

8149; Youmans, Love; F; 1907-25; -1/4; S; Head; 8031; Yes; Yes; Al. 4699 An. 7955

8150; Youmans, Iris; F; 1904-28; -1/4; S; Head; 8032; Yes; Yes; Al. 4698 An. 7956

8151; Young, Christopher; M; 1902-30; plus 1/4; S; Head; 8033; Yes; Yes; Al. 2515 An. 7961

8152; Young, Dorothy; F; 12/2/10-21; 1/4; S; Head; 8034; Yes; Yes; Al. 5583 An. 7959

8153; Young (Peck), Katie; F; 1885-47; plus 1/4; Wd.; Head; 8035; Yes; No; Al. 4361 An. 7958

8154; Young, Floyd; M; 10/25/12-19; 1/4; S; Son; 8036; Yes; Yes; Al. 6882 An. 7960

8155; Young, Amelia; F; 2/23/09-23; -1/4; S; Head; 8037; Yes; Yes; Al. 4867 An. 7965

8156; Young, Benjamin; M; 5/7/12-19; -1/4; S; Head; 8038; Yes; Yes; Al. 6901 An. 7998

8157; Young, Henry C; M; 8/22/10-21; plus 1/4; M; Head; 8039; Yes; Yes; Al. 5538 An. 7966

8158; Young, Edward; M; 1883-49; 1/4; M; Head; 8040; Yes; No; Al. 2529 An. 7962

8159; Young (Livermont), Cecelia; F; 1882-50; -1/4; M; Wife; 8041; Yes; No; Al. 2530 An. 7963

Census of the __**Pine Ridge**__ reservation of the __**Pine Ridge, South Dakota**__ jurisdiction, as of __**April 1**__, 19**32**, taken by __**James H. McGregor**__, Superintendent.

Key: Number; Surname, Given; Sex; Date of Birth-Age at Last Birthday; Tribe (Oglala Sioux, unless stated otherwise); Degree of Blood; Marital Status; Relationship to Head of Family [Last Census Roll Number]; At Jurisdiction Where Enrolled (Yes/No); (If no – Where); Ward (Yes/No, if given); Allotment, Annuity and Identification Numbers (if given).

8160; Young, Leona; F; 1/23/15-17; -1/4; S; Daughter; 8042; Yes; Yes; Al. 8186 An. 7967

8161; Young, Myrtle; F; 1/4/18-14; -1/4; S; Daughter; 8043; Yes; Yes; Al. 4866 An. 7964

8162; Young, Blaine; M; 8/8/29-2; -1/4; S; Son; 8044; Yes; Yes; Id. U-13790 An. none

8163; Young, Emery; M; 1903-29; -1/4; M; Head; 8045; Yes; Yes; Al. 4794 An. 7976

8164; Young, Frank; M; 1885-47; -1/4; M; Head; 8046; No; Rosebud, South Dakota; Yes; Al. 2506 An. 7970

8165; Young, Frank; M; 1897-35; -1/4; S; Head; 8047; Yes; Yes; Al. 5640 An. 7969

8166; Young, George; M; 1871-61; 1/4; M; Head; 8048; Yes; No; Al. 2512 An. 7974
8167; Young (no data), Ida; F; 1878-54; plus 1/4; M; Wife; 8049; Yes; No; Al. 2513 An. 7975
8168; Young, Lawrence; M; 2/1/14-18; 1/4; S; Son; 8050; Yes; Yes; Al. 8199 An. 7977
8169; Young, Lillie; F; 5/6/16-15; 1/4; S; Daughter; 8051; Yes; Yes; Al. 8200 An. 7978
8170; Young, Earl; M; 3/19/18-14; 1/4; S; Son; 8052; Yes; Yes; Id. U-10821 An. 7979
8171; Young, Verdel; F; 6/4/20-11; 1/4; S; Daughter; 8053; Yes; Yes; Id. U-10822 An. 7980

8172; Young, Henry; M; 1896-36; 1/4; M; Head; 8054; Yes; Yes; Al. 2528 An. 7981
8173; Young (Peck), Viola; F; 1903-29; 1/4; M; Wife; 8055; Yes; Yes; Al. 2466 An. 7982
8174; Young, Eddelman; M; 5/19/21-10; 1/4; S; Son; 8056; Yes; Yes; Id. U-10818 An. 7983
8175; Young, Eugene; M; 4/18/23-8; 1/4; S; Son; 8057; Yes; Yes; Id. U-13084 An. 7984
8176; Young, Glover; M; 9/11/27-4; 1/4; S; Son; 8058; Yes; Yes; Id. U-12416 An. none
8177; Young, Lyle; M; 10/17/29-2; 1/4; S; Son; 8059; Yes; Yes; Id. U-13399 An. none

8178; Young, Irvin; M; 1907-25; plus 1/4; S; Head; 8060; Yes; Yes; Al. 2522 An. 7995

Census of the **Pine Ridge** reservation of the **Pine Ridge, South Dakota** jurisdiction, as of **April 1**, 19**32**, taken by **James H. McGregor**, Superintendent.

Key: Number; Surname, Given; Sex; Date of Birth-Age at Last Birthday; Tribe (Oglala Sioux, unless stated otherwise); Degree of Blood; Marital Status; Relationship to Head of Family [Last Census Roll Number]; At Jurisdiction Where Enrolled (Yes/No); (If no – Where); Ward (Yes/No, if given); Allotment, Annuity and Identification Numbers (if given).

8179; Young, Leon; M; 11/15/11-20; 1/4; S; Head; 8061; Yes; Yes; Al. 6900 An. 7972

8180; Young, Owen; M; 2/23/10-22; 1/4; M; Head; 8063; Yes; Yes; Al. 5443 An. 7997

N.E.: Young (Roubideaux), Eva; F; -----; Rosebud Sioux; M; Wife;

8181; Young, Philip; M; 1894-38; 1/4; M; Head; 8064; Yes; No; Al. 2527 An. 7990
8182; Young (Peck), Mary; F; 1895-37; 1/4; M; Wife; 8065; Yes; No; Al. 2257 An. 7991
8183; Young, Winifred; F; 3/18/17-15; 1/4; S; Daughter; 8066; Yes; Yes; Id. U-10820 An. 7992

8184; Young, Victor; M; 1897-35; 1/4; S; Head; 8067; Yes; Yes; Al. 2514 An. 7993

8185; Young, Victor; M; 1877-55; 1/4; M; Head; 8068; Yes; Yes; Al. 2519 An. 7994

N.E.: Young (Bouvare), Louisa; F; -----; Rosebud Sioux; plus 1/4; M; Wife;

8186; Young, Walter; M; 1892-40; -1/4; M; Head; 8069; Yes; No; Al. 5042 An. 7999
8187; Young (Williams), Winnie; F; 1893-39; plus 1/4; M; Wife; 8070; Yes; No; Al. 4572 An. 8000
8188; Young, Mary; F; 10/11/19-12; -1/4; S; Daughter; 8071; Yes; Yes; Id. U-10824 An. 8001
8189; Young, Walter W; M; 3/13/22-10; -1/4; S; Son; 8072; Yes; Yes; Id. U-10956 An. 8002
8190; Young, Ray A; M; 10/9/23-8; -1/4; S; Son; 8073; Yes; Yes; Id. U-11248 An. 8003
8191; Young, Joseph A; M; 7/12/25-6; -1/4; S; Son; 8074; Yes; Yes; Id. U-11737 An. none
8192; Young, Lloyd; M; 2/14/30-2; -1/4; S; Son; 8075; Yes; Yes; Id. U-13436 An. none

8193; Young, William; M; 1882-50; 1/4; M; Head; 8076; Yes; No; Al. 2523 An. 8004
8194; Young (Richard), Louisa; F; 1882-50; 1/4; M; Wife; 8077; Yes; Yes; Al. 2524 An. 8005
8195; Young, Cornelia; F; 8/26/12-19; 1/4; S; Daughter; 8078; Yes; Yes; Al. 6903 An. 8006
8196; Young, Delbert; M; 4/25/14-17; 1/4; S; Son; 8079; Yes; Yes; Al. 7953 An. 8009

Census of the __Pine Ridge__ reservation of the __Pine Ridge, South Dakota__ jurisdiction, as of __April 1__, 19**32**, taken by __James H. McGregor__, Superintendent.

Key: Number; Surname, Given; Sex; Date of Birth-Age at Last Birthday; Tribe (Oglala Sioux, unless stated otherwise); Degree of Blood; Marital Status; Relationship to Head of Family [Last Census Roll Number]; At Jurisdiction Where Enrolled (Yes/No); (If no – Where); Ward (Yes/No, if given); Allotment, Annuity and Identification Numbers (if given).

8197; Young, Clema; F; 7/17/16-15; 1/4; S; Daughter; 8080; Yes; Yes; Al. 8240 An. 8010

8198; Young, Ilene; F; 11/26/19-12; 1/4; S; Daughter; 8081; Yes; Yes; Id. U-11108 An. 8011

8199; Young, Irene; F; 11/26/19-12; 1/4; S; Daughter; 8082; Yes; Yes; Id. U-10823 An. 8012

8200; Young, William Jr.; M; 6/15/22-9; 1/4; S; Son; 8083; Yes; Yes; Id. U-11055 An. 8013

8201; Young, Sidney; M; 5/15/26-5; 1/4; S; Son; 8084; Yes; Yes; Id. U-11963 An. none

8202; Young, Henry; M; 1908-24; -1/4; S; Head; 8085; Yes; Yes; Al. 4789 An. 8006

8203; Young, Herbert; M; 10/27/09-22; -1/4; S; Head; 8086; Yes; Yes; Al. 4790 An. 8007

8204; Young Bear, Benjamin; M; 1903-29; F; M; Head; 8087; Yes; Yes; Al. 2251 An. 8014

8205; Young Bear (Left Hand), Helen; F; 4/4/11-20; F; M; Wife; 8088; Yes; Yes; Al. 6948 An. 3793

8206; Young Bear, Kenneth; M; 9/13/31-6/12; F; S; Son; ---; Yes; Yes; U-11055

8207; Young Bear, George; M; 4/9/11-20; F; S; Head; 8089; Yes; Yes; Al. 7398 An. 8019

8208; Young Bear, Henry; M; 1901-31; F; Wd; Head; 8090; Yes; Yes; Al. 796 An. 8015

8209; Young Bear, Ernest; M; 10/19/25-6; F; S; Son; 8091; Yes; Yes; Id. U-11733 An. none

8210; Young Bear, Martin; M; 1859-73; F; M; Head; 8092; Yes; Yes; Al. 795 An. 8017

8211; Young Bear (no data), Rachel; F; 1857-75; F; M; Wife; 8093; Yes; Yes; Al. 2250 An. 8018

8212; Young Dog, Mary; F; 7/3/11-20; F; S; Head; 8095; Yes; Yes; Al. 5834 An. 8028

8213; Young Dog, Oscar; M; 1881-51; F; M; Head; 8096; Yes; Yes; Al. 637 An. 8024

8214; Young Dog (Sitting Dog), Jennie; F; 1886-46; F; M; Wife; 8097; Yes; Yes; Al. 638 An. 8025

8215; Young Dog, Amos; M; 11/29/17-14; F; S; Son; 8098; Yes; Yes; Id. U-10828 An. 8030

Census of the **Pine Ridge** reservation of the **Pine Ridge, South Dakota** jurisdiction, as of **April 1**, 19**32**, taken by **James H. McGregor**, Superintendent.

Key: Number; Surname, Given; Sex; Date of Birth-Age at Last Birthday; Tribe (Oglala Sioux, unless stated otherwise); Degree of Blood; Marital Status; Relationship to Head of Family [Last Census Roll Number]; At Jurisdiction Where Enrolled (Yes/No); (If no – Where); Ward (Yes/No, if given); Allotment, Annuity and Identification Numbers (if given).

8216; Young Dog, Dorothy; F; 6/9/22-9; F; S; Daughter; 8099; Yes; Yes; Id. U-12029 An. 8032

8217; Young Dog, Irene; F; 11/14/24-7; F; S; Daughter; 8100; Yes; Yes; Id. U-11563 An. 8033

8218; Young Dog, Isaac; M; 5/8/29-2; F; S; Son; 8101; Yes; Yes; Id. U-13198 An. none

8219; Young Skunk, ---; M; 1868-64; F; M; Head; 8102; Yes; Yes; Al. 2904 An. 8034

8220; Young Skunk (no data), Irene; F; 1860-72; F; M; Wife; 8103; Yes; Yes; Al. 3405 An. 8035

Handwritten Below Census

6043; Not used.
6051; Duplicated.
7910; Not used.
7917; Duplicated.

Limited Index

ABRAMS, --- 261
ADAM 213
ADAMS
    Ellen 25
    Lizzie 419
AFRAID OF HAWK, Fannie 124
AFRAID OF HIS HORSES, Jennie ... 53
ALLEN
    Jessie 396
    Julia 396
    Katherine 19
    Lizzie 66
    Viola 347
ALLEN-BOYER, Augusta 88
ALLMAN
    Frank 137
    Grace 245
    Julia 372
    Lillian 204
    Lillie 341
    Lydia 237
    Myrtle 71,206
AMERICAN BEAR, Mary 352
AMERICAN HORSE
    Albert 92
    Alice 269
    Leonard 92
AMIOTTE
    Belle 81
    Delma 74
    Maude 424
    Nora 65
ANGEL, Frances 385
APPLE, Jennie 199
ARAPAHOE, Lucy 168
ARMSTRONG, Cecelia 316
ARROW SIDE, Annie 157
ARROW WOUND, Sallie 224
ASK THEM SOMETHING, --- 321
BABBY
    Grace 72,421
    Irene 284
    Minnie 87
    Wilma 309
BAD BEAR, Mary 377
BAD COB, Mary 38
BAD HEART BULL, Dollie 281
BAD IRON, Winnie 252

BAD WOUND
    Agnes 287
    Emily 169
    Grace 406
    Stella 406
BAD YELLOW HAIR, Marie 413
BADGER, Alice 68
BAGGAGE, Mary 198
BAKER, Beth 282
BALD EAGLE
    Jessie 140
    Sarah 298
BALD HEAD, Amelia 413
BARDEAUX, Lulu 160
BARKER, Mabel 18
BARTLETT, Lena 318
BEAR EAGLE, Mary 199
BEAR KILLER, Bene 419
BEAR LOUSE, Amy 402
BEAR NOSE
    Julia 187
    Susie 113
BEAR ROBE
    Alice 267,342
    Annie 154
    Bessie 430
    Lena 342
    Rose 346
BEAR RUNNER, Julia 188
BEAR SHIELD
    Alice 91
    Annie 35
BEAR STOPS, Mary 164
BEAR STOPS-SHOT, Nellie 149
BEAUVOIS, Mollie 179
BELT, Sarah 47
BENT, Jessie 207
BETTELYOUN
    Alice 436
    Lillie 97
    Lucinda 341
    Martha 160
    Mary M 206
    Rene 269
    Ruby L 73
BETWEEN LODGES
    Esther 48
    Laura 48

Limited Index

Walter 48
BEUCH, Madeline 249
BEVA, Emma 314
BIG BEND, Katie 42
BIG BOY, Annie 373
BIG CROW
   Alvina 207
   Lucy 215
   Susie 433
BIG HEART, Dorothy 333
BIG OWL, Lucy 370
BIG WHITE HORSE, Julia 38
BIG WOLF, Susie 52
BINGHAM, Leon 281
BIRD, Bessie 256
BIRD EAGLE
   Agnes 434
   Mary 219
BIRDNECKLACE, Ida 177
BISSONETTE
   Amelia 4
   Angelina 39
   Bertha 406
   Eliza 191
   Jessie 383
   Lavina 232
   Lottie 293
   Sallie 220
   Sophia 39
   Susie 242
BLACK BEAR
   Agnes 290
   Ella 306
   Emma 34
   Jessie 350
   Laura 292
   Lizzie 70
   Lucy 190
   Mabel 22
   Rebecca 306
   Rosa 48,372
   Stella 117
   Susie 207
BLACK BIRD
   Moses 365
   Rebecca 365
   Rosa 365
BLACK BULL, Alice 383

BLACK CROW
   Ellen 370
   Ethel 357
   Katie 230
   Millie 63
BLACK ELK
   Ida 41
   Lucy 231
BLACK EYES, Anna 332
BLACK FEATHER, Nellie 377
BLACK FOX, Hannah 70
BLACK HORSE
   Clifford 79
   Emma 79
BLACK KETTLE, Jessie 389
BLACK ROAD, Maggie 263
BLACK SHEEP, Bessie 239
BLACK TAIL DEER
   Fannie 295
   Jennie 270
BLACK WHIRLWIND, Susie ... 92
BLACKSMITH, Rosa 6
BLUE BIRD
   Earl 64
   Sarah 120
BLUE CLOUD, Elsie 192
BLUE HORSE OWNER
   Hilda 49
   Martha 193
   Reuben 17
BLUE LEGS, Edna 315
BLUFFING BEAR, Dora 176
BLUNT HORN
   Lucy 162
   Vina 302
BONE, Helen 377
BONSER, Clara 248
BORDEAUX, Mary 325
BORES A HOLE, Dora 18
BOUILLARD, Lucy 236
BOUVARE, Louisa 439
BOWMAN, Loran 268
BOYER, Maggie 211,429
BRANDON
   Ethel 283
   Wilma 174
BRAVE
   Daisy 42

Limited Index

Maggie..................................32
BRAVE EAGLE
  Ada...17
  Bessoe................................145
  Jessie...................................35
  Lizzie...................................16
  Mary...................................192
BRAVE HEART
  Frankie...............................353
  Mary..............................261,297
  Rosa...................................237
BREAKS IN, Anna 317
BREAKS LAND, Mollie..............114
BREAST, Gertie.........................343
BREWER
  Elizabeth...........................205
  Ellen...................................309
BRINGS
  Alice...................................425
  Bessie.................................260
  Ernestine............................260
  Lucy...................................232
  Minnie..................................47
  Owen.................................425
BRINGS IT, Bertha...................188
BRINGS PLENTY, Alice............204
BRINGS WHITE...................38,216
  Ella.....................................401
BROKEN LEG
  Jessie...................................92
  Lucy...................................252
  Rosa.....................................48
BROKEN NOSE
  Lucy...................................373
  Winnie...............................408
BROKEN ROPE
  Everett...............................351
  Loranzo.............................351
  Sallie..................................351
  Vance.................................351
BROWN
  Alice...................................203
  Anita...................................374
  Florence............................244
  Harry..................................233
  Helen.................................414
  Henry.................................233
  Jennie............................99,318

  Josephine..........................366
  Julia....................................233
  Leona.................................150
  Pansy.................................345
  Rosa.....................................16
  Susie....................................19
  Susie I.................................74
BROWN CLOUD, Julia...............426
BROWN DOG, Eva....................109
BROWN EAR HORSE
  Fannie..................................22
  Katie..................................410
  Mary...................................104
BROWN EARS, Belle..................389
BROWN EYES
  Fannie................................158
  Mary...................................404
  Susie..................................414
BULL, Nancy.............................52
BULL BEAR
  Ethel M..............................260
  Helena...............................260
  Julia....................................260
  Lawrence..........................260
  Morris................................260
  Moses................................260
  Rosa...................................106
BULL TAIL
  Ada....................................407
  Lizzie.................................130
  Stella.................................107
BURNELL, Violet........................20
BUSH
  Agnes................................225
  Elizabeth...........................352
  Ellen...................................412
  Eugene..............................412
  Eva.....................................427
  Julia....................................382
  Lillie..................................225
  Lucy...................................427
BUSHY TOP PINE, Owenn........122
CALLIGO, Catherine..................110
CAMPBELL, Ida V.....................240
CARLOW
  Anna....................................54
  Jennie................................431
  Nellie C................................4

Limited Index

CATCHALL, Florence......75
CATCHES
  Eugene......217
  Everett......217
  Lucy......217
  Mary......305
  Ramona......217
  Vincent......217
CENTER
  Fannie......216
  Maggie......91
CHARGES AT......187
CHARGING
  Laura......1
  Lavon......152
  Louisa......398
  Mary......204
  Tillie......157
CHARGING BEAR, Alice......85
CHARGING CROW
  Cecelia......228
  Hattie......209
  Minnie......264
CHASE, Hilda......223
CHASE ALONE
  Margaret......143
  Rowland......143
CHASE IN SIGHT
  Garcia......409
  Winnie......409
CHASE IN WINTER
  Clara......142
  Winola......153
CHASE-IN-WINTER, Theresa......79
CHASING HAWK, Mattie......203
CHASING JUMPER, Bertha......275
CHEYENNE
  Effie......104
  Essie......224
CHIEF
  Julia......305
  Lillie......132
  Mary......137
  Nancy......389
CHIEF BEAR
  Arena......264
  Jennie......264
  Joseph, Jr......264

  Vera......264
CHIEF EAGLE
  Anna......304
  Jessie......230
  Josephine......303
  Nellie......321
  Susanna......148
CHIPS
  Alice......174
  Avena......148
  Emma......63,380
  Ethel......149
  Isabelle......383
  Lawrence......436
  Minnie......43
  Susie......173
CIAGO, Grace......129
CLIFFORD
  Alice......117
  Eleanor......395
  Hattie......385
  Irene......165
  Julia......47
  Maggie......415
  Mary......269
  Myrtle......146
CLINCHER
  Mary......1
  Naomi......21
CLOUD HORSE
  Nancy......130
  Winnie......429
CLOUD MAN, Lucy......153
COLLINS, Vina......208
COMES BACK HARD......228
COMES FROM WAR, Lucy......152
COMES WALKING, Emma......12
CONDELARIO
  Alice......215
  Lucinda......248
  Marguerite......263
  Sophia......395
CONQUERING BEAR, Jennie......215
CONROY
  Cecelia......320
  Lena......125
  Millie......149
COOK, Dorothy......195

Limited Index

CORN, Emma...248
CORNELIUS, Lottie...56
CORNETT, Olive...96
COTTIER
   Allen...147
   Elizabeth...362
   Esther...84
   Lucy...178,208
   Mabel...195
   Maggie...283
   Ollie...202
   Pearl...105
   Wm, Jr...84
COURNOYER, Agnes...152
CRAVEN
   Edith...194
   Hattie...146
   Hazel...32
   Jessie...88
   Minnie...262
CRAZY BEAR, Forine...183
CRAZY DOG, Lucy...48
CRAZY HORSE, Jennie...131
CRIBB, Elizabeth...105
CRIER, Mary...17,292
CROOKED EYES
   Rosa...271
   Susie...415
CROSS
   Daisy...157
   Sarah...34
CROW
   Annie...36
   Catherine...330
   Julia Lizzie...11
   Mary...143
CROW WOMAN, Nancy...184
CUMMINGS
   Jennie...79
   Mary...364
CUNY
   Eva...366
   Laura Pearl...64
   Louise...268
   Millie...209
   Viola...139
CUT, Lucinda...235
CUT GRASS

Louisa...109
Lucy...434
DANIELS, Ruth...96
DAVID...122
DAVIDSON
   Anna...254
   Elizabeth...46
   Julia...66
DAY BOY, Josephine...390
DEON
   Florence...173
   Mary...88
DESERA, Rosa...232
DIRT KETTLE
   Julia...79
   Marie...79
DISMOUNTS THRICE, Sophia...317
DISTRIBUTION, Minnie...424
DIXON
   Josephine...264
   Ruth...255
DOG CHIEF, Nellie...190
DONOHUE, Adeline L...327
DON'T THINK, Mary...36
DOOR, Mary...346
DORIAN, Esther...54
DREAMER
   Rosae...259
   Verbena...259
DREAMING BEAR, Lucy...359
DRIPPING
   Julia...419
   Maude...369
   Susie...369
DROP TWO, Sarah...344
DRURY
   Harry...263
   Keith...263
DUBRAY
   Irene...221
   Minnie...277
   Mollie...200
   Vivian...356
DUBRAY NELLIE, Lizzie...57
DUNLAP, Mabel...26
EAGLE BEAR
   Helen...141
   Mabel...286

Limited Index

EAGLE BIRD
  Helen 67
  Winnie 420
EAGLE BULL
  Bertha 132
  Ella 118
  Eva 139
  Jennie 132
  Lloyd 132
  Mary E 226
  Stuart 118
EAGLE DRESS, Mary 317
EAGLE ELK, Jessie 189
EAGLE LOUSE, Lizzie 290
EAGLE SHAWL
  Agnes 399
  Hattie 391
EAGLE SHIELD, Helen 285
EAGLE SHIRT, Mary 70
EAGLE TAIL, Paul 145
EAR RING, Leon 177
ECOFFEY
  Ethel 240
  Inez 146
  Louisa 186
  Nora 158
ELBOW SHIELD, Daniel 55
ELDRIDGE, Nettie 307
ELK BOY, Mary 226
ERVING, Elizabeth 114
FAST, Annie 353
FAST EAGLE
  Comer Paul 354
  Jessie 20
  Martha 354
  Mary 415
  Orlando 354
FAST HORSE
  Annie 433
  Cecelia 200
  Lucinda 69
  Rosa 341
  Wilbur 200
FAST THUNDER
  Emma 68
  Fannie 238
  Mary 264
FAST WOLF

  Cora 40
  Eva 308
  Lena 55
FEATHER, Mary 61
FILLS THE PIPE, Hattie 71
FINNEY, Virginia 379
FIRE, Nellie 389
FIRE PLACE
  Pansy 380
  Thomas 381
FIRE THUNDER
  Ambrose 79
  Angelique 94
  Annie 93
  Bertha 85
  Dorothy 79
  Louisa 328
  Lydia 43
  Martha 236
FISHER
  Anna 223
  Grace 155
  Hattie 148
  Laura 240
FLESH, Mary 409
FLOOD
  Elizabeth 203,374
  Etta 374
FLY, Josephine 432
FOG
  Fannie 164
  Mary A 187
  Pearl 100
FOOL HEAD
  Alice 181
  Jennie 172
  Lucelia 3
FOOTE, Thelma 392
FOX, Susie 158
FOX BELLY
  Eva 142
  Jennie 44
  Lucy 289
FRAZIER
  Ethel 395
  Maxine 74
FRIDAY SCARES
  Jennie 21

Limited Index

Julia 21
FROG
  Anna 33
  Febie 220
  Nora 220
FULLER
  Margaret 332
  Nora 331
GALLIGO
  Alvina 143
  Carl D 393
  Felmoor 205
  Frances 385
  Joseph 385
  Kiva 25
GARNET, Edith 211
GARNETTE
  Cynthia B 294
  Emma 294
  Frances E 294
  Theodore 294
GARNIER
  Emma 40
  Julia 233
  Sophia 179
GARREAU, Alice 289
GARTER, Bessie 430
GAY, Lizzie 135
GERRY
  Cynthia 160
  Louisa 307
  Lucy 85
GETS THERE FIRST
  Jennie 371
  Mabel 261
GHOST, Ellen 210
GHOST BEAR
  Jessie 415
  Rosa 370
GIAGO, Lucy 397
GIBBONS
  Annie 164
  Maggie 167
  Myrtle 230
GILLESPIE
  Lizzie 129
  Sarah 266
GILLISPIE

Bettie 367
Emma 373
Jennie 317
Maggie 104
GIROUX
  Lucy 202
  Martha 310
GIRTEN, May 301
GLEASON, Pearl 26
GLICK, Ione 368
GOES AFTER, Bessie 243
GOES IN CENTER, Alice 56
GOINGS
  Leta 159
  Vergie 167
GOOD CLOUD, Augusta 275
GOOD CROW
  Charles S 357
  Elizabeth 357
  Eva 357
  Frances 357
  Raymond 357
GOOD ELK, Lucy 163
GOOD LANCE, Emma 110
GOOD MEDICINE, Mattie 231
GOOD PIPE, Hail 224
GOOD SHIELD, Sophia 278
GOOD SOLDIER
  Hazel 320
  Lena 48
  Victoria 21
GOOD TEACHER, Ida 19
GOOD VOICE DOG, Katie 46
GOOD VOICE FLUTE, Louisa 274
GOOD WALKING 99
GOOD WEASEL
  Etta 107
  Nellie 197
GOODMAN, Fannie 175
GOODWIN, Julia 215
GRAHAM
  Florence A 93
  Ollie 93
GRASS
  Jennie 370
  Julia 350
  Victoria 409
GRAY BLANKET, Lizzie 68

Limited Index

GRAY GRASS, Mary 122
GREEN, Viola 249
GRESH
   Lizzie 61
   Mary 347
   Susie 60
GRIFFITH
   Eleanor 269
   Murle 422
GRIST, Ramona 182
GROUSE, Alice 157
GUARNE, Mary 28
GUERRIER, Annie 279
H BIRD, Jessie 245
HAD YELLOW HAIR, Mary 216
HAIR WOMAN, Josephine 212
HAND BOY, Allen 18
HAND SOLDIER
   Etta M 120
   Louisa 382
HARD HEART, Helen 112
HARVEY
   Julia 237
   Mary 425
   Susie 186
HAS NO HORSES, Julia 357
HAT
   Jennie 151
   Lucy N 74
HATCHET, Hazel 235
HAWK WING
   Alice 73
   Zona 177
HAWKINS
   Agnes 268
   Eva 105
   Lottie 24
   Sophia 288
   Theresa 391
HEAD, Evangeline 392
HEART HEART, Rosa 397
HEART MAN, Anna 388
HELPER, Melissa 387
HENDERSON
   Florence 138
   Lucy 407
HENRY
   Emma R 405

   Martha 311
HER DOOR, --- 364,407
HER GOOD HORSE, Fannie 212
HER HORSE, Sarah 243
HER HORSES
   Alice 365
   Julia 244
   Lucy 416
   Maggie 140
HERMAN, Winifred 86
HERNANDEZ, Catalina 77
HERNRY 217
HIGH BULL, Victoriea 342
HIGH CAT, Julia 192
HIGH CRANE
   Ella 196
   Nancy 108
HIGH EAGLE
   Alice 48
   Emily 224
   Mary 93
   Pearl 98
   Sophia 124
HIGH HORSE, Eva 300
HIGH PINE
   Berdena 411
   Reynold 138
HILL
   Esther 46
   Lizzie 392
HOLLOW BEAR, Elizabeth 162
HOLLOW HORN, Agie 2
HOLLOW HORN BEAR, Leah 288
HOLLOW WOOD, Mollie 52
HOLY BEAR, Julia 364
HOLY EAGLE, Julia 37
HOLY ELK
   Gertrude 382
   Julia 297
   Roy 297
HOLY HOCK, Julia 97
HOLY LODGE, --- 376
HOLY ROCK
   Emily 25
   Victoria 230
HOLY TRACK 182
HOOP, Alice 207
HOPKINS

Laevinia 11
Stephen 11
HORN CHIPS, Rosa 152
HORN CLOUD, Pearl 214
HORNBECK
   Elizabeth 288
   Julia 143
   Maggie 288
   Viola 75
HORSE, Jessie 172
HORSE STANDS IN SIGHT, Esther...
.... 275
HORSE WOMAN, Lizzie 336
HOWARD, Minnie 247
HOWLING HORSE, Mary 410
HUDSPETH
   Myrtle 188
   Thelma 428
HUMPHREY, Maud 121
HUNGRY, Lucy 212
HUNTER
   Alice 289
   Cornelia 176
   Victoria 335
HUNTS ENEMY
   Mamie 216
   Mollie 216
IMITATES DOG
   Andrew 434
   Belle 434
   Bessie 37
   Ella 434
   Jettie 212
   Jonas 434
   Nettie 43
   Victoria 434
INDUSTRIOUS, Jessie Annie 432
INGERSOL, Sarah 255
IRON BOY, Lottie 121
IRON BULL
   Cora 227
   Daniel 113
   Eva 113
   Louisa 246
   Olive 113
IRON CLOUD
   David 228
   Ora 229

   Seth 16
IRON CROW
   Anna 253
   Garfield 253
   Lucy 401
   Pearl 428
   Rosa 116
IRON ELK, Mary 257
IRON HEART
   Clara 335
   Elizabeth 147
   Hannah 22
   Julia 334
IRON ROAD 69
IRON ROPE, Winnie 253
IRON TAIL, --- 360
IRON TEETH
   Nancy 311
   Rosa 216
IRON WING, Maggie 105
IRVING
   Catherine 355
   Cecelia 355
   Clara 355
   Ella 278
   Ellen 378
   Eugene 355
   Julia 242
   Martha 355
   Mary 355
   Monica 355
   Seth Chas 355
   Wilbert 355
IRVINGS, Ollie 86
JACKSON, Agnes 238
JACOBS
   Celesta 380
   Wilma 334
JANDRON, Grace 20
JANIS
   Aggie 87
   Alice 134,155,320
   Bessie 50
   Cecelia 81
   Dorotha 80
   Ellen 170
   Eugene 99
   Filla 128

Frank L 99
Hermos 371
Julia 423
Kiva 138
Lizzie 256
Louisa 9
Lucy 333
Mary 281
Mary Marian 305
Rose 90
Sadie 338
Winnie 327
JANIS TWISS, Pearl 170
JANIS-SEARS, Josephine 144
JARVIS
    Julia 393
    Lizzie 286
JEALOUS OF HIM
    Alice 63
    Susie 377
    Woodrwo 63
JOHN 216
JOHNSTON, Florence 122
JONES
    Josephine 408
    Julia 131
    Louisa 333
JUMPING EAGLE, Alice 54
KEITH
    Alice 362
    Grace 205
    Jess G 114
    Marie 180
    Mary A 187
KELLY, Clara 254
KICKING BEAR, Mary 91
KILLS ABOVE, Maggie 63
KILLS AT LODGE
    Jessie 92
    Julia 258
KILLS BAD, Augusta 266
KILLS CROW
    Annie 2
    Julia 31
    Louisa 6
KILLS ENEMY
    Cecelia 123
    Jessie 416

Nellie 292
Sallie 150
KILLS ENEMY IN MORNING, Etta 340
KILLS IN LODGE, Rosa 377
KILLS IN WATER
    Eugene 91
    Martha 212
KILLS IN WINTER, Lizzie 398
KILLS INDIAN CROW, Jennie 204
KILLS ON HORSE BACK, Sallie .. 257
KILLS RED, Julia 339
KILLS REE, Carrie 165
KILLS RIGHT
    Emma 304
    Lizzie 185
KILLS SMALL
    Bessie 196
    Cornelius 17
    Mary A 178
KILLS WARRIOR, Ella 73
KILLS WELL, Ida 149
KINDLE, Emma 71
KINKADE, Rose 160
KNIFE
    Bessie 249
    Maxine 249
KNIGHT
    Helen 51,103
    Oliver 103
KNUTH, Geneva 339
KOCER, Johanna 88
LA FORCE, Mary 256
LA PLANT, Delia 56
LABEAU, Adelia 164
LABUFF
    Angelique 421
    Jeannette 286
LADEAU, Emma 151
LADEAUX
    Alice 374
    Dora 121
    Josephine 428
    Maggie 326
LAFURGE, Iris 4
LAKOTA, Amelia 417
LAMAR, Margorie 85
LAMB

Limited Index

Edith 101
Mary 379
LAME, Mary 217
LAME DOG
   Elmer 199
   Rosa 410
LAMONT, Mary 9
LANG
   Helen 368
   Mabel 368
   Myra 183
LANGDEAU, Mary A 207
LAPOINT, Grace 18
LAPOINTE
   Anna 317
   Annie 359
   Georgene Esther 24
   Vera 245
LARABEE
   Alice 315
   Mary 349
   Nellie 56
LARVIA, Helena 130
LARVIE
   Maggie 25
   Rose 50
   Susie 101
LAST HORSE
   Georgiana 379
   Jennie 193
   Kate 267
   Mary 193
   Millie 199
   Salina 24
LAYS BAD
   Cora 205
   Helen 30
LAYS BAD-SMITH, Jeanette 418
LAYS BEAR
   Clara 164
   Emma 53
   Lucy 427
   Mary 427
   Sarah 411
LAYS HARD, Dora 213
LEAF NO NECK, Mary 213
LEE
   Emma 276

Erma 333
Jessie 128
Susanna 18
Vienna 128
LEFT HAND
   Adam 171
   Helen 440
   Jacob 171
   Julia 171
LEFT HAND BEAR, Cecelia 14
LEFT HAND BULL
   Mary 290
   Nancy 325
LESSERT
   Emily 12
   Olive 355
LEVERING, Sallie 407
LIP, Katie 136
LITTLE
   Harson 243
   Sarah 311
LITTLE BALD EAGLE
   Nancy 264
   Rosa 346
LITTLE BEAR
   Alice 322
   Sarah 393
   Zuzella 287
LITTLE BIRD
   Ambrose 52
   Lucy 52
   Nettie 42
   Opal 295
   Rosa 67
LITTLE BOY
   Cecelia 122
   Mary 181
LITTLE BULL
   Jessie 259
   Julia 396
LITTLE CHIEF
   Elva 66
   Emma 289
   Jennie 242
   Lucy 189
   Mary 407
LITTLE CLOUD, Blanche 258
LITTLE CROW, Ellen 137

LITTLE DOG
　Frank 63
　Jessie 63
　Julia 392
　Rosa 241
LITTLE ELK
　Lizzie 175
　Viola 111
LITTLE FINGER, Jessie 418
LITTLE HOOP, Sallie 256
LITTLE KILLER
　Bessie 259
　Ida 361
　Mabel 288
　Owen 287
LITTLE MOON, Sarah 393
LITTLE SOLDIER
　Jennie 402
　Lizzie 426
　Nellie 127
　Sallie 110
LITTLE SPOTTED HORSE
　Fannie 198
　Mary 219
LITTLE THUNDER, Winnie 410
LITTLE WARRIOR
　Dallas 419
　Dorothy 315
　Sadie 398
LITTLE WHITE MAN, Katie 224
LITTLE WHITEMAN, Nellie 12
LITTLE WOUND
　Belle 260
　Jessie 298
LIVERMONT
　Cecelia 437
　Florence 2
　Hazel 86
　Mary Ivy 183
LIVING BEAR, Annie 340
LIVING OUT SIDE, Ida 219
LIVING OUTSIDE, Susie 291
LOAFER
　Adaline 69
　Eugene 299
LOAFER JOE
　Edna 41
　Lizzie 426

LOCATION 191
LOCKE, Annie 63
LOGAN
　Amelia 425
　Nancy 239
LONE BEAR, Susie 173
LONE DOG, Mollie 297
LONE ELK, Susie 33
LONE HILL
　Edna 408
　Florence 313
　Helen 313
　Sallie 41
　Tillie 31
LONE WAR, Lizzie 64
LONE WOLF
　Agnes 352
　Emma 193
　Marion 135
　Rosa 252
LONG BULL
　Lydia 213
　Marguerite 78
　Susie 419
LONG CAT
　Bessie 114
　Elsie 133
　Julia 29
　Lizzie 425
LONG COMMANDER, Carrie 194
LONG SOLDIER
　Bessie 97
　Emily 61
　Levi 61
　Lucy 61
　Virginia 21
LONG VISITOR, Ellen 361
LONGHORN, Hattie 244
LOOKING CLOUD, Nancy 426
LOOKING ELK
　Lester 249
　Norwood 249
LOOKING HORSE, Rosa 162
LOOKING WHITE, Jennie 8
LOOKOUT, Nora 356
LUHAN, Millie 312
MAKE SHINE
　Jessie 107

Julia 298
Louisa 64
Oliver 256
MANY HORSES
   Elizabeth 426
   Lillie 166
MARROW BONE
   Emma 321
   Jessie 207
   Victoria 322
MARSHALL
   Annie 387
   Jennie 247
   Lizzie 10
MARTIN
   Bessie 312
   Edith 240
   Frances 302
   Mattie 126
MARTINEZ
   Emma 76
   Nora 266
MATHEWS
   Aloysius 155
   Gilbert 155
   Julia 156
   Susie 155
   Vina 155
MATTHEWS, Emily 156
MCDANIELS, Paul L 112
MCDONALD, Edna 196
MCGAA, Jessie 362
MCGRESH, Maggie 223
MCMILLAN
   Mary J 243
   May 242
MCWILLIAMS, Belle 209
MEANS
   Ada 49
   Jessie 314
   Josephine 98
   Lorene 161
MEDICINE BOY
   Mary 23
   Susie 338
MEDICINE WOMAN, --- 251
MENARD, Ethel 48
MERRIVAL

Keva 249
Lema 397
Pauline 257
MERRIVALL, Laura 267
MESTETH
   Aloysius 71
   Amanda 387
   Annie 81
   Ferne Doris 312
   George L 312
   Gladys R 312
   Jennie 119
   Louis 290
   Lucille 58
   Maggie 58
   Mary 114
   Vincent 57
MEXICAN, Millie 418
MIDKIFF
   Goldie 160
   Lorraine 403
MILK
   Elizabeth 272
   Lillian 256
MILLS, Annie 74
MOCCASIN TOP, Emma 39
MONROE
   James Clifford 31
   Julia Dorothy 15
   Lena 145
   Mary 347
   Zouie 366
MONTILEAUX
   Clara 47
   Emily 408
   Julia 154
   Lottie 175
   Louisa 335
MOORE, Evaline 246
MOOSE, Mary 170
MORAN, Nancy 83
MORISETTE, Edith 251
MORRISETTE
   Bernard 233
   Madeline 233
   Sophia 71
   Zoey 71
MORRISON

Limited Index

Andrew 308
Bettie 220
Edith 245
Elizabeth 245
Emma 274
Frank, Jr. 245
Helena 86
Josie 281
Lena 57
Mabel 245
Robert E. 245
Rosa 62
MOUSSEAU
   Agnes 17
   Lucy 232
   Mary 14, 104
   Sophia 156
   Susie 36
MOVES CAMP
   Belle 273
   Clara 358
MULKEHAY, Della 190
NECK SHIELD, Martha 356
NEISS, Bernice 1
NELSON
   Ellen 240
   Grace 84
   Jennie 226
   Katie 401
   Lillian 310
   Madge 179
   Mary 201
   Pearl 300
   Rosa 284
NO BRAID
   Lizzie 171
   Mary 304
NO FLESH
   Emma 37
   Mable 181
NO LEAF, Nancy 52
NO NECK
   Ellen 353
   Grace 9
NO WATER, Mary 210
NOT HELP HIM
   Sallie 61
   Seth 62

OLD SHIELD
   Jessie 189
   Susie 132
ONE FEATHER
   Julia 258
   Nellie 299
   Rosa 391
O'ROURKE
   Agnes 89
   Georgianna 154
   Isabelle 276
   Josephine 278
   Pansy 254
   Pearl 275
OWL BULL, Mabel 151
OWNS MANY HORSES, Rosa 163
OWNS THE FIRE, Cora 427
OWNS THE MULE 141
PABLO, Agnes 128
PALMIER
   Catherine 29
   Elizabeth 29
   Ida 134
   Josephine 180
   Laura 28
   Leo 29
   Louis 28
   Lucille 29
   Mamie 431
PARKER, May 134
PARTS HIS HAIR
   Ada 217
   Bessie 260
   Emma 107
   Maggie 412
PATTON
   Susie 435
   Theresa 29
PAWNEE LEGGINS, Lizzie 154
PEANO, Hilda 318
PECK
   Dora 46
   Julia 113
   Katie 437
   Lottie 221
   Mary 439
   Nellie 404
   Viola 438

Limited Index

PEDIGO, Beth 282
PICKET PIN
  Delia 324
  Susie Aurelia 30
PICOTTE
  Cecil 45
  Kathryn 126
PINE BIRD
  Alice 281
  Jennie 361
PINE LEAF 129
PLEASES HERSELF, --- 364
PLENTY BEAR, Mabel 82
PLENTY BIRD, Nancy 376
PLENTY HARANGER, Jennie 83
PLENTY HORSES 150
PLENTY STARS, Fannie 170
PLENTY WOLF
  Emma 162
  Mary 196
  Susie 349
PLENTY WOUNDS
  Eva 242
  Louisa 298
  Nellie 31
POOR BEAR
  Allen 36
  Elsie 36
  Julia 59
POOR ELK
  Elizabeth 3
  Rosie 193
POOR THUNDER, Anna 280
POUIER, Mary P 254
POURIER
  Ella 106
  Ellen 430
  Florence 377
  Grace 264
  Helena 368
  Her Horses 365
  Josephine 175
  Mary L 94
  Rose 378
POUTING, --- 321
PRAIRIECHICKEN
  Eva Lillian 11
  Zallie Eliza 11

PRETTY BULL
  Carrie 145
  Katie 140
PRETTY CLOUD, Isabelle 45
PRETTY EAGLE, Mary 339
PRETTY FACE
  Antonia 162
  Peter 163
PRETTY WOMAN 3
  Bessie 109
PROTECTOR, Lucy 432
PROVOST
  Bessie 275
  Gertrude 255
  Hazel 65
  Josephine 148
  Julia 147,151
  Mary 248
  Maude 255
PUMPKIN SEED, Eva 153
PUMPKINSEED, Mary 301
QUICK BEAR, Eve 151
QUICK-HAWK, Lucy 215
QUIGLEY, Anna 249
QUINN, Thomasena 166
QUIVER
  Anna 420
  Fannie 273
  Julia 424
  Mike 420
  Stella 425
RABBIT-GOOD HORSE, Jennie 144
RAINBOW 118
RANDALL
  Carl Richard 22
  Gertrude 151
  Hazel 216
  Jessie 374
  Lizzie 229
  Lucy 380
  Mabel 329
  Mollie 229,239
  Nellie 306
  Opal 87
  Pearl 121
  Stella 374
  Thomas 131
RATTLING HAWK, --- 287

Limited Index

RED BEAR
  Alice 246
  Emma 92
  Mary 330
  Rosa 304
RED BIRD
  Lucy 144
  Mary 313
RED BREATH BEAR
  Ella 147
  Mildred 147
RED CLOUD, Lucy 3
RED CROW, Maggie 110
RED EAGLE 58
RED EAR HORSE
  Bessie 171
  Eva 171
  Sallie 329
RED ELK
  Augusta 227
  George 210
  Mary 269
  Mattie 44
  Millie 227
  Ruth 47
  Victoria 14
RED EYES
  Louisa 34
  Lucy 405
  Maggie 191
  Susie 92
RED FEATHER
  Claudia 305
  Eva 338
  Flent 338
  Fosa 401
  Joseph 338
  Winnie 338
RED FISH, Lizzie 110
RED HAWK
  Lucy 239
  Susie 340
RED HORSE
  --- 360
  Elizabeth 53
  Mary 232
  Sarah 375
RED KETTLE

  Lydia 370
  Nancy 43
RED OWL
  Bessie 249
  Hattie 384
RED PAINT, Mary 417
RED PLUME, Girl 261
RED RABBIT, Mary 106
RED RING 108
RED SHIRT
  Emily 214
  Evangeline 214
  Ollie 215
  Rosa G 214
  Sarah 214
  Varia 129
RED STAR
  Sallie 272
  Stella 369
RED TOMAHAWK, Julia 110
RED WOLF, Jennie 58
RICHARD
  Angeline 27
  Annie 225
  Emma 327
  Jessie 332
  Josephine 205
  Julia 152
  Leona 343
  Louisa 439
  Lucinda 287
  Mary 197
  Ollie 106
RIFF, Alice 77
RINGING SHIELD, Lucy 23
RIOS
  Delores 96
  Francis 97
ROBERTSON
  Emily 284
  Minnie 208
ROBIDEAUX, Gertrude 246
ROBINSON, Dorothy 74
ROCKS, Delia 7
ROCKY BEAR, Mamie 185
ROMERO
  Edward 145
  Leo 145

Limited Index

Lillie ...323
Mabel ...136
Maggie ...290
Rosa ...45
Stella ...413
Sussie ...145
ROOKS
   Catherine ...149
   Evelyn ...421
   Jessie ...427
   Noresta ...59
   Rebecca ...221
   Rosanna ...4
   Susie ...229
   Timothy ...169
   Zona ...310
ROSS
   Alice ...209
   Angelique ...166
   Edna ...124
ROUBIDEAUX, Eva ...439
ROUGH FEATHERS, Julia ...53
ROUILLARD
   Effie ...387
   Isabell ...252
ROUSE, Ellen ...176
ROWLAND
   Emma ...81
   Jessie ...234
   Pearl ...100
RUBEN, Hattie ...76
RUFF
   Edna ...183
   Grace ...202
   Lizzie ...26
   Mary ...326
   Vina A ...307
RULEAU
   Isabel ...318
   Leta ...126
   Louisa ...88
   Zouie ...344
RUMSEY, Sophia ...13
RUNNING BEAR, Vernice ...364
RUNNING HAWK
   Cecelia ...185
   Joseph ...389
   Maggie ...389
RUNNING HORSE
   Alice ...363
   Lizzie ...253
RUNNING SHIELD
   Anna ...168
   Bessie ...391
   Fannie ...435
   Nora ...117
RUNS ABOVE, Lizzie ...294
RUNS AGAINST
   Irene ...295
   Mabel ...168
   Sophia ...30
RUNS ALONG THE EDGE
   Alice ...169
   Christine ...194
   Julia ...178
RUNS BETWEEN ...189
RUNS CLOSE TO LODGE
   Annie ...139
   Lillie ...346
   Peter ...139
RUSSEL, Lena ...282
RUSSELL
   Julia ...254
   Marguerite ...385
RYAN, Rose ...104
SALVIS, Lillie ...4
SALVOIS ADAMS, Alice ...423
SALWAY
   Alice ...250
   Anna Christine ...215
   Cecelia ...122
   Sophia ...308
   Susie ...257
SANDERS, Millie ...326
SAUNDERS, Julia ...74
SCHOENHUT, Evelyn ...25
SCHRADER, Frances ...177
SCOUT, Cecelia ...139
SCRAPER, Lizzie ...159
SCRATCHER, --- ...383
SEARS
   Bernice ...183
   Cora ...100
   Lulu ...381
   Ollie ...101
   Pearl ...126

Limited Index

Susan 103
SERAWOP, Emma 93
SHANE, Bessie 281
SHANGREAU
   Agatha 277
   Angeline 312
   Donroy 265
   Eldine 209
   Lillie 312
   Myrtle 127
   Pacific 265
   Pearl 263
   Rosa 5
   Vesta 396
   Winnie 431
SHARP FISH, Ora 345
SHAVING BEAR, Anna 14
SHE ELK VOICE WALKING
   Ora 210
   William 210
SHE STOPS, --- 406
SHELL WOMAN, --- 291
SHIELD
   Hazel 352
   Joseph 352
   Mary 371
   Sallie 197
   Stephen 352
SHIELDS
   Cora E 100
   Dora J 100
   Gerald 100
   Wendell 100
SHORT BEAR
   Cecelia 16
   Jennie 116
   Nettie 250
SHORT BULL
   Jessie 91
   Katie 44
SHOT TO PIECES
   Annie 7
   Dora 130
   Sadie 29
SHOUT AT
   Jessie 412
   Louisa 38
SICKLER, Ruby 113

SIERRO, Hellaria 214
SIERS
   Frances 228
   Josephine 179
   Julia 129
SIREWAP, Ella 225
SITTING BULL, Nancy 187
SITTING DOG, Jennie 440
SITTING EAGLE, Winnie 141
SITTING HOLY
   George 197
   Mary 197
SITTING UP
   Ellen 434
   Emma 376
   Esther 28
   Theresa 367
SIX FEATHERS
   Mollie 406
   Sallie 121
SIX SHOOTER, Maggie 259
SKALANDER
   Edith 208
   Elsie 349
SKENANDARE, Ida 410
SLEEPS, Ruth 118
SLOW, Beulah 233
SLOW BEAR
   Amelia 39
   Tony 39
SLOW DOG
   Helen 87
   Jessie 324
SMITH
   Alice 319
   Della 299
   Marion 93
   Myrtle 239
   Sophia 52
SMOKE
   Lena 361
   Melvin 361
SOUND SLEEPER
   Bessie 274
   Lily 274
SPIDER
   Lucy 231
   Nellie 302

SPIDER BACK BONE, Stella.........400
SPOTTED BEAR
   Rosa...115
   Stella..114
SPOTTED BUFFALO, Hilda...........138
SPOTTED CROW
   Lucy...140
   Susie..420
SPOTTED EAGLE, Jessie..............343
SPOTTED ELK, Minnie...................49
SPOTTED HORSE
   Angelique.......................................218
   Frances..388
   Jo..433
   Sarah..45
SPOTTED OWL, Fannie...................36
STABBER
   Emma..354
   Julia..339
   May...117
STAHL, Esther..................................336
STAND UP, Julia..............................413
STANDING BEAR
   Angelina..125
   Esther...287
   Hattie..278
   Lillie...378
   Ora..246
STANDING BUFFALO, Emma......116
STANDING ROCK SIOUX BEAR,
   Oliver..45
STANDING SOLDIER, Mary...........45
STANDS
   Hobart..349
   Susie..348
STAR
   Kermit..339
   Lucy...370
   Rosa...66
   Susie..273
STEALS HORSE, Susanna.............172
STEWART
   Emerson..187
   Sifrey...187
STIRK
   Ellen...195
   Louisa...80
   Mildred..60

Nellie..207
Pearl...185
Rosa...10
STOVER
   Grace..311
   Hattei...394
   Laura..100
   Sarah Grace....................................367
STRIKES ENEMY
   Lizzie..69
   Susie...92
STRIKES PLENTY
   Sallie..379
   Susie..382
STRONG TALK, Jessie...................420
SUN BEAR, Talbert............................20
SURROUNDED, Grace...................123
SWADLEY, Ethel.............................322
SWAIN
   Eva...112
   Lillian..99
SWALLOW
   Ellen...138
   Geraldine..77
   Helen...336
   Ida..240
   Louisa..368
   Lucy...23
   Susan...363
SWIFT EAGLE, Mary......................239
SWORD
   Jessie...322
   Louisa..260
TAIL
   Ida..390
   Jennie..116
   Leo...159
   Mary..53
   Sarah...116
TAKES AWAY FROM THEM, Bessie
  211
TAKES ENEMY, Nancy..................394
TAKES THE SHIELD
   Clara M...291
   Josie...291
TALKS ABOUT HER, Mable.........241
TASSO
   John...79

Limited Index

Sidney 78
TEBO, One Leroy 18
TELLS HIS NAME, Isabel 34
TEN FINGERS
   Ellene 166
   Lucy 123
TERRAPIN LIGHTS, --- 426
THOMPSON
   Florence 232
   Hazel 112
   Julia 372
   Lizzie 296
THREE STARS
   Andrew 22
   Sallie 354
THUNDER BEAR
   Alice 154
   Victoria 203
THUNDER BULL
   Cora 435
   Mabel 109
THUNDER HAWK
   Andrew 374
   Francis 110
   Joseph 38
   Vincent 110
THUNDER TAIL, Edith 107
TOBACCO
   Clara 422
   Susan 385
TRIMBLE
   Ellen 154
   Eloise 57
TROTTERSCHAUD, Vernon 179
TROUBLE FRONT, Anna 213
TRUEBLOOD, Gladys 331
TURNING BEAR
   Amelia 217
   Ollie 31
TURNING HOLY
   Angelique 100
   Eliza 163
   Kenneth 83
   Tony 100
TWAY, Emma 86
TWISS
   Agatha 428
   Anna W 422

Clara 170
Florence 96
Lillian 103
Minnie 265
Naomi 15
Stella 24
TWISS-KNIGHT, Clara 103
TWO BONNETS
   Christina 241
   Helena 355
   Lulu M 355
   Violet R 355
TWO BULLS
   Dora 116
   Julia 176
   Lucy 181
   Nellie 261
TWO DOGS
   Asay 165
   Edith 165
   Helen 165
   Joe 166
   John 165
   Margaret 166
TWO EAGLES
   Eunice 416
   Katie 272
TWO ELK
   Collins 273
   Jennie 213
TWO HORSE, Anna 249
TWO LANCE
   Christine 119
   Elaine 257
TWO TAIL, Emma 161
TWO TAILS, Sarah 298
TWO TWO
   Amelia 5
   Lottie 60
   Theresa 436
TWO-TWO, Helena 190
TYON
   Ida 412
   Susan 194
UNDERSTANDING CROW, Hattie 391
USES BOW, Julia 143
VALANDRY

Hattie	12
Jennie	303
Mary Ione	305
Maude	316
Minnie	208
Stella	422
VALANRY, Mary	208
VAN WERT, Josephine	245
VIERLING, Myrle	161
WABANESCOM, Sophia	27
WAITE, Susie	77
WALKING	
Annie	128
Clarinda	127
Katie	128
WALKING BULL	
Cornelia	379
Lydia	279
WALKING ELK, Agnes	433
WALKS FAST, Rosa	69
WALKS UNDER GROUND	
Maggie	234
Millie	204
WALKS UNDER THE GROUND, Sarah	162
WALLER, Cricket Ruby	4
WALN-HILL, Lucille	195
WALTERS, Susie	205
WAR BONNET	
Jennie	108
Lizzie	144
WARRIOR	
Alice	417
Dora	158
WARTENSLEBEN, Bettie	198
WATER	
Georgette	246
Ida	197
WEARS WHITE, ---	347
WEASEL	
Edna	397
Mary	274
WEASEL BEAR	
Cora	71
Edna	300
Nancy	197
Susie	120
WEIR, Katie	72
WESTON	
Etta C	145
Grace	324
Merle	405
Myron	405
Richard, Jr	405
WHALEN, Mary	359
WHIRLWIND, Anna	158
WHIRLWIND BEAR, Susie	291
WHIRLWIND HORSE	
Agnes	123
Christine	123
Zetta	299
WHIRLWIND SOLDIER, Rachinda	201
WHITCOMB, Mary	167
WHITE	
Emma	75
Ernest	171
Evelyn	277
Florine	325
Irene	277
Louisa	270
Mary	277
Millicent	277
Rosalie	202
WHITE BEAR	
Alice	293
Jessie	323
WHITE BEAR CLAWS, Julia	20
WHITE BELLY, Mattie	280
WHITE BIRD, Emma	171
WHITE BUFFALO CHIEF, Nada	200
WHITE BULL	
Ella	410
Susan	405
WHITE BUTTERFLY	
Ellen	92
Julia	197
Louisa	401
WHITE CALF, Ella	218
WHITE COYOTE, Sophia	120
WHITE CROW, Susie	174
WHITE DRESS, Lizzie	229
WHITE EAGLE, Mary	270
WHITE ELK	
Emma	125
Hanna	125

Limited Index

Susie 125
WHITE FACE
   Agnes 182
   Psific 353
WHITE FEATHER, Mary 367
WHITE HOLLOW HORN, Florence ...
.... 414
WHITE HORSE
   Nellie 337
   Susie 337
WHITE LANCE, Lucy 104
WHITE MOUNTAIN, Mrs 306
WHITE THUNDER
   Bessie 220
   Eva 225
   Mary 399
WHITE WHIRL WIND, Jennie V ... 336
WHITE WHIRLWIND
   Alice 304
   Ellen 70
WHITE WOLF
   Frances 2
   Susie 400
WHITELANCE, Susie 10
WILCOX, Blanche 8
WILD HORSE, --- 287
WILDE, Edna 105
WILKIE, Rose 222
WILLIAMS
   Anna 345
   Charlotte 220
   Irene 400
   Jennie 55
   Lizzie 319
   Susie 265
   Winnie 439
WILSON
   Ellen 75
   May Belle 183
   Ramona 421
WITT
   May 358
   Wilbur 129
WOLF ON HILL, Alice 152
WOOD RING, Edith 180
WOODEN RING, Esther 253
WOODPECKER, Nancy 52
WOODS, Susie 240

WOUND HEAD, Joshua 227
WOUNDED
   Bessie 294
   Cecelia 420
   Mary 42
WOUNDED HEAD
   Bessie 206
   Sarah 291
WOUNDED HORSE
   Hazel 295
   Julia 209
   Mabel 2
   Mary Jane 365
Y S LITTLE BEAR, Mary 233
YANKTON
   Grace 64
   Helena 251
   Sallie 110
YANKTON WOMAN, Bird 70
YELLOW BEAR
   Mary 119
   Ruth 52
YELLOW BIRD
   Alice 112
   Charles 301
   Jo 362
YELLOW BOY
   Elizabeth 381
   Harold 340
   Jessie 40
   Lucy 58
   Mabel 124,359
   Mary 340
YELLOW BUG, --- 382
YELLOW EYES
   Belle 273
   Edna 274
YELLOW HAIR
   Esther 235
   Mary 161
YELLOW HAWK
   Julia 390
   Nancy 54
   Susie 83,255
YELLOW HORSE
   Elmer 392
   Eva 68
YELLOW HORSE WOMAN 70

YELLOW ROPE, Sallie R 351
YELLOW SHIELD, Grace...............211
YELLOW THUNDER
    Amelia..82
    Jessie..279
    Julia..108
    Louisa..30
    Winfred....................................409
YELLOW WOLF
    Nancy.......................................258
    Sallie...258
YELLOW WOOD, Mary 417
YOUMAN, Susie M........................347
YOUMANS, Mabel A.....................348
YOUNG
    Carrie..279
    Chery..344
    Florence....................................113
    Freda...147
    Lottie..111
    Louis...225
    Louise.......................................111
    Mary...268
    May Flora.................................184
    Nellie..113
    Nora..344
    Wallace.....................................297
YOUNG BEAR, Helen....................370
YOUNG DOG
    Emma.......................................428
    Nancy.......................................430
YOUNG WOLF EARS, Annie........170
ZIMIGA, Ellen.................................57
ZWIMIEGA, Sadie........................407

www.ingramcontent.com/pod-product-compliance
Lightning Source LLC
Chambersburg PA
CBHW020238030426
42336CB00010B/521